GREAT LIVES
FROM
HISTORY

GREAT LIVES FROM HISTORY

American
Series

Volume 2
Com-Ham

Edited by

FRANK N. MAGILL

SALEM PRESS

Pasadena, California   Englewood Cliffs, New Jersey

Library of Congress Cataloging-in-Publication Data
Great lives from history.
   Bibliography: v. 1, p.
   Includes index.
   Summary: A five-volume set of biographical
sketches of some 400 Americans, presenting their
contributions and impact on United States history
and development and including individual bibliog-
raphies.
   1. United States—Biography. [1. United States
—Biography] I. Magill, Frank Northen, 1907-   .
CT214.G74   1987   920'.073 [B] [920]   86-31561
ISBN 0-89356-529-6 (set)
ISBN 0-89356-531-8 (volume 2)

PRINTED IN THE UNITED STATES OF AMERICA

LIST OF BIOGRAPHIES IN VOLUME TWO

LIST OF BIOGRAPHIES IN VOLUME TWO

GREAT LIVES
FROM
HISTORY

ARTHUR HOLLY COMPTON

Born: September 10, 1892; Wooster, Ohio
Died: March 15, 1962; Berkeley, California
Area of Achievement: Physics
Contribution: Although Compton's most famous discovery was that named for him, the Compton effect, he also carried out important cosmic ray research, contributed significantly to the development of the atom bomb, and was an influential educator.

Early Life

Arthur Holly Compton was born September 10, 1892, in Wooster, Ohio, the youngest of four children. His father, Elias, was professor of philosophy and later dean of the College of Wooster. His mother, née Otelia Augspurger, was educated at the Western Female Seminary (later Western College for Women) in Oxford, Ohio, from which she received an honorary LL.D degree in 1933.

Compton grew up in a home that provided love and guidance and emphasized education, discipline, and religious training. His father was an ordained Presbyterian minister, his mother a Mennonite committed to pacifism. Both parents knew how to temper freedom with restraint, instill mental and physical discipline, and focus their children's lives on service to others. Compton's eldest brother, Karl Taylor (1887-1954), became president of the Massachusetts Institute of Technology in 1930. His sister, Mary Elesa (1889-1961), and her husband, C. Herbert Rice, spent forty years as educational missionaries in India. His brother, Wilson Martindale (1890-1967), after a distinguished career in business and government, became president of Washington State University in Pullman, Washington, in 1944. Compton himself eventually became chancellor or Washington University in St. Louis in 1945. Because of their many educational contributions, the Comptons became known as America's first family of learning.

Compton attended the Wooster elementary and grammar school (1898-1905) and Wooster Preparatory School (1905-1909); at the latter, his interest in science awakened. He became particularly fascinated with astronomy, eventually persuaded his parents to allow him to use his savings to purchase a small telescope, and with it and a camera photographed Halley's comet in 1910. He also became skilled in building model airplanes and ultimately built a triplane glider with a twenty-seven-foot wingspan which he successfully flew for about two hundred feet in 1910.

In the fall of 1909, Compton entered the College of Wooster and soon faced the decision of choosing a career. He was strongly inclined to go into the ministry, but his father sensed that his interest in science was deeper and encouraged him in that direction. His older brother Karl, too, served as a model, since Karl had studied physics at Wooster and by the fall of 1909 was working on his doctoral degree in that subject at Princeton. By the time Arthur completed his bachelor's degree in 1913, he was inclined toward a career in science, and he followed in Karl's footsteps, going to Princeton for graduate study. Still, his thoughts ran more toward some field in engineering, since he believed that by devoting his life to such a practical field he could be of more benefit to mankind. During his first term at Princeton, however, he came under the influence of Karl's thesis adviser, O. W. Richardson, a distinguished physicist who had been trained in the Cavendish Laboratory in Cambridge, England, and as a result Compton became convinced that he could achieve the end he desired more effectively by studying physics. He completed his Ph.D. degree in physics at Princeton in June of 1916. That same month, on June 28, he married Betty Charity McCloskey, a former classmate at Wooster. They had two sons, Arthur Alan (born 1918) and John Joseph (born 1928).

In the fall of 1916, Compton took up a position as instructor in physics at the University of Minnesota in Minneapolis, where he remained for one academic year. He then went into industry, working as a research physicist in the Westinghouse Lamp Company in Pittsburgh. Soon, however, he began to miss the freedom to pursue research problems of his own choosing that he had experienced at Princeton and Minnesota, and he decided to leave Westinghouse after two years there. That decision was made possible because at the close of World War I National Research Council Fellowships were established with funds from the Rockefeller Foundation. Compton was one of the first physicists in America to receive one of these fellowships, and in the fall of 1919 he left for a year's study abroad in the Cavendish Laboratory in Cambridge, England, under Ernest Rutherford. Returning to the United States in the summer of 1920, he accepted a position as Wayman Crow Professor of Physics and head of the Department of Physics at Washington University in St. Louis. Three years later, he transferred to the University of Chicago, filling a professorship in physics that had become vacant through the move of Robert A. Millikan to the California Institute of Technology in Pasadena.

Life's Work

Compton's doctoral dissertation research at Princeton had involved reflecting X rays from certain crystals, with the intent of using them as a probe to determine how the electrons are distributed about the center of the crystal atoms. During the next six years, from the fall of 1916 to the fall of 1922, at Minnesota, Westinghouse, the Cavendish Laboratory, and Washington University, Compton carried out a complex series of further experimental and theoretical investigations of how X rays and even higher-energy radiations, gamma rays, are scattered by aluminum, carbon, and other elements.

Only very gradually did he come to understand that to explain correctly the results that he and others were finding experimentally, he would have to assume that the X rays and gamma rays were behaving not like waves but like particles. Thus, for example, when an X ray struck an electron in a carbon atom, it was just as if one little billiard ball had struck another, sending it on its way by transferring some energy and momentum to it. In the process, the incident X ray loses some energy and momentum, and since the energy of an X ray is proportional to its frequency, the scattered X ray has a lower frequency or higher wavelength than the incident X ray. By using a spectroscope, Compton was able to compare the wavelength of the scattered X ray to that of the incident X ray, and he found that it had increased by just the amount he had calculated on the basis of the billiard-ball collision model. X rays in this experiment did indeed behave just like little particles possessing energy and momentum.

This conclusion came as a great surprise to most physicists when Compton published it in early 1923. Albert Einstein had argued as long before as 1905 that there were reasons to believe that in certain circumstances high-frequency electromagnetic radiation behaves like particles or quanta of energy, but Einstein's so-called light-quantum hypothesis was greeted with profound skepticism in succeeding years. Although Compton's experimental and theoretical program was not motivated by a desire to test Einstein's hypothesis, after his results were in, they were recognized as the first conclusive experimental proof of it. That forced physicists to consider anew the way radiation interacts with matter, and Compton's discovery was a crucial stimulus to the creation of modern quantum mechanics in 1925-1926. For his discovery, ever after known as the Compton effect, Compton won the Nobel Prize for Physics in 1927, sharing it with the inventor of the cloud chamber, C. T. R. Wilson. That same year he was also elected to the National Academy of Sciences.

At the end of 1930, Compton's researches turned away from X rays and toward the highly penetrating rays impinging on the earth from outer space. These rays had been discovered in 1911-1912 by the Austrian V. F. Hess, but their true nature was still unknown. Robert A. Millikan, who gave these rays their modern name, "cosmic rays," believed them to consist of extremely high-frequency light quanta, or "photons." Others, including Compton, believed them to consist of positively charged particles. A great controversy erupted, and to settle it Compton secured financial support from the Carnegie Institution and sent out nine expeditions to different parts of the globe in 1931-1934, trying to determine if the cosmic-ray intensity is different at different latitudes. He and his coworkers (who included his wife, Betty, and their teenage son Arthur) found that the intensity steadily decreased in going from either pole to the equator, proving that the incoming cosmic rays were being deflected poleward by the earth's magnetic field. This could only happen if they were charged particles, not photons; they were ultimately identified as positively charged hydrogen and helium nuclei.

Concurrently with his scientific work, Compton was giving much thought to philosophical and religious issues. A yearlong trip to India in 1926-1927 on a Guggenheim fellowship enabled him to view his own heritage in a broad cultural perspective, and it renewed his concern for humanity. Throughout the 1930's, he visited and lectured widely at colleges and universities in the United States and England, exploring the connections among science, religion, and human values, trying to illuminate ancient questions such as man's relationship to God and the nature of human free will in the light of the lessons of quantum theory and relativity. In his deep concern for these questions, he was very much following in the footsteps of his father.

When World War II broke out, Compton's great prestige as a scientist brought him into the heart of the Manhattan Project, the American atom bomb project. Nuclear fission had been discovered in Germany at the end of 1938, and scientists in the United States—both native-born Americans and Europeans who had been exiled from their homelands—feared that Adolf Hitler might come into possession of this terrible weapon. Compton was asked to chair a committee to assess the feasibility of developing atomic energy for military purposes, and his positive conclusions, which were transmitted to President Franklin D. Roosevelt in November of 1941, were decisive in moving the American project forward. Compton himself became director of the plutonium research project in 1942. It was he who brought Enrico Fermi to Chicago and oversaw Fermi's construction of the first chain-reacting pile there on December 2, 1942. Two and a half years later, Compton was appointed to the committee that advised President Harry S Truman on the use of the weapon against Japan. Few American physicists have been called upon to bear comparable responsibilities.

Summary

Compton was only the third American (after A. A. Michelson and Millikan) to win the Nobel Prize for Physics, and his achievement contributed significantly to the coming-of-age of physics in the United States in the 1920's and 1930's. Immediately after World War II, he accepted the chancellorship of Washington University in St. Louis, where more than two decades earlier he had made his famous discovery of the Compton effect. He served as chancellor from 1945 to 1953 and as Distinguished Service Professor of Natural Philosophy from 1954 to 1961, becoming one of the best-known and most influential educators in America. He received twenty-five honorary degrees and numerous awards and medals, including the United States government's Medal for Merit in 1946. In 1961, he was appointed professor-at-large, intending to divide his time among Washington University, Wooster College, and the University of California, Berkeley. He died in Berkeley of a cerebral hemorrhage on March 15, 1962, and was buried where he was born, in Wooster, Ohio.

Bibliography

Blackwood, James R. *The House on College Avenue: The Comptons at Wooster, 1891-1913*. Cambridge, Mass.: MIT Press, 1968. The early history of the Compton family.

Compton, Arthur Holly. *Atomic Quest: A Personal Narrative*. New York: Oxford University Press, 1956. Compton's account of the Manhattan Project.

_____. *The Freedom of Man*. New Haven, Conn.: Yale University Press, 1935. Compton's Terry lectures.

_____. *The Human Meaning of Science*. Chapel Hill: University of North Carolina Press, 1940. Compton's McNair lectures.

_____. *Scientific Papers of Arthur Holly Compton: X-Ray and Other Studies*. Edited by Robert S. Shankland. Chicago: University of Chicago Press, 1973. Includes a valuable introduction surveying Compton's scientific work.

Johnston, Marjorie, ed. *The Cosmos of Arthur Holly Compton*. New York: Alfred A. Knopf, 1967. Contains many of Compton's nontechnical works and includes his "Personal Reminiscences" and a bibliography of his writings.

Stuewer, Roger H. *The Compton Effect: Turning Point in Physics*. New York: Science History Publications, 1975. A historical and technical account of Compton's discovery and its influence on physics.

Roger H. Stuewer

JAMES BRYANT CONANT

Born: March 26, 1893; Dorchester, Massachusetts
Died: February 11, 1978; Hanover, New Hampshire
Areas of Achievement: Science, education, and international diplomacy
Contribution: Conant helped unravel the mysteries of the components of
  chlorophyll and hemoglobin. He served as an innovative president of Har-
  vard University, United States high commissioner to Germany after World
  War II, and ambassador to the newly created German Federal Republic.

Early Life

James Bryant Conant was born March 26, 1893, in Dorchester, Massachusetts. His father, James Scott Conant, was a photoengraver who had served
in both the Union army and navy during the Civil War and had witnessed the
famed battle between the *Monitor* and the *Merrimac*. His mother, née Jennet
Orr Bryant, was the daughter of a shoe and leather salesman. Both of
Conant's parents were greatly influenced by Swedenborgianism, which Conant claimed made him suspicious of the standard defenses of Christianity.
His father's interest in applied chemistry in his photoengraving work sparked
an interest in science for the young Conant. He was the only youngster in his
neighborhood who had his own laboratory. At an early age, he began developing formulas for almost everything, including the family's grocery buying,
which his mother claimed saved the household money.

When Conant was ten, he applied for admission to Roxbury Latin School,
a college preparatory school with a good reputation in chemistry and physics.
He failed the spelling part of his admissions test, but his strong-willed mother
managed to get him admitted. While at Roxbury, Conant came under the
influence of Newton Henry Black, who encouraged him to pursue the study
of chemistry by directing him into qualitative analysis, a subject usually reserved for college sophomores.

In 1910, Conant entered Harvard University, where he finished the undergraduate program in three years. Professor Black helped Conant obtain
credit for the work in chemistry he had done at Roxbury. His mother insisted
that he also take a course in philosophy, since she did not want him to
become a narrow-minded chemist. He later regarded this course and one in
art and culture of the Renaissance as giving him a worldview.

At Harvard, Professor Elmer Peter Kohler helped shape Conant's attitudes and opinions with a zest for detailed, difficult tasks. Conant credited
Kohler for bringing commonsense judgment to bear on human problems, an
approach which Conant later emulated in the worlds of academe and
diplomacy.

Conant edited the Harvard *Crimson* as a sophomore, which qualified him
for admission into the Signet, the school's select literary club. It was in this

circle that Conant received his general education, through the sophisticated conversations around the luncheon tables. Later, as president, Conant would tell entering students, "A Harvard education is what you will receive outside of class."

Upon graduating with an A.B. in chemistry, Conant immediately began working toward his Ph.D. at Harvard, which he received in 1916. Conant attracted the attention of his professors as a promising chemist and teacher. The lean six-footer always wore glasses and had a congenial smile. He developed the habit of sliding back his cuff and quickly glancing at his watch, as if he were always in a hurry.

Life's Work

Conant was a brilliant research chemist who did experiments in reduction and oxidation, free radicals, quantitative organic reactions, and superacid solutions. He helped in creating an understanding of the molecular structure of chlorophyll and hemoglobin, for which he was considered for a Nobel Prize. He wrote two widely used textbooks, *Practical Chemistry* (1920) and *Chemistry of Organic Compounds* (1933), and a scientific text for laymen, *On Understanding Science* (1947).

In the summer before receiving his doctorate, Conant worked as a chemist in industry at the Midvale Steel Company in Philadelphia, developing new analytical procedures. This experience taught him the inner politics and production problems of a manufacturing plant. He was given an intimate preview of the marriage of chemistry and American industry. In 1916, he worked with colleagues to open a plant to manufacture benzoic acid from toluene. A tragic fire destroyed the plant, and Conant learned the hazards of the free enterprise system when he was forced to pay off stockholders from the royalties of one of his patents.

Conant accepted an invitation to return to Harvard as an instructor in 1916, and the following summer he accepted a position with the Bureau of Chemistry in Washington, D.C. Since America had entered World War I on the side of the Allies, Conant worked on a process for manufacturing a drug which hitherto had been imported from Germany. Later he joined a research team at the American University in Washington, where he became a first lieutenant in the Sanitary Corps of the army. He advanced to the rank of major in the Chemical Warfare Service. He went to Willoughby, Ohio, where he worked in a converted auto factory on chemical weapons for the war.

Following World War I, Conant was named assistant professor of chemistry at Harvard. He worked closely with Nobel Prize winner Theodore William Richards and became enamored of his daughter, Grace, whom he affectionately called "Patty." They were married in April of 1921 and later became the parents of two sons, Theodore and James. Conant told his young bride that he had three ambitions beyond his marriage to her: to become a leading organic chemist, to be president of Harvard University, and to be named a member of the president's cabinet, possibly secretary of the interior. Conant reached the first two goals and possibly exceeded the third in government service as United States high commissioner and later ambassador to Germany.

In 1923, Conant traveled to Germany to satisfy his curiosity about German universities. He had regarded himself as too parochial, having spent most of his time in the academic environment of the Boston area. He wondered what made German science, particularly organic chemistry, so successful. After spending eight months visiting their universities, he concluded that their secret lay in their professorial organization and the rivalry among the schools, prompting them to exert their best academic efforts.

In 1929, Conant was elected the Sheldon Emery Professor of Organic Chemistry and became chairman of the department in 1931, where he also continued his research in organic chemistry. During this period, he was rejected as a trustee of his alma mater, Roxbury, because he was not sufficiently well-known. In 1933, however, at the age of forty, he was brought into prominence by being chosen as Harvard's twenty-third president, a position he held for twenty years.

Soon after his election as president, he traveled to England to observe at first hand the systems of Oxford and Cambridge. Since its founding, Harvard had looked to the English model and had followed the Oxford example of making appointments. Former president A. Lawrence Lowell had also introduced Oxford's tutorial system at Harvard.

Conant was an innovator in education and showed little regard for custom. On his office wall was a plaque which exemplified his willingness to change. It read: "Behold the turtle, he makes progress only when he sticks his neck out." He wanted the university to be a national rather than a regional school, and in 1934 he established national scholarships to enable young men of outstanding ability to attend Harvard regardless of financial circumstances or regional background. The scholarships were large enough to cover all essential expenses and were arranged on a sliding scale adjusted to the student's financial need. Conant also followed Lowell's trend of establishing strong professional schools surrounding the undergraduate college. He paid particular attention to the Department of Education, which he regarded as critical to the American public educational system. Fearing that teachers were trained more in pedagogy and less in factual content, he established the master of arts for teachers degree in 1935, which required greater concentration in the teachers' intended subject areas. Although Conant had been opposed to coeducation at Harvard when he became president, he was instrumental in 1943 in forming the agreement of the Harvard corporation with the trustees of Radcliffe College to permit women to gain credit from attending classes on the Harvard campus.

When World War II broke out in Europe, Conant became an early advocate of American intervention on the side of the Allies. Although he had been critical of the anti-German hysteria that accompanied World War I and admitted that he had voted for Woodrow Wilson in 1916 because of his promise to keep the United States out of the war, he saw that Fascism in the 1930's threatened to wipe out a free way of life in Western civilization. To remain silent was suicidal.

In 1940, President Franklin D. Roosevelt sent Conant to England to serve as a scientific liaison with the British. Roosevelt also named him as chemistry adviser to the National Defense Research Committee. One of the committee's assignments was to work on the development of synthetic rubber, since the importation of natural rubber through war zones seemed highly unlikely. Conant had worked on a synthetic rubber project with the E. I. Du Pont Company. In 1941, Conant succeeded Vannavar Bush as chairman of the National Defense Research Committee.

The American government had greater need for Conant's scientific acumen, and he was appointed to the Military Policy Committee which set the policy for the development of the atom bomb. Bush, Karl T. Compton, and Conant were often called "the grand dukes of the atomic bomb project." In addition to his role as scientific adviser, Conant also was involved as a member of the Select Interim Committee in the selection of the target in Japan for the first bomb, which was dropped on Hiroshima, August 6, 1945. He defended America's dropping the bomb on the basis that the war did not appear to be coming to an end, and the planned invasion would take many more Japanese and American lives than a minimum of atom-bomb strikes forcing Japan to surrender.

Although he received an Atomic Pioneer Award in 1970 and was commended for his work in the development of peaceful uses of the atom, Conant never considered its peaceful use nearly as important as its destructive possibilities in war. Soon after the war, he traveled with Secretary of State James Byrnes to Moscow to talk with the Soviets and the British about the international control of the atom bomb. He urged meetings between American and Soviet scientists but believed strongly that strict secrecy should be maintained by the Americans. He perceived that the Soviets were still five to fifteen years behind in developing an atomic weapon as long as they did not have access to American secrets.

In 1947, President Harry S Truman appointed Conant as general adviser to the Atomic Energy Commission. Conant served on the committee until 1952 and stoutly defended J. Robert Oppenheimer against the accusations that he was influenced by pro-Soviet and anti–United States views.

In 1953, Conant resigned as Harvard's president and was appointed by President Dwight D. Eisenhower as America's high commissioner to Germany. While in the post, he had to deal with the stream of refugees coming into the American sectors from the Soviet sector and the rebuilding of a war-torn nation. He was also caught in the crossfire between Communist rioters in East Germany and Senator Joseph McCarthy at home, who had accused him of not taking a firm enough hand against the Communists. President Eisenhower was satisfied with his conduct and appointed him America's first ambassador to the newly created German Federal Republic in 1955, a post he held for nearly two years.

Conant had a keen interest in public education. Not even the best of the universities could preserve the Jeffersonian concept of an aristocracy of talent unless the public schools formed a durable foundation. In the late 1940's, he warned against the dangers of divisiveness in nonpublic schools. His critics accused him of waging war against parochial schools. Although he saw a need for private schools, Conant was fearful of anything that weakened the support of public education and that consequently endangered the nation's future.

After returning from Germany, Conant applied for and received a grant for $350,000 from the Carnegie Foundation to examine problems in the public schools. The Soviets had launched *Sputnik*, and this caused observers to compare the American and Soviet educational systems. It appeared that the United States was lagging in the scientific fields. The Carnegie grant enabled Conant to study American education and make recommendations for improvement. His guide for reform, published under the title *The American High School Today* (1959), contained the checklist simplicity of a maintenance manual which enabled educators to implement easily his ideas. He campaigned coast-to-coast for reforms, particularly school consolidations which would provide ample scientific facilities for both rural and urban students.

Conant also became aware of the number of black Americans who dropped out of school and created a high unemployment rate. His book *Slums and Suburbs: A Commentary on Schools in Metropolitan Areas* (1961) was prophetic of the urban riots of that decade.

Active until his last years, Conant died after a long illness in a nursing home in Hanover, New Hampshire, February 11, 1978.

Summary

Conant was a man of many talents, as the title of his autobiography, *My Several Lives* (1970), implies. Although highly intelligent, he never lived in an ivory tower but was always on the cutting edge of the great movements of his time. He represented a tradition of educational leaders who perceived that American education is holistic. Having made significant changes in the structure and program of one of America's leading universities, he devoted his energies to the education of adolescents. He never forgot his own experiences as a young man and how essential it was for one to have a firm foundation before building for the future. He recognized the value of teachers as inspirers and allowed his own enthusiasm for teaching to become evident whether in a faculty meeting or a diplomatic discussion.

Conant was a prolific writer. He published twenty-two books ranging from science to politics, social problems, and education. He received honorary doctorates from many prestigious universities in the United States and Europe. He was appointed to important posts by four presidents, two Democrats and two Republicans. He was accorded high honors by political and military organizations, including Honorary Commander Most Excellent Order of the British Empire (1948), the Medal of Honor and Oak Leaf Cluster (1948), and the Great Living American Award in 1965.

Bibliography

Conant, James Bryant. *The American High School Today: A First Report to Interest Citizens*. New York: McGraw-Hill Book Co., 1959. Commonly called the "Conant Report," the book made clear the changes that needed to be made in American secondary schools in order to keep pace with the times. Contains twenty-one recommendations, some of which were quite revolutionary. An excellent insight into Conant's educational theories.

_____. *Germany and Freedom: A Personal Appraisal*. Cambridge, Mass.: Harvard University Press, 1958. An insightful account of Conant's attempts to create a better understanding between the United States and the Federal Republic of Germany. The book is based on the Godkin Lectures delivered at Harvard in 1958.

_____. *My Several Lives: Memoirs of a Social Inventor*. New York: Harper and Row, Publishers, 1970. Conant's autobiography, in which he gives intimate details of his election as Harvard's twenty-third president, his work on the atom bomb, and his confrontation with Senator Joseph McCarthy. Also included are some of his important addresses.

_____. *Scientific Principles and Moral Conduct*. Cambridge, Mass.: Harvard University Press, 1967. Since Conant had worked on developing poison gas in World War I and the atom bomb in World War II, he was aware of the moral implications involved in the application of science to war. Conant wrote as both a scientist and a concerned humanitarian.

Douglass, Paul Franklin. *Six upon the World: Toward an American Culture for the Industrial Age*. Boston: Little, Brown and Co., 1954. Conant is one of the six figures treated in this study (among the others are Walter Reuther and Francis Spellman), which presents his life and thought in overview. The book is marred by its boosterish approach to its subjects and to American culture in general. Includes bibliography.

"Obituary." *The New York Times*, February 12, 1978, sec. 1: 4. An excellent editorial on the many contributions of Conant, particularly in educational reforms.

Passow, A. Harry. *American Secondary Education: The Conant Influence.* Reston, Va.: National Association of Secondary School Principals, 1977. A perceptive look at Conant's recommendations for junior and senior high schools and the impact they had ten and twenty years later.

Raymond Lee Muncy

JAY COOKE

Born: August 10, 1821; Sandusky, Ohio
Died: February 18, 1905; Ogontz, Pennsylvania
Area of Achievement: Banking
Contribution: Cooke was the foremost investment banker during the mid-nineteenth century and pioneered new ways of mobilizing the savings of Americans for productive ends.

Early Life

Jay Cooke, born August 10, 1821, was the third son of Eleutheros and Martha Cooke. The family had relocated in several moves from New England to the Lake Erie settlement of Sandusky. Eleutheros was an ardent Whig politician and served in Congress for a term when Jay was a young boy. The family atmosphere was devoutly Protestant. Jay attended public school in Sandusky until the age of fourteen, when he ended his formal education and took a job as a clerk in a general store. After a year at work, Jay left Ohio for St. Louis, staying there a year, until the commercial disruption following the Panic of 1837 caused him to return to Sandusky. Still only sixteen, Jay left Sandusky in the spring of 1838 for Philadelphia, where he obtained work with his brother-in-law's canal transport company. The firm failed shortly after Jay's arrival in the city, and he returned once more to Sandusky, staying only a few months, until he was lured back to Philadelphia with a job offer from the banker E. W. Clark. From 1839 to 1857, Cooke worked in the Clark banking house, first as an office boy; soon, because of his head for figures and nose for profits, he became a partner at the age of twenty-one.

An early photograph taken of Cooke in the 1840's shows a young man of modest stature, clear eyes, and somber nature. He looks as if he were trying to look older than he was. This fits the character of the man: earnest, sober, deeply religious, and a family man. Jay took his older brothers Henry and Pitt into partnership when each needed money and supported them throughout numerous misadventures for most of their lives. He started his own family shortly after his 1844 marriage to Dorothea Allen, and the couple had eight children, though not all survived childhood. The Cookes did not entertain extensively, keeping the Episcopal Church at the center of their lives.

As a partner at E. W. Clark and Co., Cooke practiced mercantile banking as it existed before the Civil War. The profits of the firm came from dealing in "domestic exchange," that is, banknotes from various parts of the country that the firm discounted according to risk. The nation in those days had no official government currency except metallic money, so the paper medium of daily exchange was provided by private bankers. With the banknotes of so many banks in circulation, the banker had to judge shrewdly the worth of the paper that purported to be "good as gold." The firm also loaned money for short periods of time to Philadelphia merchants and engaged in the commodity trade. As he prospered at E. W. Clark and Co. in the 1850's, Cooke began to invest his own money in a number of outside ventures. These included a daring land speculation in Iowa and Minnesota that originated as a project to give work to his bankrupt brother Pitt. Cooke sent Pitt west to the Iowa prairies to obtain land from the government at prices below $1.25 an acre, with careful guidance about how to resell it to incoming farmers at three and four dollars an acre. The speculation made so much money that Pitt paid his debts and Cooke became even more wealthy. Growing restless as a junior partner at E. W. Clark and Co., he left the firm in 1857 and devoted his attention to private investing, particularly in railroads, for the next few years. He decided to reenter the banking business on the eve of the American Civil War and opened Jay Cooke and Co. on January 1, 1861.

Life's Work

Abraham Lincoln took office to find the Treasury nearly empty, and with the firing on Fort Sumter, he faced a greater challenge in raising money than in raising volunteers. Wars are expensive to fight and governments can finance them either by taxation, borrowing, or printing paper money. The rebel government in Richmond chose the last option and, by the end of the war, had an inflation rate of five thousand percent. The Union government of Lincoln chose to borrow to pay the war, a better strategy, but one that worked only because of the efforts of Jay Cooke.

The traditional method of government finance was to offer government bonds at competitive auction to private bankers. This practice worked well enough in peacetime, but in 1861, many bankers were unsure whether the Union would survive to pay the debt. Secretary of the Treasury, Salmon P. Chase, insisted on selling the bonds at par (one hundred cents on the dollar), but most bankers considered them to be too risky at that price. The Treasury and the nation muddled through 1861, unable to raise enough money but uncertain of any other way of doing business. Cooke, however, had an idea about how to raise hundreds of millions for the war effort. Through his older brother Henry, a Washington journalist, Cooke approached Secretary Chase and offered to be the government's sales agent for government bonds. For a small fee, Cooke promised to sell all the bonds that the government could issue. He based this confident assertion on his earlier experience as the fiscal agent for the State of Pennsylvania in selling a bond issue of three million dollars. He had simply marketed the bonds directly to the public at par, bypassing other investment bankers.

As the war turned against the Union in the summer of 1862, Chase became more receptive to Cooke's idea, if only out of desperation. In October, the secretary appointed Jay Cooke and Co. sole agent to sell fifty million dollars of government bonds at six percent interest. The bonds were due in twenty years, but the government could redeem them in five, hence the popular name of the debt was "5-20's." Cooke promised to sell a million dollars a day of 5-20's and took a fee of one half of one percent, on the first ten million dollars worth sold, and three eighths of one percent on the remainder. Cooke faced two challenges in selling the debt. First, he had to build a distribution network of retail sales agents to sell the bonds, and second, he had to convince the public to buy them. In each case, he was spectacularly successful. Cooke appointed twenty-five hundred subagents to sell bonds throughout the Union and by using the telegraph, effectively coordinated the efforts of this sales team. A heavy use of newspaper advertising and handbills worked to convince the public of the patriotic necessity of buying government bonds. Any Northern newspaper of 1863 was likely to carry a prominent ad placed by Cooke urging citizens to buy bonds. The sales campaign began in earnest in February, 1863, and by the end of June, Cooke had marketed more than $175,000,000 in 5-20's. Over the next seven months, until the loan was oversubscribed by late January, 1864, he sold more than $325,000,000. After paying advertising costs, office expenses, and commissions to the subagents, Cooke was left with a commission of perhaps one sixteeenth of one percent of the sales. He did not get rich selling the bonds; rather, he earned something even greater, the title Financier of the Union.

The government bond business made Jay Cooke and Co. the best-known banking house in the United States, and this when Cooke was still in his early forties. In 1865, he repeated his earlier coup in helping the government to finance a new issue of bonds, the so-called 7-30's. This loan drive was even more extensive and more successful than the 1863 issue of 5-20's. From January, 1865, through the end of July of that year, Cooke managed to sell more than $800,000,000 worth of new government bonds. The sales force was more than double that of the earlier sale, and for the 7-30's, Cooke even had itinerant salesmen follow the progress of the Union Army in the South to sell the Union public debt to the conquered rebels.

For several years after the war, Jay Cooke and Co. engaged in further government debt financings. By 1869, the government finance business had wound down and opportunities for profit appeared elsewhere. Cooke had some antebellum experience in railroad finance, and it was in this direction that he took his firm in 1869. That year, he agreed to be the banker and agent for the Northern Pacific Railway Company, a line projected to link Lake Superior with Puget Sound on the Pacific. The nation had just completed one transcontinental railroad in the Union Pacific–Central Pacific, linking Omaha to San Francisco, but the Northern Pacific promised to be the largest construction project in American history. Cooke was attracted to the Northern Pacific for a number of reasons. He had speculated in Minnesota lands in the 1850's and believed in the future of the Northwest. He renewed his land speculation near the tiny settlement of Duluth in 1866, and when he visited the place in 1868, he saw it as the next Chicago, a mighty future metropolis handling the produce of the American West. Early in 1869, Cooke sold bonds for the Lake Superior and Mississippi Railroad, linking Duluth to St. Paul, and the success of that venture convinced the investor to take on the Northern Pacific's tasks of raising capital to build the two-thousand-mile railroad.

The original financing plan intended for the Northern Pacific to build westward in anticipation of the traffic along the line. This, together with land sales from its magnificent fifty-million acre land grant from Congress, would finance further construction, operations, and debt service. This plan proved too optimistic, since there was almost no white settlement along the route. Cooke managed to raise five million dollars for construction in 1870, but only with great difficulty. His efforts to interest European bankers and investors failed, as they thought the Northern Pacific too risky.

In 1871, Cooke began a public campaign to sell $100,000,000 in Northern Pacific bonds at 7.3 percent interest, the goal of the drive being to raise enough money from small investors to complete the road. Cooke used the same techniques he had learned in selling government bonds during the war: a nationwide network of subagents and hundreds of thousands of dollars spent on advertising. Indeed, Cooke made the Northern Pacific bond-selling slogan, "Safe! Profitable! Permanent!" ubiquitous in the country in 1871 and 1872. The results, however, were disappointing. Cooke only sold about sixteen million dollars worth of bonds in 1871 and 1872. The investing public judged the Northern Pacific too risky an enterprise, despite the high interest rate offered and the reputation for reliability that Cooke brought as the railroad's banker.

Gradually, Cooke crossed the line between banker and promoter of the Northern Pacific. The railroad repeatedly overdrew its account with Cooke's bank and showed signs of mismanagement. The road's problem was that in its first few years, it had substantial expenses and little revenue. The Cooke banking houses in Philadelphia, New York, Washington, and London became overextended in Northern Pacific affairs by 1872, and when a tightening of the money market in 1873 pressed banks in general, Jay Cooke and Co. was forced to close its doors: It no longer had sufficient reserves to pay the demands of its depositors. The shock of the failure of the leading private bank in the United States caused a panic on Wall Street and ushered in the worst business recession Americans had experienced to that date.

Cooke declared bankruptcy in 1873, and lost most of the multimillion dollar fortune he had accumulated. He spent the next several years satisfying his creditors and by 1880, he resumed business as an investor in Western mining ventures. He made a second fortune before his death but preferred to live a quiet life as an old man devoted to family and church. He died in Ogontz, Pennsylvania, in 1905.

Summary

Jay Cooke performed three great services in his adult life as a banker. First, he earned the title Financier of the Union because he came to the rescue of an empty Treasury at a critical time in the Civil War. Had Cooke not successfully sold the 5-20's to the public in 1863, the Treasury would have probably had to resort to extensive printing of paper money, much as the Confederates did. The result would have been ruinous inflation and perhaps a different outcome to the war.

Second, even though Cooke failed in his endeavor to make the Northern Pacific a money-maker in the early 1870's, he did succeed in getting the road launched, and his vision of the Northwest as a great grain-, timber-, and coal-producing region of free and prosperous Americans did come true. Despite his 1873 bankruptcy, Cooke lived long enough to see his idea of the Northwest emerge as emigrants from eastern America and immigrants from Europe poured into the region. While Duluth never became the next Chicago, it developed into the greatest inland grain, coal, and iron port in North America, and the citizens of that city gratefully remembered Jay Cooke's part in their rise.

Third, Cooke helped change the nature of investment banking. Prior to his financing the Civil War debt, private banking consisted of discounting notes and short-term loans from bankers to merchants. The savings of average Americans were not tapped in any way except through a handful of small savings-and-loan associations. Cooke changed that by reaching out to hundreds of thousands of Americans in the war and appealing for their small holdings to support the cause. In the century following, Wall Street would devote increasing amounts of time and effort to attracting the savings of the individual investor. Without Cooke's innovation, the great financial undertakings of the day could not have taken place. Without the savings of millions of people, the government debt and the great industrial projects, such as the railroads, could not have been funded.

Bibliography

Cooke, Jay et al. "Guide to the Lands of the Northern Pacific Railroad in Minnesota." In *The Fruits of Land Speculation,* edited by Paul Wallace Gates. New York: Arno Press, 1979. This pamphlet amply demonstrates Cooke's talent as a promoter. It explains the route of the Northern Pacific and the advantages of moving to the country west of Duluth.

Hammond, Bray. *Sovereignty and an Empty Purse: Banks and Politics in the Civil War.* Princeton, N.J.: Princeton University Press, 1970. This book examines how the Treasury found itself in desperate condition in 1861, and how it mobilized itself to raise the necessary funds to prosecute the war. The author treats at length Cooke's relationship to the Treasury.

Larson, Henrietta M. *Jay Cooke: Private Banker.* Cambridge, Mass.: Harvard University Press, 1936. This is the standard biography of Cooke, concentrating on his banking career from the 1840's through the 1873 failure. Among biographies of businessmen, this is one of the most outstanding.

Minnigerode, Meade. *Certain Rich Men*. New York: G. P. Putnam's Sons, 1927. Reprint. Freeport, N.Y.: Books for Libraries Press, 1970. This book consists of biographies of wealthy Americans of the late nineteenth century. The contrast between Cooke and some of his less scrupulous colleagues is noteworthy.

Oberholtzer, Ellis Paxton. *Jay Cooke: Financier of the Civil War*. Philadelphia: George W. Jacobs and Co., 1907. Oberholtzer was the first to make use of the magnificent Jay Cooke Papers manuscript collection at the Historical Society of Pennsylvania. There is considerable emphasis on the private side of Cooke's life.

Trescott, Paul B. *Financing American Enterprise: The Story of Commercial Banking*. New York: Harper and Row, Publishers, 1961. This book has a good chapter on American railroad finance and puts the Northern Pacific episode in perspective.

James W. Oberly

CALVIN COOLIDGE

Born: July 4, 1872; Plymouth, Vermont
Died: January 5, 1933; Northampton, Massachusetts
Areas of Achievement: Politics and government
Contribution: Practicing the virtues most Americans seemed to honor in absentia, Calvin Coolidge served as president of the United States during the central years of that extraordinary decade, the 1920's.

Early Life

John Calvin Coolidge was born in Plymouth, Vermont, on July 4, 1872. His father, Colonel John Calvin Coolidge (the rank was an honorary one bestowed for service on the governor's staff), was a prominent local figure who had served several terms in the state legislature. His mother, the former Victoria Josephine Moor, died when young Calvin was twelve. It was a painful loss to the boy, and his memories of his mother were very precious to him. It was from her family that he inherited the dash of Indian blood which so charmed political pundits during his presidential years. His only sister, Abigail, who was three years younger than Calvin, died in her teens. Her death was another blow to the sensitive youth.

After a brief period spent teaching school, Coolidge entered Amherst College in 1891. There he joined the College Republican Club and, in his senior year, a social fraternity. He was one of three persons in his class chosen to speak at graduation. His was the task of presenting a humorous speech, which he completed with considerable wit and the approval of his class. In 1895, he moved to Northampton, Massachusetts, and began the study of law. At the age of twenty-five, he was admitted to the bar and settled into the quiet, sober, often dull, and always frugal life-style which he followed until his death.

Standing slightly over five feet eight inches tall, Coolidge was a slim, rather drab, and colorless figure. His once reddish hair became a sandy brown as he matured. With his broad forehead, cleft chin, and thin features, he lived up to the Washington description of him as one who was "weaned on a dill pickle." Well deserving the sobriquet "Silent Cal," Coolidge began his diligent climb through small-town politics. Always listening and working rather than talking—though he could speak effectively, with his dry, raspy voice and flat New England accent—Coolidge became a local Republican committeeman before he was thirty and not long thereafter was elected to the Republican State Committee. In addition, Coolidge served on the town council, was named vice president of a local savings bank, and, in 1900, was appointed city solicitor.

At the age of thirty-two, Coolidge courted and wed Grace Goodhue, a teacher at the local school for the deaf and dumb. Her charm and vivacious personality were a perfect foil to his lack of, and disregard for, the social graces. Theirs was a happy and contented marriage, each understanding and accepting the foibles of the other. They had two sons, John and Calvin, Jr., who completed the family.

In 1906, Coolidge was elected to the Massachusetts House of Representatives, where the same qualities that had served him so well in Northampton led to his slow but steady rise to leadership. Coolidge was elected mayor of Northampton in 1910; in 1912, he was elected to the state Senate; and two years later, was chosen president of the state Senate. The next logical step was the office of lieutenant governor, to which he was elected in 1916, and in 1918, he was elected governor of Massachusetts.

Life's Work

Events conspired to make Governor Coolidge a national figure. The labor unrest which followed the end of World War I produced the Boston police strike in 1919. Though the strike was settled largely without the intervention of the governor, Coolidge captured the imagination of the country and the convictions of the time with a dramatic phrase in a telegram sent to American Federation of Labor president Samuel Gompers: "There is no right to strike against the public safety by anybody, anywhere, any time." This statement catapulted Coolidge into national prominence and made him the popular choice for vice president among the delegates to the Republican National Convention in 1920. Safely elected with President Warren G. Harding in the Republican return to "normalcy," Coolidge gave undistinguished service in an undistinguished office.

Calvin Coolidge had no part in the scandals which pervaded the Harding Administration. He remained untouched by the revelations of bribery and misuse of high office. When he succeeded to the presidency upon the death of Warren G. Harding in 1923, he seemed to represent the incorruptible side of a tarnished Republican coin. As if to symbolize his virtues, Coolidge, visiting his home in Vermont when he learned of Harding's death, was sworn in as president by his father (a notary public) in the light of a kerosene lamp. The rugged simplicity of the swearing in was in sharp contrast to the bright urban lights and fast-paced life that seemed more typical of the 1920's. Coolidge made no changes in Harding's cabinet. He came especially under the influence of Secretary of the Treasury Andrew W. Mellon, who represented the established wealth that was, to Coolidge, the result of success in America. Coolidge particularly identified his and the country's interests with the class represented by Mellon in his most often quoted statement that "the business of America is business."

Coolidge presided over a government largely retreating from the activism and reform of the Progressive Era and from the demands of victory in World War I. He was personally honest, loyal, and frugal—and he served as the keeper of America's conscience. While the nation indulged itself in an orgy of spendthrift frivolity, the silent approval of so austere a president seemed to make virtuous an otherwise hedonistic attitude toward life.

Coolidge was personally popular and was always an adroit politician, so it was with ease that he was nominated for president in his own right in 1924. These same factors, supported by an accelerating prosperity and aided by a seriously divided Democratic Party (whose nominating convention cast 103 ballots before deciding upon John W. Davis of West Virginia as their candidate), led to a Republican victory. The Coolidge years saw decreasing governmental activity and few legislative accomplishments. Coolidge vetoed one of the few major bills of the era, the McNary-Haugen bill, which was designed to bring stability to the farm market. He continued the traditional high tariff policy supported by the Republicans, and both his policy and his pronouncements encouraged the upward movement of the stock market that characterized his years as president.

Coolidge vigorously supported economy in the operation of the government. He believed that a reduction in government costs, while beneficial in its own right, would also make possible a reduction in taxes, particularly for the business classes. He mildly favored railroad consolidation in the interest of greater efficiency and was interested in a waterways project in the St. Lawrence area (though never the Mussel Shoals project proposed during his term, which formed the base of the future Tennessee Valley Authority). In spite of a growing reputation as "Silent Cal," Coolidge held frequent and often lengthy press conferences during his years as president.

In foreign policy, Coolidge, like his party, opposed American membership in the League of Nations. He did, however, unsuccessfully support American participation and membership in the World Court. In line with his respect for business, Coolidge staunchly demanded that European nations repay to the United States their debts from World War I. He supported efforts to work out a schedule of payments (tied to the payment of German reparations), and he believed that the payment of the valid debts was necessary to provide worldwide economic stability. He was also a strong advocate of the Kellogg-Briand Pact and its effort to promote peace by outlawing the use of war as a national policy.

Coolidge's personal popularity, combined with the continuing prosperity of the nation during his administration, made him seem a logical candidate for renomination in 1928. Therefore, it was a stunning surprise when, while on vacation in 1927, he informed reporters that "I do not choose to run for President in 1928." It was a statement on which he never elaborated and from which he never deviated. Many contemporaries believed that he wanted another full term but wanted to be drafted by his party. Others believed that the decision stemmed from a reluctance to violate the two-term tradition (since he had already served the remainder of Harding's term). For others, it seemed that the death of his youngest son in the White House had taken much of the joy from public life, and he seemed tired of holding office. Whatever the reason, the decision was never effectively challenged, and the Republicans turned to Secretary of Commerce Herbert Clark Hoover as their candidate in 1928.

Coolidge and his wife left the White House in the same quiet style which had always characterized their life. Coolidge refused many offers of employment, lest his name and former position be used to advertise a business. He and Grace returned to Northampton, where, for the first time in all of their years of marriage, Coolidge finally purchased a house. He kept busy writing his autobiography, as well as a number of magazine articles, and served on several committees. He died quietly and alone of a coronary thrombosis on January 5, 1933.

Summary

With the advent of the Great Depression in 1929, the Roaring Twenties, the Coolidge Era, came to an end. Coolidge was deeply concerned about the effect of the Depression, especially so for those whose losses were heavy. Yet he had always had a clear perception of credit as another form of debt and was, himself, largely untouched by the crash. Far more a Hamiltonian than a Jeffersonian in his philosophy of government, Coolidge supported the interests of property as necessary for the stability of the government. He believed that a healthy business environment was essential to the national well-being of the United States. Coolidge was personally frugal, always saving a part of his salary no matter how small, and he carried that same commitment to frugality with him into government.

Coolidge believed that government should not intrude in the daily lives of its citizens. It is one of the great ironies of American history that his years of inactivity at the head of the nation helped to pave the way for the enlarged role of government which the New Deal of President Franklin D. Roosevelt brought about in an effort to recover from the Depression.

The decade of the 1920's was unique in American history. Presiding over this boisterous era was an essentially shy little man; competent, respectable, cautious, loyal, and honest. These were qualities of character held in high regard by Americans even as they flouted them. Coolidge was always an intensely political person—a quality often overlooked as more flamboyant personalities strutted on center stage. He had a politician's sensitivity to the public's needs and wishes. He captured in himself those qualities Americans both desired and trusted—an island of stability and old-fashioned virtue in an ocean of new values.

Coolidge Prosperity was more than simply a campaign slogan. It was a very real perception of cause and effect, and much of Coolidge's popularity stemmed from that perception. Coolidge was an enormously popular president—popular more as a symbol than as an individual whose idiosyncrasies and foibles were well-known and well loved. He was precisely suited to the public temperament in the 1920's, and perhaps he could have succeeded in no other era. His personality and philosophy could not have provided effective leadership for either the surging reforms of the Progressive Era or the demands for an enlarged government under the New Deal. Rather, he provided a period of rest and retreat from government activity.

Calvin Coolidge was not a great president; neither was he a failure. He was a man unusually suited to an unusual time. More a symbol of an imagined past—in which simplicity, honesty, and frugality were cherished—than a reflection of the roaring rush of modernity that characterized the 1920's, Coolidge gave Americans what they wanted, though the lesson of history might suggest that he was not exactly what they needed.

Bibliography
Abels, Jules. *In The Time of Silent Cal.* New York: G. P. Putnam's Sons, 1969. Excellent brief survey of Coolidge, the man, and a useful analysis of the years in which he served the United States.
Allen, Frederick Lewis. *Only Yesterday.* New York: Harper and Row, Publishers, 1931. An indispensable contemporary account of the 1920's. Has little comment on Coolidge but is valuable for the insights and the immediacy of its portrayal of those times.
Bradford, Gamaliel. *The Quick and the Dead.* Boston: Houghton Mifflin Co., 1931. With his usual wit and perspicacity, Bradford profiles Coolidge, as well as others, who marched more colorfully across the stage of American history.
Coolidge, Calvin. *The Autobiography of Calvin Coolidge.* New York: Cosmopolitan Book Corp., 1929. The length of this work certainly refutes the idea of an always "Silent Cal." It offers some insights into the mind and philosophy of this generally unknown president. Like most autobiographies, it must be read with caution and supplemented by other, more objective works.
Fuess, Claude Moore. *Calvin Coolidge: The Man from Vermont.* Boston: Little, Brown and Co., 1940. A lively, well-written account of a not-so-lively man. It is, however, very partisan toward Coolidge and needs to be balanced by other works.
Hicks, John D. *Republican Ascendancy, 1921-1933.* New York: Harper and Row, Publishers, 1960. An excellent book for background on the 1920's from a governmental and political perspective.
Hoover, Irvin Hood. *Forty-two Years in the White House.* Boston: Houghton Mifflin Co., 1934. The always lively account of life behind the scenes at the White House written by chief usher "The" Hoover. He did not particularly like Calvin Coolidge, and his comments provide a useful, though not

always to be trusted, view of Coolidge's personal life.

Murray, Robert K. *The Politics of Normalcy: Governmental Theory and Practice in the Harding-Coolidge Era.* New York: W. W. Norton and Co., 1973. Yet another excellent account of the 1920's, with an emphasis upon the part played by Coolidge. There are not many available biographies of Coolidge, and books such as this one on the 1920's are thus especially valuable to the student.

Thompson, Charles Willis. *Presidents I've Known and Two Near Presidents.* Freeport, N.Y.: Books for Library Press, 1956. Moderately useful personal view of Calvin Coolidge with less insight into his impact on his time.

White, William Allen. *A Puritan in Babylon: The Story of Calvin Coolidge.* New York: Macmillan, 1938. An excellent standard biography of Coolidge. White was well acquainted with Coolidge and admired him, so this book also should be balanced by a less admiring view. White's verbose style somewhat dates this book, but his talent and insight make it well worth reading.

Carlanna L. Hendrick

JAMES FENIMORE COOPER

Born: September 15, 1789; Burlington, New Jersey
Died: September 14, 1851; Cooperstown, New York
Area of Achievement: Literature
Contribution: Cooper pioneered the historical novel based on American themes and characters. He also wrote the first sea novel. In his fiction and nonfiction, he proved himself an astute social critic of the excesses of democracy.

Early Life

The eleventh child of William Cooper and Elizabeth Fenimore Cooper, James Cooper—he was to add the Fenimore in 1826—was born in Burlington, New Jersey, on September 15, 1789. When Cooper was thirteen months old, the family left the urban Burlington for the wilderness at the southern shore of Ostego Lake. Here William Cooper built Ostego Hall and developed the surrounding area as Cooperstown. This frontier village would serve as the model of Templeton in *The Pioneers* (1823), as the novelist's father would become the aristocratic Judge Temple in that novel and Ostego Lake turn into Lake Glimmerglass. By the time the Coopers settled in New York, the Indians had departed; Cooper's Indians derive from books, not personal knowledge. The wilderness remained, though, and figured prominently in many of his novels.

Cooperstown soon established a local academy, which Cooper attended before going to Albany to study under the Reverend William Ellison. In 1803, Cooper entered Yale. At the age of thirteen, he was more interested in pranks than studies. After blowing up a classmate's door with gunpowder, Cooper was expelled.

The following year, he was sent to sea aboard the *Stirling*, where he encountered a series of adventures he would later use in his nautical novels. Off the coast of Portugal, the ship was pursued by pirates. Entering British waters, they found themselves no safer. With the Napoleonic Wars raging, Britain was impressing American seamen into its navy; the *Stirling* was boarded and several sailors removed.

Cooper returned safely to the United States, where he was eligible for a commission as midshipman in the navy. His first assignment was to a ship in dry dock in New York; his second was to a ship still under construction on Lake Ontario. Eager to see active service in open water, he maneuvered to secure a berth aboard the *Wasp*, an eighteen-gun sloop. Again, though, he was disappointed, for the commanding officer was so impressed with the midshipman that he made him his recruiting officer, a post that required Cooper to remain onshore. Despite this series of disappointments, Cooper had learned much about ships, and this knowledge found its way into both his fiction and his nonfiction.

In December, 1809, Cooper's father died; in May, 1810, Cooper therefore requested a twelve-month furlough to attend to family business. This business included wooing Susan Augusta DeLancey, daughter of a country squire. On January 1, 1811, the two were married.

Cooper had promised Susan that he would surrender his commission in the navy, so he turned his attention to earning a living as a gentleman farmer and speculator. Between 1813 and 1819, his six siblings died, making him heir to his father's extensive land holdings but also leaving him responsible for his brothers' dependents and debts. As he struggled with these various financial difficulties, a happy accident changed the course of his life and of American letters as well.

Life's Work

In 1820, the Coopers were living in Scarsdale. Among the popular recreations of the family was reading aloud. One day, Cooper began Jane Austen's *Persuasion* (1818). After a few pages, Cooper threw the book down in disgust and announced, "I could write you a better book than that myself." Since Cooper disliked any writing, even letters, his wife expressed her incredulity and challenged him to make good his boast. The result was *Precaution* (1820).

In itself, this first book is not noteworthy, for the work is a novel of manners typical of female British writers of the period. *Precaution* is important, though, because it launched Cooper's literary career. He next turned his attention to an American theme, though he found the writing difficult. As he wrote to Andrew Thompson Goodrich, "The task of making American manners and American scenes interesting to an American reader is an arduous one—I am unable to say whether I shall succeed or not." The popular response to *The Spy* (1821) resolved any doubts. The book quickly went through three editions and was adapted for the New York stage; a French translation appeared within a year. Critical appraisals were equally favorable: The *North American Review* called Cooper "the first who deserved the appellation of a distinguished American novel writer."

The novel was based on the actual life of a spy who served under John Jay during the American Revolution. Harvey Birch's wanderings between the British and American lines in Westchester County allowed Cooper to depict the landscape and manners of New York. The book is American in more than setting, though. Unlike the heroes of British fiction, Birch is an outsider, who, despite heroism and integrity, is never integrated into society.

With his next novel, *The Pioneers*, Cooper struck an even more responsive chord. The book sold some three thousand copies on the day of publication and introduced a character as enduring as Robinson Crusoe. Natty Bumppo, the pioneer, is a mythic figure whose image was to descend through the dime novels of Erastus F. Beadle to the Lone Ranger (whose companionship with Tonto mirrors Bumppo's relationship with the Indian Chingachgook) and similar television and film heroes. In this self-reliant frontiersman, Cooper produced an archetypal American and a microcosm of the nation moving ever westward.

The Pioneers was the first of five novels collectively known as the Leatherstocking Tales, which together trace Bumppo's life from his youth (*The Deerslayer*, 1841) in the 1740's to his death on the Great Plains in 1804 (*The Prairie*, 1827). Not only did Cooper create the mythic pioneer in these works but also he painted a mythic frontier that was to reappear in the histories of Francis Parkman and Frederick Jackson Turner. This frontier is majestic and overwhelming. Armies enter the wilderness to emerge as tattered remnants. The small forts are dwarfed by their harsh, rugged surroundings.

In this setting, Cooper plays out the conflict between savage Indians and the forces of white civilization. Cooper's novels thus serve as an apology for the displacement of the American Indians, many of whom, like the Iroquois and Sioux, are portrayed as too evil to deserve survival. Not all of Cooper's Indians are bad; he incorporates the myth of the noble savage into his descriptions of the Delaware and the Pawnee tribes. These good Indians, though, are doomed by their very virtues, which render them easy prey to less scrupulous members of both the white and red races. Further, despite their nobility, they remain savage.

Though Cooper's frontier novels justify the conquest of the West, they also recognize the tragic consequences. The Indians are displaced, but so are the pioneers. Natty Bumppo's life is a series of migrations westward, because he brings a civilization that cannot tolerate his ways. Nor is Cooper unaware of the beauty of this wilderness vanishing beneath the ax of civilization. When Judith Hunter in *The Deerslayer* asks Bumppo where his love is, he replies,

> She's in the forest, Judith—hanging from the boughs of the trees, in a soft rain—in the dew on the open grass . . . and in all the other glorious gifts that come from God's Providence.

Cooper's next novel also broke new ground. At a dinner party in New York City, Cooper's companions of the Bread and Cheese Club were praising Sir Walter Scott's *The Pirate* (1822) for its realism. Scott, unlike Cooper, had never been to sea; Cooper quickly demonstrated numerous flaws in the work. When challenged to do better, Cooper responded with *The Pilot* (1824). Though Cooper is best remembered as a writer of the frontier, he was to produce eleven nautical novels, all replete with precise detail; later writers of the sea, among them Herman Melville and Joseph Conrad, praised Cooper's efforts in this area. Set, like *The Spy*, during the American Revolution, *The Pilot* was also successful.

Cooper's popularity led to his appointment to the committee that welcomed the Marquis de Lafayette when he returned to the United States in 1824. In that year, too, Columbia University recognized his achievements by awarding him an honorary master of arts degree.

The Last of the Mohicans (1826), another of the Leatherstocking Tales, further enhanced his reputation. In 1826, on the eve of his departure for Europe, Cooper was feted by the Bread and Cheese Club. Among those present were De Witt Clinton, governor of New York; General Winfield Scott; Charles King, later to be president of Columbia University; and James Kent, former chancellor and chief justice of New York. In one toast, King placed Cooper on the same level as Sir Walter Scott; in another, Kent called Cooper "the genius which has rendered our native soil classic ground, and given to our early history the enchantment of fiction."

Cooper went to Europe nominally as American consul to Lyon, but his real intent was to see Europe and to arrange for the publication of his novels abroad. While in Europe, Cooper was urged by Lafayette to dispel certain misconceptions about the United States. The result was *Notions of the Americans* (1828), a glowing account of his native land. At Lafayette's prompting, he also involved himself in a pamphlet war between French monarchists and republicans.

Despite his defense of democracy, Cooper's reputation was declining in the United States. He was criticized for intervening in the political affairs of France, and his European novels—*The Bravo* (1831), *The Heidenmauer* (1832), and *The Headsman* (1833)—were not well received back home. By the time he returned to the United States on November 5, 1833, he was no longer the hero he had been seven years earlier. Nor was he pleased with what he regarded as the excesses of democracy that had accompanied the presidency of Andrew Jackson. In *A Letter to His Countrymen* (1834), Cooper began a series of criticisms of the United States, and he announced his retirement as a novelist.

He was to return to fiction in 1838, but he was not idle during the intervening years, publishing a series of travel books and a social satire on both England and the United States, *The Monikins* (1835). In his European novels, Cooper had warned his countrymen to beware of oligarchies and not to sacrifice their freedoms to powerful commercial interests. Now that he was home, he saw greater danger to the Republic from the lower, rather than the upper, classes. *The American Democrat* (1838) offers Cooper's clearest vision of the United States, where "acts of tyranny can only proceed from the publick. The publick, then, is to be watched in this country, as, in other countries, kings and aristocrats are to be watched." He still believed in democracy as the best form of government, but his ideal democracy was Jeffersonian, not Jacksonian. Merit should have the chance to succeed regardless of pedigree, but the natural aristocrat should govern. While people should enjoy equality under the law, social distinctions should remain.

The American Democrat aroused little controversy, but the two novels issued that year to incorporate its ideas received harsh treatment: *Homeward Bound* and *Home as Found* were sharply attacked in the press. Cooper's aristocratic appearance did not help his popularity, either. In Mathew Brady's photograph he looks like a stern autocrat, with high forehead, penetrating gaze, Roman nose, and firm chin.

As the new decade began, Cooper briefly regained his popularity when he produced the last two of the Leatherstocking Tales, *The Pathfinder* (1840) and *The Deerslayer*. His next two novels, *The Two Admirals* (1842) and *The Wing-and-Wing* (1842), also mark a return to his earliest writing, in this case the sea adventure.

He could not keep away from controversy for very long, though. In 1839, the Antirent War began in New York, as tenants insisted on owning their land instead of renting it. Cooper's sympathies were with the landowners, and the Littlepage novels—*Satanstoe* (1845), *The Chainbearer* (1845), and *The Redskins* (1846)—justify their position. Cooper was as disgusted with the politicians as with the tenants, and in his preface to *The Redskins*, he wrote that if the government could not curb the antirent faction, the sooner that government was abolished, the better.

Cooper's next novel, *The Crater* (1847), allowed him to achieve that wish, at least in fiction. An island arises in the South Pacific, and at first its government is a perfect Jeffersonian democracy. With the arrival of lawyers, journalists, and Fundamentalist preachers—all of whom Cooper regarded as the bane of American life—this ideal is corrupted. As if in divine retribution, the island then sinks back into the ocean.

Despite Cooper's long-standing feud with his countrymen, after his death at Cooperstown on September 14, 1851, Washington Irving arranged a memorial tribute for him in New York City. William Cullen Bryant delivered the eulogy, Daniel Webster attended, and leading literary figures sent tributes. Whatever the editorialists and general public thought of him, these men recognized the great contribution that Cooper had made to American letters.

Summary

In *Notions of the Americans*, Cooper complained that the United States did not offer material for a national literature. In his thirty-two novels, though, Cooper gave the lie to this statement. He proved that the United States did offer the fabric for the romancer and dramatist to create a truly American literature.

Cooper's novels are American not only because of their setting but also because of their characters: pioneers, Indians, slaves, and the hero who is an outsider, shunning and shunned by society. The themes, too, are native; even when they criticize contemporary society they do so from the perspective of the ideals of the Founding Fathers.

Cooper, however, did not simply create American novels; he also created an audience for them. Early in the nineteenth century, Sidney Smith had asked in *The Edinburgh Review*, "Who reads an American book?" He might have asked, too, "Who publishes an American book?" Cooper's own publisher, Carey of Philadelphia, had issued only two American novels before 1820. Between 1830 and 1840, it published 142. Other publishers in this country followed suit, and abroad Cooper's novels were printed in more than thirty cities.

As such works as *The History of the Navy of the United States of America* (1839) demonstrate, Cooper knew history and could present it well. His historical novels are not so much history, though, as myth. They established the prevailing image of the Indian as treacherous foe or doomed noble savage. They created the fiction of the empty wilderness waiting for the white man to settle it and so fueled the imagination of those who sought to fulfill America's manifest destiny to rule from sea to sea. Drawing on the already existing stories about Daniel Boone, Cooper provided in Natty Bumppo the American hero, whom Henry Nash Smith in *Virgin Land* (1957) calls "the most important symbol of the national experience of adventure across the continent."

Quintessentially American, Cooper nevertheless saw the dangers of rampant democracy. His social criticism was not popular, but it established a literary mode that, like his frontier and nautical novels, influenced later writers. William Dean Howells, Frank Norris, and Sinclair Lewis are but three who followed in this mode. Like his most famous creation, then, Cooper was indeed a pathfinder and pioneer.

Bibliography

Boynton, Henry Walcott. *James Fenimore Cooper*. New York: Century Co., 1931. Focuses on Cooper the man rather than Cooper the writer. Boynton notes Cooper's faults but tends to gloss over them or explain them away.

Franklin, Wayne. *The New World of James Fenimore Cooper*. Chicago: University of Chicago Press, 1982. Through a close reading of five of Cooper's novels—*The Pioneers*, *The Wept of Wish-ton-Wish* (1829), *Wyandotté* (1843), *The Crater* (1847), and *The Last of the Mohicans*—Franklin examines Cooper's attitude toward the frontier. Maintains that for Cooper, the wilderness begins as a place of hope and promise but ends as the source of tragedy.

McWilliams, John P. *Political Justice in a Republic: James Fenimore Cooper's America*. Berkeley: University of California Press, 1972. Argues that Cooper remained a dedicated republican all of his life. McWilliams shows that while Cooper's views are consistent, American society changed dramatically between 1820 and 1850 and hence produced a darkening vision in the fiction.

Railton, Stephen. *Fenimore Cooper: A Study in His Life and Imagination*. Princeton, N.J.: Princeton University Press, 1978. A psychological approach to Cooper's life. Railton sees Cooper as dominated by his father and reads the life and fiction in the light of an Oedipal complex.

Spiller, Robert Ernest. *Fenimore Cooper: Critic of His Times*. New York: Minton, Balch and Co., 1931. Concentrates on Cooper's social views and sees him as a writer who sought to analyze and express as well as criticize the United States of his day.

Walker, Warren S. *James Fenimore Cooper: An Introduction and Interpretation*. New York: Barnes and Noble, 1962. A biography organized around the various themes in Cooper's writing—the frontier, the sea, American democracy. A concluding chapter reviews critical response to Cooper from 1820 to the middle of the twentieth century.

Waples, Dorothy. *The Whig Myth of James Fenimore Cooper*. New Haven, Conn.: Yale University Press, 1938. Claims that many of the attacks on Cooper during his lifetime came from Whigs who distorted his character. Stresses Cooper's political views.

Joseph Rosenblum

AARON COPLAND

Born: November 14, 1900; Brooklyn, New York

Area of Achievement: Music
Contribution: Copland advanced the cause of music in America through a lifetime of musical composition and an unending concern for and promotion of a distinctly American music.

Early Life

Aaron Copland, the fifth and youngest child of Harris and Sarah Mittenthal Copland, was born on November 14, 1900, in Brooklyn, New York, to a family neither musically gifted nor extraordinarily devoted to music. Both of Copland's parents were Jewish immigrants from Lithuania, each emigrating to the United States as a child; they met and married in Brooklyn in 1885. Two years later, Copland's father opened a family-run department store, above which the Copland family lived and where Aaron was to spend the first twenty years of his life.

Copland led a fairly typical childhood, attending public grammar school, working part-time in the family store, and attending summer camp. From 1914 to 1918, he attended and was graduated from Boys' High School. His musical training began rather late for one who was to go on to become an accomplished composer and musician. Since Copland's parents had provided each of his four older siblings with music lessons and believed that none had derived any benefit from them, they were less than willing to make a similar expenditure for their youngest child. Consequently, when Copland was eleven years old, he began to learn the piano from his older sister, Laurine. This experiment lasted no more than six months, after which Copland was left to his own devices with the piano. After more than two years of this self-study, Copland's parents finally consented to his wish to take formal piano lessons, provided he secure the teacher on his own. At age fourteen, therefore, Copland arranged to take lessons with Leopold Wolfsohn in Brooklyn, and so began the formal training of one of America's finest musicians.

After Copland expressed interest in becoming a composer, Wolfsohn helped him secure harmony lessons in Manhattan with Rubin Goldmark in September of 1917. With Goldmark, Copland received conventional theoretical training in counterpoint and composition for the next four years. Wolfsohn was eventually replaced as Copland's piano teacher by Victor Wittgenstein, also of Manhattan. In addition, Copland began at this time to attend performances by the New York Symphony and concerts held at the Brooklyn Academy of Music, taking particular interest in the new music arriving from Europe, especially the works of Maurice Ravel and Claude Debussy.

Upon graduation from high school in 1918, Copland decided against attending college in order to pursue his musical studies full-time. His parents agreed to support his interest for a short time, hoping that he would eventually tire of composing and go on to college. For Copland, however, there would be no turning back. Although still quite young, he had already developed a strong interest in French music and the modern school, and he was eager to go to France himself. When an older friend, Aaron Schaffer, went to Paris to attend the Sorbonne, Copland's desire to go to France was heightened all the more. Meanwhile, at Goldmark's suggestion, Copland left Wittgenstein to study piano with Clarence Adler in the winter of 1919. He continued to work with Adler until early 1921.

In the spring of 1921, Copland read an advertisement in *Musical America* for the Summer School of Music for American Students at Fontainebleau, France. Upon application, Copland was awarded one of nine tuition scholarships to attend the three-month summer school, to commence in June of 1921. With further support from his parents, it was agreed that Copland would spend one year in France pursuing his musical studies. The three months Copland spent at Fontainebleau, where he studied composition under Paul Vidal and piano with Ricardo Viñes, were the only months Copland spent in a formal music school. While there, a fellow student introduced Copland to the composition teacher Nadia Boulanger, who was to have considerable impact on his career and development as a composer. He began to study formally with Boulanger in August, 1921, and through her met many of the leading musicians of Paris as well as other American composers, such as Virgil Thomson, Melville Smith, and George Antheil. During the closing ceremonies of the Fontainebleau school session one month later, in September, 1921, Copland performed a piece he had written in 1920, "The Cat and the Mouse." Jacques Durand of the French publishing firm Durand and Son was in the audience and offered to buy world rights to the piece for five hundred francs (about thirty-five dollars), to which an elated Copland agreed. In December of that same year, Copland competed for the Prix de Paris at the Institut de Paris and received an honorable mention for his efforts. Soon after, his professional premiere took place at the Salle des Agriculteurs.

While in Europe, Copland took in as many concerts, films, and theater performances as possible. During holiday and summer seasons, he traveled extensively to places such as Vienna, Salzburg, Berlin, Rome, Florence, and Milan, and his projected one year in Paris extended eventually to three years abroad. By January, 1923, the Société Musicale Indépendante performed for the first time a Copland piece (his *Passacaglia*), and the student composer had entered the ranks of the professionals.

Life's Work

Before leaving Paris in 1924, Copland was introduced by his teacher, Boulanger, to the famous composer Serge Koussevitsky, who in America would become a principal mentor and support to Copland. It was Koussevitsky, as conductor of the Boston Symphony, who would conduct many first performances of Copland's work in the many years to follow their meeting in Paris.

When Copland arrived back in his native New York, he was eager to launch his professional career. Faced with the need to earn a living, he advertised his services as a piano instructor, only to find not a single student to respond to his venture. Despite this rather surprising outcome, Copland was able to secure, through a friend with connections to the board of directors of the New York League of Composers, an audition with the League. The board accepted two of Copland's piano pieces for a November, 1924, concert, which was to be the first performance in America of his work. Through this audition, Copland met music critic and writer Paul Rosenfeld, who was able to secure a year's subsidy for the young composer from Mrs. Alma Wertheim, of the Morganthau family, thus enabling Copland to concentrate wholly upon his musical compositions.

Although Copland valued his sojourn in Europe and his exposure to its music, he felt the need to develop a more specifically American sound in his own compositions. Accordingly, he turned his attention toward adopting jazz to symphonic music. One of the compositional highlights of this early phase in his career was his famous *Music for the Theater*, first performed by the Boston Symphony Orchestra in November, 1925. In it, Copland separated his manner of composition from the European style, creating what many have labeled a distinctly American style based on the jazz idiom.

The first Guggenheim fellowship in musical composition was awarded to Copland in October, 1925, providing him with a year's stipend of twenty-five hundred dollars. This fellowship was renewed in October, 1926, for another year's support. With this funding, Copland returned to Paris, in March, 1926, to participate in a concert of American music at the Société Musicale Indépendante. It was there that he met Roger Sessions, with whom he was to found, in 1928, the Copland-Sessions Concerts.

With the January, 1927, performance of Copland's *Concerto for Piano and Orchestra* to mixed reviews in Symphony Hall, Boston, he began to turn his attention away from jazz and toward a search for new mediums. His output decreased somewhat, but his musical experimentation increased as he sought new directions for his American sound. Meanwhile, with his Guggenheim stipend due to expire in October, 1927, Copland took a position as lecturer at the New School for Social Research in New York City. He was to maintain this connection with the New School for the next decade, lecturing on and arranging concerts of modern music.

To further the cause of American music and bring recognition to younger American composers, Copland and his fellow musician Sessions organized a series of concerts between 1928 and 1931 in New York City known as the

Copland-Sessions Concerts. All were dedicated to the performance of works by younger American composers of merit.

As the Depression descended upon America, not only were there fewer performances of Copland's work, but also much of his newer compositional work was of an experimental nature, difficult to play and to understand at that time for layperson and musician alike. In June, 1930, Copland received five thousand dollars in prize money from an RCA-Victor Symphonic Award, which he used to travel to Europe, Africa, Mexico, and within the United States. He also made plans for an American music festival similar to those held in Europe. These plans became reality when, from April 30 to May 1, 1932, the Yaddo Festival of American Music was held.

Copland's most prolific period as a composer began in the mid-1930's, when he began to create music useful to and enjoyed by the American public. This period is often known as his "music for use" (*Gebrauchsmusik*) phase and is characterized by music of a functional nature. In all, Copland produced nearly forty scores during this time: pieces for high school groups, folk pieces, radio commissions, ballet, film, theater, and opera scores, and even two children's piano pieces. His most popular works of this period include *The Second Hurricane* (1937) and *El Salón México* (two-piano version, 1935; orchestral version, 1937). Although his popular image soared, Copland did not forfeit completely his more abstract themes, continuing to work on his Third Symphony, which he completed eventually in 1946, as well as other works geared toward concert-hall audiences.

When the United States entered World War II, Copland turned his musical abilities to the service of his country. He was sent by the State Department as an ambassador of goodwill to Latin America in 1941 and again in 1947. His trip was financed by yet another Guggenheim grant in the early 1940's, and he succeeded in opening the American musical world to many talented Latin American musicians while at the same time exposing himself to new musical idioms which would eventually find their way into his later compositions. During this same decade, Copland also became involved with the Berkshire Music Center (at Tanglewood, Massachusetts) at the request of his friend and mentor, Koussevitsky. Copland took on the position of assistant director of the center and head of the Composition Department. He was to be associated with the intense six-week sessions at Tanglewood for nearly twenty-five years after his initial summer in 1940.

As the 1950's approached, Copland began to try his hand at conducting, not merely his own work but also the work of other American musicians. In this capacity, Copland traveled throughout the world for the next twenty years; a valuable collection of recordings of his music under his direction has been created.

After the 1960's, Copland's musical output slowed. With one exception (his *Duo for Flute and Piano*), all of his later works have been reworkings of

older compositions which remained unpublished. Recognition of his undis-
puted status as the finest of American composers was forthcoming in 1961
with the first of several invitations to visit the White House. More than
twenty years later, in 1985, Copland's unrivaled status in American musical
history was again acknowledged, when, on the occasion of the composer's
approaching eighty-fifth birthday, two Copland retrospectives were held: one
by the New York Philharmonic Orchestra, under the direction of Zubin
Mehta, and the other by the Los Angeles Philharmonic Orchestra, under the
direction of Erich Leinsdorf.

Summary

Aaron Copland would have contributed greatly to creating a world-class
American music if he had never ventured beyond his musical compositions.
Copland, however, is far more than a great American composer; he is the
guardian of music in America. What he could not convey or teach through
his compositions or lectures he would try to convey through the written
word. His extensive literary efforts, which include four books and more than
sixty articles and critical essays on music, are all geared toward promoting
the cause of music, especially music in America, to the general public as well
as to the professional music world. Copland himself stated the purpose of his
first book, *What to Listen for in Music* (1939, 1957), as an explanation to the
general public of the fundamentals of intelligent listening to music.

Copland's list of honors is the finest indicator of his place in American
music. From Guggenheim fellowships to the Pulitzer Prize in music in 1945
for his *Appalachian Spring* and the Academy Award in 1950 for his film score
for *The Heiress*, Copland has been repeatedly honored for his eclectic and
valuable contributions to American music. Although Copland never was to
give up his obsession with composing and return to his formal education, as
his parents had hoped in his youth, his skill and renown were to place him as
an instructor in both the New School for Social Research and Harvard
University and as recipient of honorary degrees from such prestigious American universities as Princeton University and Harvard University.

Bibliography

Berger, Arthur. *Aaron Copland*. New York: Oxford University Press, 1953.
    Berger attempts to familiarize the reader with both the music and the per-
    son of Aaron Copland. The book is divided into two major parts, the first
    dealing with the life and accomplishments of Copland and the second deal-
    ing with the more technical aspects of his music.
Butterworth, Neil. *The Music of Aaron Copland*. New York: Universe
    Books, 1985. Primarily an examination of Copland as composer, Butter-
    worth's monograph is meant to provide an introduction to Copland's music
    for the general reader as well as to the musically inclined, although the

sophistication of the study makes it more suitable for the latter. Well illustrated with useful appendices.

Copland, Aaron. *Copland on Music.* Garden City, N.Y.: Doubleday and Co., 1960. In this third of his four books, Copland has compiled various essays he wrote on music from the 1930's through the 1950's.

_____. *Music and Imagination.* Cambridge, Mass.: Harvard University Press, 1952. This last of Copland's books is a collection of the six lectures Copland delivered as the Charles Eliot Norton Professor at Harvard University in 1951.

_____. *Our New Music: Leading Composers in Europe and America.* New York: McGraw Hill Book Co., 1941. Copland presents here a compilation of essays on contemporary European and American composers and of the emerging American musicians.

_____. *What to Listen for in Music.* New York: McGraw-Hill Book Co., 1939, 1957. Copland wrote this book to explain clearly the fundamentals of music—rhythm, melody, and harmony—in an attempt to increase the intelligent enjoyment of music by the growing American music public.

Copland, Aaron, and Vivian Perlis. *Copland: 1900 Through 1942.* New York: St. Martin's Press/Marek, 1984. An autobiography of Copland, intended as a first volume of his life, based on the presumption that knowledge of an artist's life enhances the enjoyment and understanding of his art. This volume begins with Copland's birth and concludes with the early World War II years. Included are commentaries by various people closely associated with Copland's life and career.

Dobrin, Arnold. *Aaron Copland: His Life and Times.* New York: Thomas Y. Crowell, 1967. A simple narrative of Copland's life and musical development, covering his earliest childhood to his entry into the professional music scene and his advancement to a place of prominence in the American and international music world.

Smith, Julia. *Aaron Copland: His Work and Contribution to American Music.* New York: E. P. Dutton and Co., 1955. The first thorough study of Copland and still a reliable reference for his early life. Smith does not separate Copland's work from his life in this musical-critical study, examining instead his life and work simultaneously.

Maureen A. Harp

JOHN SINGLETON COPLEY

Born: July 3, 1738; Boston, Massachusetts
Died: September 9, 1815; London, England
Area of Achievement: Painting
Contribution: Copley achieved a striking realism in his portraits and a vibrant excitement in his historical paintings. In gaining international acclaim, he showed that America could have a distinguished cultural life.

Early Life

John Singleton Copley's English ancestors migrated to Ireland in the 1660's. His parents, Mary Singleton and Richard Copley, were married there in 1735, and then came to Boston about a year later, where they ran a tobacco shop. Richard Copley died a few years later. John Singleton Copley, who had been born in 1738, was still a small boy, and his mother was left to run the tobacco shop alone. They lived in very modest circumstances until the boy was ten.

When his mother remarried in 1748, the boy's life took a crucial turn. His new stepfather was Peter Pelham (c. 1695-1751), who already had something of an artistic career under way. He had been a moderately successful mezzotint engraver in London for some years when he decided to emigrate to Boston in 1727. There he found little public interest in his engravings for a while, but he was a versatile man who undertook various other activities to make a living, including teaching.

Pelham had a number of artistic friends, including the distinguished portraitist John Smibert (1688-1751), whom he had known in London. Smibert was the foremost of a number of painters who were in Boston at the time, doing portraits and family groups from which engravings were often made. All of them, including Robert Feke (c. 1705-c. 1750), John Greenwood (1727-1792), and Joseph Badger (1708-1765), were household acquaintances of the Pelham family. Their influence on the talented and impressionable boy can be seen in the early work he did in his own artistic career.

The young Copley was a studious, industrious, somewhat introverted person, who read his stepfather's books on art and learned to use the engraver's tools. He was rather a good-looking boy who could manage the pleasant expression and good manners expected of him, while, like many teenagers, in his private thoughts he resented the great limitations of the provincial community in which he lived. Some time later, he expressed this resentment by declaring that in Boston painting was regarded mainly as a way of preserving likenesses of favored persons. The people seemed to think of painting, he complained, as simply another trade, like that of a carpenter, tailor, or shoemaker, rather than as one of the noble arts of the world.

Into this household a son, Henry Pelham, was born, in 1749. Then, in

December, 1751, Peter Pelham died. Copley, at thirteen, again had no father. While there were older stepbrothers, Copley felt strongly that he should do all he could to support his mother and the new half brother. Within a year or two, he used Pelham's tools and studio to produce a few portraits and other pictures. Thus, his artistic career was launched at an astonishingly early age, as he was driven by a combination of natural zest and ability for the work, and by adverse personal circumstances.

Life's Work

It was natural that the young Copley's first efforts at engraving and painting should be a virtual continuation, both in subject and in style, of the work of Peter Pelham. After doing only one engraving, however, he devoted himself exclusively to painting. For some time, his work was much like that of other artists; yet, already, there were subtle but distinct differences. His idea of the painter's art, prompted by his reading about the Renaissance and the various "old masters" of European fame, went well beyond the portraiture which dominated Colonial American fashion. He experimented with paintings from prints of scenes depicting classical mythology, but no one was much interested in them. Bostonians wanted portraits, and so he worked energetically to paint them. His portraits, beginning with one of his stepbrother, Charles Pelham (1754), were well received, and he was given frequent commissions within a short time. Among those early portraits were those of Joshua Winslow (1755), William Brattle (1756), and Mr. and Mrs. Jonathan Belcher (1756), all prominent members of society whose names are familiar to historians. He was still not twenty years old.

It was in the 1760's that his talent burst forth into genuine distinction. His portraits of the Reverend Edward Holyoke (1759-1761) and of Epes Sargent (1759-1761) show a striking realism and great insight into human nature, qualities which eventually became distinguished features of Copley's work. The young John Hancock had just inherited a fortune from his wealthy merchant uncle, Thomas Hancock, when he sat for a portrait by Copley (1765). He was very pleased, and this led to his request that Copley paint a portrait of his Uncle Thomas, to be presented to Harvard College, which had been a particular interest of the late merchant. That huge canvas, more than eight feet high, was praised by many people. Copley's fame was rising.

It was in 1765 that Copley painted the picture that changed his life, a portrait of his younger half brother, Henry Pelham; it later became known as *Boy with a Squirrel*. He sent this work to a friend in London, apparently hoping that a favorable reception of it would make him known beyond the Colonies, and it did. Exhibited in 1766, it was strongly praised by the great Sir Joshua Reynolds, and also by the brilliant young Benjamin West (also born in 1738), an American whose precocious achievements as a painter had brought him to Europe a few years earlier. Both offered constructive criticisms, relatively minor ones; West, for his part, also began a correspondence with Copley, in which he repeatedly urged the Bostonian to come to London. Yet Copley was making a large amount of money by this time, for he had become much in demand as the premier portraitist of America. On Thanksgiving Day, 1769, Copley married Susanna Farnham Clarke, daughter of the well-to-do Richard Clarke, a merchant and agent for the East India Company. It was a truly loving, solid marriage, which sustained both of them during the troublesome years that were to come. Three of their six children lived, as did their mother, beyond the age of ninety.

The times had become turbulent in Boston, especially since the Stamp Act riots (1765), boycotts, demonstrations by the radical Sons of Liberty, and, finally, the arrival of British troops to keep order. There was a confrontation with the troops in which five civilians were killed, soon known as the Boston Massacre (March, 1770); then came the destruction of East India Company property, remembered as the Boston Tea Party (December, 1773). Copley probably, in a general way, shared the hostility to British policies, but he did his best to stay out of politics. His wife's family and friends were nearly all Loyalists, some of them prominent and outspoken ones.

Copley's artistic talents at this time were still growing. He was doing more and more pastels, wherein his gift as a colorist became especially impressive. He went to New York at the behest of Myles Cooper, president of King's College (whose portrait he had painted when Cooper visited Boston). There, in seven months, he painted thirty-seven portraits, which included, he believed, some of his best work. Yet, as people in all social and political ranks became ever more preoccupied with the escalating troubles over British authority in America, the commissions became fewer. Copley had long had friends on both sides of the Anglo-American quarrels, but increasingly it was difficult to maintain neutrality.

At last, he made a difficult decision: He left Boston in June, 1774, for a study trip to Europe, the move which Benjamin West had urged so long as necessary for Copley's professional growth. Copley always insisted that he left Boston only to improve his art. Along with many people of the time, he probably believed that the political troubles would blow over, and he could return in a year or two to resume remunerative work. Instead, Parliament's policy became much more severe, and Americans reacted strongly, leading to actual war by April, 1775. Late in May, Copley's wife and children sailed for England; her Loyalist father and brothers came afterward. In October, Copley returned to London from his European tour, which had indeed been enriching, and there was a joyous family reunion. His American career was finished; he never returned to his native land.

Copley's English career began in most promising circumstances. His reputation in England was high, he had friends among the most prominent men in artistic circles, his work habits were excellent and well established, and he was eager to paint. At first, he painted mostly portraits, for the sake of income. Later, he was able to do the historical paintings for which Americans had shown little interest. The first of these, *Watson and the Shark* (1778), received high critical acclaim, and it was a quick popular success. This painting was soon followed by *The Death of the Earl of Chatham* (1779-1781), a bold effort to portray on a heroic scale a recent (1778) event. It was fraught with political danger (Chatham had his enemies), the setting of the picture (the House of Lords) was known to many, and there were fifty-five portraits of public figures in it. Nevertheless, it was a great success, and it assured Copley's reputation as one of the two great historical painters of the time. The other was his friend and fellow American, Benjamin West. Other historical paintings which followed were also praised, including *The Death of Major Peirson* (1782-1784) and *The Siege of Gibraltar* (1783-1791).

In 1783, Copley was admitted to full membership in the Royal Academy. He moved his family to a fine new house. He received permission (though not a commission) to paint members of the royal family. That painting, known as *The Three Youngest Daughters of King George III* (1785) would, he assumed, bring him actual royal commissions; at the least, it would surely bring much business from the highest nobility, who would be pleased to have portraits done by one who painted for the royal family. His painting received poor reviews, however, and, while he continued to paint portraits, rarely were his sitters from the upper nobility. At this time, Copley began to be plagued with other disappointments, as well. Both of the two children who had been born in England died within two weeks, late in 1785. Another picture was severely criticized in 1786. Copley had offended the Royal Academy when he exhibited his *Death of the Earl of Chatham* privately, before it could be shown in an Academy exhibition. Then, he repeated the offense with his huge *The Siege of Gibraltar* (it was truly a spectacle, nearly eighteen feet high and twenty-four feet wide), for which he had a huge tent erected for public exhibition. Finally, a rift began to develop between him and Benjamin West, whose political sagacity at least equaled his artistic talent, for he was on his way to becoming the president of the Royal Academy.

Copley continued his assiduous labors for the remainder of his life. Many of his last paintings were excellent, although none surpassed and few equaled his earlier best work. The prolonged wars with France (1793-1815) became more and more disruptive for Copley and his circle. His living costs remained high and even increased to the point at which they exceeded his income. Some artistic decline accompanied his physical decline. He died on September 9, 1815.

Summary

Copley rose from modest circumstances to become, in a twenty-year period, the foremost painter in America. He achieved distinction in his portraits, with his close attention to exact detail, lifelike realism, and insight into personality and character. Furthermore, many of them have inestimable historical value: Paul Revere, sitting in shirt sleeves, holding his teapot, tools before him; Samuel Adams, in a good but plain suit, papers in hand, pointing to more papers before him, about to speak (one supposes) against British tyranny; these and other images make the men and women, and the times, come alive. His portrait of John Adams, painted later in England, also has this lifelike quality. In his English career, Copley became regarded as among the foremost painters of the time, virtually the peer of Sir Joshua Reynolds, Thomas Gainsborough, and George Romney. His historical paintings contain multiple masterpieces of portraiture, and they excite interest in significant events.

At a time when pride in America was crucially needed, Copley contributed importantly to it. He always denied that he was a Loyalist, and there are passages in his letters and traditional anecdotes which support him. After the war, he had cordial relationships with visiting Americans, and he painted some of their portraits. His daughter married a Boston merchant, and Copley's contacts with Boston continued. Yet his impact on a rising American culture was found in his demonstration that an American could achieve renown in the arts. This example provided inspiration to many aspiring American artists, who wanted their new country to share in full measure the richness of civilization and culture.

Bibliography

Amory, Martha Babcock. *The Domestic and Artistic Life of John Singleton Copley, R.A.* Boston: Houghton Mifflin Co., 1882. Family traditions and personal information by Copley's granddaughter. Although some information is erroneous, this book enhances one's understanding of Copley through its many anecdotes, and through the letters which are printed here. Also contains information about Copley's eminent son, Lord Lyndhurst.

Flexner, James Thomas. *American Painting: First Flowers of Our Wilderness.* Boston: Houghton Mifflin Co., 1947. Illustrated survey of Colonial American painting; especially good on problems faced by aspiring artists. Chapters 9 and 10 are on Copley, and they provide a lively story of the artist to 1774.

_____ . *John Singleton Copley.* Boston: Houghton Mifflin Co., 1948. A brief biography which is especially good reading. The author revised and enlarged his treatment of Copley in an earlier book, *America's Old Masters: First Artists of the New World* (1939). Thirty-two black-and-white plates plus a frontispiece in color.

Frankenstein, Alfred. *The World of Copley, 1738-1815.* Alexandria, Va.: Time-Life Books, 1970. Well-written text and many beautiful illustrations, many in color. This is a relatively brief account of Copley's life, but by emphasizing the art as much as the man, it conveys his artistic achievements very well. Effective portrayal of the context of Copley's work, both the "world" into which he arrived and the quite different one at the time of his death.

Jones, Guernsey, ed. *Letters and Papers of John Singleton Copley and Henry Pelham.* Vol. 71. Boston: Massachusetts Historical Society, 1914. Indispensable material for a serious study of Copley. Apt quotations from these letters appear in most of the books about Copley, but there is no substitute for perusing them on one's own terms.

Prown, Jules David. *John Singleton Copley.* 2 vols. Cambridge, Mass.: Harvard University Press, 1966. The most valuable single source of reliable, detailed information about the artist and his work. Done with impressive scholarship, this work is nevertheless delightful to read, with its mixture of biographical information and informed aesthetic commentary. Appendices are invaluable, including checklists of pictures and 678 illustrations.

Richard D. Miles

FRANCISCO VÁSQUEZ DE CORONADO

Born: 1510; Salamanca, Spain
Died: September 22, 1554; Mexico City, Mexico
Areas of Achievement: Exploration and discovery
Contribution: As leader of the 1540-1542 expedition to the Seven Cities of Cíbola and Quivira, Coronado explored what became Arizona, Texas, New Mexico, Oklahoma, and Kansas and opened the Southwest to Spanish colonization and settlement.

Early Life

Francisco Vásquez de Coronado was born in 1510, in Salamanca, Spain, the second son of noble parents, Juan Vásquez de Coronado and Isabel de Luján (his proper family name was Vásquez, but Americans mistakenly call him Coronado). Only a few details abut his childhood are known. His father became governor (*corregidor*) of Burgos in 1512, an important royal appointment. In 1520, his father created an entailed estate, whereby the family property passed to Francisco's older brother Gonzalo. Although the other children received one-time settlements, with provision made for their education, they had to make their own way in life.

Coronado decided to seek his fortune in the New World. Handsome (perhaps fair complexioned, if a portrait of his brother Juan is any indication), generous, modest, and loyal, Coronado was a favorite at court and won the friendship and patronage of Antonio de Mendoza, the first viceroy of New Spain. Coronado sailed with Mendoza, arriving in Mexico City in November, 1535.

Mendoza's patronage was invaluable. In 1537, he chose Coronado to put down a rebellion of black miners. The following year, the viceroy named his young friend to a seat on the Mexico City council without even seeking royal approval for his appointment. Meanwhile, Coronado helped found the Brotherhood of the Blessed Sacrament for Charity, which provided alms for the needy and educated orphan girls. He was also married, to Beatriz de Estrada, whose father, Alonso de Estrada, had been New Spain's royal treasurer and was rumored to have been the illegitimate son of King Ferdinand. His wife's dowry included half of a large country estate. Coronado, the fortune seeker, had become a landed country gentleman. The marriage produced five children.

Again the viceroy called on Coronado. A serious Indian rebellion had convulsed the mining towns of New Galicia (northwestern Mexico), and Mendoza sent Coronado to suppress it and act as governor of the region. Coronado surmised that the Indians had risen because of horrible abuse and exploitation at the hands of the Spaniards.

Life's Work

News had begun to filter into Mexico about rich Indian cities lying far to the north. First had come Álvar Núñez Cabeza de Vaca, who had survived Panfilo de Narváez's disastrous expedition to Florida. He staggered into Mexico in 1536, with tantalizing but enigmatic stories about seven great and wealthy cities to the north. Mendoza sent Fray Marcos de Niza to verify Cabeza de Vaca's stories in early 1539. Coronado accompanied the friar on his way through New Galicia to the Seven Cities but then returned to his duties as governor. Fray Marcos returned in the fall, claiming to have actually visited Cíbola, the land of the Seven Cities. His report was more wondrous than Cabeza de Vaca's. Mendoza and Coronado began to plan an expedition to explore and conquer Cíbola. Speed was important. Charles V had commissioned Hernando de Soto, the new governor of Cuba and Florida, to explore north from Florida, and Hernán Cortés himself had returned from Spain, anxious to claim Cíbola as his own.

While men gathered in New Galicia for the expedition, Mendoza and Coronado dispatched another scouting party to Cíbola under Melchior Díaz, who was more knowledgeable about the northern frontier than any Spaniard. Before Díaz returned, a force of more than three hundred Spaniards was ready at Compostela, along with several priests, perhaps a thousand Indian allies, and about fifteen hundred horses and pack animals. Although subject to the viceregal government, the expedition was privately financed. Mendoza invested sixty thousand ducats in it, and Coronado, fifty thousand ducats from his wife's estate. Mendoza initially hoped to lead the foray himself but eventually named Coronado on January 6, 1540, to head it. Meanwhile, a small squadron under Hernando de Alarcón was to sail up the Gulf of California and support Coronado by sea, although Alarcón never did find Coronado.

The Coronado party set out from Compostela on February 23, 1540, without waiting for Díaz's report, but met the scout at Chiametla. He secretly told Coronado that he had been to Cíbola and had found no gold, silver, or great cities. Rumors about the report upset the men, who were young adventurers and soldiers of fortune looking for gold, glory, and empire. Yet Fray Marcos reassured them that great riches awaited those with the courage to persevere.

After the force reached Culiacán, Coronado decided to push ahead quickly to Cíbola with a small party of eighty Spaniards, along with some Indian allies. The main group would follow later. During the long trek through Sonora and eastern Arizona, supplies dwindled and horses died. When Coronado reached Cíbola (Hawikuh) in July, 1540, his men were starving. Mendoza had ordered Coronado neither to abuse the Indians nor to make slaves of them. He thus tried to negotiate with the Zuni at Cíbola (there and elsewhere, most communication with the Indians was probably by sign language), but they ambushed his scouts and then attacked the whole party. Coronado besieged the fortified pueblo and was nearly killed. García López de Cárdenas, second in command, captured Cíbola but found none of the promised riches.

Recovered from his wounds, Coronado reassumed command. On July 15, 1540, he sent a small party under Pedro de Tovar to explore Tusayán to the northwest, home of the Hopi. It returned with reports of a great river and a land of giants somewhere beyond. In late August, Coronado dispatched López de Cárdenas with twenty-five horsemen to investigate: They discovered the Grand Canyon. For several days, three men tried to reach the Colorado River far below but managed to climb down only a third of the way. Disappointed but determined to press on, Coronado sent messengers, including a disgraced Fray Marcos, back to Mendoza.

Several Pueblo Indians arrived in Cíbola and invited the Spaniards to visit Cicúique (Pecos) and Tiguex, two hundred miles to the east near the headwaters of the Rio Grande. Coronado sent Hernando de Alvarado and twenty men to reconnoiter. They found pueblos of multistoried houses and friendly Indians but no riches. In late November of 1540, Coronado decided to move his force there for the winter, including the main expedition which had just arrived at Cíbola.

The Spaniards and Mexican Indians were not equipped for the harsh winter. Despite Coronado's attempts to treat the Indians humanely, the Spaniards forced one village of Indians to vacate their pueblo so that the intruders could live there. They took large amounts of food and winter clothing, and when a Spaniard molested an Indian woman and received no punishment, resentment smoldered.

Meanwhile, Alvarado found two Indian slaves, whom the Spaniards called Turk and Sopete. They told Alvarado about Quivira, a fabulously rich land farther to the east. Turk, whose fertile imagination concocted the type of reports the Spaniards wanted to hear, claimed that he had owned a gold bracelet from Quivira, which a Pueblo chieftain had stolen from him. This was the closest the expedition had come to gold, and Alvarado immediately imprisoned the chief.

Torture of the chief to locate the imaginary bracelet, together with the other abuses, transformed the previously friendly Indians into sullen and finally hostile hosts. The Tiguex War erupted. Coronado sent Cárdenas to deal with the rebellion, and he brutally suppressed it by March, 1541, mistakenly burning at the stake thirty or forty warriors who had surrendered during a truce at Arenal.

Coronado then decided to push on to Quivira, even though Sopete said that Turk's stories were lies. The expedition left for Quivira on April 23, 1541. The men found no gold, but their trek revealed huge buffalo herds and the plains Indians, including the Tejas tribe, which gave its name to Texas. With no topographical features to orient them on the flat plains, they piled buffalo chips to mark their trail. In the Texas panhandle, Coronado finally realized that Turk had deceived him. He placed Turk in chains, chose thirty-six men to continue on with Sopete as guide, and sent the remainder of the expedition back to Tiguex to wait. Sopete led them into central Kansas. There they found Quivira, land of the Wichita Indians, and final disappointment, for there was no gold or silver. In revenge, the Spaniards strangled Turk but left Sopete in his homeland as a reward for his service. Coronado then turned back toward Tiguex, arriving there in September.

A discouraged Coronado dispatched a report to the viceroy and spent the winter at Tiguex. On December 27, 1541, during a horse race, Coronado fell, and a horse stepped on his head, nearly killing him. Coronado never fully recovered. More somber and less vigorous, he consulted with his men and decided to return to Mexico. Three friars stayed to work among the Indians, however, and a few soldiers criticized him for not allowing them to remain and settle in the region. The expedition left Tiguex in April and straggled into Culiacán in June, 1542, where it disbanded.

Coronado's later years added nothing to the great explorer's fame. Despite Mendoza's disappointment over the expedition's failure, he sent Coronado back to New Galicia as governor. In 1543, Charles V ordered an inquiry into the conduct of the expedition, particularly its treatment of the Indians, and the following year, Coronado's performance as governor came under royal scrutiny. Absolved of the most serious charges, Coronado was nevertheless removed as governor by Mendoza, as much because of his poor health as for his misdeeds. Coronado thereafter lived in Mexico City, serving on the city council and administering his estates. He died on September 22, 1554.

Summary

As a leader, Coronado pales in comparison with someone such as Cortés. He owed his appointment to head the expedition to Mendoza; others, such as Melchior Díaz, were better qualified and more experienced. Perhaps his greatest weakness was his naïve acceptance of Fray Marcos' and Turk's lies. Still, Coronado endured the same hardships as his men, fought in the front ranks, and lost only about twenty men over the course of the entire expedition. Although a strict disciplinarian, he was not a tyrant but usually consulted with his men before making important decisions. Despite the Arenal atrocities, for which he was at least indirectly responsible, Coronado was remarkably humane in comparison with other Spaniards of his day.

Coronado's expedition was a major step in the exploration of North America. Although the Spaniards considered his mission a huge disappointment because it produced no gold, Coronado made important contributions by other standards. The trails he blazed, following the old Indian paths, served later Spanish parties as they moved north to settle and colonize the Southwest. He proved that the continent was much wider than previously thought and discovered the continental divide. His expedition brought back valuable information about the Indian tribes, wildlife, and geography of the region and added vast territories to the Spanish crown.

Bibliography

Aiton, Arthur S. *Antonio de Mendoza: First Viceroy of New Spain*. Durham, N.C.: Duke University Press, 1927. A scholarly biography of Coronado's patron. Discusses Coronado's expedition and provides valuable information on contemporary New Spain.

_____. "The Later Career of Coronado." *American Historical Review* 30 (January, 1925): 298-304. By Mendoza's biographer, this article analyzes the period after the great expedition. Probably too critical of Coronado.

Bolton, Herbert Eugene. *Coronado on the Turquoise Trail: Knight of the Pueblos and Plains*. Albuquerque: University of New Mexico Press, 1940. A masterpiece based on a thorough use of archival records and the accounts left by its members. Bolton traveled the entire Coronado trail.

Day, A. Grove. *Coronado's Quest: The Discovery of the Southwestern States*. Berkeley: University of California Press, 1940. A readable, documented study of the expedition, written to commemorate its four hundredth anniversary. Contains several inaccuracies as to the location of Coronado's trail. Despite evidence to the contrary, Day argues that Fray Marcos never visited Cíbola.

Hammond, George Peter, and Agapito Rey, eds. *Narratives of the Coronado Expedition, 1540-1542*. Albuquerque: University of New Mexico Press, 1940. Extremely useful collection of English translations of reports, dispatches, and correspondence by Coronado, Mendoza, Alarcón, and others relating to Coronado's expedition and trial.

Hodge, Frederick W., ed. *Spanish Explorers in the Southern United States, 1528-1543*. New York: Charles Scribner's Sons, 1907. Contains a translation of the account of Coronado's expedition written by Pedro de Castañeda, a participant, although he was not present at all the important events. Also contains a translation of Cabeza de Vaca's narrative.

Ortiz, Alfonso, ed. *Handbook of North American Indians*. Vol. 9. Washington, D.C.: Smithsonian Institution, 1979. Deals specifically with the Zuni, Pueblo, and Hopi Indians and contains historical, anthropological, and archaeological studies by experts in the various fields. Also contains an extensive bibliography.

Sauer, Carl O. *Sixteenth-Century North America: The Land and the People as Seen by the Europeans*. Berkeley: University of California Press, 1971. The leading historical geographer of sixteenth century North America includes a chapter on the Coronado expedition, focusing on the environment rather than the man.

Winship, George Parker. *The Coronado Expedition, 1540-1542.* In *U.S. Bureau of American Ethnology, 1892-1893*, vol. 14, pt. 1, 329-613. Washington, D.C.: Government Printing Office, 1896. Contains a scholarly historical introduction to Coronado's expedition, Castañeda's narrative in both Spanish and English, translations of other relevant documents, a bibliography, maps, and illustrations.

Kendall W. Brown

JOHN COTTON

Born: December 4, 1584; Derby, England
Died: December 23, 1652; Boston, Massachusetts
Area of Achievement: Religion
Contribution: One of the foremost clergymen who defined the religious practices of early New England, Cotton was one of the architects of Congregationalism.

Early Life

John Cotton was born in Derby, England, on December 4, 1584. He was the son of Roland Cotton, an attorney. Cotton attended the Derby grammar school and then entered Trinity College, Cambridge University, at about the age of thirteen. He received his B.A. in 1602. In 1603, he was elected a fellow (a member of the faculty) at Cambridge's Emmanuel College, from which he received his M.A. in 1606. While at Emmanuel, Cotton served at various times as tutor, catechist, and dean. He developed close friendships with Cambridge contemporaries with whom he cooperated later in his career, including Thomas Hooker, Richard Sibbes, Thomas Goodwin, and Thomas Weld.

These men were in part responsible for Cotton's conversion to Puritanism and his transformation into a zealous Calvinist reformer working within the Church of England. Emmanuel College was a center of Puritan activity at Cambridge, and Cotton was soon recognized as one of the movement's key spokesmen.

Cotton was ordained into the ministry in 1610, and in 1612 the corporation of St. Botolph's Church in Boston, Lincolnshire, chose him as their vicar. He was an active preacher whose popularity attracted many believers, including laypersons such as Anne Hutchinson and fellow English clergymen who traveled to Boston to hear him and study under him. His Puritan stand began to involve him in clashes with the authorities, including an incident in which he was suspected of having inspired iconoclastic vandalism against some of the statues and stained glass in the church. The support of prominent laymen, such as the Earl of Lincoln, protected him until 1632, when he was called to defend himself before Archbishop William Laud's Court of High Commission. Cotton was in contact with the leaders of the Puritan exile community in the Netherlands and had supported the Puritan migration to Massachusetts, preaching the farewell sermon to the Winthrop fleet in 1630. Fearing that he would be silenced if he remained in England, he decided to emigrate to New England.

Life's Work

On his arrival in Boston, Massachusetts, in 1633, Cotton was elected by the congregation of the Boston church to be their teacher, one of the two ministerial positions in the church. His evangelical preaching in the months that followed stirred a religious revival in which many were "born again" and shared the stories of their spiritual rebirth with their fellow believers. From this evolved the requirement of a conversion narrative from all who sought full membership in the churches of the colony. The Puritan settlers were gradually trying to shape an orthodox system of faith and a unified church structure which would be a model for England and the rest of the world. To achieve this goal, the settlers needed to achieve consensus on matters which had been subjects for speculation when the Puritans were a dissenting and largely powerless minority within the established church in England. There were continual doctrinal disputes within New England. Cotton's conflicts with Roger Williams and with Anne Hutchinson are both examples of such disputes, the resolution of which further defined the Colonial polity.

Cotton was a key figure in this definition of Massachusetts' orthodoxy. In the dispute with Roger Williams, which was carried on in print into the 1640's, Cotton was the foremost spokesman for the New England belief that the State, while institutionally separate from the Church, had a responsibility to safeguard religion by acting against those whose beliefs threatened the order of the churches. In the Antinomian controversy, Anne Hutchinson (who had followed Cotton to the New World) claimed Cotton as her inspiration when she argued that there was no connection between saving grace and human works. Hutchinson argued that because the elect had been sanctified by God, there was no need for them to devote themselves to good works in order to ensure their salvation. Salvation was contingent not upon a Covenant of Works but rather upon a Covenant of Grace. Cotton tried to maintain a middle ground which asserted God's freedom to act in various ways on men's souls. When Hutchinson's increasing radicalism threatened to divide and hence to destroy the newly established church, Cotton joined his clerical brethren in their decision to denounce her.

Despite suspicions aroused by his ambiguous position in the early phases of the Antinomian controversy, Cotton maintained and expanded his position as the foremost interpreter of Puritanism in New England. He was a principal architect of the Congregational ecclesiastical polity which allowed each congregation of believers to control its own affairs, with consultation with neighboring churches but free from the supervision of any hierarchical church authority. Cotton advanced the value of this system in a series of tracts: *The True Constitution of a Particular Visible Church* (1642), *The Way of the Churches of Christ in New England* (1645), and *The Way of the Congregational Churches Cleared* (1648). These publications were directed at an English audience that was in the process of restructuring church order as part of the Puritan Revolution. They were published in London, through the efforts of English friends, such as Thomas Goodwin and Philip Nye, who were advocates of New England Puritanism, in Britain. As the unity of English Puritanism fragmented in the 1640's, Cotton identified himself with the Congregational faction of the Independent coalition that opposed the imposition of a national Presbyterian system. His publications and those of other Colonial clergymen were intended to support Congregational Independency as advanced by clergymen, such as Goodwin, and civil leaders, such as Oliver Cromwell.

In 1651, Cotton gave evidence of his continued support for the revolutionary cause in England when he preached a sermon explaining and justifying the 1649 execution of King Charles I. In his sermon, Cotton set forth his belief in the limits of civil authority and the right of the people to resist tyranny. He believed that the events in England signaled the approach of the millennium as foretold in Scripture. Cotton died on December 23, 1652, still hopeful that New England Puritanism would prevail in England and that the millennium would soon follow.

Summary

John Cotton was one of the most influential members of the founding generation of New England Puritans, a position he achieved by his abilities but which was reinforced by his status as one of the ministers of the Boston church. He helped to define the Congregational system of church governance, and he persuaded New England to accept the Calvinist belief in man's dependence on God's grace. He defended colonial religious practices against domestic critics such as Roger Williams and against English Presbyterian authors. He was one of the clergymen who shaped New Englanders' belief that they were a people in covenant with God, a people whose example would transform the world. His views were carried on and defended to later generations by his grandson Cotton Mather.

Bibliography

Bremer, Francis J. "In Defense of Regicide: John Cotton on the Execution of Charles I." *William and Mary Quarterly*, 3d series, 37 (January, 1980): 103-124. Contains Cotton's 1651 sermon justifying the execution of Charles I, prefaced by an introduction discussing Cotton's political theory and his views on the English Puritan Revolution.

Cotton, John. *John Cotton on the Churches of New England*. Edited by Larzer Ziff. Cambridge, Mass: Harvard University Press, 1968. A well-introduced and annotated edition of some of Cotton's major works on church organization.

Emerson, Everett H. *John Cotton*. New Haven, Conn.: College and University Press, 1965. A volume in Twayne's United States Authors Series, this study focuses on Cotton's published works, summarizing them and providing worthwhile analysis.

Hall, David D. *The Faithful Shepard: A History of the New England Ministry in the Seventeenth Century*. Chapel Hill: University of North Carolina Press, 1972. The best study of the Colonies' clergy, showing the problems faced by Cotton and his colleagues and how they responded to those challenges.

Rosenmeier, Jesper. " 'Clearing the Medium': A Reevaluation of the Puritan Plain Style in Light of John Cotton's *A Practicall Commentary Upon the First Epistle Generall of John*." *William and Mary Quarterly*, 3d series, 37 (October, 1980): 577-591. Examines and explains Cotton's preaching style and relates it to his views on personal relationships.

──────────. "The Teacher and the Witness: John Cotton and Roger Williams." *William and Mary Quarterly*, 3d series, 25 (July, 1968): 408-431. Examines the debate between Cotton and Williams and relates their differing views to different forms of scriptural interpretation.

Ziff, Larzer. *The Career of John Cotton: Puritanism and the American Experience*. Princeton, N.J.: Princeton University Press, 1962. The best biography, though its interpretations should be supplemented by those in the articles above.

Francis J. Bremer

STEPHEN CRANE

Born: November 1, 1871; Newark, New Jersey
Died: June 5, 1900; Badenweiler, Germany
Area of Achievement: Literature
Contribution: Crane is best remembered for his war novel, *The Red Badge of Courage* (1895); he also wrote estimable poetry and more than a dozen other novels and collections of stories.

Early Life

Stephen Crane, the youngest son of a youngest son, was the last of fourteen children born to the Reverend Jonathan Townley Crane and his wife, Mary Peck. Crane's father was a presiding elder of the Newark, New Jersey, district of the Methodist Church (1868-1872) when Stephen was born and served in a similar capacity in the Elizabeth, New Jersey, district of the church from 1872 until 1876. Because Methodist clergymen were subject to frequent transfer, the young Stephen was moved from Newark to Paterson, New Jersey, before he was old enough to attend school and to Port Jervis, New York, shortly before he began school. His *The Third Violet* (1897) and *Whilomville Stories* (1900) are set in villages modeled after Port Jervis.

Crane's father died in 1880, when the boy was eight years old, and, in 1883, Stephen and his mother moved to Asbury Park, New Jersey, a seaside resort some sixty miles from New York City, to be near the Methodist camp community of Ocean Grove, a town adjacent to Asbury Park, which Jonathan Crane had been instrumental in establishing. Stephen's brother Townley already ran a press bureau in Asbury Park, and soon their sister Agnes moved there to teach in the public schools.

As Stephen strayed from the religious teachings of the Methodist Church, his mother became concerned about his spiritual welfare, and, in 1885, she sent him to Pennington Seminary, some ten miles from both Trenton and Princeton, in the hope that he would receive a solid academic background and would simultaneously grow closer to the Church. Crane's father had been principal of Pennington Seminary for the decade from 1848 to 1858, and his mother had spent the first ten years of her marriage at Pennington.

Stephen, a handsome, dark-haired youth with a prominent nose, sensuous lips, and deep, dark eyes, rankled under Pennington's strong religious emphasis. In 1888, he enrolled in the Hudson River Institute in Claverack, New York, a coeducational institution with a military emphasis for its male students. It was perhaps during this period that Crane became extremely interested in war.

During the summers, Crane assisted his brother in his news bureau, learning something about journalism as he went about his work. He entered Lafayette College in 1890 to study engineering, but failed in his work there and left after the Christmas holiday to attend Syracuse University, where he played baseball, managed the baseball team, and worked on the school newspaper. He was not a strong student, and he left school in 1891 to seek his fortune in New York City. His mother died on December 7 of that year.

Stephen, who had met and established a friendship with Hamlin Garland in the summer of 1891, tried to make his living as a newspaperman, but he was not initially successful in this work. In 1892, however, the serial publication of seven of his "Sullivan County Sketches" gave him the encouragement he needed to pursue a literary career diligently.

Life's Work

Buoyed up by seeing his work in print, Crane, in 1893, paid for a private printing of *Maggie: A Girl of the Streets* (1893), a book gleaned from his experience of living in New York City's Bowery during the preceding two years. This early work, highly shocking in its time because it views with sympathy a girl who becomes pregnant out of wedlock and shows the hypocrisy of her lower-class family's morality, was first published under the pseudonym Johnston Smith.

Maggie was unabashedly naturalistic, somewhat in the tradition of Émile Zola. Despite William Dean Howells's attempts to get the book distributed, it sold hardly any copies in its original edition. In 1896, however, Crane revised it, cutting out much of its offensive profanity, omitting some of its graphic description, and regularizing the grammar and punctuation. His reputation had by this time been established with the publication, the preceding October, of *The Red Badge of Courage*, a book that grew out of Crane's fascination with war, battles, and men in combat. *Maggie*, although it still was deemed shocking to delicate sensibilities, was more favorably received in 1896 than it had been three years earlier.

The Red Badge of Courage existed in some form in 1894, when it was published abridged in newspapers by the Bacheller Syndicate. *George's Mother* (1896) appeared two years later, and in its use of realistic detail it goes far beyond that of William Dean Howells, who had become Crane's friend.

With the publication of both *The Black Riders and Other Lines* and *The Red Badge of Courage* in 1895, Crane became an overnight celebrity. In March of that year, he also went to Mexico for the first time, and the trip made a substantial impression upon him. With the appearance of *George's Mother*, *Maggie*, *The Little Regiment and Other Episodes of the American Civil War* (1896), and *The Third Violet*, it was quite apparent that Crane, still only twenty-five years old, was on the way to becoming one of the leading literary figures in the United States. If readers complained because he wrote about subjects that depressed them, they could not reasonably contend that the conditions about which he wrote did not exist or that he wrote badly about them.

Although Crane was fascinated by war and by 1896 had written much about the subject, he had never known the battlefield, and he was keenly aware of this lack in his experience. Therefore, when the Bacheller Syndicate offered to send him as a correspondent to join the insurgents who were fighting against Spanish rule in Cuba, Crane enthusiastically accepted the assignment. He went first to Jacksonville, Florida, to wait for a ship, the *Commodore*, to be outfitted for the short trip to Cuba. Arriving in Jacksonville in November, he met Cora Stewart, who owned a brothel and nightclub, the Hotel de Dream.

It took until December 31 for the *Commodore* to be ready to sail, and by that time Crane and Stewart, who already had a husband, had fallen in love. Nevertheless, Crane sailed for Cuba as planned. The ship, however, got only several miles down the St. John's River before it ran aground. Crane and some of his shipmates were forced to put to sea in a small, flimsy lifeboat before the *Commodore* capsized with some loss of life.

It was fifty-four hours before Crane and his companions were able to ride the heavy surf to shore at Daytona. One of his companions was drowned as they came to shore. From his frightening experience in the lifeboat, Crane wrote what is probably his best known and most artistically confident short story, "The Open Boat." The shipwreck scuttled, for the time, Crane's plans to go to Cuba. Instead, he and Steward sailed for Greece in late March, both of them to report on Greece's war with Turkey.

In mid-1897, Crane and Stewart, who was six years older than he, went to England, where he wrote some of his most memorable short stories, including "The Monster," "Death and the Child," and his much anthologized "The Bride Comes to Yellow Sky." He introduced Cora Stewart as his wife, although the two had never been married because she was not free to do so. It was at this time that Crane met Joseph Conrad and became his close friend.

After Crane's collection *The Open Boat and Other Tales of Adventure* (1898) was published, the author returned to the United States to join the armed forces in the Spanish-American War, which the United States had just entered. He was, however, rejected for military service and instead went to Cuba as a war correspondent for Joseph Pulitzer. He was fearless in combat situations, but his health began to fail. He did some work in Puerto Rico and in Cuba for the Hearst newspapers, but in 1899, the year in which *War Is Kind* (1899), *Active Service* (1899), and *The Monster and Other Stories* (1899) were published, he returned to England, this time to live in the stately Brede Place in Sussex. While celebrating Christmas, Crane had a massive hemorrhage brought on by tuberculosis.

In the spring of 1900, the year in which *Whilomville Stories* and *Wounds in the Rain* were published, Crane's health declined, and in May, he and Cora, accompanied by a retinue consisting of their butler, maids, nurses, and a doctor, went to Badenweiler in Germany's Black Forest, hoping that the climate would benefit the ailing writer's health. There Crane died on June 5. Three of his works, *Great Battles of the World* (1901), *Last Words* (1902), and *The O'Ruddy* (1903), were published shortly after his death.

Summary

Dead at twenty-eight, Stephen Crane had just begun to come into his own as a writer. His early work, particularly the original version of *Maggie*, reflected his passionate interest in reform and his understanding of the problems of the poor, but much of this early book was seriously flawed, largely because Crane had not yet mastered the basic mechanics of expression.

Yet with *The Red Badge of Courage*, which stands as one of America's acknowledged classics, Crane demonstrated that he was getting a firm grip on his art. The classic naturalism of *Maggie* and of *George's Mother*, the conventional realism of *The Red Badge of Courage* and of *The Little Regiment and Other Episodes of the American Civil War*, and the impressionistic symbolism of *The Black Riders* suggest the great versatility of which Crane was capable.

Both in his insistence on living an action-packed life, often quite close to the edge, and in his accuracy and economy of description, Crane reminds one of Ernest Hemingway, along whose lines he might have developed had he lived a normal life span.

Bibliography

Bruccoli, Matthew J. *Stephen Crane, 1871-1971*. Columbia: Department of English, University of South Carolina, 1971. Extremely valuable bibliography, although not easily accessible.

Cady, Edwin H. *Stephen Crane*. Rev. ed. Boston: Twayne Publishers, 1980. This updating of Cady's 1962 edition is carefully researched and well reported. It is a standard critical biography of Crane. Its updated bibliography is useful.

Colvert, James B. *Stephen Crane*. New York: Harcourt Brace Jovanovich, 1984. This biography, aimed specifically at the nonspecialist, is highly readable and is enhanced by numerous illustrations. Its bibliography is limited but well selected. The author's research is impeccable.

Gibson, Donald B. *The Fiction of Stephen Crane*. Carbondale: Southern Illinois University Press, 1968. This study, although badly dated, is valuable in suggesting the sources of much of Crane's fiction and in establishing some of Crane's literary relationships.

Gullason, Thomas A., ed. *Stephen Crane's Career: Perspectives and Evaluations*. New York: New York University Press, 1972. The contributors to this book consider Crane in the light of his times and his background. They trace sources of his stories, review Crane research, consider Crane's short fiction quite thoroughly, and present some of Cora Stewart's original writing.

Katz, Joseph, ed. *Stephen Crane in Transition: Centenary Essays*. DeKalb: Northern Illinois University Press, 1972. The nine essays in this centenary edition that commemorates Crane's birth consider the novels, the stories, Crane's journalistic career, his literary style, and his radical use of language. The introduction is astute, and the afterword gives a fine overview of resources for study.

Nagel, James. *Stephen Crane and Literary Impressionism*. University Park: Pennsylvania State University Press, 1980. Nagel sees Crane in a new light that suggests his remarkable versatility. The book has especially strong insights into *The Black Riders*.

Solomon, Eric. *Stephen Crane: From Parody to Realism*. Cambridge, Mass.: Harvard University Press, 1966. A penetrating study that shows Stephen Crane's remarkably swift development as a writer who found his metier in realism despite his sallies into naturalism and impressionism.

Stallman, Robert W. *Stephen Crane: A Critical Bibliography*. Ames: Iowa State University Press, 1972. This book is now somewhat dated; it is still useful to scholars, however, and is more easily available generally than Matthew J. Bruccoli's splendid bibliography, which was completed the year before Stallman's.

Walford, Chester L., Jr. *The Anger of Stephen Crane*. Lincoln: University of Nebraska Press, 1983. Walford considers Crane a semiliterate genius and presents his work as a repudiation of the epic tradition and of conventional religion. Although the book is not always convincing, it is engaging and original in its approach.

R. Baird Shuman

CRAZY HORSE
Tashunca-uitko

Born: 1842?; Black Hills of South Dakota
Died: September 5, 1877; Fort Robinson, Nebraska
Area of Achievement: Native American leadership
Contribution: Crazy Horse, the greatest of the Sioux chiefs, led his people in
  a valiant but futile struggle against domination by the white man and white
  culture. He fought to the last to hold his native land for the Indian people.

Early Life

Little is known of Tashunca-uitko's early life; even the date of his birth and
the identity of his mother are somewhat uncertain. He was probably born in
a Sioux camp along Rapid Creek in the Black Hills during the winter of 1841-
1842. Most scholars believe that his mother was a Brule Sioux, the sister of
Spotted Tail, a famous Brule chief. His father, also called Crazy Horse, was
a highly respected Oglala Sioux holy man. Tashunca-uitko was apparently a
curious and solitary child. His hair and his complexion were so fair that he
was often mistaken for a captive white child by soldiers and settlers. He was
first known as "Light-Haired Boy" and also as "Curly." At the age of ten, he
became the protégé of Hump, a young Minneconjou Sioux warrior.

When he was about twelve, Curly killed his first buffalo and rode a newly
captured wild horse; to honor his exploits, his people renamed him "His
Horse Looking." One event in Crazy Horse's youth seems to have had a particularly powerful impact on the course of his life. When he was about fourteen, His Horse Looking witnessed the senseless murder of Chief Conquer-
ing Bear by the troops of Second Lieutenant J. L. Gratton and the
subsequent slaughter of Gratton's command by the Sioux. Troubled by what
he had seen, His Horse Looking went out alone, hobbled his horse, and lay
down on a high hill to await a vision. On the third day, weakened by hunger,
thirst, and exposure, the boy had a powerful mystical experience which
revealed to him that the world in which men lived was only a shadow of the
real world. To enter the real world, one had to dream. When he was in that
world, everything seemed to dance or float—his horse danced as if it were
wild or crazy. In this first crucial vision, His Horse Looking had seen a warrior mounted on his (His Horse Looking's) horse; the warrior had no scalps,
wore no paint, was naked except for a breech cloth; he had a small, smooth
stone behind one ear. Bullets and arrows could not touch him; the rider's
own people crowded around him, trying to stop his dancing horse, but he
rode on. The people were lost in a storm; the rider became a part of the
storm with a lightning bolt on his cheek and hail spots on his body. The storm
faded, and a small red-railed hawk flew close over the rider; again the people
tried to hold the rider back, but still he rode on. By the time he revealed this

vision a few years later, His Horse Looking had already gained a reputation for great bravery and daring. His father and Chips, another holy man, made him a medicine bundle and gave him a red-tailed hawk feather and a smooth stone to wear.

When he went into battle thereafter, he wore a small lightning streak on his cheek, hail spots on his body, a breech cloth, a small stone, and a single feather; he did not take scalps. He was never seriously wounded in battle. His Horse Looking's father, in order to honor his son's achievements, bestowed his own name, Crazy Horse, upon the young man (he then took the name Worm) and asserted to his people that the Sioux had a new Crazy Horse, a great warrior with powerful medicine.

The Grattan debacle had one immediate effect other than the vision: It resulted in brutal reprisals by the Bluecoats. On September 3, 1855, shortly after Crazy Horse had experienced the vision, General W. S. Harney attacked the Brule camp in which Crazy Horse was living with Spotted Tail's people. The soldiers killed more than one hundred Indians (most of them women and children), took many prisoners, and captured most of the Sioux horses. Crazy Horse escaped injury and capture but was left with an abiding hatred of the whites. Since the major white invasion of the West did not begin until after the Civil War, Crazy Horse spent his youth living in the traditional ways: moving with the seasons, hunting, and warring with the other plains Indians.

Life's Work

The solitary boy grew into a strange man who, according to Black Elk,

> would go about the village without noticing people or saying anything. . . . All the Lakotas (Sioux) liked to dance and sing; but he never joined a dance, and they say nobody heard him sing. . . . He was a small man among the Lakotas and he was slender and had a thin face and his eyes looked through things and he always seemed to be thinking hard about something. He never wanted many things for himself, and did not have many ponies like a chief. They say that when game was scarce and the people were hungry, he would not eat at all. He was a queer man. Maybe he was always part way into that world of his vision.

Crazy Horse and the Oglala north of the Platte River lived in relative freedom from the white man's interference until 1864. From the early 1860's, however, there was ever-increasing pressure from white settlers and traders on the United States government to guarantee the safety of people moving along the Oregon and Santa Fe trails and to open the Bozeman Road which ran through the Sioux country.

The military began preparations early in 1865 to invade the Powder River Indian country; General Patrick E. Connor announced that the Indians north of the Platte "must be hunted like wolves." Thus began what came to be known as Red Cloud's War, named for the Sioux chief who led the Sioux and Cheyenne warriors. General Connor's punitive expedition in 1865 was a failure, as were subsequent efforts to force the free Indians to sign a treaty. In 1866, General Henry B. Carrington fortified and opened the Bozeman Road through Sioux territory. By 1868, having been outsmarted, frustrated, and beaten again and again by Red Cloud's warriors, the United States forces conceded defeat, abandoned the forts, closed the Bozeman Road, and granted the Black Hills and the Powder River country to the Indians forever.

Crazy Horse rose to prominence as a daring and astute leader during the years of Red Cloud's War. He was chosen by the Oglala chiefs to be a "shirt-wearer" or protector of the people. All the other young men chosen were the sons of chiefs; he alone was selected solely on the basis of his accomplishments. Crazy Horse played a central role in the most famous encounter of this war. On December 21, 1866, exposing himself repeatedly to great danger, he decoyed a troop of eighty-one of Colonel Carrington's men, commanded by Captain William J. Fetterman, into a trap outside Fort Phil Kearny. All the soldiers were killed.

Red Cloud's War ended in November, 1868, when the chief signed a treaty which acknowledged that the Powder River and Big Horn country were Indian land into which the white man could not come without permission. The treaty also indicated that the Indians were to live on a reservation on the west side of the Missouri River. Red Cloud and his followers moved onto a reservation, but Crazy Horse and many others refused to sign or to leave their lands for a reservation; Crazy Horse never signed a treaty.

As early as 1870, driven by reports of gold in the Black Hills, many whites began to venture illegally into Indian territory. Surveyors for the Northern Pacific Railroad protected by United States troops also invaded the Black Hills in order to chart the course of their railway through Indian land. Crazy Horse, who became the war chief of the Oglala after Red Cloud moved onto the reservation, led numerous successful raids against the survey parties and finally drove them from his lands. The surveyors returned in 1873; this time they were protected by a formidable body of troops commanded by Lieutenant Colonel George Armstrong Custer. In spite of a series of sharp attacks, Crazy Horse was unable to defeat Custer, and the surveyors finished their task. In 1874, Custer was back in Indian territory; he led an expedition of twelve hundred men purportedly to gather military and scientific information. He reported that the hills were filled with gold "from the roots on down"; the fate of the Indians and their sacred hills was sealed. Not even the military genius of their war chief, their skill and bravery, and their clear title to the land could save them from the greed and power of the white men.

During the years between the signing of the 1868 treaty and the full-scale invasion of Indian lands in 1876, Crazy Horse apparently fell in love with a Sioux woman named Black Buffalo Woman, but she was taken from him through deceit and married another man, No Water. Crazy Horse and Black Buffalo Woman maintained their attachment to each other over a period of years, causing some divisiveness among the Sioux and resulting in the near-fatal shooting of Crazy Horse by No Water. Crazy Horse eventually married an Oglala named Tasina Sapewin (Black Shawl) who bore him a daughter. He named the child They Are Afraid of Her, and when she died a few years later, he was stricken with grief.

Because of the reports concerning the great mineral wealth of the Black Hills, the United States government began to try to force all the Indians to move onto reservations. On February 7, 1876, the War Department ordered General Philip Sheridan to commence operations against the Sioux living off of reservations. The first conflict in this deadly campaign occurred March 17, when General George Crook's advance column under Colonel Joseph J. Reynolds attacked a peaceful camp of Northern Cheyennes and Oglala Sioux who were on their way from the Red Cloud Agency to their hunting grounds. The survivors fled to Crazy Horse's camp.

Crazy Horse took them in, gave them food and shelter, and promised them that "we are going to fight the white man again." Crazy Horse's chance came in June, when a Cheyenne hunting party sighted a column of Bluecoats camped in the valley of the Rosebud River. Crazy Horse had studied the soldiers' ways of fighting for years, and he was prepared for this battle. General Crook and his pony soldiers were no match for the Sioux and Cheyenne guided by Crazy Horse. Crook retreated under cover of darkness to his base camp on Goose Creek.

After the Battle of Rosebud (June 17), the Indians moved west to the valley of the Greasy Grass (Little Big Horn) River. Blackfoot, Hunkpapa, Sans Arc, Minneconjous, Brule, and Oglala Sioux were there, as well as the Cheyenne—perhaps as many as fifteen thousand Indians, including five thousand warriors. The soldiers had originally planned a three-pronged campaign to ensnare and destroy the Indians. Crook's withdrawal, however, forced General Alfred Terry to revise the plan. On June 22, he ordered Colonel John Gibbon to go back to the Bighorn River and to march south along it to the Little Big Horn River. Custer and the Seventh Cavalry were to go along the Rosebud parallel to Gibbon and catch the Indians in between. General Terry, with the remaining forces, would trail them and provide whatever support was necessary. General Terry expected that Gibbon and Custer would converge and engage the enemy on June 26.

General Custer and his troops arrived on June 25, and Custer elected to attack the Indian encampment without waiting for Gibbon's column. His rash decision was fatal to him and to the Seventh Cavalry. The Sioux and Cheyenne, led by Crazy Horse and Gall, Sitting Bull's lieutenant, crushed Custer; more than 250 soldiers died. Perhaps Crazy Horse and Gall could have defeated the troops of Gibbon and Terry as well, but they were not committed to an all-out war, as were the whites, and they had had enough killing, so they moved on, leaving the soldiers to bury their dead.

The Battle of the Little Big Horn is recognized as a great moment in the history of the Sioux nation, but it also proved to be a sad one, for it confirmed the United States government's conviction that in spite of the Treaty of 1868, the free Indians must be either confined to a reservation or annihilated. In the brutal days which were to follow, Crazy Horse clearly emerged as the single most important spiritual and military leader of the Sioux.

The government's response was swift: On August 15, a new law was enacted which required the Indians to give up all rights to the Powder River country and the Black Hills. Red Cloud and Spotted Tail succumbed to what they took to be inevitable and signed documents acknowledging that they accepted the new law. Sitting Bull and Gall fought against the forces of General Crook and Colonel Nelson Miles during the remainder of 1876 but decided to take their people to Canada in the spring of 1877. Crazy Horse alone resolved to stay on his own lands in the sacred Black Hills.

General Crook led an enormous army of infantry, cavalry, and artillery from the south through the Powder River country in pursuit of Crazy Horse, and Colonel Miles led his army from the north, looking for the Oglala war chief. Crazy Horse was forced to move his village from one place to another in order to avoid the Bluecoats. He had little ammunition or food, the winter was bitterly cold, and his people were weary. In December, he approached Colonel Miles's outpost and sent a small party of chiefs and warriors with a flag of truce to find out what the colonel's intentions were. The party was attacked as it approached the outpost; only three Sioux survived. Miles's brutal intentions were made quite clear, and Crazy Horse was forced to flee again.

Colonel Miles caught up with the Sioux on January 8, 1877, at Battle Butte; in spite of his lack of ammunition and the weakened condition of his warriors, Crazy Horse was able, through bravery and superior tactics, to defeat Miles. Crazy Horse and his band escaped through the Wolf Mountains to the familiar country of the Little Powder River. The soldiers decided to cease their military operations until spring, but they redoubled their efforts to persuade the Indians to surrender. Numerous emissaries were sent throughout the northern lands with pack trains of food and gifts to tempt the suffering Sioux and Cheyenne into coming in to the security of the agencies. Many small bands yielded to these entreaties, but Crazy Horse only listened politely and sent the messengers home. His fame and his symbolic value to the Indians grew daily; the longer he resisted, the more important he became to the thousands of Indians now confined to reservations. When Spotted Tail himself came to entice them to give up, Crazy Horse went off alone into the deep snows of the mountains in order to give his people the freedom to decide their own fate. Most chose to stay with their leader, but Spotted Tail did convince Big Foot to bring his Minneconjous in when spring came.

In April, General Crook sent Red Cloud to plead with Crazy Horse and to promise him that if he surrendered, the Sioux would be given a reservation in the Powder River country, where they could live and hunt in peace. At last, Crazy Horse gave in; the suffering of his people was so great, the prospects of renewed conflict with Crook and Miles so grim, and the promise of a Powder River reservation so tempting that he led his band to the Red Cloud Agency, arriving in an almost triumphal procession witnessed by thousands on May 5, 1877. Predictably, Crazy Horse did not like living at the agency, and General Crook did not make good on his promise of a Powder River reservation. Black Shawl died, and Crazy Horse married Nellie Larrabee, the daughter of a trader. The more restive Crazy Horse became, the more concerned the government became, and the more vulnerable the chief was to the plots of his enemies. Wild rumors that Crazy Horse planned to escape or to murder General Crook circulated. The government officials decided that it would be best to arrest and confine the war chief. On September 4, 1877, eight companies of cavalry and four hundred Indians, led by Red Cloud, left Fort Robinson to arrest Crazy Horse and deliver him to the fort. Crazy Horse attempted to flee but was overtaken and agreed to go and talk with Crook. When it became clear to him that he was not being taken to a conference but to prison, Crazy Horse drew his knife and tried to escape. He was restrained by Little Big Man and other followers of Red Cloud, and Private William Gentles bayoneted him. He died in the early hours of September 5; his father, Worm, was at his side. Crazy Horse's parents were allowed to take the body; they rode into the hills and buried their son in a place known only to them.

Later that fall, the Sioux were forced to begin a journey eastward to the Missouri River and a new reservation/prison. Among the thousands of Indians were Crazy Horse's Oglala. After approximately seventy-five miles of travel, the Oglala, two thousand strong, broke from the line and raced for Canada and freedom. The small cavalry contingent could only watch as these Sioux fled to join Sitting Bull—manifesting, in their refusal to submit to the white man, the spirit of Crazy Horse.

Summary

Crazy Horse, like numerous other Indian patriots, was a martyr to the westward expansion of the United States, to the unity and technological superiority of the white culture, to its assumed racial and cultural superiority, and to the greed of white Americans. He also seems to have been a truly exceptional and admirable man; he was the greatest warrior and general of a people to whom war was a way of life. He provided a powerful example of integrity and independence for the Indians during a very difficult period of their history; he never attended a peace council with the whites, never signed a treaty, never even considered giving up his lands: "One does not sell the earth upon which the people walk." Furthermore, he seems to have been a basically selfless man who was genuinely devoted to the greater good of his people, to protecting his native land and his traditional way of life. To quote Black Elk:

> He was brave and good and wise. He never wanted anything but to save his people, and he fought the Wasichus (the whites) only when they came to kill us in our own country. . . . They could not kill him in battle. They had to lie to him and kill him that way.

When Crazy Horse was born, the Sioux were a strong, proud, and free people; they were skilled horsemen and masters of war and hunting. The rhythms of their lives were the rhythms of the seasons and of the game they hunted. They venerated nature and cherished individual freedom and achievement. When Crazy Horse died, the Sioux were still proud, but they were no longer truly strong or free. Freedom, independence, and cultural integrity were realities for Crazy Horse in his youth, but particularly after the tragic battle at Wounded Knee in December, 1890, freedom and independence and integrity as a people have only been dreams for the Sioux— dreams in which the legend and spirit of Crazy Horse, fierce, intelligent, indomitable, continue to play a vital part, as is evidenced by Peter Matthiessen's choice of a title for his angry and eloquent 1983 study of the contemporary struggles of the Sioux: *In the Spirit of Crazy Horse.*

Bibliography
Andrist, Ralph K. *The Long Death: The Last Days of the Plains Indians.* New York: Macmillan Publishing Co., 1964. The story of the military conquest of the plains Indians, the Sioux as well as others. A vivid, meticulous, and well-written survey. Excellent maps.
Brininstool, E. A. "Chief Crazy Horse: His Career and Death." *Nebraska History* 12, no. 1 (1929). Scholarly source of basic biographical information.
Brown, Dee. *Bury My Heart at Wounded Knee: An Indian History of the American West.* New York: Holt, Rinehart and Winston, 1971. A revisionist history of the West from 1860 to 1890 from an Indian point of view. Crucial to a full understanding of American history and the destruction of the culture and civilization of the American Indian. Crazy Horse's story is one of many.
Connell, Evan S. *Son of the Morning Star: Custer and the Little Bighorn.* San Francisco: North Point Press, 1984. An intelligent and thorough reconstruction of what might have happened and why at the Little Big Horn on

June 25,1876. A fascinating study of the major participants in that historic battle. Focus is on Custer.

Hinman, Eleanor. "Oglala Sources on the Life of Crazy Horse." *Nebraska History* 57, no. 1 (1976). Interviews with Oglala Indians who witnessed various events in the life of Crazy Horse. Provides particularly interesting insights into his conduct in battle, his feud with No Water, and his death.

Josephy, Alvin M., Jr. *The Patriot Chiefs: A Chronicle of American Indian Resistance*. New York: Viking Press, 1958. The life stories of outstanding Indian leaders, including Crazy Horse, Tecumseh, and Chief Joseph. A good brief biography. Places Crazy Horse's struggle in the context of the heroic and tragic resistance of Indians throughout North America to the white man.

Neihardt, John G. *Black Elk Speaks*. Lincoln: University of Nebraska Press, 1961. A fascinating document which contains the life story of an Oglala holy man as told by himself. He was a member of Crazy Horse's tribe, was present at the Little Big Horn as well as at Fort Robinson when Crazy Horse was killed. Invaluable insights into the Sioux culture and way of life.

Olson, James C. *Red Cloud and the Sioux Problem*. Lincoln: University of Nebraska Press, 1965. Well-documented appraisal of Indian affairs in the Western plains in the 1860's and the 1870's. Thorough account of relations between the Sioux and the federal government. Judicious treatment of contending leaders.

Sandoz, Mari. *Crazy Horse: The Strange Man of the Oglalas*. New York: Alfred A. Knopf, 1941. A comprehensive and authoritative biography in which the author attempts to tell not only the chief's story but also that of his people and culture. Told from Crazy Horse's point of view.

Vaughn, Jesse W. *Indian Fights: New Facts on Seven Encounters*. Norman: University of Oklahoma Press, 1966. A flawed study of seven significant battles which occurred between 1864 and 1877 in Wyoming and Montana. Vaughn's accounts of the Fetterman Massacre and Major Reno's part in the Battle of the Little Big Horn are quite useful.

Hal Holladay

HARVEY WILLIAMS CUSHING

Born: April 8, 1869; Cleveland, Ohio
Died: October 7, 1939; New Haven, Connecticut
Areas of Achievement: Neurosurgery and neurophysiology
Contribution: Cushing was the founder of modern neurosurgical procedures, introducing into general medicine and surgery the determination of blood pressure and the continuous recording of vital signs during surgery. He made fundamental discoveries about the disorders of the pituitary gland and had a profound influence on the training of surgeons in the United States.

Early Life
Cushing was born the tenth and last child to Henry Kirke and Betsey Williams Cushing. His father, grandfather, and great-grandfather were all physicians. He had a happy, secure childhood, the family comfortably provided for by his father, a highly regarded practitioner and professor at the Cleveland Medical College. Cushing grew up lean and handsome, with finely chiseled features and considerable athletic ability.

He enrolled at Yale, and, despite his father's urging not to participate on athletic teams, earned a varsity letter in baseball, the sport he loved most. Not until his senior year did he seriously entertain the idea of a medical career; in 1891, after he was graduated, he entered the Harvard Medical School, as had his brother Edward earlier. His academic performance at Harvard, in contrast to his record at Yale, was outstanding. His excellent artistic ability enabled him to draw anatomical structures with fidelity and sketch patients to fix symptoms and general appearance, which he continued to do throughout his career as part of the case history of his patients.

Harvard students received their clinical training at Massachusetts General Hospital, where Cushing made his first major contribution to medicine. He had to administer ether to a woman prior to surgery; when the surgeon opened the abdomen, the patient died. The anguished Cushing thought of leaving medical school, remaining only after being reassured by the surgeon that the patient was in such bad condition that she would probably have died anyway. With a fellow student, Ernest Codman, he investigated the administration of ether, realizing that it was done with no awareness of the depth of anesthesia. The students devised a chart whereby the surgeon and anesthetist could tell at a glance the vital signs of the patient, a major contribution to the safeguarding of the patient during surgery.

Cushing interned in surgery at Massachusetts General Hospital. Following Wilhelm Conrad Röntgen's discovery of X rays in 1895, Cushing introduced the clinical use of X rays at the hospital, which he then carried to Johns Hopkins University upon accepting a residency under the foremost surgeon in the

United States, William Halsted.

Johns Hopkins was the preeminent American medical school, and in Halsted it had a masterful, innovative surgeon. Cushing had learned in Boston that speed was the first essential in successful surgery; under Halsted, with the new German asepsis methods to prevent infection and with anesthetics to provide the gift of time, he learned to perform long, painstaking operations with the gentle handling of tissue.

Cushing advanced rapidly, doing much of the surgery between 1896 and 1900, as Halsted became increasingly ill. He performed the first removal of the spleen in the United States; he extended the use of cocaine, introduced by Halsted as a local anesthetic, to amputations for the shoulder and hip. During 1898-1899, he concentrated on a surgical approach to the treatment of tic douloureux by excising the ganglion from which the sensory nerve to the face arises. His success—he reduced mortality by fifty percent—brought him his first fame. Sufferers of this excruciatingly painful malady came to him from all over the country. During these years as resident, he learned much, proved himself, and did so many operations, including innovative ones, that it was clear he had a bright future ahead of him.

Cushing combined the temperament and sensitivity of the artist with the patience and method of the scientist. A charming and engaging person, he could also be domineering and critical as a surgeon. His associates admired him for his skill and brilliance, but his tongue-lashings upset them. The most revered clinical teacher in the United States, William Osler, warned him that his future at Johns Hopkins depended on his controlling his temper and tongue.

Cushing had been seeing Katharine Stone Crowell, a Cleveland neighbor, for several years. A close relationship developed, but marriage, as she understood and accepted, would have to wait until his future was more assured.

Life's Work

Based upon a few experiences in Boston and his tic douloureux work, Cushing decided to specialize in neurosurgery. With recommendations from his professors, he went to Europe (1900-1901) to learn from its outstanding medical scientists. In Bern, he worked with the Swiss Nobel laureate, Emil Theodor Kocher, the foremost surgeon in Europe and known to Cushing for his treatise on the lesions of the spinal cord. In Pavia, while on a one-month trip to medical centers in Italy, he was introduced to the sphygmomanometer, the blood-pressure device invented by Scipione Riva-Rocci and in routine use at the hospital there. He sketched it, was given a model of the inflatable armlet part, and, on his return to Johns Hopkins, introduced blood-pressure determination into surgery and general medicine. In England, he assisted another Nobel laureate, the neurophysiologist Charles Sherrington, who at that time was exploring the motor cortex of the brain.

From 1901 to 1912, Cushing was on the surgical faculty of Johns Hopkins, becoming the first American full-time neurosurgeon, engaging in surgical research and animal experimentation, and developing hitherto unthinkable brain operations. On June 10, 1902, he married Katharine Crowell. Their deep love made for a strong marriage, despite his having to sacrifice much of his family life to his profession. They had five children; in 1926, his first-born, William, was killed in an automobile accident. His daughter, Betsey, married James Roosevelt, son of Franklin Delano Roosevelt (and later married John Hay Whitney); another daughter, Barbara, married William Paley of the Columbia Broadcasting System.

The problems facing the neurosurgeon in the early years of the twentieth century were formidable. There had been removal of brain tumors in Europe and the United States with occasional success, but the methods were those of general surgery, and survival was unusual. Cushing succeeded in developing methods of locating the site of tumors based on diagnostic signs and physiological research, and surgical techniques delicate enough to make brain operations feasible. The number of his operations increased yearly, with corresponding reductions in mortality, to levels achieved by no others in his lifetime (from nearly one hundred percent when he began to less than ten percent).

From 1909 to 1912, he was at a peak of activity in clinical and experimental work. In 1910, he invented the silver clip to control hemorrhage, a revolutionary step in lowering the death rate and opening the way to more extensive operations on tumors that were previously inaccessible. The disorders of the pituitary gland at the base of the brain came under scrutiny. He introduced the terms hypopituitarism and hyperpituitarism for the abnormal secretion of the pituitary and the conditions of dwarfism, gigantism, and acromegaly that result. These conditions were fully studied physiologically, clinically, and surgically, and were the subject of a major monograph on the disorders of the pituitary gland in 1912, with remarkable case illustrations and histories.

Cushing had become internationally famous. Many offers from universities came; he turned them all down, reluctant to leave Johns Hopkins and its excellent facilities. In 1912, however, he decided to return to Harvard, with an opportunity to plan a new teaching hospital, the Peter Bent Brigham Hospital, under the control of the Harvard Medical School; Cushing would be the surgeon-in-chief and professor of surgery. He aroused controversy by wanting clinical work for medical students to begin immediately, at the expense of coursework. He was scornful of teachers who lived in ivory towers and refused to make reference to the clinical applications of what they taught. The controversy which developed reflected the historical background of medical education, which had been one of coursework and examinations and not laboratories and teaching hospitals. Cushing was, in fact, the first clinical teacher to give full time to the work of a teaching hospital.

During World War I, Cushing organized a Harvard volunteer unit in 1915, to serve at a Paris military hospital. From 1917, he was a lieutenant colonel at a base hospital in France, operating eleven to eighteen hours daily and drastically reducing mortality by fifty percent in serious head and brain injuries. A 1918 paper on wartime brain injuries made a major contribution to neurosurgery and was used as a reference work by surgeons in World War II. In October, 1918, Cushing suffered a disabling attack of an undiagnosed illness with symptoms of fever, double vision, and numbness in the feet; it would flare up and cause increasing disability later in his life.

Resuming his Harvard career after the war, Cushing continued to improve and expand the field of neurosurgery. He wrote monographs on the different kinds of tumors, their classification, natural history, and treatment. The medical community regarded him as the foremost American surgeon, and he found himself training assistants and students from all over the world.

Cushing also became an accomplished writer. At first an awkward and labored stylist, he honed his skills by writing and rewriting daily, and he became an outstanding example of the physician-writer. Following the death of Osler in 1919, he wrote *Life of Sir William Osler* (1925), a study not only of the man's career but also of the development of medical education during Osler's lifetime. Full of wit, love, and understanding of his dear friend, it brought to life the man and his qualities and won for Cushing the Pulitzer Prize in 1926.

Cushing had to keep track of all of his patients, since neurosurgery had no past history. He requested that they write him on every anniversary of their operation. While he needed to know their subsequent history for the sake of medicine, he also had a sincere interest in their welfare. Letters came from most of them—he eventually performed more than two thousand brain tumor operations—as well as birthday and Christmas cards with statements of gratitude and news of important events in his patients' lives; he had made every one of them his personal responsibility, and each knew that he or she was special to Cushing.

Cushing's days of surgery ended in 1931. Plagued by ill health, he nevertheless continued to contribute to medicine—especially with his identification of the disease now known as Cushing's syndrome, following a brilliant study of patients with painful adiposity of the face and increased basophilic cell activity in the pituitary gland.

In 1932, the year of his retirement from Harvard, thirty-five young associates formed the Harvey Cushing Society with his permission (later named the American Association of Neurological Surgeons). From 1933 to 1937, he was professor of neurology at Yale. An avid collector of medical classics, he left his library of about eight thousand items to Yale. The Historical Library, as a wing of the new Yale Medical School, opened two years after his death.

In retirement, Cushing resumed the role of physician-writer-biographer, focusing on Andreas Vesalius, the Renaissance physician, and producing an extraordinary bio-bibliography of the famed artist-anatomist. By the end of the summer of 1939, the project was nearly complete. In October came a fatal heart attack. Friends finished the project, which was published in 1943, on the four hundredth anniversary of Vesalius' famous treatise on human anatomy.

Summary

Cushing founded the modern discipline of neurosurgery, based on meticulous history-taking, examination, diagnosis, and painstaking operative technique. He wrote the classical descriptions of the history of various types of tumors and developed the surgical treatment to the then-inaccessible pituitary gland. He trained a generation of surgeons, gifted students who came to him, then spread his methods worldwide. He made the laboratory and animal experimentation essential to surgical advance. Exercising profound influence on medical education, he played a major role in the awakening of American medical schools to the demands of research and clinical training in the development of a proficient medical profession.

Bibliography
Cartwright, Frederick F. "The More Recent Specialties: Brain, Lung and Heart." In *The Development of Modern Surgery*, 209-221. New York: Thomas Y. Crowell, 1968. Cartwright provides a lucid historical account of modern surgery, examining Cushing's predecessors and his work in the context of surgical knowledge of the time.
Fulton, John F. *Harvey Cushing: A Biography*. Springfield, Ill.: Charles C Thomas, 1946. This is the definitive biography. More than seven hundred pages long, it presents Cushing's life and career based on the personal knowledge of a longtime associate and using Cushing's unpublished notes and letters.
Singer, Charles, and E. Ashworth Underwood. "Some Modern Surgical Advances" and "The Pituitary." In *A Short History of Medicine*, 2d ed., 366-371, 541-549. New York: Oxford University Press, 1962. The authors give a good overview of the development of neurosurgery and endocrinology and Cushing's contributions to these areas.
Thomson, Elizabeth H. *Harvey Cushing: Surgeon, Author, Artist*. New York: Henry Schuman, 1950. Written for both the general reader and the physician and making use of the Fulton biography, this is more than a shorter version of the Fulton book. Thomson provides illuminating material on Katharine Cushing, her influence on her husband and children, and on Cushing's relationships with his patients. A book of wide appeal.
Walker, A. Earl, ed. *A History of Neurological Surgery*. Baltimore: Williams

and Wilkins, 1957. For the more advanced reader. The dominance of Cushing in this discipline is reflected in many of the twenty-eight chapters, each written by an expert in neurosurgery.

Albert B. Costa

GEORGE A. CUSTER

Born: December 5, 1839; New Rumley, Ohio
Died: June 25, 1876; Little Big Horn River, Montana Territory
Area of Achievement: The military
Contribution: Although greatly obscured by the events surrounding his death at the Battle of the Little Big Horn, Custer's illustrious Civil War exploits made him one of the nation's most respected military figures and a national idol. After the war, his expeditions into the Yellowstone region and the Black Hills earned for him renown as an explorer and compiler of scientific information.

Early Life

George Armstrong Custer was born December 5, 1839, in New Rumley, Ohio. In 1849, his father sent him to live with the boy's married half-sister, Lydia Reed, in Monroe, Michigan. The elder Custer wanted his favorite son to acquire the best possible education, and he had been assured by his daughter that the private "Young Men's Academy" in Monroe would benefit George.

At the age of sixteen, "Autie," as his family affectionately nicknamed him, returned to his parents' home and began a career as a schoolteacher. Always devoted to his family, Custer faithfully presented his mother his monthly salary of twenty dollars as a token of his appreciation of their sacrifices to enable him to become educated.

Like many young men who had been swept up in the thrilling accounts of the Mexican War, Custer nurtured his boyhood love for the military and was determined to make it his profession. In 1857, Custer entered West Point, but during his four years at the Academy his academic record and numerous demerits placed him near the bottom of his class. "My career as a cadet," he recounted in his "War Memoirs" (1876), "had but little to commend it to the study of those who came after me, unless as an example to be carefully avoided." What became known as "Custer's luck" prevailed, however, and in early summer, 1861, the Union Army, desperate for officers, took Custer's entire class, and three days before the first Battle of Bull Run, Second Lieutenant Custer reported to the Army of the Potomac.

Life's Work

Serving as aide-de-camp to Generals George Brinton McClellan, Philip Kearny, and Alfred Pleasonton, Custer's enthusiasm, bravery, and dedication to duty earned for him rapid promotion to the rank of captain. While under Pleasonton, the chief of the Union cavalry, Custer gained a reputation for zeal, sound tactics, and active participation in combat. Consequently, upon Pleasonton's recommendation, on June 29, 1863, Custer, at the age of twenty-three, was made brevet brigadier general in command of the Michigan Cavalry Brigade.

As a general, Custer's initial distinction was his attire. In an attempt to achieve a look of maturity, the sad-eyed youth grew a mustache and allowed his sandy blond locks to drape nearly to his shoulders. To adorn his wiry five-foot, ten-inch, 165-pound frame, the army's youngest general chose rather foppish clothing. Unlike his more conservative fellow officers, Custer wore a broad-billed hat, blue velvet coat with a wide sailor collar, red silk tie, gold insignia tie clasp, white gloves, and loose trousers tucked inside high riding boots.

Any doubts as to the well-dressed cavalier's leadership qualities vanished quickly, as his junior officers marveled at his acts of bravado. Custer enjoyed the thrill of battle and led his men into the fray, waving either his hat or sword, and exhorting them to charge with a shrill "Come on, you Wolverines!" Unlike many Union commanders, Custer gave his troops all the credit for his victories, while shouldering all blame in defeat. This gave "Old Curly," as his men dubbed him, the reputation of being a "soldiers' general," and by the end of the war Custer ranked behind only Ulysses S. Grant, William Tecumseh Sherman, and Philip Sheridan as a beloved savior of the Union.

His combat record was outstanding, and his victories over J. E. B. Stuart's forces at Gettysburg and Yellow Tavern were instrumental in the ultimate triumph of the North. To honor his achievements, Custer, who had risen to the rank of brevet major general in 1864 and had accepted Robert E. Lee's symbolic white towel of surrender, was permitted to witness Lee's official surrender in the McLean House at Appomattox. General Sheridan then purchased the table upon which the document had been signed and presented it to Custer's wife, Elizabeth, with the notation: "There is scarcely an individual in our service who has contributed more to bring about this desirable result than your very gallant husband."

Custer's war record was sufficient to warrant his place as an American military hero. Custer differed from many of his fellow generals, however, in that he felt himself too young to retire on his laurels and had no desire to enter politics. Therefore, he remained in his chosen profession and was sent West.

In May, 1865, he was dispatched to Texas to help destroy the remnants of General Edmund Kirby-Smith's rebel forces, and the following year he was ordered to Washington, D.C., to testify before a congressional committee on conditions in Texas and western Louisiana. In 1866, he reverted to his regular army rank of captain and returned to Monroe. The remainder of that year was spent writing his memoirs and accompanying President Andrew Johnson on his campaign "Swing Around the Circle."

In late 1866, Custer was promoted to lieutenant colonel and assigned to

Fort Riley, Kansas, to head the newly formed Seventh Cavalry. The next year, he participated in General Winfield S. Hancock's campaign against the Sioux and Cheyenne. During this expedition, Custer and his men broke through a virtual siege of Fort Wallace and rescued the garrison. Finding the post ravaged by cholera, he took part of his command on a two-hundred-mile trek to Fort Harker to obtain medical supplies for Fort Wallace. He sent the medicine back with a junior officer, while he obtained permission from the commanding general at Fort Harker to return to Fort Riley to visit Elizabeth. Following the disastrous campaign, Hancock told Congress that he had been undermined by actions of his subordinates, especially Custer, and demanded that the offending junior officer be court-martialed for deserting his command. Despite saving Fort Wallace from attack and disease and having authorization for his absence, Custer was found guilty and suspended, without pay, for one year.

In September, 1868, Generals Sherman and Sheridan had Custer reinstated to lead the Seventh Cavalry on another campaign. Sheridan told Custer: "I rely on you in everything, and shall send you on this expedition without orders, leaving you to act entirely on your own judgment." This faith was rewarded, as a surprise dawn attack on an encampment of hostile Cheyenne along the Washita River resulted in one of the military's most successful Indian battles. Custer seized large quantities of ponies, blankets, weapons, and food, but found himself criticized in the Eastern press because during the daylong fighting fifty-three Indian women and children were slain.

Four years of relative inactivity ended in 1873, when Custer was named second in command for General David Stanley's fifteen-hundred-man force assigned to guard the Northern Pacific Railroad Company survey party. During this service in the Yellowstone region, Custer enhanced his reputation as an Indian fighter by defeating a war party of three hundred Sioux, while sustaining only one casualty among his ninety men.

In July, 1874, Sheridan again called upon Custer, whom he said was "the only man who never failed me," this time to lead an expedition into the Black Hills of the Dakotas. Sheridan feared that if the Sioux went to war, they would use their sacred territory in that area as a refuge. Since the Black Hills had never been explored by whites, Custer was instructed to take more than one thousand men, including soldiers, geologists, paleontologists, zoologists, botanists, and photographers, to reconnoiter the region. Custer sent back voluminous data on scientific discoveries, but the public was most interested in his finding of gold and other precious minerals. Soon a rush of miners flooded onto land reserved by treaty for the Sioux.

Ironically, Custer's downfall was his successful Black Hills expedition. As the Sioux joined with the Northern Cheyenne to repel the white trespassers, the federal government embarked upon a military campaign intended to celebrate the nation's centennial by ridding the Plains of all Indian resistance to white expansion. A coordinated three-prong attack, under the leadership of Generals Alfred Terry, George Crook, and John Gibbon, was to converge on the suspected main Indian encampment along the Little Big Horn River in the Montana Territory. Custer, commanding the only cavalry in the expedition, was sent ahead by Terry to scout the area, and he arrived at the Little Big Horn late on June 24, 1876, two days before the scheduled rendezvous. On the morning of June 25, fearing that his force had been seen and that the enemy would flee before the vise could close around them, Custer decided to launch an attack. Splitting his forces for a pincer movement, as he had done successfully in the past, Custer found himself facing between three thousand and five thousand warriors, nearly three times the number Sheridan had predicted. Cut off from all assistance, Custer and the remainder of his 225 men staved off two charges before succumbing to the superior numbers and weaponry of the Indians.

Summary

Articulate and intelligent, Custer exemplified the nineteenth century career officer by making the motto "duty, honor, country" a way of life. Although his best friends at West Point were Southerners, Custer fought against them because he believed their cause was traitorous. Personally sympathetic to the plight of Indians being driven from their land, he fought against them because his government ordered him to do so. Insubordination was intolerable to Custer, and he believed that orders, no matter how personally offensive, had to be obeyed. Contrary to allegations, Custer did not attack a day early because he sought glory, but rather because his orders from Terry permitted him to act upon his own best judgment.

In death, Custer achieved the ultimate goal of the campaign. National outrage demanded vengeance, and, to avoid possible annihilation, the Indian forces disbanded. Even defeat could not dim Custer's fame in the eyes of his adoring country.

Bibliography

Carroll, John M. *Custer in the Civil War: His Unfinished Memoirs*. Edited by John M. Carroll. San Rafael, Calif.: Presidio Press, 1977. A compilation of documents relating to Custer's Civil War career, followed by a reprinting of the seven chapters of the general's unfinished "War Memoirs," first published in *Galaxy Magazine* in 1876. These chapters, although self-centered, are significant because they represent the final works in Custer's prolific literary career.

Connell, Evan S. *Son of the Morning Star: Custer and the Little Bighorn*. San Francisco: North Point Press, 1984. A thoroughly researched examination of the personalities of Custer, government officials, and Indian leaders. A skillful blend of biography and history of the Plains Indian Wars.

Custer, Elizabeth. *Boots and Saddles: Or, Life in Dakota with General Custer*. Reprint. Williamstown, Mass.: Corner House Publishers, 1974. This facsimile reprint, without introduction, of the original 1885 edition recounts the travels of "Libbie" with her husband from the spring of 1873 through what she calls "Our Life's Last Chapter." An adoring wife, Mrs. Custer dedicated her life to the glorification of her husband. This book, like her *Tenting on the Plains* and *Following the Guidon*, is in her husband's memory and, for that reason, must be read with scrutiny.

Custer, George A. *My Life on the Plains*. Edited by Milo Quaife. New York: Citadel Press, 1962. Originally written as a two-year series of articles for *Galaxy Magazine*, this first appeared in book form in 1874. It offers a self-serving account of Custer's activities from 1867 through 1869. This edition offers the best introductory material and a faithful reprinting of the original.

Frost, Lawrence A. *The Custer Album*. Seattle: Superior Publishing Co., 1964. Former curator of the Custer Room of the Monroe County (Michigan) Museum, Frost is one of the foremost experts on his hometown hero. The text is completely sympathetic to Custer, but even those who do not share that view will be fascinated by the wealth of photographs of Custer and his family.

Graham, William A. *The Custer Myth: A Source Book of Custerania*. Harrisburg, Pa.: The Stackpole Co., 1953. An encyclopedia of events concerning Custer's last battle. Graham spent much of his life obtaining interviews with Indian and white participants of the Little Big Horn. Essential for anyone seriously interested in Custer.

Jackson, Donald Dean. *Custer's Gold: The United States Cavalry Expedition of 1874*. New Haven, Conn.: Yale University Press, 1966. A brief, scholarly account of the Black Hills expedition and its impact on both Indians and westward expansion.

Monaghan, Jay. *Custer: The Life of General George Armstrong Custer*. Boston: Little, Brown and Co., 1959. Perhaps the most balanced biography of Custer. Well-researched and written in a flowing narrative, the book is sympathetic to Custer, but Monaghan resists the temptation to gloss over the general's flaws.

Van de Water, Frederic F. *Glory Hunter: A Life of General Custer*. Indianapolis: Bobbs-Merrill Co., 1934. As the title indicates, this is a hostile biography, written to counter the image set forth by Mrs. Custer's works. Custer is portrayed as a selfish, vain glory-seeker, willing to risk his men's lives to achieve fame. Still considered by many "Custer haters" as a classic, this book should be read with Frost's or Monaghan's to gain a more accurate picture of Custer.

Bruce A. Rubenstein

CLARENCE DARROW

Born: April 18, 1857; Kinsman, Ohio
Died: March 13, 1938; Chicago, Illinois
Area of Achievement: Law
Contribution: The most renowned defense attorney of his time, Darrow won a number of important verdicts in difficult cases while espousing unpopular causes.

Early Life

The fifth of eight children (one of whom died in infancy), Clarence Seward Darrow was born on April 18, 1857, in Kinsman, a small town in northeastern Ohio. His father, Amirus Darrow, was a carpenter who increasingly supplemented his income by working as an undertaker; he was also an avid reader who scattered books on all subjects throughout the house. In addition to his own commitment to reading and self-instruction, young Darrow owed some of his later outlook to his father's unorthodoxy and skepticism toward revealed religion. His mother, Emily Eddy Darrow, bestowed much attention upon him and, until her death when he was fifteen, had great hopes for his success. He was educated at a local school and spent his summers playing baseball or working on a farm. At the age of sixteen, Darrow enrolled at Allegheny College, in Meadville, Pennsylvania; he gave up his studies there after a year and for a time was employed as a schoolteacher. In 1877, he spent a year at the University of Michigan's law school. Apparently, Darrow grew weary of formal education, and he spent a further year working and studying at a law office in Youngstown, Ohio. After a brief and apparently perfunctory oral examination, Darrow was admitted to the Ohio bar, at the age of twenty-one.

With his career now fairly started, Darrow took a fancy to Jessie Ohl, the daughter of a prosperous mill keeper, and after an involved courtship, they were married in 1880; their son Paul was born three years later. Darrow opened law offices in Andover and then in Ashtabula, Ohio; although few cases came his way, in 1884 he was elected borough solicitor, or prosecutor. Darrow had already campaigned actively for the national Democratic Party. He chafed at a small-town existence and thought it likely that his legal career would advance further in a large city. Accordingly, in 1887, he moved with his family to Chicago, where social and political strife had already given the city some notoriety.

Life's Work

For a time, Darrow served on the legal staff of the city of Chicago, and he also obtained a position as corporation counsel for the Chicago and North Western Railway. Increasingly disaffected with the venality and easy ethics of his employer, he took another job with a law firm and began to specialize in cases with social implications. After the mayor of Chicago was shot to death, Darrow tried unsuccessfully, in an appeal, to save the assassin from the gallows. In 1894, widespread disorders accompanied a massive strike of the Pullman Company's railroads; Darrow offered his services but was unsuccessful in his efforts to defend Eugene V. Debs from charges of criminal conspiracy. Darrow also attempted a sortie into national politics but was defeated when he ran for the United States Congress as a Democrat in 1896. As his professional commitments mounted, Darrow became estranged from his wife, Jessie, and they were quietly divorced in 1897. For a time, Darrow considered a literary career; he produced works that dealt with crime and social ills, as well as *Farmington* (1904), a semiautobiographical novel.

In 1898, Darrow took up another criminal conspiracy case, brought against Thomas I. Kidd and other leaders of a woodworkers' union in Wisconsin; he persuaded a jury that Kidd could not be held responsible for incidental acts of union violence that the leaders had neither foreseen nor encouraged. Elected to the Illinois legislature in 1902, Darrow continued to take labor cases, and he served as counsel for the United Mine Workers at United States Anthracite Coal Arbitration Commission hearings in Scranton, Pennsylvania. His remarriage, to Ruby Hamerstrom in 1903, seemed to put his personal life on a firmer footing. Social concerns continued to attract him; in 1907, he won acquittal for William D. Haywood, of the Western Federation of Miners, who had been charged with complicity in the bombing death of a former governor of Idaho. In 1911, in another case involving union violence, Darrow defended James B. and John J. McNamara, who had planted dynamite in the *Los Angeles Times* building; the resulting explosion had killed twenty-one people. Pleading his clients guilty and pointing out that they had not intended to cause any loss of life, Darrow prevailed upon a jury to spare the lives of the defendants; one was sentenced to life imprisonment and the other received fifteen years in prison. After this trial, Darrow himself was charged with jury bribery, and he assisted in his own defense. During the proceedings, the testimony of detectives and police informants was discredited, and he retained his freedom.

Darrow often gave the impression of studied casualness; he was tall, large boned, with prominent cheekbones, a sharp beaklike nose, and an overhanging forehead. He had light-blue eyes that, according to his contemporaries, could be animated by kindness or contracted in anger and outrage. In his gait, he seemed to slump forward; frequently during arguments, an unruly shock of hair would fall over his eyes. His clothes, though well tailored, seemed invariably unpressed, and Darrow claimed that he usually slept in them. His voice was deep, resonant, and slightly rasping. He was a born debater, skilled at the parry and thrust of cross-examination. His summations were moving and masterfully devised treatises upon morality and the law, which frequently attracted overflow audiences into the courtroom.

Darrow was a confirmed skeptic, whose views were tempered by humanity and an instinctive sympathy for the downtrodden. He inveighed against the death penalty, which he considered a barbaric relic of more intolerant ages. An openly avowed agnostic, he sometimes contended that life had no meaning. Frequently, he took controversial cases for the sake of defendants and ideas that were out of public favor. Much of his success derived neither from factual expertise nor from technical mastery of the law; rather, he was determined and generally able to sway juries and judges with deeply felt moral appeals.

As word of his prowess spread, Darrow attracted numerous clients. Many times, he took their cases simply because he did not have the heart to turn them away. About certain issues he felt deeply; in 1920, he invoked the guarantee of freedom of speech in his unsuccessful defense of twenty Chicago Communists. Abhorrence of the death penalty prompted him, in 1924, to defend Nathan F. Leopold, Jr., and Richard Loeb, who had carried out the wanton and senseless murder of a fourteen-year-old boy. Darrow pleaded his clients guilty and in a lengthy, heartfelt plea, kept them from execution. To protest the rising tide of Fundamentalism, in 1925 he took the case of John T. Scopes, who was charged with violation of a Tennessee statute against teaching evolution in the public schools. Although ultimately the defendant was fined, Darrow arranged a dramatic courtroom confrontation by examining counsel for the prosecution, William Jennings Bryan; in the process, Darrow pointed up the inconsistencies that resulted when biblical literalism was applied to the problems of science. For many years, Darrow had been outraged by racial inequality; by his own account his most satisfying case came with his defense, in 1926, of a black family in Detroit. While defending their house against an angry, rampaging mob, Dr. Ossian Sweet and his sons had fired on their assailants, killing one man and wounding another. By evoking the atmosphere of extreme prejudice against them and demonstrating the severe provocation that beset the Sweets, Darrow obtained a verdict of self-defense. In 1927, he won acquittal for two anti-Fascist Italian émigrés who had killed two of their political opponents during a quarrel in New York.

Darrow read widely and had an abiding interest in science, literature, and social thought; he also propounded his views readily and augmented his income by taking part in platform debates. Against some of the well-known figures of his day, Darrow defended agnosticism, condemned Prohibition and capital punishment, and morbidly contended that life was not worth living. He also considered retirement from the practice of law. By this time, his son Paul had established a career in business and was in no sense inclined to emulate his famous father's professional pursuits. For nine months in 1929 and 1930, Darrow and his wife traveled extensively on a vacation in Europe.

Darrow's last major case, which he claimed he took because he wanted to visit Hawaii, was a defense of Lieutenant Thomas Massie and three others in 1932. They had killed one of the men who had allegedly raped Massie's wife. At length, verdicts of manslaughter were returned against the defendants; in an agreement with the prosecution, Darrow and his colleagues obtained executive clemency for their clients in return for dismissals of the indictments still pending in the rape cases. In 1934, Darrow was called to Washington and made chairman of the National Recovery Administration Review Board. Decidedly uncomfortable in this position, he contended that the government was acting as much to sanction as to control the growth of combinations in business. After a year, he resigned. Failing health was accompanied by increasing brooding and despondency; Darrow made few public appearances, and some of those close to him felt that his death, when it came on March 13, 1938, must also have brought relief.

Summary

During his lifetime, Darrow served as defense attorney in nearly two thousand cases; more than one hundred of them were for charges of murder. At one time, Darrow estimated that he had represented one-third of his clients without payment; many other cases were taken to protest what he regarded as cruelty and injustice. His most celebrated cases have become a permanent part of the nation's legal lore, and his summations have been taken as models of expository speaking.

In important respects, Darrow was unique, and he spoke for the unpopular and the outcast during an age before legal consensus had delineated the rights of the accused. Some of his abiding concerns, such as opposition to the death penalty, are still warmly debated. Although he did little to advance the technical growth of the law, his stance of strident advocacy is still cited in recalling some of the most memorable courtroom confrontations in American legal practice.

Bibliography

Darrow, Clarence. *Crime, Its Cause and Treatment*. New York: Thomas Y. Crowell, 1922. This work constitutes the most extensive single statement of Darrow's views on crime and penology. He argues that heredity and environment create most criminals; crime would be reduced by improving social conditions. Darrow maintains that, for the most part, punishment is meant not to deter criminal acts, but to satisfy society's primal longings for vengeance.

_____. *The Story of My Life*. New York: Grosset and Dunlap, 1932. Brash, irreverent retelling of Darrow's life in law, which becomes markedly world-weary toward the end. Interspersed among accounts of his famous cases are excursions into science, religion, and criminology. This work is valuable not so much for its discussion of particular clients or trials—some are dealt with rather sketchily—as for its evocation of the issues and concerns that moved Darrow.

Leopold, Nathan F., Jr. *Life Plus Ninety-nine Years*. Garden City, N.Y.: Doubleday and Co., 1958. The memoirs of one of Darrow's most celebrated clients, this work deals largely with the author's trials and imprisonment. Early in the book, Leopold writes admiringly of Darrow's work during his Chicago murder trial of 1924; he also mentions Darrow's visits and continuing concern during his incarceration.

Ravitz, Abe C. *Clarence Darrow and the American Literary Tradition*. Cleveland: Press of Western Reserve University, 1962. Early in his career, literature was a sometime avocation for Darrow, and this study points to the relationship between his legal theories and his ventures into fiction and literary criticism. Many of his early writings dealt with crime and industrial accidents; the themes of these now nearly forgotten productions foreshadowed concerns he also voiced in the courtroom and in his later, nonfiction works.

Scopes, John T., and James Presley. *Center of the Storm*. New York: Holt, Rinehart and Winston, 1967. The defendant during the famous Tennessee trial of 1925, Scopes discusses his beliefs on evolution, science, and religion. He describes Darrow as the second most influential man in his life, after his father, and depicts at length the unusual but incisive defense his attorney offered.

Stone, Irving. *Clarence Darrow for the Defense*. Garden City, N.Y.: Doubleday Doran and Co., 1941. A popular biography on a broad canvas, this work is dated in some ways but was also written close to the events it describes. It is sufficiently thorough and detailed still to warrant consultation. Darrow's major trials and triumphs are set forth at length, at times projecting a heroic image. Darrow's personal papers, published materials available at the time, and interviews with nearly two hundred contemporaries and associates of the great advocate were used in the preparation of this work.

Tierney, Kevin. *Darrow: A Biography*. New York: Thomas Y. Crowell, 1979. A sober and clear study that assesses Darrow's limitations as well as his strengths. Factual problems in some of Darrow's cases, and also his inconsistencies as a thinker, are presented along with his many achievements. While in no way disparaging, this closely argued and well-documented work delineates the one-sided qualities that indeed contributed so much to Darrow's greatness.

Weinberg, Arthur, and Lila Weinberg. *Clarence Darrow: A Sentimental Rebel*. New York: G. P. Putnam's Sons, 1980. A thorough and well-rounded though somewhat uncritical modern biography. Darrow's own trial for jury bribery is treated at some length. The relationship between his great cases and his manner of thinking is developed through each stage of his career; along the way tribute is paid to his espousal of unpopular causes. This work draws extensively upon court records, Darrow's own writings, and unpublished papers of Darrow and several of his associates.

J. R. Broadus

JEFFERSON DAVIS

Born: June 3, 1808; Christian County, Kentucky
Died: December 6, 1889; New Orleans, Louisiana
Area of Achievement: Politics
Contribution: Davis served his country ably as senator and secretary of war; his commitment to the South led him to accept the presidency of the Confederacy and attempt to preserve Southern independence against bitter opposition and overwhelming odds. Reviled or idealized as a symbol of the Confederacy, Davis' consistency of principle and unflagging efforts balance out the fact that he was not well fitted for the demands of the times and the position.

Early Life

In the turbulent decades of the early 1700's, a son of Welsh immigrants moved his family from Philadelphia to the Georgia area; Evan Davis' son Samuel, as reward for his services as a Revolutionary guerrilla captain, was granted land near Augusta. He was chosen county clerk and in 1783 married Jane Cook. Continuing the family pattern, Samuel migrated often; in 1792 he moved to Kentucky, where his tenth and last child, Jefferson (Finis) Davis, was born at Fairview in Christian (later Todd) County, on June 3, 1808. By 1811, the family was living in Louisiana but later moved to Wilkinson County, Mississippi Territory. In these frontier areas, owners worked in the fields with their slaves; Samuel Davis was able to give only a single slave to each of his children when they married. His eldest son, however, Joseph Emory Davis, demonstrated in his life the "flush times" and upward mobility of the Lower South: He became a lawyer, the wealthy owner of a great plantation, and a "father" to his youngest brother.

In his youth, Jefferson Davis spent two years at the Roman Catholic St. Thomas' College in Kentucky and then attended local schools near home; in 1821, he studied classics at Transylvania University in Lexington, Kentucky. Just after his father's death, late in 1824, he entered West Point Military Academy. He was over six feet tall, slender, an active, high-spirited young man, with brown hair and deep-set gray-blue eyes, a high forehead and cheekbones, and an aquiline nose and square jaw. In 1828, twenty-third out of a class of thirty-three, he was graduated as a second lieutenant. For the next seven years he was on frontier duty at the dangerous and lonely posts in Wisconsin and Illinois, acquitting himself well and with initiative; in 1832, he briefly guarded the captive chief Black Hawk. In 1833, at Fort Crawford, Wisconsin, he met Sarah Knox Taylor, daughter of the commandant, Colonel Zachary Taylor; despite the latter's objections, they were married June 17, 1835, at her aunt's home in Kentucky.

Despite Davis' conviction of his aptitude for the military, he resigned his commission; Joseph gave the young couple an adjoining new plantation, Brierfield, and fourteen slaves on credit. As neither was acclimatized, they left for the Louisiana plantation of a Davis sister, but they both contracted malaria, and Knox Davis died on September 15, 1835. A grieving Davis, convalescing in Havana and New York, spent some time also in a senatorial boardinghouse in Washington, D.C., but soon returned to Brierfield. For the next eight years he led a solitary and reclusive life, reading extensively in literature, history, and the classics and associating primarily with his brother. During this period he developed the basic system of Brierfield, which was almost an ideal plantation: benevolent master, slaves trained and working according to their abilities and making many decisions concerning their labor and earnings, and Davis' personal slave James Pemberton as overseer with a practically free hand. During these years Davis developed his attachments, both theoretical and personal, to the soil, the South, and the new aristocratic society of the Lower South. His identification was completed and symbolized by his marriage on February 26, 1845, to Varina Anne Banks Howell; she was half his age, a black-haired beauty of Natchez high society, with a classical education and a vivacious temperament. Throughout her life, "Winnie" Davis was high-strung, demonstrative, and emotionally turbulent, a determined woman who fought fiercely for those she loved and who was not always either tactful or forgiving.

By this stage of his life, Davis' personality had been formed. Despite his military experience and life as a planter, he had never really had to fight for place and position; he was more of a theoretician than a realist. He was affectionate with family and friends, essentially humorless, coldly logical, with a deep-rooted egotism and a sense of his own merit; he was never able to believe that others' criticism or disagreement could be sincere or impersonal. Committed firmly to aristocracy and slavery, state sovereignty and states' rights (under the Constitution and within the American nation), always a Democrat, Davis moved into politics. In 1843, he lost an election for the state legislature to a well-known Whig; in 1844 he was a Polk elector. In 1845, he was elected to the United States House of Representatives.

Davis entered into marriage in February, 1845, and entered Congress in December; in June, 1846, on the outbreak of the Mexican War, he resigned from the House to become colonel of the volunteer mounted First Mississippi Rifles. He trained his regiment and equipped his men with the new percussion rifles, and under Major General Zachary Taylor it participated creditably in the victory at Monterrey. When, in the following February, General António Lopez de Santa Anna led fifteen thousand men across two hundred miles of desert to confront Taylor's five thousand at Buena Vista, Davis' Mississippi Rifles fought off a Mexican division in an action (the famous V-formation) that may have been decisive for the American victory. Davis led the regiment despite a wound in the foot that kept him on crutches for two years and in intermittent pain for the next decade. This episode gained for Davis a popular reputation as a military hero and reinforced his already in-eradicable conviction of his own military capability.

After Buena Vista, with Taylor's influence waning and the regiment's enlistment expiring, Davis again resigned a military commission, and in December, 1847, was appointed to a vacancy in the Senate. An expansionist, he supported President Polk on the Mexican Cession, even suggesting American acquisition of Yucatan; although he acquiesced in extending the Missouri Compromise line to the Pacific, he asserted that there was no con-stitutional power to prohibit slave property in any territory. The complex politics associated with the Compromise of 1850 included several Southern groupings: Unionists, radical states' righters (in favor of immediate seces-sion), Southern "nationalists" (or "cooperationists," anticipating possible later secession by the South as a whole). When his fellow Mississippi senator Henry S. Foote ran for governor on a Union ticket (a coalition of Whigs and some Democrats), Davis was persuaded to resign from the Senate (in September, 1851) and oppose him on the Democratic ticket; Davis lost by a thousand votes. Political defeat was offset by the birth of the Davis' first child, Samuel Emerson, on July 30, 1852.

Having aided in the campaign to elect Franklin Pierce, Davis was appointed secretary of war in March of 1853. Ironically, these four years were to be the most congenial and productive of his life. He was in good health and spirits; "Winnie" Davis was a charming and vivacious hostess and the Davis house was the social center of official Washington circles. There was a growing family: Although Samuel died on June 30, 1854, Margaret Howell (Maggie or Pollie) was born on February 25, 1855, and Jefferson, Jr., on Jan-uary 16, 1857. As secretary of war, Davis supported the concept (developed by John C. Calhoun during his tenure of the office) of an expansible army; infantry units were issued the new percussion-cap muzzle-loading rifles and Minié balls; infantry tactics were made somewhat more flexible; West Point officers were encouraged to study in Europe and to develop military theory; and the regrettable system of army departments was strengthened. Davis urged the use of camels in the Southwest, but the experiment failed. Davis was unable to influence the Administration on the issues of the *Black War-rior* seizure and the Ostend Manifesto, but as a Southern expansionist he enthusiastically organized a research expedition to the Southwest to provide data which led to the Gadsden Purchase.

The end of Davis' term in the cabinet was soon followed by his election to the Senate; he took his seat in March, 1857. Another son, Joseph Evan, was born on April 18, 1859. Davis' time as senator would have been the peak and epilogue of his political career, had it not been prologue to suffering and defeat. Nearly fifty, he was gaunt and neurotic; he suffered from dyspepsia and neuralgia and lost the sight of his left eye. He was an effective orator, aided by the obvious intensity of his convictions, and he strongly supported the South's interests in the increasingly bitter sectional confrontations of the 1850's. Within the Democratic Party, he fought the popular sovereignty position of Stephen A. Douglas and worked to prevent the latter's nomination as Democratic candidate in 1860.

Abraham Lincoln's election and nonnegotiable stand against expansion of slavery into the territories convinced Davis of the necessity and inevitability of secession; on January 21, 1861, upon learning of Mississippi's secession, he resigned from the Senate. Like few others at the time, Davis expected war, probably anticipating a command position; he was indeed appointed major general of Mississippi's troops. The Montgomery convention, which established a provisional government, however, needed a president more acceptable to the moderates (or earlier "cooperationists") and early in February, 1861, elected Jefferson Davis.

Life's Work

Davis was elected president of the Confederate States of America, for the constitutional six-year term, on October 6, 1861; on December 16, William (Billy) Howell was born. Davis was inaugurated in the official Confederate capital of Richmond, Virginia, on February 22, 1862. On March 6, 1861, the Confederate Congress had authorized a hundred thousand volunteers for a twelve-month enlistment, but even after, Fort Sumter, Davis did not move to ensure an adequate munitions supply or a financial base (for example, the use of cotton supplies to secure paper currency). The emphasis on protecting the capital at Richmond effectively divided the Eastern and Western Confederacy; Davis retained the system of military departments, their heads responsible directly to him, and therefore eliminated the possibility of unified strategy or well-coordinated action. His military strategy was only to defend, meeting Union forces wherever they might move. He failed to understand that the military situation, as well as the political situation, was a revolutionary one; he could not come to grips with the conditions and concepts of this first modern war. It is true that few at that time fully comprehended its implications; Lincoln, Ulysses S. Grant, and William Sherman were probably the only ones who realized its necessities.

Davis' long-standing quarrel with Joseph E. Johnston stemmed from the latter's failure to be ranked highest of the five Confederate full generals. Late in the war, Davis removed Johnston from command in Georgia at a critical point: General John Bell Hood's loss of Atlanta aided in Lincoln's reelection and continued Northern support of the war. Public and congressional opinion did not influence Davis: He refused to remove General Braxton Bragg despite that officer's ineffectiveness in battle, and when forced to remove Judah P. Benjamin as secretary of war, he "promoted" him to secretary of state. Davis spent too much time in battle areas; he neglected the West and refused to authorize the transfer of troops across the boundaries of military departments to areas where they were needed. Even after Antietam, he could not see that only a major offensive held any hope of victory and independence; instead, he insisted on scattering garrisons and attempting to hold every inch of territory. Robert E. Lee's offensive into Pennsylvania came too late and could not thereafter be repeated.

Close control of military policy overshadowed all other considerations in Davis' administration, although all policy in fact concerned the pursuit of the war. Davis' commitment to a "Southern nation" provoked opposition, from "fire-eaters" such as Robert Barnwell Rhett and William L. Yancey, states' righters such as Governors Joseph E. Brown of Georgia and Zebulon B. Vance of North Carolina, and Vice President Alexander H. Stephens. The influential *Richmond Examiner* and *Charleston Mercury* regularly opposed Davis' policies; his imperious approach and inability to handle the political situation gave rise to vague but frightening rumors that he was a despot who at any moment might take over the entire government and even use the army to control the people. The tension between sovereign states and an embryo national government in wartime can be seen in most of the controversial issues: general conscription was denounced as unconstitutional, attempts to suspend the writ of habeas corpus were deemed tyrannical. The "rich man's war and poor man's fight" continued with increasing military setbacks and declining supplies and morale.

During the last winter of the war, Davis remained strangely optimistic. He had always had strong faith; in May of 1862 he had joined St. Paul's (Episcopal) Church. Although devastated by the death of Joseph, who fell from a balcony on April 30, 1864, he was consoled by the birth of Varina Anne (Winnie) on June 27, 1864. He urged a draft of forty thousand slaves (to be freed after victory); he sent an agent to offer Great Britain an emancipation program in return for recognition and military alliance. Peace movements, projects to remove Emperor Maximilian from Mexico, the Hampton Roads conference: Davis would consider no compromising of Southern independence (just as Lincoln was committed absolutely to the Union). He seemed to believe that at the last moment the South might yet be saved, perhaps by one great battle led by General Lee and by himself that would sweep the Union armies from the field.

Having evacuated his family, Davis, along with several associates, left Richmond on April 3, 1865, still committed to continuing the war. News of Appomattox convinced the party to head southward; a cabinet meeting in Greensboro, North Carolina, agreed that General Johnston should ask for terms. At Charlotte, twelve days later, the group recognized Confederate defeat and dispersed, Davis moving south into Georgia to rejoin his family and attempt to leave the country. On May 10, the Fourth Michigan Cavalry came upon them at Irwinville, Georgia; Davis' brief attempt to slip away in a hastily snatched-up rain cape belonging to his wife gave rise to the story that he had tried to disguise himself as a woman to evade capture.

For the next two years, Davis remained a state prisoner in a damp casemate cell in Fortress Monroe. He was once put forcibly in irons for five days, with a lamp burning continually and the guard marching regularly outside, without adequate clothing or books, and suffering from erysipelas. His fortitude, faith, and kindliness impressed the doctors assigned to him, and finally he was placed in more comfortable quarters in the fortress, his family (which had been kept in Savannah) permitted to join him and friends permitted to visit him. On May 4, 1867, he was arraigned on a charge of treason in the federal district court in Richmond and released on bail supplied by ten men, among them Horace Greeley and abolitionist Gerrit Smith. Thereafter, he and his family traveled at various times to Canada, Cuba, New Orleans, Vicksburg, and Davis Bend, as well as to Europe. He was never brought to trial, as the complex constitutional issues surrounding secession remained too controversial and politically incendiary (especially during the Reconstruction period) to be aired in connection with the former president of the defeated Confederacy. His case was dropped on December 5, 1868.

During the remaining years of his life, Davis experienced a series of business failures, several unprofitable European trips, and a gradual recovery of his health. Maggie became Mrs. J. Addison Hayes and settled in Memphis, but Billy died of diphtheria in 1872, and the remaining son, Jefferson, Jr., having failed at Virginia Military Institute, died of yellow fever in 1878. Davis was able to salvage only part of the value of his old plantation in 1878. A friend of Varina, the widowed Mrs. Sarah A. E. Dorsey, gave him a cottage in which to work, on her plantation "Beauvoir," near Biloxi, on the Mississippi Gulf coast. Varina was finally reconciled to this cooperation, and to Davis' inheritance of the estate in 1879, and aided him in his writing of the two-volume *Rise and Fall of the Confederate Government* (1881), primarily a justification of the constitutionality of secession. In the South, Davis was largely "rehabilitated," being often invited to make speeches and dedicate memorials (including one near his birthplace). His youngest, Winnie, the "Daughter of the Confederacy," was assailed for wishing to marry a New York lawyer, grandson of an abolitionist, and died in 1898 at thirty-three, still single and grieving.

Despite financial problems, Davis, as he had done previously, continued to support both Howell and Davis relatives and several poor children and to entertain a variety of visitors. In 1889, he fell ill with bronchitis in New Orleans, Louisiana, and died there on December 6; he was buried there but, on May 31, 1893, reinterred in Richmond. He had steadfastly refused to ask for a federal pardon, even in order to be elected senator from Mississippi, averring that he had committed no legal offense. On October 17, 1978, a unanimous joint resolution of Congress restored his citizenship.

The year after Davis' death, his widow wrote her two-volume *Memoir* (1890); living in New York, she kept his reputation alive, with the help of Joseph Pulitzer and the Confederate "expatriates" in the North. She died in New York on October 16, 1906, at the age of eighty, and was given a military funeral in Richmond.

Summary

Jefferson Davis was poorly suited for the task of political leadership of the Confederacy at its birth. He had a strong will and iron self-discipline, willing to drive himself relentlessly despite failing health and personal troubles, but he could neither deal effectively with political personalities nor catch the public imagination and gain popular support. In a revolutionary situation he was a conservative and a legalist. Satisfied as to the right of secession and the constitutional basis of state sovereignty, he regarded Northern opposition as motivated only by jealousy, greed, and aggression; yet committed to the ideal of the Southern nation, he could not tolerate independent action by state governments or opposition to policies (such as drafting slaves) that the Confederate government believed were necessary to the war effort. He shared with many the delusion that cotton was king and that economic pressures would lead quickly to European aid and victory; he therefore agreed to policies that resulted in the Confederacy's economic isolation. Free to act out his lifelong perception of himself as master strategist and commanding general, Davis kept tight control over all military aspects, never freeing even Lee from it completely, and refusing sound advice at crucial moments. Up to the end of the war, Davis never believed that defeat was possible; he thought that one more major campaign would turn the tide.

Davis' policy was passive-defensive; he always expected European aid even though he was informed of the actual situation. Politically naïve, he apportioned cabinet appointments evenly among the states, thereby making bad choices and alienating the powerful radical secessionists. He dominated his cabinet, so that its able members could not act effectively, yet did not urge his cautious treasury secretary, C. G. Memminger, to be as financially audacious as necessary for real accomplishment. He himself frequently functioned as secretary of war, a position he would have preferred to the presidency or to any other except that of commanding general. He understood neither the proper role of the executive nor the exigencies of strategy, and in attempting to be both president and general, he failed to fulfill either function well.

A nationalist facing sovereign states, a logical theoretician dealing with volatile personalities and political realities, an egotist who could see only the goal but who could not believe that his political opponents also strove for ideals, a leader in revolutionary times who could not rally popular support for great sacrifices: Davis was more of a debit than a credit entry in the Confederacy's account. Yet his dedication was total and his efforts unrelenting, and in the aftermath of defeat, Davis enjoyed more popular admiration than at any other time in his life. He had been a great senator and a great secretary of war. He had never sought public office, but accepted it as a duty. He attracted intense loyalty and admiration as well as provoking bitter enmity, and with all his failings, it is impossible to imagine that any other man in the Confederacy could have done better in those circumstances. Surviving personal tragedies and the loss of an independent South, Davis died unshaken in his beliefs and conscious of his own rectitude and unswerving loyalties, in his own mind fully justified and fulfilled.

Bibliography
Davis, Jefferson. *Jefferson Davis: Private Letters, 1823-1889*. Edited by Hudson Strode. New York: Harcourt, Brace and World, 1966. Very effectively edited providing practically a condensed biography. As with the three-volume biography, strongly biased, placing even more emphasis than Strode's work on personalities.
Davis, Varina. *Jefferson Davis, Ex-President of the Confederate States of America: A Memoir by His Wife*. 2 vols. New York: Belford Co., 1890. A laudatory account, more than sixteen hundred pages; includes long quotations from Davis' speeches and correspondence as well as biographical information dictated by Davis shortly before his death and valuable information from participants in events. Apart from Davis' obvious bias, the book is detailed and usually reliable.
Dodd, William Edward. *Jefferson Davis*. Philadelphia: G. W. Jacobs and Co., 1907. Reprint. New York: Russell and Russell, 1966. Written by a professor at Randolph-Macon College, the book reflects nineteenth century biases of time and place: contented slaves, good masters, Anglo-Saxon civilization. Dodd attempts to balance his own commitment to the United States with strong attachment to the rightness of Davis and the South on the constitutional issues and the "War Between the States."
Strode, Hudson. *Jefferson Davis: American Patriot, 1808-1861*. New York: Harcourt, Brace and Co., 1955.
_____. *Jefferson Davis: Confederate President*. New York: Harcourt, Brace and Co., 1959.
_____. *Jefferson Davis, Tragic Hero: The Last Twenty-five Years, 1864-1889*. New York: Harcourt, Brace and World, 1964. This detailed, three-volume biography by a professor of creative writing is the result of painstaking research, based on both secondary sources and primary documents including a thousand previously unavailable personal letters. Neither scholarly nor analytical; detailed narrative and quotations replace the historian's generalizations. Pro-Davis with a pro-Southern, secessionist bias; often reads more as special pleading than as careful interpretation.
Tate, Allen. *Jefferson Davis*. New York: G. P. Putnam's Sons, 1969. A very

brief account by one of the Nashville "Agrarians." Emotional and often contradictory defense of Davis as representative of the stable agrarian Southern society facing the aggression of the new industrial North; simultaneously blames Davis for the Confederate defeat.

Warren, Robert Penn. *Jefferson Davis Gets His Citizenship Back*. Lexington: University Press of Kentucky, 1980. Very brief, almost a memoir of the author's boyhood in the early twentieth century South, by a master writer. Effective evocation of the war and the man.

Wiley, Bell Irvin. *Confederate Women*. Westport, Conn.: Greenwood Press, 1975. Relatively brief but informative work, based on primary sources. Excellent portrayal of the lives, ideas, and influence of Virginia Clay-Clopton, Mary Boykin Chesnut, and Varina Davis.

Marsha Kass Marks

EUGENE V. DEBS

Born: November 5, 1855; Terre Haute, Indiana
Died: October 20, 1926; Elmhurst, Illinois
Areas of Achievement: Labor and politics
Contribution: Debs's work in the organization of labor and the adoption of social welfare legislation had a significant impact on the American economy and government.

Early Life

Eugene Victor Debs was born in Terre Haute, Indiana, on November 5, 1855. He was the third child of six who survived to adulthood and the first son of Jean Daniel Debs and Marguerite Marie Bettrich Debs. His parents had emigrated in 1849 from Alsace, lived briefly in New York City and Cincinnati, and settled in Terre Haute, opening a grocery store which provided the family with a modest but sustaining income.

In his reading of Victor Hugo's *Les Misérables* (1862)—he was named by his father after Hugo and Hugo's compatriot and fellow novelist, Eugène Sue—Debs early became aware of the wretchedness of poverty and the dream of its eradication. His formal education was perhaps less influential; in 1871, against his parents' wishes, he left high school, worked for the Terre Haute and Indianapolis Railroad, and in December, 1871, was promoted to the position of fireman.

Debs was employed as a railroadman for two years. In 1873, as a result of the financial panic and the subsequent economic depression, he lost his job, moved to East St. Louis, and at first hand witnessed the realities of urban beggary and desperation. After his return to Terre Haute the next year, he secured employment in a wholesale grocery company and participated in the cultural and civic institutions of the small Midwestern city. He established, along with others, the Occidental Literary Club, served as its president, and provided a platform for such national figures as the atheist propagandist and orator Robert Ingersoll, the former abolitionist Wendell Phillips, who had embraced the cause of labor, and the poet James Whitcomb Riley. The visit to Terre Haute of Susan B. Anthony, and the refusal of the literary club to sponsor her speech, brought him into contact with the cause of women's rights and the hostility which the intrepid suffragist constantly encountered.

Life's Work

In February, 1875, although no longer involved in the industry, Debs became a member of the newly established Vigo Lodge of the Brotherhood of Locomotive Firemen, rose rapidly to prominence in union circles, and with labor support was elected first as Terre Haute city clerk and then, in 1884, as a representative to the lower house of the Indiana General Assembly. His legislative record reveals a dedication to labor issues, the sponsoring of railroad workers' safety and employers' liability bills, and the abortive support of a law extending the ballot to Indiana women.

The year 1885 was a momentous one in Debs's life and career. A photograph taken sometime later shows him clean-shaven, with a receding hairline, and smart clothes. On June 9, 1885, he married Katherine Metzel, the stepdaughter of a Terre Haute druggist. He was grand secretary of the Brotherhood of Locomotive Firemen and editor of its magazine; before the year's end, he left his positions in the grocery warehouse and as state legislator and devoted himself fully to the cause of labor organization.

In the pages of the union's official publication, Debs frequently commented on labor strategies and the structure of unionization. He was opposed to strikes except as a last resort. He believed that the use of boycott was a terrible example of economic coercion. He dissociated himself from any project that would effect an "amalgamation" of labor organizations and the dissolution of the independent craft unions.

The 1888 strike against the Chicago, Burlington and Quincy Railroad, which concluded in defeat for the union, had an important impact on Debs and modified his attitude toward labor organization. If not yet advocating the establishment of an industrial union, he urged that the railway unions develop a federation similar to the American Federation of Labor, and, by numbers and a united front, win concessions on wages and other terms and conditions of employment. His efforts and those of other railroad labor leaders reached a brief fruition in 1889, in the establishment of a Supreme Council of the United Orders of Railroad Employees, combining in a federation firemen, brakemen, and switchmen. The organization was too weak, however, to resolve disputes among its members, caused bitterness and estrangement among the railroad unions, and at its 1892 annual convention, Debs reluctantly sponsored a successful resolution dissolving this experiment in labor federation.

Disillusioned by the impotency of the Supreme Council of the United Orders of Railroad Employees, believing that a federation of craft unions would not prove effective in ameliorating labor conditions, Debs turned to the creation of an industrial railroad union. The American Railway Union (ARU) founded in Chicago in June, 1893, with Debs serving as president, represented a threat not only to railroad corporations but also to the railroad unions of craftsmen and to the American Federation of Labor. It proposed to organize all railroad workers, coal miners, and longshoremen employed in the industry, irrespective of their skills. Reflecting the racism of the 1890's, it barred black Americans from membership. (Debs, however, opposed such exclusionary language in its constitution.)

The year 1893 was an unpropitious time to form a new labor organization. There was another financial panic and another depression; the ranks of the unemployed swelled, and the breadlines in the cities grew longer. On the other hand, the depression caused railroadmen to desert the unions; before a year was over, the ARU had become the largest single labor union in the United States, with a membership of more than 150,000. In April, 1894, it won a brilliant victory and a wage increase after an eighteen-day strike against the Great Northern Railroad. Yet its triumph was transitory: A month later began the strike and lockout at the Pullman Palace Car Company outside Chicago. The employee-inhabitants of Pullman town had long been resentful of the unwillingness of the company to sell them the houses in which they lived, to accord them political rights in the selection of town officials, and to lower rents as wages were reduced in September, 1893. Against the advice of Debs and other ARU officers, in May, 1894, they struck, and, the next month, sent their delegates to the first annual convention of the industrial union which by coincidence was meeting in Chicago. Their accounts of exploitation and deprivation swayed the convention to support a boycott of all railroad companies with Chicago terminals unless they refused to link Pullman cars to their passenger trains.

The Pullman Strike of 1894 pitted the ARU against the General Managers Association, a trade organization of twenty-four railroad companies with terminals in Chicago. Allied with management were the judges of the federal courts, the Democratic Administration of Grover Cleveland, and particularly Attorney General Richard Olney. Olney was determined to crush the railroad workers and to destroy their union. He attained both objectives. Borrowed from the Chicago, Milwaukee, and St. Paul Railroad, appointed as special district attorney, Edwin Walker successfully petitioned the federal court in Chicago to grant an injunction which prohibited the ARU, its president, and other officials from any further supervision of the strike. They could not speak, write instructions, or use telegraph or telephone lines to support ARU members who had paralyzed railroad traffic, not only in and out of Chicago but also in twenty-seven Western states and territories. Unemployed railroad workers were transported from the East to replace striking employees, and on July 4, 1894, federal troops appeared in Chicago by Cleveland's order. Labor had suffered one of the most devastating defeats in its history. The ARU was wrecked, its members blacklisted, and the Pullman workers were forced to return to their jobs under the old conditions. Debs was sentenced to six months' imprisonment in Woodstock Jail for violating the federal court's injunction.

The failure of the ARU and the subsequent incarceration converted Debs to socialism as a preferable economic system. Within two years after his release, he joined the Social Democratic Party (in 1901, it became the Socialist Party of America), served on its executive board, and, in 1900, ran for President of the United States. It was the first of five campaigns. Debs used his candidacies as forums for education, attracting large crowds, arguing that socialism and democracy were compatible, standing on party platforms that advocated, among other things, women's suffrage, industrial safety legislation, shorter workdays, and the abolition of child labor. He received 96,978 votes in 1900, 402,406 in 1904, and eight years later, a climactic vote of 897,011, representing six percent of the electorate.

World War I and the entry of the United States in April, 1917, marked the end of the Socialist electoral momentum. In June, 1917, Congress passed the Espionage Act (amended the next year to include nine new federal criminal offenses) to enforce the Selective Service Act and to suppress verbal opposition to the war. Debs was angered by the imprisonment of many of his Socialist colleagues under the congressional legislation. On June 15, 1918, in Canton, Ohio, he addressed the Ohio Socialist Party Convention. In a long and sometimes eloquent speech, he expressed sympathy for his incarcerated Socialist comrades, excoriated the United States Supreme Court, and criticized conscription and the United States' participation in the European conflagration. He did not directly counsel draft resistance or illegal action in the military forces or say anything to promote the success of the German army. Nevertheless, he was arrested, indicted, and, in September, 1918, tried in a Cleveland courtroom, convicted, and sentenced to ten years' imprisonment. His appeal to the United States Supreme Court, his attorneys arguing that the Espionage Act violated the First Amendment guarantee of freedom of speech, was concluded in March, 1919, by Justice Oliver Wendell Holmes, Jr.'s opinion affirming the conviction.

Debs, sixty-three years old, confronted a decade of imprisonment. Depressed at times by his confinement in Atlanta Penitentiary, elated at others by the steady flow of sympathetic letters and visitors, in 1920 he ran once more for president, the only candidate ever to have done so while in prison.

Ironically it was Republican President Warren G. Harding who ordered Debs's release on Christmas Day, 1921. The Socialist leader was not able to unite his party, which had been torn by dissension over the war and by the emergence of two Communist political organizations. His personal popularity, however, had not waned. He spoke out against violent revolution, criticized the Soviet government, and worked to revise Socialist Party fortunes. Hampered by failing health, he continued his speaking tours throughout the country, edited the *American Appeal*, and, in a last pamphlet, pleaded the case of Nicola Sacco and Bartolomeo Vanzetti. He died on October 20, 1926, in Lindlahr Sanatorium in a Chicago suburb and was buried in his hometown of Terre Haute.

Summary

Although the ARU failed and the Socialist Party declined in influence during his lifetime, Debs left behind him important legacies in the currents of twentieth century American history. The ARU served as a model of the industrial organization of labor, emulated by the establishment of the more enduring Congress of Industrial Organizations. The Socialist Party of America, under his leadership, impelled the major political parties of Democrats and Republicans to coopt reformist elements in their rival's platform. The abolition of child labor, maximum hour and minimum wage legislation, the protection of employees in the workplace, woman's suffrage, and the graduated income tax became part of state and federal legal codes or amendments to the United States Constitution.

Debs's conviction and incarceration under the Espionage Act educated the American public and the Supreme Court about the dangers of suppressing dissent and the crucial relationship between the free speech guarantee and the preservation of democratic institutions. Perhaps most important, his dedication to the alleviation of poverty, to social justice, and to peace has inspired other Americans in later generations and has contributed to the richness of American political life.

Bibliography
Debs, Eugene Victor. *Writings and Speeches of Eugene V. Debs*. New York: Hermitage Press, 1948. A collection of Debs's works, with an introduction by Arthur M. Schlesinger, Jr., including an abridged version of the Canton speech for which the Socialist leader was convicted and imprisoned for violation of the Espionage Act. The book further exhibits the quality of Debs's rhetorical skills.
Ginger, Ray. *The Bending Cross: A Biography of Eugene Victor Debs*. New Brunswick, N.J.: Rutgers University Press, 1949. The most colorful and readable study of Debs's life, narrative in form, but perpetuating a mythic portrait of the Socialist leader.
Lindsey, Almont. *The Pullman Strike*. Chicago: University of Chicago Press, 1942. The only systematic account of the conflict between the Pullman workers and the ARU on one side and the railroad corporations and the Cleveland Administration on the other. The author emphasizes employee grievances relative to conditions in Pullman, Illinois, and, along with a careful analysis of the course of the strike, presents the reactions and recommendations of the United States Strike Commission in its aftermath.
Morgan, H. Wayne. *Eugene V. Debs: Socialist for President*. Syracuse, N.Y.: Syracuse University Press, 1952. Focuses on the five presidential campaigns as well as on the history of the party between 1900 and 1925.
Peterson, J. C., and Gilbert C. Fite. *Opponents of War: 1917-1918*. Madison: University of Wisconsin Press, 1957. One of many such studies, a wide panorama of the suppression of dissent during World War I, the closing of German-language and Socialist newspapers, the prosecutions under the Espionage Act, and the antilibertarian record of the Woodrow Wilson Administration.

Salvatore, Nick. *Eugene V. Debs: Citizen and Socialist*. Urbana: University of Illinois Press, 1982. The best and most analytic biography to date; the author argues that Debs's career can be viewed in an American tradition of radical reformism rather than as an attempt to implant into American politics an alien European ideology.

Shannon, David. A. *The Socialist Party of America: A History*. New York: Macmillan, 1955. An overview of the fortunes of the Socialist Party from its origins in 1901 to the early 1950's, placing Debs in a context of intraparty factionalism.

David L. Sterling

LEE DE FOREST

Born: August 26, 1873; Council Bluffs, Iowa
Died: June 30, 1961; Hollywood, California
Area of Achievement: Electronics
Contribution: De Forest's three hundred patents mark him as a great American inventor. For his most famous invention—the thermionic grid-triode—he was known as the "father of radio."

Early Life

Lee de Forest was born in Council Bluffs, Iowa, but grew up in Talladega, Alabama, where his parents moved when he was six. His father, Henry Swift de Forest, was a Congregationalist minister of Huguenot background who served as president (1879-1896) of Talladega College, for black students. Lee's mother, descended from the *Mayflower*'s John Alden, was among the first graduates of Iowa's Grinnell College. Lee had a sister, Mary, born 1872, and a brother, Charles, born 1878.

Even when young, de Forest was aware of his destiny as an inventor. He had a passion to understand the workings of all things mechanical and electrical, often building model foundries and even castles based on his observations. De Forest also discovered early that mechanical prowess can create happiness: On Christmas Day, 1879, he delighted the children of his poverty-stricken town by solving problems that had kept a model train from working. His creations drew the admiration of upper-class Talladega whites, who otherwise held Lee's "do-gooder" family in contempt.

As a teenager, de Forest attended Mt. Hermon School in Massachusetts, then entered a three-year course in mechanical engineering at the Sheffield Scientific School at Yale University on a scholarship endowed by a wealthy ancestor. After he was graduated in 1896, de Forest returned for graduate studies with such leading academic scientists of his time as Josiah Willard Gibbs and Henry Bunstead.

In his twenties, the intense, blue-eyed de Forest was thin, almost gaunt, shabbily dressed in shiny suit and hand-me-down straw hat. He already displayed what would become lifelong traits: a strong preference for applied over theoretical science, idealistic excitement over possible uses for his inventions, and keen disappointment at what he considered their misapplications. An introvert, he lacked the business acumen of such innovators as Nicola Tesla, Guglielmo Marconi, and Thomas Edison, all of whom he longed to emulate. Yet he protested loudly if he received less credit than he thought was his due for his inventions. Throughout his life, his companies were engaged in costly, protracted lawsuits over patent rights. Not that de Forest's work went unrecognized. As early as his first postgraduate year, he won national acclaim when the *Scientific American* for March, 1897, published a discussion of his "equationer," a machine he devised that would solve quadratic equations.

Bunstead had introduced him to Hertzian radio waves, however, and radio transmission was to become his principal life interest. In 1899, de Forest produced one of America's first doctoral theses on the subject now known as radio: "Reflection of Hertzian Waves from the Ends of Parallel Wires."

Life's Work

De Forest got his first job at a dynamo factory of Western Electric in Chicago. He spent his free hours trying to develop a Hertzian wave detector suitable for receiving radio broadcasts. Hearing of this work, his supervisors at Western Electric first gave him the use of a laboratory during nonworking hours, then released him from telephone work altogether, telling him to "Do as you damn please." For several years thereafter he concentrated exclusively on wireless data transmission, especially its journalistic applications. In 1904, his electrolytic wave detector was used by European reporters transmitting news of the Russo-Japanese war, until the Japanese put a stop to this practice. In 1906, he made good on an earlier failed attempt to transmit an on-the-spot account of the International Regatta contest.

In the meantime, he had organized his own firm, De Forest Wireless Telegraph Company. At first privately financed, the company later sold shares to the public. Two events brought the company to disaster in 1906: A patent infringement suit went against it, and de Forest's associates released questionable stories to the media in an attempt to influence the price of shares. De Forest resigned, selling a group of patents to his former partners for a mere one thousand dollars.

Painful though it was, this marked an important transition for de Forest, from telegraphy (signal transmission) to radio (voice transmission). In 1907, he patented a Hertzian wave detector, the "Audion," which was vastly superior to his earlier invention and to other scientists' inventions then in use. It was the famous thermionic grid-triode vacuum tube, similar to a two-element device invented by John Ambrose Fleming in 1904, except that de Forest had inserted a third electrode as a stabilizer between cathode and anode. Also in 1907, de Forest made experimental voice broadcasts to the public in New York City. In 1910, he broadcast a live operatic performance by Enrico Caruso.

By most accounts, however, it was not until 1912—while working at the Federal Telegraph Company in Palo Alto, California—that de Forest recognized the true potential of his device. In that year he realized that he could amplify high-frequency radio signals by "cascading" a series of Audion tubes. In so doing, he increased the device's capability above what could have been accomplished by the previous method of raising the voltage on a single tube. Starting with a radio signal that was very weak, de Forest strengthened it by placing transformers between tubes so that the signal from each tube was amplified before passing into the next one. Moreover, experimentation showed him how to produce oscillation by feeding part of the signal from his triode vacuum back into its own grid. Used with antennae, this oscillating signal greatly improved the power and quality of voice or music transmissions over what was produced by the crude transmitters of the day. Modifications made de Forest's inventions usable for either transmission, receipt, or amplification of radio signals.

These inventions were milestones for both radio and long-distance telephone communication, bringing tremendous changes in everyday life throughout the industrialized world. De Forest's success led to his becoming a charter member (and afterwards president) of the Institute of Radio Engineers in 1912; three years later, he received the Elliot Cresson Medal of Honor from the Franklin Institute. Unfortunately, as so often in de Forest's life, this triumph was alloyed by conflict and disappointment: In 1909, his second firm, the De Forest Radio Telephone Company, had begun to fall apart, again because of his associates' questionable practices. In 1912, the process culminated in the indictment of de Forest on charges of using the mails to defraud the public. Ironically in light of his triode successes, he was accused of promoting a "worthless" device, the Audion tube. Not until early 1914 was the case resolved, with two of the company's partners convicted and jailed, but with de Forest and another partner acquitted.

By now, de Forest had become highly distrustful of businessmen. Unsure of his ability to manufacture his own inventions, he began to sell his patents, sometimes at prices far below their true worth. For example, according to an early biographer, de Forest's disillusionment was intensified when in 1912 he sold his Audion patent to American Telephone and Telegraph for fifty thousand dollars—only to learn that the company had earmarked ten times that amount should it become necessary to close the deal.

Nevertheless, proceeds from this sale—in addition to ninety thousand dollars from the sale of the triode to the Bell System in 1914—enabled de Forest to organize a new company in New York. This firm, which manufactured radio tubes and other equipment for military and civilian use, brought de Forest a steady income until 1923, when he sold it to devote full time to work on sound motion pictures. For the next four years he spent much time in American theaters demonstrating what he called "Phonofilm," which recorded sound optically on the film itself. This principle is similar to the one used in motion pictures today, but de Forest, unable to achieve high-quality sound, failed to interest film producers of the time. One film critic, Karl Kitchen, wrote:

> The invention, . . . which has been perfected by Dr. Lee de Forest, does all that is claimed for it. The action and the sound synchronize perfectly—but

what of it? The music sounds like ordinary phonograph music which is very different from that of a symphony orchestra, to put it mildly. . . . Besides, the theatre-going public has not evidenced any interest in talking pictures.

As before, rival inventors brought patent litigation against de Forest, and he against them. One important case—against Elias Reis over the "film-slit" method of producing motion-picture sound—was decided in de Forest's favor, but most of the other suits ultimately went against him. During the late 1920's, he worked on another device for motion-picture theaters: a television process using a mechanical scanner, which also proved unsuccessful. His next enterprise, in the 1930's, was the production of Audion-diathermy machines for medical use. World War II saw him engaged in military research for Bell Telephone Laboratories.

De Forest was embittered by the claims of those who disputed the priority of his inventions and by the exploitation of radio by others for enormous profit. (It should be noted, however, that the work of other scientists was needed to improve on his original ideas, just as he improved on those of his predecessors; for example, H. D. Arnold and Irving Langmuir enhanced the effectiveness of de Forest's triode through their efforts to attain the highest possible vacuum.) Yet what galled de Forest far more was the insipid, commercial uses to which his inventions—especially radio—were put. In his fifties, this lifelong devotee of Beethoven and Wagner confronted a group of radio executives with these words:

> What have you done with my child? The radio was conceived as a potent instrumentality for culture, fine music, the uplifting of America's mass intelligence. You have debased this child, you have sent him out in the streets in rags of ragtime, tatters of jive and boogie-woogie, to collect money from all and sundry.

Despite his anger over "the dreary dollar-chasing uses of the ether," de Forest continued to believe strongly in the future of electronics and its value for human life. He remained involved in the field almost to his death. He was eighty-four when he received his last patent in 1957, on an automatic telephone dialing device.

Also relatively late in life, de Forest received recognition commensurate with the magnitude of his inventions. Among his many honors were the Prix Saint Tour of the French Academy, honorary doctor of science degrees from Yale and Syracuse universities and the Cross of the Legion of Honor from the French government. He was even considered for the Nobel Prize in physics. Although he never achieved that honor, he was world famous as the "father of radio" and the "grandfather of television."

De Forest was married four times. His final marriage, to film actress Marie

Mosquini in 1930, was a happy one that lasted the rest of his life. As a widow, she donated his papers and other materials to the Foothill Electronics Museum in Los Altos, California, established in 1969.

Despite the immeasurable value of de Forest's inventions—radio alone was a billion-dollar industry by the time he reached fifty—de Forest left an estate worth only twelve hundred dollars when he died in Hollywood, California, on June 30, 1961.

Summary

Although only a few of de Forest's three hundred patents are considered important today, it is impossible to overstate the significance of his thermionic grid-triode and his use of it as an oscillator and amplifier. As electronic advances, these are on a par with the much later development of the transistor (1947) and of solid-state electronics (the 1950's). Even greater is the significance of the triode as a social, educational, and cultural development. Radio, with the triode at its heart, has brought lectures, musical and dramatic performances, and news events from congressional deliberations to military battles, into the homes of millions around the world. Like television after it, radio has brought the world closer together, providing, as de Forest put it, "a new world cement."

His vision concerning the practical benefits of his inventions to humanity mark him as a quintessential American of the late nineteenth century. Also characteristic of a child of that era were de Forest's individualism and his extreme drive and discipline; often while working in his laboratory he would go without food or sleep, and at least once he fainted from illness and exhaustion.

If these are the traits that fueled his successes, he had other traits, equally typical of his period, that account for his many failures, above all a naïve faith that others shared his idealism. Once this faith was broken, de Forest mirrored ordinary citizens' growing disillusionment with and distrust of American businessmen and large corporations.

Radio and other inventions to which Lee de Forest contributed have broadened people's horizons, but it remains to be seen whether advanced communications technology will fulfill his vision of binding together

the various peoples . . . of the globe in a quickened intelligence, a livelier sympathy, a deeper understanding. This, in time, would spread the knowledge which alone will end war.

Bibliography

Carneal, Georgette. *A Conqueror of Space*. New York: Horace Liveright, 1930. An authorized biography that praises its subject uncritically and passes over de Forest's share of responsibility for business reverses. Valuable for its vivid anecdotes evoking de Forest's milieu and character, and for its technical descriptions of his experiments.

De Forest, Lee. *Father of Radio: The Autobiography of Lee de Forest*. Chicago: Wilcox and Follet, 1950. A biased and rather immodestly titled autobiography that amply reveals the character of de Forest. Contains his 1920 paper on the development of the triode, as well as a list of his other inventions.

Levine, Israel E. *Electronics Pioneer: Lee de Forest*. Milwood, N.Y.: Associated Faculty Press, 1964. A straightforward, clearly written account of de Forest's life for nontechnical readers.

MacLaurin, W. Rupert. *Invention and Innovation in the Radio Industry*. Salem, N.H.: Ayer Co., 1971. Stresses the economic consequences of major technical contributions to the development of radio.

Miessner, Benjamin Franklin. *On the Early History of Radio Guidance*. San Francisco: San Francisco Press, 1964. Contains an impartial, well-documented account of the development of the triode, including de Forest's contributions.

Thomas Rankin

CECIL B. DEMILLE

Born: August 12, 1881; Ashfield, Massachusetts
Died: January 21, 1959; Los Angeles, California
Area of Achievement: Film
Contribution: Capturing early twentieth century American values on the screen, DeMille achieved popular, if not critical, success in his film spectacles and sex comedies.

Early Life

Cecil Blount DeMille was born August 12, 1881, in Ashfield, Massachusetts. His mother, née Matilde Beatrice Samuel, was descended from an English Jewish family; his father, Henry deMille (Cecil was alone in capitalizing the "D"), was descended from Dutch immigrants who prospered in the northeast. DeMille, who was intent on advancing on social as well as artistic and financial fronts, never acknowledged his Jewish ancestry. Similarly, he maintained that his father was a "professor" who taught at Columbia University; such was not the case, but the story suited the image that DeMille sought to maintain.

DeMille's parents were particularly influential in determining the course of his life. After a brief teaching career, his father considered the ministry but, at his wife's urging, opted for a career in the theater instead and, in fact, became a successful playwright. Though he died when DeMille was only twelve, the theatrical influence continued in the person of DeMille's mother, who, after she failed at running a school for girls, became a theatrical agent in New York. DeMille credited his mother with playing the most influential role in his life, for she passed on to her favorite son her ambition and competitiveness, as well as her belief in women's rights. As a result, DeMille was left with contradictory emotions in his relationships with women: He wanted to dominate, but he also respected independent women who resisted his efforts at control.

DeMille attended the Pennsylvania Military College before he completed his education at the American Academy of Dramatic Arts. Like his father and his older brother, William, who was establishing himself as a playwright, DeMille had decided that his future was in the entertainment world. After his graduation in 1900, he took an acting job and appeared both in New York and on the road. In 1902, he married Constance Adams, an actress, and they spent several years working together in various acting troupes without much success. Nor were his playwriting ventures—first with David Belasco, then with his brother—more successful. By the end of the decade, his dramatic endeavors, which included a stint as manager of his mother's theatrical agency, had been unrewarding, both financially and critically.

Life's Work

DeMille's real career began in 1913, when he and Jesse L. Lasky, a musician friend, saw *The Great Train Robbery* (1903) and became intrigued with the possibility of telling a story through the cinematic, rather than dramatic, medium. As a result of their subsequent discussions, the Jesse L. Lasky Feature Play Company was formed: In addition to DeMille and Lasky, the partners were Arthur Friend, an attorney, and Samuel Goldfisch, who later became Samuel Goldwyn. *The Squaw Man* (1914), the company's first production, was shot in Hollywood, where the company relocated. While the company was named for Lasky, DeMille was actually in charge of the film, which was a tremendous financial success, and both the Lasky Company and DeMille were established as forces to be reckoned with in the film industry. By 1915, DeMille had expanded the company by hiring additional directors and cameramen, as well as some eighty actors and actresses. Among his recruits was his brother, William, who left the New York theater to head the fledgling company's script department. With the purchase of screen rights to ten of David Belasco's plays, DeMille gained valuable properties in addition to the prestige Belasco's name generated. In order to distribute their films, the Lasky company signed a distribution contract with the newly formed Paramount Pictures. By the end of 1915, DeMille himself had directed twenty-one films.

One of those 1915 films was *The Cheat*, a society drama about a deceitful woman who is branded by a Burmese ivory merchant who lends her ten thousand dollars on the condition that she sleep with him. The East-West sexual content (Sessue Hayakawa played the Burmese) titillated film audiences and made the film a financial as well as artistic success. With *The Cheat*, DeMille established himself as a director of quality films, and beginning in 1916 he began to direct fewer but more expensively budgeted films. In 1916, DeMille signed a five-year contract with Famous Players-Lasky (while DeMille was filming in Hollywood, Adolph Zukor's Famous Players company effected the merger with Lasky): That contract brought him a thousand dollars per week and the assurance that his films would be identified specifically as his work. A "DeMille" film had much the same box-office appeal as a film by D. W. Griffith, the acknowledged leading director. In fact, DeMille, who was a master at public relations, did much to shape the American public's image of the director as the dominant creative force in filmmaking. On the set, he was an imposing figure in boots, jodhpurs, open shirt, and Louis XV hat; to convey his commands he carried a whistle but later adopted a megaphone and then a loudspeaker. His private life was no less conspicuous: first, an appropriately ornate mansion; then a magnificent "weekend retreat" called, with DeMille restraint, "Paradise"; finally, a yacht, purchased in 1921, called *Seaward*. DeMille acted and lived the role of the Director, both in art and in life.

Before World War I, DeMille made films in several different genres: comedies, Westerns, war pictures, and society dramas. After the war, however, he sensed a growing public interest in consumerism as the lower classes began to desire to emulate the rich. Gone was the Protestant work ethic that promoted sacrifice, postponed gratification, and celebrated hard work and honesty; in its place was the ethic of the Jazz Age, with its permissive attitudes toward sex and morality and its elevation of materialism over spirituality. That postwar audience renounced Victorian values and endorsed the "fast" life of the rich and the famous, which they found in DeMille's films with their emphasis on "sex appeal" and the "modern woman." DeMille, whose mother had passed on to her son similar views about independent women, seemed particularly suited to depict "the modern woman." The most important of these popular sex comedies were *The Affairs of Anatol* (1921), *Old Wives for New* (1918), *Don't Change Your Husband* (1919), and *Why Change Your Wife?* (1920).

DeMille's film production slowed to about two pictures a year after 1922, probably because of DeMille's entrepreneurial efforts, which extended beyond filmmaking to film production: Cecil B. DeMille Productions was formed to enable him to control production of his films. After some bitter disputes with Zukor over production costs (well in excess of a million dollars) for *The Ten Commandments* (1923), DeMille broke with Famous Players. Lasky purchased the Ince Studios and arranged to have his films distributed through Producers Distributing Corporation (PDC). When, however, the Keith Albee-Orpheum circuit of theaters merged with PDC, DeMille Productions, and Cinema (the holding company), his control over production was again threatened. After subsequent mergers and consolidations further weakened DeMille's control, he signed a contract with Metro-Goldwyn-Mayer (MGM). Unfortunately, his three MGM films did not fare well at the box office, and his contract was not renewed. In fact, when he returned from an extensive overseas trip and wanted to make *The Sign of the Cross* (1932), he had difficulty financing the film until he got the necessary backing from Paramount (the old Famous Players-Lasky). The financial success of *The Sign of the Cross* established him at Paramount, where he stayed for the remainder of his career, and freed him from any anxiety over control of his films.

The Sign of the Cross, like *The Ten Commandments* and *The King of Kings* (1927), was pure spectacle heavily laced with sex, in this case featuring Claudette Colbert in a notorious milk bath, a homosexual Nero, lesbian handmaidens, and sexual images of lips, thighs, and feet. Since success breeds success, DeMille's skill with spectacle led to other similar efforts, notably *Cleopatra* (1934), *The Crusades* (1935), and a reworking of *The Ten Commandments* (1956). While DeMille made financially successful Westerns such as *The Plainsman* (1937) and *Union Pacific* (1939), spectacles were his forte, and they are the films for which he is remembered. Actually, DeMille, who was not temperamentally suited to handling details, was at home with spectacles because of the challenge they posed. In a sense, the epic poet is superior to the lyric poet because scope is important: Only a larger-than-life director could handle the larger-than-life themes and the religious/ philosophical content of the historical spectacle.

Of the seventy films he directed, less than twenty were made between 1929, when he made his first sound film, and 1956, when he made his last film, a new version of *The Ten Commandments*. One reason for his relative inactivity was the time and energy he devoted to each film; another reason involved his extracinematic political activities. A self-made man, the embodiment of the Horatio Alger myth, DeMille believed in the individual, not the State, and became active in the Republican Party and in contemporary political issues. Predictably, DeMille opposed the stand of the American Federation of Radio Artists against right-to-work legislation (DeMille himself was associated with the Lux Radio Theatre) and in retaliation organized the DeMille Foundation for Political Freedom in 1945. As a consultant for a government agency producing Cold War films, he favored loyalty oaths and opposed so-called Communist infiltration of the film industry. Although he lost the Lux Radio Theatre job in 1944, he wrote for several years a nationally syndicated column espousing his conservative beliefs. For his "patriotic" efforts, he was recognized by the American Legion, and Vice President Richard M. Nixon presented him with the Freedom Foundation Award.

Perhaps because he was such a fervid anti-Communist, perhaps because he had such a strong ego, DeMille thought that he and his films were the targets of leftist reviewers. At any rate, despite a string of box-office successes, he did not receive the acclaim he sought from serious film critics. On the other hand, he was recognized by the film industry he had helped to create: In 1953, he received an Academy Award for Best Picture for *The Greatest Show on Earth* and also the prestigious Irving Thalberg Award—both from the Academy of Motion Picture Arts and Sciences—and the first D. W. Griffith Award given by the Hollywood Foreign Correspondents Association; in 1956, the Screen Producers Guild gave him the Milestone Award for his contributions to the American film industry. Three years later, he died in Los Angeles of heart problems; he had characteristically ignored the heart attack he suffered during the filming of *The Ten Commandments*.

Summary

DeMille's film career and life were characterized by ambition, determination, and competitiveness. His sibling rivalry with his older brother, who initially outshone the younger DeMille, served to motivate him, and when William joined him in Hollywood, DeMille triumphed. In fact, his desire for control was such that his adopted sons called him "Mister." On the set he was "The Chief," "Mister DeMille," or "Boss." Because he did not want competition from the actors and actresses who worked for him, he preferred to work with lesser-known stars whom he could control and develop. Similarly, he had a stable of actors and actresses with whom he repeatedly worked in a kind of stock company; presumably, they could be counted on to cooperate.

Although DeMille never received the critical acclaim accorded Griffith, he shaped film history. Few others in the entertainment business shared his grasp of what the public wanted. DeMille knew small-town America, and he himself was torn, as were other Americans, between Victorian ideals and modern realities (a conflict epitomized in the sexual titillation of his biblical epics). If, in his films, he appealed to the concerns of his time—rugged individualism, upward mobility, and consumerism—his death in 1959 spared him from the fate of many directors in their declining years: irrelevance. The 1960's would not have been a fertile decade for a director with DeMille's conservative politics and desire for control.

Bibliography

Bodeen, DeWitt. "Cecil B. DeMille." *Films in Review* 32 (August, September, 1982): 385-397. An overview of DeMille's cinematic career, the article summarizes the plots of several DeMille films and contains a filmography.

DeMille, Agnes. *Speak to Me, Dance with Me.* Boston: Little, Brown and Co., 1973. An account by DeMille's niece of her experiences working with him on *Cleopatra* and some personal observations about DeMille's life and career.

DeMille, Cecil B. *Autobiography.* Englewood Cliffs, N.J.: Prentice-Hall, 1959. DeMille's own account, aided by Donald Hayne's editing, of his life and career is more revealing about his career than about his private life and temperament.

Ewen, Stuart, and Elizabeth Ewen. *Channels of Desire: Mass Images and the Shaping of American Consciousness.* New York: McGraw-Hill Book Co., 1982. An analysis of DeMille's sex comedies and melodramas as they shaped consumption patterns of immigrant women seeking to emulate life in films.

Higashi, Sumiko. *Cecil B. DeMille: A Guide to References and Resources.* Boston: G. K. Hall, 1985. An indispensable compendium of resources, the book contains, in addition to a comprehensive bibliography and a filmography, archival information and an excellent short biography.

Higham, Charles. *Cecil B. DeMille.* New York: Charles Scribner's Sons, 1973. The best book-length biography of DeMille, Higham's book also contains helpful critical discussions of the films.

Ringgold, Gene, and DeWitt Bodeen. *The Films of Cecil B. DeMille.* New York: Citadel Press, 1969. A lavishly illustrated (stills and photographs of Hollywood "personalities"), film-by-film treatment of DeMille's films. Information provided includes a synopsis, cast credits, and excerpts of contemporary film reviews, as well as a biographical introduction and a filmography.

Thomas L. Erskine

JACK DEMPSEY

Born: June 24, 1895; Manassa, Colorado
Died: May 31, 1983; New York, New York
Area of Achievement: Boxing
Contribution: Dempsey was one of the greatest sports personalities of the so-called Golden Age of Sports (the 1920's) and the first boxer to make major contributions to sporting life in the United States.

Early Life

William Harrison "Jack" Dempsey, one of eleven children, was born on June 24, 1895, in Manassa, Colorado, of Indian, Irish, and Scottish ancestry. The son of Hyrum and Celia Dempsey, he became accustomed to a nomadic existence early in life, a primary requisite for a boxing career. Hyrum had converted to the Church of Jesus Christ of Latter-day Saints and had moved to Manassa in 1880 because it was a center of Mormon life. Hyrum, however, never was a successful businessman and was regarded as something of a dreamer. The family began a succession of moves from Manassa when Jack was four or five years old; the longest stay was at a ranch near Montrose, Colorado, for two years.

Jack permanently left his family in 1911, when they were living in Lakeview, Utah, and he was sixteen years old. He had already been attracted to the sport which made him famous, for he had begun to fight at about ten years of age, and it had become a way of life. This was a type of boxing in which there were no holds barred, and the biggest and toughest competitors usually won. As a preventative against cuts (which might interfere with his vision and hence his ability to hit and block blows), the budding boxing great bathed his face and hands in beef brine. Cuts were lessened this way, and his hands were toughened as well.

Dempsey was never large, especially if compared to boxers of the late twentieth century. In his prime as an adult, Dempsey stood six feet, one and a half inches tall and weighed from 180 to 187 pounds; in his earlier years, he often weighed less than 150. From 1911 to 1916, Dempsey led the life of what one could legitimately call a hobo, though a hobo who worked and would accept any gainful employment. During this time he also fought and sharpened his skills and techniques. His was a rather brutal existence, an existence which forced Dempsey to remain aloof from most other hoboes because of his fear of homosexual attack from older, stronger individuals or groups. This in itself was good training for a boxer; once he is in the ring, a boxer is completely on his own, simply one individual who is pitted against another.

Dempsey was not the only man of his family to box. At one time, his older brother Bernie was fighting under the name of Jack Dempsey. This Jack was one of the more popular earlier middleweights and was known as "The Non-pareil." One night, William Harrison substituted for his older brother in the ring and used the name Jack Dempsey. This fight in Denver gave him his permanent professional name.

Dempsey needed two more ingredients for a really successful boxing career. Most successful boxing careers are shaped, if not made, by a manager, and an astute boxing promoter of matches can make or break a career. Dempsey's fights in the West gave him these, for he was introduced to the men who would be the two most important figures in his professional life. John Leo McKernan, or Jack Kearns, was the epitome of the fight manager: a master storyteller whom Nat Fleischer, editor of *The Ring*, credited with having invented the art of "ballyhoo." The promoter was George L. "Tex" Rickard, who was to develop boxing's first million-dollar gates, with Dempsey as the prime attraction.

Kearns was the most successful manager in the history of boxing, until the 1970's, for producing revenue for his boxers and himself. He managed six world champions, four of whom have been elected to *The Ring*'s Hall of Fame. Dempsey, Kearns, and Rickard were also lucky: They were at the right place at the right time. Boxing had only recently been legalized in the state of New York, opening the largest populated area of the country to mass spectator sports. For the first time, boxing was being taken from small, seedy arenas which housed only a few hundred or a thousand seats, to the sporting meccas of America.

Dempsey's first two managers were Jack Price and John "The Barber" Reisler. It was not until 1917, when he was twenty-two, that Dempsey met Kearns and began his rise to fame. By the time he met Kearns, he had knocked out practically every opponent he had faced, but without recognition and the good paydays that went with that accomplishment. By the time he won the heavyweight championship of the world in 1919 from Jess Willard, he had knocked out twenty-one opponents in the first round, and newspapers had begun calling him the "Manassa Mauler" and "Jack the Giant Killer." From 1917 until 1919, he suffered only one defeat, and by 1919 he had won more than eighty victories.

Dempsey had also married by this time. His first wife, Maxine Gates, was a saloon piano player whom he had met during his early days in the West. He then married Estelle Taylor, an actress, whom he had met after becoming heavyweight champion. They were later divorced and Dempsey married a singer, Hannah Williams. They had two daughters, Joan in 1934 and Barbara in 1936, but again he was divorced, in 1943. Dempsey was given custody of the children. He was married for the fourth time in 1958, to Deanna Piatelli, who survived him. Dempsey also adopted his fourth wife's daughter from a previous marriage, who took the name Barbara Piatelli Dempsey. She later helped him to write his 1977 autobiography, *Dempsey*.

Life's Work

Dempsey's status as a serious contender was established when he knocked out Fireman Jim Flynn in one round. In July, 1918, he knocked out Fred Fulton in twenty-three seconds of the first round. Dempsey threw the only punch, a right. This got him a title fight with Jess Willard, who had won the title in 1915 but who had defended it only once since then, in a no-decision match with Frank Moran in 1916.

The championship bout with Willard, on July 4, in Toledo, Ohio, made Dempsey a national hero. Willard was five inches taller and seventy pounds heavier, and was the overwhelming favorite. The fight was held in a specially made outdoor arena constructed of rough-hewn planks, a Rickard trademark. Although the ring was set up on the shores of Maumee Bay, it was blisteringly hot. Dempsey began to stalk Willard; he had to stand on his tiptoes in order to reach the champion. Reach the champion he did, however, for Dempsey knocked him down seven times in the first round, breaking Willard's jaw in twelve places. Both Dempsey and Kearns left the ring at the end of the first round, believing the fight won. Dempsey had to reenter the ring, but at the end of the fourth round, Willard retired, after taking a frightful beating. Dempsey was now champion.

What is not generally known about Dempsey, however, is that this time of his life was not a particularly happy one. He was not immediately accepted by the public as a champion; indeed, he did not become a real hero until he lost the crown to Gene Tunney. A large part of this lack of acclaim was because of questions concerning his role in the war effort during World War I. Supposedly doing essential work in a Philadelphia shipyard, he had posed for a news photograph while holding a riveting gun and wearing overalls. He was also, however, wearing patent-leather dress shoes. The photograph convinced many that he had evaded fighting, and the sobriquet "draft dodger" was hung on him. Partly as a result of this unfavorable publicity, Rickard matched Dempsey with Georges Carpentier, the light-heavyweight champion. Carpentier was advertised as the archetypal hero; he had been decorated while serving in the French armed forces during the war. Rickard shrewdly surmised that many fans would buy tickets hoping to see Dempsey lose. Rickard built one of his stark wooden arenas in an area of Jersey City known as Boyle's Thirty Acres. A crowd of 80,183 paid $1,789,238 to see the fight—it was the first of the legendary million-dollar gates. Carpentier, however, did not stand a chance. He was knocked out in the fourth round.

There were some unpleasantries associated even with the Willard fight. Dempsey maintained that he never received any funds from the proceeds of his share of the fight. Kearns reportedly bet ten thousand dollars on Dempsey to win in a first-round knockout. When Dempsey had to return to the ring, he lost the bet. The rest of the money supposedly went for training expenses. This was the first intimation that all was not well between

Dempsey and Kearns. Kearns later claimed that Dempsey's pounding of Willard was a result of his wrapping of Dempsey's hands with plaster of paris the previous night, actually a common ploy then used by fighters, especially those employed by circuses and traveling carnivals, who regularly took on all comers. Generally, if the challenger lasted three rounds, he was declared the winner. Most did not, thanks to such ploys.

Dempsey's next fight after Carpentier was held in Shelby, Montana. This fight is still cited as an example of what small-town promoters should not do: hock the family jewels for a bit of national recognition. Kearns had received a guarantee of $250,000 for Dempsey to fight Tommy Gibbons in Shelby. The fight was held in the oil-rich town, but very few people came to witness Dempsey's victory in a five-round decision. Nevertheless, Kearns collected the entire guarantee; one of the most fabled stories of sports and gambling concerns Kearns's foresight in hiring a locomotive and caboose to whisk the Dempsey entourage out of town.

Dempsey actually fought only six fights defending the championship. During this period, there were no boxing commissions or organizations mandating that champions defend their title at least twice a year. He won the title in 1919, then in 1920 defeated, for the second time, Billy Wiske and Bill Brennan, before meeting Carpentier in 1921. It had taken Dempsey twelve rounds to dispose of Brennan by knockout. He did not defend the title in 1922. In 1923, he defeated Gibbons and then fought the famous battle with Luis Angel Firpo of Argentina in New York City. This short fight probably contained more action than any other heavyweight championship bout. Early in the first round, Dempsey was stopped by a right to the jaw, but he was able to knock Firpo down four times. Firpo then knocked Dempsey into the press row. Reporters broke his fall and helped push him back into the ring. Dempsey then knocked Firpo down for the fifth time—and all this happened in the first round. The second round was all Dempsey's, and he finished Firpo off by knocking him down twice.

Dempsey did not fight again for three years. Then came his two losses to Gene Tunney. Tunney, an ex-marine, won the title from Dempsey on September 23, 1926. More than one hundred thousand spectators witnessed the bout. Dempsey lost by a ten-round decision. By this time, Kearns was no longer Dempsey's manager and was suing Dempsey for his share of the Tunney purse. A year later, Dempsey challenged Tunney for the title. Dempsey was soundly outboxed, except for the long-count seventh round. Dempsey knocked Tunney down but refused to go to a neutral corner as newer rules mandated. Dempsey stood over the fallen Tunney for at least four seconds before moving to a neutral corner. Only after Dempsey had done so did the referee begin his count. Tunney recovered, and any hope that Dempsey would win was lost.

Dempsey made a comeback in August of 1931, but a loss to Kingfish

Levinsky in August of 1932 convinced him to retire again. In 1940, he returned to the ring once again, but only to knock out three stiffs.

During his career, Dempsey fought sixty-nine professional bouts. He won forty-seven by knockout, seven by decision, and one by foul; in five of his fights there was no decision, and four were declared a draw; he lost four by decision and was knocked out once.

While champion, Dempsey had been attracted to the glamour and charisma of the stage and screen. His featured role in a Broadway play was, to say the least, not outstanding. The female lead was played by his second wife, Estelle Taylor, a star of silent films whom he had met while in Hollywood. His Hollywood career was a disaster, however, as was the film *Manhattan Madness* (1925), in which he appeared.

After the Tunney bouts, Dempsey refereed bouts and tended to his business interests. During World War II, he was unable to enlist in the United States Army but joined the coast guard as director of its physical fitness program. He held the rank of commander, ending his service in November, 1945.

Dempsey was the first winner of the New York Boxing Writers Association's Edward J. Weil Memorial Plaque, in 1938, and was elected to the Boxing Hall of Fame in 1954. By this time, his popularity was at an all-time high, and he was generally regarded as the best boxer in history until the postwar period. Probably the most important reason for this public acclaim was Dempsey's mellowing personality. His successful restaurant on Broadway in New York City kept him in the public eye, for he was always willing to greet a customer and have his picture taken with him or her. He died on May 31, 1983, in New York City.

Summary

Jack Dempsey is a sports legend, along with such epic American sports heroes as Harold "Red" Grange and the Four Horsemen of Notre Dame, of football fame, and the other greats of sports' Golden Age. Although his record in the ring is possibly overrated, his fights were marked by a ferocity seldom encountered elsewhere in boxing. His long life enabled him to become a genial host in the most populous city in the United States, a position which continued to keep him in the national limelight. The champ thus came to personify much that was good in American life.

Bibliography

Bromberg, Lester. *Boxing's Unforgettable Fights*. New York: Ronald Press Co., 1962. Bromberg graphically depicts the fights with Willard, when Dempsey won the championship, the Carpentier and Firpo fights, and the two Tunney fights. Interesting reading.
Dempsey, Jack, with Barbara Piatelli Dempsey. *Dempsey*. New York:

Harper and Row, Publishers, 1977. The official autobiography by Dempsey, who was assisted by his adopted daughter. Should be read with care and compared to other sources.

Fleischer, Nathaniel S. *Fifty Years at Ringside*. New York: Fleet Publishing Corp., 1958. Fleischer, editor and publisher of *The Ring* in its heyday, was considered "Mr. Boxing" after World War II. Provides an excellent evaluation of Dempsey, compared to other ring greats such as Jack Johnson and Joe Louis. Fleischer always considered Johnson to be the greatest champion.

_____. *The Heavyweight Championship*. New York: G. P. Putnam's Sons, 1949. Includes excellent comparisons between Dempsey and Tunney, and captures the reasons for which Dempsey was so popular with the public after his defeats by Tunney.

Heimer, Mel. *The Long Count*. New York: Atheneum Publishers, 1969. Focuses on the long-count knockdown in the second Dempsey-Tunney bout; provides good insights into the private life as well as the career of Dempsey.

Kearns, Jack, with Oscar Fraley. *The Million Dollar Gate*. New York: Macmillan Publishing Co., 1966. An "as-told-to" autobiography providing Kearns's version of his life with Dempsey. Anti-Dempsey, it should be read in conjunction with Dempsey's own autobiography.

Roberts, Randy. *Jack Dempsey: The Manassa Mauler*. Baton Rouge: Louisiana State University Press, 1979. The best source for beginning to understand Dempsey's problems both in and outside the ring.

Smith, Red. "Jack Dempsey Is Dead." *The New York Times*, June 1, 1983, sec. 2: 4. In-depth obituary of Dempsey, prepared by Smith, who was a noted sports columnist for *The Times*.

Henry S. Marks

GEORGE DEWEY

Born: December 26, 1837; Montpelier, Vermont
Died: January 16, 1917; Washington, D.C.
Area of Achievement: Naval service
Contribution: Dewey defeated the Spanish in the Battle of Manila Bay on May 1, 1898, and subsequently served as senior officer of the navy until his death.

Early Life

George Dewey was born December 26, 1837, in Montpelier, Vermont, the son of Julius Y. Dewey, a physician, and Mary Perrin Dewey. His mother died when he was five, but he seems to have had a happy childhood anyway, full of high spirits and practical jokes. He enjoyed a very close relationship with his father. After attending a military school in Norwich, Vermont, Dewey sought appointment to the United States Military Academy; because there were no vacancies at West Point, however, he went to the United States Naval Academy instead, graduating in 1858, fifth in a class of fifteen.

Promoted to lieutenant just as the Civil War began, he served with distinction in the blockading fleet and especially on the Mississippi, where his courage and resourcefulness earned for him positions of considerable responsibility, despite his youth. It was also on the Mississippi that he came to admire the daring Admiral David G. Farragut, later famous for the immortal, although perhaps apocryphal, words "Damn the torpedoes! Full speed ahead!" More than thirty years later, Dewey would have reason to ponder these words.

Dewey reached the rank of lieutenant commander by the war's end; then, like other career officers, he had to settle down to the dull circumstances of the peacetime navy. On October 27, 1867, he married Susan B. Goodwin, daughter of a New Hampshire governor. She died in 1872, after the birth of their son, George Goodwin Dewey. The bereaved husband remained a bachelor for the next twenty-seven years—and a very eligible one he was: trim, sporting a glorious mustache, and handsome even into advanced middle age. He was also fairly well-to-do by virtue of his holding shares in his father's life insurance company.

Life's Work

The post–Civil War navy had too many officers for its shrinking and obsolete fleet, yet Dewey managed by seniority and competence to gain his share of promotions and even more: commander in 1872, captain in 1884, and commodore in 1896. He spent fewer of these years at sea than is the norm, preferring duty in Washington, D.C. There he became head of the Bureau of Equipment in 1889 and president of the Board of Inspection and

Survey in 1895. He sometimes used these positions to encourage naval progress, but he was too senior—and too devoted to intraservice harmony— to identify fully with the younger, reform-minded officers of that era. Like many other senior officers, he cultivated political connections instead. One of his friends, Assistant Secretary of the Navy Theodore Roosevelt, along with a Vermont senator, arranged for his appointment as commodore of the United States Asiatic Squadron in 1897.

Dewey was not an advocate of imperialism, but he knew that the Philippines in general, and the Spanish fleet in Manila Bay in particular, would be likely American targets should there be war with Spain. When that war began in April of 1898, his squadron was already well advanced in its preparations for combat. With the declarations of war, Dewey's ships were suddenly deprived of the services of Hong Kong and all other neutral ports, and they had none of their own. He could perhaps have violated Chinese neutrality by using a port on her coast—and the impotent Chinese government would not have been able to stop him—but that would have been no more than a temporary expedient. Hence, his squadron either had to steam out of the Far East or conquer a base for itself in Manila Bay. Leaving was unthinkable: Apart from the psychological and diplomatic consequences of departing without a fight, the United States could hardly abandon its interests in Asia; nor could it allow Spain to keep the Philippines, valuable as they would be as bargaining chips at the peace table—or as the site of a permanent American base in the Far East to assist in the expansion of American interests there.

Flying his flag in the magnificent light cruiser *Olympia*, Dewey led five other ships out of Hong Kong on his way to battle. Spain's Admiral Patricio Montojo awaited him in Manila Bay with seven ships, but they were smaller and less well armed than Dewey's, and with fewer well-trained crews. Some of his ships were in wretched condition. Spanish weakness afloat could in theory be offset by some other factors: If Montojo could disperse his ships, he might be able to harass American commercial shipping indefinitely, or the Spanish could shelter their ships under the guns of Manila and sow mines in Dewey's path. Yet none of these options came to anything: The Spanish ships could not scatter without exposing Manila to bombardment; Manila's coast artillery was inadequate; and the Spaniards lacked insulated wire with which to arm their mines. Thus, the gloomy Montojo fully expected to go down fighting for honor's sake alone, even giving up the slight protection of Manila's guns so as to spare the civil population an enemy bombardment.

The Americans could not have been fully aware of the extent of Spanish weakness. Although the United States consul in Manila had indicated Montojo's dilemma, his information might not have been complete; it was, in any case, many days old by the time Dewey set sail. The Spaniards might yet score heavily with lucky hits from their guns or with the few makeshift mines they had managed to sow, thereby making an American victory, if it could be achieved, either incomplete or dreadfully Pyrrhic. Dewey himself, on the other hand, had nothing but contempt for the Spanish defenses. He was more than willing to "damn the torpedoes," that is, the mines. His final words on the subject were perhaps not as stirring as Admiral Farragut's, but just as decisive: "Mines or no mines, I'm leading the squadron in myself." When his ships got in range of Montojo's, he gave his soon-to-be famous order to the captain of the *Olympia*: "You may fire when you are ready, Gridley." The result was the total destruction of Montojo's squadron in the Battle of Manila Bay, May 1, 1898; there were no American combat fatalities. Dewey subsequently maintained a blockade of Manila and cooperated with the newly arrived United States Army so as to force the city's surrender.

Two long-term international problems arose during the Manila Bay campaign. One was America's relationship with the anti-Spanish Filipino insurrectionaries. Their leader, Emiliano Aguinaldo, claimed that Dewey had promised freedom for the Philippines in return for the insurgents' help in defeating the Spaniards on land. Dewey denied agreeing to anything but a purely military alliance, with no commitments regarding the future of the islands. Given his—and Aguinaldo's—political naïveté, it is perhaps likely that they had genuinely misunderstood each other. In any case, their disagreement was a minor milestone on the road to war between the United States and the Filipino rebels.

Dewey's other political problem during the blockade concerned the attitude of Germany. The kaiser's Asiatic fleet visited Manila Bay and openly displayed its sympathy for the Spaniards. Americans wondered if the Germans wanted the islands for themselves. It is true that the Germans sometimes behaved as if the rules of blockade simply did not apply to them, and their ships far outclassed Dewey's. Fortunately, the matter was resolved, but Dewey, and many other Americans, carried away from this experience a lingering suspicion of Germany's intentions all over the world.

In 1899, Dewey returned to the United States, where he was lionized to an incredible degree. There were Dewey hats, cigarettes, canes, songs, and even paperweights. Congress elevated him to the rank of admiral of the Navy, making him the senior officer of the two armed services, with the right to remain on active duty for life. In 1900, he was appointed head of the Navy Department's General Board, and in 1903, he became the chairman of the Joint Army-Navy Board.

Meanwhile, there had been a Dewey-for-president boom, looking toward the election of 1900. Disliking public adulation, Dewey nevertheless allowed himself to be talked into running; his candidacy soon fell flat, however, mostly because of his own political ineptitude. For one thing, his cause was damaged by his comment about how easy the job of president would be. For another, his political ideas were few and ill-considered: He declared himself a

Democrat, yet he despised the radical wing of that party; although he had originally wanted nothing in the Philippines but a coaling station, he nevertheless officially associated himself with the Republican president's decision to seek the annexation of the entire archipelago.

Dewey's second marriage, on November 9, 1899, also worked to his political disadvantage. He was the nation's darling, and for him to marry at all was bound to arouse popular jealousy; his choice of bride made the situation all the worse: She was Mildred McLean Hazen, a wealthy widow with the image of a snob. Worse yet, she was a Protestant who had turned Catholic, apparently for no better reason than to please the best social circles in Austria, where she had once happened to live. Anti-Catholics in the United States therefore claimed that she might someday donate Admiral Dewey's house to the Catholic Church—a house which had been purchased for him by subscription by the people of a grateful nation. It was all very silly, but the fuss engendered by his marriage nevertheless contributed to the collapse of Dewey's political hopes, such as they were, and he eventually withdrew from the presidential race. (His wife later turned Protestant again.)

Dewey's service as senior officer of the navy showed him to be a conscientious but uninspired leader. He sought compromise, no matter what the cost, to prevent arguments within his beloved navy. He tried to please both sides in the controversy between the partisans of Admiral William T. Sampson and those of Admiral Winfield S. Schley concerning the latter's role in the Caribbean phase of the Spanish-American War; but his efforts along these lines led only to an obvious self-contradiction. In another matter, he supported the young reformers who wanted to establish a general staff within the Navy Department, yet he turned against them when their tactics offended his sense of propriety. He wanted the navy to have modern battleships, yet he refused to make full public use of his prestige in order to acquire them because he disliked arguing with naval conservatives. Like many others, he suspected that the next war for the United States would be with Germany, but in this case he carelessly allowed his opinion to become public knowledge, thereby embarrassing his country.

Old age and arteriosclerosis finally took their toll on him, especially after a slight stroke in 1913. He died in Washington, D. C., on January 16, 1917.

Summary

Dewey's career from 1865 to 1897 was only somewhat more lustrous than those of many other officers. He was resourceful and courageous enough, in 1898, to make his ships ready and then to seize the opportunity for glory in Manila Bay, yet the praises and promotion that followed were all out of proportion to his achievement. Sampson and Schley, after all, had commanded more and more heavily armed ships than Dewey had ever possessed, and in a more important theater of war, the Caribbean; moreover, they defeated a Spanish fleet that was stronger than Montojo's. Dewey, it is true, had displayed a certain phlegmatic panache; clearly, however, what made him so much greater than Sampson and Schley in the public's eye was the mere fact that his triumph came at the very beginning of the war, before anyone else's victory could claim the headlines.

Nor did his postwar career provide much justification for his elevation to the highest of ranks. His judgments in the realm of politics were often ludicrous, and even in strictly naval matters they were sometimes flawed, largely because of his obsession with intraservice harmony. Perhaps Dewey's most important contribution after 1898 was his support for the modernization of the battle fleet, but even in this case he was simply on the side of an irresistible trend, and halfheartedly at that. Avoiding conflict within the navy came at the cost of a more forceful and forward-looking role as his department's most senior admiral.

Bibliography

Cosmas, Graham A. *An Army for Empire: The United States Army in the Spanish-American War*. Columbia: University of Missouri Press, 1971. Despite its title, this book sheds much light on all aspects of the Spanish-American War. It is very scholarly, but also readable.

Herrick, Walter R., Jr. *The American Naval Revolution*. Baton Rouge: Louisiana State University Press, 1966. Another scholarly and well-written book. Herrick covers the political events that led to the building of the United States' modern fleet during the 1890's; this was the program that gave Dewey the qualitative edge he enjoyed in Manila Bay.

Karsten, Peter. *The Naval Aristocracy: The Golden Age of Annapolis and the Emergence of Modern American Navalism*. New York: Free Press, 1972. This is an important book that reexamines the naval officer corps of the late nineteenth century, including the generation of reformers whose projects Dewey sometimes endorsed.

O'Toole, G. J. A. *The Spanish War: An American Epic, 1898*. New York: W. W. Norton and Co., 1984. A very enjoyable popular account.

Potter, E. B., and Chester W. Nimitz, eds. *Sea Power: A Naval History*. Englewood Cliffs, N.J.: Prentice-Hall, 1960. This is the standard textbook on all naval history, used, for example, at the United States Naval Academy. The editors are, respectively, an eminent naval historian and a great World War II admiral.

Spector, Ronald. *Admiral of the New Empire*. Baton Rouge: Louisiana State University Press, 1974. This is the only modern biography of Dewey; fortunately it is a magnificent, albeit brief, account. The author is a very prominent scholar as well as a good stylist. The brevity of his book is a result in part of a lack of existing source material.

Sprout, Harold M., and Margaret Sprout. *The Rise of American Naval*

Power. Princeton, N.J.: Princeton University Press, 1946. An older but highly respected survey of American naval history.

Karl G. Larew

JOHN DEWEY

Born: October 20, 1859; Burlington, Vermont
Died: June 1, 1952; New York, New York
Areas of Achievement: Philosophy, psychology, and reform
Contribution: In his intellectual concerns and educational interests, Dewey significantly shaped the roles of philosophy and reform in the United States.

Early Life

John Dewey was born October 20, 1859, in Burlington, Vermont. His mother, née Lucina Artemisia Rich, was twenty years younger than his father, Archibald Dewey, who owned a grocery business in the community. John was the third child in a family of four. Although the Civil War separated the family for six years when Archibald enlisted in the army, by 1866 they had returned to Burlington, where Archibald entered the cigar and tobacco business.

In the years that followed, John Dewey grew up in a middle-class world where the native-born Americans and Irish and French Canadians shaped his early social experiences. John Dewey's parents encouraged his wide-ranging reading and his outdoor activities. His mother's evangelical piety, however, influenced Dewey's values well into adulthood. On the whole, his childhood was a pleasant one, and his parents were warm and supportive, although his mother's pietistic worrying about Dewey's behavior upset him.

After a good high school education in the classics, Dewey entered the University of Vermont. In addition to the classical curriculum, he took biology courses and read widely in the literature of the emerging Darwinian controversies. His interests were moving him toward the study of philosophy. What he read and what he had experienced in his young life contributed to the philosophical issues of dualisms such as body/soul, flesh/spirit, and nature/mind, but Dewey wanted a unity of knowledge that overcame such divisions. In the meantime, Dewey was graduated from the University of Vermont in 1879. For the next two years, he taught high school in Oil City, Pennsylvania, a community much in flux from the rapid growth of the oil business.

At Oil City, two events greatly shaped Dewey's life. First, Dewey's religious doubts (or fears) came to seem foolish to him. He felt a oneness with the universe, and although he continued attending church for the next dozen years, he had left the religious faith and practice of his parents. Over the course of his long and productive life, after his abandonment of evangelical Christianity, Dewey embraced the absolute idealism of Georg Wilhelm Friedrich Hegel (1770-1831), with its emphasis on the unity of existence. Later, Dewey accepted humanistic naturalism, with its continuity of nature and man drawn from the thought of Charles Sanders Peirce (1839-1914) and William James (1842-1910).

In 1882, Dewey entered The Johns Hopkins University for graduate study in philosophy. A serious but sly student, Dewey was quietly exploring the relationship between religion and morals in late nineteenth century American life. At Johns Hopkins, Dewey accepted neo-Hegelianism. Dewey and his whole intellectual generation were seeking something new, something to explain life, a transformation of values. Dewey's fully developed naturalism was, however, in the future. He had begun the transformation of his religious beliefs by ruling out the supernatural but placing its values into the natural. In time, as a philosopher, Dewey placed in the natural world a faith that had previously been assigned to a coming Kingdom of God.

In 1884, he joined the department of philosophy at the University of Michigan. During the next four years, he broadened his interests in social affairs and educational matters, and he wrote and published. He also married, in 1886, Harriet Alice Chipman, a bright and capable woman who encouraged Dewey in pursuing his ideas. Wife, mother, and critic, she was a source of encouragement until her death in 1927. *Psychology*, Dewey's first book, was published in 1887; it combined empirical psychology with German metaphysical idealism. After a year at the University of Minnesota, he returned to Michigan as chairman of the department of philosophy. Until 1894, when he went to the University of Chicago, Dewey built up the department's faculty and cut his final ties to organized religion. His interests became increasingly secular. He accepted an appointment at the University of Chicago as chairman of the department of philosophy, psychology, and pedagogy.

Within two years, he established the Laboratory School, which provided the institutional expression of progressive education. He expressed his ideas in *The School and Society* (1899). Dewey did not neglect his other interests; he wrote *Studies in Logical Theory* (1903). At Chicago, Dewey was active in academic, civic, and reform matters. A brilliant group of scholars were on the faculty at that time. Unfortunately, both Dewey and his wife, who held an appointment in the school of education, resigned because of a misunderstanding over the terms of her position.

Life's Work

Dewey joined the department of philosophy at Columbia University in 1904, where he taught until 1930. His greatest achievements and contributions were before him. By 1910, Dewey had sketched out his mature philosophy. Although scholars disagree about the relative influences of Hegel and Charles Darwin, the judgment here is that Dewey never completely divorced himself from their influences. His philosophy was a fusion of Hegelian idealism and Darwinian naturalism, expressed in a context of reform for industrial America. Ideas had significant consequences for human life; they were instruments to shape the world and place values, albeit human ones, into human affairs. As part of the natural world, all human activity, including the use of intelligence, was a process that existed in nature and not in an independent (or dualistic) mode of being. As a biological function, reflective intelligence meant that, by naturalistic metaphysics, people adapt to environmental situations. His 1896 essay "The Reflex Arc Concept in Psychology" is indicative of his functionalism in psychology and instrumentalism in philosophy. From physical to mental, continuity was the key concept. Language, in conjunction with other cultural elements (and here the anthropologist Franz Boas influenced Dewey's thinking), contributed to the cultural transformation from the biological to the logical.

Science, or the scientific method, was the basis of Dewey's message. Within ten years, he published four major books: *Reconstruction in Philosophy* (1920), *Human Nature and Conduct* (1922), *Experience and Nature* (1925), and *The Quest for Certainty* (1929). In these books, Dewey argued that scientific truth was an instrument to control and direct human experience or culture. Means and ends were one in nature and in society, particularly a democracy. A reconstructed philosophy, "active and operative," was relevant to the twentieth century by reorganizing the environment. By scientifically removing specific trouble areas, human happiness and productivity would increase. He wanted a rational and critical mediation between the self and other human beings as expressed in *Individualism, Old and New* (1930).

During his years at Columbia, Dewey was active in reform movements and public lectures in the United States and abroad. As the years passed, the honors increased; he became America's national philosopher. As one historian remarked, he was the "guide, the mentor, the conscience of the American people... for a generation no major issue was clarified until Dewey had spoken." Dewey continued to write and lecture after his retirement in 1930. He was a real intellectual presence during the New Deal, World War II, and afterward. His political activities often drew criticism, and traditionalists saw dire social consequences in his progressive educational ideas. After his first wife died in 1927, he married Roberta L. Grant in 1946. Suffering from complications of a broken hip, Dewey died on June 1, 1952. His ashes are now buried on the campus of the University of Vermont.

Over the course of his long life, John Dewey wrote forty books and seven hundred articles on a wide range of subjects. In 1959, under the editorial leadership of Jo Ann Boydston, the Center for Dewey Studies at Southern Illinois University began an ambitious program to publish his complete works.

Summary

Dewey is a major presence in American history. Many formal expressions such as lectureships, institutes, and university buildings bear his name. A society and foundation were established to help spread Dewey's ideas on democracy and educational reform. His portrait was included in the United States Post Office's Prominent Americans series.

As a philosopher, Dewey was the creator of instrumentalism, his version of William James's pragmatism, applied more directly and completely to the industrial problems of the United States. His work made pragmatism an operative concept in American politics. His efforts, particularly late in the nineteenth century, in contributing to the concept of functionalism earned for him a permanent place in the development of American psychology. Although he was often criticized for the excesses of progressive education, his educational writings contributed to the reform of American public schools. Finally, his writing and teaching, particularly in the first half of the twentieth century, made him a leading American liberal. Concerned always about individual self-realization and reconstruction of American society for a just life for all, John Dewey practiced in his own life what he advocated for others.

Bibliography
Bernstein, Richard J. *John Dewey*. New York: Washington Square Press, 1966. The best brief account of Dewey's philosophy, critical but sympathetic.
Boydston, Jo Ann, ed. *Checklist of Writings About John Dewey: 1887-1973*. Carbondale: Southern Illinois University Press, 1974. A publication from the Center for Dewey Studies, this bibliography graphically illustrates the massive impact of the philosopher's ideas on American life.
Cahn, Steven M., ed. *New Studies in the Philosophy of John Dewey*. Hanover, N.H.: University Press of New England, 1977. A first-rate collection of essays by the leading scholars of Dewey's philosophy. They represent the best in recent writings about him.
Conkin, Paul K. *Puritans and Pragmatists*. Bloomington: Indiana University Press, 1976. In discussing eight eminent American thinkers, this book provides a solid, albeit technical, account of Dewey's place in American thought.
Coughlan, Neil. *Young John Dewey: An Essay in American Intellectual History*. Chicago: University of Chicago Press, 1975. This detailed account of Dewey's life before 1904 argues that the Hegelian orientation to Dewey's thought is greater than traditionally assumed.
Dykhuizen, George. *The Life and Mind of John Dewey*. Carbondale: Southern Illinois University Press, 1973. The best detailed one-volume biography available. It is now the standard biography.
Hook, Sidney, ed. *John Dewey, Philosopher of Science and Freedom: A Symposium*. New York: Dial Press, 1950. Although somewhat dated, this book contains observations from people who personally knew Dewey.
Kuklick, Bruce. *Churchmen and Philosophers: From Jonathan Edwards to*

John Dewey. New Haven, Conn.: Yale University Press, 1985. A major interpretative study with an emphasis on the continuing theological influences on American philosophical thought.

Marcell, David W. *Progress and Pragmatism: James, Dewey, Beard and the American Idea of Progress*. Westport, Conn.: Greenwood Press, 1974. A good account about the development of twentieth century reforming liberalism and Dewey's contributions.

White, Morton G. *The Origin of Dewey's Instrumentalism*. New York: Columbia University Press, 1943. The classic secondary account dealing with Dewey's mature philosophy. It is clearly written.

Donald K. Pickens

EMILY DICKINSON

Born: December 10, 1830; Amherst, Massachusetts
Died: May 15, 1886; Amherst, Massachusetts
Area of Achievement: Poetry
Contribution: Dickinson, living a reclusive social life, led an inner life of intense, imaginative creativity that made her one of America's greatest poets.

Early Life

The sparse facts of Emily Elizabeth Dickinson's external life can be summarized in a few sentences: She was born in the town of Amherst, Massachusetts, on December 10, 1830, spent her entire life in her family home, and died in it on May 15, 1886. She was graduated from Amherst Academy in 1847, then attended nearby Mount Holyoke Female Seminary for one year. She traveled occasionally to Springfield and twice to Boston. In 1854, she and her family visited Washington and Philadelphia. She never married and had no romantic relationships. Yet her interior life was so intense that a distinguished twentieth century poet and critic, Allen Tate, could write, "All pity for Miss Dickinson's 'starved life' is misdirected. Her life was one of the richest and deepest ever lived on this continent." It is a life which has proved a perplexing puzzle to many critics and biographers.

What led to Dickinson's monastic seclusion from society? Was it forced on her by a possessive, despotic father? Was it self-willed by her timid temperament, by rejected love, or by her neurotic need for utmost privacy while she pursued the muse of poetry? Speculation abounds, certainty eludes; nothing is simple and direct about her behavior. Perhaps the opening lines of her poem #1129 are self-revealing:

> Tell all the Truth but tell it slant—
> Success in Circuit lies
> Too bright for our infirm Delight
> The Truth's superb surprise

When Dickinson was born, Amherst was a farming village of four to five hundred families, with a cultural tradition of Puritanism and a devotion to education as well as devoutness. The Dickinsons were prominent in public and collegiate activities. Samuel Fowler Dickinson, Emily's grandfather, founded Amherst College in 1821 to train preachers, teachers, and missionaries. Edward Dickinson (1813-1874), Emily's father, was the eldest of nine children. He became a successful attorney and, at age thirty-two, was named treasurer of Amherst College, a position he kept for thirty-eight years. He served three terms in the Massachusetts legislature and one term as a member of Congress. Even political opponents respected him as forthright, courageous, diligent, solemn, intelligent, and reliable; he was the incarnation of responsibility and rectitude. In a letter to her brother, Dickinson mocked him (and her mother): "Father and Mother sit in state in the sitting-room perusing such papers, only, as they are well assured, have nothing carnal in them."

Emily's mother, Emily Norcross (1804-1882), was born in Monson, Massachusetts, twenty miles south of Amherst. Her father was a well-to-do farmer who sent his daughter to a reputable boarding school, where she behaved conventionally, preparing herself for the respectable, rational marriage that ensued after Edward Dickinson had courted her politely and passionlessly. The mother has received adverse treatment from most of Dickinson's biographers because of several statements the daughter wrote to her confidant, Colonel Thomas Wentworth Higginson (1823-1911):

> My Mother does not care for thought.
> I never had a mother. I suppose a mother is one to whom you hurry when you are troubled.
> I always ran Home to Awe when a child, if anything befell me. He was an awful Mother, but I liked him better than none.

Richard Sewall indicates in his magisterial two-volume *The Life of Emily Dickinson* (1974) that Emily's acerbic remarks should not be taken at their surface meaning in the light of the poet's continued preference for remaining in the familial home. To be sure, Dickinson's mother read meagerly and had a mediocre mind, but she was a tenderhearted, loving person who committed herself wholly to her family and to the household's management. While she never understood her daughter's complex nature, she also never intruded on Dickinson's inner life.

Dickinson's brother Austin (1829-1895) was closest to her in disposition. Personable, sensitive, empathic, and sociable, he became an attorney, joined his father's practice, and succeeded him as Amherst's treasurer in 1873. He shared his sister's wit, taste in books, and love of nature; his vitality was a tonic for her. He married one of her schoolmates, Susan Gilbert, vivacious, worldly, and articulate.

Dickinson and her sister-in-law, living next door to each other, were in each other's homes frequently during the first years of this marriage. Dickinson had a near-obsessive concern for her immediate family and greatly desired to make of her sister-in-law a true sister in spirit. She sent Sue nearly three hundred of her poems over the years—more than to anyone else. Yet a satisfyingly soulful friendship never quite materialized. To be sure, Sue's parties did keep Dickinson in at least limited circulation in her early twenties. The two women exchanged books and letters, with Dickinson occasionally seeking Sue's criticism of her poems. Dickinson, always fond of children, was particularly delighted with her nephew Gilbert; tragically, he died of typhoid fever at the age of eight; Dickinson's letter of condolence called him "Dawn and Meridian in one."

Yet the two women's paths ineluctably diverged. Sue had a husband and, eventually, three children and was an extroverted social climber. For unknown reasons, Dickinson and Sue quarreled in 1854, and Dickinson wrote her the only dismissive letter in her correspondence: "You can go or stay." They resumed their friendship, but it proved turbulent, as did Sue's and Austin's marriage. In 1866, Sue betrayed Emily's confidence by sending her poem "A Narrow Fellow in the Grass" to the *Springfield Republican*, which mutilated it by changing its punctuation. "It was robbed of me," Dickinson bitterly complained.

With her natural sister Lavinia (1833-1899), Dickinson bonded intimately all her life. Like her older sister, Lavinia remained a spinster, remained at home, and outlived her family. Dickinson and Lavinia were devotedly protective of each other. The younger sister was relatively uncomplicated, steady in temperament, pretty, and outgoing. Their only quasi-serious difference centered on Vinnie's love of cats, contrasted to Dickinson's care for birds. It was Lavinia who organized the first large-scale publication of Dickinson's poems after her death.

Outside her family circle, Dickinson had only a few friends, but they mattered greatly to her—she called them her "estate" and cultivated them intensely. While still in her teens, she established a pattern that was to recur throughout her life: She sought to attach herself to an older man who would be her confidant and mentor or, to use her terms, "preceptor" or "master." These pilots would, she hoped, teach her something of the qualities which she knew she lacked: knowledge of the outer world, firm opinions and principles, sociability, and intellectual stability.

Dickinson's first candidate was Benjamin Newton (1821-1853), only nine years her senior, who was a law student in her father's office from 1847 to 1849. He served her in the roles of intellectual companion, guide in aesthetic and spiritual spheres, and older brother. He introduced her to Ralph Waldo Emerson's poetry, encouraged her to write her own, but died of consumption in his thirty-third year, before she became a serious poet. Her letters to him are not extant, but in a letter she wrote Higginson in 1862, she probably refers to Newton when she mentions a "friend who taught me Immortality—but venturing too near, himself—he never returned—."

Dickinson's first mature friendship was with Samuel Bowles (1834-1878), who inherited his father's *Springfield Republican* and made it one of the most admired newspapers in the United States. Bowles had a penetrating mind, warmth, wit, dynamic energy, strongly liberal convictions, and an engaging, vibrant personality. Extensively seasoned by travel, he knew virtually every important public leader and was a marvelous guest and companion. He, and sometimes his wife with him, became regular visitors in both Edward and

Austin Dickinson's homes from 1858 onward. Thirty-five of Dickinson's letters to Bowles survive, and they show her deep attachment to—perhaps even love for—him, even though she knew that he was out of her reach in every way—just as her poetry was out of his, since his taste in literature was wholly conventional. In April, 1862, Bowles left for a long European stay. Shortly thereafter, Emily wrote him, "I have the errand from my heart—I might forget to tell it. Would you please come home?" Then, in a second letter, "[I]t is a suffering to have a sea . . . between your soul and you." That November, the returned Bowles called at Amherst. Dickinson chose to remain in her room, sending him a note instead of encountering him.

Life's Work

The turning point in Dickinson's career as a poet, and hence in her life, came in her late twenties. Before 1858, her writing consisted of letters and desultory, sentimental verses; thereafter, particularly from 1858 to 1863, poetry became her primary activity. As far as scholars can ascertain, she wrote one hundred in 1859, sixty-five in 1860, at least eighty in 1861, and in 1862— her *annus mirabilis*—perhaps as many as 366, of a prosodic skill far superior to her previous achievement. What caused such a flood of creativity? Most— but not all—biographers attribute it to her unfulfilled love for the Reverend Mr. Charles Wadsworth (1814-1882).

Dickinson and Lavinia visited their father in Washington, D.C., during April, 1854, when he was serving his congressional term. On their return trip, they stopped over in Philadelphia as guests of a friend from school days and heard Wadsworth preach in the Arch Street Presbyterian Church, whose pastor he was from 1850 to April, 1862. Married and middle-aged, of rocklike rectitude, shy and reserved, Wadsworth nevertheless made an indelible impression as a "Man of sorrow" on Dickinson. He was generally regarded as second only to Henry Ward Beecher among the pulpit orators of his time. A contemporary newspaper profile described him in these terms:

> His person is slender, and his dark eyes, hair and complexion have decidedly a Jewish cast. The elements of his popularity are somewhat like those of the gifted Summerfield—a sweet touching voice, warmth of manner, and lively imagination. But Wadsworth's style, it is said, is vastly bolder, his fancy more vivid, and his action more violent.

It is presumed that Dickinson must have talked with Wadsworth during her Philadelphia visit. Few other facts are known: He called on her in Amherst in the spring of 1860, and again in the summer of 1880. She requested his and his children's pictures from his closest friend. In April, 1862, Wadsworth moved to San Francisco, becoming minister to the Calvary Presbyterian Society. Dickinson found this departure traumatic: She used "Calvary" ten times in poems of 1862 and 1863; she spoke of herself as "Empress of Calvary," and

began one 1863 poem with the words, "Where Thou art—that is Home/
Cashmere or Calvary—the Same. . ./ So I may come." With probable reference to her inner "Calvary" drama of loss and renunciation, she began at this
time to dress entirely in white. By 1870, and until his death, Wadsworth was
back in Philadelphia in another pastorate, but the anguished crisis he had
caused her had ended by then.

After Dickinson's death, three long love letters were found in draft form
among her papers, in her handwriting of the late 1850's and early 1860's.
They address a "Master," and have therefore come to be called the "Master
Letters." Their tone is urgent, their style, nervous and staccato. In the second of them, "Daisy" tells her "Master": "I want to see you more—Sir—
than all I wish for in this world—and the wish—altered a little—will be my
only one—for the skies." She invites him to come to Amherst and pledges
not to disappoint him. Yet the final letter shows the agony of a rejected
lover, amounting to an almost incoherent cry of despair. For whom were
these letters intended? Thomas Johnson and most other biographers desig-
nate Wadsworth. Richard Sewall, however, argues for Bowles, on the internal evidence that some of the images in the unsent letters parallel images in
poems that Dickinson did send Bowles.

In 1861, Dickinson composed the most openly erotic of her poems, #249,
with the sea the element in which the speaker moors herself:

> Wild Nights—Wild Nights!
> Were I with thee
> Wild Nights should be
> Our luxury!
>
> Futile—the Winds—
> To a Heart in port—
> Done with the Compass—
> Done with the Chart!
>
> Rowing in Eden—
> Ah, the Sea!
> Might I but moor—Tonight—
> In Thee!

Is this poem derived from autobiographical experience—or, at least, intense
longing for such experience—or is the first-person perspective no more than
that of the poem's persona or speaker? Again, Dickinsonians divide on this
question.

On April 15, 1862, having liked an article by Thomas Wentworth Higginson, Dickinson sent him four of her poems and a diffident note, asking him if
he thought her verses were "alive" and "breathed." Trained as a minister,
Higginson had held a Unitarian pulpit in Newburyport, Massachusetts, then

resigned it to devote himself to social reforms, chief of which was abolition-ism. He had made a reputation as a representative, influential mid-century literary critic, with particular interest in the work of female writers. The four poems Dickinson mailed him were among her best to date; in his evaluative replies, however, he showed an obtuse misunderstanding of them, as well as of her subsequent submissions, which were to total one hundred.

Dickinson undoubtedly felt a strong need for another "preceptor"—Wadsworth had just departed for San Francisco—and especially for a lit-erary rather than romantic confidant. Higginson was to prove her "safest friend" for the remainder of her life. A warm, courteous, sympathetic man, he regarded her with mystified admiration. After their correspondence had been under way for several months, he asked her to send him a photograph. Her response was, "I had no portrait, now, but am small, like the Wren, and my Hair is bold, like the Chestnut Bur, and my eyes, like the Sherry in the Glass, that the Guest leaves." After Higginson had met her eight years later, he confirmed this self-portrait and added to it that Dickinson was a "plain, shy little person, the face without a single good feature."

Dickinson's poetry, unfortunately for both of them, was simply beyond Higginson's grasp. He immediately and consistently advised her not to seek its publication because it was "not strong enough." His critical judgments were invariably fatuous, showing deaf ears and blind eyes to her original lan-guage, syntax, meter, and rhyme. She resigned herself to his recommenda-tion against publication but gently yet firmly ignored his strictures concerning her poems' construction. Thomas Johnson summarizes the relationship as "one of the most eventful, and at the same time elusive and insubstantial friendships in the annals of American literature."

In the late 1870's, nearing her fiftieth year, Dickinson fell in love with Otis Phillips Lord (1812-1884). He was a distinguished lawyer who, from 1875 to 1882, served as an associate justice of the Massachusetts Supreme Court. He answered Dickinson's constant need for a settled, senior friend-tutor, in-tellectually gifted and personally impressive; he became her last "preceptor." She had first known Judge Lord when he had called on Edward Dickinson; like her father, he was vigorous, conscientious, commanding, and highly dis-ciplined. Their affection developed after December, 1877, when Lord's wife died. Fifteen of her letters to him survive and indicate that, over the objec-tion of his nieces, Lord apparently offered to marry her. With her father and Bowles now dead and her mother an invalid requiring many hours of her time each week, Dickinson found considerable solace in their correspon-dence. Yet she also knew that her reclusive life was too rigidly established for her to adapt to the major changes that marriage would require of her.

On April 1, 1882, Wadsworth, the man she had called "my closest earthly friend," died. On May 1 of that year, Lord suffered a stroke; on May 14, Dickinson wrote him a fervent letter of joy at his (temporary) recovery, assuring him of her "rapture" at his reprieve from impending death; on October 5 came news of her beloved nephew Gilbert's death; on November 14, her mother finally died, after years of serious illness. It is not surprising that Dickinson then underwent a "nervous prostration" that impaired her faculties for many weeks.

After an 1864 visit to Boston for eye treatment, Dickinson did not leave Amherst for the remainder of her life. Her withdrawal from society became gradually more marked. By 1870, she did not venture beyond her house and garden, preferring to socialize by sending brief letters, some of them accompanied by poems, flowers, or fruit. She retreated upstairs when most visitors came to call, sometimes lurking on an upper landing or around corners. While strangers regarded her eccentricities as unnatural, her friends and family accepted them as the price of her retreat into the intensity of her poetry. Perhaps her most self-revealing poem is #303, whose first stanza declares,

> The Soul selects her own Society—
> Then—shuts the Door—
> To her divine Majority—
> Present no more—

Emily Dickinson died of nephritis on May 15, 1886.

Summary

Emily Dickinson's nearly eighteen hundred poems, only seven of which saw print during her lifetime, constitute her "Letter to the World" (#441), her real life. They establish her, along with Walt Whitman, as one of this nation's two most seminal poets. Her sharp intellectual wit, her playfulness, and her love of ambiguity, paradox, and irony liken her poetry to the seventeenth century metaphysical achievements of England's John Donne and George Herbert and New England's Edward Taylor. Yet her language and rhythm are often uniquely individual, with a tumultuous rhetoric that sharply probes homely details for universal essence. She is a writer who defies boundaries and labels, standing alone as a contemporary not only of Herman Melville and Nathaniel Hawthorne but also, in the poetic sense, of T. S. Eliot, W. H. Auden, Robert Frost, Robert Lowell, and Sylvia Plath. Her work ranks with the most original in poetic history.

Bibliography

Dickinson, Emily. *The Complete Poems of Emily Dickinson*. Edited by Thomas H. Johnson. Boston: Little, Brown and Co., 1960. The text of the three-volume edition with the variant readings omitted.
_____. *The Letters of Emily Dickinson*. Edited by Thomas H. Johnson and Theodora Ward. 3 vols. Cambridge, Mass.: Harvard University

Press, 1958. The definitive editions of Dickinson's poetry and letters. They have been arranged in the most accurate chronological order possible and numbered. In 1890, the first collection of Dickinson's poems was brought out by Mabel Loomis Todd and Higginson, with two more volumes in 1891 and 1896, all in disorderly, random selections, with gross editorial violations of the poet's spelling and syntax. Johnson has therefore done an invaluable service to American literary scholarship by taking Dickinson's jottings, scribbles, and semifinal drafts and sorting them out. Even so, his choices of alternative language have sometimes been questioned by other Dickinson specialists.

_____. *The Poems of Emily Dickinson*. Edited by Thomas H. Johnson. 3 vols. Cambridge, Mass.: Harvard University Press, 1955. "Including variant readings critically compared with all known manuscripts."

Johnson, Thomas H. *Emily Dickinson: An Interpretive Biography*. New York: Atheneum Publishers, 1976. A gracefully written, authoritative critical biography by the dean of contemporary Dickinson scholars. It is the first that discusses in detail Higginson's significance in Dickinson's life and career.

Sewall, Richard B. *The Life of Emily Dickinson*. 2 vols. New York: Farrar, Straus and Giroux, 1974. By far the most comprehensive Dickinson interpretive biography. Sewall devotes his first volume to Dickinson's family, his second to her friends, and intertwines her life with both circles with great tact, sympathetic understanding, and impressive learning. The prose is clear and often eloquent. One of the most admirable modern literary biographies.

_____, ed. *Emily Dickinson: A Collection of Critical Essays*. Englewood Cliffs, N.J.: Prentice-Hall, 1963. A rich and diverse collection of critical essays, displaying an almost bewildering range of interpretive views. Such important critics and scholars as Charles Anderson, R. P. Blackmur, John Crowe Ransom, Allen Tate, and George Whicher are represented.

Gerhard Brand

JOHN DICKINSON

Born: November 8, 1732; Crosia-dore Plantation, Maryland
Died: February 14, 1808; Wilmington, Delaware
Areas of Achievement: Political science and government
Contribution: At a crucial point in the development of the American Revolution, Dickinson stated the colonists' arguments against England in a new and compelling way and became, for a while, a spokesman for all the Colonies. Later, he helped draft and win ratification of the United States Constitution.

Early Life

John Dickinson was born on November 8, 1732, on a plantation in Maryland that had been in his family for three quarters of a century. Eight years later, John's father, Samuel, moved his family to Delaware, where he hired an Irish tutor named William Killen to teach his children classics and history. Samuel Dickinson was a lawyer as well as a gentleman farmer, and Killen, too, was attracted to the law (he later became chief justice of Delaware), so it is not surprising that the young John Dickinson chose law as a career. When he was eighteen, John Moland, one of Philadelphia's leading attorneys, accepted him as a student. The three years that Dickinson spent in Moland's office introduced him to a much wider world than he had known before, and he began to meet other young men who would become important in revolutionary Pennsylvania and Delaware. His fellow students in Moland's office, for example, included Samuel Wharton and George Read.

To complete his legal training, Dickinson left America in 1753, to study at the Inns of Court in London. Five years later, he returned to Philadelphia and opened his own law office. A bookish and intelligent man, he was apparently as interested in studying and writing history, especially English constitutional history, as he was in trying cases. Nevertheless, he quickly became one of the most successful lawyers in the city. A portrait of him done years later reveals a man with the somewhat portly build typical of successful men in the eighteenth century. His mental abilities, his training, and his understanding of history and constitutional law, however, were anything but typical.

The popular, talented, and wealthy young attorney soon ran for office and won election to the Delaware legislature in 1760. Two years later, he became a delegate to the Pennsylvania Assembly, representing Philadelphia, where he opposed Joseph Galloway and Benjamin Franklin in their attempts to have King George III convert Pennsylvania from a proprietary colony ruled by the Penn family to a royal colony run by a royal governor. Dickinson had little love for the Penns, whom he (and most Pennsylvanians) regarded as a particularly rapacious clan, much too prone to place their own welfare above the public good. Yet Dickinson thought the remedy which Franklin proposed would make things worse, for it would strip Pennsylvanians of the protection that their proprietary charter afforded them from direct royal (and parliamentary) interference in their affairs.

Dickinson's stand was not popular, and he lost his seat at the next election. On the sidelines and out of public favor, he began to write about the emerging struggle between the Colonies and England. That struggle would change Dickinson's life and career and lead him away from the practice of law toward a life of revolutionary politics and public service.

Life's Work

In 1765, Dickinson published the pamphlet *The Late Regulations Respecting the British Colonies on the Continent of America Considered*. In it, he denounced both the Sugar Act (1764) and the Stamp Act (1765) as ill-advised and economically senseless attempts by Parliament to raise revenues in the American Colonies. The popular essay made Dickinson one of Pennsylvania's leading opponents of the Stamp Tax, and so when the legislature chose delegates to attend the Stamp Act Congress in New York, Dickinson was among them. That congress so closely reflected the cautious Dickinson's views, and so respected his talents as a constitutional scholar and essayist, that it permitted him to draft its formal resolutions. In them, Dickinson stated the Colonies' objections to the Stamp Act but avoided any suggestion that colonists ought to resist the law until it was (as the congress hoped it would be) repealed.

Parliament did repeal the Stamp Act in 1766, but soon a new threat to colonial liberties arose when England again tried to raise a revenue in the Colonies. The Townshend Revenue Act of 1767 imposed taxes on English goods imported into the Colonies. In December, 1767, Dickinson began publishing in the *Pennsylvania Chronicle* a series of letters signed "A Farmer in Pennsylvania," which opposed the Townshend taxes. John Dickinson was not a farmer in Pennsylvania. He was a lawyer in Philadelphia. Yet the overwhelming majority of colonists (ninety percent or more) lived in rural areas, not cities, and were not likely to be much impressed by "Letters from a Philadelphia Lawyer." Dickinson wisely chose a more appealing pen name. In any case, that he was the Pennsylvania Farmer quickly became public knowledge.

In the "Farmer's Letters," as they came to be called, Dickinson accomplished two things. First, he summarized and stated the colonists' claim that English attempts to tax them were not merely inexpedient and ill-advised, but were flatly unconstitutional—and he summarized that claim more clearly and succinctly than any colonist had yet done. "It is *inseparably essential to the freedom of a people*," he wrote at the Stamp Act Congress and repeated in Letter IV, "that NO TAX be imposed on them, *except with their own consent*, given personally, or by their representatives." Second, he pointed out that the form of any tax England attempted to lay upon American colonists to raise revenues was irrelevant. What mattered in deciding if a tax was or was not constitutional was the purpose for which it had been passed. If England taxed, for example, colonial imports in order to restrict American trade with foreign nations, then the purpose of that tax was primarily to regulate trade—and few colonists, and certainly not Dickinson, as yet challenged England's right to regulate the Colonies' trade. If England laid a tax on colonial imports in order to raise money, however (as it did in the Townshend Act), then the tax was unconstitutional. Dickinson added that it was the colonists' right to determine for themselves what Parliament's intent had been in passing any colonial tax.

The "Farmer's Letters" were immensely popular. Nearly every colonial newspaper published them. A pamphlet version appeared in Philadelphia in 1768 and was republished at least six times in American cities, while other editions came out in London, Paris, and Dublin. When most colonial assemblies endorsed Dickinson's ideas, he became the first American who could, with some justice, claim to speak for the American Colonies, rather than for only a few of them. In the "Farmer's Letters," Dickinson laid the foundation for an emerging sense of American "nationality" among the colonists. He brought much closer the day when colonists would think of themselves not as New Yorkers or Virginians or Rhode Islanders first, but as one people, sharing common ideas, interests, and goals. This was the most important contribution of the "Farmer's Letters" to the developing American Revolution and to the nation it created.

For a while, Dickinson was the most popular man in the Colonies. Praised by town meetings, toasted by county committees, honored by legislatures, Dickinson found himself hailed from Massachusetts to Georgia. In the "Farmer's Letters," he had staked out the most advanced constitutional ground and had placed himself at the cutting edge of the incipient revolution against England. Dickinson's exceptional popularity, however, did not last. He opposed, publicly and often, any open resistance to English law and especially any violent resistance. Perhaps influenced by his family's Quaker heritage, he held to that opinion, insisting that conciliation, patience, and petitions, along with trade boycotts, were the proper means of changing England's mind even after the Tea Act and the Boston Tea Party. Not even the passage of the Coercive (or, from the colonists' point of view, the Intolerable) Acts, the imposition by England of martial law in Massachusetts and the military occupation of Boston, changed his mind. By the spring of 1775, Dickinson was being denounced for his caution as a Loyalist sympathizer and a coward throughout much of New England, while many ardent rebels in Pennsylvania became suspicious, if not of his loyalty, then at least of the depth of his commitment to the rebel cause.

By late 1774, even Dickinson knew that war might be unavoidable, and that the colonists had best prepare for the worst even as they tried to avoid it. He served that year as a Pennsylvania delegate to the First Continental Congress, as chairman of his colony's Committee of Safety and Defense, and as colonel of the first battalion of revolutionary militia raised in Philadelphia. Yet even after the war began at Lexington in April, 1775, Dickinson still sought a peaceful resolution of the troubles between England and her Colonies, and he still refused to support a declaration of American independence. In December, 1775, for example, after eight months of war, Dickinson arranged to have Pennsylvania's delegation to the 1776 Continental Congress (which included himself) forbidden by the Assembly to consider independence at Congress.

By the end of 1775, Dickinson had come to fear what England's armies might do to America in a revolutionary war declared too soon, without sufficient preparation, planning, and unity and without a single guarantee of foreign assistance. He also worried about what colonists might do to themselves during such a war and after it. Dickinson was well aware of the jealousies and antagonisms among colonists that had characterized most of colonial history and which had not dissolved when the war began. He worried that thirteen petty, independent states might eventually make war on one another, and that anarchy or tyranny might follow. He worried, in short, that the liberties that colonists were fighting to preserve might be destroyed by the Revolution intended to secure them. Thus, when Congress took a preliminary vote on independence on July 1, 1776, Dickinson spoke eloquently in opposition and voted no. When the final vote came the next morning, however, it was clear that independence would pass overwhelmingly, so Dickinson abstained; he took no part in the vote that finally, after fifteen months of war, declared the American Colonies free and independent states.

Dickinson still had misgivings about the Revolution following independence, especially when Congress rejected his draft of a proposed constitution for the new nation, which would have created a relatively strong central government. Instead, Congress adopted articles of confederation which left most significant powers in the hands of the separate states. Widely suspected of being a lukewarm rebel at best, his advice ignored by Congress, and his seat there taken from him by the end of 1776, Dickinson withdrew from public life for a time, resigning his commission and his place in the legislature.

In 1779, however, Dickinson returned to Congress as a delegate from Delaware. Two years later, he became president of that state's Supreme Executive Council, and he soon won the same post in Pennsylvania, although he despised the state's radical revolutionary constitution. His troubled experience as president of the council merely reinforced his conviction that the states and the nation could neither survive nor prosper without stronger, more stable governments.

When Delaware chose him as a delegate to the Federal Constitutional

Convention at Philadelphia in the summer of 1787, Dickinson accepted. He took an active part in the convention's deliberations and played an important role in arranging the compromises among the various factions represented there (and particularly between the large and small states) that made any agreement on a new national constitution possible. Never as ardent an advocate of national government power (as opposed to state power) as James Madison or Alexander Hamilton, Dickinson nevertheless worked at the convention to create a more vigorous central government than existed under the Articles of Confederation.

After the convention presented the new national Constitution to the states for their approval, Dickinson wrote a series of letters signed "Fabius," which began appearing in newspapers in the fall of 1787. They urged ratification of the Constitution on the grounds that it would provide the stability of government that the ineffective Articles of Confederation manifestly had not, and so protect liberty, ensure the due power of each state within the Union, and guarantee stability. That done, he all but retired from public life, though he continued to follow public affairs closely and to express his opinions in letters and essays. When he died in February, 1808, he was seventy-six years old.

Summary

John Dickinson was, all of his life, a cautious, conservative man. In 1776, he did not so much embrace revolution as accept it when events left him no choice. Never much attracted by the possibilities that revolution offered to create new liberties, Dickinson instead feared the threat revolution posed to liberties he already enjoyed—liberties solidly grounded in English history, law, and tradition. The "Farmer's Letters" united the colonists behind a single constitutional doctrine in opposition to England—a necessary condition for independence and an American nation. At the same time, Dickinson upheld the power of law, peaceful persuasion, and public discourse as the proper means by which colonists might see their grievances redressed. As late as July, 1776, Dickinson opposed the Declaration of Independence, which his own writings had helped make inevitable. Yet once his fellow colonists chose to establish a new nation, he stood with them. Once he understood, as John Adams, Benjamin Franklin, and others did before him, that the fact of imminent tyranny outweighed the dangers of resistance and even independence, commitment to the Revolution did not waver. He spent the remainder of his public life helping to secure independence and working to prevent the liberties he valued from being consumed by the Revolution or undermined in its aftermath. At the Federal Constitutional Convention of 1787, he worked to enhance the power of the central government without unduly limiting the autonomy of the states. Once a stable national frame of government had been agreed upon at Philadelphia, Dickinson campaigned to have it accepted by the states. After ratification, with the Republic safe, at least for a while, Dickinson retired to his home in Delaware as one of the founders of a new republic in a world of monarchies.

Bibliography

Dickinson, John, and Richard Henry Lee. *Empire and Nation: Letters from a Farmer in Pennsylvania; Letters from the Federal Farmer.* Englewood Cliffs, N.J.: Prentice-Hall, 1962. Contains the text of all the "Farmer's Letters." Forrest McDonald's introduction is useful for putting the letters in context.

Flower, Milton E. *John Dickinson, Conservative Revolutionary.* Charlottesville: University Press of Virginia, 1983. The first full biography of Dickinson since 1891 and the only one readily available. Scholarly and not particularly easy reading. Flower portrays Dickinson in the usual manner, as a conservative, and offers few new insights. Yet Flower provides far more, and more accurate, information about Dickinson than any other single source.

Jacobson, David L. *John Dickinson and the Revolution in Pennsylvania, 1764-1776.* Berkeley: University of California Press, 1965. Not a full biography. Scholarly yet surprisingly readable. Treats Dickinson as less conservative than most historians do.

Jensen, Merrill. *The Articles of Confederation: An Interpretation of the Social-Constitutional History of the American Revolution, 1774-1781.* Madison: University of Wisconsin Press, 1959. Includes a detailed account of Dickinson's draft of articles of confederation submitted to Congress shortly after Independence. See especially chapter 4, which deals exclusively with Dickinson's draft. Places the Articles of Confederation and the debate over them within the larger context of the Revolution. Though somewhat dated, the book is still useful for understanding Dickinson and the political climate in which he lived.

Stille, Charles J. *The Life and Times of Charles Dickinson.* Philadelphia: J. B. Lippincott Co., 1891. Uncritical, occasionally inaccurate, based on limited sources and difficult to find, this work was nevertheless the only full biography of Dickinson generally available until Flower's biography appeared in 1983. Although Stille's immense respect and sympathy for Dickinson too often interfere with his judgment, the book offers some worthwhile insights into Dickinson's politics and character.

Van Doren, Carl C. *The Great Rehearsal: The Story of the Making and Ratifying of the Constitution of the United States.* Westport, Conn.: Greenwood Press, 1982. Originally published in 1948, this nicely written, largely narrative account provides a good background for understanding Dickinson's role at the Federal Constitutional Convention and in the ensuing ratification debates.

Robert A. Becker

WALT DISNEY

Born: December 5, 1901; Chicago, Illinois
Died: December 15, 1966; Burbank, California
Areas of Achievement: Animation, motion pictures, television, and theme parks
Contribution: More than any other person, Disney was an innovator in the entertainment industry, a chance-taker responsible for what he termed "imagineering," leading the way in children's amusements.

Early Life

Walter Elias Disney was born December 5, 1901, in Chicago, Illinois. His mother, née Flora Call, was German-American; his father, Elias Disney, was Irish-Canadian. Both parents had farming backgrounds. Walt Disney was the youngest of four sons by eight years but was older than his only sister, Ruth.

With little doubt, the strongest influence on Walt during his childhood was his father. The older Disney was a religious Fundamentalist and stern taskmaster who was always ready to beat his children with his belt. That practice finally led to a showdown in Walt's teen years, when he physically prevented his father from beating him, marking a turning point in their relationship. The Disney children were denied a typical childhood environment, their father refusing to provide toys, games, and sporting equipment. Added to this were the frequent job changes of the frustrated Elias Disney, who sought success in such areas as farming, railway shops, carpentry and contracting work, newspaper distributing, and factory owning. The disruption of moves from Chicago to Marceline, Missouri, to Kansas City, Missouri, and back to Chicago in the space of eleven years principally accounted for Walt's never getting past the ninth grade.

Walt's favorite childhood memories were of Marceline, where he lived from the age of four to eight. The Disneys worked a forty-eight-acre farm, a life Walt loved. It also provided him with his first acquaintance with a variety of animals, contact which his closest brother, Roy, stressed was the start of a sensitive, lifelong consideration. Marceline was also a railroad hub, and Disney was ever after captivated by trains.

Following the collapse of the farm, the Disneys rode in a boxcar to Kansas City, where Elias bought a newspaper delivery route. Seven days a week, Walt delivered early morning newspapers over a sprawling route, sometimes falling asleep in warm buildings and then waking in panic to find himself behind schedule. Nightmares of that panic affected him for the rest of his life. Tardiness at school regularly resulted, and post-school hours were occupied by afternoon paper deliveries. Paid nothing for this, Walt worked in a candy store at noontime to earn spending money.

In his teen years, Walt participated in vaudeville amateur nights, doing a prizewinning Charles Chaplin act, and took some beginning art lessons. When Elias sold his business to move back to Chicago to take over a jelly factory, the fifteen-year-old Walt stayed in Kansas City. He tutored the new owner of the newspaper distributorship and became a vendor on the Santa Fe Railroad through the summer.

Rejoining his parents in Chicago, he became a school newspaper cartoonist, pursued photography, worked at the jelly factory, took odd jobs, and joined an art class at the Chicago Academy of Fine Arts. When he finished the ninth grade, he worked for the post office through the summer and decided to enlist in the military. The United States had recently entered World War I. Disney, anxious to serve and to wear a uniform to impress the girls, was rejected by every recruiter; he was too young. With his mother's cooperation, Disney obtained forged documents which enabled him to be accepted as a driver in the Red Cross Ambulance Corps. The war ended just before Disney went overseas, but his experiences in France made an indelible mark on him. Though not yet eighteen when he returned to Chicago, he knew that he could not return to school. Disney had reached his full height (five feet ten inches) and weighed a solid 165 pounds. He was ready to strike out on his own.

Life's Work

Moving to Kansas City, Disney went through an assortment of jobs as a commercial artist and cartoonist, his work leading to an enthusiastic interest in filmed cartoons. He also met, and even tried a business partnership with, Ub Iwerks, a young man his own age who was a more gifted artist than Disney. Thus started a long and interesting, often troubling, relationship between the consummate artist Iwerks and the consummate organizer and visionary Disney.

During this period, Disney combined a live performer with cartoon figures in *Alice's Wonderland* (1923), which led to a popular *Alice in Cartoonland* (1923-1926) series after Disney had moved to Hollywood, California. Over three years, Disney produced fifty-six *Alice in Cartoonland* comedies.

Disney returned to a straight cartoon format with the *Oswald the Rabbit* (1927) series, producing twenty-six cartoons in the series in less than two years before losing the rights to Oswald in a New York contract dispute with Charlie Mintz and Universal Pictures. Oswald was tremendously popular, and Disney knew that he had to have a dynamic, new character.

Disney had by then married Lillian Bounds (July 13, 1925), an original employee in the first Disney Brothers Studio. She had accompanied Disney to New York and now faced with him the important trip back to California. Referring to a series of Ub Iwerks sketches and reminiscing with Lilly about past experiences, Disney settled on a cartoon mouse as his next star. Disney first called his character Mortimer, but Lilly thought that pompous and suggested Mickey. Soon after, Disney—with Iwerks getting prominent credit as the major cartoonist—finished two Mickey Mouse cartoons, *Plane Crazy* (1928), based on the exploits of Charles Lindbergh, and *Gallopin' Gaucho* (1928), with Mickey emulating Douglas Fairbanks. Prior to their release, however, Disney saw the first feature talkie, *The Jazz Singer* (1927), and realized that the future of films was in sound. He immediately worked on a third Mickey Mouse cartoon, *Steamboat Willie*, incorporating sound and thus revolutionizing the film cartoon industry. Its premiere on November 18, 1928, stands as a hallowed date in Disney annals. After its success, sound was added to the first pair of Mickey Mouse cartoons, and they were released.

Within three years, Mickey Mouse had captured audiences throughout the United States, and by 1936 it was said in all seriousness that the famous mouse was the most widely recognized figure in the world. Disney himself was acclaimed as one of the two top geniuses in filmmaking; Chaplin was the other. Sales of Mickey Mouse watches and windup handcars literally saved the Ingersoll Watch Company and the Lionel Corporation from bankruptcy during the Depression. Figures such as songwriter Cole Porter, conductor Arturo Toscanini, and King George VI of England were dedicated Mickey Mouse fans, while famed Russian director Sergei Eisenstein pronounced Mickey Mouse to be America's most original cultural contribution.

Most intriguing of all was the symbolic tying together of Mickey Mouse and his creator. Mickey's voice, on all sound tracks until 1946, was Disney's own. During that period, Mickey, along with the other featured characters (Donald Duck and Pluto are prime examples), had progressed from a Depression barnyard to comfortable middle-class suburbia. Mickey Mouse had ventured into dozens of occupations, from airplane pilot to polo player to orchestra conductor, and had ended as an entrepreneur. Some claimed that Disney had used Mickey to grope for his own niche—and the entrepreneur won in the end.

In 1931, Disney suffered a nervous breakdown. Fully recovered, he launched into the rest of the decade with enormous energy. He earned plaudits for innovative moves and won a string of Academy Awards. In 1932, he was the first in animated cartooning to use the Technicolor process. His Academy Award–winning *Three Little Pigs* (1933) had uplifted American morale during the Depression by supplying a theme, "Who's Afraid of the Big Bad Wolf?" *Snow White and the Seven Dwarfs* (1937), the first feature-length cartoon in history, also took an Oscar and paved the way for many later classics. Academy Awards were also won by *The Tortoise and the Hare* (1935), *The Old Mill* (1937), and *The Ugly Duckling* (1939), among other films. To Disney, the most important development of the 1930's was the growth of the studio. From a handful of employees and a garage studio had emerged many hundreds of workers in a huge complex.

The 1940's were quite different. Disney actually could have gone bankrupt.

World War II gravely affected the studio's overseas market, and American entry into the war came on the heels of two box-office disasters: *Fantasia* (1940) and *The Reluctant Dragon* (1941). *Fantasia* was not to be seen as a masterpiece until the 1960's. A traumatic labor union strike (1941) devastated Disney, whose belief that he headed one big, happy family was shattered when roughly half the cartoonists picketed. An irony through this episode was that the conservatively Republican, strongly anti-Communist Disney, who blamed the strike on the Communists, had come full spectrum from his father, who had been an active labor unionist supporter of oft-defeated Socialist presidential candidate Eugene Debs. The strike so affected Disney that, appearing close to a second breakdown, he agreed to tour Latin America for the State Department. In his absence, the strike was settled.

The surprising success of *Dumbo* (1941), the shortest feature Disney ever made, and *Bambi* (1942), as well as a United States government contract to produce training films, barely kept Disney in business. The goodwill tour of Latin America inspired *Saludos Amigos* (1943) and *The Three Caballeros* (1945), but Disney's finances had to wait for the war's end before significant recovery.

Disney's first postwar feature was *Make Mine Music* (1946), which was later cut into ten short cartoons, another innovation by Disney and one he followed with later omnibus features. *Song of the South* (1946) followed, combining live action and cartoon animation, and gaining an Academy Award for its song "Zip-a-dee Doo-dah." The National Association for the Advancement of Colored People and the National Urban League, however, criticized the work for perpetuating racial stereotyping.

Two years later, Disney produced one of his favorite films, *So Dear to My Heart*, entirely live-action. Though animated features immediately followed—*The Adventures of Ichabod and Mr. Toad* (1949) and the extremely profitable *Cinderella* (1950)—the 1950's, and especially the 1960's, saw Disney shifting emphasis to live-action films.

Disney practically took over the field of nature documentaries in the 1950's with his *True-Life Adventure* series, winning three Oscars and several international awards. The decade also witnessed Disney's entry into television, starting innocently with consecutive Christmas specials in 1950-1951, proceeding to a weekly *Disneyland* series in 1954 (during which a *Davy Crockett* serial led to a surprise multimillion dollar bonanza) and a daily *Mickey Mouse Club* show in 1955. Thereafter, Disney virtually wrote his own ticket in television.

Disney's most important accomplishment of the 1950's, however, was Disneyland, which opened in Anaheim, California, on July 13, 1955, the Disneys' thirtieth wedding anniversary. When taking his daughters, Sharon (adopted) and Diane, to amusement parks, Disney had been constantly disappointed and had determined to create a far superior park. He insisted that

Disneyland was not an amusement park, though he claimed that it was his own private amusement area. The fantastic success of Disneyland and the later Walt Disney World (1971) in Florida stood as final testimony to Disney's courage and vision. He had stood virtually alone against other Disney executives, willing to risk frightening losses against a dream, something he had done fairly often before. Controversial in this regard is what happened to his EPCOT (Experimental Prototype Community of Tomorrow) idea. Disney's intention was to have an actual live-in community of thousands of people, under an all-weather dome, with its own schools, shopping and entertainment areas, and innovative technology placing them a minimum of twenty-five years into the future. Those thoughts died when Disney died. EPCOT, as exciting as many of its projects are, and as Disney-like as its practices are, falls far short of Disney's own concept.

By the 1960's, Disney was a wealthy man in full command of a respected, diversified empire. Despite the tremendous expansion of Disney holdings, he remained in dictatorial control, as he had since the 1920's. Yet, in the 1960's, critics suggested that Disney had lost his spirit, pointing to the lack of any outstanding films. His answer was the supercalifragilisticexpialidocious *Mary Poppins* (1964). The biggest financial hit in Disney's life, the film was nominated for thirteen Academy Awards and garnered five. Though more projects followed, *Mary Poppins* proved to be his last hurrah. Disney, a heavy smoker through his career, was hospitalized for lung cancer in 1966, appeared to have recovered from major surgery, but suffered a relapse, dying on December 15, 1966, in a hospital room which overlooked his Burbank studio. An entire world mourned the loss of a man who had come to seem like a favorite uncle.

Summary

Disney was said to have the facility of seeing things no others saw, from chairs being reshaped into acrobatic animals to swamps converted into paradises. More important, he was willing to express his ideas openly, despite the risk of ridicule. Had Disney been an outstanding artist himself, it is entirely possible, even probable, that his success would have been much more limited, given the tens of thousands of talented artists who do not achieve fame. Disney learned early, however, that his own drawing skills were limited. Thus, he became the organizer, the "idea man," and exercised absolute control of his own, and hence his corporation's, destiny. Disney's attention to the most minute detail, his insistence on perfection, his enormous drive, and his need to be boss caused him to be both loved and hated by his employees. The finished product, be it feature film, cartoon short, comic book, or Disneyland ride, bore his unmistakable stamp, however, whether employees were happy or not: That was the Disney way. Disney always assumed that others were as fiercely devoted to each project as he, an assumption which often misled him into thinking that others shared his joy as well.

Disney, born in the big city and spending most of his life in major cities, nevertheless loved small-town and country life, often painting the contrast between urban ugliness and rural beauty. Indeed, his works created a Disney America, and the effects of these Disney impressions on American culture are inestimable. Presented through his films, television productions, comic and story books, and theme parks, Disney's America may well represent the nation's image to most Americans, especially given the fact that the learning process with Disney almost always begins at an early age.

The probability is that Disney never intended to create a substitute America. Instead, Disney in many ways was Everyperson. He did not cater as much to a mass public as to his own taste, which was clearly reflective of conservative American ideals. When he aimed to please the public, his objective was to entertain, to amuse, to bring smiles to his consumers, rather than to propagandize. He was his own best audience. By suiting himself— almost as if he were giving himself a childhood he had never had fulfilled— he innately satisfied the public. Certainly more creative than nearly anyone in his public, he accumulated wealth that supplied him with the potential of snobbery. Yet Disney never lost the common touch.

Disney's place in the American panorama is secure. His classic works are regularly reissued in cinemas, a Disney Channel and other television productions keep his name prominently in the limelight, copyrighted Disney materials are marketed abundantly every day, and the California and Florida theme centers easily exceed any others in attendance. Indeed, it has been suggested that Disneyland and Walt Disney World constitute America's Mecca, shrines which most Americans visit at least once in their lives.

Disney seized opportunities as they presented themselves and, though hating failure, never feared it. The greatest key to Disney's stunning success was probably his willingness to be selfish enough not only to be himself, but also to risk his own and others' bankrolls to prove that his ideas were the right way to go.

Bibliography
Apple, Max. "Uncle Walt." *Esquire* 100 (December, 1983): 164-168. A quick and basically frank look back at Disney.
Culhane, John. *Walt Disney's "Fantasia."* New York: Harry N. Abrams, 1983. A rich, sensitive study by one of Disney's most valued employees, concentrating on a film classic which caused Disney more than a few headaches. An excellent source.
Davidson, Bill. "The Fantastic Walt Disney." *Saturday Evening Post* 237 (November 7, 1964): 66-68. An interesting look into a Disney who had by then ventured into his varied nooks and crannies. Poignant in that Disney had little more than two years to live at the time of its publication.

Finch, Christopher. *The Art of Walt Disney*. New York: Harry N. Abrams, 1973. Probably the best work done on Disney. Rich with illustrations, it also contains important biographical data, as well as a number of extremely challenging premises, not the least being a defense of Disney as a great artist.

Maltin, Leonard. *The Disney Films*. New York: Bonanza Books, 1973. An excellent source by one of the best film historians. The book is compartmented into such matters as features and shorts so that a sense of continuity is somewhat missing, but still, it is clearly the best source on Disney films.

Mosely, Leonard. *Disney's World*. New York: Stein and Day, 1985. Pulling no punches, this study reveals some data never published before. The author contends with the question of whether Disney's corpse is in a cryogenic state and reaches no definite conclusions.

Munsey, Cecil. *Disneyana: Walt Disney Collectibles*. New York: Hawthorn Books, 1974. A fascinating work which seems to cover every marketed product from Disney's long career. The book's lone drawback is that, since its publication, the collector's market has experienced tremendous inflation.

Schickel, Richard. *The Disney Version*. New York: Touchstone Books, Simon and Schuster, 1985. A strong, challenging study, loaded with provocative side trips. Probably the most stimulating of the biographical studies, this latest edition is superior to the earlier works by the same author.

Thomas, Bob. *Walt Disney*. New York: Simon and Schuster, 1976. The warmest Disney biography, without being sugarcoated. The author is a dependable, fair-minded, noted biographer and his work served greatly to aid the later Mosely work.

Wallace, Kevin. "Onward and Upward with the Arts: The Engineering of Ease." *The New Yorker* 39 (September 7, 1963): 104. A well written, witty, informative, and thought-provoking treatment, typical of *The New Yorker*.

John E. DiMeglio

DOROTHEA LYNDE DIX

Born: April 4, 1802; Hampden, Maine
Died: July 17, 1887; Trenton, New Jersey
Area of Achievement: Social reform
Contribution: Dix crusaded for the building of hospitals for the insane. She played a direct role in the creation of thirty-eight mental hospitals and inspired the construction of many more. She was also superintendent of army nurses for the Union army during the Civil War.

Early Life

Dorothea Lynde Dix was born in a tiny frontier hamlet, Hampden, Maine, on April 4, 1802. She was the eldest child and only daughter of Joseph and Mary (née Bigelow) Dix. Her father had dropped out of Harvard to marry her mother, who was eighteen years older than her husband and who may have been mentally ill or retarded. Joseph Dix had moved to Maine to manage the real estate holdings of his father, Elijah Dix, a prominent Boston physician and businessman. Joseph did not succeed as a manager and became a Methodist minister and a writer of religious tracts.

Escaping from an unhappy childhood, Dorothea moved to Boston to live with her grandparents at the age of twelve. There she met her lifelong friend and correspondent, Ann Heath of Berkshire. Her grandmother, the former Dorothy Lynde, was now widowed, and after two years sent her granddaughter to live with an aunt in Worcester, Massachusetts. In Worcester, Dorothea excelled in school and, upon her return to Boston at the age of nineteen, took up schoolteaching. In 1822, an engagement to an older cousin, Edward Bangs, was broken; from that point she turned all suitors away, remaining single for the remainder of her life.

Dix suffered a physical collapse in 1824 but published the first of her many works in 1825, *Conversations on Common Things*, a book of commonsense knowledge for children. She retired from public life because of illness (apparently tuberculosis) and enjoyed the hospitality of the family of William Ellery Channing, a prominent Unitarian minister and one of her closest friends. She served as a governess in the Channing home in Newport, Rhode Island, and spent winters with the Channing family on the island of St. Croix from 1830 to 1833.

Dix returned to teaching in Boston again in 1831 but gave it up in 1836 because of ill health. In this period, she also published *American Moral Tales for Young Persons* (1832). At the urging of her physician, she embarked on a trip to England in the hope that the journey would restore her health. There she met several English reformers and philanthropists. They included Dr. Samuel Tuke, the son of the founder of one of England's best-known mental institutions, and a Liverpool Unitarian, William Rathbone, with whom she stayed for an extended period.

Dix's grandmother had died in 1836 and had left her with a small income. Depending on that and the kindness of friends, Dix, it appeared, would now take up the life of a typical spinster. Presumably, she would again teach and perhaps write another book or two to fill her days.

In 1841, however, she went to the East Cambridge Jail, where she had been asked to conduct a Sunday School class for the women. She was thirty-nine years old when she entered the jail. The scene she found there shocked her deeply and led to her resolve to work for the improvement of prison facilities, especially for the insane.

Life's Work

The inmates in the women's quarters in the East Cambridge Jail included drunkards, vagrants, prostitutes, and some unkempt and ill-clothed women who were insane. The quarters stank and lacked both furniture and heat. When Dix questioned the keepers, they told her that lunatics could not feel the cold. With the assistance of Samuel Gridley Howe, another Boston friend and philanthropist, Dix succeeded in forcing the jail keepers to clean up the women's quarters and provide the inmates with heat. Dix had found her life's work.

Her first step, characteristically, was to survey the available information. She learned that humane institutions had already been established in the United States and in Europe. Still, a complete survey of the existing institutions would show that many did not come up to the standards of the exemplary few. For the next eighteen months, Dix conducted a survey of every jail, almshouse, and house of correction in the Commonwealth of Massachusetts, taking copious notes describing the conditions she found.

The result of her survey was *Memorial to the Legislature of Massachusetts* (1843), in which she described the deplorable conditions she had found in institutions around the state. The memorial provoked a storm of controversy, but with the support of prominent figures such as Samuel Gridley Howe (who had written the introduction), Horace Mann, and Charles Sumner, Dix prevailed upon the legislature to appropriate additional money for the asylum in Worcester. Her new career had begun on a successful note.

She turned next to the neighboring states of Rhode Island and New York and was equally successful there in 1844. In 1844-1845, she moved to New Jersey, where there was no mental institution. There the opposition to her recommendations was stronger, but she prevailed and even helped to design the building which became Trenton State Hospital. Privately, she referred to it as "my first-born child," and she would later return to it to live out her days. For the next three decades, however, she threw herself into the cause of building hospitals, traveling throughout the United States to take up that cause in state after state, including Kentucky, Maryland, Ohio, Illinois, Mississippi, Alabama, and Tennessee. As a result of these labors, she became famous and honored across the country.

Besides working for better treatment of the mentally ill, Dix worked in prison reform, publishing *Remarks on Prisons and Prison Discipline in the United States* in 1845. She also worked for a school for the blind in Illinois and was sympathetic to women's rights, peace, temperance, and education.

Near the middle of the century, she worked vigorously for a policy whereby some of the public domain would be set aside for a federally funded hospital for the insane. A memorial presented to Congress argued the case, but for six years Congress took no action despite her efforts. Finally, in 1854, the measure passed both houses only to see President Franklin Pierce veto it.

A trip to Europe followed this disappointment. Dix visited England, Scotland, the Continent, and Turkey and sought an audience with Pope Pius IX to tell him of conditions near the Vatican. She returned to the United States in 1856 and again took up her familiar rounds of travel and lobbying for the mentally ill.

In 1861, when the Civil War broke out, Dix became the superintendent of army nurses for the Union army, although she had many friends in the South. She had high standards for her nurses and insisted that they be over thirty and "plain looking." Because of controversy surrounding her strict administration, she lost much of her power of appointment, but she stayed on in the job until 1866.

She resumed her familiar labors after the war, spending a large amount of time in the South, where the war had devastated not only the economy but also many institutions (and state resources). Her energies went to smaller projects rather than the great institution-building tasks of the prewar years. For example, she worked diligently for a monument to be erected at Fortress Monroe in Virginia to honor the Union soldiers who had died there; she selected the granite personally and begged a stand of arms to form a fence around the monument's base. In 1881, feeling her age, she retired to a small apartment at Trenton State Hospital in New Jersey. She died there in 1887 and was buried in Mount Auburn Cemetery in Cambridge, Massachusetts.

Summary

Dorothea Dix is best remembered as a builder of institutions: Thirty-eight hospitals constructed in the nineteenth century owe their existence in part to her efforts. She was a tireless campaigner for the rights and needs of the mentally ill, championing their cause when most people preferred to lock them away and forget that they existed.

While not the first lobbyist, Dix was surely one of the most successful advocates of all time. She overcame the obvious handicap of her sex and considerable resistance to the spending of public money for any but the most obvious purposes. She succeeded by dint of hard work, preparing herself with solid facts in support of her case, and exhibited absolute persistence.

Such a woman was unusual in the nineteenth century. Unlike most of her sisters, she never married, joining a small but growing group. Since she had a private income, she was not forced by economic circumstances to find a husband to support her. Her values and her conduct epitomized the nineteenth century cult of domesticity, which stressed the moral superiority of women. Most middle-class women, however, rarely ventured into the public sphere, while Dix made it her business to address legislatures and to persuade them to do something they probably did not want to do. Thus, Dorothea Dix was an extraordinary American who devoted her energies to the improvement of her country's humanitarian efforts.

Bibliography

Cott, Nancy. *The Bonds of Womanhood: "Woman's Sphere" in New England, 1780-1835*. New Haven, Conn.: Yale University Press, 1977. This superb work provides the necessary documentation for the female context in which Dix lived. While her spinsterhood was unusual, the strong emotional bond she enjoyed with Ann Heath was not, as Cott attests.

Flexner, Eleanor. *Century of Struggle: The Women's Rights Movement in the United States*. Cambridge, Mass.: The Belknap Press of Harvard University Press, 1966. A classic treatment of the women's rights movements, with which Dix was in sympathy.

Marshall, Helen E. *Dorothea Dix: Forgotten Samaritan*. Chapel Hill: University of North Carolina Press, 1937. Reprint. New York: Russell and Russell, 1967. Although somewhat dated, this is a fine scholarly biography. Includes a valuable one-chapter excursus on the treatment of mental illness prior to Dix's time. Well documented, with an extensive bibliography and a superb index.

Snyder, Charles M., ed. *The Lady and the President: The Letters of Dorothea Dix and Millard Fillmore*. Lexington: University Press of Kentucky, 1975. Interesting for its treatment of a brief period of Dix's life.

Wilson, Dorothy Clarke. *Stranger and Traveler: The Story of Dorothea Dix, American Reformer*. Boston: Little, Brown and Co., 1975. A readable but superficial popular biography, emphasizing Dix's role as "one of America's first and foremost women achievers." No documentation, but includes bibliography. The book is enhanced by a generous selection of illustrations.

Joseph M. Hawes

STEPHEN A. DOUGLAS

Born: April 23, 1813; Brandon, Vermont
Died: June 3, 1861; Chicago, Illinois
Area of Achievement: Politics
Contribution: Endowed with a vision of nationalism, Douglas worked to develop the United States internally and to preserve the Union.

Early Life
Born on April 23, 1813, in Brandon, Vermont, Stephen A. Douglas spent his early life in Vermont and western New York State. His father died when Douglas was only two months old, and he lived on a farm with his widowed mother until he was fifteen. At that point, he set off for Middlebury, Vermont, to see "what I could do for myself in the wide world among strangers." He apprenticed himself to a cabinetmaker, but a dispute developed and he returned home after eight months. His mother remarried in late 1830, moved with her new husband to his home in western New York near Canandaigua, and Douglas accompanied them.

His early schooling in Vermont had been of the sketchy common-school variety, but in New York he entered the Canandaigua Academy, where he boarded and studied. There, he began to read law as well as study the classics, until he left school on January 1, 1833, to devote himself to full-time legal study. Early interested in politics, and particularly that of Andrew Jackson, Douglas associated himself for six months with the law office of Walter and Levi Hubbell, prominent local Jacksonians. New York State requirements for admission to the bar being very stringent—four years of classical studies and three of legal—Douglas decided to move. He was a young man in a hurry, and in June, 1833 (at twenty years of age), he moved west to seek his fortune.

He went first to Cleveland, Ohio, before finally settling further west in Illinois. Douglas taught school briefly in Winchester, Illinois, and then decided to apply for his law certificate. Requirements for admission to the bar were far easier to satisfy on the frontier than they were in the settled East, and in March, 1834, Douglas was examined by Illinois Supreme Court Justice Samuel D. Lockwood and received his license to practice. At age twenty-one, he had a vocation as a licensed attorney and could pursue his real love, which was politics. Douglas was not physically imposing, standing only five feet, four inches, with a head too large for his body, but he possessed tremendous energy. He would later receive such nicknames as the "Little Giant" and "a steam engine in britches."

Douglas' rise up the political ladder was meteoric. In 1835, he was elected state's attorney for the Morgan (Illinois) Circuit, and his political career was launched. He held a series of elective and appointive offices at the state level and was elected to the United States House of Representatives for the first time in 1843, at age thirty. He held that position until he resigned in 1847, having been elected to the United States Senate, a post he held until his death in 1861 at age forty-eight.

Life's Work

Douglas' life work was clearly political in nature. He had a vision of America as a great nation, and he wanted to use the political system to make his dream of "an ocean bound republic" a reality. He was willing to do whatever was necessary to develop and expand the United States and to preserve what was sacred to him, the Union. He expended enormous amounts of energy on his dream of developing the West by working to organize the Western territories and by urging the construction of a transcontinental railroad to bind the nation together.

Two of the highlights of Douglas' career in the Senate involved the Compromise of 1850 and the Kansas-Nebraska Act of 1854. There is a certain irony in the fact that the former was thought to have saved the Union while the latter destroyed it. Upon the acquisition of a vast amount of territory in the Mexican War, the nation was on the verge of disunion in 1849-1850 over the question of whether slavery should be allowed to expand into the area of the Mexican concession. It was Douglas, taking over from an ailing Henry Clay, who put together the package which has come to be called the Compromise of 1850. That compromise, which required months of intense political maneuvering, included such items as California's entry into the Union as a free state, the organization of New Mexico and Utah as territories without restriction on slavery, a stronger fugitive slave law, the abolition of the slave trade in the District of Columbia, and the settlement of the Texas Bond issue. That this legislation was passed is a testimony to Douglas' ability to put together what appeared to be impossible voting coalitions.

With that compromise widely acclaimed as the "final settlement" of the nation's problems, Douglas sought but failed to get the Democratic nomination for the presidency in 1852. It went instead to Franklin Pierce, who defeated General Winfield Scott in the general election and who is regarded in retrospect as one of the weakest American presidents. Pierce, fearing Douglas' unconcealed political ambitions, excluded him from the inner circle of presidential power, and that exclusion compounded the great despair into which Douglas was plunged following the death of his first wife in January, 1853. His wife was the former Martha Martin of North Carolina, and her short life ended from the complications of childbirth. In an effort to overcome his grief, Douglas left the United States for a tour of Europe in the spring of 1853, and when he returned for the opening of the Thirty-third Congress that fall, he was out of touch with political developments in this country.

In the preceding session of Congress, Douglas' Senate Committee on Territories had reported a bill to organize Nebraska Territory with no mention of slavery. By the time he returned from Europe, the political dynamics had changed, and the pressure mounted to organize two territories and to include a section dealing directly with the slavery question. Kansas-Nebraska lay wholly within the area acquired by the Louisiana Purchase in 1803, where slavery had been forbidden by the Missouri Compromise of 1820. Convinced that it was crucial to the national interest to get these territories organized as quickly as possible, and firmly believing that the slavery question was a phony issue, Douglas rewrote his organization bill. The new version called for two territories, Kansas and Nebraska, and included a sentence which stated that the 36°30' section of the Missouri Compromise was inoperative as it had been "superseded by the principles of the legislation" passed in 1850, which had made no reference to slavery. Such a statement was consistent with Douglas' long-standing belief in popular sovereignty, the idea that the people of a given territory should determine for themselves the institutions they would establish.

When the bill passed after months of the most hostile infighting in the United States Congress, and the president signed it into law in May, 1854, a storm of protest swept over the United States the likes of which had not been seen before and has not been seen since. The Kansas-Nebraska Bill split the Democratic Party and occasioned the rise of the Republican Party as the vehicle for antislavery sentiment. Douglas had misjudged the growing moral concern over slavery, and the nation was aflame; the flame would not be extinguished for more than a decade of controversy and bloody war. The situation was so critical as to make impossible an effective concentration by the government on other issues deserving of attention. The man who in 1850 and 1853 wanted to avoid the slavery issue and sought to consolidate and unify the United States became an instrument of its division.

His association with the Kansas-Nebraska Bill and his consistent failure to perceive the moral nature of the slavery question would haunt the rest of Douglas' abbreviated political career. It would frustrate his efforts to secure his party's nomination for the presidency in 1856 and would cost him dearly in the momentous election in 1860 which Abraham Lincoln won. In between, in 1858, Douglas defeated the Republican Lincoln for the United States Senate from Illinois, but that was a small victory in the overall scheme of national life.

Summary

If ever a man represented the best and the worst of his times, it was Stephen A. Douglas. He was born in 1813 as the nation moved into an intensely nationalistic period; he lived through the Jacksonian period with its turbulent trends toward democracy; he died just as his beloved Union came apart in the Civil War. Douglas was devoted to the concept of democracy, but it was a democracy limited to white adult males. Given his view (widely held at the time) that blacks were inferior beings, he saw no reason to be concerned about their civil rights—they simply had none. His political career was shaped by his love for the Union and by his desire to see the United States grow and expand, for he was truly a great nationalist. He thought in terms of the West and of the nation as a whole and did not constrict himself to a North-South view.

Douglas was, perhaps, the most talented politician of his generation, but his moral blindness, while understandable, was his tragic flaw. He alone among his contemporaries might have had the capacity and the vigor to deal with sectionalism and prevent the Civil War, but his fatal flaw kept him from the presidency. Once the war broke out, Douglas threw his support to his Republican rival Abraham Lincoln and in an attempt to rally northern Democrats to the cause of Union he said, "We must fight for our country and forget our differences."

Beset by a variety of infirmities at the age of forty-eight, Douglas hovered near death in early June, 1861. On June 3, 1861, with his beloved second wife Adele by his bed, he died. His last spoken words, passed through Adele as advice for his young sons, suggest Douglas' ultimate concern as a politician: "Tell them to obey the laws and support the Constitution of the United States."

Bibliography
Capers, Gerald M. *Stephen A. Douglas: Defender of the Union*. Boston: Little, Brown and Co., 1959. As the title suggests, this volume is generally pro-Douglas and forgives his moral blindness. It is fairly brief and is well written.
Hamilton, Holman. *Prologue to Conflict: The Crisis and Compromise of 1850*. New York: W. W. Norton and Co., 1966. A valuable work and one which was a pioneering effort in quantitative history. Hamilton uses statistics to analyze voting patterns and to clarify the way Douglas put the compromise together. The writing is excellent, as one might expect from a former newspaper man. Hamilton was the first historian to give Douglas the credit he deserved.
Johannsen, Robert W. *Stephen A. Douglas*. New York: Oxford University Press, 1973. This volume is the definitive work on Douglas. Johannsen is meticulous in his research, fair in his assessment, and thorough in his coverage.
Nichols, Roy Frank. *The Democratic Machine: 1850-1854*. New York: Columbia University Press, 1923. While Nichols' book is dated, it is still worth reading. The author probably knew more about the politics of the 1850's than any single individual.

Potter, David M. *The Impending Crisis: 1848-1861.* New York: Harper and
Row, Publishers, 1976. This major interpretation puts Douglas' political
activity in the context of his times and provides many insights into his
character.

Charles J. Bussey

FREDERICK DOUGLASS

Born: February, 1817?; Tuckahoe, Talbot County, Maryland
Died: February 20, 1895; Washington, D.C.
Areas of Achievement: Oratory, writing, and reform
Contribution: Douglass' lifelong concerns were with freedom and human rights for all people. He articulated these concerns most specifically for black Americans and women.

Early Life

Frederick Douglass was born a slave in Tuckahoe, Talbot County, Maryland, and originally was named Frederick Augustus Washington Bailey. He was of mixed African, white, and Indian ancestry, but other than that, he knew little of his family background or even his exact date of birth. Douglass believed that he was born in February, 1817, yet subsequent research indicates that he may have been born a year later in February, 1818. Douglass never knew his father or anything about him except that he was a white man, possibly his master. Douglass' mother was Harriet Bailey, the daughter of Betsey and Isaac Bailey. Frederick, his mother, and his grandparents were the property of a Captain Aaron Anthony.

In his early years, Frederick experienced many aspects of the institution of slavery. Anthony engaged in the practice of hiring out slaves, and Douglass' mother and her four sisters were among the slaves Anthony hired out to work off the plantation. Consequently, Douglass seldom saw his mother and never really knew her. The first seven years of his life were spent with his grandmother, Betsey Bailey, not because she was his grandmother but because as an elderly woman too old for field work she had been assigned the duty of caring for young children on the plantation.

The boy loved his grandmother very much, and it was extremely painful for him when, at the age of seven, he was forced by his master to move to his main residence, a twelve-mile separation from Betsey. It was there, at Anthony's main residence, that Douglass received his initiation into the realities of slavery. The years with his grandmother had been relatively care-free and filled with love. Soon, he began to witness and to experience personally the brutalities of slavery. In 1825, however, Douglass' personal situation temporarily improved when Anthony sent him to Baltimore as a companion for young Tommy Auld, a family friend. Douglass spent seven years with the Aulds as a houseboy and later as a laborer in the Baltimore shipyards. The death of Anthony caused Douglass to be transferred to the country as a field hand and to the ownership of Anthony's son-in-law. Early in 1834, his new owner hired him out to Edward Covey, a farmer who also acted as a professional slave-breaker. This began the most brutal period of Douglass' life as a slave.

After months of being whipped weekly, Douglass fought a two-hour battle with Covey that ended in a standoff, and the beatings stopped. Douglass' owner next hired him out to milder planter, but Douglass' victory over Covey had sealed his determination to be free. In 1836, Douglass and five other slaves planned an escape but were detected. Douglass was jailed and expected to be sold out of state, but the Aulds reprieved him and brought him back to Baltimore, where he first served as an apprentice and then worked as a ship caulker. However improved Douglass' situation might be in Baltimore, it was still slavery, and he was determined to be a free man. On September 3, 1838, Douglass borrowed the legal papers and a suit of clothes of a free black sailor and boarded a train for New York.

In New York, he was joined by Anna Murray, a free black woman with whom he had fallen in love in Baltimore. Douglass and Anna were married in New York on September 15, 1838, and almost immediately moved further north to New Bedford, Massachusetts, where there were fewer slave catchers hunting fugitives such as Douglass. It was also to elude slave catchers that Douglass changed his last name. He had long abandoned his middle names of Augustus Washington; he now dropped the surname Bailey and became Frederick Douglass. The move and the name change proved to be far more than symbolic; unknown to Douglass, he was about to launch on his life's work in a direction he had never anticipated.

Life's Work

New Bedford was a shipping town, and Douglass had expected to work as a ship caulker; however, race prejudice prevented his working in the shipyards and he had to earn a living doing any manual labor available: sawing wood, shoveling coal, sweeping chimneys, and so on. Anna worked as a domestic when she was not caring for their growing family. Anna bore Douglass five children: Rosetta, Lewis, Charles, Frederick, Jr., and Annie. Unexpectedly, the abolition movement of the 1830's, 1840's, and 1850's changed both Douglass' immediate situation and his whole future.

Within a few months of his escape to the North, Douglass chanced on a copy of William Lloyd Garrison's abolitionist newspaper, *The Liberator*. *The Liberator* so moved Douglass that, in spite of his poverty, he became a subscriber. Then, on August 9, 1841, less than three years after his escape, Douglass and Garrison met. This and subsequent meetings led to Garrison offering Douglass an annual salary of $450 to lecture for the abolitionist movement. Douglass was so convinced that he would not succeed as a lecturer that he accepted only a three-month appointment. In fact, he had begun his life's work.

Scholars have debated whether Douglass' greatest accomplishments were as an orator or a writer; both his speaking and his writing stemmed from his involvement with the abolition movement, and both were to be his primary activities for the remainder of his life.

From the beginning, Douglass was a powerful, effective orator. He had a deep, powerful voice which could hold his audiences transfixed. Moreover, Douglass was an impressive figure of a man. He had a handsome face, bronze skin, a leonine head, a muscular body, and was more than six feet in height. He stood with dignity and spoke eloquently and distinctly. Indeed, his bearing and speech caused critics to charge that Douglass had never been a slave; he did not conform to the stereotypic view of a slave's demeanor and address. Even Douglass' allies in the abolition movement urged him to act more as the public expected. Douglass refused; instead, he wrote his autobiography to prove his identity and thus began his career as a writer. The *Narrative of the Life of Frederick Douglass: An American Slave* (1845) remains his most famous and widely read book. It was an instant success. Yet in the narrative, Douglass had revealed his identity as Frederick Bailey, as well as the identity of his owners, making himself more vulnerable than ever to slave catchers. Anna was legally free, and because of her their children were free also, but Douglass was legally still a slave. To avoid capture, he went to England, where he remained for two years.

In England, Douglass was immensely successful as a lecturer and returned to the United States, in 1847, with enough money to purchase his freedom. By end of the year, he was legally a free man. Also in 1847, Douglass moved to Rochester, New York, and began publication of his own newspaper, *North Star*. While editing *North Star*, Douglass continued to lecture and to write. In 1855, he published an expanded autobiography, *My Bondage and My Freedom*; he also published numerous lectures, articles, and even a short story, "The Heroic Slave" in 1853. Much later in life, he published his third, and most complete, autobiography, *Life and Times of Frederick Douglass* (1881).

In all of his writings and speeches, Douglass' major concerns were civil rights and human freedom. As a person born in slavery, and as a black man living in a racially prejudiced society, Douglass' most immediate and direct concerns were to end slavery, racial prejudice, and discrimination. Yet he always insisted that there was little difference between one form of oppression and another. He proved the depth of his convictions in his championing of the women's rights movement at the same time he was immersed in his abolitionist activities. In fact, Douglass was the only man to participate actively in the Seneca Falls Convention which launched the women's rights movement in the United States in 1848. Moreover, his commitment was lasting; on the day of his death, in 1895, Douglass had returned only a few hours earlier from addressing a women's rights meeting in Washington, D.C.

By the 1850's, Douglass was active in politics. He also knew and counseled with John Brown and was sufficiently implicated in Brown's Harpers Ferry raid to leave the country temporarily after Brown's capture and arrest. From the beginning of the Civil War, Douglass urged President Abraham Lincoln not only to save the Union but also to use the war as the means to end slavery. Douglass also urged black men to volunteer and the president to accept them as soldiers in the Union armies. By the end of the Civil War, Douglass was the most prominent spokesman for black Americans in the country. With the end of the war and the advent of Reconstruction, Douglass' work seemed to have reached fruition. By 1875, with the passage of the Civil Rights Act of that year, not only had slavery been ended and the Constitution amended but also the laws of the land had guaranteed black Americans their freedom, their citizenship, and the same rights as all other citizens. Yet the victories were short-lived. The racism, both of North and of South, that had dominated the antebellum era triumphed again in the 1880's and 1890's. According to the Constitution, black Americans remained equal, but it was a paper equality. In fact, prejudice and discrimination became the order of the day across the whole United States.

For Douglass personally, the years following the Civil War contained a number of successes. He was financially solvent. He served in a number of governmental capacities: secretary of the Santo Domingo Commission, marshal and recorder of deeds in the District of Columbia, and United States minister to Haiti. For twenty-five years, he was a trustee on the board of Howard University. Nevertheless, these personal successes could not alleviate Douglass' bitter disappointment over the turn of public events, and he never ceased to fight. He continued to write, to lecture, and even began another newspaper, *New National Era.*

Summary

Frederick Douglass' career and his personal life were all the more remarkable when one considers the times in which he lived. His life was an example of the human will triumphing over adversity. Born into slavery, by law a piece of chattel, surrounded by poverty and illiteracy, he became one of America's greatest orators, an accomplished writer and editor, and for more than fifty years he was the most persistent and articulate voice in America speaking for civil rights, freedom, and human dignity regardless of race or sex. Douglass, more than any other individual, insisted that the ideals of the Declaration of Independence must be extended to all Americans.

Douglass' personal life reflected the principles for which he fought publicly. He always insisted that race should be irrelevant: Humanity was what mattered, not race, and not sex. In 1882, Anna Murray Douglass died after more than forty years of marriage to Frederick, and in 1884, Douglass married Helen Pitts, a white woman who had been his secretary. The marriage caused a storm of controversy and criticism from blacks, whites, and Douglass' own family. Yet for Douglass there was no issue: It was the irrelevance of race again. His own comment on the criticism was that he had married from his mother's people the first time and his father's, the second.

Douglass is most frequently thought of as a spokesman for black Americans and sometimes remembered as a champion of women's rights as well. Up to a point, this is accurate enough; Douglass was indeed a spokesman for black Americans and a champion of women's rights, because in his own lifetime these were among the most oppressed of America's people. Douglass' concern, however, was for all humanity, and his message, for all time.

Bibliography

Douglass, Frederick. *Frederick Douglass: The Narrative and Selected Writings*. Edited by Michael Meyer. New York: Vintage Books, 1984. In addition to being a readily accessible, complete edition of *Narrative of the Life of Frederick Douglass*, this book includes excerpts from Douglass' two later autobiographies and twenty selected writings by Douglass on various topics which are not easily obtainable.

_____. *Narrative of the Life of Frederick Douglass: An American Slave*. Boston: Anti-Slavery Office, 1845. Reprint. Garden City, N.Y.: Doubleday and Co., 1963. Originally published in 1845, the work covers Douglass' life up to that time; it was his first book and remains the most widely read of his three autobiographies.

_____. *My Bondage and My Freedom*. New York: Miller, Orton and Mulligan, 1855. Reprint. New York: Dover Publications, 1969. Originally published in 1855, this is the least read of Douglass' autobiographies.

_____. *Life and Times of Frederick Douglass*. Hartford, Conn.: Park Publishing Co., 1881. Reprint. New York: Citadel Press, 1984. First published in 1881 and reissued in 1892. The 1892 edition is the most commonly reproduced and the most complete of the three autobiographies.

Foner, Philip. *Frederick Douglass*. New York: Citadel Press, 1969. A thorough biography, unfortunately out of print, but available in libraries.

Factor, Robert L. *The Black Response to America: Men, Ideals, and Organization from Frederick Douglass to the NAACP*. Reading, Mass.: Addison-Wesley Publishing Co., 1970. Factor offers an interesting theoretical interpretation of Douglass as a black spokesman and informative comparison of Douglass with other black spokesmen and leaders.

Huggins, Nathan Irvin. *Slave and Citizen: The Life of Frederick Douglass*. Boston: Little, Brown and Co., 1980. Brief and readable, this is among the later publications on Douglass.

Meier, August. *Negro Thought in America: 1880-1915*. Ann Arbor: University of Michigan Press, 1963. Meier offers a good account of the varieties of thought among black Americans for the period covered and suggests an intriguing, plausible thesis regarding shifts of opinion in the black community. Although the era dealt with by Meier covers only the last fifteen years of Douglass' life, it is still worth reading the book for insight into Douglass and especially for any comparison or contrast of Douglass with later black spokesmen such as Booker T. Washington and W. E. B. Du Bois.

Quarles, Benjamin. *Frederick Douglass*. Washington, D.C.: Associated Publishers, 1948. Reprint. New York: Atheneum Publishers, 1976. Originally published in 1948, this an easily available, thorough biography.

D. Harland Hagler

THEODORE DREISER

Born: August 27, 1871; Terre Haute, Indiana
Died: December 28, 1945; Hollywood, California
Area of Achievement: Literature
Contribution: Combining a strong social conscience, a frankly deterministic view of life as a struggle for survival, and an honest representation of human sexuality, Dreiser's fiction helped to shape a generation of American writers and to mute the voice of censorship in American culture.

Early Life

Theodore Herman Albert Dreiser was born August 27, 1871, in Terre Haute, Indiana, the eleventh of a dozen children. His father, John Paul Dreiser, was a German Catholic immigrant who eloped with and married, in 1851, the teenage Sarah Schanab, daughter of a Moravian farm family living near Dayton, Ohio. A weaver by trade, John Paul prospered in Sullivan, Indiana, where, in 1870, the family's initial good fortune disastrously ended. A fire destroyed John Paul's woolen mill; while he was rebuilding the mill, a heavy beam fell on his head, seriously injuring him. During his convalescence, the family lost virtually everything they owned.

Nearly penniless, the Dreisers moved to Terre Haute, where Theodore was born. The father's fortunes never improving, Theodore was reared in grim poverty as the family underwent a succession of moves. His early education came in Catholic parochial schools and the public schools of Warsaw, Indiana, where his family settled in 1884. The most telling aspects of Dreiser's boyhood were the persistent financial hardship, the numerous family removals, and the ardent asceticism of his father's German Catholic orthodoxy. Consequently, Dreiser came to resent bitterly his social and economic status, to develop a sense of insecurity, and, ultimately, to reject Catholicism and later religion itself.

At age sixteen, Dreiser left home to seek his fortune in Chicago. Awkward and tall, spindly and weak, he hardly cut a dashing figure. Edgar Lee Masters, in *The Great Valley* (1916), described him in a poetic portrait:

> Jack o'Lantern tall shouldered,
> One eye set higher than the other,
> Mouth cut like a scallop in a pie,
> Aslant showing powerful teeth.
> Swaying above the heads of others.
> And the eyes burn like a flame at the end of a funnel.
> And the ruddy face glows like a pumpkin
> On Halloween!

This unlikely caricature of a man had little success in Chicago at first, but he eventually landed a steady job in a warehouse. There he became an avid reader through the efforts of an older friend and former teacher. Encouraged to make something of himself, he attended Indiana University for a year but returned in 1890 to Chicago and various menial jobs. His imagination had been fired, however, his tireless reading continued, and he burned to improve his lot.

Life's Work

Hoping to become a writer, Dreiser began the application rounds at Chicago newspapers. In 1892, he obtained a position as a reporter with the *Chicago Globe*. Shortly thereafter, Dreiser accepted a job at the St. Louis *Globe-Democrat*, left Chicago, and began the journalistic career which he followed from city to city for nearly a decade. His experiences in such cities as St. Louis, Toledo, Cleveland, and Pittsburgh helped form his maturing social views. Reporting on the activities of impoverished strikers who battled against the economic and social inequities preserved by such robber barons as John D. Rockefeller, Andrew Carnegie, and Jay Gould, Dreiser was assembling the raw material from which would spring his novels, with their bleak realism, their pessimistic determinism, and his own rejection of capitalism and subsequent conversion to Communism.

The 1890's were pivotal years for Dreiser. Not only did he become a successful journalist and free himself from material need, but he also took a wife and embarked on his fiction-writing career. In 1893, he met and began to court Sarah (Sallie) Osborne White, whom he married on December 28, 1898. The marriage proved disastrous, and Dreiser and his wife were separated in 1909. (In 1919, Dreiser met and became intimate with Helen Richardson, a distant cousin, though the couple were unable to marry until 1944 because Sarah, to her death in 1942, refused to grant a divorce.) Also in the 1890's, Dreiser began to write commercial short stories and articles with some success, and, in 1899, he began his first novel, *Sister Carrie*, completed in 1900 and accepted by Doubleday, Page and Company.

Sister Carrie introduced the major themes and social attitudes that characterize Dreiser's powerful fiction. A study of Carrie Meeber, a small-town innocent who comes to Chicago and falls into temptation, *Sister Carrie* clearly draws upon Dreiser's memories of the similar fate of two older sisters. Weary of her shoe-factory job (depicted in the muckraker style of the 1890's, with lascivious bosses and inhuman working conditions), Carrie slips into a romantic liaison and becomes a kept woman. Eventually, after playing mistress to several others, she achieves great success as an actress. In contrast to the authors of typical "fallen woman" stories of his era, Dreiser refused to punish Carrie. Instead, he presents no clear villains or heroes and offers no moral judgments. Through a combination of fate, character weaknesses, and a corrupt capitalistic society, Carrie and her principal lover lead heartbreaking lives.

Sister Carrie also marked the start of Dreiser's lifelong battle with censorship. Recommended by the well-known naturalistic author Frank Norris, *Sister Carrie* was contracted for publication by Frank Doubleday, though he had not read the manuscript. Later (supposedly because Mrs. Doubleday read the proofs and expressed stunned horror), Doubleday tried to avoid publication. Stubbornly insisting on the contractual terms, Dreiser forced publication, but Doubleday printed only a minimum run, sent no review copies, and made no advertising effort. Selling fewer than five hundred copies, the novel passed almost unnoticed. In 1907, a second edition, brought out by B. W. Dodge, met with considerable success, but the pattern had been established, and Dreiser would fight a running battle against censorship for the remainder of his career.

Despondent over *Sister Carrie*'s failure to achieve either critical or financial success and plunged back into personal economic chaos, Dreiser apparently suffered a mental breakdown and became suicidal. After a sanatorium confinement, he regained his balance and his passionate drive for success. Accepting an editorial position at Street and Smith, publisher of cheap magazines and dime novels, Dreiser's business fortunes rapidly improved until, in 1907, after several job changes, he assumed a significant editorial post at an excellent salary with Butterick Publishing Company. His personal drive, meticulous attention to detail, imaginative leadership, and friendly relations with his talented staff resulted in Dreiser's great success at Butterick, with which he remained until 1910, when he left to pursue his creative writing.

With the publication of *Jennie Gerhardt* (1911), Dreiser began a burst of creative energy that lasted fifteen years and witnessed the bulk of his finest literary achievement. Like *Sister Carrie*, *Jennie Gerhardt* traces the fortunes of a kept woman. Nobler than Carrie, Jennie is a lower-class working girl who leaves her wealthy lover when she realizes that she is an impediment to his career. The novel details the social barriers between the classes, belying the American notion of a classless society. Also like *Sister Carrie*, though it was not suppressed, *Jennie Gerhardt* won the attention of a Puritanical readership that regarded its depiction of illicit love and illegitimate birth as a menace to the moral standards of the country.

Next came *The Financier* (1912), the first book in Dreiser's "trilogy of desire," a series tracing the activities of Frank Cowperwood, a businessman and financier based on street-railway magnate Charles Tyson Yerkes. The second novel of the trilogy, *The Titan* (1914), focuses on Cowperwood's ruthless stock manipulations and sexual appetite. After printing and promoting the novel, Harper and Row refused to publish it, but with his recent successes, Dreiser was able to find another publisher. *The Stoic* (1947) was the final book of the trilogy which, though begun much earlier, was published posthumously.

The "Genius" (1915) again brought Dreiser into conflict with censorship.

The story of Eugene Witla, a sensitive dreamer and a gifted realistic artist who disregarded social conventions in pursuit of his painting and sexual variety, the novel is based on Dreiser's own career, a kind of self-portrait of the artist. Though the novel's central concern is Dreiser's favorite thematic motifs, the individual pitted against society's conventions and the notion of life as a struggle for survival, reviewers and the Puritanical element of the reading public instead focused their attention on the frank details of marital discord and sexuality. Condemned for its so-called obscenity and blasphemy by both the Western (Cleveland) and the New York societies for prevention of vice and threatened with lawsuits, in 1916 the novel was withdrawn by publisher John Lane. After protracted litigation, Dreiser gave up the battle, and The *"Genius"* remained out of print until 1923.

Dreiser's next novel, and perhaps his finest, was *An American Tragedy* (1925). It follows the grim life of the hapless Clyde Griffiths, who rises from his slum birth to achieve material success and the prospect of a fortunate marriage into a wealthy, upper-class family. Yet a pregnant mistress stands in his way. Determined to murder her, he botches the preparation, loses his nerve at the critical moment, but then is ironically tried, convicted, and electrocuted for her murder when she accidentally drowns. The novel combines all the central concerns of Dreiser's art. It is a Socialist indictment of the American capitalist economic system. It is a naturalistic depiction of man struggling feebly against the massive victimizing forces of environment, heredity, and fate. It also relies upon Dreiser's mechanistic theory of life, in which chemical forces compel man to act in prescribed ways. Dreiser based much of *An American Tragedy* on the court records of an actual trial of Chester Gillette, who, in 1906, murdered his pregnant girlfriend when their relationship threatened his economic and social prospects. The novel, in a unique blend of fact and fiction, uses substantial sections of the trial transcript, sometimes verbatim. Though banned in Boston for corrupting the morals of youth, *An American Tragedy* was clearly the most publicly successful of Dreiser's novels, gaining for him a wide reading audience and later being made into a film.

Dreiser's reputation as a major author firmly established, he wrote only one more novel, *The Bulwark* (1946), published posthumously. Yet though his finest achievements lay in novel writing, Dreiser produced work in various genres. Most notable are several short-story collections, *Free and Other Stories* (1918), *Twelve Men* (1919), *Chains* (1927), and *A Gallery of Women* (1929); a number of plays, *Plays of the Natural and Supernatural* (1916), *The Hand of the Potter* (1918); essays collected in *Hey Rub-a-Dub Dub!* (1920); the autobiographical *A Book About Myself* (1922) and *Dawn* (1931); and the poetry of *Moods: Cadenced and Declaimed* (1926).

After his success with *An American Tragedy*, Dreiser traveled to the Soviet Union, the trip resulting in a political book, *Dreiser Looks at Russia* (1928), and in a swing toward Communism. A witness to Depression-bred social despair and misery, he began to turn most of his public attention to aiding the economically and socially disadvantaged. In 1931, he even accepted the chairmanship of the National Committee for the Defense of Political Prisoners, and, for the next ten years, he championed the underdog at every opportunity.

In 1944, Dreiser was honored by the American Academy of Arts and Letters when he became the recipient of that organization's Award of Merit for his fiction. He also married Helen Richardson on June 13. On July 20, 1945, Dreiser applied and was accepted for membership in the Communist Party. Only months later, on December 28, at his home in Hollywood, California, Dreiser died of a heart attack. On February 1, 1946, Dreiser's will was filed for probate. In a final gesture, in keeping with his social activities and deep sensitivity toward the disadvantaged, Dreiser left his estate to his wife Helen, requesting that upon her death she bequeath the bulk of the estate to a black orphanage.

Summary

Since his death, Dreiser's reputation has steadily ascended, reaching a significant and secure place in the twentieth century American scene. Perhaps it is the raw power that springs from the pages of his novels in unsparing honesty and realism that has earned greatness for him and has most influenced American culture.

The principal theme in Dreiser's work is the conflict between the individual and society, a theme which is not unique. Yet Dreiser's focus was an especially modern application of the theme to the largely urban, industrialized America that had sprung up after the Civil War to replace the former agrarian society. He was the first American novelist to depict powerfully and with startling directness the modern world of business and capitalism, the first to depict the appalling depersonalization of the individual caught in the pressure to conform in an urban society. In uncompromising detail and frankness, he revealed an America in which the measure of a person's success was the pursuit and acquisition of material possessions and status. Inevitably confronting the powerful, unyielding forces of a class-structured society, his characters and their bleak fates gave the lie once and for all to the American myth of a classless society. As Alfred Kazin tellingly observes of the attempted suppression of and shocked critical reaction to *Sister Carrie*'s publication, the novel "did not have a bad press; it had a frightened press, with many of the reviewers plainly impressed, but startled by the concentrated truthfulness of the book."

Dreiser was also significant as a major influence on the American naturalist school of writers. Shaped largely by scientific evolutionary theorists such as Herbert Spencer, Aldous Huxley, and Charles Darwin, Dreiser's philosophy of life was developed in the novels as a mechanistic and deterministic struggle for survival. Relentlessly, he depicted the pathos of human behavior directed by the twin compulsions of biological and environmental forces which he labeled "chemisms." Among the writers strongly influenced by Dreiser were Sinclair Lewis, James T. Farrell, and John Steinbeck.

Finally, in insisting upon the author's duty to treat sex as a major force in human lives and in refusing to cave in to the repressive forces in American society, Dreiser led the struggle to shatter the influence of the narrow, mean-minded minority who were the self-appointed arbiters of American moral standards. In 1900, *Sister Carrie* was effectively suppressed; in 1925 *An American Tragedy*, though similarly attacked, not only was published but also gained numerous critical proponents and a wide reading public. More than any other writer, Dreiser was responsible for the changed attitudes in the United States which arose during the twenty-five years between these two novels. Undoubtedly, his long and often bitter struggles against prurient, Puritanical, would-be censors helped to smooth the way for the even more frank and similarly honest treatment of sex in the next generation of writers.

Bibliography
Elias, Robert H. *Theodore Dreiser: Apostle of Nature*. New York: Alfred A. Knopf, 1948. Rev. ed. Ithaca, N.Y.: Cornell University Press, 1970. A critical biography that follows the events in Dreiser's life that most directly influenced his literary production. Emphasizes Dreiser's social concerns and sympathy for the individual. Contains an excellent annotated survey of research and criticism.
Gerber, Philip L. *Theodore Dreiser*. Boston: Twayne Publishers, 1964. An objective critical biography that relates Dreiser's life experiences to his literary achievements. First major biographer to have access to Dreiser's published letters.
Kazin, Alfred, and Charles Shapiro, eds. *The Stature of Theodore Dreiser*. Bloomington: Indiana University Press, 1955. This collection gathers a wide, representative selection of significant essays on Dreiser, ranging from personal reminiscences to critical evaluations.
Lehan, Richard. *Theodore Dreiser: His World and His Novels*. Carbondale: Southern Illinois University Press, 1969. Systematically discusses the elements of Dreiser's life that helped to influence the genesis, evolution, pattern, and meaning of his novels.
Lydenberg, John, comp. *Dreiser: A Collection of Critical Essays*. Englewood Cliffs, N.J.: Prentice-Hall, 1971. This collection gathers fifteen critical essays, ranging from early to modern appraisals. A balanced sampling of reactions to Dreiser's art.
Matthiessen, F. O. *Theodore Dreiser*. New York: William Sloane Associates, 1951. Principally a book of detailed literary criticism. Thoughtful and

perceptive analysis of Dreiser's artistic virtues.

Pizer, Donald, Richard W. Powell, and Frederic E. Rusch. *Theodore Dreiser: A Primary and Secondary Bibliography*. Boston: G. K. Hall and Co., 1975. The most comprehensive bibliography on Dreiser, this book provides a quick, accurate guide to a sweeping list of writings by and about Dreiser.

Shapiro, Charles. *Theodore Dreiser: Our Bitter Patriot*. Carbondale: Southern Illinois University Press, 1962. A careful critical analysis of the novels, based on their varying thematic concerns.

Swanberg, W. A. *Dreiser*. New York: Charles Scribner's Sons, 1965. A pure biography, this book does not attempt literary criticism but brings together more materials and sources than any other. The most comprehensive biography.

Peter P. Remaley

W. E. B. DU BOIS

Born: February 23, 1868; Great Barrington, Massachusetts
Died: August 27, 1963; Accra, Ghana
Areas of Achievement: Civil rights and journalism
Contribution: One of the principal founders of the National Association for the Advancement of Colored People and editor of several influential journals, Du Bois was for many years the leading black intellectual in the United States. Through his teaching, writings, and speeches he advocated economic, political, and cultural advancement of blacks not only in the United States but also abroad.

Early Life
William Edward Burghardt Du Bois (pronounced "du boyce") was born of mixed African, French Huguenot, and Dutch descent in Great Barrington, Massachusetts, on February 23, 1868. His father, Alfred Du Bois, was the son of Alexander Du Bois, a light-skinned man born of a union between a mulatto slave girl in Santo Domingo and a wealthy American of French Huguenot descent. He lost his father early and was reared by his mother, Mary Burghardt, whose family traced its roots to a freed slave in the days of the American Revolution. The Burghardts were proud of their long, stable residence in Massachusetts as free farmers, but because they were black they remained outside the social elite.

Du Bois grew up as part of a small black community of about fifty people among some five thousand whites in Great Barrington. Though his childhood was basically happy, he learned early that blacks were not fully accepted as equal, even in New England. Determined to be a leader of his people, Du Bois studied hard and dreamed of getting a degree from Harvard. Books and writing interested young Du Bois more than athletics, although he did enjoy games and socializing with his friends. When he was graduated from high school in 1884 at the age of sixteen, he was the only black in his class of twelve and was already urging blacks to take advantage of their opportunities to advance through education and other forms of self-help.

The death of his mother shortly after his graduation, lack of funds, and his young age forced deferment of his plans to attend Harvard. After working several months and receiving scholarship aid from some interested churches, however, he was able to enter Fisk University in Nashville, Tennessee, in the fall of 1885. Because of his superior academic background, he was admitted at the sophomore level. Fisk was a radically different world from that of Great Barrington, and, significantly, it provided him with the long-sought opportunity to relate to blacks his own age. Now living among the two hundred blacks at Fisk, he felt a stronger sense of identification with his people and continued his instinctive efforts to make his fellow blacks more conscious of what they could accomplish. He also learned more about the deep-rooted racial discrimination of the South after Reconstruction. Summers were spent teaching in small western Tennessee schools, adding to the profound influence of his Fisk years.

Du Bois was graduated from Fisk in 1888 and at last was able to attend Harvard. With financial aid he matriculated that fall at the junior level. In 1890, he earned a second baccalaureate degree, and the next year a master's degree. From 1892 to 1894, he interrupted his Harvard doctoral program to take advantage of a fellowship to study at the University of Berlin. There he came into contact with some of Europe's most prominent scholars, such as sociologist Max Weber, Heinrich von Treitschke, and Rudolf von Gneist. Like George Santayana and the famous psychologist-philosopher William James at Harvard, these seminal thinkers left a deep mark on his formative mind. Again, he used his summers to good advantage by traveling on the Continent. This European experience did not lessen his commitment to uplifting his race, but it did, he recalled, help him emerge "from the extremes of my racial provincialism . . . and to become more human."

Du Bois returned to Harvard in 1894 and completed his dissertation, *The Suppression of the African Slave Trade to the United States* (1896). That it was accepted for publication by Harvard proved to be the beginning of a career in writing and scholarship. When he was graduated in 1895—the first black to earn a Ph.D. at Harvard—he was ready to enter the academic world and become part of what he called the Talented Tenth—the intellectual elite which, he believed, was the key to the advancement of blacks. He was chosen to speak at the commencement ceremonies and was recognized for his oratorical abilities.

Life's Work

Du Bois' first appointment was at Wilberforce College in Ohio as an instructor in classics, a field in which he had excelled both at Fisk and at Harvard. He was not happy there, however, and in 1896 took a position at the University of Pennsylvania in Philadelphia, where his primary responsibility was to undertake a study of black society in the city's Seventh Ward slums. His experience in Philadelphia was another disappointment. His apartment in the slum area brought him close to the worst effects of poverty, and he felt slighted by the university leadership. On the positive side, his year there produced his second major work and the first serious sociological study of American black social life, *The Philadelphia Negro: A Social Study*, which was published in 1899 after he moved to Atlanta.

From 1897 to 1910, Du Bois headed the economics and history program at Atlanta University, and for the first time settled into a rewarding job. During that crucial period when black Americans were going through many important changes, Du Bois developed his ideas in *Atlanta University Studies* and wrote for prominent journals such as the *Atlantic Monthly*. In 1903, he compiled his thoughts in his best-known work, *The Souls of Black Folk*. By then he was openly challenging the ideas of his fellow black, Booker T. Washington, head of the Tuskegee Institute in Alabama. Washington had rapidly risen to prominence after his Atlanta Exposition Address of 1895, in which he urged blacks to acquire industrial education, property, and good personal habits rather than push immediately for political rights or social equality.

The Washingtonian approach has been called accommodationism, while Du Bois' strategy emphasized immediate acquisition of rights such as voting, education, and access to public facilities. Known as a "radical" at that time, in contrast to the more conservative Tuskegee mentality, Du Bois became an intense rival of Washington, who nevertheless remained the most influential black spokesman until his death in 1915. In 1905, Du Bois led a group of like-minded people in the formation of an organization to counter the Tuskegee approach. Meeting on the Canadian side of Niagara Falls in July, they established the Niagara Movement, a short-lived group that never attracted much popular support. Its program was in some ways the opposite of Washington's. It emphasized integration of education, voting rights for black men, and more rapid development of blacks' economic resources. Washington had urged blacks: "Cast down your bucket where you are." Du Bois and the Niagara Movement insisted that they must actively protest against inequality and seize every opportunity to move into the mainstream of American life.

The Niagara Movement failed by 1909, but that same year Du Bois worked with Mary White Ovington and other interested whites in formally establishing the National Association for the Advancement of Colored People (NAACP). It grew out of an interracial meeting triggered by the violent racial disturbances in Springfield, Illinois, in 1908. Du Bois left Atlanta University in 1910 to become director of publicity and research for the NAACP. He also established a new journal, *The Crisis*, which became a semiofficial organ of the NAACP and afforded Du Bois larger opportunities than the Niagara Movement's journal, *The Horizon*, to promulgate his ideas on the Talented Tenth, racial solidarity of blacks, and many other issues. *The Crisis* became essentially self-supporting, and Du Bois often argued with other NAACP leaders about its content. Regarding it essentially as his, he felt that *The Crisis* was actually the spearhead of the movement rather than of the parent NAACP organization.

Du Bois' career after 1910 went through many changes that reflected the varying conditions of race relations in the United States. He retained his editorial position until his break with the NAACP in 1934, but he frequently departed from official NAACP positions. Increasingly he advocated black separatism in the economic sphere, a modified version of Marxist socialism, and Pan-Africanism. Du Bois organized the first important Pan-African congress in Paris in 1919 and became a major rival of Marcus Garvey, the famous Jamaican who led the "back to Africa" movement between the world wars. Until the end of his life, Du Bois advocated various versions of Pan-Africanism and became known in Africa for both this and his many involvements in peace organization. A light-skinned, distinguished looking man with a mustache and goatee, he contrasted physically with most Africans but, nevertheless, identified with them. By the time his book *Black Reconstruction* (1935) was published, he was openly supporting socialism and racial separatism.

A third stage of his career began in 1934 as he returned to teaching at Atlanta University. From then until 1944, he resumed his academic work and added to his growing list of publications: *Black Folk: Then and Now* (1939); his autobiographical *Dusk of Dawn: An Essay Toward an Autobiography of a Race Concept* (1940); after returning to an NAACP job in 1944, *Color and Democracy: Colonies and Peace* (1945); and *The World and Africa* (1947).

After World War II, Du Bois continued to change as the history of blacks in the United States and the world evolved. The persistence of colonial rule after the war disturbed him, and he frankly criticized the great powers for not totally freeing their dependencies. While he continued to see the Soviet Union as a model in some respects, he did not refrain from criticizing that country's domination of Eastern Europe and other areas. His displeasure with American foreign policy further alienated him from his own country, and in 1951 he was charged with failing to register as an agent for a foreign power because of his pivotal position in the Peace Information Center. Although he was acquitted, he never felt at home in the United States after that. He was invited by Kwame Nkrumah to the 1957 ceremonies marking the end of British colonial rule in Ghana, but was not allowed to go— although Vice President Richard Nixon and black leader Martin Luther King, Jr., were present. Eventually, in 1961, he joined the Communist Party and left his native land for Ghana. Du Bois became a citizen of Ghana and died there, at age ninety-five, in 1963.

Summary

The life of W. E. B. Du Bois was a mirror of the growing independence of black thought. On the surface he embodied many contradictions: capitalism and socialism, separatism and integration, militancy and accommodationism. Yet the common thread of his evolving thought was his awareness of the racial question and the necessity to resolve it. "The problem of the Twentieth Century," he wrote in *Souls of Black Folk*, "is the problem of the color-line." To him, it would yield only to determination and information. His commitment to scientific sociological research was so profound that some have said that he relied too much upon it.

Du Bois, however, was not merely a social scientist. He took pride in his blackness even as he recognized its complexity. He sensed in himself and all black Americans a dual identity.

> One ever feels his two-ness,—an American, a Negro; two souls, two thoughts, two unreconciled strivings; two warring ideals in one dark body, whose dogged strength alone keeps it from being torn asunder.
>   The history of the American Negro is the history of this strife,—this longing to attain self-conscious manhood, to merge his double self into a better and truer self.

Thus, science and poetry flowed together in Du Bois' mind as he wrestled with the universal problem of racism and ways to deal with it.

Du Bois anticipated several salient themes of modern black history, including the emphasis upon development of capital resources by blacks and cultural identification with Africa. Although he left the United States, he was widely respected among mainstream black reformers for his literary and personal contributions to black liberation. Ironically, his death occurred on August 27, 1963, as more than 200,000 people were assembling to march on Washington. They paused to honor Du Bois, and on the next day NAACP head Roy Wilkins paid tribute to him at the Lincoln Memorial, where Martin Luther King, Jr., delivered his historic "I Have a Dream" speech.

Bibliography
Broderick, Francis L. *W. E. B. Du Bois: Negro Leader in a Time of Crisis*. Stanford, Calif.: Stanford University Press, 1959. An older work still valuable for understanding the evolving views of Du Bois. It contains much biographical information and is especially incisive in capturing the troubled spirit of Du Bois through his many difficult transitions. The seemingly surprising changes such as his break with the NAACP in 1934 are seen as flowing naturally from certain racist tendencies he had from his youth. Credits Du Bois with two major accomplishments: emphasis upon equal rights for blacks and his service to black Americans' morale.
Du Bois, W. E. B. *The Autobiography of W. E. Burghardt Du Bois: A Soliloquy on Viewing My Life from the Last Decade of Its First Century*. New York: International Publishing Co., 1968. One of two major autobiographies by Du Bois. Along with his *Dusk of Dawn*, provides a useful overview of his life, especially his periodic challenges to other points of view about racial advancement.
_____. *Color and Democracy: Colonies and Peace*. New York: Harcourt Brace and Co., 1945. A short work that reveals the beginnings of Du Bois' postwar perspective. There is an urgency in his insistence that the United States and Europe can no longer determine the destiny of all peoples. Du Bois argues that genuine democracy calls for education and economic advancement of the developing nations. Democracy can work, he

insists, although many fear a world of free, peaceful people governed on a
basis of equality.

_____. *The Philadelphia Negro: A Social Study*. New York: Schocken
Books, 1967. A new edition of the Du Bois classic, with a useful introduction by E. Digby Baltzell. Established Du Bois as a serious social analyst of racial problems. Historically based and well-documented, remains a
valuable examination of what was the oldest and largest northern black
community.

_____. *The Souls of Black Folk: Essays and Sketches*. Chicago: A. C.
McClurg, 1928, originally published in 1903. Du Bois' best-known work,
partly autobiographical. Gives insight into his views of the dual nature and
citizenship of the black American. The economic, social, and psychological conditions of blacks are explored by an insider torn by his own
conflicting drives. Each section is preceded by "sorrow songs" showing the
painful struggle of blacks for dignity and self-esteem despite the burdens of
slavery and lingering discrimination.

Rampersad, Arnold. *The Art and Imagination of W. E. B. Du Bois*. Cambridge, Mass.: Harvard University Press, 1976. One of the few good treatments of Du Bois' creative genius. Essentially a biography, this work traces
Du Bois' life from his New England beginnings to his last years in Ghana.
Not so much concerned with controversies and rivalries as with his literary
accomplishments, especially his fiction. Du Bois comes through as a concerned man, not a self-styled propagandist.

Ross, Barbara Joyce. *J. E. Spingarn and the Rise of the NAACP, 1911-1939*.
New York: Atheneum Publishers, 1972. A valuable tool for seeing Du Bois
in perspective in the formative stages of the NAACP. Shows relationship
with Spingarn and the administrative structure of the organization. Clari-
fies many of the disputes between Du Bois and the NAACP.

Rudwick, Elliott M. *W. E. B. Du Bois: Voice of the Black Protest Movement*.
Champaign: University of Illinois Press, 1982. Previously published as
W. E. B. Du Bois: A Study in Minority Group Leadership. Philadelphia:
University of Pennsylvania Press, 1960. A well-documented study; covers
the full sweep of Du Bois' career from his youth to his later involvements
in Pan-Africanism and peace promotion. Presents Du Bois as both a realist
and an idealist, a skilled propagandist, and a devoted believer in equality.
Rudwick suggests that although Du Bois erred in predicting socialism as
the answer to the needs of black Americans, he accurately forecast the
strong African orientation of contemporary black culture.

Tuttle, William M., ed. *W. E. B. Du Bois*. Englewood Cliffs, N.J.: Prentice-
Hall, 1973. The first section offers a good selection of Du Bois' writings
and his basic ideas such as the Talented Tenth, Pan-Africanism, and socialism. The second part includes articles by A. Philip Randolph, Kelly Miller,
Marcus Garvey, E. Franklin Frazier, and others reacting to Du Bois' ideas

and impact. The final section comprises essays by August Meier, Truman Nelson, and other scholars. An outstanding work for viewing Du Bois in his historical context.

Thomas R. Peake

JAMES BUCHANAN DUKE

Born: December 23, 1856; Durham, North Carolina
Died: October 10, 1925; New York, New York
Area of Achievement: Business
Contribution: From modest beginnings, Duke organized and built up the largest conglomerate of tobacco companies in the nation, comprising the American Tobacco Company and its subsidiaries; he also founded power and textile companies and established the Duke Endowment in support of Duke University as well as other educational and charitable institutions.

Early Life

James Buchanan Duke was born on December 23, 1856, in a six-room farmhouse near Durham, North Carolina. He was the youngest in the family: There were two half brothers from his father's first marriage, and a brother and a sister had also preceded James. In 1858, his mother, Artelia Roney Duke, died from typhoid fever, which also claimed his older half brother. His father, Washington Duke, owned about three hundred acres of land, on which he grew corn, wheat, oats, and some tobacco. During the Civil War, he served for two years with the Confederate artillery; in 1865, Union soldiers looted his farm and left behind little but leaf tobacco. Immediately thereafter, however, demand for tobacco mounted, and prices rose; between 1866 and 1872, the Duke family's production increased from 15,000 to 125,000 pounds. James took part in the planting and preparation of their crop. His early education took place in local schools. Evidently he learned quickly, but preferred mathematics to the humanities. In 1872, he enrolled in the New Garden Academy, near Greensboro, North Carolina; quite abruptly, he gave up his courses there and left for the Eastman Business College in Poughkeepsie, New York, where he studied bookkeeping and accounting.

By 1874, Washington Duke felt sufficiently confident in the industry's future that he sold his farm and bought a tobacco factory in downtown Durham. Although he originally intended to go into business on his own, James Duke accepted with alacrity his father's offer that made him, and his brother Benjamin Duke, one-third partners in the new concern. Leaving correspondence and other official functions to the others, James Buchanan Duke kept their financial records and devised numerous means by which to economize on the operations of their tobacco firm.

Somewhat daunting in bearing if not precisely handsome, as he entered manhood Duke gave an impression of strength and energy. He was six feet, two inches tall and powerfully built; his features were distinguished by a broad brow, a straight, thick nose, and piercing blue eyes. His lank red hair, parted at the side, showed a tendency to thinness in his later photographs. He spoke in a gentle drawl; often among others he would remain silent for protracted periods, and then hold forth at some length on matters of concern to him.

Life's Work

Although the Dukes seemed overwhelmed by their competitors, notably the massive Durham Bull Company in their native city, they began to advertise on local billboards. They also began to promote cigarettes, which hitherto had not sold well but were peculiarly suited to the bright tobacco leaf that was grown in abundance across parts of North Carolina and Virginia. They launched promotional campaigns in many states; they obtained permission from a touring French actress to use her picture in the company's cigarette advertisements. The Dukes also readily adopted another innovation: In 1884, they had the newly invented Bonsack cigarette-rolling machine installed in their plant. While it was sometimes inclined to clog during use, this device could produce more than two hundred cigarettes a minute, or about fifty times as many as an expert artisan working by hand.

Sensing that a national market might exist for the company's cigarettes, in 1884 Duke moved to a small apartment in New York City and opened an office there. After two years, this branch was also turning a profit, in part because of Duke's meticulous familiarity with all aspects of the tobacco trade, and in part as a result of his flamboyant innovations in advertising. The company offered complimentary cigarette packs to immigrants coming into New York harbor; it sponsored sporting events; it issued coupons, enclosed in its cigarette cartons, which could be redeemed for cash. Billboards, posters, and advertisements in newspapers and magazines promoted the various brands the company offered. By 1889, of some 2.1 billion cigarettes produced in the United States, about 940 million had come from the factories of W. Duke and Sons. Its sales were well over $4 million, of which $400,000 was profit.

After prolonged and tortuous negotiations, Duke persuaded the presidents of four other leading tobacco concerns to form the American Tobacco Company; to win over his erstwhile rivals, Duke obtained a contract with the Bonsack company restricting sales of their rolling machines to the new trust. As president, Duke expanded upon his promotional methods: New coupon schemes were devised, and pictures of attractive women in tights were issued in packs of some of the company's brands. Moreover, the trust's vast resources allowed it to absorb smaller concerns, many of which were bought up outright or controlled through subsidiaries or holding companies. Duke also turned on the few powerful corporations that had remained independent. The Durham Bull Company was taken over, and the trust acquired a controlling interest in the Liggett and Myers Company and the R. J. Reynolds Company. By 1900, the American Tobacco Company accounted for 92.7 percent of American cigarette production and 59.2 percent of the nation's output of pipe tobacco. By 1901, James B. Duke added the American Cigar Company to this business empire, and became its president; with this stroke, one-sixth of the country's cigar trade came under his control.

With annual sales of about $125 million, the American Tobacco Company was in a position to determine prices and wages as it saw fit. During the Spanish-American War of 1898, Congress had imposed a surtax on tobacco, and repealed it three years later; Duke's trust held their cigarette prices at the previous levels and kept the balance as profits. Competitive bidding for tobacco was curtailed; prices to farmers were held as low as three cents per pound, spawning organized violent outbreaks by "night riders" operating in Kentucky and Tennessee. Foreign markets were also exploited. The trust acquired subsidiaries in Australia and New Zealand; in 1895, it obtained several Canadian firms. In 1901, a two-thirds interest was obtained in one of the leading German cigarette dealers. It also opened offices in Japan and built factories in China to accommodate the demand for its products. Seeking to reduce competition in international markets, in 1902 the American Tobacco Company reached agreement with representatives of the Imperial Tobacco Company, which delimited the areas where each company could do business. The British-American Tobacco Company was formed, with assets of about thirty million dollars and an established network in the British Empire; Duke became its president.

In the course of his work, Duke had occasionally seen Mrs. Lillian McCredy, a divorced woman with a dubious reputation. In 1904, after some years of intermittent and rather surreptitious courtship, they were married in 1904 in a small private ceremony. It was a troubled and tempestuous union; after ten months, Duke claimed that his wife had been unfaithful and sued for divorce. In a sensational trial, he offered the evidence of company detectives and intercepted messages from his wife's paramour. In 1906, the court found in Duke's favor. He was later introduced to Mrs. Nanaline Holt Inman, the widow of a cotton merchant from Atlanta. Duke was captivated by her expressive, classical features. She responded to his attentions, and in 1907 they were married in a small church in Brooklyn. Their daughter and only child, Doris, was born in 1912; during his later years, Duke displayed a pronounced fondness for her.

Shortly before his second marriage, Duke was confronted with the most serious challenge of his business career. The American Tobacco Company, which was estimated to control eighty percent of all tobacco production in the United States, was brought to court in antitrust litigation by the Department of Justice. In 1908, Duke himself was required to testify. A federal court found that the American Tobacco Company had indeed operated in restraint of trade. The Supreme Court upheld this ruling, and in 1911 the defendants were ordered to dissolve the trust. Accordingly, snuff and cigar companies were cut loose. R. J. Reynolds and Liggett and Myers were severed from the American Tobacco Company, which after reorganization held perhaps two-fifths of its previous assets.

Already Duke had diversified his business interests, and after the antitrust suits he turned with redoubled attention to concerns in his native region. In 1905 he had provided support for hydroelectric works along the Catawba River, which flows through the western portions of North and South Carolina. Between 1907 and 1925, eleven plants were built for the Southern Power Company, which in 1924 was rechristened the Duke Power Company. In short order, Duke also came to own textile mills that used the electricity his plants supplied. Against the advice of others in the business, Duke also underwrote the construction of a hydroelectric complex along the Saguenay River in Upper Quebec, and in time this venture became profitable.

Over the years, the Duke family contributed in increasing amounts to Trinity College, a small Methodist institution in North Carolina; in 1892 a subvention from Washington Duke supported work on a campus in Durham. James Buchanan Duke, though possessing only a limited formal education, increasingly had come to believe that institutions of higher learning held out the best hopes for widespread social progress. In 1918, he became one of Trinity's trustees. In collaboration with the college's president, William P. Few, plans were devised for a series of gothic buildings, including a magnificent chapel and tower. Duke personally supervised the selection of the local stone that was used; he took great interest in plans for a new medical center. In all, Duke contributed nineteen million dollars to the college, of which eight million dollars were offered when Few agreed to change its name to Duke University. (There is no substance to stories that previously Duke had made similar, unsuccessful, offers to Princeton, Yale, or other universities.) During the year before he died, Duke composed a will establishing the Duke endowment, which in all comprised about eighty million dollars in securities and at that time was the largest permanent foundation of its sort in the nation. In addition to providing continuing support for Duke University, it also left substantial sums for other colleges, hospitals, orphanages, and Methodist churches in North Carolina. Much of the remainder of his estate was left to Duke's wife Nanaline and their daughter Doris. Duke himself suffered from pernicious anemia; after his health declined for several months he died, rather suddenly, on October 10, 1925, at his home in New York. Ultimately, he was buried in the chapel of the university to which he had given his name.

Summary

Duke was an accomplished businessman; it was said that for years he would work twelve hours a day in his office, and then visit tobacco stores to learn more about the retail trade. He was able to capitalize upon three major developments: He realized early the potential popularity of cigarettes; he utilized advertising nearly to the limit of its effectiveness; in an age in which manifold business combinations became possible, he proved to be a shrewd, hard-bitten bargainer able to form and direct massive industrial organizations to his own advantage. Even when antitrust proceedings compelled its reorganization, Duke was able to retain control of more parts of his original company than his opponents had thought possible. His persistent exploitation of the opportunities that existed in his day, in the tobacco industry and in power and textiles, indicated the combination of business sense and ruthlessness which accompanied his rise. His philanthropic endeavors, which have left lasting monuments to the Duke family fortune in his native state, were inspired by his own notions of social betterment. Although he owned several magnificent houses, and in his later years enjoyed the pleasures his wealth could buy, Duke seemed intent on achieving recognition that, as he expressed it to the university's president, would last for a thousand years. Driven by personal imperatives to achieve business supremacy, and then to provide philanthropic support for an institution and an endowment bearing his name, Duke left an enduring legacy which attests the curious and complementary duality of his ambitions.

Bibliography
Cunningham, Bill. *On Bended Knees: The Night Rider Story*. Nashville, Tenn.: McClanahan Publishing, 1983. Vivid though awkwardly written history of the armed bands that arose to resist farmers' collaboration with the American Tobacco Company. Despite its somewhat melodramatic tone, this work reflects extensive research.
Durden, Robert F. *The Dukes of Durham: 1865-1929*. Durham, N.C.: Duke University Press, 1975. Sound scholarly study which uses a number of manuscript collections at Duke University. Avoiding extremes of adulation or debunking, this work considers both the business activities and the philanthropic concerns of the family; particular attention is paid to their support for educational institutions.
Jenkins, John Wilber. *James B. Duke: Master Builder*. New York: George H. Doran Co., 1927. Admiring biography which ascribes Duke's success to business acumen and hard work; his marketing innovations are credited, but relatively little is said about the personal or corporate conflicts that affected his life and work. The last chapters provide a sympathetic overview of his philanthropic activities.
Kroll, Harry Harrison. *Rider in the Night*. Philadelphia: University of Pennsylvania Press, 1965. Although brisk and informal, this work on conflict in the tobacco-growing regions of Kentucky and Tennessee is well informed and steeped in local color. While evoking the plight of the farmers, the author does not explicitly take sides in the confrontations he discusses.
Porter, Earl W. *Trinity and Duke, 1892-1924: Foundations of Duke Univer-*

sity. Durham, N.C.: Duke University Press, 1964. The most complete work on the creation of Duke University, this study traces its formative years as Trinity College and considers the involvement of educators and administrators in securing support from the Duke family.

Tilley, Nannie May. *The Bright-Tobacco Industry: 1860-1929*. Chapel Hill: University of North Carolina Press, 1948. Massive treatment of the subject which is important for the general context of Duke's business activities. Both the technical and the economic aspects of tobacco marketing during this period are discussed in great detail.

Winkler, John K. *Tobacco Tycoon: The Story of James Buchanan Duke*. New York: Random House, 1942. Detailed biography which is somewhat derogatory in tone, and which relies heavily upon earlier works, such as that of Jenkins. Provocative in its treatment of the more scandalous periods of Duke's life, such as his divorce and his reaction to antitrust litigation.

J. R. Broadus

JOHN FOSTER DULLES

Born: February 25, 1888; Washington, D.C.
Died: May 24, 1959; Washington, D.C.
Area of Achievement: Diplomacy
Contribution: As secretary of state from 1953 to 1959, a period marked by major crises in Asia and Europe, Dulles advocated a policy of firmly countering Soviet and Chinese Communist advances; in doing so, he enunciated a diplomatic doctrine that had great influence in the Cold War era.

Early Life
Born in his parents' home in Washington, D.C., on February 25, 1888, John Foster Dulles was the first son of Allen Macy Dulles, a Presbyterian minister of modest means, and Edith Foster Dulles, who came from a family of prominent business and political figures. The boy's given names were taken from his maternal grandfather, John Watson Foster, an experienced diplomat who became secretary of state under President Benjamin Harrison. Another son and three daughters were later born to the Dulles family, two of whom, Allen and Eleanor, later became well-known for government work and authorship. When the family moved to upstate New York, young Dulles was educated in local schools, including Watertown High School; he read widely in literary classics but was also a budding outdoorsman, spending his summers fishing and sailing. In 1903, with his mother and his sister Margaret, Dulles spent some time in Lausanne, Switzerland, where he acquired a knowledge of French; the following year, at the age of sixteen, he entered Princeton University.

He performed creditably in his schoolwork; an important interlude came in 1907, when, at the invitation of John Watson Foster, who was then a special counsel to the Chinese delegation, Dulles served as a general secretary to the Second Hague Peace Conference. He returned to Princeton and was graduated second in the class of 1908. His bachelor's thesis earned for him a fellowship to support a year's study at the Sorbonne in Paris; he took courses in international law and, at this point, evidently decided upon a legal career instead of entering the ministry. Dulles spent two years at the law school of George Washington University, in Washington, D.C. He had great powers of concentration and a remarkably retentive memory; seemingly with slight effort he was able to complete his coursework a year early, in 1911.

Dulles returned to his father's home, and while he was there, he renewed his acquaintanceship with Janet Avery, who had visited Paris while he was at the Sorbonne. When he took his bar examination, Dulles, working rapidly, answered many of the questions and then left early; he caught a train to meet Janet for a canoeing date. It was there that he proposed marriage to her. He learned later that he had been admitted to the practice of law. With the assistance of John Watson Foster, Dulles obtained a clerk's position at the reputable and established firm of Sullivan and Cromwell in New York. In 1912, Dulles and Janet Avery were married; for many years he was to value her companionship and advice and to find her supportive during troubled periods of his career. During the six years that followed, two sons and one daughter were born to them.

Life's Work

With his knowledge of international law, Dulles was given several Latin American assignments; early in 1917, he was entrusted with a mission to Central America involving the defense of the Panama Canal. During World War I, he received a commission in the Army General Staff and served with the War Trade Board in Washington; he was rejected for combat duty because of his poor eyesight. Later, with his maternal uncle, Secretary of State Robert Lansing, he accompanied the American delegation to the Paris Peace Conference of 1919. As chief counsel on reparations and other financial matters, Dulles vigorously opposed the Allies' demands on Germany. His warning that burdensome reparations would produce further instability and international turmoil went unheeded. Upon his return to private practice, Dulles took on a number of international cases; on several occasions, he was called back to Washington to assist in the government's negotiation of foreign loans.

Dulles was a burly, strongly built man with a somewhat ponderous, deliberate manner. He had broad oval features, a wide mouth, and a blunt, protruding nose. His strong, heavy jaw, heavy eyebrows, and penetrating blue eyes behind wire-rimmed glasses gave an impression of firm determination. Even in his impromptu speeches, Dulles spoke incisively and in a well-organized manner, but his voice was often described as flat, and he had a tendency to slur some consonants.

As his professional career developed, Dulles, as a Presbyterian elder, remained active in church work. In 1940, he became chairman of the Commission on a Just and Durable Peace, an organization created under the auspices of the Federal Council of Churches. He acted as well as an adviser to Thomas E. Dewey when the Republican governor of New York ran for president in 1944. Dulles' experience in foreign policy was also appreciated by the Democratic Administration in power; he was made a State Department adviser to the San Francisco Conference of 1945, which led to the foundation of the United Nations. He served on several other diplomatic assignments; he also entered politics again when, in 1949, he was appointed to the seat of a retiring senator from New York. He lost the ensuing by-election, and then was called back to the State Department. In one of the major achievements of his career, Dulles, in 1951, concluded negotiations which, while circumventing the Soviet Union and Communist China, led to a formal peace treaty with Japan and widened the United States' security arrangements in the Pacific.

In 1952, Dulles served as an adviser to Dwight D. Eisenhower in his campaign for the presidency; his own views were expressed in articles calling for "a policy of boldness" and the "rollback" of Soviet power in Europe. In a press interview, Dulles stated his belief that the United States should "go to the brink of war" to reverse Communist advances, and the phrase "brinkmanship" was widely used to describe his views on foreign policy. Upon Eisenhower's victory in the election, Dulles was made secretary of state; forthwith he concerned himself with negotiations to end three years of conflict in Korea. Dulles issued veiled warnings about the bombing of Chinese airfields and the use of nuclear weapons shortly before an armistice was concluded, in July, 1953. Another crisis loomed in Indochina, where Communist guerrillas in Vietnam threatened to displace French forces who were fighting to preserve their colonial outposts. Although he was unable to obtain support elsewhere for a proposed American military intervention, Dulles exerted his influence to limit Communist gains in territory during the negotiation of the Geneva Accords of 1954. France then granted independence to Laos and Cambodia and accepted the partition of Vietnam between Communist and non-Communist factions.

Dulles urged the United States' allies to improve their military preparations and enunciated a doctrine of "massive retaliation," with nuclear weapons, as a means of deterring Soviet ventures. When European leaders could not agree on the creation of a multinational army, he announced his approval for the formation of a West German army, to be used in conjunction with the Atlantic alliance. In May, 1955, Dulles took part in the negotiations by which the United States, Britain, France, and the Soviet Union ended their occupation of Austria and guaranteed that country's independent, neutral status; some of the secretary's admirers maintained that his insistence on a rapid resolution of this issue forced the Soviet representatives to make concessions otherwise not forthcoming. During the summer and autumn of 1955, allied leaders met their Soviet counterparts at summit conferences held in Geneva; disarmament and European security problems were discussed there. During the meetings, Dulles was decidedly more wary of Soviet officials than were the other Western participants.

Problems of a different order arose in the Middle East, where Dulles promoted regional defense organizations to counteract Soviet ambitions. In 1955, Egypt began to buy military equipment from the Soviet bloc; the next year, Dulles rejected Egypt's request for financial assistance in building the Aswan Dam. President Gamal Abdul Nasser of Egypt retaliated by nationalizing the Suez Canal Company. Britain and France, which depended upon oil supplies from the Middle East, argued for international sanctions against Egypt and attempted to obtain Dulles' support against Nasser. In October,

1956, Israel launched a surprise invasion of the Sinai peninsula, and British and French forces occupied the Suez Canal zone. There was profound dismay in London and Paris when Dulles openly condemned the attack and urged the invading powers to withdraw. Although the crisis subsided, the Atlantic alliance had undergone serious strain.

Another crisis broke out within days of the Suez war: An insurrection in Hungary led to a massive invasion of that country by Soviet armored forces. In spite of Dulles' proclaimed policy of the "liberation" of Eastern Europe, President Eisenhower was compelled to acknowledge that the United States was in no position to challenge the Soviet Union's domination of small nations within its orbit.

More vigorous responses were possible elsewhere. To combat political instability in the Middle East, where it was feared that Nasserist or pro-Soviet influence was spreading, marines were sent to Lebanon in July, 1958. An acute crisis arose when Communist China began shelling islands situated between Formosa and the mainland; the American Seventh Fleet was then stationed in the Formosa Straits, and Dulles bluntly warned against any further hostile actions. European concerns arose once again in the last crisis of Dulles' life. In November, 1958, Soviet premier Nikita Khrushchev demanded a change in the status of Berlin. On behalf of his government, Dulles insisted that American forces would remain in the divided city.

Dulles had recurrently been troubled with ill health, which he tolerated with remarkable courage and good humor. During the Suez crisis of 1956, he had been hospitalized for treatment of a cancerous colon; this condition hampered him during later years, and eventually further operations were necessary. In February, 1959, he was treated for a hernia; the cancer also was found to have spread. Dulles later offered his resignation as secretary of state, which was accepted on April 15. After a gallant struggle with his illness, he succumbed finally on May 24, 1959, at the Walter Reed Hospital in Washington, D.C.

Summary

During his tenure as secretary of state, Dulles was alternately regarded as a defender of free nations or a threat to peace; he explained his policy as the calculation of means short of war by which Communist powers might be constrained to yield. His diplomatic style was forthright and audacious. Many of his statements were couched in moral and religious summons to combat Communist encroachments around the world. On the other hand, his participation was important for the conclusion of major international agreements, such as the Korean armistice and the Austrian State Treaty. Summit meet-. ings with Soviet leaders went ahead. Dulles warned of difficult and prolonged periods of international rivalry, but, upon many occasions, he also practiced the art of negotiation with his adversaries.

Dulles was, on the whole, favorably regarded by Western observers while he was in office and for some time thereafter; since the Vietnam War, historians critical of him have contended that his insistence on the monolithic unity of aims among Communist states left American foreign policy in an excessively rigid and unyielding position. According to this line of argument, Dulles unnecessarily intensified the Cold War and burdened the United States with commitments to resist Communism on a global scale. For others, however, it is possible to regard Dulles' diplomacy as the expression of views that were held in the United States during a specific period, before Soviet or Chinese aims in the Cold War had become manifest. In this view, Dulles formulated an approach to foreign policy that stated American interests and aims in bold and definite terms and thus answered the anxieties of his times without the actual resort to war.

Bibliography

Berding, Andrew H. *Dulles on Diplomacy*. Princeton, N.J.: Van Nostrand, 1965. Sympathetic recollections of a professional diplomat who for two years was assistant secretary of state under Dulles. Based on Dulles' speeches and the author's lengthy conference notes.

Dulles, Eleanor Lansing. *Chances of a Lifetime: A Memoir*. Englewood Cliffs, N.J.: Prentice-Hall, 1980. The reminiscences of Dulles' sister, who led a varied life of authorship combined with travel and some diplomatic functions. There are a number of useful passages about her brother's early years and about the crises he confronted as secretary of state.

Dulles, John Foster. *War or Peace*. New York: Macmillan, 1950. A tract for the times, this work sets forth Dulles' views concerning Communism and the relative balance of forces at midcentury. He discusses the extent of Communist aims while expressing his hopes for reversing Soviet and Chinese advances without causing a world war.

Gerson, Louis L. *John Foster Dulles*. New York: Cooper Square Publishers, 1967. Volume 17 of the series "The American Secretaries of State and Their Diplomacy," this is well-rounded and generally sympathetic study of Dulles' diplomacy by a leading authority on American foreign policy. On balance, the author upholds Dulles' judgments on Communism and international security.

Goold-Adams, Richard. *John Foster Dulles: A Reappraisal*. New York: Appleton-Century-Crofts, 1962. Sprightly account by a well-informed British journalist who sifts apart the problems of substance and style in Dulles' approach to international relations; while critical in some respects, in others, Goold-Adams acknowledges Dulles' strengths as a negotiator.

Guhin, Michael A. *John Foster Dulles: A Statesman and His Times*. New York: Columbia University Press, 1972. A topical examination of Dulles' pronouncements on foreign policy, this work contends that he was neither so inflexible nor so doctrinaire as many have claimed.

Hoopes, Townsend. *The Devil and John Foster Dulles*. Boston: Little, Brown and Co., 1973. A full-scale biography, this work was written at the end of the Vietnam War, and the author implies that Dulles cast American foreign policy in a rigid mold that unduly emphasized anti-Communism. Particular attention is paid to Dulles' positions on Middle Eastern and Asian crises; the moral and religious elements in his diplomacy are stressed and commented upon unfavorably.

Mosley, Leonard. *Dulles: A Biography of Eleanor, Allen, and John Foster Dulles and Their Family Network*. New York: Dial Press, 1978. A lengthy popular work, somewhat fast and loose in its presentation of facts, which deals as much with Allen Dulles and his career in government intelligence, as with John Foster Dulles' diplomatic work. For all of the Dulleses, matters of personality are emphasized as much as their actual political concerns.

Pruessen, Ronald W. *John Foster Dulles: The Road to Power*. New York: Free Press, 1982. The most detailed single account of Dulles' life before he became secretary of state, this work is written from a new leftist standpoint, but it fully acknowledges the complexity of its subject's character. The contrapuntal influences of his legal career and his religious beliefs are discussed in relation to Dulles' political work and government service from the early years through the onset of the Cold War.

Toulouse, Mark G. *The Transformation of John Foster Dulles: From Prophet of Realism to Priest of Nationalism*. Macon, Ga.: Mercer University Press, 1985. A study of the years until 1952, this work contends, perhaps too strongly, that Dulles' political views were intertwined with his theological outlook. His church-affiliated work during World War II and his relations with religious groups during the early Cold War are explored at length.

J. R. Broadus

ELEUTHÈRE IRÉNÉE DU PONT

Born: June 24, 1771; Paris, France
Died: October 31, 1834; Philadelphia, Pennsylvania
Area of Achievement: Business
Contribution: Combining sharp business acumen with innovative technical methods and tenacious moral principles, Du Pont founded E. I. Du Pont de Nemours and Company, which became a powerful American empire.

Early Life

Eleuthère Irénée Du Pont was born on June 24, 1771, in Paris, France. He was named in honor of liberty and peace (after the Greek words for these ideals) at the insistence of his godfather, Turgot, who was also his father's benefactor. His father, Pierre Samuel Du Pont, served the corrupt French throne for many years and was rewarded with nobility. His mother, Nicole Charlotte Marie Le Dée, died when Irénée was fourteen years old. He also had an older brother, Victor, to whom he was very close. Irénée grew up at the family estate at Bois-des-Fosses, about sixty miles south of Paris.

Irénée spent all of his young life in the harsh and oppressive political atmosphere of France during the epochs of Louis XVI, of the revolutionary mobs whose favorite instrument was the guillotine, and finally of Napoleon Bonaparte. After the death of his mother, Irénée's life became closely interwoven with that of his politically active father. In 1788, when Irénée was seventeen years old, the popular rebellion took place. As the nation's ideology was more and more identified with the political Left, Pierre remained on the Right. He and the Marquis de Lafayette, with whom he shared the title of commander of the National Guard, founded the Société de 1789, an organization composed of the most conservative wing of the bourgeoisie, which favored a constitutional monarchy. Pierre and Irénée began to attack the Jacobins, the radical party of the petite bourgeoisie, from their newly acquired publishing house in Paris. On August 10, 1792, they led their sixty-man private guard to defend the king's palace from a Jacobinian assault that was demanding an end to the monarchy. During this period, at the age of twenty, Irénée married Sophie Madeleine Dalmas, with whom he had seven children during the course of their marriage.

After the uprising, Irénée served as apprentice to the chemist Antoine Lavoisier, the greatest scientist of his day and a close friend of his father. Lavoisier was the head of the French monarch's gunpowder mills and it was there that Irénée learned the craft of gunpowder-making and acquired a precise sense of the scientific method. The revolution struck, however, and the king and Lavoisier were guillotined per the orders of Robespierre. Pierre was arrested shortly thereafter and would have also been guillotined had not the bourgeoisie, now convinced that their revolution was irreversible, asserted their control over the revolution by seizing power from the radicals. Robespierre was executed and Pierre was granted his freedom.

At this point, Irénée was making a precarious living operating the publishing house. The print shop, which was the main source of his income, had once been wrecked by the mob during a political uproar and there was no guarantee that the same thing might not happen again. His newspaper, *Le Républicain*, carried a revolutionary theme. Pierre's new newspaper, *L'Historien*, was a vehicle for reviving royalism and opposing Napoleon's appointment as commander-in-chief of the French forces in Italy. The bourgeoisie, however, struck and backed Napoleon's coup. Pierre and Irénée were imprisoned. With the help of a friend who was a member of the commission that prepared lists for deportation, Pierre regained their freedom under a plea of senility, but he had to pledge to leave France.

So it was that the Du Pont family set sail aboard the *American Eagle* and arrived on the shores of Newport, Rhode Island, on December 31, 1800. It was in the United States that Irénée's individuality, creativity, innovative spirit, and strong character began to emerge. His physical appearance—he was small in size, with a cleft chin, a long sharp nose, and weak lips—belied the strength and courage he later displayed as he built his empire. His ability to restrain his emotions and his instinctive caution in befriending anyone who was not family also contributed to the building and solidifying of his dynasty in years to come.

Life's Work

Du Pont found in the United States a political climate that was very different from that of France. Insistence on freedom had led to the Declaration of Independence and the American Revolution. The American economy encouraged initiative, and the door of advancement was open to all.

Gunpowder was a much-needed commodity on the American frontier. It was needed for protection from Indians and wild animals, to shoot game for meat and skins, and to help clear land to build new homes and roads. American powder makers during the Revolution had made some acceptable powder, although ninety percent had been bought from France. By 1800, explosions and British competition had put most of the domestic mills out of business.

Shortly after his arrival in the United States, Du Pont went to purchase some gunpowder for hunting. His expert eye recognized its poor quality and its inability to meet the urgent needs of the American frontier. This discovery sparked his ingenuity and his dream was born. On July 19, 1802, at the age of thirty-one, he purchased land on the Brandywine Creek near Wilmington, Delaware, on the site of what had been the first cotton mill in America. He had originally planned to call his plant Lavoisier Mills out of respect for his mentor. He reconsidered, however, and decided to name it Eleutherian

Mills, in honor of freedom, as a happy portent to political refugees. In the spring of 1804, the first Du Pont gunpowder went on public sale.

Du Pont spent thirty-two years on the Brandywine Creek as president of E. I. Du Pont de Nemours and Company. Throughout these years, the shortage of liquid capital was a constant problem for him. Although his original investors had pledged funds to build and run the mills, they did not give the amount promised, and he was forced to raise the difference through notes. When the mills began to show a profit, the stockholders demanded the earnings in dividends instead of reinvesting a portion to increase production and sales as he wanted to do. Du Pont had the business acumen of a twentieth century entrepreneur, while his investors were stagnating in eighteenth century procedures. His way out of the impasse was to purchase their stock. They demanded exorbitant prices, so he signed more notes to meet them. In this way, he assured himself that only he and other family members would control the company, and by the time of his death, most of these notes had been paid off.

During his tenure with the company, Du Pont established the technical, methodological, and ethical principles to which the company still adheres. With regard to the technical and methodological aspects, Du Pont addressed the need to give careful attention to raw material preparation. Charcoal was made from willow trees because they always grew new branches and had an inexhaustible supply. Saltpeter was always thoroughly cleaned regardless of its state of cleanliness when it was received. Sulphur was always pure and clear in color. Du Pont also had the foresight to install a labor-saving device for kerneling powder. In times of prosperity as well as in times of adversity, Du Pont always sought out means to improve the quality of his product and improve his methods. This was the forerunner of the product and process improvement approach of modern industry. He even anticipated the modern principle of enlarging a company's income and usefulness through diversification. Du Pont provided one of the earliest examples of industrial integration by growing grain for the horses which transported the gunpowder in fields adjacent to the mills.

Du Pont was a man who abided by an exemplary code of ethics. The most salient example of this manifested itself during the tragedy which befell his mills in March, 1818. Explosions ruined much of the plant and killed forty men. At that time, there were no laws which committed the company to compensate the families of the victims, but Du Pont pensioned the widows, gave them homes, and took responsibility for the education and medical care of the children. He paid these costs and those of rebuilding the plant by renewing his notes and signing more. Another example of Du Pont's strong social and moral consciousness involved his principle that quality was a matter of pride, with which no compromise could be made. He constantly refused offers to manufacture inferior powder for shipping. He was once approached by the government of one of the states, which was irritated at a new federal tariff law and had threatened to resist its reinforcement by force of arms. Du Pont replied that he had no powder for such a purpose.

Du Pont's unyielding adherence to these principles brought him rewarding results. In 1804, during the first year of production, he made 44,907 pounds of gunpowder, which sold for $15,116.75. In 1805, both amounts had tripled. In 1808, an additional mill and new facilities accounted for the annual production of 300,000 pounds. In 1810, the profits exceeded thirty thousand dollars. In 1811, with a profit of forty-five thousand dollars, the Du Pont mills were the largest in the Western Hemisphere. The War of 1812 brought government orders totaling 750,000 pounds of gunpowder. Although this would appear to be a profitable assignment, the business realities proved to be the contrary. The company had to risk its cash and borrow heavily to extend the capacity of the mills. Du Pont purchased an adjoining property called the Hagley Estate, erected additional facilities, renamed it the Hagley Yards, and thereby completed the first major expansion in the company's history. By the time of his death on October 31, 1834, the output of corps of workmen, with constantly improving machinery and equipment, exceeded one million pounds. The Brandywine mills had become a major American enterprise.

Summary

Du Pont created much more than a family business; he bred a tradition which still endures. This tradition espoused his code of business honor which was inseparable from his code of personal honor. His guiding principle was that privilege was inextricably bound to duty, and this principle ruled his entire life. He had a sense of obligation to his customers which was a rarity in the business world of his time. He staked personal fortunes on many occasions in order to fulfill a pledge. His commitment to technological innovations and increased productivity never undermined his commitment to top-quality products. His foresight and ingenuity antedated his century in technological and moral consciousness. These precepts, which originated from the Brandywine mills, still guide the Du Pont Company. The Du Pont family empire is a global one which has expanded to include real estate, arms and defense industries, computers, communications, media, utilities, oil, food industries, banks, aviation, chemicals, rubber, insurance, and many other businesses.

When Du Pont came to the United States in 1800, he was a strange man in a strange country. Yet he recognized that the United States was a land of opportunity, and the Du Pont Company grew because the fledgling nation's needs, and free traditions encouraged progress. America grew because people such as Du Pont contributed the seeds of growth that bloom in risk, courage, and innovation. He may have been forced to come to the United States, but he died as Delaware's most valuable citizen.

Generations of men and women contributed to the development of the Du Pont Company from a single gunpowder mill to a company which is international in scope and significance. The original Du Pont mills have been replaced by more modern and efficient buildings and procedures, but it is the spirit of Du Pont which remains and reigns: His code of business honor and his code of personal integrity, of privilege and duty, still pervade his business empire.

Bibliography

Dorian, Max. *The Du Ponts: From Gunpowder to Nylon*. Boston: Little, Brown and Co., 1961. Concentrates on the Du Pont genealogy and the way in which each family member contributed to the building of the empire. Stresses the role of Pierre Du Pont, his service to Louis XVI, his title of nobility, and the political connections which enabled him to migrate to America.

Dujarric de la Rivière, René. *E. I. Du Pont de Nemours: Élève de Lavoisier*. Paris: Librairie des Champs-Élysées, 1954. Focuses on the period of Du Pont's life during which he served as apprentice to Lavoisier, who taught him the craft of gunpowder-making. This expertise served him well in the United States, where he established the first gunpowder mill, which later evolved into the Du Pont dynasty.

Du Pont de Nemours, E. I., and Co. *Du Pont: The Autobiography of an American Enterprise*. Wilmington, Del.: E. I. Du Pont de Nemours and Co., 1952. The best book on Du Pont's life and ingenuity. Also explores the century and a half that followed the first gunpowder mill on the Brandywine in terms of the parallel development of the Du Pont Company and the United States.

Du Pont de Nemours, Pierre Samuel. *Irénée Bonfils*. Wilmington, Del.: E. I. Du Pont de Nemours and Co., 1947. Discusses the religious beliefs of the Du Pont family, which were somewhat redefined after the death of Du Pont's mother, who was a Catholic. The tone is one of tolerance toward other religions and a strong appeal is made for a united church.

Winkler, John K. *The Du Pont Dynasty*. New York: Reynal and Hitchcock, 1935. Explores the Du Pont family history from their early days in France to their early days in Delaware. It also details the advancements and expansion of the company from its inception.

Zilg, Gerard Colby. *Du Pont: Behind the Nylon Curtain*. Englewood Cliffs, N.J.: Prentice-Hall, 1974. Chronicles the life of the Du Pont family from France, their migration to America, the success of Du Pont's first gunpowder mill, and the expansion of the Du Pont dynasty.

Anne Laura Mattrella

JAMES BUCHANAN EADS

Born: May 23, 1820; Lawrenceberg, Indiana
Died: March 8, 1887; Nassau, New Providence Island, Bahamas
Areas of Achievement: Business, invention, and engineering
Contribution: Eads revolutionized long-span bridge construction; the Eads
   Bridge, spanning the Mississippi River at St. Louis, is the only such struc-
   ture bearing an engineer's name. He was a highly successful capitalist and
   an inventor of note, with more than fifty patents credited to him.

Early Life

James Buchanan Eads was born on May 23, 1820, in Lawrenceburg, Indiana, an Ohio River town. His family was of moderate means, moving in
search of better fortune to Cincinnati, Ohio, then to Louisville, Kentucky.
As a result of economic difficulties, between the ages of nine and thirteen
Eads had only minimal formal education. Nevertheless, by the time he was
eleven years old, Eads, working from observations made during family moves
on steamers, had already constructed a small steam engine and models of
sawmills, fire engines, steamboats, and electrotype machines.

In Louisville, Eads's father experienced serious business reverses, so at
only thirteen Eads traveled to St. Louis, working passage on a river steamer
and seeking employment. After suffering hardships, Eads found well-paying
work in a St. Louis mercantile establishment. Recognizing Eads's abilities, an
employer opened his library (reportedly one of the Mississippi Valley's finest)
to him, and Eads used it intensively to study civil engineering, mechanics,
and machinery. When he was nineteen, his family moved to Dubuque, Iowa,
where young Eads signed as second clerk aboard the river steamer *Knicker-
bocker*, which operated between Dubuque and Cincinnati. In the next few
years, having risen to purser, he served aboard several Mississippi steamers
and became intimately acquainted with the navigational characteristics of the
river with which his life became intimately linked.

Life's Work

In 1842, now an attractive, industrious, tactful, ingenious, and personable
man, Eads placed his savings into copartnership with Case and Nelson, a
firm of St. Louis boat builders, in order to help the company to expand into
the salvage of river wrecks. Hundreds of steamers were lost annually during
the mid-nineteenth century because of boiler explosions, contact with bars or
snags, and other accidents, and millions of dollars were lost to river pirates
and to the unpredictabilities of the river itself. As a consequence, Eads and
his partners extended their salvage operations the length of the Mississippi
and to the Gulf countries of Central America, profiting greatly. Nevertheless,
Eads sold his shares and established the first glass manufactory west of the

Mississippi, an equally profitable enterprise.

Drawing upon his vast experience with the Mississippi and its tributaries, Eads founded his own salvage company in 1847. His success lay in his design and construction of a series of "submarines," diving bells raised and lowered by derricks and supplied with compressed air, which revolutionized salvage work. Not only were sunken cargoes recovered, but also vessels themselves could be refloated. His final salvage boat, bought from the American government and redesigned, was the largest, most powerful of its type ever built. Eads was so successful with his diving bells and snag boats that in 1856-1857 he proposed a federal contract to clear obstructions and maintain free navigation of the Mississippi and other Western rivers over subsequent years. His proposal was defeated, however, chiefly by the opposition of Senators Judah P. Benjamin of Louisiana and Jefferson Davis of Mississippi, the former to serve in several capacities in Davis' Confederate Cabinet. Thwarted, but already wealthy, at the age of thirty-seven Eads retired with his second wife to the comfort of a St. Louis suburb, ostensibly to recover from his latest bout with tuberculosis

Yet the most significant phases of his career lay ahead. Edward Bates, a friend of the Eads family who had entered Abraham Lincoln's cabinet as attorney general, alerted Eads to the possible need for his services as secession of the South threatened in 1860; the Administration was anxious to preserve free navigation of the Mississippi. Shortly after war erupted in 1861, Eads won federal contracts for construction of seven six-hundred-ton armored steamers to be ready for action in sixty-five days. Greatly handicapped by his illness, Eads still assembled men and materials from ten states and from the mills of half a dozen cities, successfully completing his first delivery in forty-five days. Within one hundred days he designed and constructed an aggregate of five thousand tons of military shipping. These vessels contributed to Union victories at Forts Henry and Donelson and at Island No. 10, thereby opening the northern Mississippi. Indeed, at the time of these victories, Eads actually owned the vessels, having paid for them with his own funds (he had not yet been reimbursed by Washington). Before 1865, Eads built fourteen heavily armored gunboats, four mortar boats, and seven armored transports, all delivered on time and to specifications. Furthermore, his revolving gun turrets later became standard. For this and other inventions, Eads was elected a Fellow of the American Academy for the Advancement of Science. Devoid of engineering training, Eads had amply demonstrated not only a mastery of novel shipbuilding but also a profound knowledge of iron and steel potentials. Combined with his grasp of the Mississippi's peculiarities, his ingenuity, tenacity, high civic esteem, and organizational abilities, he was brilliantly equipped for his next enterprise: bridging the Mississippi at St. Louis.

With canal-building and the era of the river steamer waning, railway expansion dominated the postwar period. From 1865 until Eads's death in 1887, railway mileage increased from about forty thousand to more than 200,000 miles. Concurrently, need for bridges (hitherto of wooden or iron truss constructions) of long spans and heavy bearing capacities became imperative. Proposals for a St. Louis span had been made earlier than 1867 by Charles Ellet, Jr., as well as by John Augustus Roebling, engineers of distinction, but Eads's plan won the vital approval of the St. Louis business community and of the city's officials.

For his unprecedented scheme, Eads employed unprecedented means. Aware of his own weaknesses, he created a superb staff: Charles Shaler Smith joined him as chief engineering consultant; two other able men were chosen as assistant engineers; and the chancellor of Washington University served as mathematical consultant. With Bessemer steel then available, Eads selected steel as his basic construction material. This ran against the advice of many engineers; indeed, the British Board of Trade banned the use of steel for bridges until years later. Moreover, Eads helped transform Bessemer steel into chrome steel, that choice alone altering subsequent major bridge construction, in which special steels came to supersede iron. Foundations created special problems. Eads knew the Mississippi, and by treading its bottom in his diving bell he confirmed that three or more feet of sand and silt moved along the river bed at speed of flow. Winter ice jams and the necessity of keeping navigational channels open further complicated planning. The pneumatic caissons devised for foundation work were not new in principle but they had seldom been tested and never on the scale or at the depths required to reach bedrock: 123 feet below the mean water level on the Illinois side and eighty-six feet at St. Louis. Moreover, these iron-shod timber caissons were seventy-five feet in diameter and designed to sink under their own weight as work progressed. Consequently, several lives were lost, others frequently endangered and cases of "bends" from depths and pressures were numerous.

Double-decked for trains and for normal traffic, the bridge featured unique arches that had been cantilevered into position, the central sections coming last. Moreover, the three arched spans were of unprecedented length: 1,560 feet overall. Notwithstanding distinguished assistance, Eads designed and oversaw, as his engineers testified, every one-eighth of an inch of the structure, and his aesthetic sense produced a masterwork of great beauty, one still in service. It was completed in 1874, just as the nation's first and longest industrial depression struck. Bondholders foreclosed on the bridge's mortgage. Eads's own bank proved to be one of the great financial disasters of the day. By 1877, the financier and speculator Jay Gould assumed control of the bridge.

Eads, however, swiftly recovered from this crash. By 1875 he had begun overriding congressional opposition to a $5,250,000 contract for permanently clearing major bars at the mouth of the Mississippi and extending its South

Pass jetties into deep Gulf waters. Again through ingenuity developed after study of European river jetties, Eads designed an inexpensive "mattress" construction, successfully completing the job and recouping his fortune. Indeed, he offered seventy-five million dollars of his own money if Congress would charter his company for construction of a ship-railway across the Mexican isthmus at Tehuantepec, thereby bringing the Pacific twelve hundred miles nearer to the Mississippi than Ferdinand de Lesseps' ongoing Panama project. Even as Congress moved to accept his proposal, however, Eads's health failed. He died on March 8, 1887, in Nassau, the Bahamas.

Summary

Either as a great capitalist or as a great engineer, Eads would have enjoyed distinction. Essentially filling the ideal of the American self-made man, he combined both roles, distinguishing himself in both. He revolutionized the salvage business with his inventions, notably with his design of steam-driven centrifugal pumps and his diving bells. He revolutionized bridge construction with his arch designs and, above all, with his introduction of steel for such structures. He resolved through financial, political, and engineering inventiveness and skill the freeing of the river around which so much of his life revolved. In 1884, he became the first American recipient of the Albert Medal from the British Royal Society of Arts. Further, of the eighty-nine persons elected to the Hall of Fame for Great Americans, Eads (elected in 1920) was the sole engineer or architect chosen during the institution's first sixty years of existence.

Bibliography

Condit, Carl W. *American Building: Materials and Techniques from the Beginning of the Colonial Settlements to the Present.* 2d ed. Chicago: University of Chicago Press, 1982. Sweeping and expert analysis. Chapter 12, "Long-Span Bridges in Iron and Steel," treats Eads in proper technical context.

Kouwenhoven, John A. "The Designing of the Eads Bridge." *Technology and Culture* 23 (1982): 535-568. Scholarly work in a widely available, learned journal.

_____. "James Buchanan Eads: The Engineer as Entrepreneur." In *Technology in America: A History of Individuals and Ideas*, edited by Carroll W. Pursell, Jr. Cambridge, Mass.: MIT Press, 1981. Chapter 8 on Eads is excellent; scholarly and well written.

Scott, Quinta, and Howard S. Miller. *The Eads Bridge: Photographic Essay.* New York: Columbia University Press, 1979. The fullest description of the bridge; less useful for the general context of Eads's other activities.

Woodward, Calvin M. *A History of the St. Louis Bridge: Containing a Full Account of Every Step in Its Construction and Erection.* St. Louis: Janes and Co., 1881. This account of the building of the Eads Bridge is old but is the most exhaustive.

Yager, Rosemary. *James Buchanan Eads: Master of the Great River*. New York: Van Nostrand Reinhold Co., 1968. Interesting overview of Eads's life and activities, but not the final word on Eads's work.

Clifton K. Yearley
Kerrie L. MacPherson

THOMAS EAKINS

Born: July 25, 1844; Philadelphia, Pennsylvania
Died: June 25, 1916; Philadelphia, Pennsylvania
Area of Achievement: Art
Contribution: Eakins produced a handful of major paintings which were to add to the reputation of the United States as a center of art independent of Europe. He was also an important influence on art education in the United States.

Early Life

Thomas Eakins was born in Philadelphia on July 25, 1844, and was to die in the family home in that city in 1916. Eakins' father, Benjamin Eakins, of Scottish-Irish parentage, was a writing master in the Philadelphia school system, and Thomas had early ambitions to follow his father into that work. His mother was of English and Dutch descent. It was a close, middle-class family with a modest private income which was to help support Eakins throughout his life, since his teaching and painting did not always do so. He was particularly close to his three sisters, and they often appear in his paintings.

He evidenced early talents in draftsmanship and drawing and was to study them formally from high school onward, but he also had strengths in science, mathematics, and languages. Eakins was to use his knowledge of science and mathematics extensively in the preparation of his more complicated paintings.

Eakins studied at the Pennsylvania Academy of Fine Arts in Philadelphia, from 1861 to 1866. Drawing from casts of fine antique sculpture was the center of the technical studies at the school, and to Eakins' dissatisfaction, little drawing was done from live models. He supplemented his work by enrolling in anatomy classes at Jefferson Medical College, where he was allowed to watch surgeons operating, and where he began a practice which he admitted he disliked, but which he considered essential to the student artist—the study of anatomy—by taking part in dissection classes. By the end of his time at the academy, he had done very little painting. In September, 1866, he left for France in order to study in Paris.

He entered the conservative École des Beaux-Arts, choosing to study under the painter Jean-Leon Gérôme, who was himself somewhat conservative and old-fashioned, but who gave Eakins a thorough grounding in drawing, with emphasis on the use of live models. Eakins again added anatomy classes to his studies, and when he started to paint seriously in his second year, he took a studio where he could work alone while continuing his instruction under Gérôme. His correspondence evidences little interest in what was going on about him in Paris, although it was a time of considerable ferment in the art world, and the early work of the painters who were to become the Impressionists was being shown and discussed. At the end of his three years in Paris, he toured the galleries of Spain, showing particular enthusiasm for the technique and realistic subject matter of José Ribera and Diego Velázquez. On July 4, 1870, he returned to Philadelphia, where he was to live and work for the remainder of his life.

Life's Work
There had been indications of a fully formed skill in a few of Eakins' paintings in the late 1860's, and that maturity was soon confirmed in his work in the 1870's. A solid and stocky young man (he can be seen hovering in the middle-background of some of his paintings) with an active interest in rowing and hunting, he brought the world of his athletic pleasures into his paintings, and he is best known for a group of stunningly forceful studies of rowers which exemplify the American love of high athletic skill and outdoor life. *John Biglin in a Single Scull* (1873) and *Max Schmitt in a Single Scull* (1871) are the most popular examples of these intense, imploded moments of athletic focus, in which the subjects, patently modest, convey an aesthetic rightness, a kind of metaphysical truth about life which connects them with the earlier tradition of American paintings celebrating the rugged men working the rivers of America.

This paean to personal skill is explored again in his pictures of surgeons at work, musicians at play, and prizefighters in action. Eakins was, however, to run into trouble with the public, who found his paintings of surgeons at work in the operating theaters too gruesome and bloody, and his paintings of male and female nudes were often considered too crudely unblinkered. He could, on the other hand, be quietly tender in his paintings of musicians, particularly in his studies of his sisters.

As a result, he established a reputation as one of the foremost realists of the latter half of the nineteenth century, but he did not sell many pictures. In his later years, he turned more and more to portraits, generally using friends and acquaintances as subjects, and he rarely was commissioned to do so. He showed little inclination to idealize his portraits. Rather, he tended to catch his sitters in the introspective moment, and he was often successful in getting something of their character on the canvas. His later portraits often went further and revealed physical and emotional vulnerabilities which did not always please his subjects.

It is possible to think of him as a portraitist from beginning to end with the athletes and men of action showing the best of prime human endeavor, and some of the latter sitters revealing the cruel, inexorable nature of time passing. Yet it is those early pictures of sportsmen which are, quite rightly, best remembered.

This mixed reputation that he developed as a painter, of being enormously talented but a bit crude, carried over into his parallel career as an art teacher and administrator. In 1876, he joined the Pennsylvania Academy of Fine Arts as their instructor in the life classes; gradually he became so important to the school's work that in 1882 he became the director. As he did in his own painting, he put heavy emphasis upon drawing from life, not because he did not appreciate the greatness of ancient sculpture but because he saw the naked human form as the best subject for the young artist. He also urged his students to take anatomy classes with medical students. Over the years, opposition built up, inside the school and outside, over his insistence that students, male and female, should draw from life. In 1886, his exposure of a male model, completely nude, before a class of female students caused such an avalanche of protest that he was asked to resign. He took a large group of male students with him, and they formed the Art Students League of Philadelphia with Eakins as the sole, unpaid instructor. The school lasted for six years but foundered eventually for financial reasons. Eakins continued to teach in art schools as a guest lecturer, but his insistence on using nude models often got him into trouble, and by mid-life, he ceased to teach.

He had a continuing interest in sculpture and left a few pieces which show considerable skill, but the later years were in the main confined to doing portraits, with occasional returns to his studies of athletes and nudes.

Summary

Eakins made a double contribution to American culture. As an educator, he championed, to his own detriment, the need to repudiate the sometimes prurient sexual morality of the late nineteenth century in favor of an intelligent acceptance of the human body as the basis for study in art colleges. His fight, often played out in public, made it easier for such artistic and educational freedoms to become a common aspect of American art instruction.

He was also the first prominent art teacher to bring science into the classroom and studio. His personal use of, and instruction in the preparation of mathematically precise preliminary studies, his use of scale models, and particularly his pioneering use of photography were to become commonly applied tools.

Despite his training in France and his admiration for Spanish painters, he was peculiarly American. His choice of subjects and his refusal to idealize them are examples of his solid, down-to-earth approach to art. Other painters romanticized the portrait; Eakins used it to record reality, however uncomplimentary. He has been called antiartistic, but he proved that art could be made out of life as it was seen. His refusal to compromise for profit and popularity is an example of his American forthrightness, and his affection for science, for mathematics, for photography, for sport, for high professional endeavor may also be seen as marks of his American character.

Possessed of abundant painterly skills, he often seems too skeptically stolid to make use of them, but at his best, particularly in his sporting pictures, he can make the simple moment accumulate a splendor which links him with painters such as Paul Cézanne and Jean-Baptiste-Siméon Chardin. At those moments of pastoral innocence, the paintings achieve a poetic density which transcends and glorifies the simplicity of the mundane act of living. Then, he is at his best—and his most American.

Bibliography

Goodrich, Lloyd. *Thomas Eakins*. Cambridge, Mass.: Harvard University Press, 1982. An updated look at Eakins, including interviews with Eakins' widow, students, and sitters. Good bibliography of articles on Eakins.

_____. *Thomas Eakins: His Life and Work*. New York: Whitney Museum of American Art, 1933. A major study combining critical biography and catalog in which the reviving reputation of the artist is assessed in conjunction with the neglect which followed his death.

_____. *Thomas Eakins: Retrospective Exhibition*. New York: Whitney Museum of American Art, 1970. A paperback monograph, prepared for the major retrospective show at the Whitney Museum of American Art by the scholar most involved with putting Eakins into the mainstream of American art. Good, with numerous reproductions and an excellent short essay.

Hendricks, Gordon. *The Life and Work of Thomas Eakins*. New York: Grossman Publishers, 1974. An obsessively detailed study, provocative in its assumptions.

Johns, Elizabeth. *Thomas Eakins: The Heroism of Modern Life*. Princeton, N.J.: Princeton University Press, 1983. An interesting study of specific subjects painted by Eakins, putting them into the context of how other artists have used the same subjects.

Porter, Fairfield. *Thomas Eakins*. New York: George Braziller, 1959. An edition of "The Great American Artists" series, this inexpensive paperback includes a generous selection of his paintings, some in color, and a short, sensible critical comment upon Eakins' life and career.

Siegl, Theodor. *The Thomas Eakins Collection*. Philadelphia: Philadelphia Museum of Art, 1978. A careful assessment of Eakins' individuality as a painter and a sympathetic consideration of his personality.

Charles H. Pullen

AMELIA EARHART

Born: July 24, 1898; Atchison, Kansas
Died: July 2, 1937?; near Howland Island in the Pacific Ocean
Area of Achievement: Aviation
Contribution: By being the first woman to fly across the Atlantic and by establishing numerous other flying records, Earhart helped to promote commercial aviation and advance the cause of women in aviation.

Early Life

Amelia Earhart, the daughter of Amy Otis and Edwin Stanton Earhart, was born in the home of her maternal grandparents in Atchison, Kansas. Her grandfather was Alfred G. Otis, a pioneer Atchison settler who became a prominent lawyer, banker, and federal district court judge. Her father worked for a railroad as an attorney and claims agent.

Her early childhood was spent in Kansas City, Kansas, where she and her younger sister learned to ride horseback. When her father accepted a job in Des Moines, Iowa, in 1905, Amelia and her sister remained for a year in Atchison, where she later recalled, "There were regular games and school and mud-ball fights, picnics, and exploring raids up and down the bluffs of the Missouri River." After joining her father in Des Moines, Amelia attended school and began reading the books that further encouraged her spirit of adventure. Sir Walter Scott, Charles Dickens, George Eliot, and William Makepeace Thackeray were her favorite authors, and she and her sister made up imaginary journeys while they played in an abandoned carriage.

When her father went to work for the Great Northern railroad, the Earharts moved to St. Paul, Minnesota, but Edwin's alcoholism grew worse and her mother took her daughters to Chicago, where Amelia was graduated from Hyde Park High School in June, 1916. She attended the Ogontz School in Rydal, Pennsylvania, then went to Toronto, Canada, where her sister was in school. In Toronto, she saw wounded veterans of World War I and became a Red Cross volunteer. She worked at Spadina Military Hospital, where she came to know and admire the young flyers of the Royal Flying Corps. In 1918, she was ill with pneumonia and went to live with her sister in North-ampton, Massachusetts. While her sister was enrolled at Smith College, Amelia took a course in automobile repair. In 1919, she moved to New York City to study medicine at Columbia University but left after a year to join her parents in Los Angeles.

The aviation industry was just beginning to develop in Southern California, and Amelia was attracted to the air shows and flying demonstrations at local airports. She took her first airplane ride at the Glendale airport and soon convinced her parents to help her take flying lessons with a pioneer woman pilot, Neta Snook. In June, 1921, Amelia made her first solo flight in a Kinner Airster. A year later, she had saved two thousand dollars to buy a three-cylinder Kinner Canary, a plane in which she set a woman's altitude record of fourteen thousand feet. Her career as a pilot was launched.

Life's Work

Even in 1922, however, flying was expensive, and paid employment for women in aviation was limited. When her parents were divorced, Amelia sold her plane and returned to Massachusetts, where she taught English to immigrants and became a social worker at Denison House, a Boston settlement. She was able to combine her interests in social work and aviation, on one occasion flying over Boston and dropping leaflets announcing a Denison House street fair and on another, judging a model airplane contest for the National Playground Association.

In 1928, she was selected by the publisher George P. Putnam to fly with pilot Wilmer Stutz and mechanic Lou Gordon in a Fokker trimotor across the Atlantic. The plane, named *Friendship*, had been purchased from the explorer Richard Byrd by Amy Phipps Guest, an American flying enthusiast who had married and settled in England. When Mrs. Guest was unable to make the flight herself, she asked Putnam to find a young woman to represent her in the promotion of women in aviation. On June 3, *Friendship* left Boston for Halifax, Nova Scotia, and Trepassy, Newfoundland. Delayed by bad weather for several days, the plane left Trepassy on June 17 and landed the following day at Burry Point, Wales. Earhart was given a hero's welcome on her return to New York.

Because her flight came only a little more than a year after the solo flight by Charles Lindbergh, and because of her tall, slender build and short, blonde hair, she was nicknamed "Lady Lindy," but she preferred to be called "AE." Within a few months Putnam rushed her account of the flight, *Twenty Hours Forty Minutes* (1928), into print. The book is part autobiography, part journal of the flight, and part advocacy of flying in general. It is the third part that is most interesting because of her observations on the future of flying and on the role of women in aviation.

After stating that the remarkable thing about flying is that it is not remarkable, Earhart goes on to discuss the need for more attractive airports, a review of safety regulations, and better weather reporting. Women will have a role to play in all these areas, she asserts, because they have already had a major impact on the automobile industry. The airplane will be used for leisure and recreation, and the growing purchasing power of American women will help to shape the airline industry. Earhart concludes her book with a characteristically honest assessment of the ways in which her life has been changed by her sudden fame.

For the remainder of her life, Earhart campaigned tirelessly for the cause of women in flying. She participated in many cross-country air races, flew an autogyro (a forerunner of the helicopter), and was one of the founders of an organization of licensed women pilots, the Ninety-nine Club. In 1932, she was elected a member of the Society of Women Geographers. She also wrote a column on aviation for *Cosmopolitan* magazine. Her advice was sought by many airlines and airplane manufacturers, and she became a model for young women throughout the country.

In 1931, she married Putnam, who had been managing her career. Her second book, *The Fun of It*, was published in 1932. In it Earhart adds details about her childhood and further explains her attraction to flying, especially to unusual aerial maneuvers known as "stunting."

> I had fun trying to do [stunts] . . . so much so, in fact, I have sometimes thought that transport companies would do well to have a "recreation airplane" for their pilots who don't have a chance to play in the big transports or while on duty. If a little stunt ship were available, the men could go up 5000 feet, and "turn it inside out" to relieve the monotony of hours of straight flying.

Her assurance that flying was safe and fun and her example as the first woman to fly the Atlantic alone increased her popularity with the public. Earhart's solo flight from Harbor Grace, Newfoundland, to Culmore, Ireland, May 21-22, 1932, won for her the Distinguished Flying Cross from the Congress of the United States, an award from the French Legion of Honor, and a medal from the National Geographic Society.

In 1935, she became the first person to fly alone from Hawaii to California and the first to fly nonstop from Mexico City to Newark, New Jersey. The trustees of Purdue University purchased a twin-engine Lockheed Electra for her, and she began to plan a round-the-world flight. After several false starts and minor accidents, Earhart and her navigator, Fred Noonan, took off from Miami, Florida, on June 1, 1937. A month of flying brought them across the Atlantic, Africa, and southern Asia to Lae, New Guinea. She and Noonan took off July 2, intending to land and refuel on tiny Howland Island in the middle of the Pacific Ocean. Several hours later, the Coast Guard cutter *Itasca*, anchored off Howland Island, heard a radio message from Earhart that she was lost and running low on fuel. Neither the plane nor its pilot and navigator were ever found.

Because the Japanese claimed many of the islands in the mid-Pacific, rumors grew that Earhart and Noonan had crashed on a Japanese-held island and been captured and killed. After World War II, attempts were made to find the wreckage and confirm the rumors, but no convincing evidence has come to light.

Summary

Earhart was one of the most appealing heroes in an age of American hero worship. Like Charles Lindbergh and Richard Byrd, Amelia Earhart pioneered air travel by establishing flying records and opening new routes. Like Babe Didrikson the athlete and Louise Arner Boyd the Arctic explorer, Earhart showed that women had a place in fields that were generally restricted to men.

Although she was criticized during her life for using her fame for profit—at various times she promoted Lucky Strike cigarettes, luggage, and sports clothes—Earhart remained essentially a private person. Because her parents believed that girls should have the same opportunities as boys, she was able to learn to fly. Because she believed that she should help others by sharing her experiences, she maintained a hectic schedule of flying and lecturing.

Once she had been given the opportunity to be the first woman to fly across the Atlantic, Earhart dedicated herself to flying. She was able to combine pleasure with business, and she worked hard at both. Success brought her into contact with other notable women from Eleanor Roosevelt to film star Mary Pickford. Earhart was also a celebrity, and her untimely death at the age of thirty-nine enshrined her in the hearts of her generation.

Amelia Earhart was a product of the social changes in the United States between the world wars. In many ways she epitomized her generation's desire to break with the past and to create a better world. She captured something of that spirit in one of her poems, which begins:

> Courage is the price that life exacts for granting peace.
> The soul that knows it not, knows no release
> From little things;

> Knows not the livid loneliness of fear
> Nor mountain heights, where bitter joy can hear
> The sound of wings.

Bibliography
Backus, Jean L. *Letters from Amelia: 1901-1937*. Boston: Beacon Press, 1982. A candid biography with quotations from letters to family members and friends. Backus was a friend of Amelia's mother and the owner of the house in Berkeley, California, where Mrs. Earhart lived in 1949. The book supplements the biographies by Amelia's sister, Muriel Earhart Morrissey, and her husband, George P. Putnam.
Earhart, Amelia. *The Fun of It: Random Records of My Own Flying and of Women in Aviation*. New York: Harcourt Brace and Co., 1932. Reprint. Detroit, Mich.: Gale Research Co., 1975. The most complete autobiographical account of Earhart's life and the most interesting of her books. Earhart depicts herself as a tomboy who loved books.
_____. *Last Flight*. New York: Harcourt Brace and Co., 1937.

Reprint. Detroit, Mich.: Gale Research Co., 1975. Her last writings, compiled and annotated by her husband.

──────────. *Twenty Hours Forty Minutes*. New York: G. P. Putnam's Sons, 1928. Reprint. New York: Arno Press, 1980. Her first book, hastily written after her Atlantic flight, June 17-18, 1928. Interesting details from her log kept during the flight.

Loomis, Vincent V. *Amelia Earhart: The Final Story*. New York: Random House, 1985. An attempt to prove that Earhart and Noonan survived the crash of the Electra in 1937. Loomis was a pilot in the South Pacific during World War II and adds many interesting technical details about Earhart's round-the-world flight, but his evidence for Earhart's capture and death in a Japanese prison camp is circumstantial.

Morrissey, Muriel Earhart. *Courage Is the Price*. Wichita, Kans.: McCormick-Armstrong, 1963. A brief biography by Earhart's younger sister.

Pellegreno, Ann Holtgren. *World Flight: The Earhart Trail*. Ames: Iowa State University Press, 1971. The story of the author's successful completion in 1967, using a reconstructed Lockheed Electra, of Earhart's attempted round-the-world flight. Good technical details and a discussion of the mystery of Earhart's disappearance.

Putnam, George Palmer. *Soaring Wings*. New York: Harcourt Brace and Co., 1939. A biography by Earhart's husband. It is good on her attitude toward marriage and women in aviation and business.

Bernard Mergen

GEORGE EASTMAN

Born: July 12, 1854; Waterville, New York
Died: March 14, 1932; Rochester, New York
Areas of Achievement: Photography, invention, business, and philanthropy
Contribution: Through his introduction of his simple-to-operate roll-film Kodak camera, Eastman made photograph-making accessible to virtually all people. He built the Eastman Kodak Company into the world's largest photographic manufacturing establishment by dominating world markets and by pioneering in organized industrial research and development.

Early Life
George Eastman was born in the small, upstate New York town of Waterville. Both his maternal and his paternal ancestors had arrived from England to settle in New England in the 1630's. From the 1840's, his father, George W. Eastman, operated a commercial business college in Rochester, New York, and commuted to the family home in Waterville; his mother, Maria Kilbourn, cared for her young son and two older daughters. When George was six years old the family removed to Rochester, and in 1862 his father died. Maria Kilbourn Eastman, a devout Episcopalian, had to support her family by taking in boarders. George sought to assist as he could. After seven or eight years of private and public education, George left school at the age of fourteen to work first in an insurance office and later as a bookkeeper in a bank.

During his formative years, Eastman enjoyed working with tools, kept detailed accounts of his income and expenditures, carefully saved money, and revealed increasing interest in photography as a hobby. By the late 1870's he began to investigate the new gelatin emulsion dry plates that allowed factory production of photographic plates, unlike the traditional awkward, costly, and time-consuming production of photosensitive plates by each photographer at the site and at the time of taking the photograph. Gelatin emulsions were to simplify and revolutionize the practice of photography in the 1880's, and Eastman, as a serious amateur, came to photography with this new perspective.

The short, trim Eastman was austere and shy in personal relations and no doubt incorporated values and sought to convey a demeanor that was fostered both within a home where his father had operated a business college and in the banking community where he worked. He also already displayed what was to be this bachelor's lifelong devotion to his mother and to her memory.

Life's Work
The young Eastman brought to photographic production a combination of

strong interest in technology and science, a deep commitment to business values (especially the role of impersonal market forces), great personal ambition, and a deep-seated need to be independent and in control of his environment. He entered upon commercial production of photographic plates about 1880, while still employed at the bank. He entered with a strategy, perhaps encouraged by his good friend, the Rochester patent attorney and inventor George Selden. Eastman invented and patented a plate-coating machine. He sought to raise capital for his American enterprise by selling rights for its use in Great Britain. While he did not succeed in raising capital in this way, it is clear that from the beginning he pursued sophisticated technical-marketing-financial plans.

In 1881, Henry Strong, an older gentleman with a successful buggy whip factory, joined in partnership with Eastman in the dry plate business. While the company was initially successful, it soon became clear that Eastman had no particular marketing advantage and that prospects for growth were dim. In 1884, William Hall Walker, a local camera maker, joined Eastman and Strong and a small number of other local investors in forming a company to pursue not only production of dry plates but also development of a new film system of photography. Walker and Eastman invented a commercial paper-film system, but it did not attract extensive usage by professional photographers—the principal photographers of the day.

In 1887, Eastman reconceived the market for the tightly patented system: amateurs rather than professionals. By making the camera very simple to use and by providing factory service for developing and printing the photographs, Eastman made it possible for the average person to pursue photography for the first time. The simple camera was named the "Kodak" (a word created by Eastman, who used the letter "k" twice in honor of the "k" in Kilbourn, his mother's maiden name) and was first marketed in mid-1888. Eastman and his emulsion-maker, Henry M. Reichenbach, soon developed thin celluloid film to replace the paper film that was used at first.

Employing the slogan, "You press the button, we do the rest," the Kodak camera system of film photography transformed photography and the industry. Having an international perspective from the beginning, Eastman successfully marketed film photography to the world. By the mid-1890's, the success of the product attracted many imitators and Eastman's patent strategy began to falter. At that time he employed people to work full-time, constantly making improvements in cameras and film so that every year the company would have improved products—an additional strategy to place the company ahead of the competition and therefore capable of dominating the market. Over the years, the Eastman Kodak combination of high-quality and reliable film and a continuing stream of improved cameras made the Kodak trademark of enormous value.

By the turn of the century, Eastman sought to control not only film photography but plate cameras, photographic print papers, and motion-picture film as well. Like many American and European entrepreneurs of that era, he began to buy out competing companies and to acquire exclusive control of key materials or technical processes. These tactics, along with the company's strategy of continuous product innovation, soon made Eastman Kodak the overwhelmingly dominant photographic company in American and also in many markets worldwide.

Three challenges soon faced Eastman as he ran his company: antitrust action from the government, concern that some other company might develop a commercially successful color film, and concern that other companies might attract key employees from Eastman Kodak and thereby gain valuable trade secrets. During the 1910's and early 1920's, Eastman and his attorneys fought the antitrust issue—especially trying to defend Eastman's earlier acquisition of competing dry plate, camera, and photographic paper companies. Eastman finally sold some of these companies as part of a consent decree.

Eastman's concern that some European company or inventor would develop an important color process preoccupied him throughout the 1910's. He had full-time people in Europe whose primary responsibility was to seek out such possibilities. When, in 1911, during a tour of European facilities, he visited a German chemical company with a large research laboratory and an officer of the company asked Eastman about his laboratory, Eastman was embarrassed to admit that he did not have one. Within days of this event, he began planning such a facility and finding a suitable director for it. In 1912, the Eastman Kodak research laboratory was established with C. E. Kenneth Mees as director. The laboratory was charged with the responsibility for the future of photographic science and technology at Kodak. The laboratory was the culmination of Eastman's career-long strategy of seeking to maintain Eastman Kodak control of the market through dominance of photographic technology. It also met the need to pursue color photography and to give George Eastman something further to boast about.

Eastman also addressed the potential loss of employees by introducing a number of highly innovative employee benefit programs. Early in the 1910's he established a profit-sharing program for employees, and during the next decade he pioneered many other benefit programs—to many of which he personally contributed. These benefit programs also developed at a time that he began an active but low-profile philanthropic program. During the 1910's and 1920's, he donated more than $100 million dollars to educational, medical, and civic organizations. Especially notable were his contributions to the Massachusetts Institute of Technology, the University of Rochester, and the Hampton and Tuskegee institutes. The Eastman School of Music, which is a part of the University of Rochester, is one of the few organizations to which he contributed that carries his name.

Summary

From the turn of the century, Eastman's personal education and interest in music and art grew. An Anglophile, he actively supported American involvement in World War I. He also promoted progressive municipal reforms—largely based on arguments of efficiency. Not a member of an established church, not a highly sociable person, not involved deeply in national politics (he was a Republican) and business circles, he devoted himself largely to his company, his city, and his philanthropies. Despite a certain isolation and insularity, he participated in international movements that created large-scale business corporations, wedded science and technology to many of them through institutionalized research and development, and sought to create a new relationship between employee and employer. He built his life and his company on independence and control. At the age of seventy-eight, as his body and mind began to fail him, he took his own life, leaving a simple note: "My work is done."

Bibliography

Ackerman, Carl W. *George Eastman*. London: Constable and Co., 1930. This book-length biography quotes extensively from Eastman's correspondence, tells a good heroic story, details his philanthropy, but is not very critical or analytical. Eastman himself is reputed to have helped to edit this authorized biography.

Chandler, Alfred D., Jr. *The Visible Hand: The Managerial Revolution in American Business*. Cambridge, Mass.: Harvard University Press, 1977. This major study of the history of American business emphasizes the changing economic environment and the changing role of corporate managers as large-scale enterprise emerged in the latter part of the nineteenth century and the early twentieth century. It provides an excellent context for understanding Eastman's business career.

Coe, Brian. *The Birth of Photography: The Story of the Formative Years, 1800-1900*. New York: Taplinger Publishing Co., 1977. This popular history of early photography includes discussion of Eastman's influence. Many striking photographs in the book highlight the changes in photography from 1840 to 1900.

Eastman, George. *Chronicles of an African Trip*. Rochester, N.Y.: Privately printed, 1927. Consisting of letters written by Eastman and photographs taken by him and his traveling companions, this book provides an intimate view of Eastman "at leisure" at age seventy-two, during his African safari in the spring and summer of 1926.

Jenkins, Reese V. "George Eastman and the Coming of Industrial Research in America." In *Technology in America: A History of Individuals and Ideas*, edited by Carroll W. Pursell, Jr., 129-141. Cambridge, Mass.: MIT Press, 1981. This brief essay describes Eastman's approach to research and development and how his technical strategy changed as his company grew. It describes the establishment of the Eastman Kodak research laboratory and the cultural context out of which this institution emerged.

_____. *Images and Enterprise: Technology and the American Photographic Industry, 1839-1925*. Baltimore: Johns Hopkins University Press, 1975. This detailed history of the entire American photographic industry provides both an analytical account of Eastman's business career and the context within which it occurred. Emphasizing business and economic aspects, it does not place Eastman or his photographic developments in a larger social and cultural context.

_____. "Technology and the Market: George Eastman and the Origins of Mass Amateur Photography." *Technology and Culture* 16 (January, 1975): 1-19. This brief but detailed account of the invention and introduction of the Kodak camera during the late 1880's emphasizes technological, economic, and business considerations and argues that Eastman's technical innovations created amateur photography as it is known today.

Johnson, Osa. *I Married Adventure: The Lives and Adventures of Martin and Osa Johnson*. Philadelphia: J. B. Lippincott Co., 1940. This popular story includes significant testimony and photographs of George Eastman as he hunted and photographed wild game with the Johnsons in Africa in the mid-1920's. It gives a good glimpse of Eastman in his early retirement years.

Newhall, Beaumont. *The History of Photography from 1839 to the Present*. New York: Museum of Modern Art, 1982. This outstanding general history of photography provides an excellent art-historical perspective but underemphasizes the technical, economic, and social dimensions. Having been frequently revised, this book is well written and handsomely illustrated.

Reese V. Jenkins

MARY BAKER EDDY

Born: July 16, 1821; Bow township, New Hampshire
Died: December 3, 1910; Chestnut Hill, Massachusetts
Area of Achievement: Religion
Contribution: Eddy founded the Church of Christ, Scientist.

Early Life

Mary Baker Eddy was born Mary Morse Baker on July 16, 1821, in Bow township, New Hampshire. Her father, Mark Baker, was a farmer. Mary Baker was a sickly child and attended school irregularly. As a young girl she began writing poetry, a habit which continued throughout her life.

Mary Baker's parents were Congregationalists and at a young age she joined their church. She rebelled, however, against her father's stern Calvinism, preferring to think of God as loving and kind, like her mother, Abigail.

In December, 1843, Mary Baker married George Washington Glover, a builder from New England who was then living in the South. She traveled with him to Charleston, South Carolina, and then to Wilmington, North Carolina. In June, 1844, Glover died of yellow fever. Mary, a widow after six months of marriage, returned to her parents in New Hampshire. In September her son, George Washington Glover II, was born.

After the birth of her son, Mary was in ill health for years, suffering from dyspepsia and nervous ailments. The doctors she went to could not relieve her. She lived as a dependent in her parents' home and was unable at times to care for her son. In November, 1849, her mother died. When her father remarried in December, 1850, Mary moved in with her sister's family. Shortly thereafter, her son went to live with his old nurse and her husband in another town.

Mary's periods of illness worsened. To make her feel better her family devised rockers and swings and sometimes hired neighbor boys to push the swings for hours on end. Despite her ill health, she remained a pretty woman, slender, with curly brown hair and blue-gray eyes. When she felt well, she could be a vivacious conversationalist.

In June, 1853, Mary married Dr. Daniel Patterson, a dentist. She later insisted that her primary motivation in marrying Dr. Patterson was to reestablish a home and reclaim her son. This aim failed; in 1856, George moved west with his foster parents. His mother did not see him again until 1879. Her marriage to Dr. Patterson was not a success. As a dentist, he traveled from town to town, leaving his wife at home; her illnesses grew more severe.

In 1862, Dr. Patterson, on a mission to help Union sympathizers in the South, was captured by Confederate forces and imprisoned. His wife, preoccupied with her bad health, journeyed in October, 1862, to Portland, Maine, to visit Phineas P. Quimby, a clockmaker turned doctor who healed by mental application. Quimby healed Mary, and her life was changed.

Quimby had been a hypnotist and a "magnetic doctor." In 1862, he was treating patients with mental healing. He influenced Mary's development of Christian Science, and was also the source of other "mind cure" therapies. Mary was enthusiastic about Quimby's teachings; yet she looked for a spiritual, biblical reason for his cures.

When Quimby died in January, 1866, Mary was living with her husband in Lynn, Massachusetts. In February, she was injured in a fall on ice. She cured her own injuries, she believed, through the power of God.

Life's Work

Mary's life for the next decade looked exceedingly bleak to the outside world. Her husband deserted her and they were divorced in 1873. She lived for years in boardinghouses in various New England towns before settling in 1875 at 8 Bond Street, Lynn. Yet these years of poverty were immensely productive for her, for during this time she worked out her theories and theology of healing and began to teach. From 1872 to 1874, she labored on her book, published in October, 1875, as *Science and Health*. In 1877, she married Asa Gilbert Eddy and assumed the name under which she would become famous, Mary Baker Eddy.

Eddy's *Science and Health* served as a textbook for her classes and as part of the scriptures for the Church of Christ, Scientist, founded in 1879. *Science and Health* was to go through many editions and to be polished repeatedly by Eddy and her editors. It became the core of Christian Science theology.

Eddy contended that matter was nonexistent and that disease was also unreal, a false belief held by the sufferer. Christian Science practitioners were taught that they could heal by calling on divine power.

Eddy's following grew in the 1870's. In 1876, the Christian Science Association was formed, and in 1879 the Church of Christ, Scientist, was chartered. Eddy moved her headquarters to Boston in 1882.

During the 1880's, Eddy, already in her sixties, spent her time working for the growth of Christian Science, teaching classes and writing. Her fame spread and her congregation grew. The revenues from her books began to come in; eventually she became a wealthy woman.

Throughout these years, Eddy faced opposition from conventional clergy and irate medical doctors. Disgruntled students who found her autocratic left her church to form their own healing groups. Eddy put these and all other afflictions down to "malicious animal magnetism," which, she argued, could be used to injure or even to kill. When her husband died in 1882, she insisted that her enemies had used such powers to kill him.

In 1889, concerned that the growing church she had founded would slip from her control, she dissolved the church's institutional forms and left Boston for Concord, New Hampshire. For three years she worked on revisions of *Science and Health* and on the reorganization of her church. In 1892, she completed her reorganization, founding The Mother Church in Boston and structuring the church government so as to be under her sole control. She was then past seventy years old.

In her later years, Eddy became increasingly reclusive and only rarely emerged from her home in Concord. At the same time, her world reputation grew so that even critics such as Mark Twain referred to her as the most famous woman of her time. Her followers came close to deifying her; her critics referred to her as a pope in petticoats.

Her last years were troubled by lawsuits fomented by sensation-seeking newspapers on behalf of her relatives, who feared that she had lost control of her considerable fortune. The lawsuits were unsuccessful. Despite these troubles, Eddy lived to see her church grow to eighty-five thousand members by 1906. She died on December 3, 1910, at the age of eighty-nine.

Summary

Eddy was the foremost of a number of Americans in the nineteenth century to explore the possibilities of mental healing. Historians have argued that the mind cure movement's strength in New England was rooted in a rebellion against the Calvinist image of God as stern, all-powerful sovereign. While this rebellion took many forms, few were as successful, or as controversial, as that led by Mary Baker Eddy.

Eddy's insistence that God, the Father-Mother, was All, that matter did not really exist, and that disease and illness could be cured through this realization drew public attention and, in some cases, public ire. By the end of her long life, she was very famous, the subject of both reverence and derision. It was, and is, possible to interpret her life in different ways. To some members of her church, she was a saint, the bearer of a new revelation, an addition to the inspired word of God. To others, such as the cynical Mark Twain, she was a money-grubbing, dictatorial woman who wrote poorly besides. Her supporters saw her as a courageous figure who won health and power after years of illness, poverty, and heartbreak. Her detractors believed that her illness was largely psychosomatic, and that she was deeply disturbed, even paranoid.

Whether Eddy is seen as saint or charlatan, her accomplishments remain monumental. She founded a religion, providing scriptures and a unique theology. She was at once a mystic and a brilliant administrator. Her monument, the Church of Christ, Scientist, still stands and has outposts all over the world.

Bibliography

Dakin, Edwin Franden. *Mrs. Eddy: The Biography of a Virginal Mind*. New

York: Charles Scribner's Sons, 1929. This popular biography offers an extremely critical look at Eddy's life. While acknowledging Eddy's accomplishments, Dakin labels her neurotic, grasping, and paranoid. Includes a bibliography which lists her works and a number of contemporary articles about her.

Gottschalk, Stephen. *The Emergence of Christian Science in American Religious Life*. Berkeley: University of California Press, 1973. This scholarly work puts Eddy's theology into the context of the American religious tradition. Documents the reaction of conventional American Protestants, Catholics, and Jews to the emergence of Christian Science, and explains how her theology differed from theirs.

Meyer, Donald. *The Positive Thinkers: A Study of the American Quest for Health, Wealth and Personal Power from Mary Baker Eddy to Norman Vincent Peale*. Garden City, N.Y.: Doubleday and Co., 1965. The title sums up the book. Eddy is one of a number of positive thinkers examined.

Peel, Robert. *Mary Baker Eddy*. 3 vols. New York: Holt, Rinehart and Winston, 1966, 1971, 1977. This massive, scholarly trilogy is the accepted authoritative work on the life of Eddy. Peel, a professional historian and a Christian Scientist, provides a balanced yet sympathetic account of her life.

Twain, Mark. *Christian Science*. New York: Harper and Brothers, 1907. Twain's famous attack on Eddy and her church; not one of his best works, yet it illustrates some of the impact her doctrines had on the popular mind.

Jeanette Keith

THOMAS ALVA EDISON

Born: February 11, 1847; Milan, Ohio
Died: October 18, 1931; West Orange, New Jersey
Area of Achievement: Invention
Contribution: With his successful incandescent electric lighting system, Edison transformed the world of American electrical technology. With his myriad other inventions, including a stock ticker, duplex and quadraplex telegraph, phonograph, telephone transmitter, motion-picture camera, and storage battery, he symbolized the ingenious, prolific, heroic, and professional American inventor in an age of invention, innovation, and industrialization.

Early Life

Thomas Alva Edison grew up in America's Midwestern industrial heartland during this country's transformation from an agrarian to an industrial nation. Born in Milan, Ohio, on February 11, 1847, the seventh and last child of Samuel and Nancy (née Elliot) Edison, Edison was reared in Port Huron, Michigan, near Detroit. He found formal schooling disagreeable, so his mother, a former teacher, tutored young Tom at home. Gifted with a natural inquisitiveness, a love of science and experimentation, and access to the Detroit Free Library, he largely educated himself.

As a teenager, Edison worked, first selling newspapers and candy on the train between Port Huron and Detroit, and later as a telegraph operator in the Midwest. In both jobs he managed to find time to perform various chemical and electrical experiments and to continue his lifetime reading habit. By 1868, he had moved to Boston, where he came under the intellectual influence so strong in that city at the time. There his reading of Michael Faraday's work on electricity, with its heavy emphasis on experimentation and conceptualization of physical models, strengthened his own strong preference for applied science with its testing of hypotheses, its pragmatic approach to problems, and its interest in practical application. Inventing for profit became a goal for Edison as he directed his genius toward the industrial and economic climate of post–Civil War America.

Seeking fame and fortune, Edison moved to New York City in 1869, having neither a job nor money. A combination of luck and acumen at the Law's Gold Indicator Company resulted in his appointment as plant superintendent. Edison's working in Wall Street during an age of enterprise provided him with the basis for his first commercially successful invention, an improved stock ticker. His additional improvements of stock ticker technology brought Edison forty thousand dollars for his patent rights, a princely sum in 1870. With a small fortune and some fame, Edison turned to electrical technology, an arena which consumed much of his life's work.

Life's Work

Like so many of his fellow pioneers in the world of electrical invention, Edison was well versed in telegraphy. His many years as a first-rate telegraph operator, his familiarity with electrical devices and experiments, and his vision of an industrial, urban America directed his various endeavors. In the period from 1872 to 1874, he turned his attention to duplex and quadruplex telegraphy, the process of sending two or four simultaneous signals, respectively, over a single wire. His commercial success with these two processes led him to improvements with the telephone, itself a special type of telegraph.

In 1876, Edison sought and found a more efficient transmitter for the telephone. His carbon button device in the mouthpiece provided a stronger signal which would travel farther on transmission lines. With this success, he demonstrated his legendary ability to improve existing inventions. In this same year, he moved to Menlo Park, New Jersey, and established a research and development laboratory complete with support personnel and several workshops. Edison realized the central role of systematic inquiry for new enterprises, and Menlo Park became the prototype for the industrial research laboratories which have been so important for innovation in a technological society.

The phonograph was another Edison invention with its origins in telegraphy. The embossed paper tape which recorded the dots and dashes of telegraph messages gave off a musical sound when Edison moved the tape quickly through a repeater mechanism. From this stimulus he devised a tinfoil-covered cylinder which would record vibrations of sound entered through a recording diaphragm. A quickly conceived idea became a patented reality in 1877, although the phonograph required substantial modification before it became a commercial success. Edison's ability to invent a "talking machine" enhanced his reputation as a genius. His most prolific years of work on the phonograph came in the period 1887-1890, when he developed the wax-coated flat record and separate recording and playback components.

Success with the early phonograph led Edison to another challenge in the world of electricity: an incandescent electric lighting system. From 1878 to 1882, he and his Menlo Park staff devoted much of their time to the invention and innovation of a system which would subdivide the electric arc light. In this task, Edison was an entrepreneur as well as a pioneer developer of a new technology. He used the full resources of the Menlo Park laboratory and workshops to attack the problems of incandescent lighting and to seek commercially successful solutions to those problems, which required many painstaking hours of research and development; he relied on the best talent in Menlo Park, the scientific method of inquiry, and the systematic empirical approach to problem-solving.

When Edison began his quest to provide a workable lighting system, he built on an awareness of arc lighting developments and on the achievements of other inventors seeking an incandescent system. He realized that he needed a high resistance lamp filament which would burn for several hours, an efficient generator, a distribution network with wires, switches, meters and fuses, and a central power station. A heavy reliance on a skilled and knowledgeable staff provided the successful lighting elements: a carbonized cotton filament, the "long legged Mary Ann" generator, and the prototype Pearl Street central station. He set his sights on the market place, used the familiar terminology and methods of gas illumination in his system, and displayed his entrepreneurial talents by promoting his own system, a promotion helped greatly by his reputation as an inventive genius (a reputation which Edison made no attempt to dispel). So successful was he in this enterprise that to generations of Americans, Thomas Edison was *the* inventor of the electric light.

Although Edison's business acumen was greater than most people believed, his chief interest was not the ledger book, and he soon tired of the business of electric lighting and turned to other areas of invention. By 1892, the Edison General Electric companies became part of a larger conglomerate known simply as the General Electric Company. With his name no longer associated with the operation, Edison lost interest in electric lighting developments and sold his stock in General Electric. He now had millions of dollars to use for new inventive challenges.

By 1887, Edison had moved his laboratories to West Orange, New Jersey, in a more extensive physical plant. With this move, he could engage in large-scale invention and innovation, as he did in the 1880's and 1890's with two major projects: the motion picture camera and a magnetic ore separation process. The former was a commercial success; the latter was an economic disaster.

Although he began his work on the motion picture camera in 1887, Edison performed most of the developmental work on it in the years from 1889 to 1891. His invention of a camera that took a series of still photographs in rapid succession resulted from mechanical insight rather than any electrical or chemical knowledge which was so important in almost all of his other inventions. That he could successfully devise a practical motion picture camera through the strength of his mechanical ability attests his inventive talent.

From 1894 to 1899, Thomas Edison devoted his attention to another chiefly nonelectrical project: magnetic ore separation. Sensing that a market for low-grade Eastern iron ore existed if it could be extracted cheaply, he invested several years and millions of dollars in creating huge ore-crushing machines. These machines would pulverize the ore deposits and the resulting powder would pass by electromagnets which separated the ore from the dross. Although a technical success, the process never could compete with the low-cost ores of the Mesabi range; Edison found himself deeply in debt by 1900 and finally abandoned the scheme.

At the turn of the century, Edison returned to electrical technology with his invention of a durable storage battery. From 1899 to 1909, he and his West Orange technical staff developed an alkaline-iron-nickel storage battery as an improvement over the widely used lead-acid battery. Edison envisioned this lighter, more durable battery for use in the growing automobile industry, especially in electric cars. By the time Edison had a commercially successful battery available in 1909, however, electric cars had lost favor with the public, which preferred the internal combustion vehicles being promoted by men such as Henry Ford. The Edison battery proved unreliable for intermittent automobile uses, was ineffective in cold temperatures, and never replaced the lead-acid storage battery in motor car applications. Edison's battery did find successful use in marine and railroad applications which required a durable, long-lived battery.

The storage battery was Edison's last major invention. In 1914, a fire destroyed most of the West Orange laboratories; World War I diverted his attention as he served as chairman of the Naval Consulting Board to direct the nation's inventive talent into the war effort. As he grew older, Edison spent the winter months at his home in Fort Myers, Florida, and established a modest laboratory there. In 1927, he began work trying to create artificial rubber but did not complete that endeavor. His fertile mind was active until his death at West Orange, New Jersey, on October 18, 1931.

Summary

With the death of Thomas Alva Edison, America lost a legendary and heroic inventor. The example of his life and personality—simplicity, pragmatism, hard work, self-education, linked to inventive genius—appealed to the egalitarian spirit of Americans in an age of enterprise. Edison was a self-made man whose mental capacity, ambition, and dedication brought him success in the tradition of the American spirit of private enterprise. In an age of invention and industrialism, he stood as a symbol of the modern spirit in the United States with his contributions of electrical inventions and innovations: duplex and quadraplex telegraphy, incandescent lighting, telephone transmitter, phonograph, motion picture camera, and storage battery. These contributions alone guarantee his place among great Americans.

Yet, Thomas Edison the heroic inventor is as much myth as reality. His strong determination to conquer a problem or task and his ability to work long hours in his laboratory are characteristic of the lone inventor, but Edison was much more complex than might be suggested by the familiar image of the simple genius at work alone. He was among America's foremost professional inventors. His success was a result in large measure of his prescience about changes in an urban, industrial America and the need for new technological systems to serve that new society. Edison's technique matched his vision; he excelled at improving on existing designs, assessing the commercial potential of a device. He also relied heavily on a systematic and rational approach to invention and innovation and on a highly trained staff, as his Menlo Park and West Orange laboratory complexes attest. Edison's early use of the industrial research laboratory provided a model for American industry in the twentieth century. Further, Edison's talent for understanding complex processes, for seeing the need for technological systems, and for focusing on practical application mark him as a highly organized professional who was a pioneer inventor-innovator and entrepreneur. Just as his image as a heroic inventor appealed to the average American of his time, so his success as a professional inventor who held nearly eleven hundred patents should appeal to students of America's technological, social, and economic history.

Bibliography

Conot, Robert. *A Streak of Luck*. New York: Seaview Books, 1979. The most recent full-scale biography of Edison; this account of Edison's personal life and technological achievements is well written, contains a useful Edison chronology, and treats Edison's successes and failures in a thorough and objective manner.

Dyer, Frank Lewis, and Thomas Commerford Martin. *Edison: His Life and Inventions*. 2 vols. New York: Harper and Brothers, 1910. The first authorized biography of Edison. Limited because it was published during Edison's lifetime. Praises Edison and lacks objectivity.

Hughes, Thomas P. *Thomas Edison: Professional Inventor*. London: Her Majesty's Stationery Office, 1976. An excellent brief treatment of Edison as professional inventor by a leading American historian of technology.

Jehl, Francis. *Menlo Park Reminiscences*. 3 vols. Detroit: Edison Institute, 1936. Although written by an Edison associate and very subjective, this is an excellent source of material on the workings of the Edison laboratories and of Edison himself. Many useful illustrations.

Jenkins, Reese V. "Elements of Style: Continuities in Edison's Thinking." In *Bridge to the Future: A Centennial Celebration of the Brooklyn Bridge*, edited by Margaret Latimer, Brooke Hindle, and Melvin Kranzberg, 149-162. New York: New York Academy of Sciences, 1984. Jenkins explores the fascinating subject of style as a factor in Edison's inventions; well worth considering.

Josephson, Matthew. *Edison: A Biography*. New York: McGraw-Hill Book Co., 1959. An excellent full-scale biography of Edison which treats his professional and personal life in detail. Contains cogent discussions of Edison's inventions, innovations, and relationships with financial figures such as Jay Gould and J. P. Morgan.

Passer, Harold C. *The Electrical Manufacturers, 1875-1900*. Cambridge, Mass.: Harvard University Press, 1953. Passer treats Edison as a pioneer inventor-entrepreneur and places his work in the context of the economic changes of late nineteenth century America. An excellent and often-cited work.

Harry J. Eisenman

JONATHAN EDWARDS

Born: October 5, 1703; East Windsor, Connecticut
Died: March 22, 1758; Princeton, New Jersey
Area of Achievement: Theology
Contribution: The greatest Puritan theologian in America, Edwards tried to establish an intellectual foundation for Puritanism, to find a rational interpretation of predestination, and to justify the ways of God to man.

Early Life

Jonathan Edwards was born in East Windsor, Connecticut, on October 5, 1703. Sited on the Connecticut River, East Windsor was still frontier, where worshipers carried muskets to church. Edwards was the only boy among ten sisters, but there were seven boy cousins living next door and a number of boys attending school under Edwards' father, the Reverend Timothy Edwards. Educated by his father, Edwards was a precocious boy who was ready for college at the age of thirteen. When he was eleven, he wrote a paper on flying spiders that is remarkable for both its scientific observation and its literary skill. As a teenager, Edwards was already dedicated to religion as his unquestioned calling. Sober and meditative by temperament, he had a private place of prayer deep in the woods.

In 1716, he entered Yale College, founded only fifteen years earlier, with a freshman class of ten. At this time Edwards experienced an intense religious struggle, which he later described in his "Personal Narrative"; in particular, he had been "full of objections against the doctrine of God's sovereignty, in choosing whom he would to eternal life, and rejecting whom he pleased; leaving them eternally to perish, and be everlastingly tormented in hell." This doctrine appeared horrible to him, but somehow he managed to accept it and to delight in God's absolute sovereignty. After graduating from Yale at seventeen, in 1720, Edwards studied theology for two years in New Haven, after which he served for a year and a half as pastor to a Presbyterian church in New York City. For the next two years, Edwards was a tutor at Yale. On February 22, 1726, he was ordained at Northampton, Massachusetts, as assistant minister to his eighty-four-year-old grandfather, Solomon Stoddard. About twenty-five miles north of East Windsor, on the Connecticut River, Northampton was then an isolated frontier village, cut off by forests from the wider world. In July of 1727, Edwards married Sarah Pierrepont, the daughter of a founder of Yale. Edwards was then twenty-three, his bride seventeen. She was apparently the ideal wife for him, a capable manager, a devoted mother to their surviving three sons and seven daughters, a deeply religious person able to share her husband's spiritual life. When the famous evangelist George Whitefield visited the Edwards family in 1740, he was so impressed with Mrs. Edwards that he wished he could marry someone like her. When Solomon Stoddard died in 1729, Edwards, at twenty-six, became the minister of the chief parish of western Massachusetts.

Life's Work

Coming of age when the Puritan oligarchy had crumbled and when Puritan theology was being challenged by Deism and by more liberal Christian denominations, Edwards tried to create a philosophical justification for Calvinist dogma. Calvinism can be summed up in the acronym TULIP: total depravity, unconditional election, limited atonement, irresistible grace, and perseverance of the saints. First proclaimed in John Calvin's *Institutes of the Christian Religion* (1536), these doctrines had been the backbone of Puritanism. The most thorny of them were the ideas that humanity is not merely in a state of Original Sin (which is not total and is balanced by human goodness) but is totally depraved; everyone deserves damnation, and most will receive it; only a limited few will be saved by God's inscrutable mercy. Along with this doctrine is the idea of predestination; there is no free will, and every detail of each individual's life is predetermined by God, including salvation and damnation, which are ordained before birth, so that no amount of good works can merit salvation for one who is not among the elect.

Calvin offered no proof of these grim doctrines; he merely maintained that God's majesty is so great that humanity is nothing beside it. By Edwards' time, the Puritans had lost their monopoly on the northern colonies; other denominations preached a more merciful creed, according to which salvation was available (though not guaranteed) for everyone, while Deism threw out Christianity altogether, denying miracles, original sin, the incarnation and resurrection, and proclaiming that "whatever is is right."

Edwards has been maligned as the quintessential "hell-fire and brimstone" preacher, chiefly because of a sermon entitled "Sinners in the Hands of an Angry God," which he gave at Enfield, Connecticut, on July 8, 1741. In it he dramatized the concept of total depravity, arguing that everyone deserves to be cast into Hell, so that divine justice never stands in the way, for sinners are already under a sentence of condemnation and only God's restraints keep them out of Hell. Yet people cannot count on those restraints, for "the God that holds you over the pit of hell, much as one holds a spider, or some loathsome insect over the fire, abhors you, and is dreadfully provoked." The flaming mouth of Hell gapes wide, "the bow of God's wrath is bent," the wrath of God is like great waters damned but ready to be released. Edwards piles up more metaphors for God's wrath but then urges his congregation to repent so that they may receive divine mercy.

Indeed, it is that mercy which Edwards stressed in most of his work. In his entire career, he gave only two sermons on hellfire, the other being "The Justice of God in the Damnation of Sinners" (1734). Edwards was no ranter; he was slender and shy, with a thin, weak voice; he spoke his sermons with quiet intensity. What made them eloquent was his immense preparation, his ability to paint pictures that made the abstract visible in terms of familiar experience, and the sense of authority that made him seem merely the mouthpiece for God. He was not a fiery preacher, nor was he an ecclesiastical scold giving lurid exposés of community sins and laying down blue laws.

The problem that Edwards tried to cope with was that of reconciling a loving and merciful God with a God who predestined most of mankind to Hell before they were even born. If salvation or election is already determined, why should individuals strive for salvation, when they have no free will? Why should ministers call sinners to repentance?

Nevertheless, Edwards tried, stressing "the excellency of Christ," and in 1734, he preached so eloquently that a revival broke out in Northampton (though he had not calculated to start one) and quickly spread to other towns. Seemingly wholesome at first, it turned to frenzied hysteria, with numerous suicides and attempted suicides. Edwards tried to tone down such bizarre behavior and "bodily manifestations," writing in *A Faithful Narrative of the Surprising Work of God* (1737) that "multitudes" felt suicide "urged upon them as if somebody had spoke to them, 'Cut your own throat. Now is a good opportunity.' "

The Northampton revival foreshadowed a much broader one, ushered in in 1740 by the visiting evangelist George Whitefield, who, unlike Edwards, was an itinerant preacher using the devices of theatrical showmanship; Lord Chesterfield said Whitefield could make people weep simply by the way he said "Mesopotamia." Following Whitefield, a revival frenzy broke out all over New England, called the Great Awakening. After its initial inspiration passed, novelty took over, with ecclesiastical juvenile delinquents trying to take over services and with zeal considered more important than knowledge, so that there was danger that fanaticism would triumph.

In response, Edwards wrote one of his major works, *A Treatise Concerning Religious Affections*, preached in 1742-1743 and published in 1746, in which he tried to distinguish between genuine and false religious experiences. Edwards said that the Church should be concerned with souls, not bodily symptoms. He did not study the bizarre details but tried to examine the laws of human nature behind such behavior. Turning to John Locke's *An Essay Concerning Human Understanding* (1690), Edwards denied innate ideas and said that all knowledge comes through sensation, whereby one apprehends those ideas that God has willed to communicate. Accordingly, the imagination conjures up things that are not present objects of sense, and here is "the devil's grand lurking place." Edwards divided the mind into the Understanding and the Will; Reason belongs to the former, and though it is important, it is not, as the Deists maintained, sufficient, for Edwards believed that true religion comes from "holy love," which is not in the Understanding but in the Will. Thus, echoing Saint Paul, Edwards wrote that "he that has doctrinal knowledge and speculation only, without affection, never is engaged in the business of religion." The man who has received a divine light does not merely notionally believe that God is glorious, but he has a sense of the gloriousness of God in his heart. Rational understanding alone is insufficient. There is, then, an essential emotional element in religion.

Edwards attempted to distinguish between the false emotionalism of revivalism, generated by mass hysteria, and a true religion whereby regenerate individuals receive a supernatural light from divine grace and are touched by the Holy Ghost, which acts within them as an indwelling vital principle. Therefore, enthusiastic delusions and bodily manifestations are merely from the imagination, not of love from and for God.

For modern readers, *Religious Affections*, which has been greatly condensed here, is likely to be the most meaningful of Edwards' works. In his day, *Freedom of Will* (1754) was thought to be his masterpiece. In it he tries to reconcile human choice with the doctrine of predestination. Briefly, his reasoning is that each act of the will depends upon a preceding act of the will, back to the original act of creation in the mind of God. Accordingly, he concluded that one is free to do what one will but not to will what one will.

In 1747, when David Brainerd, missionary to the Indians, died, Edwards edited his life and diary, producing a popular book that spurred missionary activities. Then in June of 1750, Edwards' congregation dismissed him after twenty-three years as minister. He had been too aristocratic for Northampton tastes, but the actual break came over the question of whether the unconverted should be admitted to Communion. When Edwards refused to admit those who would not acknowledge faith, he was defeated by a rigged election. Afterward, he moved to Stockbridge, Massachusetts, as missionary to the Indians. He did not consider the Indians depraved; he respected their customs, was an able administrator, and earned the friendship and trust of the Stockbridge Indians, who protected him when the French and Indian War broke out in 1754. At Stockbridge, Edwards wrote *Freedom of Will* and "The Nature of True Virtue" (1765), in which he argues that true virtue must be disinterested benevolence. Unlike his contemporary, Benjamin Franklin, a Deist who tried to make himself morally perfect by a thirteen-point program of good works, Edwards argued that true virtue comes not from repeated good choices but only from the grace of God.

In 1757, Edwards was offered the presidency of the College of New Jersey (which later became Princeton). A week after his induction on February 16, 1758, he allowed himself to be inoculated against smallpox; a month later, he died of smallpox at age fifty-four. A week later, his daughter Esther Burr also died of smallpox, and the following autumn, Mrs. Edwards died in Philadelphia. One of Edwards' grandsons, Timothy Dwight, became a poet and president of Yale; another, Aaron Burr, became vice president of the United States.

Summary

Though Perry Miller has traced a line of influence from the Puritan Edwards to the Transcendentalist Ralph Waldo Emerson, most leading nineteenth century thinkers reacted against Edwards; Herman Melville, Oliver Wendell Holmes, Leslie Stephens, and Harriet Beecher Stowe were all hostile to his Puritan doctrines, chiefly predestination, total depravity, and limited atonement. Among other things, Moby Dick (of Melville's novel of the same title, 1851) symbolizes the Puritan God of wrath and vengeance; to Captain Ahab, this God is a tyrant whose "right worship is defiance." Nathaniel Hawthorne never wrote directly about Edwards, but his somber theology and psychology may have influenced such Hawthorne tales as "The Minister's Black Veil." The twentieth century, with its horrors, has in some measure rediscovered original sin ("from whose visitations," wrote Melville, "in some shape or other, no deeply thinking mind is always and wholly free. For, in certain moods, no man can weigh this world without throwing in something, somehow like Original Sin, to strike the uneven balance"), and Edwards has had a reappraisal, though few scholars any longer accept Calvinism uncritically. In the age of the late twentieth century, with its militant Fundamentalism and biblical literalism as well as its cults and gurus, Edwards' *Religious Affections* takes on a new relevance, and though his reasoning in *Freedom of Will* may seem logic-chopping, many modern doctrines— behaviorism, Freudianism, communist dialectical materialism, to name a few—deny free will on secular but similar grounds. Edwards is now recognized not only as a writer of poetic prose but as the major philosophical and psychological thinker and writer of the Colonial era in America.

Bibliography

Cherry, C. Conrad. *The Theology of Jonathan Edwards: A Reappraisal*. Garden City, N.Y.: Doubleday Anchor Books, 1966. Sees Edwards as a major figure in American literary and intellectual history in his application of philosophy to explicate his theology.

Davidson, Edward Hutchins. *Jonathan Edwards: The Narrative of a Puritan Mind*. Cambridge, Mass.: Harvard University Press, 1968. A slim volume (161 pages) in the Riverside Studies in Literature; presents Edwards struggling against and rejecting the rationalism of the Enlightenment.

Edwards, Jonathan. *Representative Selections*. Edited by Clarence H. Faust and Thomas H. Johnson. New York: American Book Company, 1935. An anthology of the best of Edwards' work, with an in-depth introductory essay.

Elwood, Douglas J. *The Philosophical Theology of Jonathan Edwards*. New York: Columbia University Press, 1960. Explores Edwards' response to the problem of evil and his consuming awareness of God's majesty and the ecstasy of divine grace.

Fiering, Norman. *Jonathan Edwards's Moral Thought and Its British Context*. Chapel Hill: University of North Carolina Press, 1981. A study of seventeenth century moral philosophy and its influence on Edwards.

Griffin, Edward M. *Jonathan Edwards*. Minneapolis: University of Minnesota Press, 1971. A forty-page pamphlet in the University of Minnesota series on American writers; a condensed study of Edwards' life and works.

Levin, David. *Jonathan Edwards: A Profile*. New York: Hill and Wang, 1969. Contains Samuel Hopkins' book *The Life and Character of the Late Rev. Mr. Jonathan Edwards* (1765), eight articles (including a chapter each from Miller, Parkes, and Winslow) by twentieth century writers, and two poems by Robert Lowell.

McGiffert, Arthur Cushman. *Jonathan Edwards*. New York: Harper and Brothers, 1932. A portrait of Edwards as a religious psychologist.

Miller, Perry. *Jonathan Edwards*. New York: William Sloane Associates, 1949. The chief interpretive biography, by the leading scholar on American Puritanism; perhaps overstates Edwards' modernity.

Parkes, Henry Bamford. *Jonathan Edwards: The Fiery Puritan*. New York: Minton, Balch and Co., 1930. Though Parkes is an important observer of the American experience, both the title and text of his study are somewhat misleading, failing to comprehend the range and complexity of Edwards' thought, and perpetuating the caricature of the hellfire preacher.

Tracy, Patricia J. *Jonathan Edwards, Pastor*. New York: Hill and Wang, 1980. A brief biography that focuses on Edwards' pastoral role in Northampton.

Winslow, Ola Elizabeth. *Jonathan Edwards, 1703-1758*. New York: Macmillan Publishing Co., 1940. A Pulitzer Prize–winning biography; the most detailed study of Edwards' life and times.

Robert E. Morsberger

ALBERT EINSTEIN

Born: March 14, 1879; Ulm, Germany
Died: April 18, 1955; Princeton, New Jersey
Area of Achievement: Theoretical physics
Contribution: Einstein was the principal founder of modern theoretical physics; his theory of relativity fundamentally changed man's understanding of the physical world. His stature as a scientist, together with his strong humanitarian stance on major political and social issues, made him one of the outstanding men of the twentieth century.

Early Life

Albert Einstein was born on March 14, 1879, in Ulm, Germany, to moderately prosperous Jewish parents. His early childhood did nothing to suggest future greatness; he was late learning to speak, and his parents feared that he might be backward. He was apparently fascinated at the age of five by the mysterious workings of a pocket compass, and at the age of twelve he became enthralled by a book on Euclidean geometry. In his childhood, he also learned to play the violin and so acquired a love of music which was to last throughout his life.

In 1888 Einstein was sent to the Luitpold Gymnasium in Munich, but he disliked the regimented and authoritarian atmosphere of the school. Even at this young age he seems to have exhibited the independence of mind, the ability to question basic assumptions and to trust in his own intuition, which were to lead him to his brilliant achievements. He left the gymnasium in 1895, without gaining a diploma. His father tried to send him to a technical school in Zurich, but he failed the entrance examination, in spite of high scores on mathematics and physics. The following year he was more successful, and in 1900, he received the diploma which qualified him to teach. To his disappointment, however, he failed to obtain a teaching position at the school.

In 1901, Einstein became a Swiss citizen. (He had renounced his German citizenship in 1896.) In 1902, after temporary positions at schools in Winterthur and Schaffhausen, he secured a post as a technical expert in the Swiss patent office in Berne, where he was to remain for seven years. In the following year, he married Mileva Maric, a friend from his student days in Zurich, and in 1904 the first of their two sons was born.

Einstein's first scientific paper had been published in 1901, and he had also submitted a Ph.D. thesis to the University of Zurich. While he was working quietly in the patent office, however, isolated from the mainstream of contemporary physics, there was little to suggest the achievements of 1905, which were to shake the scientific world to its core.

Life's Work

In 1905, Einstein published three major papers, any one of which would have established his place in the history of science. The first, which was to bring him the Nobel Prize for Physics in 1921, explained the photoelectric effect and formed the basis for much of quantum mechanics. It also led to the development of television. The second concerned statistical mechanics and explained the phenomenon known as Brownian motion, the erratic movement of pollen grains when immersed in water. Einstein's calculations gave convincing evidence for the existence of atoms.

It was the third paper, however, containing the special theory of relativity, that was to revolutionize man's understanding of the nature of the physical world. The theory stated that the speed of light is the same for all observers, and is not dependent on the speed of the source of the light, or of the observer, and that the laws of nature (both the Newtonian laws of mechanics and Maxwell's equations for the electromagnetic field) remain the same for all uniformly moving systems. This theory meant that the concept of absolute space and time had to be abandoned because it did not remain valid for speeds approaching those of light. Events that happen at the same time for one observer do not do so for another observer moving at high speed in respect of the first. Einstein also demonstrated that a moving clock would appear to run slow compared with an identical clock at rest with respect to the observer, and a measuring rod would vary in length according to the velocity of the frame of reference in which it was measured.

In another paper published in 1905, Einstein stated, by the famous equation $E = mc^2$, that mass and energy are equivalent. Each can be transferred into the other because mass is a form of concentrated energy. This equation suggested to others the possibility of the development of immensely powerful explosives.

Such was Einstein's achievement at the age of twenty-six. There had not been a year like it since Newton published his *Principia* in 1687. The scientific world quickly recognized him as a creative genius, and in 1909 he took up his first academic position, as associate professor of theoretical physics at the University of Zurich. After two more positions, one in Prague and the other in Zurich, he became a member of the Prussian Academy of Sciences and moved to Berlin in 1914.

In the meantime, Einstein had been working to extend the special theory of relativity to include new laws of gravitation, and the general theory of relativity was published in 1916. It was one of the greatest intellectual productions ever achieved by one man, and its picture of the universe as a four-dimensional space-time continuum lies at the foundation of all modern views of the universe. The theory stated that large masses produce a gravitational field around them, which results in the curvature of space-time. This gravitational field acts on objects and on light rays; starlight, for example, is deflected when passing through the gravitational field of the sun.

In 1919, the general theory received experimental confirmation from a team of British astronomers. Suddenly, the world awoke to the implications of Einstein's work, and he found himself internationally celebrated as the greatest scientist of the day. During the early 1920's, he traveled extensively in Europe, the Far East, and the Americas, hailed everywhere as genius, sage, and hero. With his untidy shock of hair—formerly black, now graying—rising from a high forehead, his deep brown eyes, and small moustache, he made a striking figure. It was not only his superior intellect which aroused public recognition and respect, but also his simple good nature, nobility, and kindliness. Yet Einstein, always a modest man, was genuinely astonished at the attention he received.

It was during his travels in the 1920's that the other great concerns of Einstein's life came to the fore. A man of deep humanitarian instincts, he did not isolate himself from the turbulent political events around him. During World War I, he had spoken out against militarism and nationalism. Now, as a famous man, he once more took up the cause of pacifism, expressing his opinion openly, caring nothing for popularity.

Einstein's other lasting concern was the promotion of Zionism, and his tour of the United States in 1921 was undertaken in part to raise funds for the Hebrew University. These activities made him a target for fierce abuse from the Nazis, and even outside Germany, his radical political views made him a controversial figure.

When Hitler came to power in 1933, Einstein was on his third visit to the United States, and he resolved not to return to Germany. After brief stays in Belgium and England, he left Europe for the last time, to become a professor at the Institute for Advanced Study at Princeton. He continued to lend his support to the cause of justice and freedom, helping Jewish refugees whenever he could, and he modified his former pacifism in the face of the threat of Nazi domination. In 1939, he was persuaded to write a letter to President Roosevelt, alerting him to the military potential of atomic energy. (Einstein played no part, however, in the research which led to the development of the atomic bomb, which merely verified the truth of his famous equation.) After the war, he remained tirelessly devoted to the cause of world peace, and proposed a world government in which all countries were to agree to forfeit part of their national sovereignty.

His later scientific career took two main directions. First, he was so deeply convinced of nature's fundamental simplicity that he labored unsuccessfully for thirty years in an attempt to construct a unified field theory. Second, he could not accept one of the fundamental results of quantum theory, that the interaction of subatomic particles could be predicted only in terms of probabilities. "God does not play dice with the world," he remarked. Many of his colleagues thought him stubborn, but nevertheless he remained a revered figure; his reputation as a genius who also possessed wisdom and saintliness never left him, neither in life nor in death.

Summary

Einstein's scientific achievements entitle him to be placed alongside such figures as Copernicus, Galileo, and Newton, as a man who vastly enlarged the scope of human knowledge about the physical universe. In this respect he is a universal figure and belongs to no country. It is perhaps appropriate, however, that this German Jew, to whom destiny had decreed a nomadic existence, eventually found a permanent home in America. His links with his adopted country—he became an American citizen in 1941—are profound. He was the most illustrious of the hundreds of intellectuals who fled from Europe before World War II, and his presence at the newly formed Institute for Advanced Study, which marked a new period of development for American research and education, played a key role in attracting other eminent scholars.

Einstein had always viewed America as a bulwark of democracy and individual freedom, and in the debates which divided the country in the postwar decade—particularly the Cold War and the use of nuclear energy—his was a consistent voice for sanity and decency in the affairs of men. He spoke out for freedom of thought and speech in the McCarthy era, when he feared that the United States was betraying its own ideals, and he continued to urge scientists to consider the social responsibilities of their work in the atomic age. In his final year, he and a group of leading scientists signed a statement, known as the Russell/Einstein Declaration, warning about the terrible consequences of nuclear war. This led to the Pugwash conference on science and world affairs in 1957, in which for the first time scientists from East and West met to discuss nuclear arms. A series of influential conferences followed, and the Pugwash movement has continued its activities ever since.

Bibliography

Bernstein, Jeremy. *Einstein*. New York: Viking Press, 1973. First published in *The New Yorker* magazine this biography includes a historical survey of the scientific issues of Einstein's life. Hampered by lack of an index.

Clark, Ronald W. *Einstein: The Life and Times*. New York: World Publishing Co., 1971. Lengthy, authoritative, and readable. Gives a balanced treatment of Einstein's life, although the author tends to see Einstein as an idealist who was out of his depth when he entered practical politics.

Einstein, Albert. *Out of My Later Years*. New York: Philosophical Library, 1950. Collection of Einstein's writings, including articles, letters, appeals, and miscellaneous papers, from 1934 to 1950, on the philosophical, political, social, and scientific issues of the period.

Einstein, Albert, and Leopold Infeld. *The Evolution of Physics*. New York:

Simon and Schuster, 1938. Covers the period from the rise of the mechanical philosophy to relativity and quanta. Einstein's clarity of thought and expression is apparent throughout, and this remains one of the best popular expositions of his thought. No mathematics.

French, A. P., ed. *Einstein: A Centenary Volume*. Cambridge, Mass.: Harvard University Press, 1979. Beautifully designed, lavishly illustrated. Includes personal reminiscences from Einstein's friends and colleagues, expositions of many aspects of his scientific, political, and educational thought, and extracts from his writings.

Pais, Abraham. *"Subtle is the Lord . . .": The Science and the Life of Albert Einstein*. New York: Oxford University Press, 1982. A learned, well-documented, and illustrated work, written by one of Einstein's postwar colleagues at the Institute for Advanced Study. Presents the development of Einstein's ideas in the context of the main issues of twentieth century physics. The science is presented in-depth, and is not intended for the beginner.

Sayen, Jamie. *Einstein in America: The Scientist's Conscience in the Age of Hitler and Hiroshima*. New York: Crown Publishers, 1985. A well-researched, detailed account of Einstein's nonscientific activities from 1933 to 1955. Gives political and historical background on issues such as Palestine, the Cold War, and McCarthyism. Useful corrective to Clark, cited above.

Schartz, Joseph, and Michael McGuiness. *Einstein for Beginners*. New York: Pantheon Books, 1979. Amusing, entertaining, comic-book format, useful for those with no scientific background. Clear explanation of special relativity, and some biographical background.

Bryan Aubrey

DWIGHT D. EISENHOWER

Born: October 14, 1890; Denison, Texas
Died: March 28, 1969; Washington, D.C.
Areas of Achievement: The military and politics
Contribution: During World War II, Eisenhower served with distinction as
Allied Commander for the invasions of North Africa, Italy, and France.
He won the presidential elections of 1952 and 1956 and guided the country
through eight years of peace and prosperity.

Early Life

Although born in Texas, where his parents lived briefly, Dwight David Eisenhower grew up in the small town of Abilene, Kansas. The Eisenhowers
were a close-knit family and belonged to the Brethren Church, part of the
heritage of ancestors who had immigrated to Pennsylvania from Germany
during the eighteenth century. The third of seven sons (one of whom died as
an infant), Dwight Eisenhower enjoyed a secure childhood, completed high
school, and worked in a creamery for two years before entering West Point
on the basis of a competitive examination. West Point appealed to him
because it offered a free college education.

As a cadet, Eisenhower excelled briefly at football until a knee injury
ended that career. He proved a conscientious but not exceptional student and
was graduated sixty-first in a class of 164. At graduation in 1915, he stood
five feet, eleven inches tall and weighed 170 pounds. His classmates remembered and respected "Ike," as did his boyhood friends, as likable, honest,
and confident, a person with a quick temper but a quicker infectious grin. He
had an expressive face, blue eyes, and light brown hair that thinned and
receded when he was a young man.

Eisenhower's early military years were uneventful except for his marriage
in 1916 to Mamie Geneva Doud of Denver, Colorado. The two had met in
Texas during his first assignment at Fort Sam Houston. They became parents
of two sons, the first of whom died as a child.

Life's Work

During the 1920's and 1930's, Eisenhower demonstrated exceptional organizational skill and an ability to work with others. In 1926, Eisenhower, who
had been merely an average student at West Point, finished first among 275
in his class at the army's elite Command and General Staff School. When
General Douglas MacArthur served as the army's chief of staff, Eisenhower
assisted him, and then served as his senior assistant in the Philippines. Mac-
Arthur once evaluated Eisenhower as the most capable officer in the army.

Eisenhower's personality and his performance during maneuvers in the
summer of 1941 impressed the army's chief of staff, General George C. Mar-

shall. Both in 1941 and in 1942, Eisenhower won two promotions, jumping from lieutenant colonel to lieutenant general. In June, 1942, Marshall appointed Eisenhower European Theater Commander. The next year, as general, Eisenhower became Supreme Allied Commander and won fame as the leader of the multinational invasion of Europe in June, 1944.

After accepting Germany's surrender, Eisenhower served as the army's chief of staff. He retired in 1948 and became president of Columbia University. His book *Crusade in Europe*, published the same year, sold millions of copies and gave him financial security. Two years later, President Harry S Truman recalled Eisenhower to active duty as Supreme Commander of the North Atlantic Treaty Organization forces.

In May, 1952, Eisenhower retired from the army to seek the Republican Party's nomination for president, an office leaders in both parties had urged upon him for years. With his decisive victory in the November election, Eisenhower embarked upon a second career, one even more important than the first.

As president, Eisenhower set his primary foreign policy objective as maintaining the international role the United States had assumed during the previous decade. More specifically, he intended to end the fighting in Korea, reduce military spending, and lessen the intensity of the Cold War while still adhering to the policy of containment. Militarily, Eisenhower pursued a policy of strategic sufficiency rather than superiority. This policy, as well as a reduction of the capacity to fight limited wars, made possible cuts in the defense budget.

In 1953, Eisenhower approved an armistice in Korea and the next year rejected the advice of his secretary of state and the chairman of the Joint Chiefs of Staff, among others, and refused to intervene in the French war in Indochina. The United States took the lead, however, in establishing the Southeast Asia Treaty Organization as an attempt to accomplish in a region of Asia what the North Atlantic Treaty Organization had accomplished in Europe. During this same period, Eisenhower also approved Central Intelligence Agency covert activity that helped overthrow the governments of Iran and Guatemala and thereby contributed to the growing acceptance of undemocratic action in the name of freedom.

In 1955, he helped terminate the post–World War II occupation of Austria and then, at Geneva, Switzerland, became the first president to meet with Soviet leaders in a decade. That same year and again in 1956, Eisenhower reacted to crises in the coastal waters of the People's Republic of China, in Hungary, and in Suez in a manner that helped prevent these crises from escalating into greater violence.

On the domestic side, Eisenhower followed a moderate path. He accepted the New Deal programs and even expanded those covering labor, Social Security, and agriculture. Although he cut the budget of the Tennessee Valley Authority and reduced federal activity and regulations regarding natural resources, Eisenhower championed the nation's largest road-building project (the Federal Aid Highway Act of 1956) and federal development of the Saint Lawrence Seaway. He also approved spending increases in health care. Fiscally, Eisenhower cut taxes and controls, and each year balanced or nearly balanced the budget. The nation's gross national product, personal income, and house purchases all climbed. Inflation proved negligible, averaging one and a half percent per year. Fundamental to Eisenhower's public philosophy was his belief that only a sound economy could sustain a credible, effective foreign policy.

In the presidential election of 1956, Americans gave Eisenhower a second, even greater, landslide victory over his Democratic opponent Adlai E. Stevenson, despite Eisenhower's major heart attack in 1955 and his operation for ileitis in 1956. Voters approved his moderate policies and, like the friends of his youth and the military personnel with whom he worked, responded positively to his famous grin. His dislike of politics and his lifelong refusal to discuss personalities in public also struck responsive chords. Even his hobbies of golf, fishing and hunting, bridge and poker, and cookouts embodied widespread American values.

Eisenhower's second term continued the basic policies and themes of the first. He steadfastly resisted demands from Democrats and from conservative Republicans to increase defense spending, although he expanded the ballistic missile program after the Soviets launched the world's first human-made earth-orbiting satellite (*Sputnik*) in 1957. In 1958 (in Quemoy) and in 1958-1959 (in Berlin), Eisenhower again handled crises with deliberation. After he hosted the visit of Soviet leader Nikita Khrushchev, Eisenhower looked forward to a Paris summit meeting in May, 1960, and to a visit to the Soviet Union as his final contribution to promoting peace. On the eve of the conference, the Soviets shot down an American spy plane over Soviet territory. The U-2 incident, named after the plane, ruined the conference, canceled Eisenhower's planned visit to the Soviet Union, and dashed his hopes to improve relations between the two superpowers.

Domestic highlights of Eisenhower's second term included his ordering troops to Little Rock, Arkansas, to maintain order while the high school racially integrated its classes. In the same year, 1957, Eisenhower signed the first civil rights act in eighty-two years. Important symbolically, the act produced little change in the lives of black Americans. The same proved true of another civil rights act in 1960. In response to *Sputnik*, Eisenhower established the National Aeronautics and Space Administration (NASA) and approved the National Defense Education Act, providing the first substantial federal aid to higher education in almost a century.

Criticism of Eisenhower dealt mostly with three subjects. First, he refused to exercise any public leadership in response to Senator Joseph McCarthy's excessive unsubstantiated accusations of disloyalty directed against numerous Americans, including General George C. Marshall. Second, after the Supreme Court ruled in 1954 that separate-but-equal facilities were unconstitutional, Eisenhower refrained from lending his moral or political support for implementation of the ruling or for promotion of civil rights in general. The third area of criticism concerned his sparse defense budget and the limited range of responses it permitted in time of crisis. Eisenhower's confidence and public support, however, kept him from altering his positions because of such criticism.

In his presidential farewell address, Eisenhower warned the nation of the threat to democracy from the influence of the military-industrial complex, which benefited from massive military budgets. He retired to his Gettysburg, Pennsylvania, farm and wrote his memoirs. Most contemporary observers agreed that, had the Constitution permitted and had he been willing to run, Eisenhower easily would have won a third term.

Summary

Eisenhower, the career military officer, curtailed defense spending, pursued a foreign policy that emphasized conciliation rather than conflict, and presided over eight years of peace. An advocate of gradual domestic change, Eisenhower watched his most prominent appointee, Supreme Court Chief Justice Earl Warren, use his position and influence to bring sweeping changes to society. As a Republican president, Eisenhower, who disliked politics and favored limitations on the terms of senators and representatives, proved the most able politician of his generation. He adhered to definite policies, faced a Democratic Congress for six of his eight years in the White House, and suffered domestic and foreign setbacks, yet he gave the country eight years of economic growth and prosperity and left office with undiminished popularity.

Eisenhower obviously was a capable, complex man, but the key to his success seems to have been his ability to radiate straightforward honesty and uncomplicated common sense. The events of the decades following his presidency—the international arms race, war, riots, Watergate, inflation, declining standard of living, and uncontrollable budget deficits—have greatly enhanced respect for Eisenhower's accomplishments. Indeed, according to many, he has joined the ranks of the nation's ten greatest presidents.

Bibliography
Ambrose, Stephen E. *Eisenhower: Soldier, General of the Army, President-Elect, 1890-1952*. New York: Simon and Schuster, 1983. The most comprehensive book covering Eisenhower's life and career before he entered the White House. Based on an unequaled mastery of archival material, Ambrose provides an insightful and readable narrative. The book is especially strong on the influences that shaped Eisenhower's personality and career.

The book's highlight is Eisenhower's tenure as Supreme Allied Commander during World War II.

_____. *Eisenhower: The President*. New York: Simon and Schuster, 1984. This authoritative volume presents a detailed chronology of Eisenhower's presidency. The coverage of personalities and events, both foreign and domestic, is broad. Ambrose, the leading Eisenhower scholar, concludes with a favorable assessment of his subject. He awards higher grades in foreign than in domestic affairs.

Burk, Robert F. *The Eisenhower Administration and Black Civil Rights*. Knoxville: University of Tennessee Press, 1984. The most important book about Eisenhower and civil rights. Although Burk concentrates on events, he also discusses Eisenhower's attitudes and beliefs. The bibliographical essay is especially valuable.

Divine, Robert A. *Eisenhower and the Cold War*. New York: Oxford University Press, 1981. A clear, brief summary of several problems and themes in Eisenhower's foreign policy. In four essays (dealing with the presidency, Asia and massive retaliation, the Middle East, and Russians), Divine offers a favorable view of Eisenhower and of his handling of international crises.

Eisenhower, David. *Eisenhower: At War, 1943-1945*. New York: Random House, 1986. This massive study (nearly a thousand pages long) provides an indispensable account of Eisenhower's wartime leadership. The author (who is the grandson of his subject) emphasizes Eisenhower's awareness of long-range strategic considerations that would shape the postwar era.

Eisenhower, Dwight D. *The Eisenhower Diaries*. Edited by Robert H. Farrell, New York: W. W. Norton and Co., 1981. This 445-page volume presents the diary that Eisenhower started in 1935 and continued sporadically until late in life. Among other things, the diary records Eisenhower's frustration with individuals whom, as a matter of policy, he refrained from criticizing publicly. Farrell's introduction is excellent.

Greenstein, Fred I. *The Hidden-Hand Presidency: Eisenhower as Leader*. New York: Basic Books, 1982. This influential revisionist book examines Eisenhower's leadership techniques. Drawing heavily from the files of the president's personal secretary, political scientist Greenstein explains Eisenhower's behind-the-scenes domination of his administration. In doing so, he also reveals much about Eisenhower's personality.

Griffith, Robert. "Dwight D. Eisenhower and the Corporate Commonwealth." *American Historical Review* 87 (February, 1982): 87-122. A long, interpretative article that analyzes and synthesizes the components of Eisenhower's political philosophy (view of society, responsibility of government, role of economics) and the influence of this philosophy on his domestic and foreign policies. Griffith also describes the influences that shaped Eisenhower's philosophy.

Mayer, Michael S. "With Much Deliberation and Some Speed: Eisenhower and the Brown Decision." *The Journal of Southern History* 52 (February, 1986): 43-76. An assessment that portrays Eisenhower's civil rights record as more complex and, at times, more ambiguous than previous scholars have judged it to be. This article is broader in its concerns than the title suggests and is valuable for its account of Eisenhower's view of equality and blacks.

Reichard, Gary. *The Reaffirmation of Republicanism: Eisenhower and the Eighty-third Congress*. Knoxville: University of Tennessee Press, 1975. A careful study of Eisenhower's relationship with Republicans in Congress during his first two years in office, the only period of his presidency during which the Republicans controlled Congress. By focusing on key domestic and foreign policy issues, Reichard evaluates Eisenhower as a party leader and as a Republican.

Keith W. Olson

CHARLES WILLIAM ELIOT

Born: March 20, 1834; Boston, Massachusetts
Died: August 22, 1926; Northeast Harbor, Mount Desert, Maine
Area of Achievement: Education
Contribution: Combining administrative skill with a readiness to undertake novel and irregular ventures, Eliot transformed the structure and function of higher education in the United States.

Early Life

Charles William Eliot was born on March 20, 1834, in Boston, Massachusetts. The only son of Mary Lyman and Samuel Atkins Eliot, who were both from prominent New England families, Charles attended the Boston Latin Grammar School.

Upon graduation from Boston Latin, he entered his father's alma mater, Harvard College, in 1849. He became especially interested in mathematics and science and profited greatly from his study with a number of notable professors, among which were Louis Agassiz, Asa Gray, and Josiah Parsons Cooke. It was under Cooke, in fact, that the young Eliot was given the then unique opportunity for an undergraduate student to conduct laboratory and field work in science.

Eliot graduated in 1853, among the top three students in his class of eighty-eight, and the following year became a tutor in mathematics at Harvard. In 1858 he married his first wife, Ellen Derby Peabody, and in that same year he received a five-year appointment as assistant professor of mathematics and chemistry. While in this position, he introduced a number of curricular innovations at Harvard, including the first written examination and placing a greater emphasis on laboratory exercises as a learning tool.

Failing to secure promotion at the end of his five-year appointment as assistant professor, Eliot left Harvard in 1863 and even considered abandoning the teaching profession. The governor of Massachusetts offered him an appointment as lieutenant colonel of cavalry in the state's militia, but poor eyesight and family financial reverses forced Eliot to decline the offer. Instead, he embarked upon the first of two voyages to Europe for the purpose of further study. During his first trip abroad, Eliot was appointed to the faculty of the newly founded Massachusetts Institute of Technology, where he began teaching upon his return from Europe in September, 1865. Eliot gave four years of distinguished service to that institution. He not only organized the chemistry department in collaboration with Francis Storer but also collaborated with him in writing the Eliot and Storer manuals of chemical analysis, the first textbooks to feature laboratory and experimental work along with theoretical principles.

Eliot's study of European education while abroad and his experiences as a teacher at Harvard and MIT convinced him that American colleges and high schools were inadequate for the needs of individual students and American society. His thoughts about secondary and higher education were presented in two notable articles on "the new education," which appeared in the *Atlantic Monthly* early in 1869 and were widely read and quoted. These articles brought him to the attention of Harvard's Board of Overseers, which was seeking a new president for the school. Despite initial opposition to his election by some board members, Eliot was inaugurated as the twenty-second president of Harvard on October 19, 1869.

Life's Work

Photographs of the beardless, bespectacled middle-aged Eliot show a profile befitting that of a late nineteenth century college president: a receding hairline, firmly set chin, and mutton-chop sideburns. His presidency marked a new era at Harvard. Under Eliot's leadership, Harvard's faculty grew from sixty to six hundred and its endowment increased from a mere two and one-half million dollars to more than twenty million. He restructured Harvard into a university, concentrating all undergraduate studies in the college and building around it semiautonomous professional schools and research facilities. In 1872, he developed graduate M.A. and Ph.D. programs, followed in 1890 by the establishment of a Graduate School of Arts and Sciences. In the schools of medicine, law, and divinity, he formalized entrance requirements, courses of study, and written examinations. He assisted reformers who were interested in providing higher education for women, which led to the founding in 1894 of Radcliffe College.

Among Eliot's policies affecting Harvard, none was more fundamental than the improvement of faculty working conditions. He raised faculty salaries and introduced a liberal system of retirement pensions which Harvard maintained independently until 1906, when the Carnegie Foundation made provisions for this purpose. His introduction of the sabbatical year as well as French and German exchange professorships provided faculty with greater opportunities for contact with European scholars and greater leisure for research.

The most radical and far-reaching innovation introduced during Eliot's administration was the elective principle. This reform grew out of Eliot's conviction that college students needed more freedom in selecting courses so that they might acquire self-reliance, discover their own hidden talents, rise to a higher level of attainment in their chosen fields, and demonstrate a greater interest in their studies. Eliot also believed that modern subjects such as English, French, German, history, economics, and especially the natural and physical sciences should have equal rank with Latin, Greek, and mathematics in the college curriculum.

Gradually under Eliot's leadership, Harvard adopted the elective principle.

In 1872, all course restrictions for seniors were abolished. Seven years later, all junior course restrictions were abolished. In 1884 sophomore course restrictions came to an end, and the following year those for freshmen were greatly reduced. By 1897, the required course of study at Harvard had been reduced to a year of freshman rhetoric.

Eliot's influence was felt in other areas of college life. The long-standing rule requiring student attendance at chapel was abolished, and participation in all religious activities was made voluntary. Eliot demonstrated a keen interest in athletic policy, too. He established a general athletic committee, composed of alumni, undergraduates, faculty, and administrators. In addition, Eliot played an important role in the introduction of stricter eligibility requirements for college athletes at Harvard and other American colleges.

Although higher educational reform occupied most of his energies, Eliot used his position to influence primary and secondary schools as well. His numerous published articles and addresses covered a wide range of subjects. He argued for better training and greater security of teachers and for improved sanitary conditions in schools; he supported Progressive Era educators' efforts to improve schooling; and he emphasized the need for teachers and schools to train the senses, the body, and the imagination of the student. At the same time, he raised and diversified admissions requirements at Harvard to exert pressure upon schools to improve the quality of their instruction.

After Eliot resigned from the presidency of Harvard in 1909, he continued to participate in a wide range of activities. As a member of Harvard's Board of Overseers, Eliot maintained an interest in campus affairs. He was influential in shaping the policies of the General Education Board, the Rockefeller Foundation, and the Carnegie Foundation for the Advancement of Teaching. Eliot devoted the remainder of his time to writing, speech-making, and correspondence. Fully active until the last year of his life, he died at Northeast Harbor, Mount Desert, Maine, on August 22, 1926.

Summary

In countless ways, Eliot exerted a powerful influence upon the development of higher education in the United States. During his long and productive career, the university emerged as a preeminent force in Americans' lives. It became the primary service organization which made possible the function of many other institutions in society. The university not only brought coherence and uniformity to the training of individuals for professional careers but also provided a formal structure for the techniques Americans employed in thinking about every level of human existence.

Eliot was able to accomplish so much because, to an extraordinary degree, his own outlook mirrored the hopes and fears of many other late nineteenth century Americans. Eliot's contribution to change in higher education made a difference in American history at a crucial moment, when aspiring middle-class individuals were struggling to define new career patterns, establish new institutions, pursue new occupations, and forge a new self-identity. The university was basic to this struggle; it became a central institution in a competitive, status-conscious society. Eliot played a key role in this process by giving vitality to the American college at a time when its remoteness from society imperiled the whole structure of higher education in the United States.

Bibliography

Bledstein, Burton J. *The Culture of Professionalism: The Middle Class and the Development of Higher Education in America*. New York: W. W. Norton and Co., 1976. The best single book about the activities and ideology of Eliot and other leaders of late nineteenth century American higher education. Although somewhat overcritical, offers a needed corrective to other accounts.

Eliot, Charles W. *Charles W. Eliot and Popular Education*. Edited by Edward A. Krug. New York: Teachers College Press, 1961. This short anthology includes nine of Eliot's articles, addresses, and reports on education in the United States during the late nineteenth century and early twentieth century. It also contains a lengthy introduction which discusses and analyzes his contribution to the educational reform movement.

_____. *Educational Reform: Essays and Addresses*. New York: Century Co., 1898. Reprint. New York: Arno Press, 1969. Contains some of Eliot's early essays and addresses. Provides readers with a sample of his thinking on American education's problems and their solutions.

_____. *A Late Harvest: Miscellaneous Papers Written Between Eighty and Ninety*. Boston: Atlantic Monthly Press, 1924. This volume contains typical products of Eliot's thought during the last years of his life. In addition to a brief autobiographical piece, it includes papers on a wide range of subjects. Of particular note is a partial bibliography of Eliot's publications from 1914 to 1924.

Hawkins, Hugh. *Between Harvard and America: The Educational Leadership of Charles W. Eliot*. New York: Oxford University Press, 1972. The best single book on Eliot's tenure as president of Harvard. It analyzes his efforts to make the university ideal a reality in the changing, sometimes hostile social environment of late nineteenth century and early twentieth century America.

James, Henry. *Charles W. Eliot, President of Harvard University, 1869-1909*. 2 vols. Boston: Houghton Mifflin Co., 1930. Marred by its uncritical perspective, this nevertheless well-written, highly detailed biography of Eliot remains indispensable; all subsequent studies of James's life have drawn on it.

Rudolph, Frederick. *The American College and University: A History*. New York: Alfred A. Knopf, 1968. Provides a rich analysis of Eliot's early years as president and reformer at Harvard. Generally balanced and well researched, it provides a clear, objective account of the elective system's revolutionary impact on higher education in the United States.

Tyack, David B. *The One Best System: A History of American Urban Education*. Cambridge, Mass.: Harvard University Press, 1974. This highly readable, well-documented study only briefly discusses Eliot's activities on behalf of public schooling, but it provides a detailed account of the social milieu in which he worked and shaped his ideas about education.

Veysey, Laurence R. *The Emergence of the American University*. Chicago: University of Chicago Press, 1965. A massive study that includes more references to Eliot than to any other person. Valuable chiefly for its background information and incisive analysis of the social and intellectual context within which late nineteenth century American higher educational reform proceeded.

Monroe H. Little, Jr.

DUKE ELLINGTON

Born: April 29, 1899; Washington, D.C.
Died: May 24, 1974; New York, New York
Area of Achievement: Music
Contribution: As a pianist, composer, and band leader, Ellington made one of the most pervasive contributions to the development of jazz music in the United States.

Early Life

Edward Kennedy Ellington was born in Washington, D.C., on April 29, 1899. His parents, James Edward and Daisy Ellington, were moderately well-to-do middle-class blacks. James Edward was a popular butler and caterer in Washington, often serving at the White House, and later he worked as a blueprint reader and tracer at the Navy Yard. Both he and Daisy were cultured, well-read, and musically inclined, traits that Edward and his younger sister, Ruth, would share in the future. Neither of the Ellington children would suffer from a lack of creature comforts or social opportunities. Edward would later write that his father "spent and lived like a man who had money, and he raised his family as though he were a millionaire."

Young Edward was both musically and artistically gifted. He began taking piano lessons at the age of seven, quickly displaying a genuine talent for improvisation and originality. His talent as a composer surfaced when he was only fourteen: He wrote a piece called "Soda Fountain Rag," quickly followed by "What You Gonna Do When the Bed Breaks Down?" It was during his adolescence, moreover, that the nickname "Duke" came into play. As Ellington himself told the story, one of his friends ("a fancy guy who liked to dress well") bestowed the name on him. "He was socially uphill and a pretty good, popular fellow around, with parties and that sort of thing. I think he felt that in order for me to be eligible for his constant companionship I should have a title. So he named me Duke." The nickname stuck for the remainder of Ellington's life, constantly being reinforced by his handsome presence, charm, and almost regal manner and bearing.

Interestingly, Ellington's musical progress took a backseat to his interest in art during his elementary and early high school days. His forte was drawing, and he won first prize in a poster competition sponsored by the NAACP in 1917. Perhaps unfortunately for the art world, Ellington never took advantage of the prize, a scholarship to the Pratt Institute of Applied Art in Brooklyn. By the time he was graduated from Washington's Armstrong High School in 1917, his interests definitely had shifted to playing and composing. Yet, as evidenced by a number of subsequent Ellington compositions entitled "Portraits," he never completely lost touch with his love of art. His portraits, however, were to be of sound, not of pencil or paint, and they clearly would reflect his genuinely artistic soul. His son, Mercer Ellington, maintained that Duke "was born an artist . . . he had the typical ways of an artist from birth. Basically, anything that didn't move or inspire him didn't exist, regardless of how it could be explained in philosophical terms."

Life's Work

During World War I, Ellington served as a messenger for the State Department and the Navy Department and, in 1918, formed a small ragtime band which accepted engagements in the Washington vicinity. In that same year, he married Edna Thompson, who bore him a son, Mercer Kennedy Ellington, in 1919. The marriage was shaky from the beginning, falling apart after only a few years. Duke and Edna were permanently separated in 1925, but never formally divorced, despite Duke's subsequent romantic liaisons with other women.

In 1922, Ellington traveled to New York, where he played the piano in several bands before organizing his own five-man group in 1923. The "Washingtonians," as the band was called, first played at Barron's, a Harlem nightclub, and then in midtown at the Hollywood (later Kentucky) Club, where it would remain for nearly five years. During this period, the distinctive "Ellington sound," characterized by "jungle-like" growls, grunts, and wahwahs, came into existence. The "sound," coupled with masterful improvisation, ensured the band's subsequent popularity and success. Especially impressed was Irving Mills, the noted music publisher. Mills signed Ellington to an exclusive contract, subsidized the expansion of the band to twelve members, arranged for a recording contract, and, perhaps most significant, booked the band into the Cotton Club in Harlem.

During the Cotton Club years (1927-1932), Ellington achieved national and international recognition and fame as a pianist and band leader—long before Benny Goodman "launched" the Big Band Era in 1935. In fact, Ellington not only preceded the "big bands" but would ultimately outlast most of them, testament to the fact that his jazz orchestra was the most outstanding and enduring in the history of American music, playing well into the 1970's.

Ellington himself wrote more than a thousand musical compositions. Among his most noted pieces were "Mood Indigo" (a perpetual audience pleaser), "Sophisticated Lady," "Solitude," and "Don't Get Around Much Any More." His rendition of Billy Strayhorn's "Take the A Train," along with "Mood Indigo," became thematic trademarks of the Ellington sound. In addition, Ellington successfully experimented with both formal concert and sacred music during the course of his career. His one-hour orchestral suite, *Black, Brown, and Beige* (1943), was the first of many symphonic works performed at Carnegie Hall and elsewhere. His sacred music concerts, beginning in 1965, were well received and poignant, reflecting his deep religious feeling. In dedicating his sacred music, he said this: "Every man prays to God in his own language, and there is no language which God does not understand." Less than a year following the performance of his third sacred music concert in Westminster Abbey, Duke Ellington died of cancer in New York City on May 24, 1974.

Summary

Regarded by many as the greatest musical composer in American history, Duke Ellington exerted one of the most unique and pervasive influences on the development of jazz music in the United States. If, as it has been argued, jazz music reflects the essence of America, then Ellington surely was one of the nation's most influential spokesmen and ambassadors.

It was the rare big jazz or dance band in twentieth century America that was not in some way influenced by Ellington's style, "sound," and, especially, innovation. Ellington pioneered in the use of the human voice as a musical instrument; he revolutionized the role of the brass section with his popular "jungle" sound; he elevated the role of both tenor and baritone saxophones in orchestral arrangements; he successfully adapted jazz to both the formal concert idiom and sacred music; he was instrumental in breaking the traditional "three-minute rule" of commercial recording companies; and he more or less invented the echo chamber.

It is not surprising that Ellington's success and achievement was widely acclaimed and rewarded during his lifetime. He received gold medals from many cities, including New York and Paris; he was granted no less than fifteen honorary doctoral degrees from American universities, including Yale and Columbia; he received the Presidential Medal of Freedom (the United States' highest civilian award) from President Richard M. Nixon in 1969, and was decorated with the French Legion of Honor by President Georges Pompidou in 1973; and a number of countries, including the United States (1986), have issued postage stamps in his honor.

Worldwide tributes, acclamations, and eulogies followed the death of Ellington in 1974. President Nixon, genuinely moved by the Duke's passing, reflected the sentiments of most Americans: "The wit, taste, intelligence, and elegance that Duke Ellington brought to his music have made him in the eyes of millions of people both here and abroad, America's foremost composer. His memory will live for generations to come in the music with which he enriched his nation."

Bibliography

Ellington, Edward Kennedy. *Music Is My Mistress*. Garden City, N.Y.: Doubleday and Co., 1973. Published a year before his death, Ellington's work is more of a rambling memoir than a formal autobiography. Containing biographical sketches of his friends and associates, poems, and bits of personal philosophy, it nevertheless is an important source for those interested in the real Duke Ellington.

Ellington, Mercer, and Stanley Dance. *Duke Ellington: An Intimate Memoir*. New York: Da Capo Press, 1979. An honest, sometimes hard-hitting account of Ellington's life and music by his son. Especially good for the private side of a very public man.

Gammond, Peter, ed. *Duke Ellington: His Life and Music*. New York: Da Capo Press, 1977. More than a dozen thoughtful essays, arranged chronologically, about the man and the musician. Very good for sketches of Ellington's many sidemen. Also includes a detailed record guide.

George, Don. *Sweet Man: The Real Duke Ellington*. New York: G. P. Putnam's Sons, 1981. An honest and affectionate memoir by one of Ellington's longtime collaborators and companions. Provides much personal data and insight to which only an insider would be privy.

Jewell, Derek. *Duke: A Portrait of Duke Ellington*. New York: W. W. Norton and Co., 1977. Although not formally documented, this is probably the best biography of Ellington available. Contains both an elaborate chronology of Ellington's life and a select discography and bibliography.

Toppin, Edgar A. *A Biographical History of Blacks in America Since 1528*. New York: David McKay Co., 1971. Based on a series of articles that appeared in *The Christian Science Monitor* in 1969, Toppin's book includes a good narrative section on black American history in general and a well-written biographical essay on Ellington himself.

Ulanov, Barry. *Duke Ellington*. London: Musicians Press, 1946. Although dated, this early biography is historically and sociologically significant. The argument is made that Ellington was being held back from complete commercial success because of his race.

Robert R. Davis, Jr.

RALPH WALDO EMERSON

Born: May 25, 1803; Boston, Massachusetts
Died: April 27, 1882; Concord, Massachusetts
Area of Achievement: Literature
Contribution: Emerson was a spokesman for a peculiarly American culture.
  His writings contributed to that culture and encouraged others to add still
  further to it.

Early Life

The fourth child of Unitarian minister William Emerson and Ruth Haskins
Emerson, Ralph Waldo Emerson was born in Boston, Massachusetts, on
May 25, 1803. His father's death in 1811 left the family poor, and his mother
had to maintain a boardinghouse to support the family of six young children.

Despite this poverty, Emerson's education was not neglected. He attended
the prestigious Boston Latin School (1812-1817) and in 1821 was graduated
from Harvard. Even when he was an undergraduate, his interest in philosophy and writing was evident. In 1820, he won second prize in the Bowdoin
competition for his essay "The Character of Socrates," and the following
year, he won the prize again with "The Present State of Ethical Philosophy."
In these pieces he demonstrated his preference for the present over the past,
praising the modern Scottish Common Sense philosophers more highly than
Aristotle and Socrates.

This preference derived largely from his belief that the modern philosophers offered more guidance in how to live. Despite the mysticism that
informs much of Emerson's writing, he remained concerned with daily life.
Thus, his purpose in *Representative Men* (1850) was to draw from the lives of
great men some lessons for everyday behavior, and in the 1850's he gave a
series of lectures collected under the title *The Conduct of Life* (1860).

After graduation from Harvard, Emerson taught school for his brother
William before entering Harvard Divinity School in 1825. In 1826, he delivered his first sermon in Waltham, Massachusetts; typically, it dealt with the
conduct of life. Emerson warned that because prayers are always answered,
people must be careful to pray for the right things. One sees here another
strain that runs through Emerson's writings, the optimistic view that one gets
what one seeks.

Three years later, in 1829, Emerson was ordained as minister of Boston's
Second Church, once the Puritan bastion of Increase and Cotton Mather. In
the course of his maiden sermon there, he spoke of the spiritual value of the
commonplace. He reminded his audience that parables explain divine truths
through homey allusions and noted that if Jesus were to address a nineteenth
century congregation, he "would appeal to those arts and objects by which
we are surrounded; to the printing-press and the loom, to the phenomena of

steam and of gas." Again one finds this love of the commonplace as a persistent theme throughout his work. As he states in *Nature* (1836), "The meal in the firkin; the milk in the pan; the ballad in the street; the news of the boat" all embody universal truths.

In the same year that Emerson became minister of the Second Church, he married Ellen Louisa Tucker. Her death from tuberculosis in 1831 triggered an emotional and psychological crisis in Emerson, already troubled by elements of Unitarianism. In October, 1832, he resigned his ministry, claiming that he could not accept the church's view of communion, and in December he embarked for a year in Europe. Here he met a number of his literary heroes, including Samuel Taylor Coleridge, William Wordsworth, and Thomas Carlyle. He was less impressed with these men—Carlyle excepted—than he was with the Jardin des Plantes in Paris. At the French botanical garden he felt "moved by strange sympathies. I say I will listen to this invitation. I will be a naturalist."

Returning to Boston in 1833, Emerson soon began the first of numerous lecture series that would take him across the country many times during his life. From the lectern he would peer at his audience with his intense blue eyes. Tall and thin, habitually wearing an enigmatic smile, he possessed an angelic quality that contributed to his popularity as a speaker. The subject of his first lectures was science, a topic to which he often returned. His literary debut came, however, not from a scientific but from a philosophical examination of the physical world.

Life's Work

In 1835, Emerson married Lydia Jackson (rechristened Lidian by Emerson), and the couple moved to Concord, where Emerson lived the rest of his life. The next year Waldo, the first of their four children, was born. In 1836, too, Emerson published a small pamphlet called *Nature*. Condemning the age for looking to the past instead of the present, he reminded his readers that "the sun shines to-day also." To create a contemporary poetry and philosophy, all that was necessary was to place oneself in harmony with nature. Then "swine, spiders, snakes, pests, madhouses, prisons, enemies" will yield to "beautiful faces, warm hearts, wise discourse, and heroic acts . . . until evil is no more seen. . . . Build therefore your own world."

The volume was not popular: It sold only fifteen hundred copies in America in the eight years following its publication, and a second edition was not published until 1849. It served, though, as the rallying cry for the Transcendentalist movement. In literature this group looked to Carlyle and Johann Wolfgang von Goethe; indeed, Emerson arranged for the publication of Carlyle's first book, *Sartor Resartus* (1836), in the United States some years before it found a publisher in England. In philosophy the Transcendentalists followed Immanuel Kant in believing that man can transcend sensory experience (hence the movement's name); they thus rejected the view of John Locke, who maintained that all knowledge comes from and is rooted in the senses. In religion it rejected miracles and emphasized instead the Bible's ethical teachings.

Addressing the Phi Beta Kappa Society at Harvard on August 31, 1837, Emerson returned to his theme in "The American Scholar." He warned against the tyranny of received opinion, particularly as it appeared in books: "Meek young men grow up in libraries, believing it their duty to accept the views, which Cicero, which Locke, which Bacon have given," but "Cicero, Locke, and Bacon were only young men in libraries, when they wrote these books." The American scholar should, therefore, read the book of nature. He should do so confidently, believing that in him "is the law of all nature, . . . the whole of Reason."

Thus guided by his own insight and revelation rather than by outdated cultures, the scholar would lead others to a union with the spiritual source of life. This enlightened individual was to be American as well as scholarly, for the nature he was to take as his mentor was that of the New World rather than the Old.

In 1838, Emerson presented the controversial "Divinity School Address." To his audience of intellectual, rational Unitarians he preached the doctrine of constant revelation and called each of his listeners "a newborn bard of the Holy Ghost." Once more he was urging the rejection of the past—in this case historical Christianity—in favor of the present and trust in personal feelings rather than doctrine and dogma. His criticism of what he saw as the cold lifelessness of Unitarianism so shocked his listeners that he was barred from Harvard for almost three decades.

Such a reaction, though, was what Emerson was seeking; he wanted to shock what he saw as a complacent nation into regeneration through an appreciation of the present. "What is man for but to be a Reformer," he wrote. First a person was to reform, that is remake, himself; hence, Emerson took little interest in political parties or the many Utopian experiments— some started by members of the Transcendental Club—of the 1840's. When enough individuals reformed themselves, society would necessarily be improved.

Among those who shared Emerson's vision were a number of neighbors: Bronson Alcott, Ellery Channing, Margaret Fuller, Elizabeth Peabody, Jones Very, and Henry David Thoreau. From 1840 to 1844, this group published *The Dial*, a quarterly magazine rich in literature that expressed the Emersonian vision. Emerson frequently contributed to the journal, and for the magazine's last two years he was its editor also.

His new philosophy spread well beyond Concord. In his journal in 1839, Emerson recorded that "a number of young and adult persons are at this moment the subject of a revolution [and] have silently given in their several adherence to a new hope."

In 1841, he published *Essays*, which includes what is probably Emerson's most famous piece, "Self-Reliance." The themes of the essays were by now familiar, but the expression was forcefully aphoristic. Attacking contemporary religion, education, politics, art, and literature for their adherence to tradition, he declared, "Whoso would be a man must be a nonconformist." In 1844 appeared *Essays: Second Series*, with its call for an American poet who would sing of "our logrolling, our stumps, . . . our fisheries, our Negroes, and Indians, . . . the northern trade, the southern planting, the western clearing, Oregon, and Texas." The American poet would not care for "meters, but metermaking argument."

Emerson attempted to fill this role himself. His aunt Mary Moody had encouraged his youthful efforts in this area, and at the age of ten he had begun a poetic romance, "The History of Fortus." His early efforts had earned for him the role of class poet when he was graduated from Harvard in 1821. *Poems* (1847) suggests, however, that he lacked the ability or inclination to follow his own advice. The poems often remain tied to meter and rhyme rather than the rhythms of natural speech. In "Days," one of his more successful pieces, he described himself as sitting in his "pleached garden" and forgetting his "morning wishes." In "The Poet" he lamented, "I miss the grand design." Shortly before his second marriage, he had written to Lidian that though he saw himself as a poet, he knew he was one "of a low class, whose singing . . . is very husky." Some poems, though, like "The Snow Storm," reveal the power and beauty of nature through language that is fresh and immediate. Others, such as "Brahma" and "The Sphinx" (Emerson's favorite), use symbols well to convey spiritual messages and suggest the correspondence among man, nature, and the spiritual world that is one of the tenets of Transcendentalism.

In the next decade, Emerson published three important works based on his lectures: *Representative Men* (1850), *English Traits* (1856), and *The Conduct of Life* (1860). His lectures were not always well attended, even though he was in great demand. One course of lectures in Chicago brought only thirty-seven dollars; another audience in Illinois quickly left when it found a lecture lacking in humor.

The books that emerged from these lectures are more sober than his earlier writings. His youthful idealism is tempered by a darker sense of reality. In "Fate," the first chapter of *The Conduct of Life*, he recognizes the tyrannies of life and notes that man is subject to limitations. In the concluding essay of the book, he reaffirms liberty and urges again, "Speak as you think, be what you are," but he concedes, too, the power of illusion to deceive and mislead.

After the Civil War, Emerson published two more collections of his essays, *Society and Solitude* (1870) and *Letters and Social Aims* (1876), this second with the help of James Elliot Cabot. Much of the contents of these books is drawn from lectures and journal entries written decades earlier.

Although he was reusing old ideas, his popularity continued to grow. In 1867, he was invited to deliver the Phi Beta Kappa address again at Harvard; the previous year the school had indicated its forgiveness for the "Divinity School Address" by awarding Emerson an honorary doctorate. When he returned from a trip to Europe and the Middle East in 1873, the church bells of Concord rang to welcome him back, and the townspeople turned out in force to greet him.

Emerson recognized, however, that his powers were declining. As he wrote in "Terminus," "It is time to be old/ To take in sail/ . . . Fancy departs." John Muir saw him in California in 1871 and was amazed at the physical transformation, one mirrored by his fading mental abilities as his aphasia worsened. After John Burroughs attended a lecture by Emerson in 1872, he described the address as "pitiful." When Emerson attended the funeral of his neighbor Henry Wadsworth Longfellow in March, 1882, he could not remember the famous poet's name. A few weeks later, on April 27, 1882, Emerson died of pneumonia and was buried near his leading disciple, Thoreau.

Summary

Emerson said that Goethe was the cow from which the rest drew their milk. The same may be said of Emerson himself. Walt Whitman derived his poetic inspiration from "The Poet," as Whitman acknowledged by sending a copy of the first edition of *Leaves of Grass* (1855) to Concord. Emerson was among the few contemporary readers of the book to recognize its genius. Thoreau, though an independent thinker, also took much from Emerson. In "Self-Reliance," Emerson had written, "In the pleasing contrite wood-life which God allows me, let me record day by day my honest thoughts without prospect or retrospect. . . . My book should smell of pines and resound with the hum of insects." Here is a summary of *Walden* (1854). Emerson's emphasis on the miraculous within the quotidian may even have influenced William Dean Howells and other American realists later in the century.

As an advocate of literary nationalism, of a truly American culture, he urged his countrymen to look about them and celebrate their own surroundings. His was not the only voice calling for an intellectual and cultural independence to mirror the country's political autonomy, but it was an important and influential one. Oliver Wendell Holmes, Sr., referred to "The American Scholar" as "our intellectual Declaration of Independence."

In calling for a Renaissance rooted in the present of the New World rather than the past of the Old, Emerson was paradoxically joining the mainstream of the American spirit. Like John Winthrop in his sermon aboard the *Arbella* in 1630, he was advocating a new spirit for a new land.

Like his Puritan forerunners, too, Emerson stressed spiritual rather than material salvation. Having grown up poor, he harbored no illusions about poverty. He knew that "to be rich is to have a ticket of admission to the masterworks and chief men of every race." Because of such statements, H. L. Mencken said that Emerson would have made a fine Rotarian. This misreading of Emerson ignores the view that he expressed near the end of his life: "Our real estate is that amount of thought which we have." For Benjamin Franklin, the American Dream meant the opportunity to earn money. For Emerson, as for the Puritans, it meant the opportunity to live in harmony with oneself, to save not one's pennies but one's soul. Emerson's lectures and essays forcefully articulate a vision of America that has continued to inform American thought and writing.

Bibliography
Allen, Gay Wilson. *Waldo Emerson: A Biography*. New York: Viking Press, 1981. The definitive biography of Emerson, at once scholarly and readable. Allen is concerned with the personal as well as the public side of his subject. He also shows the evolution of Emerson's ideas by citing the stages of their development in journal entries, letters, lectures, essays, and poems.
Bode, Carl, ed. *Ralph Waldo Emerson: A Profile*. New York: Hill and Wang, 1969. How did Emerson's contemporaries view him? How has that view changed since his death? Bode offers a selection of biographical sketches by friends and scholars. Some of the earlier pieces are not readily available elsewhere.
Leary, Lewis Gaston. *Ralph Waldo Emerson: An Interpretive Essay*. Boston: Twayne Publishers, 1980. Offers an intellectual biography with a thematic arrangement. The focus is on understanding Emerson's ideas and their relationship to his life.
McAleer, John J. *Ralph Waldo Emerson: Days of Encounter*. Boston: Little, Brown and Co., 1984. Each of the eighty short chapters treats a stage in Emerson's growth as a person, thinker, or writer. Much of the book deals with actual encounters between Emerson and his contemporaries to illustrate their mutual influence.
Matthiessen, Francis Otto. *American Renaissance: Art and Expression in the Age of Emerson and Whitman*. London: Oxford University Press, 1941. Investigates the intellectual climate that produced so much significant American literature between 1850 and 1855. Focus is on literary criticism of the works themselves. Appropriately, Matthiessen begins with Emerson and explores all of his major works, not simply his publications in the early 1850's.
Miller, Perry. "From Edwards to Emerson." In *Errand into the Wilderness*, 184-203. Cambridge, Mass.: The Belknap Press of Harvard University Press, 1956. An insightful essay exploring Emerson's intellectual debt to

the Puritans at the same time that it shows the radical newness of Emerson's ideas.

Rusk, Ralph Leslie. *The Life of Ralph Waldo Emerson*. New York: Charles Scribner's Sons, 1949. Rusk's was a pioneering study, the most detailed biography of Emerson up to that time and still useful for its meticulous detail. Rusk carefully examined unpublished material to present an authoritative picture of Emerson's life. Concentrates more on the man than on his ideas.

Joseph Rosenblum

DAVID G. FARRAGUT

Born: July 5, 1801; Campbell's Station, Tennessee
Died: August 14, 1870; Portsmouth, New Hampshire
Area of Achievement: The naval service
Contribution: The first admiral in the United States Navy, Farragut is most
noted for his victory over Confederate forces in the Battle of Mobile Bay.

Early Life

The son of George Farragut and the former Elizabeth Shine, David Glasgow Farragut was born James Glasgow Farragut at the site of Campbell's Station, near Knoxville, Tennessee, on July 5, 1801. His mother was a native of Dobbs County, North Carolina, while his father was an immigrant of Spanish ancestry from the British (later French) island of Minorca. George Farragut served as both an army and then a naval officer during the American Revolution, then moved his family to Tennessee and again westward.

In Louisiana after 1807, George Farragut was a sailing master in the navy who, the following year, suffered the loss of his wife to yellow fever at their home on the shore of Lake Pontchartrain. Since he did not expect to remarry and thought that he could no longer give proper care and attention to his children, the elder Farragut arranged for his son's adoption by his friend, Commander David Porter. Porter was the commandant of the naval station at New Orleans.

Porter took his adopted son with him to Washington in 1809, and there and at his later home in Chester, Pennsylvania, he gave him better schooling than he had hitherto known. He also introduced him to Paul Hamilton, Secretary of the Navy, who promised him a commission as a midshipman. This was issued December 17, 1810, although Farragut was only nine years of age. From 1811 through 1815, Farragut served under Porter aboard the frigate *Essex*, saw action in the Atlantic and the Pacific in the War of 1812, and even had the brief opportunity at the age of twelve to command a captured prize ship, the *Barclay*. Although finally made a prisoner of war after an unsuccessful battle with the British ship *Phoebe*, the thrill of this early service and the pride he took in his adoptive father's growing reputation caused Farragut, upon release in 1814, to change his name legally to David. This was also the name of his foster brother, David Dixon Porter; the two maintained a healthy rivalry and friendship down through the years.

At home, in Chester, Farragut added to his education. He then served briefly apart from Porter following a paroled prisoner of war exchange, and concluded the war aboard the brig *Spark*. With never a thought toward a civilian occupation, Farragut immediately took service aboard a ship-of-the-line, the *Independence*, which sailed to the Mediterranean Sea to back up Commodore Stephen Decatur's squadron against the Barbary pirates in what was called the Algerine War. After this he served aboard a similar ship, the *Washington*, until he was afforded the opportunity to study under the American consul at Tunis, Charles Folsom. In addition to diplomacy, polite manners, and foreign languages, he was able to develop an understanding of English literature and mathematics. He was a bright young man, though impressive only in demeanor as he was five feet, six and a half inches tall and of average build. With his formal education complete late in 1818, Farragut embarked upon his naval career in earnest.

Life's Work

Duty was undertaken aboard the *Franklin* and the *Shark*, and while aboard the latter brig, Farragut was recommended for promotion to the rank of lieutenant at the unusually young age of eighteen. Recalled to Norfolk, Virginia, he was ordered to sea again in the sloop-of-war *John Adams*; in 1823 he volunteered for duty aboard the *Greyhound* when he heard that this ship was to be placed under the command of Captain Porter's brother, Lieutenant John Porter, and that the captain himself was to command the squadron of which it was a part. The squadron was prepared to fight pirates in the Caribbean Sea, and this was especially welcome duty to Farragut, who had come to detest piracy.

Confiscating the booty of numerous pirates and burning their ships, the "Mosquito Fleet," as the squadron was known, did effective service over the next two years. British forces then arrived to finish the job, and piracy was virtually eliminated as a common practice in Caribbean waters. An incident which occurred in the town of Foxardo, Puerto Rico, however, while he was in command of the squadron, led to Commodore Porter's court-martial and resignation from the navy. In later years he would serve his country as a diplomat.

After six months' service in the Caribbean in 1823, Farragut returned to Norfolk to marry a young woman he had met there. On September 24, 1823, Susan C. Marchant became his wife.

With formal promotion to lieutenant in 1825, Farragut was ordered once again to active duty aboard the frigate *Brandywine*, which carried the celebrated old hero of that Revolutionary battle, the Marquis de Lafayette, back to France. When he returned to the United States, Farragut found his wife suffering greatly from neuralgia. Despite a convalescence at New Haven, Connecticut, she continued to decline from the disease until her death on December 27, 1840.

While in New Haven, Farragut had come to attend lectures at Yale and reflect on the lack of educational opportunities available to young boys aboard ships. Upon returning to Norfolk, he organized a school for "ship's boys," said to be the first of its kind.

From 1828 to 1829, from 1833 to 1834, and again from 1841 to 1843, Farragut served in the South Atlantic waters off South America. He rose from first lieutenant (executive officer) of the sloop-of-war *Vandalia* to captain of the schooner *Boxer*. Several years of shore duty were then followed by orders to Pensacola, Florida, in 1838, where he was placed in command of the sloop-of-war *Erie* and given duty off Vera Cruz, Mexico. He was then advanced to the rank of commander in 1841.

Returning to Norfolk early in 1843, Farragut met and married Virginia Loyall, a native of that community, on December 26, 1843. They would have one child, a son, Loyall, born in 1844. As war with Mexico approached, Farragut anxiously requested duty off Vera Cruz and pressed his ideas for an attack on its fort, Castle San Juan de Ulloa, upon George Bancroft, Secretary of the Navy. His overzealousness in doing so, however, delayed his being given a proper command. Finally, in February, 1847, almost a year after the war got under way, he was given the sloop-of-war *Saratoga* and sent to the port. By that time, however, Vera Cruz had already been captured by army forces under General Winfield Scott. Nothing came of his service in this war except frustration, a bout with yellow fever, bitterness, and ill feelings.

Assignment to the Norfolk Navy Yard followed the Mexican War in 1848. Posted in California in 1854, Farragut was responsible for the establishment of the soon-to-be-important navy yard at Mare Island. In 1855, he was promoted to the rank of captain. Returning to the east three years later, he was named to command a new steamship, the wooden sloop-of-war *Brooklyn*. From 1858 to 1860, he remained her captain, assigned primarily to the Gulf of Mexico.

With the election of Abraham Lincoln, the secession of Southern states began in late 1860. As his native state of Tennessee and adopted state of Virginia threatened to follow others and join the Confederacy, Farragut had the same mixed feelings which struck Scott and other Southern unionists; like them, however, he professed his loyalty and stood by the same colors he had served so long.

The war's beginning, on April 12, 1861, with the firing upon Fort Sumter, was formalized by Lincoln's call for seventy-five thousand volunteers and establishment of a naval blockade of the Confederate coast. Farragut took his family out of Norfolk and established a home for them at Hastings, New York. On December 21, 1861, Farragut met the assistant secretary of the navy, Gustavus Vasa Fox, and received from him orders to take command of the Western Gulf Blockading Squadron, gather all available vessels, and proceed to capture New Orleans. Farragut designated the steam sloop-of-war *Hartford* his flagship and departed Hampton Roads in February, 1862, for Ship Island in the Gulf. Seventeen vessels, mostly gunboats, were brought in and sailed up the Mississippi; on April 18, 1862, Farragut, as his orders directed, set his mortar boats to work bombarding Fort Jackson. The fort, however, was too strong to be reduced in this manner, and so Farragut took it upon himself to run past this fort, and Fort St. Philip upstream, at night. After 2:00 A.M. on August 24, the run was successfully completed, Confederate vessels sent against them were destroyed, and New Orleans was taken through the instrument of Benjamin Butler's army. Farragut then passed Vicksburg on June 28. Instantly he became a national hero and was promoted to rear admiral on July 16, 1862. He added little to his fame with further actions on the Mississippi, which was soon in the capable hands of David Dixon Porter.

In August, the admiral made his headquarters in the evacuated harbor of Pensacola. His blockade of the Gulf Coast was now complete save for the fortified Confederate port of Mobile. This was a hornets' nest of blockade runners and Farragut's last objective. Receiving added ships and support from Secretary of the Navy Gideon Welles, he took a fleet of nineteen ships into Mobile Bay on August 5, 1864, past the Confederate batteries of Fort Morgan and through a mine field. When his lead ship, the *Brooklyn*, hesitated upon spotting the mines, and the monitor *Tecumseh* was sunk by one (then called a "torpedo"), Farragut ordered his flagship to take the lead and not to slow down. "Damn the torpedoes!" he said, and ordered the *Hartford* ahead at full speed. Successful at moving by the fort and through the mine field, Farragut's fleet defeated all Confederate vessels easily except for the *Tennessee*, a ram which held out through a desperate battle until it had suffered so badly that it surrendered at last. Soon Fort Morgan was in Union hands and the Confederate coast was closed.

As his health, ravaged by many tropical diseases, was declining, Farragut was recalled to New York in November, 1864. There he became a communicant of the Episcopal Church. A month later, as of Christmas, he was promoted as the first to hold the rank of vice admiral of the navy. The people of New York claimed him as a citizen of their city and bestowed a gift of fifty thousand dollars upon him as the war drew to a close.

On July 25, 1866, Congress created the new rank of admiral for him. He served aboard the flagship *Franklin* in command of the European Squadron, returning to New York in 1868. He then traveled to California the following year, but suffered a heart attack on the return via Chicago. Taken by steamship to be the guest of an admiral at the Portsmouth, New Hampshire, naval yard, Farragut died there on August 14, 1870.

Summary

David Farragut is regarded by many twentieth century historians as an ideal example of the nineteenth century career naval officer. Despite numerous disappointments while in uniform, his adoptive father's court-martial, and his roots in the South, Farragut remained constant in his allegiance to the United States Navy and the government it represents. His patriotism, coolness and courage under fire, thorough preparation, and belief in education are part of the heritage he and others like him left for later generations of naval officers.

His career of fifty-nine years in the service of his country has been equaled by very few men. What is more, it was a career featuring promotion as the first American to hold the rank of admiral, and it was crowned with the glory of the preeminent naval victory of the Civil War—the Battle of Mobile Bay. Had his health been better at the war's close, and had he been so inclined, virtually no appointive or elective office would have been beyond his reach.

As it was, he died, like Lincoln, near the peak of his fame and at the high tide of his fortunes. His passing was not so dramatic, but neither was much of his life. It was simply a life of dedicated service.

Bibliography
Barnes, James. *David G. Farragut*. Boston: Small, Maynard and Co., 1899. This book is a passable turn-of-the-century substitute for the Mahon book written by a then-popular biographer.
Farragut, Loyall. *The Life of David Glasgow Farragut: First Admiral of the United States Navy, Embodying His Journal and Letters*. New York: D. Appleton and Co., 1879. Reprint. New York: D. Appleton and Co., 1907. The author, Farragut's only child, has written a hagiography greatly improved by his use of Farragut's letters and journal.
Latham, Jean L. *Anchor's Aweigh: The Story of David Glasgow Farragut*. New York: Harper and Row, Publishers, 1968. The best of the modern juvenile works on Farragut, this book is well illustrated and contains useful maps.
Lewis, Charles Lee. *David Glasgow Farragut*. 2 vols. Annapolis: United States Naval Institute, 1941-1943. Reprint. Salem, N.H.: Ayer Co., 1980. The author of several excellent books on naval officers has here produced the most scholarly biography available, one enriched by original research.
Mahon, A. T. *Admiral Farragut*. New York: D. Appleton and Co., 1892. A classic work on the subject written by another famous admiral, this biography nevertheless is dated and deemed unnecessarily laudatory.
Nash, Howard P., Jr. *A Naval History of the Civil War*. Cranbury, N.J.: A. S. Barnes and Co., 1972. Concise and to the point, this is an outstanding one-volume history of the naval struggle between the North and the South. Many references are made to Farragut.
Spears, John R. *David G. Farragut*. Philadelphia: G. W. Jacobs and Co., 1905. Essentially an early juvenile biography written by a prolific author of nautical adventures, this book has some unique insights to share with the reader. It is also remarkably well illustrated with maps and charts.

Joseph E. Suppiger

WILLIAM FAULKNER

Born: September 25, 1897; New Albany, Mississippi
Died: July 6, 1962; Oxford, Mississippi
Area of Achievement: Literature
Contribution: Using the South as his inspiration and setting, Faulkner wrote a series of novels and stories which reflect universal human truths and conditions; he won the Nobel Prize for Literature in 1951 and is regarded as one of the greatest of American novelists.

Early Life

William Cuthbert Faulkner was the eldest son of Murry and Maud Butler Falkner (he changed the spelling of the family name). The Falkner family traced its heritage back across the South, through Tennessee and the Carolinas, but its most outstanding member was William Clark Falkner, grandfather of the novelist.

Known as the "Old Colonel," William Clark Falkner was the object of his grandson's rapt attention and emulation. The Colonel was a warrior who fought in the Mexican War and in the Civil War; a successful businessman who built railroads and owned plantations; a writer, whose novel *The White Rose of Memphis* (1881) was a best-seller; and a martyred hero, shot down in the street by a political enemy. His larger-than-life statue stood among the ruins of the family plantation when William Faulkner was a boy.

By contrast, Murry Falkner was a well-meaning but ineffectual man, drifting from job to job, largely on the strength of the family name, and overshadowed by his strong-willed wife. William Faulkner took after his mother in physical appearance: He was a light, short man with fine features and dark eyes. Although small, he was not frail; he was later active in sailing and flying and was an avid horseman to the very end of his life. He developed a tenacious determination to pursue his own course; in later years, his confidence would be badly shaken by disappointments, but never destroyed. As a youth he had a natural tendency toward isolation, detachment, and observation, which was later to serve him well as a writer.

Shortly before Faulkner was five, the family moved to Oxford, Mississippi. Faulkner started off well in school but soon began to decline in performance; he was never graduated from high school. He retreated into observation: For example, he preferred to watch, rather than dance, even at parties with his sweetheart, Estelle Oldham.

Faulkner's courtship of Estelle was desultory, his prospects were poor, and she married another man. Two months later, Faulkner joined the Royal Air Force in Canada, giving false information about his nationality and adding a "u" to his name. Although he later claimed combat experience and a wound from action over France, he was still in training in Toronto when the war ended. By December, 1918, he was back in Oxford.

Faulkner enrolled at the University of Mississippi at Oxford as a veteran. He did not fit in with the other students—they mocked him as "Count No-Count" because of his affectations and poverty—and his only interest was writing for campus literary journals. Within a year, he had withdrawn from the university and had drifted through a series of part-time jobs.

During this time, he continued to write, mostly poetry. In 1924, his first book, *The Marble Faun*, was published; Faulkner had to pay a subsidy to the publisher. The next year, he moved to New Orleans, where his career as a writer truly began.

Life's Work

In New Orleans, Faulkner met the author Sherwood Anderson, who encouraged his development and recommended his first novel, *Soldiers' Pay* (1926), for publication. The book was followed by *Mosquitoes* (1927). Neither volume did particularly well, but Faulkner's next novel, although not published as written until after his death, changed his career.

In 1927, he completed *Flags in the Dust* (1973; published posthumously), a long, densely populated work about the aristocratic Sartoris family in mythical Yoknapatawpha County, Mississippi. This mythical county was Faulkner's great discovery as a writer, his own "postage stamp of soil" that would be the source for some of the greatest writing of the first half of the twentieth century. Ironically, *Flags in the Dust* was rejected by the publisher.

Stung, but increasingly sure of his talent, Faulkner continued to write. His next work was his first masterpiece, *The Sound and the Fury* (1929). The novel concerns the tangled, flawed history of the Compson family, residents of Jefferson, the county seat of Yoknapatawpha. In the work a characteristic obsession of Faulkner emerges: the need to tell and retell the events of the past, from several different points of view, and with versions by several characters. Using stream-of-consciousness narrative (new at the time) and daring to employ an idiot as one of the principal narrators, *The Sound and the Fury* was a dense, sometimes difficult, but powerful work, dealing with a sense of loss and a longing for the past. The character Quentin Compson yearns for faded family glory and wrestles with incestuous desire for his sister Caddie; later a suicide in Boston, he also appears in other Faulkner tales of Yoknapatawpha. The novel was generally well received but did not earn for Faulkner much money.

In 1929, Faulkner also published a revised, shortened version of *Flags in the Dust*, entitled *Sartoris*. The novel was not as technically adventurous as *The Sound and the Fury*, but it added to the rapidly growing population of Yoknapatawpha County and established themes and plots that Faulkner would develop for the remainder of his career.

Estelle Oldham Franklin, Faulkner's early love, had returned to Oxford with her two children; in May, 1929, her divorce was granted, and she and Faulkner were married on October 7. They bought a large, dilapidated antebellum house near Oxford and named it Rowan Oak. They would have two daughters: The first would die in infancy; the second, Jill, was Faulkner's greatest pleasure from the marriage, which was destined to be a troubled one; on their honeymoon, Estelle attempted to drown herself. Throughout the years, both Faulkner and his wife were afflicted with problems, stemming from alcoholism, adultery, and lack of money.

Faulkner attempted to meet his financial burdens through writing. He sent "commercial fiction" to popular magazines such as the *Saturday Evening Post* and *Collier's*, but these pieces never brought enough steady income to meet expenses. His next novel, *As I Lay Dying* (1930), was another well-written but poorly selling work. In despair, he concocted a work designed for mass appeal: *Sanctuary* (1931), a lurid tale of abduction, corruption, and rape, set in Yoknapatawpha. Before its publication, however, Faulkner extensively revised the novel, putting sensationalism aside for artistic integrity. Despite this effort, *Sanctuary* brought him notoriety but no great income.

In 1932, Faulkner took the first of several scriptwriting jobs in Hollywood. He was not comfortable with the work, disliked California, and believed that his talent was being abused and perhaps irretrievably wasted. He was unhappy, drank heavily, and had affairs but had to continue with the scriptwriting jobs because of financial pressures. In 1932, his father died, and Faulkner assumed responsibility for the entire family.

The publication of *Light in August* (1932) deepened and expanded the Yoknapatawpha saga and was Faulkner's first major meditation on the tangled relationships of blacks and whites in the South. The book did little to relieve Faulkner's financial situation. He continued to work, on and off, in Hollywood but returned to Oxford whenever he could. Faulkner found writing increasingly difficult during this period. He published two volumes of short stories and a novel, *Pylon* (1935), but made slow progress on his major work, which would become the novel *Absalom, Absalom!* (1936). When Dean Faulkner, his younger brother, was killed in an airplane crash in 1935, Faulkner added Dean's family to his other financial obligations.

Faulkner continued work on *Absalom, Absalom!*, which finally appeared in 1936. The novel is his most dense and compact, taking titanic events from the past and recounting them through multiple narrators in the present. The tale of Thomas Sutpen, his effort to carve out a kingdom and found a dynasty in the Mississippi wilderness, is approached from several points of view, and the repetition and interplay between the stories that are told and the lives of the tellers (among then Quentin Compson, from *The Sound and the Fury*) give the novel the enduring, archetypal aspect of myth and fable. Adding to this resonance are echoes from the Bible, Greek myths, and Southern history. The novel can be difficult to read, because it demands that the reader participate in its development by piecing together the puzzling strands of the plot; still, it is Faulkner's greatest single work.

For the next six years, Faulkner divided his time between Hollywood work and his own writing. He published four novels during this period: *The Unvanquished* (1938), drawn together from short stories; *The Wild Palms* (1939); *The Hamlet* (1940), which was the first of a trilogy dealing with the Snopes family, an innumerable clan of rapacious poor whites who threaten to overwhelm Yoknapatawpha County; and *Go Down, Moses* (1942), another novel written as a set of interconnected stories, dealing with the McCaslin family, whose members include both blacks and whites in an intricate knot of kinship. After this work, Faulkner published no new novels for six years, working in Hollywood in an attempt to pay off his massive debts. His literary reputation declined: In 1939, he had been on the cover of *Time* magazine; by 1946, only *Sanctuary* remained in print.

His reputation was revived in 1946, with the publication of *The Portable Faulkner*, edited by Malcolm Cowley. Faulkner contributed new material, including a map of Yoknapatawpha County and a genealogy for his characters. Two years later, he published *Intruder in the Dust* (1948), not his greatest novel, but his first to sell really well: His chronic money problems were ended.

Faulkner's writing had always been admired in Europe, particularly in France, and in 1951, his achievements were recognized with the Nobel Prize. Earlier, in 1948, he had been elected to the American Academy of Arts and Letters. The appreciation his writing had long deserved was at last being granted.

Published in 1954, *A Fable* cost Faulkner the most effort of any of his novels, but emerged as the least effective. He returned to the land and people he knew best with *The Town* (1957) and *The Mansion* (1959), thus completing the Snopes trilogy. The approach in these works was expansive and leisurely, the narrative straightforward and traditional, in contrast to his earlier experimentation.

Increasingly recognized at home and abroad, Faulkner toured Japan, South America, and Greece for the State Department and was not afraid to involve himself with the growing crisis over segregation in his native South, urging racial understanding and cooperation. In 1962, he published his final work, *The Reivers*. On July 6, 1962, Faulkner died in Oxford, Mississippi.

Summary

Faulkner is a giant figure in American literature. His greatest novels deal with the people of Yoknapatawpha County, its town of Jefferson, and the Mississippi countryside, yet their themes and characters are not limited to any one place or time but touch universal human needs and emotions.

Faulkner has been termed a regional writer, a "Southern" writer. While it is true that his own creation is set in a vividly real South, Faulkner's strength goes beyond any one locality. As he wrote to Malcolm Cowley:

> I'm inclined to think that my material, the South, is not very important to me. I just happen to know it, and don't have time in one life to learn another one and write at the same time. Though the one I know is probably as good as another, life is a phenomenon but not a novelty, the same frantic steeplechase toward nothing everywhere and man stinks the same stink no matter where in time.

Faulkner was able to achieve this universality through his knowledge and re-creation of a specific place, the South, and through his specific, always individual, characters. More than any other American writer in this century, he has established and peopled a world that is so real that it continues to live off and outside the printed page.

As a writer, Faulkner excelled in several areas: He was adept at the creation of character and the development of plot; his technical mastery was established early and made his method of narrative as important, and as interesting, as his content. He was equally skilled at recounting dramatic, passionate events and spinning the tall-tale humor of frontier American literature.

Faulkner's greatest gift and his greatest accomplishment was his use of language, particularly powerful, cadenced, hypnotic rhetoric. More than any other American writer of the twentieth century, he explored and exploited the vast range and variety of American English in all its forms, features, dialects, and tones, and through language he crafted a series of works that will long endure.

Bibliography

Blotner, Joseph. *Faulkner: A Biography*. 2 vols. New York: Random House, 1974. The most exhaustive and definitive life of Faulkner. Blotner was a friend and associate while Faulkner was writer-in-residence at the University of Virginia. Contains an enormous amount of background material covering all aspects of Faulkner's life and career.

Brooks, Cleanth. *William Faulkner: The Yoknapatawpha Country*. New Haven, Conn.: Yale University Press, 1963. A distinguished literary critic gives an informed and thoughtful view of Faulkner's writings and accomplishments.

Cowley, Malcom, ed. *The Faulkner-Cowley File: Letters and Memories, 1944-1962*. New York: Viking Press, 1966. A collection of letters to and from Faulkner and Cowley during their association, with explanatory material by Cowley. Faulkner provides many hints and suggestions as to the intent of his works and how he created his characters.

Friedman, Alan W. *William Faulkner*. New York: Frederick Ungar Publishing Co., 1985. Part of the "Literature and Life" series, this is a good, basic introduction to Faulkner's life and career and makes an excellent starting point for the beginning student of Faulkner.

Hoffman, Frederick. *William Faulkner*. 2d rev. ed. Boston: Twayne Publishers, 1966. Introductory volume which covers the main works quickly, touching on the highlights. Short on biographical information.

Howe, Irving. *William Faulkner: A Critical Study*. 3rd rev. ed. Chicago: University of Chicago Press, 1975. Updating of an early and generally perceptive study of Faulkner's work, with special emphasis on the social settings and situations of his novels.

Kenner, Hugh. *A Homemade World: The American Modernist Writer*. New York: Alfred A. Knopf, 1975. Has only one section on Faulkner but is especially good at explaining his techniques in creating a world of written text. Offers some intriguing suggestions for further study.

Minter, David. *William Faulkner, His Life and Work*. Baltimore: Johns Hopkins University Press, 1980. A chronological study of the man and his works. The critical readings illuminate the novels, especially the lesser-known works.

Wagner, Linda, ed. *William Faulkner: Four Decades of Criticism*. East Lansing: Michigan State University Press, 1973. Useful collection of writings on Faulkner's novels and stories; helpful in showing the growing appreciation of his work by critics.

Warren, Robert Penn, ed. *Faulkner: A Collection of Critical Essays*. Englewood Cliffs, N.J.: Prentice-Hall, 1966. A good survey of the response to Faulkner by the major literary critics; touches on most of the major novels.

Michael Witkoski

ENRICO FERMI

Born: September 29, 1901; Rome, Italy
Died: November 29, 1954; Chicago, Illinois
Area of Achievement: Physics
Contribution: Fermi's experiments utilizing neutron bombardment led to the production of the first controlled chain reaction, critical to the United States' development of the atom bomb.

Early Life

Enrico Fermi was born September 29, 1901, in Rome, Italy, to Alberto Fermi, an administrator in the Italian railroad system, and Ida de Gattis, an elementary schoolteacher. Enrico learned to read and write at an early age, probably instructed by his older brother and sister. At six years of age, Enrico entered public school and soon displayed a talent for mathematics. By the age of ten, the young boy, by this time exhibiting a remarkable memory, entered a school that emphasized Latin, Greek, French, history, mathematics, natural history, and physics, courses that would prepare him for entrance into the university. Enrico led his class in scholarship and, in his spare time, studied science and built electrical motors and toys.

In 1918, after receiving his diploma from the *liceo* (high school) and winning on a competitive examination, Fermi was admitted as a fellow in the Scuola Normale Superiore, a college of the University of Pisa. The young scholar earned his doctorate, graduating magna cum laude in 1922 at age twenty-one, and obtained a postdoctoral fellowship to study physics under Max Born in Göttingen in 1923. During the academic year of 1923-1924, Fermi held a temporary position at the University of Rome as an instructor of mathematics. In September, 1924, Fermi began a three-month fellowship at the University of Leyden. He then accepted a nontenured position as *incaricato* (instructor) at the University of Florence, teaching mechanics and mathematics.

Fermi's physical appearance at this time, according to his future wife, was not as impressive as his mental abilities. His rounded shoulders, short legs—he was five feet six inches tall—thin lips, a neck thrust forward when he walked, and a dark complexion were in sharp contrast to his gray-blue, close-set, cheerful eyes. A vital, energetic man, he particularly enjoyed skiing and hiking.

Life's Work

In November, 1926, Fermi won the *concorso* (competition) for a new chair in theoretical physics at the University of Rome, a result, in part, of the publication of his paper "On the Quantization of the Perfect Monoatomic Gas." This paper calculated the behavior properties ("Fermi's statistics") of an ideal gas composed of particles of half integral spin (electrons, protons, and so on).

In 1928, Fermi published a book on modern physics for upper-level university students, *Introduzione alla fisical atomica*. During this period as professor at the university, he successfully recruited talented students to study physics with him and other faculty members. On July 19, 1928, the young physicist married Laura Capon in Rome. Two children were born of the union, Nella in 1931 and Giulio in 1936. In 1929, Fermi was appointed as the youngest member of the Royal Academy of Italy with a government salary as part of the honor, and in the summer of 1930, he was invited to teach theoretical physics at the University of Michigan, Ann Arbor, lecturing on the quantum theory of radiation.

In 1933, Fermi wrote a famous paper on the explanation of beta decay. After the announcement of Frédéric Curie and Irène Joliot-Curie in Paris that alpha particle bombardment of aluminum produced artificial radioactivity, the Italian physicist experimented with neutrons as the bombarding source. He was able to produce artificial radioactivity in fluorine in March, 1934, using a radon-plus-beryllium source of neutrons. Seven months later, in October, 1934, Fermi discovered a principle of nuclear physics that was to have far-reaching effects upon the future of science. Placing a piece of paraffin in front of a neutron source, he observed increased radioactivity in the silver target. He surmised that the paraffin slowed the neutron "bullets" and increased the neutron-proton collision cross section. This allowed the silver nuclei to capture the slow neutron, eject a proton, and become temporarily radioactive. Fermi and his coexperimenters, Bruno Pontecorvo, Edoardo Amaldi, Franco Rasetti, and Emilio Segre, also noted that water produced almost the same slowing-down effect as paraffin. The theory was proposed that neutrons lose energy in repeated collisions with hydrogen nuclei. Anticipating possible commercial applications, the scientists took out an Italian patent on this neutron-bombardment process of producing radioactive substances in October, 1935.

Fermi's reputation in scientific circles in the United States grew, and in the summer of 1936, he was invited to give a course on thermodynamics at Columbia University in New York. On previous teaching trips in 1933 and 1935, Fermi was impressed by the freedom and kindness of the American people. This appreciation had prompted him earlier to consider moving to the United States to escape the dictatorship of the regime of Benito Mussolini in Italy. Although Fermi had little interest in politics, he did understand that free and open scientific investigation was more desirable than that practiced under the dictates of an oppressive government. In 1938, Italy, influenced by the anti-Semitism sweeping Germany at that time, passed laws against persons of Jewish ancestry. Since Fermi's wife was Jewish, he decided to leave Italy. He accepted a teaching position at Columbia University and obtained an immigration visa in November, 1938. The next month, Fermi was awarded the Nobel Prize in Stockholm, Sweden, for his work with slow neutrons, and on December 24, 1938, the Fermi family left Europe for the United States (Enrico Fermi became an American citizen in July, 1944).

Events in nuclear physics were rapidly developing in late 1938. On December 22, 1938, Otto Hahn and Fritz Strassmann in Germany published the results of their experiments on the neutron bombardment of uranium. They had discovered radioactive barium among the products of that bombardment. In January, 1939, Otto Frisch and Lise Meitner theorized that the presence of radioactive barium indicated the fission (splitting) of the uranium nucleus into two nuclei of approximately equal size, barium and krypton. Fermi then surmised that if enough excess neutrons were released in the fission process, and if enough uranium atoms were present, a chain reaction, with the release of enormous amounts of energy, might result.

In early 1939 at Columbia, Fermi exchanged experimental information with two Hungarian emigrant scientists, Leo Szilard and Edward Teller. In August, 1939, Albert Einstein, the most famous physicist in the world, informed President Franklin D. Roosevelt by letter that the work of Fermi and Szilard demonstrated the possibility that a powerful bomb might be constructed, utilizing the nuclear chain-reaction principle. Roosevelt formed a Committee on Uranium to keep him apprised of the progress of the experimentation.

In the spring of 1940, Fermi and others discovered the use of graphite as a moderator in slowing down neutrons. This principle would be vital in future chain-reaction experiments involving a nuclear reactor ("pile"). Fermi also observed that lumping natural uranium would permit the start of a chain reaction without the need of isotope separation—a process which, given the technology of the time, seemed to be an almost impossible task.

By the summer of 1940, scientists at the University of California identified the product of the fission of natural uranium 238 as neptunium 239. Neptunium decays and produces plutonium 239, which fissions when bombarded with slow neutrons. If a chain reaction utilizing uranium 238 could be sustained, then enough fissionable plutonium 239 could be obtained for use in the manufacture of an atom bomb.

During 1941, Fermi experimented with a small atomic pile at Columbia University. He showed that a self-sustaining nuclear chain reaction could be achieved if the proper amount of uranium was placed in a graphite pile. By the spring of 1942, Arthur H. Compton, professor of physics at the University of Chicago, had been placed in charge of all work pertaining to the chain reaction. Compton brought physicists to Chicago to coordinate the experimental effort under the code name "Metallurgical Laboratory." Fermi supervised the construction of a large pile under the stands of the university's football stadium beginning in October, 1942. On December 2, 1942, cadmium control rods were slowly withdrawn; a twenty-eight-minute, self-sustaining chain reaction occurred, producing one half watt of energy. This was the first nuclear reactor to produce energy that would eventually be used for peaceful purposes. Several months later, a second pile (one hundred kilowatts) was built at the Argonne Laboratory outside Chicago. This success led to the construction, with Fermi's consultation, of the large water-cooled, natural-uranium-fueled, plutonium-production reactor at Hanford, Washington in 1944.

Near Los Alamos, New Mexico, in an isolated mesa area, a new laboratory was constructed for the purpose of building an atom bomb. The best minds in nuclear physics were brought to Los Alamos or consulted regarding the bomb construction. The first experiments began in July, 1943, under the direction of J. Robert Oppenheimer of the University of California. Fermi was still conducting work in Chicago and traveling to Oak Ridge, Tennessee, the site of a plant that produced uranium 235, a fissionable isotope that would be used in the manufacture of yet another bomb. He came to Los Alamos in August, 1944, and was appointed as an associate director of the laboratory by Oppenheimer. During this period, Edward Teller was working on the hydrogen bomb under Fermi's direction.

By July, 1945, enough reactor-produced plutonium had been delivered to Los Alamos to allow for the production of the first atom bomb. The testing of this weapon occurred on July 16, 1945, at Alamogordo, New Mexico. Fermi was responsible for measuring the energy levels produced by the explosion and for collecting sand and soil samples to be analyzed for radioactivity.

The first atom bomb was dropped on Hiroshima, Japan, on August 6, 1945, and the war ended shortly thereafter. In January, 1946, Enrico Fermi returned to Chicago as Distinguished-Service Professor of Physics at the Institute of Nuclear Studies, and in that year, he and four other scientists were awarded the Congressional Medal of Merit by President Harry S Truman for their work in developing the atom bomb. For the next eight years, Fermi continued his experiments in high-energy physics. During this period, he also served on the General Advisory Committee of the Atomic Energy Commission and on other advisory bodies in need of his scientific knowledge and counsel. In April, 1954, Fermi testified at the security risk hearing of J. Robert Oppenheimer, whose loyalty to the United States had been questioned because he had opposed the program for developing the hydrogen bomb. (Fermi himself, as well as other influential scientists, including Albert Einstein, had opposed the development of this thermonuclear weapon on ethical grounds.) At the hearing, Fermi pointed out Oppenheimer's service to the United States and suggested that there should be no question of Oppenheimer's loyalty.

By the summer of 1954, Fermi's health was deteriorating. An undiagnosed illness that later proved to be cancer drained his energy. He died in Chicago on November 29, 1954, at the age of fifty-three.

Summary

Enrico Fermi epitomized the popular image of the scientist, the diligent experimenter in lab coat surrounded by the apparatus of discovery. Yet he was much more. He was a talented mathematician and theorist who was able, if necessary, to build analytical instruments with his own hands. His keen mind searched for simple alternatives to problems that others thought impossible. He was an immigrant to the United States, imbued with a spirit of gratitude and loyalty to his new country. He was a devoted husband and father. Although he helped develop the atom bomb as a weapon of war, a weapon that he hoped would not be used on a civilian population, his name is primarily associated with the controlled chain reaction that is the basis of the peaceful use of atomic energy in nuclear power plants. Fermi the immigrant, like so many immigrants to America before him, brought to this nation a new knowledge, a new prestige, influence in world politics, and the basis of a new power. Fermi has entrusted future generations with the responsible use of that power.

Bibliography

Amaldi, Edoardo. "Personal Notes on Neutron Work in Rome in the Thirties and Post-War European collaboration in High-Energy Physics." In *Proceedings of the International School of Physics: "Enrico Fermi,"* edited by C. Weiner, 294-325. New York: Academic Press, 1977. Technical account of the experimental techniques and early research on the properties of the neutron by Fermi's Rome-based team, during the year between 1934 and 1935. Excellent photographs of the early handmade apparatus used as neutron sources.

Fermi, Laura. *Atoms in the Family: My Life with Enrico Fermi.* Chicago: University of Chicago Press, 1954. This biography, written by Fermi's wife, provides a personal portrait of the scientist as husband and father. The first three chapters deal with the period before 1924, the year Enrico and Laura met.

Jaffe, Bernard. "Enrico Fermi." In *Men of Science in America,* 571-628. New York: Simon and Schuster, 1958. Brief but informative account of Fermi's work before and after he came to the United States as well as descriptions of the work of other physicists leading up to the development of the atom bomb. Particularly useful diagrams illustrating the theory of nuclear fission.

Jones, Vincent C. *Manhattan: The Army and the Atomic Bomb.* Washington, D.C.: Center of Military History, United States Army, 1985. A well-documented account of the history of the development of the atom bomb.

Describes the collaboration between American science and industry under the direction of the United States Army.

Latil, Pierre de. *Enrico Fermi: The Man and His Theories*. Translated by Len Ortzen. New York: Paul S. Ericksson, 1966. Readable biography of Fermi's life with simplified explanations of complex nuclear theories. Useful as an introduction to the scientific methods of the physicist.

Libby, Leona Marshall. *The Uranium People*. New York: Crane, Russak and Co., 1979. Fascinating account of the production of the first controlled chain reaction for the manufacture of plutonium and the use of plutonium in bomb construction; the author was the only woman scientist on the project. Includes photographs of the people who were involved in the work and diagrams of the first nuclear reactor at the University of Chicago and the plutonium-production reactor in Hanford, Washington.

Segrè, Emilio. *Enrico Fermi: Physicist*. Chicago: University of Chicago Press, 1970. A well-documented, concise historical narrative written by Fermi's lifelong friend and colleague. Particular emphasis is given to the scientific background and to theories developed by Fermi.

Charles A. Dranguet, Jr.

MARSHALL FIELD

Born: August 18, 1834; near Conway, Massachusetts
Died: January 16, 1906; New York, New York
Areas of Achievement: Retailing and philanthrophy
Contribution: Founder of Marshall Field and Company, which became the
largest wholesale and retail dry-goods store in the world, Field introduced
many retailing concepts that set the standard for modern merchandising.

Early Life

Marshal Field was born near the town of Conway, Massachusetts, on
August 18, 1834, to John and Fidelia (née Nash) Field. His family had lived
in Massachusetts since 1629, when his ancestor Zechariah Field had come
over from England. Although his father was a farmer, the agrarian life did
not appeal to young Marshall. Instead, he left home at the age of seventeen
and took a job in a dry-goods store owned by Deacon Davis in Pittsfield,
Massachusetts. He worked there for five years, but, even though Davis
offered him a partnership in the business, Field had other plans. He saw the
West as the site of his future, as the place where huge fortunes could be
made by those ambitious and talented enough to take advantage of the tremendous opportunities caused by its rapid development and population
growth. Accordingly, he left New England in 1856 and moved to the rude and
dirty, but potentially thriving, city of Chicago, Illinois.

Field arrived in Chicago with little money and secured a job as a clerk with
Cooley, Wadsworth and Company, the largest wholesale dry-goods firm in
the city at the time. His starting salary was four hundred dollars a year and,
as an indication of his future business sense, he managed to save half of this
amount by living and sleeping in the store. A small, handsome young man
with a serious and polite demeanor and a large handlebar mustache, Field
also displayed a true flair for the dry-goods business and a unique appeal to
and concern for the customer. As a result, he rapidly advanced through the
hierarchy of the firm. Within a year of his arrival in Chicago, he was made a
traveling salesman for the company, and in 1861 he became general manger
of the Chicago store. His rapid rise culminated in 1862 when he was invited
to be a full partner in the company, which changed its name to Cooley, Farwell and Company. In 1864, when the financial wizard Levi Z. Leiter joined
as a new partner, Field finally had his name added to the company's title,
Farwell, Field and Company. Impressed by the entrepreneurial and financial
skill of Field and Leiter, the millionaire Potter S. Palmer offered to sell them
his retail and wholesale dry-goods business in 1865. The two men jumped at
the chance and, with money borrowed from Palmer himself, they formed the
new firm of Field, Palmer, and Leiter. Palmer dropped completely out of the
business two years later in order to concentrate exclusively on his hotel inter-

ests, leaving Field and Leiter in sole control of the growing firm. In only eight years, and by the age of thirty, Marshall Field had risen from a lowly clerk to the co-owner of one of the largest dry-goods operations in Chicago.

Life's Work

After Palmer retired from the firm in 1867, Field invited his two younger brothers, Henry and Joseph Field, to join as partners, thus consolidating his control of the business at Leiter's expense. Nevertheless, Leiter remained a partner until he sold his interest to Field in 1881, after which the business assumed the name Marshall Field and Company. Wholesale and retail sales, which had stood at approximately ten million dollars annually at the time of Palmer's withdrawal, climbed to nearly thirty-five million dollars by the early 1890's and had surpassed sixty-eight million dollars by the time of Field's death in 1906. Not even such catastrophes as the Chicago fire of 1871 (which completely destroyed his retail store and wholesale warehouse), the financial panic of 1873 (which ruined many Chicago merchants), or another fire in 1877 in his main retail outlet at the corner of State and Washington streets significantly slowed this pattern of expansion. As an example of this powerful drive to succeed, Field led Chicago in its recovery from the 1871 fire by establishing a temporary store in a horse barn at State and Twentieth streets only two weeks after the flames had died out.

At first, the wholesale aspect of the business interested Field more than the retail side. As time went on, however, and Field realized the immense profit potential of quality retailing, he devoted more and more of his energy to it, to the exclusion of the wholesale part of the firm. In 1873, the retail branch was physically separated from the wholesale branch with the opening of a new store at State and Washington streets. A program of continual expansion followed, culminating in the creation of the magnificent, city-block-square entrepôt in 1912, six years after Field's death. This massive structure still stands and serves as the flagship store of the Field Company as well as a familiar landmark in the heart of downtown Chicago.

Field was not a merchandising innovator, but he was very adept at adopting the newest methods in retailing that had been pioneered by others. His store plainly marked the price on all goods, so that the customer knew exactly what the cost of an item was when he or she first looked at it. He established resident buyers in England, France, and Germany in order to ensure his store a steady supply of quality foreign-made goods and frequently made it a practice to become the exclusive agent of popular products in Chicago—thus making sure that if customers wanted a certain product, they had to come to Fields to buy it. His reputation for honesty and courtesy was legendary, and he is credited with coining the motto The Customer Is Always Right. He also was among the first to adopt what is now the accepted practice in retailing marketing: He purchased products at wholesale for cash before there was any real customer demand for them and then, through advertising and attractive window displays, created that demand. This practice allowed Field to undersell his numerous competitors, who waited for demand to materialize before placing an order with a manufacturer, thus paying a higher wholesale price for the time. Marshall Field and Company was also the first retail outlet in the Midwest to employ window displays, to offer such personal services as gift-wrapping to customers, to establish a "bargain basement," and to open a restaurant within the store.

Field recognized ability when he saw it and often promoted talented managers to partners in his firm as a reward for their dedicated service. Former employees such as Harlow N. Higinbotham, Harry Gordon Selfridge, and John Shedd all became millionaires as a result of this practice. Once they had earned their fortunes as Field's partners, however, he then frequently proceeded to buy out their interest in the company in order to provide room for younger up-and-comers. The achievement of the American Dream was a real possibility for those who worked for Marshall Field, as long as they demonstrated the ambition, imagination, and ability he admired.

The American Dream was certainly good to Marshall Field as well. By the time of his death, he had amassed a fortune of $120,000,000. He did not waste this wealth on ostentatious display, as did so many other self-made millionaires of his era. Although he did build himself a grand mansion on Chicago's prestigious Prairie Avenue (constructed in 1873, at a cost of $100,000, by Richard Morris Hunt, the famous architect who had designed the fabulous palaces of William Vanderbilt and John Jacob Astor in New York), he otherwise lived a rather simple life dominated by his devotion to his work. He preferred to walk to his office and frequently ridiculed the pretensions of the wealthy. For example, when he was informed that a clerk was dating his daughter, he responded, "Thank God, there is no disgrace in being a clerk."

Field was not a prolific philanthropist, but when he did give, he made his gift count. After he first arrived in Chicago, he became active in such diverse organizations as the Chicago Relief and Aid Society, the Young Men's Christian Association, the Chicago Historical Association, the Art Institute, and the Civic Federation. Yet, as the years went by, business concerns monopolized an increasing portion of his time, and he let his membership in most of these organizations lapse. The year 1889 saw the rejuvenation of his charitable generosity. In that year he donated a ten-acre parcel of land, valued at $125,000, to serve as the site of the new University of Chicago. He later supplemented that gift with a $100,000 endowment to the school. In 1891, he gave $50,000 worth of land to the Chicago Home for Incurables, and, in 1893, he gave $1,000,000 to create the Columbian Museum at the Chicago World's Fair. A provision in his will for a further $8,000,000 allowed this museum to construct a permanent building on Chicago's Lake Shore Drive and to enlarge its collection. In appreciation of his support, the institution took the name the Field Museum of Natural History; it remains one of the best museums of its type in the United States.

Field's personal life contained a large share of tragedy. His first wife, Nannie Scott (they were married in January, 1863), left him in the late 1880's and took up permanent residence in France. After she died in 1896, he secretly courted Mrs. Delia Spencer Caton and married her shortly after her husband's death in 1905. Then, in November, 1905, his only son, Marshall Field, Jr., accidently shot and killed himself while preparing for a hunting trip. This last blow proved to be too much for the elderly multimillionaire. He came down with pneumonia in late December, 1905, and died on January 16, 1906. The bulk of his huge estate was left in trust to his two grandsons, Henry Field and Marshall Field III. The latter would become the founder and first publisher of the *Chicago Sun-Times*.

Summary

Marshall Field embodied those characteristics of ambition, business sense, hard work, and simplicity that Americans of his era valued so highly. The fact that a New England dry-goods clerk could become one of the wealthiest men in the United States suggested that success was within the grasp of anyone willing to work hard enough. Although there were thousands of failed clerks for every Marshall Field, Field nevertheless served as a shining example for every ambitious young man who entered the business world.

His impact on the American retail trade was equally striking. Although not an innovator himself, Field was willing to gamble on the innovations of others. He thus introduced many ideas first pioneered on the East Coast to Chicago and made his store the most progressive in the city throughout the nineteenth and early twentieth centuries. His emphasis on fairness and "the customer is always right" also won for him millions of loyal customers. As a result, in Chicago the name Marshall Field is still associated with honesty, courtesy, and high-quality merchandise at a fair price.

Finally, Field also had a profound influence on the history and institutions of the city of Chicago. Without his generosity, it is doubtful that the University of Chicago and the Field Museum of Natural History would exist. The prosperous State Street business district grew up around his State and Washington store and thus owes its life to Field's initial decision to locate there in 1873. His descendants, notably Marshall Field III, would play prominent roles in local politics and the press. Finally, several generations of Chicagoans have grown up with fond memories of Christmas trips to Field's to talk to Santa Claus, to gaze at the gigantic Christmas tree towering from the center of the Walnut Room, and to be dazzled by those magical Christmas window displays. Christmas and Field's go hand in hand in the hearts of Chicagoans and in the memories of ex-Chicagoans. Perhaps it is this feeling that represents Marshall Field's most profound gift to his beloved adopted city.

Bibliography
Cromie, Robert. *The Great Chicago Fire*. New York: McGraw-Hill Book Co., 1958. A detailed account of the holocaust that destroyed a good portion of the city in 1871. Also provides an informative description of Field's efforts to get both his business and the city back on their feet again after the fire.

Drury, John. *Old Chicago Houses*. Skokie, Ill.: Rand McNally and Co., 1941. Includes drawings, photographs, and an accurate description of Field's mansion on Prairie Avenue.

Pierce, Bessie Louise. *A History of Chicago*. Vol. 3, *The Rise of a Modern City, 1871-1893*. New York: Alfred A. Knopf, 1957. An excruciatingly minute history of the city during the late nineteenth century which includes numerous, and often colorful, anecdotes on the life, business, and contributions of Field.

Twyman, Robert W. *Marshall Field and Company, 1852-1906*. Philadelphia: University of Pennsylvania Press, 1906. Based on the author's doctoral dissertation, the book provides an excellent, although occasionally dry, analysis of the rise of Field's retailing empire.

Wagenknecht, Edward C. *Chicago*. Norman: University of Oklahoma Press, 1964. A brief, rather impressionistic, portrait of the history of the city that also presents a spotty but productive investigation of Field's influence during the late nineteenth century.

Wendt, Lloyd, and Herman Kogan. *Give the Lady What She Wants*. Skokie, Ill.: Rand McNally and Co., 1952. An exciting and well-written history of Marshall Field and Company up until 1950.

_____. *Chicago: A Pictorial History*. New York: Bonanza Books, 1958. Although brief on text, this visual history contains photographs of Field, his stores, and his mansion.

Christopher E. Guthrie

STEPHEN J. FIELD

Born: November 4, 1816; Haddam, Connecticut
Died: April 9, 1899; Washington, D.C.
Area of Achievement: Constitutional law
Contribution: In the last quarter of the nineteenth century, Justice Field's brilliant and ingenious legal opinions protected the United States' entrepreneurs from what they perceived to be the destructive power of popular government.

Early Life

Stephen Johnson Field was the sixth child of nine (seven boys and two girls) born to David and Submit Field. His father was an austere Congregational minister. His mother, whose Puritan father had given her the name "Submit" as an expression of Christian virtue, imbued her son with an independence of mind and motives which graphically demonstrated that she had been misnamed. Field's earliest education was the product of his parents' unchangeable convictions. "Our whole domestic life," wrote his brother, "received its tone from this unaffected piety of our parents, who taught their children to lie down and rise up in that fear of the Lord, which is the beginning of wisdom." At thirteen, Field's hearthside education ended when he accompanied his older sister and her husband to Greece, where they were to establish a school for young women. Two and a half years later, Field returned to Massachusetts with a less provincial view of the world and a determination to enroll at Williams College. In 1833, he entered Williams and was graduated valedictorian four years later.

Faced with the problem of choosing a vocation at the age of twenty-one, Field joined his brother's law firm in New York City. In 1841, he passed the New York bar. After ten years of service in the family law firm, however, he was anxious to set off on his own; with his brother's encouragement, he moved to San Francisco to try his luck at gold mining and lawyering. In California, it soon became apparent that he was a better lawyer than a miner. San Francisco was much too expensive for his meager purse, however, so he made his way up the Sacramento River to the frontier town of Marysville. In Marysville, he had the good fortune of rendering legal services to General John Augustus Sutter, on whose land gold had been discovered in 1849. With Sutter's help, he was elected the *alcalde* (the Mexican equivalent to the justice of the peace) of the Marysville township. A year later, with the installation of the newly drafted California constitution, he exchanged his position of *alcalde* for a seat in the legislature. In 1853, he ran for the California senate but was defeated by two votes and, with the defeat, never again sought a political position in the state.

The next six years were devoted to establishing a successful law practice and becoming financially independent. Indeed, by 1857 he had acquired enough influence with the rich and powerful people in California to be nominated and appointed to the state supreme court.

A few years later, as a result of his brilliantly reasoned and orderly *laissez-faire* legal opinions, he became the chief justice of the court. In 1863, although a Democrat, Field was appointed by the Republican President Abraham Lincoln to the United States Supreme Court.

Life's Work

Field's judicial activities covered more than forty years, thirty-four of which were on the federal bench, and during which time he wrote more than one thousand opinions. It was not the number of opinions but rather their quality which was to become his national legacy, a legacy in defense of the entrepreneurial class that was to last for more than half a century. Often he was the minority voice in his own court, yet long after majority decisions had lost their influence and had grown silent, his opinions directed the course of law in the United States.

Field's appearance, when he sat on the Supreme Court bench, was reported by some to be reminiscent of that of a Hebrew prophet. He was, in fact, short and stout, with a rounded body and an oval face covered with a white flowing beard that curled around the back of his neck and ears; yet this profusion of hair was wholly missing from the top of his head.

It is not difficult to find the foundations for Field's arguments in his religious training as a child. It was the inexorable propositions of the Bible that solidified his moral convictions and were later to mold his notions of natural and inalienable rights. As a mature judge, he found easy the transition from the God of the Bible to the Creator of inalienable rights. These autonomous, God-given rights became the bedrock conviction of nineteenth century American judicial conservatism. In his earliest opinions, Field was hard put to find precedent for his inalienable rights arguments. While the Declaration of Independence mentioned inalienable rights, the Constitution itself, which was the primary document for legal decisions, had nothing to say about such rights. With the drafting of the Fourteenth Amendment, however, Field finally had a federal document wholly adequate to his legal mission.

The critical passage in the Fourteenth Amendment read:

No state shall make or enforce any law which shall abridge the privileges or immunities of citizens of the United States; nor shall any state deprive any person of life, liberty, or property without due process of law; nor deny to any person within its jurisdiction the equal protection of the laws.

In later years, the "due process" and "equal protection of the laws" clauses were to become the most quoted words in the amendment, but for Field the "shall [not] abridge the privileges or immunities" clause was exactly the terminology he was looking for to secure his doctrine of inalienable rights.

In his earliest opinions, Field consistently applied the "privileges or immunities" clause to those cases in which individuals were seeking redress from the intrusion of government into their private lives. Eventually, however, as his influence and leadership in the Court grew, so also did his more collective definition of inalienable rights grow.

Soon he transposed and expanded his doctrine so as to accommodate the concept of citizen to include "citizens in the aggregate." Ostensibly, he argued that natural or inalienable constitutional rights applied to groups *qua* groups, and specifically to corporations. Business institutions and corporations had the same rights of protection from the invidious usurpation of privileges as did the individual citizen. This transposition from private to public rights was dramatically exhibited in a series of landmark opinions he wrote between 1865 and 1885. The earliest of these opinions was concerned with the abridgment of rights that individuals suffer at the hands of majoritarian legislation; but by 1875 he was applying the rationale he had employed in private rights cases to corporate business and industry.

For example, in 1865 there was a series of cases commonly described as "test-oath" cases that came before the Court. *Cummings v. Missouri* was one such case. In this case, the state of Missouri had required those seeking public office to declare under oath that they had not been disloyal to the United States or to the state of Missouri. This was divisive legislation since, in this border state, roughly half the population's sympathies lay with the South during the Civil War. It was legislation clearly intended to punish those who had backed the wrong side. As a consequence, anyone refusing to take this oath was to be prohibited access to various public stations and privileges. For example, they could not vote, hold public office, teach, preach, practice law, or administer public trusts.

Field was unequivocally opposed to test-oath restrictions. He argued that the requirement was punitive and in no manner tested the fitness or unfitness of citizens. Such a law, he continued, was *ex post facto*, intended to punish people without trial for past allegiances—punishment, in fact, for behavior that at the time committed was not a prosecutorial offense. Field joined a majority of the Court in striking down this legislation on the grounds that it was an abrogation of a citizen's inalienable right not to be subjected to sanctions for an act performed before the institution of a statute.

A second set of so-called due process cases was known as the "Chinese immigration" laws. Soon after the gold rush of 1849, enterprising shipping merchants began importing Chinese workers into California to do the menial labor brought on by the rapid industrial growth. In order to complete the transcontinental railroad, greater and greater numbers of Chinese were brought into California, and by 1869 government authorities were devising ways to limit the influx of these immigrants into the state. They enacted a series of laws that were unabashedly discriminatory. The Supreme Court had the task of determining the constitutionality of these laws. One law, for example, declared in the most general terms that "undesirable" Chinese were forbidden entry into the port of San Francisco, leaving the definition of undesirable up to city officials. Undesirables might mean prostitutes, or the poor, or unbonded workers. Another particularly pernicious law required that imprisoned Chinese men have their hair shorn, even though the cutting off of their plaited hair (*queue*) was for them an act of religious degradation. Again, there was a law requiring those Chinese wishing to establish a laundry business to obtain in writing the support of at least twelve taxpayers in the same city block. This was obviously a law intended to restrain the trade of the Chinese. In almost all these cases, Field argued that these laws accomplished nothing worthwhile and were merely acts of "hostility and spitefulness," clearly intended to deprive the Chinese of their natural and inalienable rights.

By 1870, Field was ready to transfer his inalienable rights doctrine from individuals to corporations and to expand his definition of persons to include "bodies of persons with a common interest." One of the earliest constitutional cases in which he argued in this fashion was *Hepburn v. Griswald*. *Hepburn v. Griswald* was a "legal-tender" or "greenback" case. Greenbacks referred to paper money, and many people had no confidence in paper money, particularly in its inflated state immediately after the Civil War. Despite private protest, however, the government insisted on paying its postwar debts with paper currency; creditors of the government regarded this practice as unstable because the government could print currency as it was needed, thus making it less and less valuable. For this reason, creditors began demanding payment *special basis*, that is, in gold and silver. In most of these legal-tender cases the Court majority supported the right of the government to pay its debts in greenbacks. Field, however, at times single-handedly, supported the creditors' right not to be required to accept these highly fluctuating, unstable paper notes. These creditors, he argued, had the right to payment special basis: They had the right to assess the worth of the payment, once it could be shown that the debtor had agreed to the value of the original contract. Legal-tender cases were clear evidence of Field's defense of his inalienable rights doctrine applied not only to aggrieved individuals but also to aggrieved groups of individuals, specifically, to corporations and industry.

Some of Field's most noteworthy "corporate citizen" arguments revolve around a series of cases pertaining to the country's railroads, and particularly to the railroad interests of some of Field's most influential California friends, men with controlling interests in Midwestern and far-Western railroads (Leland Stanford, Collis P. Huntington, Charles Crocker, and Mark Hopkins). In the 1840's and 1850's, in order to stimulate the growth of railroad building across the continent, Congress had provided railroad companies with enormous financial subsidies, tax exemptions, and outright land donations. As a result, these companies grew at an unbounded pace with powerfully unfair economic advantage over other commercial institutions. This advantage grew even larger during the next two decades because the railroads were able to escape the country's rising tax burden. The railroads also demonstrated an arrogance indicative of their power. They charged exorbitant and discriminatory rates, undercut their competitors, and refused to service the communities that they judged antirailroad. In due course, legislators, with popular support, began to introduce initiatives whose express purpose was to reduce the power and influence of these companies. In an effort to regain years of lost tax revenue, for example, the California Constitutional Convention of 1878 introduced a provision that would levy a tax against these companies' vast housing and equipment holdings. It was clear to everyone that this legislative maneuver was discriminatory since most of the inventory held by railroads was mortgaged inventory, and mortgage holdings were tax-exempt for private citizens in California.

The railroads refused to pay what they perceived as an inequitable tax and brought the disputed provision before the Supreme Court in 1882 (*San Mateo v. Southern Pacific*). This case gave Field an unambiguous opportunity to defend his "corporate citizen" argument once again. The Fourteenth Amendment, he declared, is intended to protect corporations in the same manner that individual citizens are protected. "Due process" requires that railroads, despite their vast wealth and holdings, are entitled to the same provisions of justice afforded the humblest citizen. Congress, he argued, fully intended that corporate interests receive "equal protection of the laws," and those lawyers who argued that this amendment was intended solely for black Americans were interpreting the amendment much too narrowly.

Field had considerable personal charm and was known as an enjoyable party guest. Yet he was also intensely disliked by many—with good reason, for he had some very unlikable character traits. He was a constant public moralizer, insatiably ambitious, at times vindictive, and not above making ethical compromises. Two of his brothers, David Dudley Field and Cyrus Field, became powerful, influential industrialists, and Stephen Field was accused, and not without some provocation, of tailoring his legal judgments to fit his brothers' financial interests. Off the bench, Stephen Field was intimate with Stanford, Huntington, J. P. Morgan, Jay Gould, and other wealthy industrialists, and on one occasion he even attended a private dinner party with them the night before he was to hear legal arguments in his court against their business holdings.

Stephen Field's tenure on the Supreme Court was longer than that of any justice who had gone before. He finally stepped down as a result of failing health at age eighty-two. While his devotion to individual rights was not always steadfast (he later ruled against private citizens such as women, laborers, and even the Chinese), his commitment to the interests of corporations and business never faltered. He died in Washington, D.C., on a cold, gray day in April, 1899, with the wealthy and powerful in government and business close at hand. There was also his wife, Sue Virginia, to whom he had been devoted for more than forty years.

Summary

Stephen Field's significant contribution to American society was unquestionably his brilliant legal opinions in defense of private rights. This defense was consistently sustained in support of private over public jurisdictions, opposition to loyalty oaths, opinions against the government's "legal tender" arguments, and his antislavery sympathies manifested in the "Chinese immigration" decisions. This fearless independence of mind set the direction of the Court for many years.

Bibliography

Black, Chauncey F. *Some Account of the Work of Stephen J. Field*. New York: Samuel B. Smith, 1881. This book is a systematic collection of Field's legal opinions. It includes his work as a member of the California supreme court as well as his decisions on the United States Supreme Court. There is a long introduction by John Norton Pomeroy, who was a law professor at the University of California during Field's lifetime. The introduction is of high scholarly quality but overly favorable to Field. One must, however, expect this from a volume put together by Field's political and legal friends during his lifetime.

Field, Stephen J. *California Alcalde*. Oakland, Calif.: Biobooks, 1950. This is Field's personal record of his reasons for coming to California, how he became the administrative judge of Marysville and eventually ran for the newly formed California legislature. There is also a description of his stormy struggle to obtain various political and judicial appointments, culminating in an appointment to the California supreme court.

_____. *Personal Reminiscences of Early Days in California*. Washington, D.C.: Privately printed, 1893. Reprint. New York: Da Capo Press, 1968. Field produces, in lively fashion, personal sketches of his early days in California, his first few days in San Francisco, his success and good luck in Marysville, his legislative years, and his membership on the California supreme court. Also included is his version of what he describes as an attempt to assassinate him by former chief justice of the California supreme court, David S. Terry, in 1889.

McCloskey, Robert Green. *American Conservatism in the Age of Enterprise*. Cambridge, Mass.: Harvard University Press, 1951. This is a provocative, albeit unsympathetic analysis of Field's legal influences in the post–Civil War era. McCloskey attempts to show a conceptual line of influence, from the Social Darwinism of William Graham Sumner through the legal conservatism of Field to the entrepreneurial, *laissez-faire* ideology of the capitalist Andrew Carnegie. McCloskey argues that Sumner and Field produced the moral and legal foundation for American capitalism.

Swisher, Carl Brent. *Stephen J. Field: Craftsman of Law*. Washington, D.C.: Brookings Institution, 1930. This is the best account of Field's career. It offers a rich record of his early years, his appointment as a Democrat from California to the United States Supreme Court by the Republican President Abraham Lincoln, and his political aspirations to be the Democratic nominee for president in 1880. Field had a dramatic and strenuous career, and Swisher's book covers it with literary skill.

Warren, Charles. *The Supreme Court in United States History*. 2 vols. Boston: Little, Brown and Co., 1926. This two-volume work is one of the greatest treatments of American constitutional history available. The fact that it was published in 1926 is irrelevant. In volume 2, chapters 30-34, Warren offers a concise record of the constitutional period between 1863-1888, the period during which Field's legal decisions so indelibly influenced the bench. Readers may find Warren's style excessively juridical, but the work is an invaluable account of Field's and other justices' supporting and dissenting opinions.

Donald Burrill

MILLARD FILLMORE

Born: January 7, 1800; Summerhill, New York
Died: March 8, 1874; Buffalo, New York
Area of Achievement: Politics
Contribution: In 1850, President Fillmore pushed for legislation designed to resolve a deadlock between Northern and Southern states over the admission of California to the Union and extension of slavery into new territories. Fillmore's support of the compromise legislation cost him the Whig presidential nomination in 1852; it also may have postponed the Civil War for a decade.

Early Life

Millard Fillmore was born January 7, 1800, in a long cabin on the farm in Locke township, New York, that his father, Nathaniel, and his uncle Calvin had purchased in 1799. Nathaniel and his wife, Phoebe Millard Fillmore, had come to the western frontier from Vermont, prompted by the prospect of more fertile land in the Military Tract set aside by New York State after the American Revolution in order to pay bonuses to veterans. In time, there were nine children in the Fillmore family; Millard was the second child and first son.

In 1815, Millard Fillmore was apprenticed to a wool carder and cloth-dresser at New Hope, near the farm in Niles, New York, that Nathaniel Fillmore had leased after title to the property in Locke proved invalid. He attended the district school in New Hope, teaching there and in Buffalo schools after 1818, and there he met his future wife Abigail Powers. Fillmore spent the years between this first acquaintance and their marriage, on February 5, 1826, establishing himself as a lawyer. He studied law from 1820 under Judge Walter Wood in Montville, New York, and in 1822 began work as a clerk in the Buffalo, New York, law firm of Asa Rice and Joseph Clary. Even though he had not completed the usual seven-year period of study, Fillmore was admitted to practice before the Court of Common Pleas and opened his own law practice in East Aurora, New York, in 1823. He moved to Buffalo in 1830 and in time went into law partnership with Nathan K. Hall and Solomon G. Haven.

Fillmore's appearance and public manner marked him for a career in politics. Just under six feet tall, he had broad shoulders, an erect carriage, and bright blue eyes. His hair was thick and yellow, but by middle age it had turned snowy white. His voice was deep and masculine. Never an orator like Daniel Webster or Edward Everett, both of whom served him as secretary of state, Fillmore struck juries and audiences as carefully prepared, sincere, and unaffected. An associate of Thurlow Weed in formation of the Anti-Masonic Party, he was elected three times to the New York State Assembly (1829-

1831). Fillmore's chief accomplishment in the legislature was authorship of a law eliminating the imprisonment of debtors and providing for a bankruptcy law. Characteristic of his mature political style was the careful balancing of individual and business interests that this legislation achieved.

Life's Work

Since the chief impetus behind the formation of the Anti-Masonic Party was reelection of John Quincy Adams and defeat of Andrew Jackson in the election of 1828, the party lost strength when Jackson was elected, although it retained local influence chiefly in New York, Pennsylvania, and New England. Fillmore was elected to the House of Representatives as an Anti-Mason (1833-1835), but he followed Thurlow Weed into the newly formed Whig party in 1834. Subsequently, he was sent to Congress as a Whig (1837-1843) after William Henry Harrison was elected president in 1840. Fillmore served as chairman of the House Ways and Means Committee, and in that position he engineered congressional approval of protective tariff legislation in 1842.

Mentioned as a senatorial or vice presidential candidate prior to the 1844 election, Fillmore accepted Weed's advice—perhaps intended to keep the vice presidential prospects of William H. Seward alive—that he run for governor of New York. He was defeated by the popular Democrat Silas Wright but came back in 1847 to win election as New York's comptroller. Fillmore and Seward were both favorite son prospects for the Whig vice presidential nomination in 1848. The presidential candidates were Henry Clay, General Winfield Scott, and General Zachary Taylor. When the convention chose Taylor, and some delegates objected to Abbott Lawrence of Massachusetts as his running mate, the antislavery Clay delegates put their votes behind Fillmore and assured him the vice presidential slot. He was not assured of influence within the Taylor Administration itself when, having won the election, the new president took office in 1849. William H. Seward, Weed's ally and the newly elected senator for New York, worked to minimize Fillmore's influence on the new president. Unable to control party patronage in his home state, Fillmore was limited chiefly to his constitutional duty of presiding over the debates of the United States Senate.

California had petitioned for admission to the Union. There were thirty states at the time, fifteen slave and fifteen free, and California would tip the balance in the debate over slavery. The same issue complicated discussion of territorial governments for Utah and New Mexico, acquired at the end of the Mexican War, and an outstanding Texas–New Mexico border dispute. Abolitionists and Free-Soilers campaigned to limit the expansion of slavery into new states and territories, even trying to prohibit the slave trade in the District of Columbia, while Southern political leaders argued for the extension of slavery and for more vigorous enforcement of laws requiring the capture and return of fugitive slaves.

Senator Henry Clay, the support of whose delegates at the Whig convention of 1848 had assured Fillmore the vice presidential nomination, proposed an omnibus package of compromise legislation to deal with these issues. President Taylor, though a slaveholder from Louisiana, indicated that he would veto the bill if it extended slavery into the territories gained from Mexico. He also claimed he would use federal troops to resolve the Texas–New Mexico boundary dispute. Initially, Fillmore supported Taylor's position on Clay's omnibus bill, but, in 1850, he advised the president that he would vote to accept the package if required to cast a tiebreaking vote in the Senate. Fillmore never had to cast that vote. Taylor became ill after attending ceremonies at the Washington Monument on July 4, and died on July 9, 1850, making Millard Fillmore the thirteenth President of the United States.

After taking the oath of office and accepting the resignations of Taylor's entire cabinet, Fillmore moved to occupy a pro-Union political position. He appointed Daniel Webster as secretary of state and John Crittenden as attorney general, and he filled the rest of the cabinet with equally moderate men. Fillmore repeatedly insisted that slavery was morally repugnant to him, but he also said that he intended to be the president of the entire United States. He was prepared to make compromises in the interest of national unity. When Senator Stephen A. Douglass, a Democrat, took over Senate management of Clay's stalled "omnibus bill," Fillmore indicated his willingness to sign the provisions of the omnibus as separate pieces of legislation. Between September 9, and September 20, 1850, he signed five measures designed to hammer out a compromise between Northern and Southern interests. California was admitted as a free state; Utah and New Mexico were given territorial status, with the citizens eventually to determine the status of slavery there; and Texas was compensated for the loss of territory in the adjustment of its border with New Mexico. Fillmore also signed a tougher law dealing with fugitive slaves and another prohibiting the slave trade, but not slavery itself, in the District of Columbia.

This reversal of Taylor's position achieved a political solution to a conflict threatening to erupt into military action. Fillmore had to send troops into South Carolina to deal with threats of secession and threatened to use them in the North to enforce the Fugitive Slave Act before there was general acceptance of these measures. While moderate men of all political parties supported Fillmore's position, both the Southern and New England factions of his own Whig party blamed him for those parts of the compromise package of which they disapproved. Therefore, Fillmore did not get the Whig presidential nomination in 1852 and retired to Buffalo in 1853, turning over the powers of the office to the Democrat Franklin Pierce.

In the face of the virtual dissolution of the Whigs as a national political party, Fillmore accepted the presidential nomination of the American, or

Know-Nothing Party in 1856. He attempted to distance himself from the proslavery, anti-Catholic, nativist principles of the party and to run his campaign on the Unionist basis he had advocated while president. The strategy did not work. In a three-way race against Democrat James Buchanan and Republican John C. Frémont, Fillmore came in a poor third.

With the election of Buchanan in 1856, Fillmore's national political career came to an end. Abigail Powers Fillmore died in Washington, D.C., on March 30, 1853, only a few weeks after her husband had left the White House. On February 10, 1858, Fillmore married Caroline Carmichael McIntosh, a widow, in Albany, New York. He died in Buffalo, New York on March 8, 1874; Caroline McIntosh Fillmore died there on August 11, 1881.

Summary

During the Civil War and in the years following, the popular press depicted Millard Fillmore as a Southern sympathizer. He supported the candidacy of General George B. McClellan in 1864, and he also expressed approval of Andrew Johnson's efforts to achieve reconciliation with the South at the war's end. Properly speaking, Fillmore's positions were not so much pro-Southern as conservative, exactly as they had been when he accepted the compromise legislation of 1850 in the name of preserving the Union. His role in passage of that legislation was the central achievement of his term as president.

Fillmore's initiatives in foreign policy were modest, but they too reflected his unwillingness to adopt extreme positions. Fillmore resisted moves to annex Cuba and Nicaragua; he expressed disapproval of Austria's handling of the Hungarian uprising led by Lajos Kossuth, and he blocked French attempts to make the Hawaiian Islands a protectorate. Fillmore's administration moved to normalize relations with Mexico and opened negotiations to build a canal connecting the Atlantic and Pacific oceans through Nicaragua. He sent Commodore Matthew Perry on his mission to open the ports of Japan to merchant ships of the United States.

Like Taylor, Pierce, and Buchanan, Fillmore's reputation has been affected by the failure of nineteenth century American politics to avert the Civil War. The administration of each of these presidents struggled to control the forces that led to military conflict. The legislation passed in 1850 was the most significant attempt to defuse the sectional conflict, and Millard Fillmore's role in its passage is his chief claim to historical importance.

Bibliography

Barre, W. L. *The Life and Public Services of Millard Fillmore.* New York: Burt Franklin, 1971. Reprint of a campaign biography originally published in 1856, Barre's book provides an undocumented contemporary account of Fillmore's life and tenure as president.

Fillmore, Millard. *Millard Fillmore Papers*. Edited by Frank H. Severance. 2 vols. Buffalo, N.Y.: Buffalo Historical Society, 1907. Reprint. New York: Kraus Reprint Co., 1970. These volumes contain the only printed collection of Fillmore's public papers.

Goodman, Mark. *High Hopes: The Rise and Decline of Buffalo, New York*. Albany: State University of New York Press, 1983. While Goodman's book deals with Fillmore only in passing, it contains a fascinating account of local reactions to his 1856 campaign as the presidential nominee of the American, or Know-Nothing, Party.

Holt, Michael F. *The Political Crisis of the 1850's*. New York: John Wiley and Sons, 1978. Reprint. New York: W. W. Norton and Co., 1983. Holt argues that disintegration of the Whig-Democrat two-party structure was a cause and not an effect of the political crisis of the 1850's.

Potter, David M. *The Impending Crisis, 1848-1861*. Edited by Don E. Fehrenbacher. New York: Harper and Row, Publishers, 1976. This excellent history of the period places the various conflicts Fillmore dealt with squarely within the ideological framework of Manifest Destiny.

Rayback, Robert J. *Millard Fillmore: Biography of a President*. Buffalo, N.Y.: Henry Stewart, 1959. The book explains the complex factors that drew Fillmore into the Anti-Masonic Whig, and American parties and the effects of these associations on his political career.

Schelin, Robert C. "A Whig's Final Quest: Fillmore and the Know-Nothings." *Niagara Frontier* 26, no. 1 (1979): 1-11. Schelin focuses on Fillmore's 1856 campaign for president against the background of Whig decline and Know-Nothing appeals to prejudice.

Snyder, Charles M., ed. *The Lady and the President: The Letters of Dorothea Dix and Millard Fillmore*. Lexington: University Press of Kentucky, 1975. The correspondence of Fillmore and Dix, the chief nineteenth century American advocate for reform in the treatment of the mentally ill; gives insight into Fillmore's personality as well as his actions as a public official and political candidate.

Robert C. Petersen

F. SCOTT FITZGERALD

Born: September 24, 1896; St. Paul, Minnesota
Died: December 21, 1940; Hollywood, California
Area of Achievement: Literature
Contribution: With a poetic style and an insight into the lure of and the fallacies within the American Dream, Fitzgerald created some of the most distinctively American fiction.

Early Life

Francis Scott Key Fitzgerald was born September 24, 1896, in St. Paul, Minnesota. His father, Edward Fitzgerald, was a furniture manufacturer, and his mother, Mollie McQuillan Fitzgerald, the daughter of a wealthy St. Paul businessman. After Edward Fitzgerald's business failed in 1898, he became a wholesale grocery salesman for Proctor and Gamble in Buffalo, New York. Edward was transferred to Syracuse, New York, in 1901 (when Scott's sister Annabel was born) and back to Buffalo in 1903 before losing his job in 1908. The family then returned to St. Paul to live off the money Mollie had inherited from her father.

Edward Fitzgerald, who had cowritten a novel when he was young, read from the works of Lord Byron and Edgar Allan Poe to his son and praised the boy's attempts at writing, but he hoped that Scott would become an army officer. Mollie did not encourage his literary interests and wanted him to be a successful businessman like her father, to make up for Edward's failure and to live up to the illustrious ancestors on his father's side of the family, a long line of wealthy Maryland landowners, politicians, and lawyers. (Francis Scott Key was a distant relative.)

Because Scott's family believed that he needed discipline, he was sent in 1911 to the Newman School, a Catholic preparatory school in Hackensack, New Jersey. At Newman, Fitzgerald met Father Sigourney Fay, a wealthy intellectual who introduced him to Henry Adams and other well-known literary figures. Fay became the boy's surrogate father and is the model for Monsignor Darcy in *This Side of Paradise* (1920).

In 1913, Fitzgerald enrolled at Princeton University. He dreamed of becoming a college football star but did not make the team. He had worked on school publications throughout high school and began writing for the *Princeton Tiger*, the college humor magazine. He also wrote the books and lyrics for musical productions of the prestigious Triangle Club, and through such literary endeavors he made friends with fellow students Edmund Wilson, who became one of America's most important critics, and John Peale Bishop, later a successful poet. Fitzgerald and Wilson wrote *The Evil Eye* for the Triangle Club in 1915. After a publicity photograph for that production of Fitzgerald dressed as a girl ran in *The New York Times*, he received an offer to become a female impersonator in vaudeville.

Earlier that year, Fitzgerald had met sixteen-year-old Ginevra King of Lake Forest, Illinois, at a party in St. Paul. For him, she was the embodiment of the perfect woman: beautiful, rich, socially prominent, and sought-after. Ginevra, the model for many of the young women in Fitzgerald's short stories, rejected him eventually because he was not wealthy.

That disappointment was not Fitzgerald's only one in 1915. He was elected secretary of the Triangle Club, meaning that he would be its president during his senior year, but bad grades made him ineligible for campus offices. Fitzgerald had neglected his studies almost from his arrival at Princeton. At the end of the fall semester, poor grades and illness forced him to drop out of school.

Fitzgerald returned to Princeton in the fall of 1916 to repeat his junior year, and he continued to write stories for the campus literary magazine. He was never graduated, however, since the United States entered World War I, and he joined the army as a second lieutenant in October, 1917. On weekends, he began writing "The Romantic Egotist," an early version of *This Side of Paradise*. In June, 1918, he was sent to Camp Sheridan, near Montgomery, Alabama. At a country club dance that July, Fitzgerald met eighteen-year-old Zelda Sayre, and they fell in love two months later. Zelda came from a prominent Montgomery family, her father being a justice of the Alabama Supreme Court. Zelda, considered the most popular girl in Montgomery, was attracted to Fitzgerald because they wanted the same things: success, fame, and glamour.

The war ended just as Fitzgerald was to go overseas. He was disappointed because he wanted to test himself in battle and because he saw the war as a romantic adventure. Yet more disappointments were the rejection of his novel by Charles Scribner's Sons and the disapproval of Zelda's parents, who believed that Scott was not stable enough to take proper care of their high-strung daughter. Nevertheless, Zelda agreed to marry him if he went to New York—where she desperately wanted to live—and became a success.

Fitzgerald began working for the Barron Collier advertising agency in February, 1919, writing advertisements which appeared in trolley cars. That spring, he sold his first short story, "Babes in the Woods," to *The Smart Set*, the sophisticated magazine edited by H. L. Mencken and George Jean Nathan. Zelda, however, was too impatient for his success and broke off their engagement that June.

Life's Work

Fitzgerald quit his job in July, 1919, and returned to St. Paul to live with his parents while revising his novel. Maxwell Perkins, the legendary Scribner's editor, accepted *This Side of Paradise* that September, despite objections to what his very conservative employer considered a frivolous novel. Perkins, whose suggestions helped Fitzgerald improve the book, said he would resign if Scribner's did not publish it.

Shortly after the novel was accepted, Fitzgerald became a client of agent Harold Ober and began publishing stories in the *Saturday Evening Post*, at that time the highest-paying magazine in the field. Unfortunately, he also began a lifelong pattern of drinking and wild spending. He and Zelda seemed made for each other because of their youth, beauty, ambition, and excesses. They were married April 3, 1920, a few days after *This Side of Paradise* was published.

Scribner's published three thousand copies of Fitzgerald's autobiographical novel about a college student's coming of age, and the book was sold out in three days. By the end of 1921, it had gone through twelve printings of 49,075 copies, a huge success for a serious first novel. *This Side of Paradise*, considered the first realistic American college novel, was read as a handbook for collegiate conduct. By presenting the new American girl in rebellion against her mother's values, the novel also created the prototype of the flapper. Novelist John O'Hara later claimed that a half million Americans between the ages of fifteen and thirty fell in love with the book.

The Fitzgeralds quickly became major celebrities in New York because of Scott's success and the young couple's good looks and flamboyant personalities. (Unfortunately, few photographs capture the charismatic good looks of Zelda, with her wavy hair, almond-shaped eyes, and oval face, and blond, blue-eyed, stocky Scott, whose impact is widely attested in contemporary accounts.) Zelda went from the center of attention she had been in Montgomery to the wife of a famous novelist, and she resented the change. She remained jealous of her husband's artistic success and attempted, in the course of their marriage, to become a ballerina, a painter, and a novelist. *Save Me the Waltz* (1932), her highly autobiographical novel, was written to compete with Scott's *Tender Is the Night* (1934). This sense of competition increased Zelda's drinking and contributed to her mental problems. The birth of their only child, Frances Scott (Scottie) Fitzgerald, in 1921 did little to slow down the Fitzgeralds.

The couple had to lead extravagant lives to live up to their press clippings, and Fitzgerald's work suffered for it. He borrowed from his publisher and agent and wrote short stories to finance the writing of his novels. (Of Fitzgerald's 178 stories, 146 published during his lifetime, or about two-thirds, are of inferior quality, written primarily to pay bills.) Whenever he got ahead, he spent himself into debt again.

Fitzgerald's early success was followed by two failures. *The Beautiful and Damned* (1922), while actually selling more copies than *This Side of Paradise* because of Fitzgerald's reputation, was not as well received by the critics as his first novel. This examination of how greed corrupts a marriage is Fitzgerald's bleakest, most cynical, least effective novel. Because he had long loved the theater, Fitzgerald wanted to be as good a playwright as he was a novelist. *The Vegetable* (1923), a political satire, opened in Atlantic City, New Jersey, in November, 1923, and closed quickly, leaving Fitzgerald's aspirations as a dramatist unfulfilled.

In 1924, the Fitzgeralds made their second trip to Europe; Zelda had an affair with a French aviator on the Riviera and attempted suicide, events that her husband used in *Tender Is the Night*. In Paris, Scott was introduced to Gertrude Stein and other prominent American expatriates. He met the then-unknown Ernest Hemingway and recruited him for Scribner's. Their friendship was a close but rocky one, for both writers were temperamental and suspicious of each other.

Fitzgerald's masterpiece, *The Great Gatsby* (1925), is one of the most widely read serious American novels, but this poetic look at love, wealth, innocence, illusions, corruption, and the American Dream was, ironically, a failure when it first appeared, selling half as many copies as either of Fitzgerald's previous novels. He blamed this failure on the lack of the strong women characters necessary to please the predominantly female reading public. The genius of this almost perfect novel, however, was recognized by many serious readers, including T. S. Eliot, who wrote Fitzgerald that "it seems to me to be the first step that American fiction has taken since Henry James."

Almost a decade would pass before Fitzgerald's next novel appeared. He spent that time writing stories, twice attempting unsuccessfully to become a Hollywood screenwriter, moving back and forth between the United States and Europe, seeing Zelda's mental instability and his own drinking increase. Zelda entered psychiatric clinics in France and Switzerland in 1930 and was in and out of institutions for the remainder of her life.

Fitzgerald's account of the disintegration of fragile Americans living on the French Riviera in *Tender Is the Night* is autobiographical, as is most of his fiction. The novel is considered a masterpiece but was yet another failure in 1934; both readers and critics were puzzled by the flashback structure. Fitzgerald hoped that the novel would be republished with the events rearranged into chronological order, and such an edition finally appeared posthumously, in 1951, but most critics regard it as inferior to the original version.

In the mid-1930's, Fitzgerald reached his nadir. Between 1935 and 1937, he wrote nine stories that no one would publish, and he constantly begged Harold Ober for money. His drinking became so bad that he finally had to be hospitalized. Hemingway offered to have his friend killed so that Zelda and Scottie would receive insurance money.

Fitzgerald's fortunes began improving in the month of July, 1937, when Metro-Goldwyn-Mayer hired him as a screenwriter at a salary of one thousand dollars a week, allowing him to pay off many of his debts. That same month, he met gossip columnist Sheilah Graham, and they fell in love. Fitzgerald spent his spare time educating the young Englishwoman while she tried to save him from himself, sticking by him even when he resumed drinking and mistreated her.

Fitzgerald took his film work seriously and even entertained hopes of becoming a director, but the assemblyline system of creating scripts at that time was unsuitable for someone of his talent and fragile ego. He received screen credit for only one script, *Three Comrades* (1938), an adaptation of an Erich Maria Remarque novel, but even then the finished product differed greatly from what Fitzgerald had conceived. He protested to producer Joseph L. Mankiewicz, "Oh, Joe, can't producers ever be wrong? I'm a good writer—honest. I thought you were going to play fair." He was sent to Dartmouth College with young writer Budd Schulberg in February, 1939, to research a film about the school's winter carnival, only to spend the entire trip drunk, and he was fired.

By October, 1939, Fitzgerald had decided to ignore his personal, financial, and professional problems as much as possible and began writing *The Last Tycoon* (1941), the story of an idealist film producer—based on himself and Irving Thalberg, the late head of Metro-Goldwyn-Mayer—who falls in love with a young woman much like Sheilah Graham. The novel was about half finished when Fitzgerald died of a heart attack at Graham's apartment on December 21, 1940.

Edmund Wilson assembled the unfinished novel and Fitzgerald's outline for the remainder of the book for publication in 1941. Fitzgerald's other posthumous book is *The Crack-Up* (1945), also edited by Wilson, a collection of autobiographical essays about his problems which first appeared in *Esquire* in the 1930's. Zelda Fitzgerald died in a fire at a sanatorium in Asheville, North Carolina, on March 10, 1948, and was buried beside her husband in Rockville, Maryland.

Summary

Like his friend Hemingway, Fitzgerald had the misfortune to live such a colorful existence that it has almost overshadowed his work. For many, the names Scott and Zelda Fitzgerald evoke images of an attractive but drunk couple jumping into the fountain in front of the Plaza Hotel in Manhattan. For all of his weaknesses as a human being, however, Fitzgerald is recognized as one of America's best, most perceptive writers. He produced two great novels and dozens of good-to-excellent short stories, the best being "The Ice Palace," "May Day," "The Diamond as Big as the Ritz," "Winter Dreams," "The Rich Boy," "Babylon Revisited," "Crazy Sunday," and "The Lost Decade."

One of the great subjects in American literature is failure, and Fitzgerald knew as much about this subject as any writer. He created his art to make up for his father's failure, for his not making the Princeton football team, for not living up to his potential in college, for losing Ginevra King, for missing out on the war, for not continuing to be the successful author of *This Side of Paradise*, for not working out in Hollywood, for Zelda's madness and his drinking, for not being the husband Zelda needed or the father Scottie should have had—for not proving himself to himself. Few Americans have understood the thin line between success and failure as well as Fitzgerald.

He is one of the major delineators of the American Dream, perhaps being more closely identified with this mythical concept than any other twentieth century artist. In *The Great Gatsby*, Jay Gatsby reinvents himself to fit his romantic idea of the American Dream, ending up both betraying and being betrayed by it. Throughout his fiction, Fitzgerald mourns the loss of innocence and youthful ideals while recognizing the inevitability of this loss. The great American paradox, as posed by Fitzgerald, is that holding on to illusions is both destructive and necessary. As the poet of the Jazz Age, a term he created to describe the 1920's, Fitzgerald will forever be associated with that time. In *Tender Is the Night*, he shows America's self-destructive urges in that decade and their painful consequences.

What matters most about F. Scott Fitzgerald, however, is not the tawdry details of his sad life, not any themes he examines in his art, not his place in American letters. What matters is that he could write beautifully. Nowhere in American fiction are there as many heartbreakingly lovely passages as in *The Great Gatsby*. The most moving tragedy of Fitzgerald's life was that he died believing that he was a failure and would be forgotten.

Bibliography
Bruccoli, Matthew J. *Some Sort of Epic Grandeur: The Life of F. Scott Fitzgerald*. New York: Harcourt Brace Jovanovich, 1981. The most complete biography of Fitzgerald; separates facts from myths. The culmination of thirty years of research by the leading authority on the writer. Includes an account by Fitzgerald's daughter of their Colonial ancestors.
Bruccoli, Matthew J., Scottie Fitzgerald Smith, and Joan P. Kerr, eds. *The Romantic Egoists*. New York: Charles Scribner's Sons, 1974. A pictorial autobiography of Scott and Zelda Fitzgerald taken from their scrapbooks and photograph albums. Includes letters and selections from their writings. A fascinating document.
Callaghan, Morley. *That Summer in Paris: Memories of Tangled Friendships with Hemingway, Fitzgerald, and Some Others*. New York: Coward-McCann, 1963. The Canadian novelist's memoir perfectly captures the American expatriate life in France.
Graham, Sheilah, and Gerold Frank. *Beloved Infidel*. New York: Holt, Rinehart and Winston, 1958. Graham's account of her rise from an English orphanage to a position of influence in Hollywood, with the emphasis on her romance with Fitzgerald. First of her three books about Fitzgerald.

Hoffman, Frederick J. *The Twenties: American Writing in the Postwar Decade*. Rev. ed. New York: Collier Books, 1962. Explores the relationship between literature, history, politics, science, and culture in general in the 1920's. Relates all this specifically to *The Great Gatsby*. Perhaps the best such study of the period.

Latham, Aaron. *Crazy Sundays: F. Scott Fitzgerald in Hollywood*. New York: Viking Press, 1971. This detailed account of Fitzgerald's screenwriting career has many facts and rumors but insufficient analysis.

Le Vot, Andre. *F. Scott Fitzgerald: A Biography*. Translated by William Byron. Garden City, N.Y.: Doubleday and Co., 1983. This biography by a French critic emphasizes Fitzgerald's European experiences. Inconsistent in analyzing the fiction.

Milford, Nancy. *Zelda: A Biography*. New York: Harper and Row, Publishers, 1970. Very sympathetic look at Zelda's life with much material not previously published. Presents Zelda as a woman with undeveloped talents and unused abilities.

Mizener, Arthur. *The Far Side of Paradise: A Biography of F. Scott Fitzgerald*. Rev. ed. Boston: Houghton Mifflin Co., 1965. The first full-length biography of Fitzgerald (originally published in 1951); achieves a balance between an account of his life and an analysis of his work. Re-creates the composition of each novel.

Turnbull, Andrew. *Scott Fitzgerald*. New York: Charles Scribner's Sons, 1962. Wonderful biography by a very talented writer who, as a child, knew and admired Fitzgerald. Emphasizes the artist's personality and is written almost as if it were a Fitzgerald novel.

Michael Adams

ABRAHAM FLEXNER

Born: November 13, 1866; Louisville, Kentucky
Died: September 21, 1959; Falls Church, Virginia
Area of Achievement: Education
Contribution: Successfully blending scholarship and administrative ability with reformist zeal, Flexner was responsible for major transformations of American elementary, secondary, medical, and postgraduate education.

Early Life

Abraham Flexner was born November 13, 1866, in Louisville, Kentucky. He was the son of Jewish immigrants, Esther Abraham and Moritz Flexner, who were successful Louisville hat merchants. The depression of 1873 destroyed their business, however, and reduced the family to poverty. Yet like most Jews, the Flexners placed great importance on schooling and did whatever they could to ensure that Abraham, as well as his brothers and sisters, received an education.

In 1884, Flexner entered The Johns Hopkins University with the assistance of a thousand-dollar loan from his oldest brother, Jacob. He majored in the study of ancient Greece and Rome, receiving his bachelor's degree in 1886. After graduation, Flexner returned to his hometown, where he taught for four years at the local high school. Recognizing a need to educate wealthy but unruly youths, he founded an academy that prepared them for college through brief but intensive work. His unorthodox teaching methods included the absence of rules, examinations, records, and reports. The success of Flexner's graduates brought him to the attention of president Charles W. Eliot of Harvard, which led to an article in *The Atlantic Monthly* describing his methods, entitled "The Preparatory School."

At the urging of his wife, Flexner left Louisville the following year for graduate work in psychology at Harvard. After receiving his master's degree, he traveled overseas to study comparative education at the University of Berlin. He was convinced by his experiences at Johns Hopkins, Harvard, and Berlin that American institutions of higher education should restructure themselves along the lines of the German university. In 1908, Flexner published *The American College: A Criticism*, a critique of the nation's colleges that called for more attention to scholarship and less attention to extracurricular activities. This book was the turning point in his career.

Life's Work

Flexner's book attracted the attention of Henry S. Pritchett, a former president of the Massachusetts Institute of Technology and head of the Carnegie Foundation for the Advancement of Teaching. The foundation was about to begin a major evaluation of medical education in the United States and Canada, and Pritchett commissioned Flexner to undertake the study. Undertaking his duties with a seemingly boundless energy and attention to detail, Flexner visited each of the 155 American and Canadian medical schools then in operation and described each in detail.

The results of his research were published by the Carnegie Foundation in 1910, under the title *Medical Education in the United States and Canada.* Using the minimum criteria by which European medical schools were allowed to operate, Flexner found that seventy-five percent of their American counterparts would be closed. He described many teaching hospitals as outdated and unsanitary; some he called death traps. Most medical schools, Flexner charged, existed solely for the profit of their owners. Any unqualified student could gain admission to them and be graduated if he only paid the tuition. Even reputable medical schools often lacked the most rudimentary facilities. Flexner recommended that no less than 120 of the medical schools included in his study be closed.

Flexner's study became front-page news. Two years later, he completed another study, entitled *Medical Education in Europe* (1912). Together, the two works established his reputation as the world's foremost authority on medical education. In 1913, largely as a result of these two studies, Flexner was hired by the General Education Board, a philanthropic foundation established by millionaire John D. Rockefeller to improve education in the United States. Beginning as assistant secretary, he advanced to become head of its Division of Studies and Medical Education. While working at the board, he authored and coauthored several reports, including *Prostitution in Europe* (1914), *Public Education in Maryland* (1916), *The Gary Schools* (1918), and *Public Education in Delaware* (1919). He also awarded grants to stimulate humanistic research and is credited with playing a major role in founding the Lincoln School, which is remembered as the crowning achievement of the Progressive Era's education movement.

Despite the diversity of his interests while at the General Education Board, Flexner remained interested in the improvement of medical education. In addition to the publication of a 1925 report, *Medical Education: A Comparative Study*, he devoted attention to the development of full-time, basic science research faculties at medical schools. Before his retirement from the board in 1928, Flexner disbursed fifty million dollars to medical schools.

A photograph of the beardless, balding, and bespectacled Flexner taken during his mature years shows a face of a man seemingly tailor-made for the role of a Progressive Era intellectual, with a high forehead, furrowed brow, and imperious countenance. By this time, Flexner was in great demand as a lecturer abroad. He traveled to England, where he presented the Rhodes Trust memorial lectures in 1927, and was the 1928 Taylor lecturer at Oxford University. The following year, he lectured before the Foundation Universitaire in Belgium. In 1930, his Rhodes lectures were published in revised and expanded form as *Universities: American, English, German*, in which he restated his belief in the superiority of German universities, especially in their emphasis upon conceptual research and the graduate seminar.

The Great Depression and a lack of enthusiasm for his reforms among educators thwarted Flexner's plans to direct American higher education along the lines of the German university. His ideas did find partial fulfillment, however, when he persuaded department-store magnate Louis Bamberger and his sister, Mrs. Felix Fuld, to give five million dollars to establish the Institute for Advanced Study in Princeton, New Jersey. As its first director, from 1930 to 1939, Flexner brought a small number of select scholars to the institute and gave them complete freedom, as well as virtually unlimited resources and personnel, to pursue conceptual research. An early fellow of the institute was Albert Einstein; the addition of other noted scholars, such as John von Neuman, in later years made it famous.

After leaving the institute, Flexner devoted his remaining years to writing. He wrote an autobiography, *I Remember* (1940), biographies of higher education leaders Henry S. Pritchett and Daniel Coit Gilman, and a historical-contemporary study of foundations, *Funds and Foundations* (1952). Flexner died September 21, 1959, in Falls Church, Virginia.

Summary

Over the course of his long public service career, Flexner served as a catalyst for change in many areas of American education. He was responsible, perhaps to a greater degree than any other individual, for raising educational standards in United States and Canadian medical schools. The Lincoln School, which he helped found, exerted a profound influence on the subsequent history of American elementary and secondary education. Less successful, but no less important, were his efforts to raise scholarly standards in postgraduate education, as exemplified by the Institute for Advanced Study.

Flexner was able to accomplish so much because his own thinking and behavior were in harmony with that of most early twentieth century, Progressive Era Americans. He crusaded against waste and inefficiency, bringing to public attention, for example, the deplorable state of medical education in North America. Certainly, this sense of moral outrage was one key to his success. Yet he also placed great faith in the power of science to remedy society's ills. Not science in the narrow, physical sense, but the study of any problem according to scientific principles. Indeed, Flexner's professional career was characterized by the painstaking collection and analysis of data about social problems.

This is not to say that Flexner was without his faults. His desire to generate public support for his reforms sometimes led him to dramatize and exaggerate the severity of social problems. Moreover, his lifelong conviction that efficiency and professional expertise were the only objective standards by which society could operate effectively reflected an antipathy toward democracy and a haughty elitism that devalued the role of the ordinary citizen in the decision-making process.

Certainly, no human being is perfect, and Flexner was, after all, only human. Yet from his first efforts in Louisville, he had grasped a vision of excellence in education that he pursued throughout his professional life. For all of his faults, the vision was his, and he never lost it.

Bibliography
Cremin, Lawrence A. *The Transformation of the School: Progressivism in American Education, 1876-1957.* New York: Alfred A. Knopf, 1961. The best single history of the Progressive education movement. Provides a useful, though somewhat uncritical, discussion and analysis of Flexner's frequently overlooked contribution to American school reform.

Flexner, Abraham. *Abraham Flexner: An Autobiography.* New York: Simon and Schuster, 1960. The revised edition of Flexner's *I Remember.* New York: Simon and Schuster, 1940. Somewhat self-serving, this firsthand account of Flexner's life and work nevertheless remains indispensable; all historians of medical and educational reform have drawn on it.

Floden, Robert E. "Flexner, Accreditation, and Evaluation." *Educational Evaluation and Policy Analysis* 2 (March, April, 1980): 35-46. A brief examination of Flexner's *Medical Education in the United States and Canada.* Useful primarily for challenging the widely accepted notion that Flexner's observations and conclusions were based on objective, scientific principles and method.

Hine, Darlene Clark. "The Anatomy of Failure: Medical Education Reform and the Leonard Medical School of Shaw University, 1882-1920." *Journal of Negro Education* 54 (Fall, 1985): 512-525. Traces the history and failure of the Leonard Medical School, one of several black educational institutions given a negative rating by Flexner. Examines the responses.

King, David J. "The Psychological Training of Abraham Flexner, the Reformer of Medical Education." *Journal of Psychology* 100 (September, 1978): 131-137. Examines the impact of Flexner's graduate training on his later career as a reformer. The major intellectual influences of the field of psychology on Flexner's thinking are discussed and related to his emphasis on the importance of basic science in medical education.

Parker, Franklin. "Ideas That Shaped American Schools." *Phi Delta Kappan* 62 (January, 1981): 314-319. Superficial but useful discussion of ten books or series of books that represent major turning points in American educational thought in the last seventy-five years. Useful primarily for placing Flexner within the larger context of reform in American education.

Rosen, George. *The Structure of American Medical Practice, 1875-1941.*

Edited by Charles E. Rosenberg. Philadelphia: University of Pennsylvania Press, 1983. This well-written book mentions Flexner only in passing, but it places his reforms within the context of the larger effort to restructure the medical profession in the early twentieth century United States.

Shryock, Richard Harrison. *Medical Licensing in America, 1650-1965*. Baltimore: Johns Hopkins University Press, 1967. Well-documented study of efforts to regulate medical practice in the United states. It not only discusses the impact of Flexner's reforms on this process but also provides a detailed account of the social and professional milieu in which he undertook his reform of medical education.

Monroe H. Little, Jr.

GERALD R. FORD

Born: July 14, 1913; Omaha, Nebraska

Area of Achievement: Government

Contribution: Becoming president after Richard M. Nixon's resignation in disgrace, Ford restored integrity to the office of President of the United States and a sense of decency and unity to the nation.

Early Life

Gerald Rudolph Ford, Jr., was born July 14, 1913, in Omaha, Nebraska, the son of Leslie and Dorothy King. When the boy was two, his parents were divorced and his mother presently married Gerald R. Ford, Sr., who adopted her son as his own. Jerry Ford grew up in the conservative environment of Grand Rapids, Michigan, in a warm family in which the emphasis was on integrity and hard work. These traits helped Ford, Sr., to maintain his paint manufacturing business through the Depression of the 1930's, which must have been a lesson for his sons. A good student in high school, Jerry was also an exceptional athlete both in high school and at the University of Michigan, where he earned a B.A. degree in 1935 with a B average. He then enrolled in the Yale Law School, also working full-time at Yale as a football and boxing coach. He earned his law degree in 1941, also with a B average, despite his full-time work. By this time he was more than six feet tall, powerfully built, with ruggedly handsome features which allowed him to model sports clothing in *Look* magazine. As years passed, his full blond hair slowly receded from his forehead.

Admitted to the Michigan bar in 1941, Ford and a friend founded their own law firm. Ford specialized in labor cases, always important in Michigan. When the United States entered World War II, he entered the navy as an ensign, on April 20, 1942. After a year of giving aviation cadets physical training, he went first to gunnery school and then to the *Monterey*, a new, small aircraft carrier in the Pacific. He received the highest ratings possible for an officer while serving in ten battles and through one of the worst typhoons in history, his commander describing him as an "excellent leader... steady, reliable, resourceful." He was released from active duty early in 1946 with the rank of lieutenant commander and returned to Grand Rapids. There Gerald Ford, Sr., had become Republican Party chairman for Kent County, elected by reformers who wanted to clean up the local political machine. There, too, was Republican senator Arthur Vandenberg, a leader of the Senate's internationalists and a believer in a bipartisan foreign policy. Young Ford's military experience had convinced him that prewar isolationism had been disastrous. He also believed in honest government and ran for the local seat in the United States House of Representatives in 1948, campaigning hard and winning the Republican nomination with 62.2 percent of the vote, and the general election with 60.5 percent. The same year, on October 15, he married Elizabeth "Betty" Bloomer; they had three sons and a daughter.

Life's Work

Gerald Ford represented Michigan's Fifth District for more than twenty-four years, never winning less than 60.3 percent of the vote in general elections and usually winning far more. In the House, he served on the Central Intelligence Agency and Foreign Aid subcommittees of the Committee on Appropriations and was soon regarded as an expert on drafting defense budgets. Such budgets are infinitely complex; his expertise made him one of the significant members among the 435 representatives. Hoping to become Speaker of the House one day, he turned down chances to run for the Senate or for governor of Michigan.

With the election of Dwight D. Eisenhower to the presidency in 1952, there seemed a chance of an era of Republican control of government, but Eisenhower's popularity did not have enough impact on congressional elections. Apart from 1953-1955, Ford always served in a Congress with Democratic Party majorities. His record was one of enlightened conservatism with some liberal tendencies, supporting foreign aid and military appropriations, the reform of House rules, civil rights bills, and caution in government spending. In 1966, Americans for Democratic Action rated his voting record liberal sixty-seven percent of the time. By the 1960's, he was making hundreds of speeches each year to raise money for Republican candidates.

He also began to have formal leadership roles, being elected chairman of the Republican caucus in the House in 1963 and serving on the Warren Commission to investigate the assassination of President John F. Kennedy. In 1965, he was the House Republicans' choice to become the new minority leader, replacing the older, more conservative, and less effective Charles Halleck of Indiana. This meant that if the Republicans had won control of the House, Ford would have become the Speaker. As minority leader, Ford listened to the views of congressmen of all opinions, respected others' principles, accepted differences, and tried to avoid enforcing party loyalty on every vote. He helped to shape legislation in fields ranging from education to crime control. He became a national figure and a leading spokesman for his party on major issues. He continued to support civil rights legislation, tried to keep government spending down in President Lyndon B. Johnson's Great Society programs, and supported Johnson's actions in Vietnam.

Ford had first visited Vietnam in 1953, becoming a "hawk" in his support for American intervention. In the 1960's he urged more effort to win the war, not less, telling a group of Nixon campaign strategists in 1968 that the proper response to that year's "Tet" offensive was to Americanize the war. He later defended Nixon's bombing of Cambodia and served as a channel to the

House for the views of the Administration. Critics accused him of being an unthinking "hawk" who merely reacted patriotically rather than analyzing the problem.

His loyalty to an administration already haunted by "Watergate" probably made Ford Nixon's choice for vice president under the Twenty-fifth Amendment when Spiro T. Agnew, under indictment, resigned the office. Allegedly, Nixon's first choice had been John Connally, a recent convert from the Democratic Party, but the Texan was too controversial to win congressional confirmation. The Senate confirmed Ford by a vote of 92 to 3; the House, by 385 to 35. As vice president, Ford remained doggedly loyal to Nixon while the Watergate cover-up became ever more obvious, but with the House Judiciary Committee about to vote articles of impeachment, the president resigned. On August 9, 1975, Gerald Ford became president, an office he had never contemplated holding or even seeking.

His presidency was made difficult by the lack of time for a proper transition, such as occurs after an election, and by the presence in the White House of many Nixon men whose loyalty remained to their old leader. Some critics and even some friends asserted that Ford was not really in command of his administration. Moreover, he inherited an economy caught in the grip of "stagflation" (recession accompanied by inflation, supposedly an impossible combination) and the aftermath of both the Vietnam War and the Watergate scandal. He did have widespread public approval, but that dropped from seventy-one percent to fifty percent, according to the Gallup poll, after he gave Nixon a pardon. Yet, this was something that Ford believed he "must" do in mercy to Nixon and his family and to end a "nightmare" for the country. He also divided his own party by naming the often controversial Nelson Rockefeller, governor of New York for several terms, as vice president.

The Ford Administration was unable to end either the recession or inflation, in part because of a difficult global economic situation and in part because of advisers' belief that "tight money" and a "slump" would soon end inflation. The slogan Whip Inflation Now (WIN) and presidential exhortations became subjects of ridicule. Ignorant of foreign policy matters, Ford was virtually the captive of the able but egocentric Henry A. Kissinger, who served as both secretary of state and presidential adviser. Ford's "summits" with Soviet leaders accomplished little but to associate the United States with the Helsinki Accords on human rights and Eastern Europe, which left that region under Soviet control without ending Soviet human rights violations. Worse, South Vietnam fell during Ford's time in office, its impending collapse leading him to ask Congress for massive aid for the Saigon regime, using such 1960's rhetoric as South Vietnam's "fighting for freedom." He was bothered by congressional refusal, apparently not grasping the Vietnam War's impact on the country, which included widespread distrust of Saigon.

In 1976, Ford was defeated for reelection by Democrat Jimmy Carter, former governor of Georgia. Probable reasons include Carter's imaginative and relentless campaigning, Ford's choice of the capable but then acid-tongued Senator Robert J. Dole of Kansas as his running mate, and voters' perception of Ford himself as a good man but an inept one. Retiring from the presidency on January 20, 1977, Ford wrote his memoirs, in 1981 represented the United States at the funeral of assassinated Egyptian President Anwar el-Sadat, along with fellow former Presidents Nixon and Carter, and later joined Carter in sponsoring conferences for serious discussion of major international issues.

Summary

Gerald Ford's presidency was that of a man of integrity, character, and modesty, in important contrast to his imperious predecessors of questionable honor, Lyndon B. Johnson and Richard M. Nixon. Johnson and Nixon had divided the nation; Ford sought to heal it and to some extent succeeded. Americans were relieved to find an honest man in the highest office and also to find that the "imperial presidency" of Johnson and Nixon was not permanent. Ford thus redressed the balance in American public life, making the president once more a part of the federal government rather than its tyrant. Voters also, however, perceived him as less than imaginative and forceful in a time of economic trouble; at such times Americans have customarily demanded strong leadership. Ford's speaking style, adapted to pretelevision party rallies, made him seem inarticulate, even fumbling, when exposed to the new medium nationwide and to comparison with anchormen and actors. The length of his presidency and his impact on the country were thus limited by his own characteristics.

Bibliography

Ford, Gerald R. *A Time to Heal: The Autobiography of Gerald R. Ford*. New York: Harper and Row, Publishers, 1979. Like the man himself, calm, unpretentious, straightforward; the honesty contrasts sharply with memoirs of Lyndon Johnson and Richard Nixon. Ford admits some mistakes but does not go beneath the surface to analyze his motives and decisions.

Hartmann, Jerry. *Palace Politics: An Inside Account of the Ford Years*. New York: McGraw-Hill Book Co., 1980. Ford's chief of staff's revealing if egocentric account, emphasizing the interplay of personalities between the Ford men and the Nixon men. Blames the failures of Ford's presidency on the held-over Nixon staff members.

Hersey, John. *The President*. New York: Alfred A. Knopf, 1975. A brilliant writer's diary of a week in Ford's presidency, well illustrated, but useful mostly for personal glimpses of Ford interacting with others. Avoids policy issues.

Mollenhoff, Clark R. *The Man Who Pardoned Nixon*. New York: St. Martin's Press, 1976. An investigative reporter's harshly critical account, accusing Ford of deception behind his promises of openness. Includes attacks on Ford's appointments, policies, and use of executive privilege.

Reeves, Richard. *A Ford, Not a Lincoln*. New York: Harcourt Brace Jovanovich, 1975. The most informative critical book, analyzing Ford's personality and political techniques, including the best explanation of the Nixon pardon. Reeves finds Ford decent but ignorant, overdependent on his staff, not really a leader.

Sidey, Hugh. *Portrait of a President*. New York: Harper and Row, Publishers, 1975. Evocative of the "feel" of the Ford presidency through pictures and tales of Ford's dealing with his staff and with congressmen, voters, and chiefs of state.

Vestal, Bud. *Jerry Ford, Up Close: An Investigative Biography*. New York: Coward, McCann and Geoghegan, 1974. A friendly account of Ford's early years, family, schooling, navy service, years in Congress, and the vice presidency. One can see emerging the kind of president Ford would be.

Robert W. Sellen

HENRY FORD

Born: July 30, 1863; Springwells township, Michigan
Died: April 7, 1947; Dearborn, Michigan
Area of Achievement: Automobile manufacture
Contribution: Combining ruthlessness with concern for the average worker, Ford revolutionized the early automobile industry by creating a low-priced car, the Model T, through the now famous assembly-line method. He also created the Ford Foundation, a nationwide philanthropy.

Early Life

Using money that belonged to his wife Mary (née Litogot), William Ford, an Irish immigrant, bought a farm in Springwells township, near Dearborn, Michigan, and on July 30, 1863, Henry Ford was born there. In those years, the nation was divided by civil war: Abraham Lincoln was president of the twenty-four states of the Union, while Jefferson Davis was president of the eleven states of the Confederacy. Although content as a boy on the prosperous family farm, Henry did not want to spend his life as a farmer, and his independence and mechanical skills steered him in other directions. His interest in machines began early. He was never an inventor but rather someone who loved to tinker with anything that had moving parts. He would disassemble anything in the home to find out how it worked and then put it back together. At thirteen, Henry repaired his first watch, and he became obsessed with watch repair, fixing more than three hundred without ever charging a fee. Once he took a shingle nail and sharpened it on a grindstone to create a screwdriver. Then he made a pair of tweezers from one of his mother's discarded corset stays. With these homemade tools, he took a watch apart, discovered the problem, and fixed it. Throughout his life he enjoyed repairing watches, and even as president of Ford Motor Company he delighted in repairing the watches of his visitors.

Henry had little use for school and learned almost nothing there except for the epigrams found in McGuffey's readers. He never learned to spell, to write a formed hand, to read freely, or to express himself well in the simplest written sentence. Throughout his life, Ford rarely took notes, kept no diary, and refrained from most writing.

In 1876, the Ford family was shocked by the death of Henry's mother, Mary Ford, at thirty-seven, a few days after giving birth to a stillborn child. The same year, however, also brought something magical to Henry: He saw his first self-propelled machine. While he and his father rode to Detroit on the farm wagon, Henry noticed ahead of them a machine with a portable engine and boiler mounted on wheels with a water tank. This huge iron monster could be operated by one man who stood on a platform behind the boiler, shoveled coal, operated the throttle, and steered.

In 1879, at the age of sixteen, Henry quit school, helped his father bring in the summer harvest, and moved to Detroit. In Detroit he lived with his aunt, Rebecca Ford Flaherty, whose daughter Jane had been a surrogate mother to the Dearborn Fords since the death of Mary Ford.

Henry began work at the James Flower and Brothers Machine Shop, not far from his aunt's house. The machine shop was a perfect environment for the young Henry, since the Flower brothers manufactured everything in the line of brass and iron—globe and gate valves, gongs, steam whistles, fire hydrants, valves for water pipes, and the huge machinery for Detroit's first waterworks. The shop also had a variety of machines to make and repair what was sold.

The machine shop paid $2.50 a week. Henry returned to his partiality for working on watches and made fifty cents a night working for a jeweler who hid him from customers so that they would not know how young the person was who repaired the watches. Thus, Henry had managed to combine his two main interests, and he dreamed of the future.

In 1880, in the following fall, Henry returned home to help his father with the harvest. Although he disliked the farm work, early in life he learned the values of hard work and responsibility. When he returned to Detroit late in the same year, he began working for the Detroit Drydock, where he came in contact for the first time with the internal-combustion engine. Henry stayed at the shipbuilding firm until 1882, when he was hired by Westinghouse to service steam engines. During the next few summers, he traveled all over Michigan servicing the Westinghouse engine, a machine that could be used for threshing or sawing wood. During this period, Henry's dream of a vehicle moving under its own power began to take shape.

In winter, when the roads were snowed in, he experimented in a shop he set up on the farm. After several winters, he created a small "farm locomotive," a pioneer tractor that had an old mowing engine for its chassis and a homemade steam engine. Later, Ford realized that the steam engine was too dangerous for an automobile.

On April 11, 1888, Ford married Clara J. Bryant, who remained his wife throughout his life. In 1891 the couple moved to Detroit, and two years later Ford was made chief engineer of the Edison Illuminating Company. On November 6, 1893, the Fords' only child, Edsel Bryant, was born. Ford now had the responsibility of a family to add to his dreams for the future.

Life's Work

In 1895, Ford, by then a chief engineer at Edison, attended a banquet at which Thomas Alva Edison himself was present. Ford told him about his work and the dream of the automobile and asked the nearly deaf Edison if he thought there was a future in the internal-combustion machine. Edison replied, "Yes, there is a big future for any light-weight engine that can develop a high horsepower and is self-contained. . . . Keep on with your engine. If you can get what you are after, I can see a great future." Ford's morale skyrocketed and the "Wizard of Menlo Park" became his idol. Later, Ford and Edison would become good friends.

On a spring night in 1896, Ford completed his first car. Mounted on bicycle wheels, the automobile was too big to get out the door, so an excited Ford took an ax and knocked down a wall. At four o'clock in the morning, Ford made a test run around the block. His wife and the baby, Edsel, joined him; the Ford motor car was born.

In 1899, Ford began to organize the Detroit Automobile Company with a number of associates. Disagreements broke out among the backers, and Ford was forced to resign. After this initial debacle, Ford turned to building racing cars, a decision which apparently contradicted his belief in the primacy of two things: mechanical perfection and the common man. Building a race car may have served his search for mechanical perfection, but it had nothing to do with providing the common man with a car. Or did it?

Ford gained fame in 1901 when the "999," driven by Barney Oldfield, broke all records over a three-mile course. Ford's name became a household word, and a Detroit coal dealer named Alex Malcomson soon sought out Ford to make an investment in Ford's company, a move that would attract other investors.

Ford did not like the idea of having partners, but he had no other choice in 1903, when the Ford Motor Company was launched. It was Malcomson's support that had attracted others, such as James Couzens and Charles Woodall, the lawyer John Anderson, the banker John Gray, the Dodge brothers, Horace Rackham, and Albert Strelow. Strelow turned over a shop he owned for stock, and the Dodge brothers received stock for making motors and transmissions, something they did for the Olds Company. Control—fifty-one percent of the shares—was divided between Ford and Malcomson. Ford was able to raise twenty-eight thousand dollars, and he would never need to augment that from any outside source.

The assembly line was still down the road, but the first car, the Model A (sometimes called the Fordmobile), was built by twelve men in 1903 and rolled out of Strelow's garage within a month. It sold for eight hundred dollars; the detachable tonneau cost an extra hundred dollars. By 1904, at the New York Car Show (at which Ford's car was placed in the basement), Ford realized that the Model A's time had passed. Upon his return to Michigan, Ford began to build different models, attempting to come up with what America wanted. He believed he had built such a car when the Model T was developed in late 1908 (although his associates had made contributions to the design of the Model T, Ford himself was responsible for its overall concept).

When Strelow's shop became too small to serve as a plant, the company moved to the Piquette-Beaubien plant. By 1907, that plant had also become too small, and Ford bought the sixty-acre Highland Park racetrack, anticipating larger production and sales than ever. The Highland Park plant would be totally financed by company profits and would eventually mass-produce the Model T on what would become the famous assembly line.

Malcomson disagreed with Ford and wanted an expensive car built. He needed money for other investments and sold his $12,000 original stock for $175,000. Albert Strelow and three other minor stockholders also sold out. Strelow received $25,000, lost it all in a gold mine investment, and later returned to Ford Motor begging for a job in a company he had once partially owned. Ford was now the majority stockholder and president.

Ford announced to the world in biblical hyperbole, "I will build a motor car for the great multitude," and he proceeded to do precisely that. Others tried to talk him out of mass-producing the Model T, stating that the public would want diversity. Ford, however, held fast to his plan: The idea for the Model T had been conceived in 1907; machinery to produce it was built in 1908; and production began in 1909. Eventually forty thousand Model T's rolled out of the plant in one year. By 1913, mass production had lowered the price of the Model T to five hundred dollars. Orders flooded the company, and headquarters had to notify dealers that the demand could not be met. In 1927, the last of fifteen million Model T's was built.

The assembly line was not constructed overnight; it took seven years to perfect. It began simply enough at Highland Park, when work commenced to improve subassembly of the flywheel magneto. In the past, one man had done the job of assembling the magneto in twenty minutes. Ford divided the work into twenty-nine operations. The growing magneto was carried on a conveyor belt, and the assembly time was cut to four minutes. That worked so well that the system was adapted to the construction of the entire car, which was divided into forty-five operations. The total time required for building a car was eventually lowered to ninety-three minutes.

On January 9, 1911, a long court fight over patent rights finally came to an end. In 1877, a clever patent attorney, George Selden, had built an engine and in 1895 had established a patent for it, forcing automobile builders to pay royalties. A group called the Association of Licensed Automobile Manufacturers (ALAM) was formed to oversee the patent. Ford had ignored the patent and was sued in late 1903. Now, seven years later, the Circuit Court of Appeals upheld the validity of the patent but maintained that it covered only the Brayton engine. Ford as well as other manufacturers, most of whom had been paying royalties, used the Otto engine; the claim was disallowed, and ALAM ceased to exist. It was one of many Ford victories that combined luck with old-fashioned intuition.

In 1914, the average American worker in the manufacturing industries was making about eleven dollars a week. Ford stunned the working man and made front-page news when he announced that every Ford worker would receive a minimum of five dollars a day. Thus did Ford reward loyal workers who had endured unbelievable monotony and who were not allowed to smoke or drink on the job—and were encouraged to abstain from these practices off the job. Later the workers were allowed to buy shares in the company, but Ford ruthlessly fought to prevent unionization.

In 1917 the stockholders filed suit because Ford had failed to pay dividends. He lost that suit and in December, 1918, in a cunning move, resigned the presidency and made his son Edsel president. From vacation in California, Ford announced in vague terms a new car that would compete with the Model T and cost only $250. The stockholders began selling out, except for Couzens. He raised the price of his shares and then sold.

Ford now had what he wanted: complete control. The stockholders were owed seventy-five million dollars, and even Ford did not have that. Ford distrusted bankers but was forced to borrow the money from bankers in New York. He produced ninety thousand cars in record speed and shipped them, unordered, to the dealers. They balked, but Ford warned them to take them or lose their franchises. Cash was demanded on delivery, and panic-stricken dealers were forced to borrow from the banks to pay Ford. Thus, Ford had transferred his burden to his dealers and quickly paid off the New York banks.

Summary

Aldous Huxley in *Brave New World* (1932) satirizes Ford by referring to his age as the Year of Our Ford, thus pointing to the dangers inherent in a near-perfect system of mechanization under the control of one man.

Henry Ford's famous 1933 picture reveals the kind-looking face of a man very out of place in a suit and tie. In a way, he looks like everybody's grandfather: His combed hair and clean-shaven face and half-smile betoken a patriarchal goodness; his status as a folk hero rests on the fact that he wanted to make cars for the multitude and did. Nevertheless, Ford's life was filled with contradiction and ruthlessness: He made fun of the rich but was himself a billionaire; by mass-producing a reliable car that everyone could afford, he became one of the richest men in America.

Created in 1936, the Ford Foundation, which received the nonvoting stock of the Ford Motor Company upon Ford's, Edsel's, and Clara Bryant Ford's deaths, became an agency which controlled resources in excess of half a billion dollars. Until 1950, it granted funds for charitable activities of special interest to the Ford family. Then, as a result of substantially increased funds from the estates of its founders, it became a nationwide philanthropy.

Bibliography
Arnold, Horace L., and Fay L. Faurote. *Ford Methods and Ford Shops*. New York: Engineering Magazine Company, 1915. A classic that describes

Ford's techniques in nontechnical language. Includes the design and installation methods of the Model T.

Brough, James. *The Ford Dynasty: An American Story*. Garden City, N.Y.: Doubleday and Co., 1977. Very well written biography. Contains the detailed story of all the members of the Ford family, as well as two pages of acknowledgments of sources upon which the book was based.

Burlingame, Roger. *Henry Ford: A Great Life in Brief*. New York: Alfred A. Knopf, 1955. A good, if dated, overview of Ford's life. Omits some of the Ford warts. Contains an annotated bibliography.

Dahlinger, John Côté, and Frances Spatz Leighton. *The Secret Life of Henry Ford*. Indianapolis: Bobbs-Merrill Co., 1978. A view of the Henry Ford family from Ford's illegitimate son. Ford took care of the Dahlinger family and the scandal was not really known until 1976, upon publication of David Lewis' *The Public Image of Henry Ford*.

Ford, Henry, and Samuel Crowther. *My Life and Work*. New York: Doubleday, Page and Co., 1922. Ford's memory was extremely unreliable, and since he dictated much of this book, it is filled with errors. Yet it gives great insight into Henry Ford, the man.

Gelderman, Carol. *Henry Ford: The Wayward Capitalist*. New York: Dial Press, 1981. A thoroughly researched biography, based on the Ford Archives. Particularly well-researched coverage of the Dodge and *Chicago Tribune* lawsuits; sources include the Labor Archives, previously unavailable to biographers.

Lacey, Robert. *Ford: The Men and the Machine*. Boston: Little, Brown and Co., 1986. An excellent biography of Henry Ford, Edsel Ford, Henry Ford II, and Lee Iacocca. Claims that Henry Ford hounded Edsel Ford to an early grave when Edsel served as president of Ford Motor Company. Details are given of Henry Ford's mistress and illegitimate child. Contains an exhaustive, twenty-four-page bibliography.

Lewis, David L. *The Public Image of Henry Ford: An American Folk Hero and His Company*. Detroit: Wayne State University Press, 1976. This book is devoted solely to the life of Henry Ford. Lewis published a million words about Ford prior to this book. States that he probably knows more about Ford than any other writer. An exhaustive set of notes is provided for each chapter. Lewis' sources include the Ford Archives and the Henry Ford Museum.

John Harty

EDWIN FORREST

Born: March 9, 1806; Philadelphia, Pennsylvania
Died: December 12, 1872; Philadelphia, Pennsylvania
Area of Achievement: Theater
Contribution: Despite early obstacles, Forrest became the first great American actor, the first to gain international acclaim.

Early Life

Both by temperament and circumstance, Edwin Forrest typified the rough, self-reliant individualism of the early nineteenth century pioneer.. Though he was born into a comfortable middle-class environment, his choice of an acting career compelled him to leave the security of his home and to learn his craft in some of the wildest places amid some of the wildest men in the country.

His father, a bank clerk, died when Forrest was thirteen but had already made plans for him to enter the safe, prestigious career of the ministry. The boy's remarkable memory, gift for mimicry, and already distinctive voice, however, were better suited to the playhouse than the pulpit. At ten, he was a member of an amateur theatrical troupe, playing female roles. Tradition suggests that he was shrieked and laughed at on the stage, but this early failure only cemented his determination to act.

By his early teens, Forrest had held a number of jobs, including one as an apprentice printer. In the meantime, he was studying, reading, running his own juvenile acting company, and performing his first recitations in a neighbor's old barn.

Forrest's early commitment to the stage was abetted by the fortuitousness of geography, for Philadelphia, his native city, was a vital cultural hub, a theatrical center whose playhouses were among the oldest, liveliest, and most important in the country. It seems likely that the young actor enjoyed easy access to the many plays both produced and published in Philadelphia, as well as ample opportunity to study the styles and techniques of many actors in a variety of roles.

What is certain is that one of his youthful recitations so impressed several well-to-do citizens that they supported him in his studies for the next few years. Incredibly, Forrest made his professional debut at the Walnut Street Theatre in Philadelphia on November 27, 1820, playing Young Norval, a popular juvenile lead in John Home's *Douglas* (1756). The part was perfect for him, requiring an amount of physical action which allowed him to show his grace and agility, and declamatory speech which showed to advantage his already impressive timbral voice. His success was unqualified; Forrest was only fourteen.

Life's Work

Though he performed in several plays over the next few months, Forrest was convinced that he had to break the image of a juvenile actor and gain broader experience. To do this, he decided to travel west, across the Allegheny Mountains, where he would have more freedom to learn the profession, to experiment, to grow. Thus, in 1821, having been engaged by the theatrical company of Collins and Jones, Forrest embarked on a career as a strolling player for eight dollars a week.

By October, 1822, he was in Pittsburgh, once again playing Young Norval, developing the rugged physique and booming voice that were to become the crucial ingredients in his acting style. A few months later, he and his fellow strollers sailed a flatboat down the Ohio, stopping at Lexington, Kentucky, for several performances, and then traveling overland by covered wagon to Cincinnati, opening there in February, 1823.

The experience gained in these Western cities was decisive in shaping Forrest's career. He learned the importance of holding an audience under exacting and restrictive conditions—theaters with poor lighting, a paucity of props and scenery, and a change of bill nightly. Each member of the small troupe was expected to play a variety of parts: the dramatic lead in one play, the clown in the other, the dancer in the encore or afterpiece.

In 1823, the troupe went bankrupt and Forrest was out of a job. Broke, he stayed on in Cincinnati, living with a theatrical family who admired his work. He spent the next few months in poverty, reading the works of William Shakespeare.

Finally, he accepted an offer to play in New Orleans, a key city in the Southern and Western circuit. By the winter of 1824, just short of his eighteenth birthday, Forrest opened there in a Restoration tragedy, but his leisure time in that city was spent carousing with James Bowie (who gave the young man one of his famous knives), with a roustabout steamboat captain, and with "domesticated" Indian chiefs and other frontier types. Such figures comported with his robust, hot-tempered, and impulsive spirit, complementing his basically unrefined education.

Throughout the spring of 1825, Forrest played a variety of roles in New Orleans, including Iago in Shakespeare's *Othello, the Moor of Venice* (1604) and the title role in John Howard Payne's *Brutus: Or, the Fall of Tarquin* (1818), one of his most popular portrayals. His persistence was finally rewarded. The following year, he obtained an engagement in Albany, New York, playing with Edmund Kean, the famous British actor. Shortly thereafter, he arrived in New York City, still poor but rich in experience and in a deepened understanding of his craft.

The turning point of his career was this New York debut. Opening at the Bowery Theater in November, 1826, playing Othello, he brought to the role all the experience his life on the road and in the Western playhouses had given him. He was a brilliant success. At the age of twenty, Edwin Forrest had conquered the American stage. His New York triumph was the beginning of a reputation that was to last for the next thirty years. In less than a year, he became the most famous and highest paid American actor of the period, advancing from a salary of twenty-eight dollars a week in 1826 to two hundred dollars per night in 1827-1828 to five hundred dollars per night in the late 1830's.

At this point in his career, Forrest dedicated himself to the production of American plays. To encourage the development of a national drama and, shrewdly, to find just those plays in which he could use his tall, powerfully built body to advantage, Forrest sponsored a yearly competition to attract the best work. Among the many plays submitted, two in particular became important contributions to American dramatic literature of the nineteenth century. *The Gladiator* (1831), by Robert Montgomery Bird, and *Metamora: Or, the Last of the Wampanoags* (1829), by John A. Stone, were significant examples of the history play and the play on Indian themes, respectively. Both were well suited to Forrest's gifts, containing sonorous, orotund poetry which displayed his powerful voice and quick, physical action which demonstrated his athletic prowess. Both supplied him with his most famous and popular roles to the end of his career.

Twice during the 1830's he went to England, becoming the first great American actor appearing on the London stage. With nationalistic zeal, he opened his London engagement with *The Gladiator*, playing the role of Spartacus. In England, he met Catherine Sinclair, an actress, marrying her in 1837, at the peak of his fame. It was eventually an unhappy relationship. Often rash, jealous, and increasingly petulant, Forrest sued her for divorce in 1850. The trial was nasty and scandalous, becoming more notorious by Forrest's frequent exercises in public self-justification. Though the episode did little damage to his career as an actor, it did reveal the weaker side of his character as a man.

Even before this public squabbling about his domestic life, however, Forrest's role in one of the most infamous events in the history of the American theater gave further proof of a truculence that characterized much of his professional life. For years, Forrest was the chief American rival of William Macready, the noted British actor; the two were barely civil to each other. When Forrest was hissed on opening night in his second London tour of 1845, he bluntly attributed the heckling to a Macready faction, and when, in turn, Macready played in America and Forrest bitterly denounced him in the press, the feud took on a nationalistic, patriotic hue. On the night of May 7, 1848, supporters of Forrest stormed the Astor Place Opera House in New York City, where Macready was playing. Before the police broke up the riot, some thirty people had been killed. This so-called Astor Place Riot was the beginning of Forrest's decline.

His decline was assured, as well, by his body. Riddled with gout and arthritis, he was by the 1850's in great pain; his imposing, muscular frame, which had been in large measure responsible for his success, now became an impediment to his active, robust acting style. His retirement was imminent.

Trying to recapture his past glories, Forrest accepted an invitation to visit California. He played Cardinal Richelieu, a favorite role, but the audience saw only a gouty, ill-tempered old actor, and a month later, the play closed.

California having been for him a failure, Forrest returned to Philadelphia, now taking any engagement, anywhere, that would keep him going. At this point in his career, just before the Civil War, he was living on his reputation, but it was steadily eroding as younger actors such as Edwin Booth began to eclipse him.

By the late 1860's, he was in virtual, enforced retirement, living alone in his gloomy Philadelphia mansion. Few engagements were left him. His last performance was as Richelieu in Boston, April, 1872. A few public readings closed his career, though he never stopped exercising, trying to keep his failing body in shape. On the morning of December 12, while pursuing rigorous exercise, Edwin Forrest sustained a massive stroke and was found dead later that day. In his will, he had made a provision for the establishment of a home for aged actors, but his estranged wife and an army of lawyers dismembered the will, and the provision died with Forrest.

Summary

Edwin Forrest's rise to fame and fortune was a phenomenon characteristic of the period in American history when the country was just beginning to recognize its nationalistic aspirations and to realize its political identity. The country was ready to take a native cultural hero to its heart, especially one who could compete favorably with the British and with the rest of Europe. For the American theater, Forrest came along at the right time. He had a physical dynamism that projected an image of strength, agility, and forthrightness, those traits which Americans most cherished. Critical opinion of his ability has varied, ranging from William Winter's famous remark about Forrest's being "a vast animal bewildered by a grain of genius" to more recent studies which appraise Forrest's contributions from the vantage point of history and his influence on generations of later actors.

Forrest was intensely patriotic, and his efforts to promote the American drama at a time when English drama and English actors held preference on the stage constituted a pioneering achievement from a man who had the strengths—and the moral weaknesses—of the pioneer spirit.

Bibliography

Barrett, Lawrence. *Edwin Forrest*. Boston: J. R. Osgood and Co., 1881. A fine early biography. Written less than a decade after Forrest's death, the book is valuable as an accurate and brief account by a contemporary fellow actor. The style is often laden with Victorian circumlocutions and overripe delicacies, but the assessment of Forrest that emerges is largely sympathetic and well balanced.

Csida, Joseph, and June Bundy. *American Entertainment: A Unique History of Popular Show Business*. New York: Billboard Books, 1978. A largely pictorial panorama of American theatrical history, with reproductions of playbills, posters, and advertisements, as well as portraits of famous actors and actresses. The book contains a lively assessment of Forrest's character and acting ability by fellow actor John W. Blaisdell. Also treats the theatrical milieu of the Forrest era.

Hughes, Glenn Arthur. *A History of the American Theatre: 1700-1950*. New York: Samuel French, 1951. Discusses, sometimes too sketchily, the theatrical times, customs, and personalities during Forrest's rise. A good overview rather than a specific treatment.

Moses, Montrose J., and John Mason Brown, eds. *The American Theatre as Seen by Its Critics: 1752-1934*. New York: W. W. Norton and Co., 1934. Contains William Winter's famous critique of what he called Forrest's "ranting" style. Winter dismissed Forrest as an actor who lacked intellectual depth but possessed a "puissant animal splendour." An important anti-Forrest assessment.

Wilson, C. B. *A History of American Acting*. Bloomington: University of Indiana Press, 1966. Provides an incisive account of Forrest's acting style, emphasizing the influence of Edmund Kean; rich in detail and quite readable. Most of the more important critics are cited.

Edward Fiorelli

STEPHEN COLLINS FOSTER

Born: July 4, 1826; Lawrenceville, Pennsylvania
Died: January 13, 1864; New York, New York
Area of Achievement: Music
Contribution: Working within the most popular, sometimes vulgar, style of the day, Foster wrote works of unaffected simplicity and melodic beauty that became among the finest representatives of the American folk song.

Early Life

In one of history's notable coincidences, Stephen Collins Foster, "America's troubadour," was born precisely fifty years after the signing of the Declaration of Independence, on the same day also as the deaths of Thomas Jefferson and John Adams. The ninth child of William and Eliza Collins, "Stephy," as he was sometimes called, was the baby of the family, nurtured in a warm and loving environment. His father, one of the pioneers in the establishment of Pittsburgh as a thriving "Western" city, was a middle-class businessman, would-be entrepreneur, and minor public official whose fortunes were always tottering between solvency and indigence, a condition that would carry over into Stephen's own later life.

Tutored first by his older sisters, he was educated at a number of private academies in and around Pittsburgh and in Towanda in northern Pennsylvania. Gentle, sensitive, and often pensive, he was never the scholar, and he chafed under the discipline of academic life. His only real interest was in music, a subject that he studied on his own and for which he early showed a rare ability. Even his father, who wished a business career for his youngest son, could not help but observe the boy's "strange talent." Family anecdotes describe the seven-year-old boy as picking up a flute for the first time and in a few minutes playing "Hail Columbia" and of his teaching himself to play the piano. Sent to Jefferson College in Canonsburg, Pennsylvania, Foster dropped out after a week, homesick, and returned to his family in the summer of 1841.

For the next few years, Foster lived at home, visiting relatives with his mother and occasionally attending theatrical events and concerts with his favorite brother, Morrison, his first official biographer. During this tranquil period, Foster became increasingly absorbed in his music. In December, 1844, he published his first composition, the music to a poem, "Open Thy Lattice, Love." Derivative and harmonically awkward, the song was a creditable piece of work for a boy of sixteen and already bore the naturalness, the spontaneity that was to be its composer's trademark.

Life's Work

Home life was thus somehow a catalyst to Foster's inspiration. Even after the publication of his first song, Foster continued living with his family despite efforts on their part to find him some employment. "Stephy" was always the dreamer, though the only photograph of him, taken years later when he had become famous, shows a strong face, with prominent brow, large, dark eyes, and full, almost pouting lips.

In 1845, Foster joined the Knights of S.T., a club of young men who met twice weekly at the Foster home. The members wrote verses and sang popular songs of the day. Membership in this club was probably crucial in determining Foster's career, for it provided the young composer with both a ready audience for his work and a further source of inspiration. Through the club, he came into contact with examples of the minstrel song, or, as it was then called, the "Ethiopian" melody.

Additionally, the minstrel show was just coming into its prime as a popular American form of entertainment. Pittsburgh, in fact, had, in the fall of 1830, been the scene of one of the earliest minstrel shows when a twenty-two-year-old Thomas "Daddy" Rice, the father of American minstrelsy, first put on blackface and cavorted on the stage as Jim Crow, a good-humored, illiterate black man. Whether Foster had seen this first performance is uncertain, but it is clear that by the 1840's he had become friends with Daddy Rice and had submitted to him a number of pieces in the minstrel style, which Rice politely refused.

Foster kept composing, however, and the Knights kept singing his songs "in almost every parlor in Pittsburgh," so that by 1847 Foster's songs were being circulated largely from singer to singer, a fact which explains their success as authentic creations of a basically oral folk culture rather than as products of a formal musical tradition. Emerging from this oral culture was the first of his great songs. "Oh! Susanna," a nonsense song in the American minstrel manner, was first sung in Andrews' Eagle Ice Cream Saloon in Pittsburgh in September, 1847, though it was not published until the following year.

"Oh! Susanna" made Foster famous, not only because minstrel companies all over the country appropriated it and publishers and other songwriters altered and rearranged it, but also because thousands of pioneers carried the song along with their hopes to the gold fields of California.

Curiously, Foster was at first somewhat blasé about payment for his early work. In a letter dated 1849, for example, he mentions that he gave manuscript copies of "Oh! Susanna" to "several persons" before submitting a copy to W. C. Peters for publication. Scores of pirated editions of this and later songs point out the laxity in those days with regard to copyrights, but it is clear also that Foster at first regarded songwriting as a questionable occupation for a gentleman. That he was at least partially embarrassed by or indifferent to fame as a songwriter is evident in the fact that he gave permission to the famous minstrel impresario Edwin P. Christy to perform and publish his

"Old Folks at Home"—popularly known as "Swanee River"—as Christy's own. In return, Foster was paid fifteen dollars and was encouraged to submit further work.

His association with Christy, in fact, was crucial to Foster's career. The Christy Minstrels were among the most popular theatrical troupes before the Civil War, and Foster's connection with Christy assured him of both a steady income and a ready market. Christy's Minstrels performed all over the country, transmitting Foster's songs orally months before they were ever published.

The early 1850's were Foster's most prolific period and the happiest of his life. In July, 1850, he had married Jane McDowell, daughter of an eminent Pittsburgh physician who had treated Charles Dickens on his stopover in Pittsburgh during his famous American tour in the 1840's.

Always close to his family, Foster took his young wife to live with his parents, and once again the surroundings of familial love and contentment fueled his creative powers. Often locking himself in his study for hours—a labor which belied the spontaneity of the finished compositions—he produced dozens of his best songs during the next two or three years, securing Firth and Pond of New York as his principal publisher. During this period, Foster composed "Camptown Races" (1850), "Ring de Banjo" (1851), "Old Folks at Home" (1851), "Massa's in de Cold, Cold Ground" (1852), "My Old Kentucky Home" (1853), "Jeanie with the Light Brown Hair" (1854)—inspired by his wife—and "Come Where My Love Lies Dreaming" (1855), all masterpieces which have never lost popular appeal and which have secured for their composer a preeminent place in nineteenth century American music.

The year 1855 marked a turning point in Foster's life and career. At the peak of his fame and at the height of his creative powers, Foster could now command unusual prerogatives from his publishers, one of which was to prove disastrous. He was temperamentally unfit for the plodding routine of the businessman, but songwriting was a joy, and he soon convinced himself that he could live comfortably on his *potential* as a composer. In effect, Foster pawned his future for a secure present. He developed the practice of drawing advances from his publishers, selling outright all future royalties from his published songs. As soon as a song was printed, he would calculate its future value and sell its royalties.

Living thus beyond his means, and having to write songs to live, Foster composed over the next few years scores of works, most of which were markedly inferior to his early material. "Come Where My Love Lies Dreaming" was written in 1855, but not until 1860, with "Old Black Joe," did he write a song with the powerful simplicity of his best work. In between were temperance songs and sentimental ballads, the spontaneous gaiety of his minstrel style all but gone. Not unexpectedly, Foster was experiencing domestic problems as well. His relationship with Jane became strained, and on several occasions the couple separated because of Foster's inability to support her.

By the advent of the Civil War in 1860, Foster had moved to New York City to be nearer his publishers. From this time on, he became a sort of song factory, churning out to order virtual potboilers for a public eager to hear anything new from him. Deeper in debt, he produced work that was facile, commercial, and dull: saccharine hymns, topical comic pieces, patriotic war songs, and the usual sentimental ballads of mother, home, and sloe-eyed love. Little of this work is of any importance in the canon of Foster's songs. It represents, rather, a pitiful decline in the composer's art and fortunes.

Eventually, Foster received less and less for his work—work which he must have sensed was inferior to his earlier compositions. He began drinking heavily, getting steadily weaker and falling into states of depression. Poor and in ill health, Foster was taken to Bellevue Hospital in January, 1864, where he died three days later. Found in his pockets were a few scraps of paper and a few coins totaling thirty-eight cents. In March of that year, a last great song was published from among his final papers. Called "Beautiful Dreamer," it was a final return to the gentle lyricism and honesty of his greatest work.

Summary

It is ironic that the man whose music is richly evocative of the Old South never traveled below the Mason-Dixon line. Such irony suggests the most telling characteristic of Foster as a composer—his instinctive, unschooled, spontaneous lyricism. Foster was a self-taught composer whose lack of formal, technical knowledge of the rules of composition hampered the success of his instrumental pieces, his dozen or so attempts to write "serious" music. For simple, unaffected melody, however—for "parlor" songs sung by respectable, middle-class folks—Foster's songs are unsurpassed among the works of nineteenth century composers.

Though at first reluctant, Foster steadfastly held to his commitment to become the best of the "Ethiopian" melodists. He produced songs that in effect reformed the American minstrel style. His best work bore none of the vulgarity common to the minstrel show; there was no coarseness, no crudity even in his nonsense and comic songs. His work reveals the honest, home-spun simplicity that was the strength of the oral folk tradition.

Bibliography

Foster, Morrison. *My Brother Stephen*. Indianapolis: Hollenbeck Press, 1932.
   A brief account of the composer's life, particularly his relationship with his family. Not totally objective, it ignores much of the less flattering aspects of Foster's life and character but does provide, as the earliest biography, some important information about his music.

Howard, John Tasker. *Stephen Foster: America's Troubadour*. New York: Thomas Y. Crowell, 1934, 1953. The definitive biography, well researched and unbiased. Drawing almost too minutely on private collections of Foster material, including family papers, Howard recounts Foster's schooling, travel, relationships, and financial habits. A thorough appendix includes a complete list of Foster's compositions.

Milligan, Harold Vincent. *Stephen Collins Foster: A Biography of America's Folk-Song Composer*. New York: G. Schirmir, 1920. The first objective biography. Pays particular attention to Foster's early life and to what its author perceives as a major drawback to Foster's cultivation of serious musical taste. Also treats Foster's final days and his undramatic death.

Walters, Raymond. *Stephen Foster, Youth's Golden Gleam: A Sketch of His Life and Background in Cincinnati, 1846-1850*. Princeton, N.J.: Princeton University Press, 1936. Treats a period of Foster's life while the composer was a bookkeeper for his brother, Dunning. Suggests that the Cincinnati waterfront, with its wharves and its black music, was a profound influence on Foster's creative achievements. Both Howard and Milligan also discuss this period, though both regard it as somewhat "sketchy."

Wittke, Carl. *Tambo and Bones*. Durham, N.C.: Duke University Press, 1930. An accurate and entertaining history of the American minstrel show, the book provides a clear perspective through which to appreciate Foster's success and his contribution to American music.

Edward Fiorelli

FELIX FRANKFURTER

Born: November 15, 1882; Vienna, Austria
Died: February 22, 1965; Washington, D.C.
Area of Achievement: Constitutional law
Contribution: Throughout Frankfurter's tenure on the United States Supreme Court, he was committed to the principle of judicial restraint; as a teacher at Harvard Law School for more than twenty-five years, he was one of America's greatest constitutional scholars.

Early Life

At the age of twelve, Felix Frankfurter emigrated from Vienna to New York City with his father, Leopold, his mother, Emma, three brothers, and two sisters. It was 1894. His father was an outgoing, gregarious man, something of a romantic dreamer, not very ambitious but always likable. His mother was hard-driving and serious, instilling in her children a sense of responsibility and obligation. "Hold yourself dear," she told her children, by which she meant: Set for yourself worthy goals and be proud of your cultural roots in Judaism. Frankfurter had the skills necessary to do well in the best schools in New York, but his family's means were so meager that he had to be content with a public education. He started at Public School 25 in the heart of the city and completed school at City College of New York (CCNY) in 1902. He was third in his class at CCNY and was graduated at the age of nineteen. At the urging of friends, he competed for admission to Harvard Law School, was accepted in 1903, and was graduated in 1906, having been editor of the *Harvard Law Review*. Though he began his career with a prestigious Wall Street law firm, within the year his penchant for social causes led him to accept a government job with Henry Lewis Stimson, Theodore Roosevelt's federal attorney for the Southern District Court of New York. Henry Stimson was later to become Franklin D. Roosevelt's secretary of war. Because of the close connection Frankfurter had with these powerful and influential governmental leaders and his extraordinary skills in administrative law, his alma mater soon sought to entice him back to the law school.

He returned to Harvard in 1914, where he established himself as an outstanding constitutional lawyer. He remained there until 1939, when he was appointed to the United States Supreme Court by President Roosevelt. Many conservative members of the United States Senate were fearful of his appointment, for during his years at Harvard he had a history of supporting unpopular Progressive causes. He was a legal adviser to both the National Association for the Advancement of Colored People (NAACP) and the American Civil Liberties Union (ACLU). In addition, he was a major contributor to Roosevelt's New Deal policies during their formative years in the Depression.

Three specific events led political conservatives to conclude that Frankfurter was a dangerous radical not to be trusted to sit on the highest court in the land—his *Bisbee* and *Mooney* opinions and his defense of Nicola Sacco and Bartolomeo Vanzetti. Bisbee was a small copper-mining town in Arizona. One hot day in July, 1917, on the orders of the mine owners, the sheriff of Bisbee rounded up nearly twelve hundred striking mine workers and hauled them away in trucks to a remote spot in the Arizona desert, where they remained without food or shelter for two days. Frankfurter, as a member of the United States commission investigating the incident, wrote a scathing report accusing the mine owners of acting without legal authorization. His report eventually led to the trial, although not the conviction, of many mine owners.

The *Mooney* opinion arose from the activities of Tom Mooney, a radical labor agitator accused of exploding a bomb that killed nineteen people in a labor parade in San Francisco in 1916. Because of Mooney's history of violent labor agitation, he was falsely convicted and served twenty years in prison for a crime he did not commit. Frankfurter's stinging condemnation of the San Francisco authorities rested on the argument that they had convicted Mooney not on the basis of evidence but on the basis of his political views. Conservatives perceived this report as clear evidence of his bias in favor of the labor union movement.

Yet it was Frankfurter's book *The Case of Sacco and Vanzetti* (1927), written while he was still at Harvard, which most incensed his critics. In the book, he accused Judge Webster Thayer, the presiding judge at the Sacco-Vanzetti trial, of distorting the proceeding's legal perspective. In 1920, Sacco and Vanzetti had been charged with the robbery and murder of the paymaster and guard at the Slater Morrill Shoe Company in South Braintree, Massachusetts. Sacco was an employee of the shoe factory, and Vanzetti was a fish peddler; more important, both were Communists, anarchists, draft dodgers, labor radicals, and, perhaps worst of all, Italians. According to Frankfurter, Thayer presided over a legal lynching in which the grounds for conviction were not evidence beyond reasonable doubt but public dislike for foreigners and political radicals. Despite Frankfurter's efforts, both men were convicted and executed, and as in the case of Mooney, Frankfurter's defense of these two Italians gave him a reputation as a "radical," even "Communist," law professor. This he clearly was not: He was a jurist with an unwavering commitment to the rule of law and the institutions of constitutional democracy.

Life's Work

Those who might have hoped for radicalism on the bench were quickly disappointed, and those who had feared radicalism had very little to trouble them. From the moment he took his place on the Court, it was evident that

Frankfurter did not have the doctrinaire passions of a radical. In private life, Frankfurter was an energetic, vivacious, ebullient personality, constantly in demand at social functions. He was a voluminous correspondent and an incessant, albeit captivating, conversationalist. It is fair to say, even though while on the Court he took a narrow view of the judiciary's role in government (a view often dismaying to civil libertarians), his legal influence as a jurist, a scholar, and a teacher made as great an impact on American lawyers and public officials as any justice in the twentieth century. On the Court, he became an advocate of what he called "judicial restraint." Senators and congressional legislators make the laws, he declared, and however unwise judges might think them to be, judges have only the limited obligation to interpret them. A Supreme Court justice must cultivate, he argued, "disinterest and detachment" on the bench.

Frankfurter maintained that it is the judge's responsibility to seek "judicial balancing." This meant that it was the Court's duty to find a balance between the collective interests of government represented by legislators and the individual citizen's personal liberties and aspirations, and to find this balance without doctrinaire juridical presuppositions or biases. "He must not step into the shoes of the lawmaker," he wrote, nor, he maintained, should it be the judge's role to act as the individual's personal advocate.

The history of Frankfurter's decisions on the Court reflects a lifelong commitment to the concept of judicial balancing. In 1951, on the issue of loyalty versus security, he supported the government's contention that it was unconstitutional to advocate the forcible overthrow of the United States (*Dennis v. United States*). Many opponents of the government's position had argued that taking overt action against the government was a constitutional prohibition, but merely advocating its "overthrow" was protected by the First Amendment right to free speech. Unless there was a "clear and present danger," as Justice Oliver Wendell Holmes had argued in 1919—and advocacy in peacetime was not such a danger—then a person's liberty to speak in favor of changing the government was to be constitutionally protected. People have a right to advocate their "fighting faiths," Holmes said.

Frankfurter also supported the right of the Congress to hold people in criminal contempt for refusing to answer questions about their alleged subversive affiliations (*Uphaus v. Wyman*, 1959). Nor could government employees refuse to answer questions about their political views and affiliations (*Beilan v. Board of Education*, 1958). In these cases, Frankfurter came down on the government's side, insisting that the right to free speech, the right to assemble, and the Fifth Amendment right not to be a witness against oneself had not been abrogated. Yet against these positions he balanced his opinions in favor of the individual's freedom from government interference when he believed that the constitutional protections of one citizen were being sacrificed to meet the personal preferences of others. For example, he held as unconstitutional a Michigan obscenity law banning the sale of all books judged "inappropriate for children" as much too ambiguously defined (*Butler v. Michigan*, 1957). He also voted to uphold the doctrine of academic and political freedom as protected by the framers of the Constitution (*Sweezy v. New Hampshire*, 1957). He defended the notion of placing limits on the congressional investigation of subversion (*Watkins v. United States*, 1957) and took a strong stand in favor of the Fourth Amendment's restriction against "unreasonable search and seizure" (*Harris v. United States*, 1947).

On the question of racial equality, he consistently supported the demands of black Americans for constitutional protection under the "equal protection clause" in the Fourteenth Amendment. He, along with Chief Justice Earl Warren, led the legal fight against the doctrine of "separate but equal" for racial minorities (*Brown v. Board of Education*, 1954). Moreover, it was Frankfurter who authored the "all deliberate speed" clause in *Brown II* (1955), a clause intended to prevent states and school boards from obstructing and delaying the implementation of the law (*Cooper v. Aaron*, 1958). The elected leaders of democratic government, he declared, are not to inflame public feeling by obstructive measures but are to help lead the public into compliance with the supreme law of the land.

Dedication to constitutional balancing is also to be found in Frankfurter's opinions on religious freedom. On the one hand, he supported the controversial notion that compulsory flag saluting laws do violate the First Amendment right to the freedom of religion, even though the religious beliefs of some citizens forbid saluting the flag because it violates God's injunction against taking "oaths" (*Minerville v. Gobitis*, 1940). He concurred with the State of Maryland's so-called blue law provision forbidding certain kinds of Sunday commerce (*McGowan v. Maryland*, 1961). On the other hand, he had no aversion to balancing these opinions off against a very strict interpretation of the "separation of Church and State doctrine" in 1947, when he opposed payments from the State for the transportation of parochial schoolchildren (*Everson v. Board of Education*, 1958). He also objected to the release-time programs for religious indoctrination for public school children (*McCollum v. Board of Education*, 1948).

Frankfurter's concern with the balance of powers among the three branches of government is vividly illustrated in one of the last opinions he handed down before retiring from the Supreme Court, *Baker v. Carr* (1962). In this case, voters in the state of Tennessee had asked for Court assistance in redressing unjust congressional district representation. Citizens in various counties throughout the state were receiving unequal representation. One state official, for example, might represent one million people and have one vote in the state legislature, while another official representing ten thousand votes would have the same one vote. Generally speaking, rural areas were overrepresented, while city dwellers were vastly underrepresented. Justice William J. Brennan, Jr., who had been Frankfurter's student at Harvard, spoke for the majority of the Court in 1962, when he argued that such population imbalances denied "equal protection of the laws" for large population centers in the United States. Frankfurter disagreed passionately with this legal conclusion and wrote a vehement minority report, declaring that the judiciary had not been granted the constitutional power to order the legislative branch of government to correct its own malapportionment mistakes. Usurpation of such power by the judiciary could only have the effect of undermining public confidence in the Court's role as wholly detached from political influences. Taking on tasks that were not its inherent responsibility could only serve to drag the courts into political entanglements that would eventually end in compromising political settlements.

Baker v. Carr, coming at the end of Frankfurter's long tenure on the bench, represented his lifelong commitment to the principle of judicial restraint. It is true that both liberals and conservatives talk much about judicial restraint, particularly when they lack a voting majority in their favor on the Court. Yet for Frankfurter, there was no posturing; his constant allegiance was to the principle:

> There is not under our Constitution a judicial remedy for every political mischief . . . for every undesirable exercise of legislative power. The Framers carefully and with deliberate forethought refused so to enthrone the judiciary.

On April 5, 1962, in his court chambers, the justice suffered a stroke; and although he anticipated returning to the Court, his health never permitted it. With regret, President John F. Kennedy accepted his resignation August 28, 1962. The justice and his wife, Marion Denman Frankfurter, continued to live in Washington, D.C., until his death of a heart attack three years later.

Summary

It is generally true that liberal and conservative politicians alike talk much about judicial restraint (particularly when their viewpoint lacks a favorable majority on the Court), but for Felix Frankfurter there was never any posturing; his constant allegiance was to the principle. It was at times a narrow, almost noninterventionist, view of juridical power—a view frequently dismaying to civil libertarians—but, be that as it may, his influence as a jurist, scholar, and teacher made as great an impact on public officials and lawyers as any American justice in the twentieth century.

Bibliography

Baker, Liva. *Felix Frankfurter*. New York: Coward-McCann, 1969. This biography is a detailed account of Felix Frankfurter's life and career, with much of the emphasis on those years before his appointment to the United States Supreme Court. Particular attention is paid to tracing his youthful beginnings, his law school days, and his contributions to Franklin D. Roosevelt's New Deal policies.

Hirsch, H. N. *The Enigma of Felix Frankfurter*. New York: Basic Books, 1981. This text attempts to explain Frankfurter's complex personality in psychological terms. Hirsch finds the ideological core of Frankfurter's judicial personality rooted in his poor and struggling beginnings and his later need for acceptance and belonging. It is difficult not to be somewhat dubious about this sort of interpretation.

Jacobs, Clyde E. *Justice Frankfurter and Civil Liberties*. Berkeley: University of California Press, 1961. This book concentrates on Frankfurter's view of the democratic rights embodied in the First Amendment to the Constitution. In particular, his perception of the freedom of religion, speech, press, and assembly clauses. There is an extended analysis of Frankfurter's stand on the notion of personal liberty and national security.

Kurland, Philip B. *Mr. Justice Frankfurter and the Constitution*. Chicago: University of Chicago Press, 1971. This is a condensed version of Justice Frankfurter's opinions on the Supreme Court. It also includes Kurland's marginalia. It is a helpful, efficient guide to those wishing a concise, accurate account of Frankfurter's most important cases.

Lash, Joseph P., ed. *From Diaries of Felix Frankfurter*. New York: W. W. Norton and Co., 1975. One-third of this volume is a personal biographical sketch by Lash. The other two-thirds contains Frankfurter's reflections in diary form of his days at Harvard, his encounters with President Harry S Truman and General Douglas MacArthur. He also discusses his view on the relation between Church and State.

Parrish, Michael E. *Felix Frankfurter and His Times: The Reform Years*. New York: Free Press, 1982. This book concentrates on Frankfurter's years as a Harvard law professor and the specific events that led to conservative distrust and liberal disappointment. Parrish offers interesting analyses of the Bisbee and Mooney reports, the Sacco and Vanzetti trial, and Frankfurter's interests in Zionism and the New Deal.

Donald Burrill

BENJAMIN FRANKLIN

Born: January 17, 1706; Boston, Massachusetts
Died: April 17, 1790; Philadelphia, Pennsylvania
Areas of Achievement: Public affairs, science, and literature
Contribution: Franklin helped shape most of the important political, social, and intellectual developments in eighteenth century America. He became a veritable symbol of America by the end of his life, both at home and abroad, and he remains an influential folk hero.

Early Life

Among Benjamin Franklin's English ancestors, one had owned a bit of land only twelve miles from the English ancestral seat of the Washingtons. His father, Josiah, had repudiated the Church of England and removed from England to Boston in the 1680's; his mother's forebears had arrived somewhat earlier. When Franklin was born on January 17, 1706, the modest household was already teeming with children, for he was a tenth son—and, incidentally, the youngest son of the youngest son for five generations back. The salient facts of Franklin's life were extraordinary from the start.

Although his father was a struggling tradesman (a candle maker and soap boiler), there was much in the way of reading, thinking, and discussing as well as hard work in his home. Franklin learned to read when very young, and by the age of twelve he had progressed through the Bible, the works of John Bunyan, Plutarch's *Parallel Lives* (105-115), and certain essays of Daniel Defoe and of Boston's Cotton Mather. He had very little formal schooling, and his family could not afford to send him to Harvard College.

Instead, an effort was made to bring him into the family business. He disliked the work, and he hated the smell. At that point, an older brother, James, returned from London, where he had been trained as a printer. Thus, the restless, bright, bookish twelve-year-old Benjamin Franklin was apprenticed to his high-spirited brother, who in 1721 started a newspaper, *The New England Courant*. It was the fourth newspaper in the colonies. These years were supremely important in shaping the man who later became so famous. He learned a trade which would bring him profits and prominence. He had access to many books, especially those loaned by patrons and friends. He discussed and debated matters with men who loitered in the shop and also with friends after hours. The principal subjects were the two which would be commonly avoided centuries later: religion and politics. He worked hard at learning to write and he experienced the thrill of seeing his first piece, an anonymous letter to the editor, in print. When the pugnacious James got into trouble with the authorities and was jailed, his brother, then sixteen, functioned as the editor.

The brothers often quarreled and the younger Franklin, a mere apprentice, was often treated severely. He resented this and decided to run away. He arrived in Philadelphia in October, 1723, munching on a large roll, with one Dutch dollar and a copper shilling in his pocket. The scene became a memorable passage in the memoir he later wrote, which included the fact that his future wife happened to see him and laughed at the ridiculous sight he made. He soon found work, for he was an excellent printer, and he soon found adventure as well. An eccentric governor of the province, William Keith, proposed that Franklin go to England to purchase equipment for a new printing business which Keith hoped would outdo all competition. He would send letters of credit and letters of introduction.

Franklin was in London by Christmas, 1724, but no letters came from the governor. The eighteen-year-old did find work, however, in a printing house, and as always he read intensively and grappled with ideas. After setting type for a religious book, he became convinced that the author was all wrong. In response, Franklin composed and printed a pamphlet which set forth a radical refutation. He later regarded this as a mistake, but it did gain him some attention and some new acquaintances, a few of them prominent writers of the day.

Franklin returned to Philadelphia in 1726, and he was soon employed again in his old shop. Before long, he left it to form a new business with a partner, on credit. By dint of very long hours of work, ingenious planning, and excellent workmanship, they survived—barely. Then the partner wanted to leave, and Franklin, borrowing money, bought him out. By July, 1730, he was the sole proprietor of a promising business, which included the printing of a newspaper begun the year before, *The Pennsylvania Gazette*. Six weeks later, he married Deborah Read, the daughter of his first landlady. Though she was uneducated and ignorant (thus never an intellectual companion), she was frugal, industrious, and loving. Franklin, at twenty-four, had become a solid Philadelphia burgher.

Life's Work

The foundation of Franklin's renown was his success as a businessman. Both he and Deborah worked very hard, and they lived frugally for some time. It was, however, more than routine drudgery, for new projects were always appearing: Franklin established a stationery shop; Deborah collected and prepared rags for the papermakers; he imported books in both English and foreign languages; he printed almanacs for those who compiled them— and then decided to compile his own. *Poor Richard's Almanack*, begun in 1732 and published between 1733 and 1758, was ultimately to become the best known of the many which were printed in eighteenth century America. Franklin enjoyed borrowing and reworking phrases from his reading and sometimes wrote new adages, which delighted his readers. For many, he and his fictional wise man, Richard Saunders, became one. The central themes of

Richard's concern were thrift, industry, and frugality, and Franklin at the time appeared to be practicing what "Poor Richard" preached.

Political connections quickly became an important feature of Franklin's business success. He printed much of the provincial government's work: laws, records of legislative voting, and even the new paper currency in favor of which Franklin had argued in his first political pamphlet, *A Modest Enquiry into the Nature and Necessity of a Paper Currency* (1729). He became clerk of the Pennsylvania Assembly in 1736. The following year, he secured an appointment as postmaster for Philadelphia, a position which gave him immediate access to the latest news—very helpful in his newspaper business. Later, he was deputy postmaster general for all the colonies (1753-1774), and under his administration the governmental department showed a profit. He was always heavily involved with public affairs and often managed to influence their course.

It was during his years as a businessman that Franklin's remarkable flair for civic improvement by private initiative appeared. In 1727, he founded a discussion group, or club, of tradesmen, clerks, and mechanics, which he called the "Junto." Often Franklin would first propose to his friends at the Junto for discussion an idea for a public project, and then follow his proposal with an article in his newspaper. Soon the project would be under way. He was prominent in the founding of a circulating library, a fire company, a hospital, and an academy which evolved into the University of Pennsylvania, among many other projects. Ever the keen observer of daily life in his beloved city, he was always alert to possibilities for improvement.

Franklin was also a particularly astute observer of nature itself, and this ultimately led him to the forefront of certain branches of the science of his day. On an early transatlantic voyage, he kept careful records of temperatures, of the flora and fauna of the sea, of the positions of the moon and the stars; later he made a map of the Gulf Stream. He believed that knowledge must be useful, and actual inventions came out of many of his studies, including the improved Franklin stove, bifocal spectacles, a glass harmonica (a musical instrument for which even Wolfgang Amadeus Mozart wrote music), and other lesser gadgets. His main interest, though, was electricity. His famous kite experiment in 1752 demonstrated the identity of lightning and electricity and gave him an international reputation. He was, as always, interested in practical application, which in this case became the lightning rod. Nevertheless, he was also responsible for naming the concept of polarity, negative and positive, to describe the behavior of electricity.

In 1748, Franklin was able to retire from business, expecting to devote himself to his favorite scientific pursuits. Public affairs, however, became the dominant force throughout the remainder of his life. When the threat of war with France led to a gathering of delegates at Albany in 1754, Franklin was there representing Pennsylvania. He proposed a plan for an inter-Colonial union which the Albany Congress approved, only to see it rejected by both the various Colonial governments and the imperial authorities in London. Franklin always believed that if these governments had not been so short-sighted, the American Revolution might have been avoided. In 1757, as a result of a quarrel between the Pennsylvania Assembly and the proprietors of the colony, he was sent to London as spokesman for the Assembly, the members of which wanted the authorities there to intervene. In this he achieved a partial success. While in England, he received honorary degrees from St. Andrews and Oxford. He was very happy in England and seriously considered a permanent move, but he came home to Philadelphia in 1762.

Another political quarrel in Pennsylvania led to Franklin's return to England in 1764, where he soon became involved in efforts to forestall the new imperial policies toward the Colonies, which Americans regarded as outrageous. For ten years, Franklin was torn between his profound pride in America and things American, and his enthusiasm for English culture. As the foremost American of his day, he was looked to for the preservation of American rights: He became an agent for Georgia, New Jersey, and Massachusetts, as well as the Pennsylvania Assembly. As Anglo-American relations deteriorated, Franklin revealed in private his growing conviction that the American colonists' claims were sound and that their resistance was justified, while he continued to make every diplomatic effort possible for accommodation.

Early in 1774, however, news arrived of the destruction of tea at Boston Harbor: the "Boston Tea Party." This was quickly followed by a mighty personal attack on Franklin, occasioned by his part in obtaining and circulating certain letters written by Governor Thomas Hutchinson of Massachusetts, the contents of which inflamed opinion against Hutchinson and led to a petition for his recall. Franklin was dismissed by the royal government from his postal appointment and subjected to a searing public humiliation before a committee of the Privy Council (January, 1774). For another year he tried in many ingenious ways to achieve a reconciliation, but to no avail. He sailed for America in March, 1775.

When Franklin arrived home, the Continental Congress, which had first convened during the preceding fall, was now into its second session at Philadelphia. The deliberations were now becoming extremely anxious because the unthinkable had happened: Actual fighting had broken out with British soldiers at Lexington and Concord. Franklin was made a member of the congress the day after he arrived, and he immediately undertook important work. He drew up a plan of Colonial union—something similar to an early version of a national constitution. He organized a post office and became postmaster general. He served on a number of important committees, including one which in 1776 was to draft the Declaration of Independence. He was, at the age of seventy, the oldest signer. Toward the end of that year, he was sent by the congress, along with Arthur Lee and Silas Deane, to solicit French support for the American cause.

Franklin was well-known in France. He had visited that country before, but more important was his reputation as a scientist, writer (Poor Richard's witticisms had been translated), and apostle of the latest ideas of the Age of Reason. He played the part well, with fur hat and simple clothes, a genial manner, and appropriate *bons mots*, and he exuded the spirit of liberty— a veritable backwoods Socrates spreading the truths of nature. Following the American victory at Saratoga (October, 1777), the French became receptive to American suggestions, and by February of 1778 France had become a formal ally. This meant that France was now at war with Great Britain.

Franklin became the sole American ambassador in September of 1778 and, as always, found many interests beyond his principal work. He managed, nevertheless, to keep Franco-American relations good; France provided America with material aid, an army, and, in the crucial autumn of 1781, a navy. After the British defeat at Yorktown (October, 1781), peace negotiations with Britain began. Franklin was joined by John Adams and John Jay in the final talks, but on several occasions the wily old Philadelphian's role was decisive. It was an excellent treaty for Americans, gaining them a formal acknowledgment of independence and generous boundaries.

When Franklin returned to Philadelphia in September, 1785, he was nearly eighty years old. Yet he was chosen president of the executive council of Pennsylvania, and he became the president of an antislavery society. He was chosen as a Pennsylvania delegate to the Philadelphia Convention, which drew up the United States Constitution in 1787, and he gave his prestigious support to its ratification. His last public act was signing a petition to Congress for the abolition of slavery. He died on April 17, 1790.

Summary

Franklin's life was so varied and his achievements so diverse that it seems as though there were several Franklins, though one tends to overlap the other. The most familiar is the successful businessman who rose from humble circumstances to dine with kings, substantially by his own efforts. His life symbolized the rags-to-riches success of a self-made man, a theme of great importance in American thought. His version of his life, as presented in the didactic *Autobiography* (1791) and in the sayings of Poor Richard, stressed thrift, industry, and frugality—important elements of his own Puritan heritage, rendered in secular, easily understood forms. His zest for useful knowledge became the main style of American science and technology, yet he had great respect for learning and for intellectual curiosity, and he believed that educational opportunity was indispensable for a great future nation.

He was civic-minded from the start. He demonstrated what could be done by private, voluntary community effort to care for human needs, but he also stressed the importance of alert participation in the prevailing political system. His style was egalitarian, tolerant, and democratic before such a style was expected and common; yet he understood well the importance of dignity and deference in human affairs. Americans, during his later years, repudiated kings and hereditary aristocrats, but they also yearned for heroes. Franklin provided them with a hero unlike any other known before.

Bibliography

Aldridge, Alfred Owen. *Benjamin Franklin: Philosopher and Man*. Philadelphia: J. B. Lippincott Co., 1965. An effort to explain Franklin's human qualities as much as his achievements, this is a judicious, authoritative biography by one who has done much to expand knowledge of Franklin and who has written extensively about him. Some unconventional frankness, but without debunking.

Cohen, I. Bernard. *Franklin and Newton*. Cambridge, Mass.: Harvard University Press, 1966. In this reprint of the excellent 1956 study of eighteenth century scientific thought, Cohen, distinguished historian of science, places Franklin in the context of prevailing notions about scientific method; he appreciates Franklin as a scientist without overstating the case. Especially good depiction of human qualities which affect scientific work.

Conner, Paul W. *Poor Richard's Politics: Benjamin Franklin and His New American Order*. New York: Oxford University Press, 1965. Systematic discussion of Franklin's political ideas. This is a thoughtful, well-informed book, filled with materials regarding Franklin's intellectual world. Strong effort to arrive at balanced judgments about Franklin as a thinker.

Crane, Verner W. *Benjamin Franklin and a Rising People*. Boston: Little, Brown and Co., 1954. Succinct, extremely informative, and reliable. Neither very short nor very long, this book gets to the essentials about Franklin in a commonsense way reminiscent of the good Dr. Franklin himself. Especially strong on philosophical, social, and political ideas.

Franklin, Benjamin. *The Autobiography of Benjamin Franklin*. Edited by Leonard W. Labaree et al. New Haven, Conn.: Yale University Press, 1964. Franklin's memoirs (the word "autobiography" was not used in the eighteenth century) have been printed a bewildering number of times, and most readers may well believe that they are familiar with them. It is one of those classics, however, which deserve repeated readings, even though it presents only one of the several Franklins.

Granger, Bruce I. *Benjamin Franklin: An American Man of Letters*. Ithaca, N. Y.: Cornell University Press, 1964. Skilled presentation of Franklin's literary achievements. Each chapter is devoted to a kind of writing, such as essays, letters, almanacs, and so on. Strong claims are made for Franklin, many of them persuasive.

Lopez, Claude-Anne. *Mon Cher Papa*. New Haven, Conn.: Yale University Press, 1966. Unusually charming account of Franklin's life in France during the American Revolution by one of the editors of the Franklin papers. The author does a good job of dispelling some of the myths and the nonsense about Franklin and the ladies and makes a strong case for his greatness as a diplomat. A very entertaining book.

Stourzh, Gerald. *Benjamin Franklin and American Foreign Policy*. Chicago: University of Chicago Press, 1954. Searching, learned analysis of some major features of Franklin's thought. This account begins with a review of prevailing currents of thought in the eighteenth century, featuring the Great Chain of Being, the belief in progress and in reason, and other basic notions; then it proceeds with the way Franklin developed such materials in the course of his diplomatic career.

Van Doren, Carl C. *Benjamin Franklin*. New York: Viking Press, 1938. Magisterial biography, massive and still impressive. This is the kind of book to which one might turn for reliable information about nearly anything regarding Franklin's life. An excellent literary achievement containing profound, extensive scholarship.

Wright, Esmond. *Franklin of Philadelphia*. Cambridge, Mass.: Harvard University Press, 1986. A lively, well-written biography. Much new knowledge about Franklin has come to light since Van Doren's biography, and even since that of Aldridge, and this work incorporates it gracefully. In some ways, Wright says, Franklin was " the most modern-minded of all the Founding Fathers."

Richard D. Miles

JOHN C. FRÉMONT

Born: January 21, 1813; Savannah, Georgia
Died: July 13, 1890; New York, New York
Areas of Achievement: Western exploration, politics, and the military
Contribution: John C. Frémont's exploits as an explorer helped to propel the
American people westward toward Oregon and California. When the con-
tinental nation he helped to create was faced with civil war, he fought to
maintain the Union and end slavery.

Early Life

When John Charles Frémont was born on January 21, 1813 in Savannah,
Georgia, his parents were not married. In 1811, Ann Beverly Whiting had left
her elderly husband John Pryor to run away with Charles Frémon, a young
French emigrant who taught dancing and French. For several years the struggling Frémon family traveled the South, but after the father died they settled
in Charleston, South Carolina, where John Charles grew to maturity.

At age fourteen, Frémont clerked in the law office of John W. Mitchell,
who soon sent the young man to Dr. John Roberton's academy. In 1829, Frémont entered the junior class of the College of Charleston. Showing promise, he nevertheless fell behind in his studies from a lack of diligence as well
as the distraction of a young love. In 1831, the faculty reluctantly dismissed
him for "incorrigible negligence," three months short of his graduation.

In 1833, saved from obscurity by Joel Poinsett, former minister to Mexico,
Frémont taught mathematics on the USS *Natchez* on a South American
cruise and then earned an appointment in 1835 as professor of mathematics
in the navy. He nevertheless declined this position to join Captain William G.
Williams in surveying part of a proposed railroad route from Charleston to
Cincinnati. This first assignment earned for him a second as Williams' assistant in 1836-1837, surveying the lands of the Cherokee Indians in Georgia.
Frémont showed little concern for the forced removal of the Cherokees
across the Mississippi, but he did discover a longing to pursue a life in un-
explored lands.

With the help of Secretary of War Poinsett, Frémont was assigned in 1838
to assist Joseph Nicolas Nicollet, a respected French scientist mapping the
region between the Mississippi and Missouri rivers. He was commissioned a
second lieutenant in the United States Topographical Corps and from
Nicollet received valuable experience in frontier survival, as well as rigorous
training in mapmaking and scientific observation. As Nicollet's protégé, Frémont stood ready to replace the gravely ill scientist on future missions.

Bright and inquisitive, Frémont already possessed the knowledge of surveying, mathematics, and natural sciences, as well as the impulsiveness, that
would shape his later career. Bearded and slightly but sturdily built, he was

able to endure great physical and personal hardships. His dark hair, olive skin, and piercing blue eyes attracted the friendship and affection of men and women alike. In 1841, he won the lifelong admiration and love of the young and talented Jessie Benton, acquiring not only a bride but also another powerful benefactor in her father, Senator Thomas Hart Benton of Missouri.

Life's Work

Frémont received his first independent assignment in 1841 to survey the Des Moines River region. On his return, he secretly married Jessie, soon benefitting from his family connection with Senator Benton: Advocates of American expansion, led by Benton, were eager to encourage emigration to the Oregon country, and Frémont was thus given command of his first western expedition, assigned to examine part of the trail to Oregon while gathering information useful to emigrants and the government.

In Missouri, Frémont enlisted Kit Carson as his guide and set off from the Kansas River in June, 1842. Following the Platte to the Sweetwater River, he went on to cross the Rocky Mountains at South Pass in Wyoming, later describing the route as no more difficult than the ascent up Capitol Hill. He then explored the headwaters of the Green River in the Wind River Range, unfurling an American flag atop one of its loftiest peaks. Returning, Frémont led six men in a collapsible boat down the Platte. When the current became swift and dangerous, he rashly decided to run the rapids, resulting in an accident that destroyed much of his equipment and part of the expedition's records.

Frémont's second expedition of 1843-1844 was more ambitious. With a large, well-equipped party (including an unauthorized howitzer cannon), he was to complete his survey of the overland trail all the way to Oregon. Setting off in May, the explorer first sought a new pass through the Colorado mountains but soon rejoined the Oregon Trail. Crossing at South Pass, he pushed on to the British forts in the Oregon country, finally reaching Fort Vancouver on the Columbia. On this expedition, Frémont made the first scientific investigation of the Great Salt Lake; his reports inspired Brigham Young to lead his Mormon followers to settle there and make the region bloom, as Frémont had predicted.

From Oregon, Frémont embarked on a perilous journey southward, exploring and naming the Great Basin and then attempting a risky winter crossing of the Sierra Nevada into California, successfully leading his men to Sutter's Fort in the Sacramento Valley. Inspired in part by American interest in the Mexican province of California, Frémont's adventures intensified American passions to possess this valuable Pacific prize. Returning via the old Spanish Trail, Utah Lake, and Bent's Fort on the Arkansas River, Frémont emerged in August, 1844, a national celebrity.

With Jessie's valuable help, Frémont prepared reports of his first and second expeditions that captured the excitement and promise of the new land. Congress ordered the reports published for public distribution, providing emigrants a guide for western travel. The popular reports helped to dispel the notion that the Plains region was an arid wasteland, showed the Oregon Trail passable, and praised the fertile valleys of Oregon and California.

With a well-armed party of sixty men, the brevet captain's third expedition would place him in California just as relations with Mexico worsened. Starting in June, 1845, the party followed the Arkansas and then crossed the central Colorado Rockies. Frémont paused to examine further the Great Salt Lake, then led his party across the desert to the west. While the main party followed a safer route, Frémont led a smaller group directly across the Great Basin and then attempted another winter crossing of the Sierra. Encountering less difficulty than on the previous trip, he arrived once again at Sutter's Fort, eager to play a role in California's future.

Frémont's formidable force earned the suspicion of Mexican officials, who ordered the party to leave the province. Although war with Mexico was months away, Frémont defied the order, raised the American flag, and prepared for a confrontation. When none developed, he slowly moved toward Oregon but retraced his steps after the arrival of a messenger from Washington. Marine Lieutenant Archibald Gillespie had carried important dispatches to Consul Thomas O. Larkin at Monterey, directing him to conciliate the native Californians to accept American rule. Gillespie repeated these instructions to Frémont and relayed news of trouble with Mexico. Frémont misinterpreted the government's instructions to mean that he should return to California and act to protect American interests there. After a bloody clash with Indians, he returned to the Sacramento Valley, assuming command of the "Bear Flag" revolt of American settlers in June, 1846.

Frémont's actions secured northern California for the United States, but were contrary to the government's wishes to win the province peacefully with the aid of its citizens. Once hostilities with Mexico began, American naval forces seized the ports of Monterey and San Francisco in July, 1846. Frémont's frontiersmen and settlers then formed the "California Battalion" to assist Commodore Robert F. Stockton in securing southern California. San Diego and Los Angeles were quickly occupied, but a revolt by Californians forced the Americans to retake the south. Assembling a large force in the north, Frémont arrived too late to join in the battle for Los Angeles, but he did accept (without authority) the Californians' surrender at Cahuenga.

In January, 1847, Stockton appointed Frémont governor of California. This position embroiled the current lieutenant colonel in a bitter dispute over proper authority between the commodore and General Stephen Watts Kearny, who had arrived from Santa Fe only to be bloodied by Californians at San Pasqual. As governor in Los Angeles, Frémont recognized Commodore Stockton's authority while unwisely resisting General Kearny's com-

mands, resulting in his arrest and return east virtually a prisoner. In a celebrated court-martial defense, he won public sympathy, but in January, 1848,
was found guilty of mutiny, disobedience, and conduct prejudicial to military
order. He was sentenced to dismissal from the service. President James K.
Polk disallowed the mutiny conviction but upheld the lesser charges while
suspending the punishment. Frémont spurned Polk's gesture and resigned his
commission instead, ending his career as an explorer for the United States
Army.

To regain his injured honor, Frémont organized a privately funded fourth
expedition in late 1848. Intended to locate suitable passes for a central
railroad route to the Pacific, the expedition attempted a midwinter passage
of the severe San Juan Mountains in southern Colorado. Disregarding the
advice of mountain men and perhaps misled by his guide "Old Bill" Williams, Frémont plunged into the snowy mountains, only to find disaster. Cold
and starvation eventually took the lives of ten of his thirty-three men, while a
few survivors may have resorted to cannibalism. Frémont withdrew to Taos,
New Mexico, sending a relief party to his surviving men. With a smaller
party, he pushed on to California by the Gila River route, arriving in early
1849.

Frémont's fortunes revived once more as gold had just been discovered in
California. In 1847, he had directed Consul Larkin to buy a tract of land near
San Francisco; instead Larkin had secured a large grant in the interior. At
first apparently worthless, the Mariposa grant yielded immense wealth in
gold and became the Frémonts' California home. Then in December, 1849,
Frémont was selected one of California's first United States senators, serving
a short term from 1850 to 1851 as an antislavery Democrat.

Not chosen to lead one of the five government parties surveying the best
route for a Pacific railroad, Frémont in late 1853 undertook his fifth and final
expedition to prove the superiority of a central route. On this venture, Frémont found less hardship in attempting another winter crossing of the Colorado mountains. Crossing into Utah, however, his men were again on the
brink of starvation, whereupon he swore them not to resort to cannibalism.
The party was finally saved in February, 1854, when it arrived at a Mormon
settlement in Parowan. The route was not adopted for the Pacific railroad.

As tension grew between North and South, Frémont emerged as a candidate for president in 1856, first for the Democratic party and then for the
newly organized Republican party. Hostile to slavery, he favored the Republican position, opposing slavery's westward expansion, and in June, 1856,
accepted the first presidential nomination of the young party. In the general
election he faced both Democrat James Buchanan and the candidate of the
Know-Nothing Party, Millard Fillmore. The "Pathfinder" made few campaign utterances, but his illegitimate origins and false campaign charges that
he was a Catholic virtually overshadowed his opposition to the spread of slav-

ery to Kansas. While he carried eleven free states, lack of campaign organization and money in critical states such as Pennsylvania and Indiana probably cost him the election. Perhaps Frémont was not the best man to lead his nation in time of crisis, but his popularity helped to establish the Republican party and thus contributed to the election of Abraham Lincoln four years later.

After his disappointing defeat, Frémont temporarily retired to private life, absorbed in developing the Mariposa, by now encumbered with debt. When the Civil War erupted in April, 1861, he was in Europe on business. Born a Southerner, he did not hesitate to support the Union in its greatest crisis. On his own authority he purchased arms and ammunition for the Union in England and France, and then returned home to accept an appointment as a major general commanding the Western Department based in St. Louis.

Beginning in July, 1861, Frémont's challenging task was to pacify the divided state of Missouri while raising an army to undertake an offensive down the Mississippi. He received little support from Washington, and his duties were overwhelming. While he reinforced the strategic Illinois town of Cairo, he did not act quickly enough to aid Nathaniel Lyon, who was defeated and killed at Wilson's Creek on August 10. Charges of favoritism and corruption in government contracts haunted Frémont's command, but most controversial was his sudden order of August 30 declaring martial law in Missouri, threatening to shoot captured guerrillas, and freeing the slaves of rebel masters.

While antislavery advocates praised Frémont's emancipation edict, Lincoln feared its effect on the border states and directed him to modify the order. The general stubbornly refused to heed Lincoln, forcing the president to reverse the measure publicly. With Frémont's command assaulted by powerful political enemies, Jessie went east to present his case, but her stormy interview with Lincoln did more harm than good. As Frémont sought to lead his troops to victory in southwestern Missouri, Lincoln removed him from command of the Western Department in November, 1861.

Outcry over Frémont's removal induced Lincoln to appoint him in March, 1862, to command the newly formed Mountain Department, designed to capture an important railroad at Knoxville, Tennessee. Abandoning this effort, Frémont was also outmarched by Stonewall Jackson in the Virginia Valley Campaign of 1862. At the battle of Cross Keys on June 8, Frémont proved ineffective against Confederate troops, and when Lincoln added Frémont's force to the command of John Pope, Frémont asked to be relieved. In 1864, Frémont was nominated to the presidency by some Democrats and radical Republicans dissatisfied with Lincoln. At first accepting the nomination, he soon feared a Democratic victory and withdrew from the race, helping to ensure Lincoln's reelection.

As the war came to an end, Frémont lost much of his wealth as well as control of his beloved Mariposa. His ambitions turned to railroad finance, as he still hoped to realize his dream of a Pacific railroad. He became involved with unscrupulous business associates, however, squandering the remainder of his fortune and a good portion of his reputation when the Southwest Pacific failed in 1867 and the Memphis & El Paso did so in 1870.

From 1878 to 1883, Frémont served as governor of Arizona Territory. With Jessie's help he wrote his memoirs, published in 1887. Belated gratitude from his nation came in April, 1890, when he was restored to his rank as major general and placed on the retired list with pay. Death came in New York in July, 1890, from a sudden attack of peritonitis.

Summary

Frémont's exploits as an explorer exemplified the restless energy and unbounded ambition of mid-nineteenth century America. Proud and self-reliant, Americans resented restraints and the rulings of authority. Frémont's career also reflected the lack of discipline and wisdom born of experience that led the young and sometimes careless American people into such tragedies as the brutal treatment of American Indians, the war on Mexico, and the spilling of brothers' blood in the Civil War. Like his nation, Frémont climbed heights of adventure and opportunity, but also found failure, conflict, and injustice.

Frémont never claimed to be a "Pathfinder"; his mapping expeditions usually followed paths already worn by fur traders and early emigrants. Yet his romantic journeys spurred American expansion to the Pacific, his reports encouraging western emigration while providing travelers with useful information. Frémont's mapping and scientific work rivaled that of earlier explorers, improving knowledge of the vast interior region from the Rockies to the Sierra, while helping to clarify the true natures of the Continental Divide and the Great Basin.

As politician, soldier, and financier, Frémont found less glory. His unauthorized actions in the California revolt remain controversial, while his service during the Civil War provoked charges of political opportunism and military ineffectiveness. His mining and railroad schemes typified the boom period of American industrial expansion, but left him almost destitute. His death in 1890 coincided with the end of the romantic age of the American West, where he left his name and his mark.

Bibliography

Allen, John Logan. "Division of the Waters: Changing Concepts of the Continental Divide, 1804-44." *Journal of Historical Geography* 4 (October, 1978): 357-370. This article helps to clarify Frémont's contributions to geographical knowledge of the American interior.

Dellenbaugh, Frederick S. *Frémont and '49*. New York: G. P. Putnam's Sons,

1914. An old but detailed account primarily of Frémont's expeditions. The author traces the explorer's routes and includes several useful maps.

Egan, Ferol. *Frémont: Explorer for a Restless Nation.* Garden City, N.Y.: Doubleday and Co., 1977. By focusing on Frémont's career to 1854, this work praises his accomplishments more than most.

Frémont, John Charles. *Memoirs of My Life.* Chicago: Belford, Clarke and Co., 1887. Frémont's own memoirs are the only source for much of the available information on his personal life as well as his career. An intended second volume was not published.

Goodwin, Cardinal L. *John Charles Frémont: An Explanation of His Career.* Stanford, Calif.: Stanford University Press, 1930. This is perhaps the most critical account of Frémont's life. It views the explorer as a "drifter" who entered into corrupt financial dealings.

Harlow, Neal. *California Conquered: War and Peace on the Pacific, 1846-1850.* Berkeley: University of California Press, 1982. Much of this work examines Frémont's controversial role in the California conquest. It also discusses his dispute with Kearny and subsequent arrest.

Jackson, Donald, and Mary Lee Spence, eds. *The Expeditions of John Charles Frémont.* 3 vols. Champaign: University of Illinois Press, 1970-1984. This multivolume collection of documents is an invaluable source of information for Frémont's expeditions. It includes his reports, important correspondence, and the record of his court-martial.

Nevins, Allan. *Frémont: Pathmarker of the West.* 2 vols. New York: Frederick Ungar Publishing Co., 1961. Perhaps the best study of Frémont, this work by a famous American historian portrays the explorer as a flawed hero of American expansion.

Rolle, Andrew. "Exploring an Explorer: Psychohistory and John Charles Frémont." *Pacific Historical Review* 51 (May, 1982): 145-163. This article presents an interesting if speculative psychological interpretation of Frémont's often erratic career.

Vernon L. Volpe

MARGARET FULLER

Born: May 23, 1810; Cambridgeport, Massachusetts
Died: July 19, 1850; at sea, off Fire Island, New York
Areas of Achievement: Women's rights, social reform, literary criticism, and antebellum intellectual life
Contribution: As author of *Woman in the Nineteenth Century* (1845), Margaret Fuller established herself as the nation's leading feminist theoretician. As a reporter for Horace Greeley's *New York Tribune*, she became one of the country's first female journalists; she was also a leading figure in the Transcendentalist movement and edited its journal, *The Dial*.

Early Life

Born to Timothy and Margarett Crane Fuller, Sarah Margaret Fuller was the first of nine children (during early adolescence she dropped her first name). Her father, a Harvard-educated lawyer and Jeffersonian politician, in 1817 served a term in Congress and, in 1824, passionately supported the election of John Quincy Adams. Timothy Fuller's disappointment in failing to secure a patronage job from Adams began the decline of his career. He quit his law practice in 1833 and adequately provided for his family as a farmer until his untimely death in 1835. Margaret took over as head of the family, as the eldest child and apparently because her mother proved emotionally weak.

Disappointed by the birth of a female child, Timothy Fuller nevertheless had determined to give his daughter the best possible education. He had read Mary Wollstonecraft's *A Vindication of the Rights of Woman* (1792), and he supplied Margaret with the kind of education that any Harvard-bound male child might receive. Indeed, Timothy Fuller's educational discipline proved extreme, leaving his precocious daughter emotionally overwrought, suffering from nightmares (in which immense faces came at her in the dark), sleepwalking, and lifelong migraine headaches. Still, Margaret progressed with remarkable speed. By age five, she had learned to read; at six, she began reading Latin and Greek; and at twelve, French and Italian. Before reaching adolescence, she possessed a formidable education, having read voraciously, including the works of Adam Smith, Sir Walter Scott, Lord Byron, and Jean-Jacques Rousseau. Living in Cambridge afforded the young girl the best intellectual environment the nation could offer. She attended a private school with boys such as Oliver Wendell Holmes and Richard Henry Dana, who would become part of the country's intellectual elite. Even as a young girl, she had earned a reputation as a scholar, and she became the first woman to receive library privileges at Harvard. By age twenty-two, she was studying German with the future Transcendentalist editor, James Freeman Clarke, and within three months, she was reading the works of Johann Wolfgang von Goethe and Friedrich Schiller and soon translated portions of Goethe's works into English. Envious gossip circulated that Fuller could rock a cradle, read a book, eat an apple, and knit a stocking simultaneously.

Forced into maturity at an early age, Fuller, while hardly in her teens, looked and acted like a woman in her twenties. Her finespun blonde hair adorned a pleasing face with wide-set blue-gray eyes and exceptionally white teeth. She possessed a shapely figure, but her long neck and habit of squinting, a result of nearsightedness, gave ammunition to her detractors, who mocked her as homely and unmarriageable. These criticisms arose more from disapproval of her unorthodox life, opinions, and late marriage, than from her actual physical attributes. To her enemies, Fuller was ugly and arrogant, but her friends considered her beautiful and brilliant.

When her father gave up his legal practice in Cambridge and moved his family to rural Groton, Massachusetts, she was deprived of the stimulating and vivacious social and intellectual life upon which she had come to depend. Between 1833 and 1837, she endured the death of her father and suffered tremendous stress resulting from the recognition that she could find no satisfactory role in life, from the burden of her responsibilities as head of the family, from disappointment in love, and from a prolonged religious crisis. By 1836, however, Fuller had met the great Transcendentalist philosopher, Ralph Waldo Emerson, and she soon began teaching at Amos Bronson Alcott's controversial Temple Street School. The following year, she secured a teaching position in Providence, Rhode Island (where she met John Neal, an early feminist), and began a career in writing. Between 1839 and 1844, Fuller conducted a series of conversations for women, addressing such subjects as art, literature, philosophy, ethics, the family, women, and education, a project which provided her with a creative outlet and a way to provide for women what the culture generally denied them. From 1840 to 1842, she edited *The Dial*. In 1843, Fuller traveled west, an experience which sensitized her to the plight of the American Indian and the horrid conditions afflicting the nation's prisoners, the poor, and the insane. In 1844 she accepted work as literary and social critic for Greeley's *New York Tribune* and, the following year, published a radical critique of women's social role, *Woman in the Nineteenth Century*. In 1846, dissatisfied with American culture and seeking personal independence, Fuller traveled to Europe, where she would find her own liberation, participate in the Romantic revolution that had swept across the Continent in 1848, bear a son, secretly marry the Marchese Giovanni Angelo Ossoli, the child's father, and adopt the socialist politics that led to the abortive Italian revolution of Giuseppe Mazzini and Giuseppe Garibaldi.

Life's Work

Nathaniel Hawthorne considered Fuller to be a great "humbug," and when she died in a shipwreck in 1850, he believed that she had received her just reward. The poet James Russell Lowell lampooned her as a silly know-it-all. Transcendentalist-turned-Catholic Orestes Brownson considered Fuller a dangerous and foolish heretic who sought to deny men's natural dominance over women. Edgar Allan Poe, who actually admired much of Fuller's writing, nevertheless ridiculed her and declared that she might find relief from her trials in a husband. Poe considered her ideas so extreme that he announced that the world might be divided into three categories: "men, women, and Margaret Fuller." Although the first edition of *Woman in the Nineteenth Century* sold out in a week, howls of protest went up against the author throughout the country. Her virtue came under attack, and Brownson denounced her as Boston's greatest source of corruption. Many critics dismissed her convictions by announcing that they amounted to unhappiness at being born female. English critics proved equally harsh: One British magazine referred to the author as "a he-woman."

After Fuller's death, family and friends attempted to rehabilitate her by publishing versions of her letters, diaries, and writings that stressed her desire for family and home. In the attempt to make Fuller respectable, her letters and personal manuscripts were brutalized and censored, and others were completely destroyed. A personal friend and the most sympathetic of the early biographers, Thomas Wentworth Higginson, completely misconstrued her life, painting it as a struggle between her desire for a family and her desire for a career. In their rehabilitation of Fuller, Higginson, Emerson, and the Fuller family bled Margaret of all color and complexity, virtually ignoring her significant contributions to American culture. In their hands, she became a squinty-eyed pedant with an "I-turn-the-crank-of-the-universe" attitude who, like any normal woman, performed at her best as a "conversationalist," thus denying her any authority as a serious author. Near the end of the nineteenth century, Henry James used Fuller's life as a model for the frustrated female protagonists in his novels, as Hawthorne had done earlier. Even modern historians have considered her an exotic, someone who met all the people worth knowing and found "no intellect comparable to my own." To avoid the disturbing questions Fuller's life and career posed to American society, her contemporaries and many historians turned her into a freak, half man and half woman, so unattractive that no intelligent man could marry her.

Nineteenth century Americans believed in the "doctrine of separate spheres." God and biology dictated that women remain in the home, rear children, and exert their moral influence, founded upon their assumed peculiar sensitivity to religion, upon men and society. Woman's smaller brain and predisposition to excitability were said to render her unfit for positions of authority in social and political life. Men, with greater strength and larger brains, were to occupy the sphere of public life. Fuller's greatest contribution to American history and life lies in her telling demolition of that doctrine in

Woman in the Nineteenth Century. She blasted the cultural stereotype of women, especially when that image led to a subservient role in marriage. Equally unsettling, she denounced Christianity's influence upon women and declared that Christianity had done absolutely nothing to improve women's plight. She sought compassion for prostitutes, whom she characterized not as disgusting fallen women but as victims of male lust and exploitation. She called for the economic liberation of women and demanded that they be permitted to enter any profession that they found attractive, even as sea captains.

Fuller had been nurtured on Jeffersonian liberalism and humanitarianism by her father, but Emerson proved the more crucial influence. His Transcendentalism aimed at the general elevation of society; Fuller addressed the needs of women that Emerson ignored. He expressed American democratic ideals; Fuller applied them to women. He spoke of self-reliance; she advocated self-dependence as a necessary step for liberation. He wrote of the organic relationship of all things to all people, while she reminded the nation that God had created men and women equal and interdependent, two halves of one thought. Fuller's 1845 book helped spur the 1848 Seneca Falls Convention, the first meeting advancing women's rights in the United States, and led some Americans to become aware of the bondage of all women, black and white. *Woman in the Nineteenth Century*, which remained continually in print until 1893, became a wellspring of the women's rights movement.

Rejected by her country as a heretic and a threat to civilized life, Fuller retreated to Europe in August, 1846. When she arrived in London, the astounding amount of poverty and the enormous disparity in levels of wealth made socialist ideas compelling to her. In Italy, she became a personal friend and ally of Mazzini and other European radicals. On the eve of the Italian Revolution, she published articles in the *New York Tribune* denouncing American slavery and siding with the hated abolitionists. She had always opposed slavery but never sympathized with abolitionist societies; in 1848, she publicly apologized for condemning them. She even denounced the recently concluded Mexican War, the first and most popular of America's foreign wars. Thanks to Europe, Fuller had found herself.

While in Italy, she took a lover, Giovanni Angelo Ossoli, eleven years her junior, and bore a son out of wedlock. When the Italian Revolution broke out in 1848 and French, Austrian, and Italian Bourbon forces closed in on Rome, Fuller and Ossoli threw themselves into the fight. Ossoli manned the parapets, and Fuller tended the wounded, all the while sending back to the United States a most perceptive analysis of Italian politics and collecting materials for a history of the short-lived republic. When the revolt collapsed, Fuller and Ossoli, who secretly married after the birth of their son, gained passage to the United States.

Leaving Italy in June, 1850, on the *Elizabeth*, they did not arrive off the coast of New York until early on the morning of July 19. A gale threatened the vessel and confused the inexperienced mate who captained the ship. About 4:00 A.M., the bow struck sand off Fire Island, New York. Winds violently swung the stern around, sending a load of marble, and Hiram Power's statue of John C. Calhoun, through the hull. By dawn, the ship had broken up, and Fuller, Ossoli, their child, and the manuscript history of the Italian republic were lost.

Summary

At age ten, Fuller had written that she was foredoomed to sorrow and pain. Furthermore, she knew that the source of that fate resided within her. Perceptive beyond her years, even as a child, Fuller had some sense that she had been prepared for a life which she could not lead. Brilliant, extraordinarily well-educated, and bustling with energy, Fuller found no outlets within American society for her creative force. What place existed in America for so powerful a female mind? Fuller had written in *Woman in the Nineteenth Century* that humans could not remain content and repressed. People, she asserted, naturally seek expansion, and they will get it one way or another. The primary thrust of her famous book aimed at breaking the bonds that male-dominated society placed upon all women. Fuller cared little for the ballot (although she would not have refused it); her desire for emancipation operated at a more profoundly personal level. She sought liberation of the soul and the freedom—of which Emerson spoke—for the individual to develop every talent and ability which lay within. Fuller found her true self and the greatest level of contentment after escaping the confines of American society and the expectations of family and friends. Enemies of Fuller noted that she found true happiness in a husband and a child after all, but she did so by choice, not compulsion. She remained a radical until her death off Fire Island and, according to Greeley, she was the greatest American woman of the nineteenth century.

Bibliography

Allen, Margaret Vanderhaar. *The Achievement of Margaret Fuller*. University Park: Pennsylvania State University Press, 1979. An intellectual study of the sources of Fuller's thought, with special attention to Emerson and the German Romantic Goethe.

Blanchard, Paula. *Margaret Fuller: From Transcendentalism to Revolution*. New York: Delacorte Press/Seymour Lawrence, 1978. The best and most comprehensive full-scale biography of Fuller. Based on a sensitive reading of all surviving Fuller correspondence and writings. Sets the framework for understanding Fuller's career. Especially illuminating when exploring Fuller family tensions and the influence of her father.

Deiss, Joseph Jay. *The Roman Years of Margaret Fuller: A Biography*. New

York: Thomas Y. Crowell, 1969. Deiss concentrates on Fuller's life in Italy and her work for Mazzini. Deiss lived in Italy and gained access to Italian sources that permitted him to unravel Fuller's complex personal life and solve the riddle of her marriage and the birth of her only child. Remarkably compassionate assessment of the Fuller ordeal.

Fuller, Margaret. *The Letters of Margaret Fuller*. Edited by Robert N. Hudspeth. Ithaca, N.Y.: Cornell University Press, 1983-1984. In this multivolume, ongoing work, Hudspeth has labored arduously to restore the integrity of the Fuller legacy from "admiring" editors and family members who butchered her literary remains. Where gaps exist, Hudspeth has supplied relevant material from correspondence to Fuller. Remarkably good at revealing Fuller's personal side, usually ignored and often distorted.

_____. *Woman in the Nineteenth Century*. Introduction by Bernard Rosenthal. New York: W. W. Norton and Co., 1971. Anyone interested in Fuller must read this book, originally published in 1845. The volume is not as lively as its predecessor, Wollstonecraft's *A Vindication of the Rights of Woman*, but is indispensable for understanding Fuller and the rise of the women's rights movement.

Myerson, Joel, ed. *Critical Essays on Margaret Fuller*. Boston: G. K. Hall, 1980. A gold mine of contemporary opinions of Fuller. Includes assessments by historians. Brutal attacks by Poe, Lowell, Brownson, and Hawthorne are included, as well as more sympathetic ones from Caroline Healy Dall and Lydia Maria Child.

Urbanski, Marie Mitchill Olesen. *Margaret Fuller's "Woman in the Nineteenth Century": A Literary Study of Form and Content, of Sources and Influence*. Westport, Conn.: Greenwood Press, 1980. The only book-length study of Fuller's primary work. Especially good on the varied sources of Fullers' thought, explaining how society trivialized Fuller and her ideas.

Donald Yacovone

R. BUCKMINSTER FULLER

Born: July 12, 1895; Milton, Massachusetts
Died: July 1, 1983; Los Angeles, California
Areas of Achievement: Engineering, architecture, and invention
Contribution: Fuller heightened Americans' awareness of how to employ
  natural resources to full advantage—a principle exemplified in his design
  of the geodesic dome.

Early Life

Richard Buckminster Fuller was born on July 12, 1895, in Milton, Massachusetts. His parents were Richard Buckminster and Caroline Wolcott Andrews Fuller, both of prominent New England families. Mrs. Fuller's ancestors included Roger Wolcott, a royal governor of Connecticut. Mr. Fuller's
family had arrived from England in the 1630's; his aunt was the feminist and
Transcendentalist, Margaret Fuller.

Buckminster Fuller's father was a successful merchant of leather and tea.
Young Fuller, or "Bucky" as the family called him, was one of four children.
They enjoyed a comfortable childhood in Newton, Massachusetts, in a large
house with servants. Fuller, however, had very poor eyesight; he was fitted
with powerful glasses at age four and for the first time in his life saw clearly.
He claimed to have been delighted at his wonderful new sense (he maintained that sense of delight throughout his life).

One of the boy's early triumphs occurred when he was six and a kinder-
garten student. Given dried peas and toothpicks with which to sculpt, he
constructed three squares that combined into eight triangles to complete his
first tetrahedronal octet truss. He entered Milton Academy as a day student
and did well in his studies, but not outstandingly so. His tenure at the academy was from 1904 to 1913.

Next, the young scholar entered Harvard, where he did not fare well. The
snobbery of the all-important university clubs upset Fuller, more so because
they had not accepted him. One of the reasons that the Harvard clubmen did
not embrace Fuller was his unusual physical appearance. He was five feet,
two inches tall with a head too large for his body. In addition, he wore
extremely thick-lensed glasses, and because one leg was shorter than the
other, he walked with a pronounced limp. He rebelled against his peers at
Harvard by withdrawing his tuition money from his account while still in his
first year; he spent it all in one night in New York City. His exploits that
night included a lavish dinner for the cast of the Ziegfeld Follies. Fuller may
have impressed his fellow students with this caper, but the Harvard administration was not amused, and he was expelled.

The Fuller family decided in 1914 to send him for several months to work
in a relative's textile mill in Sherbrooke, Canada. There, the young man

served as an apprentice mechanic, gained the respect of his fellow workers, and was happy. His mother (his father was by then deceased) decided, however, that her son should have a formal university education, and so, he was sent back to Harvard. His second stay there was also a failure, and he was expelled for good in 1915.

Not all of Fuller's early years were full of disappointments. His extended family summered each year at Bear Island, Maine, where he fell in love with boats and sailing. One of his first inventions was a push-pole to help propel his rowboat more efficiently than oars did. In 1917, when American involvement in World War I seemed imminent, Fuller entered the United States Naval Academy; there, he successfully completed an accelerated, three-month training period and was commissioned an ensign. This was an era during which the navy first began to fly airplanes into combat. In working with these new machines, Fuller was again inspired to invention. Seeing pilots drown in their cockpits when the airplanes flipped over in the water, Fuller devised a grappling hook, which hoisted downed airplanes quickly above the water while the pilot was pulled free.

Fuller was married to Anne Hewlett, the daughter of a prominent architect, on Rock Hall, Long Island, on July 12, 1917. Fuller then worked for a time for the Armour Meat Company and then the Kelly-Springfield Truck Company, but when his job was eliminated during the firm's reorganization, Fuller was offered a position by his father-in-law, J. Monroe Hewlett. Hewlett had invented a new building material filled with fibrous centers and put it to commercial use, creating the Stockade Building System Company. In order to accept his job of managing his father-in-law's company, Fuller, with his wife, moved to Chicago. Fuller did well in this firm from 1922 to 1927, until he ran into difficulty with the stockholders. Never interested in achieving high profits, Fuller had earned the distrust of the company hierarchy. His interest during these years had been in refining the product, but his superiors did not agree with his inclinations. Fuller's lack of interest in accumulating wealth continued throughout his life; he usually requested that people hiring his architectural and engineering services only pay him the cost of erecting the structure.

Fuller and Anne suffered a tragedy during their early life together. After a series of grave illnesses, their firstborn child, Alexandra, died at age four. Grief-stricken by the girl's death and by his business failure, Fuller fell into a period of heavy drinking and depression. He so despaired over the course of his life that he contemplated suicide. Instead, he began a two-year period of silence, seclusion, and meditation, during which he read widely and slept little.

Life's Work

From this period of intense contemplation, Fuller later claimed, he began to see the universe in new ways. He decided that he had to reeducate himself completely, that he would reject that which he could not prove to himself was true. He rejected traditional geometry, which concentrated on rectangles and planes, and substituted his own, which concentrated on triangles. From this new geometry, Fuller developed his geodesic dome—his best-known and most widely used invention. The geodesic dome has as its base numerous adjoining tetrahedrons. The alloy metals used to build the domes have high tensile strength by which force is dispersed away from the dome's surface; the result is a maximum-strength structure made from a minimum of light-weight materials. The first uses of a prototype Fuller dome were for advertising exhibits in such places as the Marshall Field's department store in Chicago in 1929. It was then that an agent of that store coined the term "dymaxion" to describe an early dome; the word is an amalgam of "dynamic" and "maximum." On the basis of the public's interest in his designs and inventions, Fuller began to appear as a lecturer before architectural and engineering societies. He also founded his Dymaxion Corporation and received some modest financial support to back his projects. Prior to this time, Fuller, his wife, and a second infant daughter, Allegra, had been living in poverty; they had received some family inheritances which had paid for their shabby apartment, but food had not always been easy to obtain, and they had often eaten only one meal a day.

Unfortunately, Fuller's domelike house did not prove to be a success in the 1930's. A number of factors caused its early demise. First, Fuller had developed the dymaxion house in the early period of the Great Depression, which held Americans in a tight grip for almost a decade; bounteous funds to develop and promote new products (which had been available in the 1920's) were almost nonexistent in the 1930's. Also, the Fuller dome was accepted with curiosity and interest by architects, but rejected by the construction industry. While Fuller saw this dymaxion house as an inexpensive home for young and poor families, the construction unions viewed it as a way of undercutting their various trade jobs. With these factors against it, the Fuller house did not find further employment until the early 1950's.

A second Fuller invention of the 1930's that enjoyed only a brief life was the dymaxion car. In order to produce prototypes of this vehicle, Fuller moved to Bridgeport, Connecticut, where a large factory building and good mechanics were available. Fuller's financial backer in this project was Philip Pearson, a wealthy Philadelphian, and the consulting engineer was W. Starling Burgess. Together, Fuller and Burgess manufactured a car which had a streamlined body similar to that of an airplane. The car, with a rear engine, was energy-efficient, getting some thirty or forty miles to one gallon of gasoline. It had a three-wheel design with front-wheel drive, so it could maneuver much more easily than a four-wheel vehicle. In tests, the dymaxion car achieved a speed of 120 miles per hour; it also held eleven passengers. Fuller himself drove the car in the New York and Connecticut area, creating a stir among spectators. Again, however, this invention was to fail. In 1933, the car was involved in a crash in which its driver was killed. Although another, "regular" car had caused the accident, publicity focused on the odd dymaxion car and pronounced it a failure. Fuller closed his factory in Bridgeport and began to concentrate on other inventions.

His next major innovative product was not a failure, but again it was an unusual item. In the early 1940's, Fuller developed a new map of the world: a flat map which avoided the exaggeration of land masses that round globes had always contained. Fuller termed his map the "dymaxion airocean" world map; the public first saw it printed in *Life* magazine in 1943.

In 1953, when the Ford Motor Company commissioned Fuller to build a ninety-three foot dome to cover the rotunda at their Dearborn, Michigan plant, he had his first overwhelming success with one of his inventions. In 1954, Fuller constructed a series of "radomes" for the Arctic Circle, where the United States Air Force had established its Distant Early Warning (DEW) Line of radar stations. The radomes were flown to their destinations and quickly assembled between Arctic storms. The results were small but unusually strong domes that withstood wind gusts of up to two hundred miles per hour.

Throughout the 1950's and the early 1960's, Fuller's domes were in demand: Corporations ordered them for their plants, cities for their theaters, and the United States government for its overseas exhibitions of new technology. One of the most famous Fuller domes was constructed in 1959 in Moscow, where it was used to house the United States Pavilion at the American Exchange Exhibition. It was two hundred feet in diameter and was built by the Kaiser Aluminum Company. This dome caused Fuller's reputation to soar and led, in part, to his appointment as a professor of generalized design at Southern Illinois University in 1959. In the years following his teaching career, Fuller lectured as a goodwill ambassador overseas and at most major American universities; he won numerous academic awards, including more than forty honorary degrees. In 1972, a nonprofit organization, The Design Science Institute, was formed in Washington, D.C., to perpetuate Fuller's designs and ideas. He died of a heart attack in Los Angeles on July 1, 1983.

Summary

Fuller accomplished much in his lifetime as a world-famous lecturer, inventor, engineer, mathematician, and architect, but his greatest influence on Americans may have come from his philosophy. Fuller advocated using the world's resources wisely and fairly so that all mankind could live in comfort. To promote this ideal, he invented the World Game in 1969, which employed computers to show how the natural environment could serve all men equally well. This game, in addition to his boisterous, enthusiastic lecturing style, endeared Fuller to established world leaders and rebellious college students alike.

Fuller's buoyant energy and fervent, optimistic conviction that man could solve his environmental problems came at a time when widespread pollution and the deep pessimism that it inspired were first developing on American soil and shore. Fuller served as a catalyst to spur younger inventors and scientists to careful, productive study of man's uses and misuses of his resources. Fuller also left a legacy of many engineering and architectural designs that will probably be developed in the future. Always ahead of his time, Fuller saw the need for entire cities covered by domes to ensure stable climatic conditions for their inhabitants. Similarly, he designed domes to be used as permanent housing on the ocean floor and on moon colonies. It is for Fuller's belief in the positive role of design and engineering for the future of America and mankind—and his vital contributions to that future—that he will be remembered best.

Bibliography

Banham, Reyner. *Age of the Masters: A Personal View of Modern Architecture*. New York: Harper and Row, Publishers, 1975. Banham places Fuller in perspective as a modern architect, seeing him as influenced by vaultworks, an ancient architectural design. The author also includes an interesting piece on how it feels to enter a Fuller dome with its open and airy spaciousness, and laments the fact that the geodesic dome is not yet widely used.

Cort, David. *Is There an American in the House?* New York: Macmillan, 1960. A book of topical essays by a noted journalist. He discusses the Fuller phenomenon of popularity as it emerged from overseas dome exhibits for the United States government. "Darkness Under the Dome" includes an amusing look at foreigners' enthusiastic response to the dome, particularly in Afghanistan.

Hatch, Alden. *Buckminster Fuller: At Home in the Universe*. New York: Crown Publishers, 1974. A warm and personal biography written by a longtime friend of Fuller. In interviews with Fuller and other friends and associates, Hatch provides fascinating highlights of his subject's life. A good balance between the personal life of Fuller and his scientific achievements.

Kenner, Hugh. *Bucky: A Guided Tour of Buckminster Fuller*. New York: William Morrow and Co., 1973. Includes a helpful annotated bibliography. Kenner also provides his own drawings of some of Fuller's inventions. He likes Fuller personally and presents him in a good light, but he does not hesitate to refute Fuller's philosophy when it seems disjointed or obscure.

McHale, John. *R. Buckminster Fuller*. New York: George Braziller, 1962. This book is one of a series on contemporary architects. The text itself is only about forty pages long, but it is followed by generous notes and a bibliography. Fuller's buildings (or structures) are shown in photographs. Perhaps too much emphasis on the functional aspect of the domes and not enough on their aesthetics.

Marks, Robert W. *The Dymaxion World of Buckminster Fuller*. Carbondale: Southern Illinois University Press, 1960. This book is devoted more to Fuller's professional life and achievements than to his personal life. Detailed, multiple pictures of all the major designs are given. Also, the author reproduces the patent pictures for several of the most famous inventions by Fuller. Photos display domes being erected in sequence.

Snyder, Robert. *R. Buckminster Fuller: An Autobiographical Monologue/ Scenario*. New York: St. Martin's Press, 1980. A unique and fascinating look at Fuller. Snyder, the inventor's son-in-law, includes in his book numerous pictures as well as Fuller's monologues from the several motion pictures in which he was featured (and which were directed by Snyder). In these films, Fuller described his designs and explained the World Game in his own special style.

Patricia E. Sweeney

ROBERT FULTON

Born: November 14, 1765; Little Britain Township, Pennsylvania
Died: February 24, 1815; New York, New York
Areas of Achievement: Engineering and invention
Contribution: Fulton built the first profitable steamboat, established the traditions that distinguished American steamboats for the remainder of the century, and laid the groundwork for future submarine and torpedo warfare.

Early Life

At the beginning of 1765, Robert Fulton, a successful tailor and leading citizen of Lancaster, Pennsylvania, sold most of his possessions and borrowed money in order to purchase a large farm, thirty miles to the south in Little Britain Township. There, on November 14, 1765, his first son, Robert Fulton, Jr., was born. Nothing else went well for the inexperienced farmer. Six years later, the elder Fulton returned to Lancaster, a bankrupt and dispirited man. He died in 1774, leaving his wife and six children without means of support other than the charity of relatives. Thus, at the age of nine, Robert Fulton learned the meaning of failure and poverty. For the remainder of his life, he struggled to achieve financial success and social status.

With the outbreak of the American Revolution, Lancaster changed from a small, isolated agricultural community to a bustling military. and economic center. The population swelled with refugees, soldiers on the march, military prisoners and gunsmiths. As young Fulton's curiosity attracted him to the new inhabitants, his quick intelligence and enthusiasm induced strangers to give time to the dark, handsome boy. Fulton spent an increasing amount of time with the gunsmiths, for whom he made mechanical drawings and painted signs. Perhaps he was having too good a time: His mother apprenticed him to a Philadelphia jeweler.

Little is known about Fulton's Philadelphia years. His master was a former London jeweler named Jeremiah Andrews. Fulton's talent at drawing and painting prepared him to produce miniature portraits on ivory lockets. By 1785, Fulton was listed in a city directory as a "miniature painter." The following year saw Fulton struck with two burdens that characterized the remainder of his life. He borrowed money to help his mother and sisters purchase another farm. At the same time, Fulton was ill with respiratory ailments. Despite his debts, the young man borrowed money and took the waters at Bath, a spa in northern Virginia favored by the upper class. There, Fulton recovered his health and doubtlessly heard about the steamboat experiments of a local man named James Rumsey. Upon his return to Philadelphia, Fulton found another steamboat pioneer, John Fitch, running his strange vessel across the Delaware River. At this time, however, Fulton displayed no interest in steam engines. He was a painter who desired to improve his skills and status. That meant that he, like other American painters before and since, had to work in Great Britain. Thus, in the summer of 1787, Fulton sailed for England. He would be absent from the United States for the next thirteen years.

Thanks to a letter of introduction, Fulton settled in London as a student of Benjamin West, an American painter popular with Britain's upper class. Fulton was not a gifted painter: He was, however, very successful at cultivating wealthy friends and patrons. Thus, Fulton managed to survive for several years as a painter. By the early 1790's, Fulton turned toward machines and canals. He devoted considerable time to studying canals and, in 1796, wrote *Treatise on the Improvement of Canal Navigation*. Many of his ideas were quite dated, but the volume was distinguished by its format. Fulton demonstrated details with excellent drawings, attempted to base designs upon mathematical calculations, and focused all canal features toward the concept of an inexpensive and national transportation system. The book established Fulton as a canal engineer.

Life's Work

With France and Great Britain at war in the mid-1790's, the patents of citizens of one nation were freely copied by the citizens of the other nation. Fulton believed that his canal ideas were valuable and ought to be patented in France. He arrived in France in 1797 and soon abandoned canals. After all, that nation had been building canals for more than a century and had little use for experts who lacked experience. Anyway, Fulton already had a new patron and a new mechanical passion.

Benjamin West had given Fulton an introduction to Joel Barlow, a Yale graduate who was making much money by running American ships through the British blockade and into French ports. Barlow and his wife, Ruth, welcomed Fulton into their Paris residence. The three lived together for the next seven years. The educated Barlow tutored Fulton in science and mathematics, and it was probably Barlow who introduced Fulton to the subject of submarine warfare. Barlow had been at Yale when another student, Robert Bushnell, designed *Turtle*, a submarine that had engaged in unsuccessful attacks upon British warships during the American Revolution. Bushnell, living in seclusion in Georgia, had sent Thomas Jefferson a detailed description of his submarine efforts, and the latter made the material available to Barlow. By the end of 1797, Fulton was working on submarines.

Within three years, Fulton completed a submarine, and in late 1800, he launched several unsuccessful attacks against British warships off French ports. His submarine *Nautilus* was an enlarged and refined version of the craft that Bushnell had built more than twenty years before. The method of attack was similar: The submarine carried a mine (called a torpedo by Fulton) to the enemy vessel. If the intended victim moved, it was safe from the slow, awkward submarine. Nor could the hand-cranked *Nautilus* overcome contrary tides or currents. In one attempt, however, Fulton and his crew of two remained submerged for more than six hours. That record was unequaled until the late nineteenth century. Fulton reached the obvious conclusion that *Nautilus* was inadequate as a weapon; he dismantled the submarine—perhaps to protect its secrets from imitators and its weaknesses from critics.

While still trying to collect funds from the French government for past submarine activities and future proposals, Fulton opened negotiations with British agents. In exchange for a substantial monthly payment, Fulton agreed to develop plans for small rowboats to tow torpedoes against French ships. In the midst of this scheme, Robert Fulton found a new patron.

Robert R. Livingston was one of the wealthiest men in America. Since helping to draft the Declaration of Independence, he had been active in public service. In 1801, Livingston became the American minister to the French government. For the past three years, the wealthy New Yorker had tried to promote steam navigation. While his brother-in-law, John Stevens, had set up a machine shop in New Jersey to conduct steamboat experiments, Livingston had secured a monopoly to steam navigation on New York waters. The two men, however, were not suited as partners. Hence Robert Fulton, the engineer anxious to win fame and fortune, and Livingston satisfied each other's needs. They became partners.

Fulton first studied the design of earlier steamboats and their engines. Next, he built models to test his own designs. Finally, in 1803, he placed a British engine aboard a craft of his own design, but the vessel moved too slowly. Fulton then left France, telling Livingston that he would return within two weeks. Fulton remained in England for two years working on his favorite project, undersea warfare. Fulton finally left England and sailed for New York.

The tall, handsome man who landed in America after nearly twenty years abroad was often mistaken for a foreign aristocrat. The boy from Lancaster had come a long way. Robert Fulton wasted no time: In the remarkably brief space of eight months, Fulton assembled the first steamboat to earn money for its owners. Fulton hired one of the best builders, Charles Brown, to construct the hull. The boat was supposed to have been designed in accordance with Fulton's study of water and wind resistance. Still, the vessel looked like an enlarged British canal boat. The engine was the best that could be bought, a Boulton and Watt from England. After a brief trial run, Fulton informed Livingston that the vessel was ready.

On August 17, 1807, *The North River Steamboat* left New York City with forty passengers, mostly apprehensive relatives of Livingston. On its way up the Hudson River to Albany, the vessel stopped at Livingston's river estate,

Clermont, the origin of the steamboat's unofficial but popular name, *Clermont*. Only a few passengers ventured aboard the steamboat for its first commercial run several weeks later. Public acceptance of the vessel increased, however, as it maintained a regular schedule. By the time river transportation closed for the winter, Livingston was earning a small but steady return on his investment.

During the winter of 1807-1808, Fulton rebuilt the steamboat with more comfortable accommodations. Because the vessel lacked sails to roll her about and voyaged on the relatively smooth waters of the Hudson River (locally called the North River), Fulton could install furniture that a sailing vessel could not accommodate. In the remaining seven years of his life, Fulton completed twenty more steamboats, each with fancier fittings than its predecessor. Thus, Fulton established the tradition of steamboat luxury. This tradition distinguished steam vessels from sailing vessels and attracted passengers.

In January, 1808, Fulton married Harriet Livingston, the beautiful niece of Robert Livingston. Once again, Fulton was working on torpedoes. In 1810, he published *Torpedo War and Submarine Explosions*, the first "do-it-yourself" book on that subject. Besides an expanding transportation system, a growing family, and torpedo work, Fulton was spending much time defending the steamboat monopoly that Livingston had pushed through the legislature years earlier. Other builders saw no more reason for a steamboat monopoly than one for sailing ships. Further, New Jersey citizens resented the Livingston-Fulton claim that New York's waters extended to the Jersey shore. The lawsuits dragged on for years.

When the War of 1812 began, Fulton concentrated on naval weapons. In marked contrast to his numerous letters and public demonstrations that characterized his earlier work in France and England, Fulton now worked in secret. He built a semisubmersible vessel to tow torpedoes against British warships off New London, Connecticut. A storm washed the vessel ashore, and the British later blew it up. Fulton's major work during the war was *Demologes*, a steam-driven battery. With its heavy cannon and thick sides, people (including British officers) expected the warship to destroy British blockaders near New York. Yet on February 24, 1815, shortly before the vessel was finished and just as news of peace reached the United States, Robert Fulton died. Exhausted by rushing the steam battery toward completion, by court actions over the steamboat monopoly, and by overexposure to a cold winter, he was too weak to resist another bout with respiratory problems.

Summary

The achievement of Robert Fulton was in developing a commercially successful steamboat. Other men may vie for the honor of inventing the steamboat, but their work failed to alter marine transportation. Robert Fulton and

The North River Steamboat ended the dependence of ships upon the wind. Moreover, whereas travel had always involved varying degrees of hardship, Fulton developed the concept of voyaging in comfort. Finally, in an age suspicious of change, Fulton introduced the modern practice of continual product development.

It is ironic that Fulton's fame in steamboats came so easily when compared to the brief time involved. That he succeeded in steam navigation was because of his willingness to build upon the work of others, to cooperate with financial backers, and to follow a logical pattern. Research, conceptualization, scale models, and mathematical calculations distinguished his work method. As a result of Fulton's efforts, the vision of steamboat pioneers became a reality.

In turn, Fulton's pioneering work in submarines and torpedoes had to wait upon further advances in technology. Yet his vision of undersea warfare fascinated contemporaries and inspired people throughout the nineteenth century. Fulton's ideas were employed with some success by the Confederacy during the Civil War, and Jules Verne named his imaginary submarine after Fulton's *Nautilus*. The United States Navy completed Fulton's *Demologes*, the world's first steam warship, renamed it *Fulton*, and then left the vessel to rot.

Robert Fulton belonged to a select group of Americans. Along with Francis Cabot Lowell and Eli Whitney, Fulton introduced technology to American society and laid the foundation for the nation to become the industrial leader of the world.

Bibliography
Chapelle, Howard I. *Fulton's Steam Battery: Blockship and Catamaran*. Washington, D.C.: Smithsonian Institution Press, 1964. Most detailed account of the steam battery based upon plans located in Denmark in 1960. Although the author is best known for his many books on American sailing vessels, he devoted the same care and expertise to collecting and analyzing the plans of steamships. Using copies of the steam battery's plans that were located in Danish archives, the author has produced the lost detailed account of Robert Fulton's last work.
Flexner, James T. *Steamboats Come True: American Inventors in Action*. Boston: Little, Brown and Co., 1978. An excellent account of steamboat pioneers before Fulton.
Fulton, Robert. *Torpedo War and Submarine Explosions*. New York: W. Elliot, 1810. Fulton's descriptions of underwater warfare not only guided the efforts of Americans who attempted to attack British warships during the War of 1812 but also became required reading for British officers aboard those same ships.
Hutcheon, Wallace, Jr. *Robert Fulton: Pioneer of Undersea Warfare*.

Annapolis, Md.: Naval Institute Press, 1981. The best account of Fulton's underwater work. Draws on many different sources for its information.

Morgan, John S. *Robert Fulton*. New York: Mason/Charter, 1977. A good overview of Fulton's life and work. The author provides the reader with a clear and well-written summary of Fulton's life and work. This book meets the needs of the general reader.

Philip, Cynthia O. *Robert Fulton*. New York: Franklin Watts, 1985. This well-researched biography is particularly good for its thoughtful analysis of Fulton's character and behavior. The author's conclusions about the relationship between Fulton and the Barlows are not accepted by all scholars.

Taylor, George R. *The Transportation Revolution: 1815-1850*. New York: Harper and Row, Publishers, 1951. This standard history examines the role of the steamboat in the expansion of the American economy and society during the first half of the nineteenth century.

Joseph A. Goldenberg

ALBERT GALLATIN

Born: January 29, 1761; Geneva, Switzerland
Died: August 12, 1849; Astoria, New York
Areas of Achievement: Politics, banking, and science
Contribution: Drawing upon the social philosophy of the French Enlightenment, Gallatin contributed, as secretary of the treasury to the administrations of Presidents Thomas Jefferson and James Madison, to the fiscal stability of the new nation and, as the first president of the American Ethnological Society, to the development of American anthropology.

Early Life

Abraham Alfonse Albert Gallatin was born January 29, 1761, in Geneva, Switzerland. Both his mother, née Sophie Albertine Rolaz, and his father, Jean Gallatin, died when Albert was an infant, so his care was entrusted to a distant relative of his mother, Mlle Catherine Pictet. The Gallatin family, part of the Geneva aristocracy and supplier of lords and councillors to the city-state, saw to it that young Gallatin was provided an excellent education. Despite access to the rich cultural heritage of his family, who counted Voltaire as a close friend, and a fine education at the academy, from which he was graduated in 1779, Gallatin resisted the aristocratic trappings of his family and identified with a growing number of students who supported Jean-Jacques Rousseau's Romantic call of "back to nature."

When his grandmother successfully gained for Gallatin an appointment as lieutenant colonel in the army of her friend Frederich, the Langrave of Hesse, then preparing to fight as mercenaries for England against the American Colonies, Gallatin rebelled and with a friend fled Geneva at the age of eighteen for America. He arrived in Massachusetts in 1780 and, without much money, set off for the frontier of Maine. After spending a year there, he returned to Boston, where he eked out a living as a tutor teaching French to students at Harvard College. Finding the atmosphere in Boston too cold for his tastes, Gallatin moved to the back country of Pennsylvania in 1782. Through business dealings, he acquired land in the region and, as a good Romantic, settled down to devote his life to farming. At one point, Gallatin hoped to establish a Swiss colony on the American frontier, but these plans came to nothing. Gallatin was successful as neither farmer nor land speculator. Personal tragedy also touched him when his wife of a few months, Sophia Allegre, whom he had met in Richmond, Virginia, died at his farm, Friendship Hill. Despondent, Gallatin contemplated returning to Geneva, but an inability to sell his farm and the fighting in Geneva triggered by the French Revolution caused him to remain in America.

His intelligence and gregariousness led him to politics, first in Pennsylvania as a member of the Harrisburg conference of 1788, which met to consider ways in which the United States Constitution could be strengthened, and then as a member of the convention that met in 1789-1790 to revise the Pennsylvania constitution. In 1790, he was elected representative of Fayette County to the Pennsylvania state legislature.

Life's Work

Gallatin had three careers: politics, business, and science. Although he believed that his investigations in science, rather than his work in government, would cause his name to be remembered in history, the reverse, ironically, proved to be the case. Western Pennsylvania elected Gallatin twice to the state legislature, and then he was elected by the legislature to the Senate of the United States. There, his eligibility was challenged because he had not been a citizen for nine years. Removed from the Senate, Gallatin returned to Pennsylvania, taking his new bride Hannah, daughter of Commodore James Nicholson of New York. His stay in Pennsylvania proved short, for in 1794 the voters of western Pennsylvania sent him to the House of Representatives, in which he served three terms. A Republican, Gallatin defended the farming interests of western Pennsylvania; at the same time, his grasp of international law and public finance and his reasoning ability and cogent arguments made him a valuable legislator at a critical time in America's early history.

In May of 1801, Thomas Jefferson appointed Gallatin secretary of the treasury. Gallatin held this post through Jefferson's two administrations and through part of James Madison's first administration. Accusations that his financial policies hindered American efforts to fight the British in the War of 1812 prompted Gallatin to leave the treasury in 1813 and accept an appointment as a special envoy to Russia, which had offered to mediate the conflict between Great Britain and the United States. Great Britian, however, refused to accept mediation and, thus, frustrated Gallatin's mission. Rather than returning to the treasury, as Madison expected, Gallatin chose to remain in Europe in diplomatic service. So began Gallatin's career as diplomat.

Along with John Quincy Adams and Henry Clay, Gallatin drew up the Treaty of Ghent, which ended the War of 1812. With the work on the treaty concluded, Gallatin, Adams, and Clay traveled to England and negotiated a commercial treaty with the British. On his return to the United States, Gallatin accepted the post of minister to France, which he held from 1816 to 1832. Upon his return from France, he intended to retire from government service and to devote the rest of life to being a gentleman farmer at Friendship Hill, but, although Gallatin was increasingly upset with the emphasis on gain in American politics, he allowed his name to be put forward for vice president. Henry Clay's ultimate acceptance of the nomination allowed Gallatin happily to withdraw his name. Life at Friendship Hill proved boring for the Gallatins after seven years in Paris, and so Gallatin once again accepted diplomatic assignment, his last, in 1826, as minister to England.

The America to which Gallatin returned in 1827 seemed foreign to him. The robust activity of Jacksonian America seemed to make a shambles of the Jeffersonian idealism to which Gallatin subscribed. So disorienting did the new United States seem to him that he seriously considered leaving the country and returning with his family to Geneva. Although he did not return to Europe, he did retire from government service, beginning a new career in business.

Gallatin moved to New York City, where John Jacob Astor urged him to accept the presidency of Astor's new National Bank. In this position, which Gallatin held from 1831 to 1839, he not only wrote on fiscal reform in articles such as *Considerations on the Currency and Banking System of the United States* (1831) but also protested slavery, the annexation of Texas by the United States, and the war with Mexico. In addition, he found time to indulge his interests in ethnology and, especially, linguistics.

While Gallatin had been living in Paris, he had made the acquaintance of the famous German scientist Alexander von Humboldt. Gallatin's knowledge of several European languages and his interest in linguistics complemented Humboldt's study of linguistics and American Indian languages. Humboldt prevailed upon Gallatin to write on Indian languages, and thus, even before Gallatin left public service, he had begun his scientific career. His first major publication in this field was *A Synopsis of the Indian Tribes Within the United States East of the Rocky Mountains and in the British and Russian Possessions in North America* (1836), followed by *Notes on the Semi-Civilized Nations of Mexico, Yucatan, and Central America* (1845) and *Indians of North-west America* (1848). Besides writing in the field of ethnology, Gallatin served as president of the American Ethnological Society, an organization he helped to found in 1842.

Summary

Although sometimes indulging in Romantic notions, Gallatin was first and foremost a gentleman of the Enlightenment. With his superb forensic skills and his ability to remain calm under personal attack, Gallatin proved a consummate politician, negotiator, and diplomat. His brilliance of mind led Jefferson to rely on Gallatin not only to oversee national finance but also to proofread his speeches and act as personal confidant. As secretary of the treasury and disbursing agent, Gallatin assumed a major role in promoting the exploration of the West and settlement of the Western frontier.

Governed by an Enlightenment philosophy that emphasized idealism and humanism in politics, learning, and society, Gallatin became uncomfortable with the raw commercialism of Jacksonian America, which seemed to him to promote only the base side of human potential. By the time of his death,

Gallatin was out of step with his time: an Enlightenment figure in Jacksonian America. Yet for many he remained the Enlightenment conscience of America's idealistic beginnings.

Bibliography
Adams, Henry. *The Life of Albert Gallatin.* Philadelphia: J. B. Lippincott Co., 1880. Still a classic account of Gallatin's life. Henry Adams, the grandson of John Adams, provides an intimate glimpse into Gallatin's life and values and places both in the context of Gallatin's European experience and a rapidly developing American society.
Allen, John Logan. *Passage Through the Garden: Lewis and Clark and the Image of the American Northwest.* Urbana: University of Illinois Press, 1975. Logan's work discusses Gallatin's economic contribution as secretary of the treasury and his intellectual contribution to the exploration of the West.
Balinky, Alexander. *Albert Gallatin: Fiscal Theories and Policies.* New Brunswick, N.J.: Rutgers University Press, 1958. An extensive study of Gallatin's theories and policies on public finance.
Bieder, Robert E. *Science Encounters the Indian, 1820-1880: The Early Years of American Ethnology.* Norman: University of Oklahoma Press, 1986. Contains a chapter on Gallatin, his study of American Indians, and his place in the early development of American ethnology.
Gallatin, James. *The Diary of James Gallatin, Secretary to Albert Gallatin, a Great Peace Maker, 1813-1827.* Edited by Count Gallatin. New York: Charles Scribner's Sons, 1931. A highly intimate and entertaining account of Gallatin's years in Paris and London, written by his son, who served as Gallatin's secretary.
Smelser, Marshall. *The Democratic Republic: 1801-1815.* Edited by Henry S. Commager and Richard B. Morris. New American Nations Series. New York: Harper and Row, Publishers, 1968. Mentions Gallatin in the larger context of the growth of the American republic.
Walters, Raymond, Jr. *Albert Gallatin: Jeffersonian Financier and Diplomat.* New York: Macmillian Publishing Co., 1957. Walters differs from Balinky in emphasizing Gallatin's Jeffersonian ties and diplomatic career.
White, Leonard D. *The Jeffersonians: A Study in Administrative History, 1801-1829.* New York: Macmillan Publishing Co., 1951. Now dated but still useful in its consideration of Gallatin's administration of the treasury.

Robert E. Bieder

JAMES A. GARFIELD

Born: November 19, 1831; Orange Township, Ohio
Died: September 19, 1881; Elberon, New Jersey
Areas of Achievement: Education, religion, politics, and law
Contribution: During his almost two decades, first as congressman, then
briefly as president, Garfield played a key role in every issue of national
importance. As party leader, he helped resolve the factionalism within the
Republican Party and enabled the Republicans to lead the United States
into the twentieth century.

Early Life

James Abram Garfield was born in a log cabin on November 19, 1831, to
Abram and Eliza Garfield, members of the Disciples of Christ church.
Abram died in 1833, thus leaving Eliza a widow, the sole provider for her
family.

Next to hunting, reading was young Garfield's greatest interest. He liked
history and fiction, especially stories of the American Revolution and stories
of the sea. At the age of sixteen, Garfield went to Cleveland, where he was
shocked and disappointed by a drunken captain to whom he had applied for
work. On that same day, August 16, 1848, Garfield secured a job as driver
with his cousin on a canal boat that carried goods between Cleveland and
Pittsburgh. After six weeks of working on the canal, Garfield became quite
ill and returned home. During his recuperation, his mother and Samuel
Bates, a schoolteacher, convinced Garfield of the importance of education.

Garfield enrolled and studied at Geauga Academy in Chester, where he
became the academy's prize Latin student. Originally, Garfield planned to
spend the winter months at the academy and the spring and summers on the
canal, but after he absorbed himself in his studies, he decided to forget the
canal life.

In the fall of 1851, Garfield enrolled in the newly established Western
Reserve Eclectic Institute at Hiram, Ohio, where he plunged into his studies
with a fierce determination to excel. Garfield's popularity and prominence at
the Western Reserve Eclectic Institute were based on his scholastic ability as
well as his physical prowess. His commanding physical appearance—he
stood almost six feet tall, with broad shoulders and a massive head topped by
a shock of unruly tawny hair—and his ability to outrun and outwrestle his
schoolmates instilled automatic respect. This, combined with his serious
demeanor, which gave an impression of quiet dignity, and his unaffected
friendliness contributed to Garfield's popularity. Enjoying success as a debater, Garfield discovered that he possessed the ability to sway an audience,
and the oratorical techniques which he learned during this period prepared
him to become one of the most effective political speakers of his time.

In 1853, Garfield began preaching at neighboring churches. The following year, having completed his studies at the Eclectic Institute, he enrolled in Williams College. There, he was elected president of two major campus organizations—the Philogian Society, a literary society, and the Equitable Fraternity, an organization designed to combat the influence of the Greek fraternities. In addition, in spite of his Campbellite beliefs, Garfield was elected president of the Mills Theological Society, a Calvinist organization. He was also elected editor of the *Williams Quarterly*, a pioneer college journal of exceptional quality, to which he contributed extensively. Indeed, Garfield never lost an election at Williams College, nor any election in which he was a candidate for the rest of his life. On August 7, 1856, he was graduated from Williams College with honors in a ceremony that included his delivering an oration on the conflict between matter and spirit.

Life's Work

As an inspiring and electrifying evangelist, Garfield preached continually during the last of the series of so-called Great Awakenings—periodic religious revivals that had begun in the Colonial era. In 1857, at the age of twenty-six, Garfield was elected president of Western Reserve Eclectic Institute, defeating his former teacher, the institute's oldest and most distinguished faculty member. As president, Garfield made the Eclectic Institute the educational center of the region, changing a sectarian academy into an institution that welcomed students of all denominations.

He believed the curriculum should reflect the trends of the time and serve as a medium through which students could prepare for successful living. He sponsored teacher-training workshops and seminars on teaching methods and school administration, and he prepared a series of lectures on American history, a subject which had not been included in the curricula of American colleges.

Garfield did not confine himself to administrative duties; he taught a full load of classes in a style designed to encourage students to think independently. Garfield's kindness and immense vitality, his readiness to praise, his deep concern for the overall welfare of his students, his enthusiasm, his ability to introduce his students to the meaning of education and the high ideals of life, and his participation with them in the extracurricular activities, especially athletic events, inspired great loyalty. The Eclectic Institute prospered under Garfield's leadership. On November 11, 1858, Garfield married Lucretia Rudolph, daughter of Zeb Rudolph, a pioneer Hiram Disciple and one of the school's most prominent trustees.

On August 23, 1859, based on his prominent background and popularity, the Republican Party of the Twenty-sixth Ohio Senatorial District nominated him for the state senate, a seat he handily won, October 11, 1859. This feat ultimately led him to the center stage of the national political arena. Garfield distinguished himself on a number of key issues, especially those pertaining to slavery and the impending crisis—the Civil War. He stood strong against slavery and, shedding his pacifism, believed that war was the best solution to the problem of slavery. When the war began, he took an active role in raising troops, influencing the governor of his state to appoint him lieutenant colonel in the Twenty-fourth Ohio Infantry; later, he was put in charge of the Forty-second Ohio Volunteer Infantry as a full colonel. Learning about Garfield's commission, the young men of Hiram, who held Garfield in the highest esteem, enthusiastically joined the Forty-second Ohio Volunteer Infantry to follow and fight with their hero.

At the outset of Garfield's military service, General Don Carlos Buell assigned him command of the Eighteenth Brigade and gave him the responsibility of planning the campaign to drive the Confederate army out of eastern Kentucky. In spite of the fact that Garfield had no military education or military experience, he accepted the task, presenting a plan which Buell accepted. Under Garfield's leadership, the Confederate forces were driven out of Kentucky.

Assuming control of the administration of eastern Kentucky, Garfield pursued a policy of reconciliation. Promoted to brigadier general, he served outstandingly as chief of staff under General William S. Rosecrans, commander of the Army of the Cumberland. Garfield reached the peak of his military career in the Chattanooga campaign, fighting in one of the epic battles of military history, the Battle of Chickamauga. Garfield's outstanding achievements in the Kentucky campaign led his friends and the Republican Party of the Nineteenth Congressional District to nominate him as their representative to Congress, September 2, 1862. While still in the army carrying out his military duties and without participating in the campaign, he won the right to represent the Nineteenth District by an impressive victory, in the congressional election of October, 1862.

Beginning with the election of 1862, Garfield easily won nine consecutive terms, splendidly serving the people of the Nineteenth District for the next eighteen years as chairman of the Military Affairs Committee (in which capacity he was the first to introduce a bill that proposed an ROTC program for the colleges), chairman of the Banking and Currency Committee, and chairman of the powerful and prestigious Appropriations Committee.

When the Democratic Party won a majority of the seats in the House of Representatives in the congressional election of 1874, Garfield assumed the leadership of the Republican minority in the House. Having lost his chairmanships, he skillfully and relentlessly spoke out against the policies of the Democratic Party. As a member of a bipartisan committee selected to investigate the 1876 presidential election in the state of Louisiana, Garfield submitted a thorough report based on data presented to him by the election board and interviews he held with those who participated in the election and those denied participation, especially voters who were terrorized by white secret societies such as the Ku Klux Klan, the Knights of the White Camellia, and the Rifle Clubs. His report helped influence the election board to nullify Samuel Tilden's majority, and Rutherford B. Hayes was granted the electoral votes of Louisiana.

The 1876 election ended in an intense controversy involving the returns of Florida, Louisiana, and South Carolina. This situation produced a political stalemate that set the stage for a potential crisis that might have led the opposing parties back to the battlefields in a new civil war. Garfield served as a member of a special Electoral Commission to elect the president and participated in the historic conference that led to the compromise between the leaders of the Republican Party and the Southern Democrats. These actions resolved the impending crisis, and Hayes became the nineteenth president of the United States.

On March 29, 1879, Garfield established himself as the outstanding leader of the Republican Party when he delivered one of the most dynamic speeches in the history of Congress. The Democrats' dogged advocacy of the principle of states' rights motivated Garfield to present his greatest speech—a speech that upheld the principle of federalism and inspired the Republicans to quit squabbling and act together as a strong united party. This speech influenced his state's legislature to elect him to serve in the United States Senate, and ultimately led to his nomination and election as President of the United States.

In 1880, Garfield was elected to serve as a delegate to the Seventh National Nominating Convention of the Republican Party, which met in Chicago. He came to the convention without any intention of seeking the nomination, but because of his great popularity, he was considered a dark-horse candidate. On the thirty-sixth ballot, the deadlocked delegates chose Garfield, hoping that he could unify the party. In a move that displeased a large number of Republicans, but as a means of placating the highly disappointed Stalwarts, who had supported Ulysses S. Grant for a third term, the imperious political boss of the New York Republican Party, Chester Alan Arthur, was selected as the party's candidate for vice president.

In November, Garfield's ability to control the various factions of his party and brilliantly manage his campaign, resulted in his winning the presidency in the closest presidential election of the century. In view of the fact that he did nothing either before or during the convention to obtain his party's nomination (he strongly opposed the effort that culminated in his nomination) and the fact that his party had all but self-destructed since the assassination of President Abraham Lincoln, Garfield achieved a magnificent victory.

On July 2, 1881, only a few months after his inauguration, Garfield was shot by a crazed office-seeker, Charles Guiteau. He died on September 19, 1881.

Summary

Garfield's election to the presidency was the crowning achievement of a spectacular and glorious career that began as the driver of a towboat on the Ohio Erie Canal. His was a classic American success story, brought to a tragically premature end.

The legacy of Garfield's brief term suggests what he might have accomplished had he lived to complete it. He laid the foundation for the development of a more independent and vigorous presidency that proved vital for a nation destined to become one of the most powerful nations in the world. The Pendleton Act of 1883, which led to the end of the spoils system in the federal government, was the logical conclusion of his efforts.

Bibliography

Brisbin, James S. *From the Tow-Path to the White House: The Early Life and Public Career of James A. Garfield*. Philadelphia: J. C. McCurdy and Co., 1880. A flattering campaign biography, written in a romantic style shortly after Garfield's nomination. Although hurriedly written, Brisbin's work vividly recounts the story of a leader who exemplified fundamental American values. Includes illustrations.

Caldwell, Robert G. *James A. Garfield, Party Chieftain*. New York: Dodd, Mead and Co., 1934. An exhaustive scholarly chronicle of the life of Garfield that, in effect, summarizes American political history from 1861 to 1881. Includes an excellent bibliography.

Doenecke, Justus D. *The Presidencies of James A. Garfield and Chester A. Arthur*. Lawrence: University Press of Kansas, 1981. This is one of the volumes of the American Presidency Series, intended to present historians and the general public with interesting, scholarly assessments of the various presidential administrations. Includes excellent notes and bibliographical essays.

Hinsdale, Mary L., ed. *Garfield-Hinsdale Letters: Correspondence Between James Abram Garfield and Burke Aaron Hinsdale*. Ann Arbor: University of Michigan Press, 1949. The correspondence between James A. Garfield and his lifelong friend, Burke A. Hinsdale, a former pupil of Garfield, superintendent of Cleveland's Public School System, outstanding teacher at the University of Michigan, and president of Hiram College. The letters between Garfield and Hinsdale discuss the various issues that confronted American between 1857 and 1881, as well as the most popular books of the period; they also reveal the writers in their lighter moods. Their correspondence, which began when Hinsdale was nineteen and continued until Garfield's death, provides graphic self-portraits of Garfield and Hinsdale, and is a significant resource for scholars of Garfield.

Leech, Margaret, and Harry J. Brown. *The Garfield Orbit*. New York: Harper and Row, Publishers, 1978. An absorbing story of the life of Garfield, showing him as a man of complex and contradictory character, in whom ambition and desire warred with firm principle. The book reveals more of the man and less of the vital issues that he confronted. Includes a Garfield genealogy; a selection of Garfield's letters; notes and references; sixty-three illustrations, mainly photographs and sketches; and maps of the Western Reserve and the military campaigns of Garfield during the Civil War.

Riddle, Albert G. *The Life, Character and Public Services of James A. Garfield*. Chicago: Tyler and Co., 1880. This is a classic biography of Garfield that covers the period from his birth to his nomination as the standard-bearer of the Republican Party.

Smith, Theodore Clarke. *The Life and Letters of James Abram Garfield*. 2 vols. New Haven, Conn.: Yale University Press, 1925. Smith's biographical study is principally based on Garfield's own words contained in his letters, journals, school and college notes, speeches, and memorabilia. The author's masterful selection and arrangement of the materials produces the effect of Garfield himself interpreting his life.

James D. Lockett

WILLIAM LLOYD GARRISON

Born: December 10, 1805; Newburyport, Massachusetts
Died: May 24, 1879; New York, New York
Areas of Achievement: Abolitionism and antebellum reform
Contribution: A crucial figure in the demise of American slavery and the coming of the Civil War, Garrison combined Protestant Evangelicalism, Jeffersonian liberalism, and Quaker humanism into a radical antislavery doctrine that called for the immediate end of the institution of slavery.

Early Life

In his 1913 biography of William Lloyd Garrison, John Jay Chapman described his subject's emergence as a radical abolitionist in 1830 as a streaking, white-hot meteorite crashing into the middle of Boston Commons. Little in Garrison's background, however, foretold of his career as a professional reformer and as the father of the radical antislavery movement. His parents, Abijah and Frances (Fanny) Maria Lloyd Garrison, had once lived simply and obscurely in wealthy Newburyport, Massachusetts. By the summer of 1808, however, President Thomas Jefferson's embargo had nearly destroyed New England's merchant marine, inflicting immense suffering upon lower middle-class sailing masters such as Abijah. That same summer, the Garrisons' five-year-old daughter died from an accidental poisoning. Abijah Garrison could not withstand the pressure and grief of this period. He took to heavy drinking and then deserted his struggling family of three. The childhood of young William Lloyd was then an even greater ordeal, and he often had to beg for food from the homes of Newburyport's wealthy residents.

In 1815, Lloyd, as he was called, was apprenticed to a Maryland shoemaker, but the young boy simply lacked the physical strength to do the work. In 1817, Lloyd found himself back in Newburyport, alone and apprenticed to a cabinetmaker. That work also proved unsuitable. When he was thirteen, his luck began to change when he secured an apprenticeship with the editor of the Newburyport *Herald.* Lloyd feared another failure, but within weeks he displayed remarkable skill and speed. The editor quickly made him shop foreman. Garrison had found his life's work.

After mastering the mechanics of the trade, Lloyd was eager to print his own writing. Like Benjamin Franklin a century before, he submitted editorials under a pseudonym (Garrison used "An Old Bachelor") which his boss liked and published. "An Old Bachelor" gained much attention, even from conservative political leaders. In 1826, with a loan from his former employer, Garrison purchased his own newspaper, which he immediately named the *Free Press.* Seeking respectability and entrance into the ruling elite of Massachusetts, Garrison advocated the conservative politics and social ideas of the Federalist Party. The *Free Press* became bellicose in its political stands, denouncing everything that smacked of Jeffersonian democracy. During his brief tenure at the paper, Garrison discovered the poet John Greenleaf Whittier, published his first poetry, and also made some oblique criticisms of the institution of slavery, but he revealed nothing that gave the slightest indication of what lay only four years in the future.

Following this relatively conservative initiation into his journalistic career, Garrison became more and more strident in his style and radical in the opinions he voiced in editorials, to the extent that he lost subscribers, defaulted on his loan, and lost his paper. In 1828, he drifted to the *National Philanthropist*, a temperance paper, and attacked dancing, theatergoing, dueling, and gambling. The fiery editor denounced war and began to display a more thoroughgoing disdain for the institution of slavery by decrying a South Carolina law outlawing black education. Garrison soon repeated his familiar pattern and within six months found himself without a job. He managed to secure a position at the *Journal of the Times* in Bennington, Vermont, and there railed at intemperance and advanced his ideas concerning peace and gradual emancipation.

In 1829, Garrison had become radicalized on the issue of slavery, about one year after reading Benjamin Lundy's newspaper, the *Genius of Universal Emancipation*. Garrison had met Lundy, a Quaker abolitionist, in 1828 and had adopted his views on the gradual emancipation of American slaves. On July 4, 1829, again unemployed, Garrison delivered his first antislavery speech, indicting the North for its racism and declaring that gradual emancipation was the only possible way to end slavery. Then, after reading the works of black Americans such as David Walker and English abolitionists such as James Cropper, Garrison decided to dedicate his life to ending what he viewed as the greatest abomination in American history. He went to work for Lundy and moved back to Baltimore, Maryland, where he coedited the *Genius of Universal Emancipation*.

Before the end of 1829, Garrison had abandoned gradual emancipation— Lundy had not—and called for the immediate end of slavery. He lashed out against slaveholders and even against New Englanders who countenanced the institution. On April 17, 1830, he was confined to a Baltimore jail for criminal libel against a New England merchant. Word of Garrison's imprisonment circulated throughout the North and eventually reached the ears of the wealthy New York merchants and reformers, Arthur and Lewis Tappan. They bailed Garrison out of jail and paid his fines. He wandered back to Boston and decided to set up a new paper there.

On October 16, 1830, Garrison advertised a series of public lectures on the subject of slavery and the American Colonization Society. The ACS, established in 1817, claimed to oppose slavery and favored black uplift and the evangelization of Africa, but Garrison sought to expose it as a tool of the slaveocrats who actually perpetuated slavery. At the October lectures, Garrison denounced the ACS as a racist organization that intended to expel free black Americans if they refused to leave voluntarily. Boston's liberal and conservative clergy alike reacted to the lectures with disgust. Other thinkers, such as Samuel Joseph May, a renegade Unitarian minister and reformer, Bronson Alcott, a Transcendentalist educator and May's brother-in-law, and Samuel E. Sewall, May's cousin, became captivated by Garrison's moral vigor and earnestness. They instantly converted to radical abolitionism and pledged to aid the young editor. Emergence of the *Liberator* the following year established Garrison as the leader of the radical antislavery movement.

Life's Work

William Lloyd Garrison stood about five feet, six inches tall. His slender, almost fragile frame supported a massive bald head, and his powerful blue eyes were framed by tiny, steel, oval-shaped spectacles. Although relentless on the lecture platform, in private Garrison comported himself with great dignity and grace. Like many reformers, he married late. While lecturing in Providence, Rhode Island, in 1829, he met Helen Benson, the daughter of the Quaker philanthropist, George Benson. Timid in the presence of women and lacking a stable career, Garrison initiated a long courtship, finally marrying Helen on September 4, 1834.

On January 1, 1831, Garrison published the first issue of the *Liberator*. It angered Northerners as irrational and incendiary and struck fear in slaveholders as an uncompromising condemnation. Garrison, as a pacifist, eschewed violent rebellion, but his strident language—something entirely new in the long history of American antislavery thought—inaugurated a new era in American history. He denounced slavery as sin, called upon all true Christians immediately to abandon it no matter what the cost to the Union, and blasted those who thought slavery might be gradually abandoned. What, gradually stop sin? Tell a man to rescue his wife from a rapist gradually? Garrison thundered. Why complain of the severity of my language, he cried, when so unutterable an evil abounded. Ignoring his critics, Garrison lashed out: "I *will be* as harsh as truth, and as uncompromising as justice. . . . I will not excuse—I will not retreat a single inch—AND I WILL BE HEARD."

Garrison's antislavery appeal fused the evangelical fervor of the Second Great Awakening, which had begun in the 1790's, with the long-standing Quaker opposition to slavery. He had tapped an essential root of American thought, and if he could convince Americans that slavery was, in fact, sin, then they would have to accept his second proposition that it be immediately abandoned. Southerners understandably recoiled from his rhetoric, but they were horrified when, eight months after appearance of the *Liberator*, Nat Turner turned Virginia inside out by fomenting a slave rebellion and killing dozens of whites, including women and children. Southerners connected the two events, blamed Garrison for the killings, put a price on his head, and demanded that Massachusetts suppress the newspaper and its editor.

In January, 1832, Garrison and twelve men—antislavery apostles— founded the New England Anti-Slavery Society. In June, he published his influential *Thoughts on African Colonization* (1832), and, for the next three years, Garrison and his associates dedicated themselves to destroying the credibility of the American Colonization Society. He helped found the American Anti-Slavery Society on December 4, 1833. Between 1833 and 1840, two hundred auxiliaries of the American Anti-Slavery Society were organized from Massachusetts to Michigan with about 200,000 members. They sent antislavery agents throughout the North to whip up controversy and support for the cause.

The growth of radical antislavery thought caused great consternation. Between 1830 and 1840, abolitionists suffered from personal and physical abuse. Rocks, bricks, and the contents of outhouses were thrown at them. They were denounced as anarchists who would destroy the Union if it suited their whim. In 1836, Southern states requested Governor Edward Everett of Massachusetts to suppress Garrison and his friends. On November 7, 1837, Illinois abolitionist editor Elijah P. Lovejoy was assassinated by a rampaging mob determined to destroy his newspaper, the *Alton Observer*. The attacks on abolitionists and the murder of Lovejoy sparked unprecedented sympathy for the antislavery advocates, who could now justifiably claim that abolitionism and a defense of a free press and free speech were inseparable.

To Garrison, abolitionism was only the most important of a collection of reforms, from women's rights to temperance, connected by a liberal Christian faith in a benevolent God and the rejection of all forms of force and violence. In 1836, Garrison learned of two extraordinary women from Charleston, South Carolina. Sarah and Angelina Grimké, born into a slaveholding family, had rejected their home and human bondage, converted to Quakerism, and moved north. In 1837, Garrison arranged a speaking tour for them in New England. Huge crowds turned out for the sisters, who risked their reputations to ignore the social restrictions against women speaking in public. Indeed, during the course of their tour, the Grimkés became ardent exponents of women's rights, having seen how prominent clergymen denounced their violation of women's restricted sphere. Garrison supported the sisters and opened up the Massachusetts Anti-Slavery Society to women, urging his conservative colleagues to do the same.

Garrison's support for women's rights brought howls of protest from other abolitionists, who urged him to avoid "extraneous" issues and stick to antislavery work. He refused to compromise and answered his critics by becoming even more radical. At the September, 1838, meeting of the American Peace Society, Garrison, May, and Henry C. Wright, a radical Garrisonian, attempted to gain the society's acceptance of nonresistance thought. They wanted to outlaw as utterly unchristian all forms of war, force, and violence, even denying one's right to defend oneself. When faced with an attacker, according to nonresistance thought, one could only respond with Christian meekness and manifestations of love. Garrison, May, and Wright all claimed that they had personally disarmed robbers or criminals with love. Conservatives refused to accept the new doctrine or to permit women to participate in their society, and they left the meeting. In response, Garrison and his friends formed the New England Nonresistance Society to spread what they saw as true Christian principles.

Garrison's extreme ideas fractured his own Massachusetts Anti-Slavery Society in 1839 and the American Anti-Slavery Society in 1840. Although the antislavery movement seemed to be crumbling, Garrison responded in typical fashion. While many of the best young male abolitionists avoided Garrison's organizations and went into politics, Garrison damned the political system. In 1842, he advocated the dissolution of the Union. The nation had become so corrupt, so dominated by slave power that no hope existed for slavery's end so long as the South remained in the Union. Although his critics argued that no hope for the end of slavery existed if the South left the Union, Garrison ignored them. In 1843, the *Liberator* adopted its most radical stand yet. The "compact which exists between the North and the South is 'a covenant with death, and an agreement with hell'—involving both parties in atrocious criminality; and should be immediately annulled." Beginning March 17, 1843, Garrison placed the slogan "NO UNION WITH SLAVE-HOLDERS!" on the masthead of his newspaper, where it remained until the Civil War.

Split over women's rights and nonresistance ideas, the antislavery movement nearly ended by the mid-1840's. Little money flowed in and few Americans could accept disunionism, no matter how much they hated slavery. Passage of the Fugitive Slave Act in 1850 boosted the American Anti-Slavery Society's prospects, since most Northerners came to hate the law as an infringement of constitutionally protected rights. As the nation moved toward civil war during the 1850's, Garrison increased his attacks on slavery, the Constitution, and the Union. With the firing on Fort Sumter in April, 1861, however, he supported Abraham Lincoln and the Union cause. Although many of his associates thought the South ought to leave the Union peacefully, Garrison saw the war as perhaps the only opportunity to end slavery, even if it did violate his peace principles. He thus supported the Lincoln Administration's war policy, all the while urging the president to abolish slavery. When Lincoln signed the Emancipation Proclamation in 1863, Garrison was ecstatic, and when the nation adopted the Thirteenth Amendment, abolishing slavery, in 1865, he felt vindicated. Believing his life's purpose fulfilled, Garrison retired from activism, though he continued to support the Republican Party and causes such as temperance and women's rights. He died in New York City on May 24, 1879.

Summary
Although Garrison harbored some racial prejudice, he was a pioneer of racial justice. He argued that racism and slavery worked hand-in-hand and that Northern prejudice and Southern intransigence shared equally in the responsibility for perpetuating slavery. Garrison's message of racial justice and abolitionism threatened the nation's class system, which exploited free Northern blacks as well as Southern slaves and endangered the tenuous bonds that had kept the Union together since the formation of the Constitution. Public reaction to Garrison did not change until passage of the Emancipation Proclamation in 1863. Before the war's end, he became a prophetic figure to Americans. The Boston mobs that tried to lynch him in 1834 raised statues to him in 1865. Modern historians have recognized Garrison's indispensable role in the ending of American slavery and have hailed him for his simple claim that the Declaration of Independence ought to speak for everyone, black and white, male and female.

Bibliography
Chapman, John Jay. *William Lloyd Garrison*. New York: Moffat, Yard and Co., 1913. A sympathetic early biography by the son of one of Garrison's associates.
Friedman, Lawrence J. *Gregarious Saints: Self and Community in American Abolitionism, 1830-1870*. New York: Cambridge University Press, 1982. Representative of the best modern studies of the abolitionist movement. Gives an inside look at the subtle distinctions the reformers made on a variety of topics related to voting, the Constitution, and how distinct groups of reformers sprang up around charismatic figures such as Garrison, Gerrit Smith, or the Tappan brothers.
Garrison, William Lloyd. *The Letters of William Lloyd Garrison*. Edited by Walter M. Merrill and Louis Ruchames. 6 vols. Cambridge, Mass.: Harvard University Press, 1971-1981. The best way for the student to become acquainted with Garrison is to read the activist's own work. These are copiously annotated personal and public letters that fully display the thinking and the sometimes idiosyncratic personality of the *Liberator*'s chief editor.
Kraditor, Alieen S. *Means and Ends in American Abolitionism: Garrison and His Critics on Strategy and Tactics, 1834-1850*. New York: Pantheon Books, 1969. Far and away the best book on Garrison's movement and thought. Kraditor fully explores the controversy of the "woman question" and argues convincingly that, in order for Garrison to gain acceptance of a minimum of antislavery thought, he had to remain more radical than the nation and many of his antislavery brethren.
Merrill, Walter M. *Against Wind and Tide: A Biography of William Lloyd Garrison*. Cambridge, Mass.: Harvard University Press, 1963. A thorough and often critical examination of the abolitionist's career. The text empha-

sizes Garrison's personality, which could be extremely abrasive and unforgiving. The author recognizes, however, that it took an abrasive personality to challenge the foundations of American society.

Perry, Lewis. *Radical Abolitionism: Anarchy and the Government of God in Antislavery Thought*. Ithaca, N.Y.: Cornell University Press, 1973. The most sophisticated treatment of antislavery thought, concentrating on Garrison and his nonresistance colleagues. Perry examines the origins of Garrison's thinking and connects it to wider trends in Western Christian thought.

Stewart, James B. *Holy Warriors: The Abolitionists and American Slavery*. New York: Hill and Wang, 1976. A good, readable survey of the antislavery movement, emphasizing Garrison's role and the religious nature of the movement that stemmed from the influence of the Second Great Awakening.

Thomas, John L. *The Liberator: William Lloyd Garrison, A Biography*. Boston: Little, Brown and Co., 1963. The best study of Garrison; it appreciates his central role in the movement but remains critical of his tactics and personality. Thoroughly researched, and more detailed than Merrill's biography.

Donald Yacovone

MARCUS GARVEY

Born: August 17, 1887; St. Ann's Bay, Jamaica
Died: June 10, 1940; London, England
Area of Achievement: Civil rights
Contribution: Combining his talents of effective journalism and charismatic oratory, Garvey organized the first black mass-protest movement in the history of the United States.

Early Life

Marcus Moziah Garvey was born in St. Ann's Bay, Jamaica, British West Indies, on August 17, 1887. His parents, Marcus and Sarah Garvey, were both full-blooded blacks of African descent. As such, the family, including young Marcus, suffered under the racial caste system prevalent in Jamaica at the time—a system which relegated pure blacks to a lower socioeconomic status than either mulattoes or whites. This fact may explain why Garvey subsequently would emphasize black racial purity, denouncing mulattoes as mere pawns or tools of the white man.

During his childhood and adolescence, Garvey was precocious, an avid reader, a gifted speaker, and a bright student. His formal education, however, did not extend beyond his fourteenth year. Family financial difficulties forced him to quit school and accept employment as a printer's apprentice, an experience which would later prove to be invaluable to his career in journalism and to the movement he came to lead. Nevertheless, Garvey's failure to complete a formal education seriously influenced his thinking and behavior for the remainder of his life, explaining, in part, his future antagonism toward the intellectual community in general and black intellectuals in particular.

As a young black journalist in the early twentieth century, Garvey became increasingly aware of and concerned with the humiliating plight of fellow blacks throughout the Caribbean. Moreover, through extensive reading, research, and travel, including a trip to England, where he was influenced by a number of African nationalists, Garvey finally came to believe that white discrimination against and exploitation of black people was a serious worldwide problem which demanded an immediate solution. Toward this end, he decided to become a leader of his race in order to unite blacks throughout the world in a nation and government of their own.

Life's Work

Following his two-year sojourn in England, Garvey returned to Jamaica in 1914, where he established the Universal Negro Improvement and Conservation Association and African Communities League, usually called the Universal Negro Improvement Association (UNIA). The initial goals of UNIA centered on universal black unification, the enhancement of black racial pride worldwide, and black development of and control over the continent of Africa. Achieving only moderate success in Jamaica, Garvey decided to seek support for his infant organization in the United States. He arrived in New York on March 23, 1916, and quickly proceeded to establish a branch of the UNIA in Harlem, which had a relatively large West Indian enclave. Two years later, he founded a newspaper, *Negro World*, which became the propaganda arm of UNIA. Coupled with a lengthy and flamboyant speaking tour throughout the United States, Garvey's editorials in *Negro World* succeeded in attracting thousands of native converts to UNIA. In a matter of months, thirty branches of the organization were established throughout the country. By 1920, Garvey claimed to have four million followers and, in 1923, six million. Although these figures were probably exaggerations, even Garvey's most critical opponents admitted that there were at least a half million members in UNIA at its height.

At the heart of Garvey's ideology was his fervent desire to mobilize the black peoples of Africa, the West Indies, the Americas, and elsewhere, for the spiritual, historical, and physical redemption of Africa and Africans, at home and abroad. "The faith we have," he declared, "is a faith that will ultimately take us back to that ancient place, that ancient position that we once occupied, when Ethiopia was in her glory." Notwithstanding this pronouncement, it is mistaken to suppose that Garveyism was simply another "Back to Africa" movement. Garvey was realistic enough to appreciate the fact that a mass black exodus to Africa, in the physical sense, was impossible. Although he did believe that black leaders had an obligation to return to their ancestral homeland to assist in its development and liberation from white colonialists, his basic argument revolved around the concept of a spiritual return to Africa for the majority of American blacks. He maintained that white racism in the United States had created a sense of self-hatred in blacks, and that the only way to purge themselves of self-contempt was through a spiritual identification with Africans and Africa. By stressing Africa's noble past, Garvey declared that American blacks should be proud of their ancestry and, in particular, proud of their blackness. Concurrently, American blacks should strive to achieve black community pride, wealth, culture, and independence in the United States by creating and maintaining a nation-within-a-nation. The struggle for African redemption, he stated, did not call for blacks to surrender their domestic struggle for political justice and economic independence.

In 1921, Garvey established a provisional government-in-exile for Africa, with himself as president. In addition, he established a black cabinet, a black army (the Universal African Legion), attired in resplendent uniforms, a corps of nurses (the Universal Black Cross Nurses), and even an African Orthodox Church, with a black God and a black Christ. Earlier, Garvey had created the Negro Factories Corporation (NFC), an experiment designed to promote black economic independence by providing loans and technical assistance to aspiring black small businessmen. The NFC reflected Garvey's acceptance of Booker T. Washington's late nineteenth century philosophy of black self-help as a stepping-stone to genuine black emancipation. Although the NFC rarely had enough working capital, it did succeed in establishing a number of independent black businesses, including a restaurant, a chain of cooperative grocery stores, and a publishing house.

Garvey's pet project was his Black Star Line, a steamship company designed to engage in commerce with and transportation to Africa. Garvey was convinced that a black-owned-and-operated "link" with the African motherland would not only promote black self-help and economic opportunity but also visibly enhance black pride and self-awareness. Thousands of urban blacks heeded the call, buying up more than a half million dollars of Black Star Line stock (inexpensively priced at five dollars a share and limited to black investors) during the first year of the company's existence. The fact that Garvey and his associates purchased (many say were hoodwinked into purchasing) ships that were hardly seaworthy did not detract from the enthusiasm this venture generated among the black urban masses. Financially, however, the Black Star Line proved to be a disaster for the UNIA. The organization was unable to raise enough money to repair steamships which, in some cases, were beyond repair. By late 1921, the company was more or less defunct.

The elaborateness, flamboyance, and, above all, the promise and the dream of Garveyism, coupled with Garvey's own charismatic personality, had a profound effect upon the black urban masses, who were drawn to their "messiah" as if he were a magnet. On the other hand, black intellectuals denounced Garvey as a buffoon (he often wore elaborate academic gowns and uniforms) and a demagogue. W. E. B. Du Bois, for example, described him as "a little, fat black man, ugly, but with intelligent eyes and a big head . . . the most dangerous enemy of the Negro race in America." For his part, Garvey shunned intellectuals such as Du Bois, whom he called a "lazy dependent mulatto," as well as the black bourgeois establishment, which, in his mind, had betrayed the black race by cooperating with whites.

Garvey's sincere. but inept management of the Black Star Line finally put an end to his meteoric rise. In 1922, he was indicted on mail-fraud charges concerning the sale of Black Star Line stock. Convicted in 1923, he was confined in prison for two years and then, in 1927, deported as an undesirable alien. In his absence, Garveyism (or Black Zionism) in the United States lost much of its appeal. Moreover, faced with a decade of economic depression during the 1930's, most urban blacks became much more concerned with their own personal survival than with the grandiose schemes of a deported Jamaican.

Unable to resurrect the UNIA in Jamaica, Garvey moved to London in 1935. Following several bouts with pneumonia in the late 1930's, Garvey suffered two severe strokes in 1940. He subsequently died in relative obscurity in London on June 10, 1940. Garvey was fifty-two years old.

Summary

Regarded by some as an egotistic, self-serving charlatan and by others as a black messiah or a black Moses, Marcus Garvey proved to be the embodiment of pent-up black nationalism in the United States during the early twentieth century. By organizing the first black mass-protest movement in the history of the United States, and by emphasizing self-help, black pride, racial purity, and the resurrection of a great black empire in Africa, Garvey unwittingly became the spiritual father of many black nationalist movements of subsequent years. Organizations such as the Black Muslims and the Black Panthers and slogans such as "black is beautiful" and "black power" would later emerge as manifestations of a revived Garveyism.

Bibliography

Brisbane, Robert H. *The Black Vanguard: Origins of the Negro Social Revolution, 1900-1960*. Valley Forge, Pa.: Judson Press, 1970. Contains a well-written, lengthy chapter on the Garvey era, placing Garvey in the mainstream of American black radicalism.

Cronon, Edmund David. *Black Moses: The Story of Marcus Garvey and the Universal Negro Improvement Association*. Madison: University of Wisconsin Press, 1962. Generally considered the most authoritative, scholarly account of Garvey and Garveyism, Cronon's book is balanced, well documented, and especially well written. Contains both a bibliographical essay and a list of primary and secondary references.

Garvey, Amy Jacques. *Garvey and Garveyism*. New York: P. F. Collier, 1970. Useful, firsthand reminiscences by Garvey's second wife and widow. Especially good for the postdeportation era in the West Indies and London.

Garvey, Marcus. *Philosophy and Opinions of Marcus Garvey*. Edited by Amy Jacques Garvey. New York: Universal Publishing House, 1923-1925. Reprint. New York: Atheneum Publishers, 1969. This is one of several reprinted volumes of Garvey's original writings edited by his widow. A supplemental volume (*More Philosophy and Opinions of Marcus Garvey*) was published by Frank Cass (London) in 1977.

Levine, Lawrence. "Marcus Garvey and the Politics of Revitalization." In *Black Leaders of the Twentieth Century*, edited by John Hope Franklin and August Meier, 105-138. Urbana: University of Illinois Press, 1982. This indispensable essay offers an analytical overview of the Garvey movement and its legacy.

Toppin, Edgar, A. *A Biographical History of Blacks in America Since 1528*. New York: David McKay Co., 1971. Based on a series of articles originally appearing in *The Christian Science Monitor* in 1969, Toppin's work contains both a chronological chapter on black American history during the Garvey era and, more important, a formal biographical essay on Garvey himself.

Vincent, Theodore G. *Black Power and the Garvey Movement*. Berkeley, Calif.: Ramparts Press, 1971. Stresses the historical link between Garveyism and American black radicalism in general, and shows how Garvey paved the way for subsequent black protest groups in the United States.

Robert R. Davis, Jr.

LOU GEHRIG

Born: June 19, 1903; New York, New York
Died: June 2, 1941; New York, New York
Area of Achievement: Sports
Contribution: Gehrig was the bulwark of the New York Yankees baseball
  dynasty of the 1920's, including the famed Murderer's Row team of 1927,
  and he played in 2,130 consecutive major league games, an endurance
  record unequaled in baseball history.

Early Life

Henry Louis Gehrig was born June 19, 1903, in New York's Upper East
Side. His parents, Heinrich and Christina Gehrig, were German immigrants
whose two other children died at a very young age. They spoke no English
upon their arrival in New York, and their lives were filled with deprivation
and poverty. Lou's father was never able to work consistently at his craft and
often drank beer and played pinochle at the neighborhood tavern. Lou's
mother was the dominating force of his life. She worked at many jobs, such
as domestic, cook, and laundress, and Lou often helped and ran her errands.
Christina Gehrig's driving ambition was to provide Lou with an education so
that he might become an engineer and escape the cycle of poverty that had
engulfed her and her husband.

As he grew up on the East Side, Lou was a profoundly shy "momma's
boy." He wore hand-me-down clothes and spoke with a German accent, leading his peers to taunt him. This formative period of his life left him with a
lack of self-confidence that he would never overcome completely. His mother,
however, emphasized the idea that hard work and dedication to his studies
were keys to success in America. Lou was so proud of his perfect attendance
record in elementary school that he would not allow pneumonia to keep him
out of school.

Gehrig was a good and attentive student, but he excelled in sports. At this
time, his father gave him a right-handed catcher's mitt for Christmas.
Although he was a southpaw, Gehrig was very proud of the glove and played
ball with neighborhood children. He was big and awkward, not a natural-
born baseball player. Yet his father helped him to build up his physique and
muscle coordination, and Gehrig became very active in school sports, particularly track, shot put, and baseball. His proudest moment occurred when he
helped his team win New York's Park Department League baseball championship.

At the High School of Commerce, and despite his mother's fears that
sports would distract her son from his studies, Gehrig became the star of the
school's basketball, soccer, and baseball teams. Commerce's soccer team, for
example, won the city's championship three consecutive years. Gehrig played

first base for the baseball team and became the team's leading slugger. During his senior year, the baseball team won the city's championship, which entitled them to play Lane High School, the champions of Chicago. Gehrig hit a grand-slam home run to help his team emerge victorious.

Gehrig's baseball exploits at Commerce enabled him to enter Columbia University in 1921 on an athletic scholarship. His parents were employed at a fraternity house, and Gehrig helped out by waiting on tables. When he had some spare time, he played baseball with members of the fraternity. He inadvertently jeopardized his scholarship, however, when he signed a contract with the New York Giants under manager John McGraw, who sent him to Hartford, Connecticut, in the Eastern League. When Gehrig's professional contract became known, Columbia University officials attempted to strip him of his amateur status. Friends intervened on behalf of Gehrig, however, and his amateur ranking was restored on the condition that he sit out his freshman year.

Life's Work

By this time, Gehrig was six feet tall with massive shoulders and weighed two hundred pounds. He played fullback on Columbia's football team and pitched and played first base on the baseball team. He was called "Columbia Lou" as his hitting exploits received increasing attention from fans. During the spring of 1923, Paul Krichell, a scout for the New York Yankees, was so impressed with Gehrig's hitting that he predicted that he would become another Babe Ruth. Gehrig was offered a bonus and a contract to complete the 1923 season with the Yankees. The money was so good that even his mother approved of his withdrawal from Columbia. Thus, at the age of twenty, Gehrig began his professional baseball career.

During the early 1920's, Yankee manager Miller Huggins sought to build a nucleus for a baseball dynasty. Babe Ruth was the heart of the team, and Gehrig found it difficult to find a place for himself. First base was Gehrig's position, but veteran Wally Pipp was at the height of his career and had a lock on it. Accordingly, Gehrig spent most of the 1923 and 1924 seasons in Hartford, where he hit well over .300 and drove out sixty-one home runs over two years.

In 1925, Gehrig's break finally came. On June 1, 1925, he pinch-hit for the shortstop. On June 2, 1925, Pipp was hit in the head by a fastball during batting practice and was unable to start the game. Huggins inserted Gehrig into the starting lineup, and Pipp never played first base for the Yankees again. Gehrig started every game for fourteen years, a total of 2,130 consecutive games, an endurance record which has yet to be approached. He became the Iron Horse of the New York Yankees.

Gehrig enjoyed a solid rookie year. He hit .295, with twenty home runs, twenty-three doubles, nine triples, and sixty-eight runs-batted-in (RBI's), for a seventh-place team. In 1926, the Yankees won the American League pennant, and Gehrig proved to be a major factor in that season with a .313 average, 107 RBI's, and twenty triples. Gehrig hit cleanup, between Ruth and outfielder Bob Musil. In 1927, that trio formed part of Murderer's Row, perhaps the greatest baseball team in history. The team's statistics were awesome: a 110-44 won-lost record, a .307 team batting average, and an earned-run-average of 3.20.

What also caught the fans' imagination were the exploits of Ruth and Gehrig. For good or ill, Ruth was the dominant personality on the team. In many ways, he was an oversized boy who challenged authority to its limits. Gehrig, in contrast, was the organization man, obedient, quiet, noncontroversial, and hardworking. Gehrig's quiet, passive personality may explain his inability to escape Ruth's shadow fully. In 1927, Gehrig hit .373 and Ruth .356; Gehrig led the league with 175 RBI's, and Ruth came in second. Yet Ruth led Gehrig in slugging percentage; in the most spectacular race of all, he and Gehrig were neck-and-neck for the home-run title. Finally, in the last weeks of the season, Ruth pulled ahead to hit sixty home runs, a record that was to last until Roger Maris of the Yankees hit sixty-one in 162 games in 1961. Few people recall that Gehrig finished second with forty-seven home runs.

During the early 1930's, the Yankees were once again in the process of reconstructing their team under manager Joe McCarthy. Ruth was desperately unhappy under McCarthy's discipline, and age began to blunt his skills. By 1935, Ruth was gone, traded to the Boston Braves. Gehrig thrived under McCarthy and, at last, emerged from Ruth's shadow. Moreover, he became more independent of his mother when he married Eleanor Twichell of Chicago late in December, 1933. Eleanor Gehrig provided her husband with a happy and contented home life. The results were obvious: In 1934, Gehrig had his best year, winning baseball's coveted Triple Crown: forty-nine home runs, 165 RBI's, and a .363 batting average.

Gehrig's days in the Yankee sun, however, were few. In 1935, his performance did not match that of 1934. In 1936, the Yankees acquired center fielder Joe DiMaggio from the Pacific Coast League, and DiMaggio would dominate the team through the 1940's. Even so, 1936 was one of Gehrig's best years, as he hit .354 and led the league in home runs (forty-nine). He came through again in 1937, with 159 RBI's, thirty-seven home runs, and a .351 average. The following year, however, was extremely disappointing. Only thirty-four years old, he appeared to be on the decline, although his .295 batting average and 114 RBI's were quite respectable. His defensive play at first base was below his usual standards; he played in constant pain, pain so severe that he had to leave games in the late innings. Gehrig suspected that he had lumbago, but his doctors diagnosed the problem as a gall-bladder condition. He was treated on that basis during the winter months.

The 1939 spring training season in St. Petersburg, Florida, revealed that Gehrig was a very ill man. His muscle coordination had deteriorated over the winter. During the early part of the regular season, Gehrig had only four hits in twenty-eight times at bat for a .143 average. Finally, in Detroit in early May, he requested that McCarthy take him out of the lineup, thus terminating his legendary consecutive-game streak. Gehrig later flew to the Mayo Clinic in Rochester, New York, where doctors diagnosed his condition as amyotrophic lateral sclerosis, an incurable and deadly form of paralysis. At the insistence of his wife, Eleanor, doctors did not inform Gehrig of the implications of his disease.

Gehrig ultimately returned to the Yankees as a coach for the remainder of the 1939 season. On July 4, 1939, the team held a Lou Gehrig day in Yankee Stadium, and more than sixty thousand fans came out to honor the Iron Horse. Gehrig was deeply moved by the fans' display of affection and respect; in a moving and heartfelt speech, he declared that he was "the luckiest man on the face of this earth." Eleanor made the last days of Gehrig's life as useful and happy as possible. She arranged to have New York Mayor Fiorello La Guardia appoint Gehrig as a member of the parole board. They attended as many cultural events as they could. Finally, on June 2, 1941, Gehrig died at home, quietly, at ten o'clock in the evening, only two weeks short of his thirty-eighth birthday.

Summary

Lou Gehrig played in 2,164 major league games, of which 2,136 were at first base, nine in the outfield, and one at shortstop. He had 8,001 official at bats and collected 2,721 hits, including 525 doubles, 162 triples, and 493 home runs. He hit a home run every 6.2 times at bat. His lifetime batting average was .340. He scored 1,888 runs, batted in 1,191 runs, struck out 789 times, and walked to first base 1,528 times. His lifetime slugging percentage was .632. In World Series play, his record was equally impressive. Gehrig played in thirty-four World Series games; in 119 at bats, he had forty-three hits, of which eight were doubles, three were triples, and ten were home runs. He scored thirty runs and knocked in thirty-five runs against the best teams that the National League had to offer. His career World Series batting average was .361, and his slugging percentage, .731.

For all their impressive effect, these statistics do not reveal Gehrig, the human being. He represented the American dream to hard-pressed citizens of the late 1920's and 1930's. He was an inspiring role model for the American youth in a way that Babe Ruth could never have been. He represented basic American values that were the bedrock of the baseball mystique: honor, sportsmanship, duty, and work. Yet Gehrig fulfilled this role without visible effort. It was as much a part of his character and personality as were the grace and dignity of his play in a child's game. He never complained that life had been unfair to him. The courage and humility of his last days were so inspiring that amyotrophic lateral sclerosis became popularly known as "Lou Gehrig's disease." In 1939, the Baseball Writers Association of America did him honor by waiving the required waiting period to vote Lou Gehrig into baseball's Hall of Fame.

Bibliography

Allen, Mel, and Ed Fitzgerald. *You Can't Beat the Hours: A Long, Loving Look at Big League Baseball, Including Some Yankees I Have Known.* New York: Harper and Row, Publishers, 1964. A general and popular account of the New York Yankees by their radio broadcaster of a quarter of a century. Covers the team from the era of Ruth and Gehrig to the era of Mantle and Maris. A very readable and entertaining book.

Anderson, Dave, Murray Chass, Robert Creamer, and Harold Rosenthal. *The Yankees: The Four Fabulous Eras of Baseball's Most Famous Team.* New York: Random House, 1979. A fascinating account of the Yankee dynasties from the perspectives of the dominating players of each era. Enough photographs to please any Yankee fan.

Fleming, G. H., ed. *Murderer's Row.* New York: William Morrow and Co., 1985. A collection of photographs, newspaper clippings, and articles by the major sportswriters of the 1920's, linked by Fleming's commentary to form a day-by-day narrative of the 1927 season. A major theme is the home-run duel between Ruth and Gehrig.

Gehrig, Eleanor, and Joseph Durso. *My Luke and I.* New York: Thomas Y. Crowell, 1976. A moving, personal account of the public and private lives of Lou and Eleanor Gehrig. Particularly revealing are insights into Gehrig's personality, the rivalry between Gehrig's mother and his wife for his affections, and the stability of Gehrig's life following his marriage.

Rubin, Robert. *Lou Gehrig: Courageous Star.* New York: G. P. Putnam's Sons, 1979. An admiring popular biography of the Iron Horse. Written by a Miami, Florida, newspaper sportswriter. Emphasizes the impact of Gehrig's formative years and his struggle to emerge from the shadow of Babe Ruth, only to be overshadowed by the young Joe DiMaggio.

Stephen P. Sayles

HENRY GEORGE

Born: September 2, 1839; Philadelphia, Pennsylvania
Died: October 29, 1897; New York, New York
Area of Achievement: Social and economic reform
Contribution: George's writings and lectures on land, labor, and economic policies expressed a popular radicalism that challenged established economic doctrines and dominant political practices, exercising a profound influence for reform both in the United States and abroad.

Early Life

An oldest son, Henry George was born into a large, devoutly Episcopalian family on September 2, 1839, in Philadelphia, Pennsylvania, close to Independence Hall, a source of lifelong inspiration to him. His father, Richard Samuel Henry George, was a sea captain's son whose once prosperous resources were depleted prior to his death. Accordingly, throughout his life Richard earned a steady, but modest, income working variously as a schoolteacher, a dealer in religious books, and for a longer period as a clerk in Philadelphia's United States Customs House—a Democratic Party political appointment. Catharine Vallance, Henry's mother, was as devout as her husband; also a former schoolteacher, she bore nine children and was proud of her descent from a close friend of Benjamin Franklin. Overall, the George household was warmly Christian and modestly comfortable. Henry George remained attached to his family all of his life.

Though receiving some primary instruction at home, the young George's formal education was brief. What there was of it failed to impress him. At six, he entered a small private school, and at nine moved on to Philadelphia's famed Episcopal Academy but performed poorly and withdrew. He was subsequently coached for admission to the city's esteemed public high school—this tutoring, he later believed, providing his best educational experience. Once enrolled, however, he quit almost immediately, thus ending his formal education at thirteen. When fully mature, he was to praise only vocational or practical learning, but in his early years there were other cultural advantages which derived from his regular use of the libraries of the Franklin Institute, the American Philosophical Society, and a small, convivial literary society.

Regardless of his formal deficiencies, they were never a handicap. Largely self-taught, reflective, ambitious, and combative, with a romantic sense of individuality and a slowly acquired ability to concentrate his energies, George would eventually meet many of the Western world's best-educated, most learned, and most politically important figures, either directly or by debating them; at such times, George was equal to his discussion partners or debating adversaries in maintaining his own faith—and, almost without exception, he gained the respect of these men.

Two sets of events brought Henry George to youthful independence and helped pave a path toward his life's work. In 1855, through family connections, he sailed as foremast boy on a sixteen-month voyage from New York to Melbourne and Calcutta. Returning to Philadelphia, he secured a job from which he rose to journeyman typesetter, a skill which carried a number of his famous contemporaries into journalism or writing. In the depressed economy of 1857, however, his friends and relatives were already living on the Pacific Coast, and he determined to join them. With an offer for a job in his pocket, he thus started his journey west. Again, thanks to parental persuasions, he sailed as an ordinary seaman on a government lighthouse vessel, which, upon arrival in San Francisco, he deserted. He would remain in the new and bustling state of California from 1858 to 1880.

Life's Work

Initially there was an unsteady quality to George's California days, especially during the Civil War. Like many, he caught "gold fever" and explored northward as far as British Columbia. He weighed rice, served as a foreman, dabbled in journalism, joined in the operation of a San Francisco newspaper, and even abandoned the Democratic Party for California's liberal brand of Republicanism, at least through the Grant Administrations. Such ventures or allegiances, however, were either short-lived or failures. Consequently, along with many young Eastern emigrants during the 1860's, he suffered economic hardships, at one point verging on desperation. Nevertheless, he was establishing mature foundations.

In 1861, George married Annie Fox, a Catholic orphaned by a broken British colonial marriage, and they started a family of their own. Moreover, in March, 1865, by his own account, he determined to devote his life to writing, exploring social issues through the economic contrasts and conflicts that appeared so stark in California. Between 1866 and 1879, he pursued this course as editor variously of eight San Francisco, Oakland, and Sacramento newspapers. Editorially he advocated (and sometimes joined) movements toward free trade and public ownership and regulation of railroads, the telegraph, and municipal utilities. He sought revisions in the state's land policies, as well as revisions in national land policy under the Morrill Act, thus encouraging more equitable land distribution both in California and in the nation.

Generally George favored trade unionism, the eight-hour day, and strikes as a last resort. He believed that high wages, leading to a greater respect for labor, would help lead to an economy of abundance. Favoring competition, he staunchly opposed its excesses or monopolies in any form. Similarly, on the then hotly debated "currency question," he proposed an end to credit manipulations by bankers and by government and a gradual restoration of wartime greenbacks (inflated currency) to equivalency in gold: a gradual return to a hard-money policy. Distressed by the cornering of California lands by a handful of speculators and wealthy individuals and anxious to see the state continue as a utopia for the common man, he urged restrictions on immigration, particularly Chinese immigration. The issues with which he dealt were current ones, engaging wide popular attention and commentary by American and British political economists of whom George was aware and whom he acknowledged, but his faith, common sense, keen personal observations, and experienced reflections lent special force to his writings.

His editorials and lectures brought George notoriety. It was two books specifically, however, that won for him national and even international recognition. In 1871, he published *Our Land and Land Policy, National and State* (really a 130-page pamphlet) in San Francisco. In it he argued that public lands should be made more available to ordinary homesteaders (eighty-acre or forty-acre allotments rather than 160-acre allotments); that existing enormous landholdings should be divested and their future restricted chiefly through the fairest and most collectible of all taxes: a tax on land. Barring the rapid drift toward land monopolies and a reopening of accessibility, he predicted revolutions in Europe and America which would begin among the dispossessed peoples of their growing and spreading urban areas. Thus spoke the frail, bald, but bearded, mustachioed, flashing-eyed Prophet of San Francisco, a man by then inspiriting pragmatic land reform movements.

Then, in 1879, George published *Progress and Poverty: An Inquiry into the Causes of Industrial Depressions, and of Increase of Want with Increase of Wealth—The Remedy*. Injustices were explicit in the subtitle. The remedy was nationalization of land and imposition of one single tax (later The Single Tax). Land values, George argued, as personal knowledge of stark contrasts between extraordinary wealth and dire need in San Francisco and New York convinced him, were communal, societal creations inherent in the scarcity of land. Pressures of population, production necessities, or monopolitistic urges thus raised land and rental values and depressed wages. The mere possession of land often made millionaires of nonproducers or noncontributors to human welfare. A tax, therefore, on such socially created rents would allow government to redistribute such gains to alleviate want and enhance community life. George was no socialist. Indeed, since the basis of local revenues was a general property tax and since George abhorred centralization over local responsibilities, he expected local governments to fulfill these necessary functions.

Progress and Poverty earned for George international fame even greater than the fame he was enjoying at home. In 1880, he moved to New York City, there to write, lecture, and carry his message abroad. He was active among reformers, land restoration leaguers, and labor and economic circles in England and Ireland in 1882 and again in England and Scotland (with particular success in the latter) in 1884. By the end of the 1880's, he had been active on the Continent as well as in Australia. In fact, he had, with some justice, come to believe that *Progress and Poverty* was the most influential work of its kind since Adam Smith's *The Wealth of Nations* (1776). Even Karl Marx, while critical, regarded George's work as a significant assault upon economic orthodoxy.

Inevitably George's prominence brought him into the political forum. After the Civil War and Reconstruction era, he had returned to the Democratic Party, though not uncritically. While many reformers championed him for the nation's and for New York State's highest political offices, he either avoided selection or lost the votes. In fact, it was the politics of New York City that claimed him. His prolabor positions were well-known. So too were his urban progressive reforms: an end to bossism, municipal ownership of utilities, and the secret ballot, among others. His idea for a single tax and his other economic proposals, such as free trade and antipoverty activities, also had wide currency. Attuned to rural dissents, he was recognized also for his awareness that the future of America lay with the consciences of its growing urban citizenry. Nominated by New York's Central Labor Union for the mayoralty in 1886, he lost in a hotly disputed three-way race. Afterward, he continued with his mission, writing and lecturing, until he tried once more to become New York's mayor in 1897 as the candidate of The Democracy of Thomas Jefferson. Indefatigable to the end, but exhausted from campaigning, he died on October 29, 1897.

Summary

No American reformer loomed larger in his generation nationally and internationally than Henry George. *Progress and Poverty* was widely translated and received a degree of attention that few other books ever have; it was in its time far more influential than the first volume of Karl Marx's *Das Kapital* (1867). George's idealism and devotion to democracy, though professional economists found his Single Tax idea flawed, did more to shake economic thinking by directing it to profound social and related political problems than anyone else's. In a narrow economic sense, he came close to developing the idea of marginal productivity. More practically, his ideas linked land questions with taxation and helped spawn tax reforms that were placed in effect not only in parts of the United States but also in Canada and Australia. If George represented popular radicalism, his roots were natively American, drawing from the best of the Jeffersonian and Jacksonian traditions. He was firmly procapitalist and a believer in fair competition. Despite flirtations with socialism, he had little regard for any type of governmental centralization. Rather, the somewhat utopian visions of democracy in which he placed his faith emphasized local government and local responsibilities. Finally, as he carried his ideas into the heart of the world's greatest city, his forceful Christianity influenced most major reformers of the Progressive era that followed his death.

Bibliography

Barker, Charles Albro. *Henry George*. New York: Oxford University Press, 1955. The richest, most exhaustively researched, perhaps definitive biography. Coverage is meticulously chronological, but Barker makes his own careful evaluations of George's development and ideas, both in the context of his time and in historical perspective.

DeMille, Anna George. *Henry George: Citizen of the World*. Edited by Don C. Shoemaker. Chapel Hill: University of North Carolina Press, 1950. George's daughter concentrates upon her father as a family man and devotes more attention to her mother's role than is to be found in any other work.

Dorfman, Joseph. *The Economic Mind in American Civilization*. Vol. 3. New York: Viking Press, 1959. Chapter 6 places George, with depth and excellence, in a context of the economic history of Popular Radicalism between 1865 and 1918.

Geiger, George Raymond. *The Philosophy of Henry George*. New York: Macmillan, 1933. A close, if pedantic and somewhat ahistorical analysis. Stresses George's pragmatism.

George, Henry, Jr. *The Life of Henry George By His Son*. New York: Doubleday, Page, and Co., 1905. Much material later incorporated in George, Jr.'s *The Complete Works of Henry George*. 10 vols. Garden City, N.Y.: Fels Fund Library Edition, 1906-1911. An associate of his father from his adolescence onward, George, Jr., later a congressman, faithfully reflects paternal decisions and ideas in this memoir.

Nock, Albert Jay. *Henry George, an Essay*. New York: William Morrow and Co., 1939. A brilliant analysis of George's character and mind.

Seligman, Edwin R. A. *Essays in Taxation*. 9th rev. ed. New York: Macmillan Company, 1921. Still readily available, this work by America's foremost authority on taxation concludes that on political, social, economic, and moral grounds, the Single Tax was a mistake. Yet Seligman freely acknowledges its great usefulness in drawing attention to abuses of medieval land systems abroad, to inequities in the general property tax in the United States, and to unjust privilege.

Thomas, John L. "Utopia for an Urban Age: Henry George, Henry Demarest Lloyd, Edward Bellamy." *Perspectives in American History* 6 (1974): 135-166. A lucid comparison of George's utopian strains with those of two famous contemporaries.

Clifton K. Yearley
Kerrie L. MacPherson

GERONIMO
Goyathlay

Born: c. 1827; near modern Clifton, Arizona
Died: February 17, 1909; Fort Sill, Oklahoma Territory
Area of Achievement: Native American leadership
Contribution: For two decades the most feared and vilified individual in the
   Southwest, Geronimo, in his old age, became a freak attraction at fairs
   and expositions. His maligned and misunderstood career epitomized the
   troubles of a withering Apache culture struggling to survive in a hostile
   modern world.

Early Life

While the precise date and location of his birth are not known, Geronimo
most likely was born around 1827 near the head of the Gila River in a part of
the Southwest then controlled by Mexico. Named Goyathlay (One Who
Yawns) by his Behonkohe parents, the legendary Apache warrior later came
to be called Geronimo—a name taken from the sound which terrified Mexican soldiers allegedly cried when calling on Saint Jerome to protect them
from his relentless charge.

Geronimo's early life, like that of other Apache youth, was filled with
complex religious ritual and ceremony. From the placing of amulets on his
cradle to guard him against early death to the ceremonial putting on of the
first moccasins, Geronimo's relatives prepared their infant for Apache life,
teaching him the origin myths of his people and the legends of supernatural
beings and benevolent mountain spirits that hid in the caverns of their homeland. Through ritual observances and instruction, Geronimo learned about
Usen, a remote and nebulous god who, though unconcerned with petty quarrels among men, was the Life Giver and provider for his people. "When
Usen created the Apaches," Geronimo later asserted, "he also created their
homes in the West. He gave to them such grain, fruits, and game as they
needed to eat. . . . He gave to them a climate and all they needed for clothing
and shelter was at hand." Geronimo's religious heritage taught him to be self-
sufficient, to love and revere his mountain homeland, and never to betray a
promise made with oath and ceremony.

Geronimo grew into adulthood during a brief period of peace, a rare interlude that interrupted the chronic wars between the Apache and Mexican
peoples. Even in times of peace, however, Apache culture placed a priority
on the skills of warfare. Through parental instruction and childhood games,
Geronimo learned how to hunt, hide, track, and shoot—necessary survival
skills in an economy based upon game, wild fruits, and booty taken from
neighboring peoples.

Geronimo also heard the often repeated stories of conquests of his heroic grandfather Mahko, an Apache chief renowned for his great size, strength, and valor in battle. Like his grandfather, Geronimo had unusual physical prowess and courage. Tall and slender, strong and quick, Geronimo proved at an early age to be a good provider for his mother, whom he supported following his father's premature death, and later for his bride, Alope, whom he acquired from her father for "a herd of ponies" stolen most likely from unsuspecting Mexican victims. By his early twenties, Geronimo (still called Goyathlay) was a member of the council of warriors, a proven booty taker, a husband, and a father of three.

Life's Work

In 1850, a band of Mexican scalp hunters raided an Apache camp while the warriors were away. During the ensuing massacre, Geronimo's mother, wife, and three children were slain. Shortly after this tragedy, Geronimo had a religious experience that figured prominently in his subsequent life. As he later reported the incident, while in a trancelike state, a voice called his name four times (the magic number among the Apache) and then informed him, "No gun can ever kill you. I will take the bullets from the guns of the Mexicans, so they will have nothing but powder. And I will guide your arrows." After receiving this gift of power, Geronimo's vengeance against Mexicans was equaled by his confidence that harm would not come his way.

While still unknown to most Americans, during the 1850's, Geronimo rose among the ranks of the Apache warriors. A participant in numerous raids into Mexico, Geronimo fought bravely under the Apache chief Cochise. Although wounded on several occasions, Geronimo remained convinced that no bullet could kill him. It was during this period that he changed his name from Goyathlay to Geronimo.

War between the United States government and the Apache first erupted in 1861 following a kidnaping-charge incident involving Cochise. The war lingered for nearly a dozen years until Cochise and General O. O. Howard signed a truce. According to the terms of the agreement, the mountain homeland of the Chiricahua (one of the tribes which made up the Apache and Geronimo's tribe) was set aside as a reservation, on which the Chiricahua promised to remain.

Following Cochise's death in 1874, the United States attempted to relocate the Chiricahua to the San Carlos Agency in the parched bottomlands of the Gila River. Although some Apache accepted relocation, Geronimo led a small band off the reservation into the Sierra Madre range in Mexico. From this base, Geronimo's warriors conducted raids into the United States, hitting wagon trains and ranches for the supplies needed for survival.

In 1877, for the first and only time in his life, Geronimo was captured by John Clum of the United States Army. After spending some time in a guardhouse in San Carlos, Geronimo was released, being told not to leave the reservation. Within a year, however, he was again in Mexico. While a fugitive, he was blamed in the American press for virtually all crimes committed by Apache "renegades" of the reservation.

Upon the promise of protection, Geronimo voluntarily returned to the San Carlos Agency in 1879. This time, he remained two years until an unfortunate incident involving the death of Noch-ay-del-klinne, a popular Apache religious prophet, triggered another escape into the Sierra Madre. In 1882, Geronimo daringly attempted a raid into Arizona to rescue the remainder of his people on the reservation and to secure for himself reinforcements for his forces hiding in Mexico. This campaign, which resulted in the forced abduction of many unwilling Apache women and children, brought heavy losses to his band and nearly cost Geronimo his life. The newspaper coverage of the campaign also made Geronimo America's most despised and feared villain.

In May, 1883, General George Crook of the United States Army crossed into Mexico in search of Geronimo. Not wanting war, Geronimo sent word to Crook of his willingness to return to the reservation if his people were guaranteed just treatment. Crook consented, and Geronimo persuaded his band to retire to San Carlos.

Geronimo, however, never adjusted to life on the reservation. Troubled by newspaper headlines demanding his execution and resentful of reservation rules (in particular, the prohibition against alcoholic drink), Geronimo in the spring of 1885 planned a final breakaway from the San Carlos Agency. With his typical ingenuity, Geronimo led his 144 followers off the reservation. Cutting telegraph lines behind him, he eluded the cavalry and crossed into Mexico, finding sanctuary in his old Sierra Madre refuge. Although pursued by an army of five thousand regulars and five hundred Apache scouts, Geronimo avoided capture until September, 1886, when he voluntarily surrendered to General Nelson Miles. (He had agreed to a surrender to General George Crook in March but had escaped his troops.)

Rejoicing that the Apache wars were over, the army loaded Geronimo and his tribesmen on railroad cars and shipped them first to Fort Pickens in Florida and then to the Mount Vernon Barracks in Alabama. Unaccustomed to the warm, humid climate, so unlike the high, dry country of their birth, thousands of the Apache captives died of tuberculosis and other diseases. In 1894, after the government rejected another appeal to allow their return to Arizona, the Kiowa and Comanche offered their former Apache foes a part of their reservation near Fort Sill, Oklahoma.

Geronimo spent the remainder of his life on the Oklahoma reservation. Adapting quickly to the white man's economic system, the aged Apache warrior survived by growing watermelons and selling his now infamous signature to curious autograph seekers. While the government technically still viewed him as a prisoner of war, the army permitted Geronimo to attend, under guard, the international fairs and expositions at Buffalo, Omaha, and St.

Louis. In 1905, Theodore Roosevelt even invited him to Washington, D.C., to attend the inaugural presidential parade. Wherever Geronimo went, he attracted great crowds and made handsome profits by selling autographs, buttons, hats, and photographs of himself.

In February, 1909, while returning home from selling bows and arrows in nearby Lawton, Oklahoma, an inebriated Geronimo fell from his horse into a creek bed. For several hours, Geronimo's body lay exposed. Three days later, the Apache octogenarian died of pneumonia. As promised, no bullet ever killed him.

Summary

The Industrial Age of the late nineteenth century altered the life patterns of American farmers and entrepreneurs, women and laborers. No groups, however, were more effected by the forces of modernization than were the Native American Indians. Geronimo's tragic career as warrior and prisoner epitomized the inevitable demise of an ancient Apache culture trapped in a web of white man's history.

While a stubbornly independent and uncompromising warrior, Geronimo symbolized to countless Americans the treacherous savagery of a vicious race that could not be trusted. Highly conscious of his wrath and unrelenting hatred, the American public never knew the deeply religious family man who yearned to abide in his mountain homeland.

During his last twenty-three years of captivity, the legend of Geronimo grew, even as the public's hatred of the once-powerful Apache mellowed into admiration. Always a good provider, Geronimo established for himself a profitable business by peddling souvenirs and performing stunts at Wild West shows. A living artifact of a world that no longer existed, Geronimo became the comic image of the tamed American Indian finally brought into white man's civilization.

Bibliography

Adams, Alexander B. *Geronimo: A Biography*. New York: G. P. Putnam's Sons, 1971. A well-researched history of the Apache wars that contains much material on Mangas Coloradas, Cochise, and other warriors as well as Geronimo. Replete with documentation of the connivances, blunders, and savagery that characterized the removal of the Apache from their homelands, this biography exposes the limitations of General Nelson Miles and the inexperience of the white leadership in Indian affairs.

Betzinez, Jason, with Wilbur Sturtevant Nye. *I Fought with Geronimo*. Harrisburg, Pa.: Stackpole Co., 1960. Another firsthand narrative account of the Apache wars written by the son of Geronimo's first cousin. Includes stories told more than half a century after the event. An entertaining primary source, but it must be used with caution.

Brown, Dee. "Geronimo." *American History Illustrated* 15 (May, 1980): 12-21; 15 (July, 1980): 31-45. The best article-length introduction to the life of Geronimo. A lively and sympathetic overview of the career of this clever Apache warrior.

Clum, Woodworth. *Apache Agent: The Story of John P. Clum.* Boston: Houghton Mifflin Co., 1936. Reprint. Lincoln: University of Nebraska Press, 1978. A story of the only man who ever captured Geronimo. Written from the notes of John Clum, a man who hated Geronimo with a passion. Biased yet entertaining account.

Davis, Britton. *The Truth About Geronimo.* New Haven, Conn.: Yale University Press, 1929, 1963. An entertaining narrative filled with humorous and thrilling incidents written by an author who spent three years in the United States Army attempting to locate and capture this Apache warrior.

Debo, Angie. *Geronimo: The Man, His Time, His Place.* Norman: University of Oklahoma Press, 1976. The best of the many Geronimo biographies. Carefully researched and documented, this balanced account portrays Geronimo neither as villain nor as hero, but as a maligned and misunderstood individual trapped in an increasingly hostile environment. Highly recommended.

Faulk, Odie B. *The Geronimo Campaign.* New York: Oxford University Press, 1969. A reassessment of the military campaign that ended with the surrender of Geronimo in 1886. Includes much information collected by the son of Lieutenant Charles B. Gatewood, who arranged the surrender and was one of the few white men Geronimo trusted.

Geronimo. *Geronimo: His Own Story.* Edited by S. M. Barrett and Frederick Turner. New York: Duffield and Co., 1906. The personal autobiography dictated by Geronimo to Barrett in 1905. A chronicle of Geronimo's grievances, in particular against the Mexican nationals. Includes informative sections on Apache religion, methods in dealing with crimes, ceremonies, festivals, and appreciation of nature.

Terry D. Bilhartz

GEORGE GERSHWIN
Jacob Gershvin

Born: September 26, 1898; Brooklyn, New York
Died: July 11, 1937; Los Angeles, California
Area of Achievement: Music
Contribution: With a relatively untrained but intuitive sense of music tech-
niques, Gershwin composed some of the most lasting popular and serious
music of the twentieth century.

Early Life

Jacob "George" Gershvin was born September 26, 1898, in Brooklyn,
New York, the second son of recent Russian Jewish immigrants. Moishe
Gershovitz had changed his name to Morris Gershvin upon immigrating to
America just as his future wife went from Rosa Brushkin to Rose Bruskin.
They named their son Jacob but called him George, and he later changed his
last name to the more melodious Gershwin. By the time Gershwin was eighteen, the family, which eventually consisted of three sons and a daughter, had
lived in twenty-five residences in Manhattan and three in Brooklyn because
Morris preferred to live within walking distance of his business activities,
which included restaurants, bakeries, Russian and Turkish baths, a cigar
store and pool parlor, a rooming house, a summer hotel, and a bookmaking
establishment.

Growing up, Gershwin was more interested in athletics than anything else
and excelled at almost every sport he attempted while ignoring academics as
much as possible. His skill at roller-skating helped his musical development
since he became interested in jazz while skating outside Harlem nightclubs.
His interest in the classics was stimulated by hearing one of his schoolmates,
eight-year-old prodigy Maxie Rosenzweig, play the violin. Under the influence of Maxie (later known professionally as Max Rosen), Gershwin tried to
play his friend's piano. When Gershwin's parents bought a piano for his older
brother, Ira, George soon monopolized it. Gershwin's first significant music
teacher, Charles Hambitzer, improved his student's technique and introduced
him to the works of Frederic Chopin, Franz Liszt, and Claude Debussy and
to the importance of harmony in musical composition.

Despite Hambitzer's preferences for serious music, young Gershwin continued to be interested primarily in popular tunes and wrote his first songs in
1913. That summer, he worked as a pianist at a Catskill Mountains resort and
made his professional debut as a composer-pianist in 1914 by playing a tango
he had written at a social given by Ira's City College of New York literary
club.

At fifteen, Gershwin quit school to work as a pianist and song plugger for
Remick's, a prominent publisher of popular music. Through this job, he

discovered the sometimes unscrupulous business practices of Tin Pan Alley while learning more about music and refining his performing skills.

In 1916, Gershwin's first song, "When You Want 'Em, You Can't Get 'Em, When You've Got 'Em, You Don't Want 'Em," with lyrics by Murray Roth, was published, and another song, "Making of a Girl" (lyrics by Harold Atteridge), was performed in a Broadway show. Gershwin left Remick's in 1917 hoping to become a composer as good and as successful as Jerome Kern. He soon had a contract with T. B. Harms, perhaps America's most important publisher of sheet music, and by 1919, he had written his first complete score for a Broadway musical, *La, La Lucille*. The most significant development in Gershwin's early career was his writing, with lyricist Irving Caesar, "Swanee" in 1919. When Gershwin played the song at a party, Al Jolson heard it, put it into his Broadway show, and recorded it in 1920. The enormous success of "Swanee" clearly indicated Gershwin's potential as a composer of popular songs.

Life's Work

One of the first indications of Gershwin's ambition to combine serious and popular music came in 1922 with *Blue Monday*, a twenty-five-minute jazz opera about life in Harlem, with a libretto by G. B. "Buddy" De Sylva. *Blue Monday* (later retitled *135th Street*) was considered a failure but showed Gershwin's determination to write a black opera—a determination which eventually led to *Porgy and Bess* (1935). Gershwin realized part of his vast ambition in 1924 when bandleader Paul Whiteman asked him to compose a jazz concerto for an elaborate New York concert intended to display the diversity of contemporary popular music. *Rhapsody in Blue* was the hit of the concert, established that Gershwin was much more than a facile composer of popular tunes, and has remained the composition most associated with the Gershwin name.

That same year saw Gershwin's first hit Broadway musical *Lady Be Good*, with his brother Ira as lyricist. Ira Gershwin (1896-1983) continued to write the words to accompany George Gershwin's music for the remainder of his brother's life as well as for some compositions unused at the time of the younger Gershwin's death. George Gershwin established a pattern of alternating between writing for Broadway or films and the concert stage for the rest of his career.

The Gershwins wrote the scores of several Broadway musicals which flopped, but about half the shows they worked on succeeded either in their original productions or in revivals. The successes included *Oh, Kay!* (1926), *Funny Face* (1927), *Strike Up the Band* (1930), *Girl Crazy* (1930), and *Of Thee I Sing* (1931). The most interesting of these are *Strike Up the Band* and *Of Thee I Sing*, both with books by George S. Kaufman and Morrie Ryskind, since they dared to present cynical political satire as musical comedy.

The Gershwins also wrote the scores for such films as *Shall We Dance* (1937) and *Damsel in Distress* (1937).

Not all of Gershwin's more serious compositions succeeded. *Second Rhapsody for Orchestra with Piano* (1932), which the composer expected would be the equal of *Rhapsody in Blue*, and *Cuban Overture* (1932) were not well received. More successful and lasting have been *Concerto in F* (1925) and *An American in Paris* (1928), the tone poem Gershwin described as a "rhapsodic ballet" and his first large-scale work not centered on the piano.

Gershwin's wish to compose a jazz opera about black Americans was increased when he read *Porgy* (1925), DuBose Heyward's best-selling novel about poor blacks in Charleston, South Carolina. Gershwin's desire to turn *Porgy* into an opera was only heightened by the successful 1927 stage adaptation by Heyward and his wife, Dorothy. After many delays, Gershwin's dream was realized in 1935 with a libretto by Heyward and lyrics by Ira Gershwin and Heyward. Gershwin explained that he was compelled to write such an opera because of his belief that "all modern jazz is built up on the rhythms and melodic turns and twists which came directly from Africa." Yet despite his considering *Porgy and Bess* "the greatest music composed in America," the opera's original production flopped. Reviewers complained that it was an awkward blend of opera, operetta, and standard Broadway musical, that it was more a succession of popular songs than a unified opera, and that it was excessively long. *Porgy and Bess* was also criticized by both blacks and whites, including Duke Ellington and Virgil Thomson, for presenting stereotyped impressions of black life created by patronizing whites.

Despite such criticism, Gershwin continued to believe in what he called his "folk opera," but he did not live to see this faith vindicated. A 1942 Broadway revival of *Porgy and Bess* was an enormous success, running for eight months. It has gone on to become the most often performed American opera in this country and throughout the world.

Ruggedly, if unconventionally, handsome with a nose broken in a childhood fight, a low-slung jaw, a heavy lower lip, and an ever-present cigar, Gershwin was lean and well muscled, keeping in shape through golf, tennis, swimming, skiing, hiking, calisthenics, and weight lifting. His healthy appearance belied a permanent case of constipation which he called "composer's stomach" and which may have resulted from insecurity. Beginning in 1934, he was treated by a psychiatrist for this problem as well as for anxiety and depression.

Gershwin was a complicated and contradictory man. Anti-intellectual, he rarely read anything. He seemed relaxed only when talking about himself and his work. He could be rude and arrogant, never allowing those around him to forget that they were in the presence of a creative genius, yet he could also be charming and rather naïve. He was socially ambitious and imitated the behavior of the rich and sophisticated who fawned on him. His admiration for his friends' accumulation of art works led him to amass an important collection of paintings by such artists as Marc Chagall, Paul Gauguin, Pablo Picasso, Henri Rousseau, and Maurice Utrillo. After establishing himself as a composer, Gershwin began painting and sketching whenever he had the time and inclination. His paintings are mostly portraits of such friends as DuBose Heyward, Jerome Kern, and Arnold Schoenberg, as well as self-portraits.

Gershwin was a dynamic performer both on the concert stage and at parties. Rouben Mamoulian, the director of *Porgy and Bess*, described Gershwin at the piano as a "sorcerer celebrating his Sabbath." Gershwin's charisma and fame made him very attractive to women, and he had innumerable romances, many with well-known actresses. He was apparently too self-absorbed to consider marriage seriously.

Living in Los Angeles while he and Ira worked on film scores, Gershwin was performing his *Concerto in F* with the Los Angeles Philharmonic in February, 1937, when his mind went blank momentarily. He began experiencing headaches and dizziness that June. Five hours after being operated on for a brain tumor on July 11, he died.

Summary

Critics have found many defects in Gershwin's music. His songs have been called pleasing but too much alike, and he wrote dozens of tunes which have not lasted. His serious works have been criticized for repeating rather than developing melodies and motifs and for having sections separated by abrupt pauses. His most famous motif, the clarinet glissando which opens *Rhapsody in Blue*, was improvised by Ross Gorman, Paul Whiteman's clarinetist, as a joke. Gershwin has had little influence on other composers, although *Rhapsody in Blue* may have encouraged other composers to incorporate popular elements into serious music. His weaknesses, however, have been overshadowed by the beauty of his melodies.

Gershwin had surprisingly little technical knowledge of music. His composing style was primarily improvisational: He went to the piano confident that something would happen. The composer explained that he began *Rhapsody in Blue* with "No set plan . . . in my mind—no structure to which my music would conform." Gershwin made up for a lack of formal understanding of harmony with an exceptionally fine harmonic sense. He could duplicate immediately almost any chordal combination he heard. Even improvising while playing his own music, Gershwin rarely harmonized a tune the same way twice.

Together with Ira, Gershwin elevated the art of Broadway musical-comedy material. Refusing to be satisfied emulating the styles of composers he admired such as Jerome Kern and Irving Berlin, Gershwin created a distinctively original popular sound which perfectly captured his time and place and has continued to be representative of the American musical spirit throughout the world. His music in particular evokes the flashiest elements of that period F. Scott Fitzgerald called the Jazz Age: speakeasies, flappers, sporty roadsters, raccoon coats, the Charleston, hedonism, iconoclasm, and a seemingly endless optimism.

Gershwin's art is enhanced by the wit and charm of his brother's lyrics, with their emphasis on repetition, alliteration, and metaphor. Ira Gershwin's lyrics are usually equal to his brother's music in quality and sometimes even superior. As much as for *Rhapsody in Blue* and *Porgy and Bess*, Gershwin's genius is epitomized by the songs he wrote with his brother. The best of these include "But Not for Me," "Embraceable You," "A Foggy Day," "I Got Rhythm," "It Ain't Necessarily So," "Let's Call the Whole Thing Off," "Nice Work If You Can Get It," "'S Wonderful," "Someone to Watch Over Me," "Summertime," and "They Can't Take That Away from Me." It is more appropriate than ironic that the last song Gershwin wrote is "Love Is Here to Stay."

Bibliography

Armitage, Merle. *George Gershwin: Man and Legend*. New York: Duell, Sloan and Pearce, 1958. Reminiscences of Gershwin's last years by the manager of his final concerts. Contains considerable information about *Porgy and Bess*.

_____, ed. *George Gershwin*. New York: Longmans, Green and Co., 1938. Collection of tributes to the composer by such friends as DuBose Heyward, Jerome Kern, Rouben Mamoulian, and Paul Whiteman. Includes Ira Gershwin's account of his brother's life.

Ewen, David. *George Gershwin: His Journey to Greatness*. Englewood Cliffs, N.J.: Prentice-Hall, 1970. The writer's third biography of Gershwin emphasizes the facts of his life and is a primary source of much information. Has been criticized for some inaccuracies.

Gershwin, Ira. *Lyrics on Several Occasions*. New York: Alfred A. Knopf, 1959. The songwriter presents a selection of one hundred of his lyrics with witty, informative comments about their creation.

Goldberg, Isaac. *George Gershwin: A Study in American Music*. New York: Simon and Schuster, 1931. The earliest study of the composer explores his relationship to the development of jazz. Devotes equal attention to Gershwin's work and personality. Supplemented by Edith Garson in 1958.

Jablonski, Edward, and Lawrence D. Stewart. *The Gershwin Years*. Garden City, N.Y.: Doubleday and Co., 1973. A pictorial biography of both Gershwins based on Ira's archives.

Kimball, Robert, and Alfred Simon. *The Gershwins*. New York: Atheneum Publishers, 1972. A scrapbook biography of the brothers with many lyrics, photographs, and reminiscences by their friends, relatives, and admirers.

Levant, Oscar. *A Smattering of Ignorance*. Garden City, N.Y.: Doubleday, Doran and Co., 1940. The composer-pianist-actor-wit's first autobiography includes a lengthy, humorous view of Gershwin as seen by one of his closest friends.

Schwartz, Charles. *Gershwin: His Life and Music*. Indianapolis: Bobbs-Merrill Co., 1973. Perhaps the most complete and objective of the numerous biographies of the composer. Contains the most information about Gershwin the man.

Smith, Cecil M. *Musical Comedy in America*. New York: Theatre Arts Books, 1950. A very complete history of Broadway musicals. Places Gershwin in the context of his fellow composers.

Michael Adams

ARNOLD GESELL

Born: June 21, 1880; Alma, Wisconsin
Died: May 29, 1961; New Haven, Connecticut
Area of Achievement: Child development
Contribution: Gesell was a pioneer in the study of the physical and mental development of children and the author of a series of popular books that influenced both psychologists and parents for more than thirty years.

Early Life

Arnold Lucius Gesell was born in Alma, a small village on the Wisconsin bank of the Mississippi River; he was the eldest of five children. His mother was an elementary schoolteacher, and both parents encouraged his intellectual curiosity. In an autobiographical sketch written when he was in his seventies, Gesell recalled that his childhood was filled with pleasures "accentuated by the everchanging, yet enduring river." Roustabouts and riverboat crews gave Alma a diversity lacking even in many larger towns. Violence, alcoholism, and crime were not unknown in Alma, and Gesell felt that his childhood experiences sensitized him, thus preparing him for his later career.

Gesell was a precocious student, who was graduated from high school at age sixteen. For his commencement exercises, Gesell ignited a tubeful of hydrogen, startling the audience. He also made a large electromagnet with the help of the village blacksmith and demonstrated its power by attaching a flatiron and hanging suspended from its handle. For the next three years, he attended the teachers college at Stevens Point, Wisconsin, where he studied, played football, edited the student newspaper, and participated in oratorical contests. Upon graduation, he taught American history, ancient history, German, accounting, and commercial geography in the Stevens Point high school.

After two years of teaching, he entered the University of Wisconsin at Madison, where he studied history under Frederick Jackson Turner and wrote a thesis titled "A Comparative Study of Higher Education in Ohio and Wisconsin." Gesell then spent a year as principal of a high school in Chippewa Falls, Wisconsin.

In 1904, he received a scholarship to Clark University in Worcester, Massachusetts, and earned a Ph.D. in psychology in 1906. At Clark, he studied under a number of important scholars in the new fields of psychology, psychiatry, and anthropology, including the founder of the field of child development in the United States, G. Stanley Hall. Gesell's doctoral dissertation was on the manifestations of jealousy in animals and in man at ascending age periods, beginning with infancy. In the months following his graduation from Clark, Gesell worked as a counselor in a boys' camp, as an elementary schoolteacher and settlement worker at East Side House in New York City, and as an instructor in psychology at the State Normal School in Plattesville, Wisconsin. An invitation from Lewis M. Terman, an innovator in intelligence testing, took him to a teaching position at Los Angeles State College, where he met and married a colleague, Beatrice Chandler, in 1909. With his wife's encouragement, Gesell returned to Wisconsin and began to study medicine, anatomy, and histology. In 1911, he was appointed assistant professor of education at Yale University, where he completed his M.D. degree in 1915.

Life's Work

Even before he completed his medical degree, Gesell helped to organize the Yale Clinic of Child Development. The clinic provided laboratories, playrooms, and offices where Gesell, his colleagues, and graduate students carried out their studies. Gesell also served as school psychologist for the State Board of Education in Connecticut and as a member of the governor's Commission on Child Welfare in 1919. These activities on behalf of Progressive reform led to the establishment of a Division for Educationally Exceptional Children under the State Board of Education.

Although Gesell never lost interest in handicapped and exceptional children, it is for his studies of normal children that he is best known. As part of his teaching technique, Gesell invited mothers to bring their infants into the classroom for observation and testing. Infants of different ages were given objects and their responses noted. Gesell also used photographs to illustrate his studies. In 1924, he began to use motion pictures to record infant and child behavior in the clinic. In 1930, a grant from the Laura Spelman Rockefeller Memorial allowed him to build a homelike studio where babies' daily activities—sleeping, walking, feeding, bathing, playing, body motions—and their social behavior were filmed. Over the years, a photographic research library of more than 300,000 feet of thirty-five millimeter and sixteen millimeter film was established.

As interest in child development grew throughout the United States, Gesell and the Yale Clinic added a nursery school that made it possible for the staff to follow children from infancy through adolescence to adulthood. These studies were the basis of Gesell's best-known and most important work. In 1934, he published *Infant Behavior: Its Genesis and Growth* with coauthors Helen Thompson and Catherine S. Amatruda. Five years later, he and the same collaborators joined Burton M. Castner in writing a work in two volumes entitled *Biographies of Child Development: The Mental Growth Careers of Eighty-four Infants and Children*. The title is indicative of Gesell's approach. Focusing on the life histories of the children, Gesell discussed the differences in physical and mental development among normal, superior, atypical, and premature infants.

In his conclusions, Gesell stressed that the growth characteristics of children are determined primarily by hereditary and constitutional factors, but that these factors do not operate independently of postnatal environmental influences. Heredity determines the direction and scope of the environmental influences. Every individual, Gesell argued, has a distinctive complex of growth, but each infant goes through fundamental sequences. Developmental norms are useful for comparison and diagnosis, but not as a unit of absolute measurement. Because of the rapidity of behavior growth, norms change at frequent age intervals.

As Gesell refined these concepts in his later work, he produced books that were popular because they both reassured parents and challenged them to stimulate their children's development. *Infant and Child in the Culture of Today*, written with Frances L. Ilg, went through seventeen editions in the United States between 1943 and 1974. Originally published during World War II, the message of the book is affirmative and optimistic: The family is the basis of a democratic culture, a culture that respects individual freedom. This book, like several of Gesell's works, was translated into dozens of languages. In 1946, Gesell and Ilg published *The Child from Five to Ten*, a book that provided parents with further norms for their growing children and recommended books, records, and games to stimulate their mental and physical growth. In the aftermath of the war, Gesell asserted that the intrinsic goodness of children offered the best hope for the perfectibility of mankind. In 1956, he, Ilg, and Louise B. Ames concluded their child development studies with *Youth: The Years from Ten to Sixteen*.

In addition to his work on normal children, Gesell wrote on Kamala, a child raised by wolves in India; on twins; and on the development of vision in children. In 1948, he retired from Yale University but continued to work in his field, first at Harvard, then again at Yale. He died in 1961, leaving a permanent legacy of studies that show the importance of prenatal and infant care.

Summary

Gesell began his work on infants and children during a period of reform directed at protecting children and their families. The American Pediatric Society was founded in 1889, Judge Ben Lindsey began working with juveniles in the courts in Denver in 1894, John Dewey founded an experimental school at the University of Chicago in 1896, the National Playground Association was created in 1906, and the Boy Scouts and Campfire Girls were established in the United States in 1910. Gesell was typical of his time in that he believed strongly that every child had a right to the opportunity to live up to his or her hereditary potential. Repeatedly, he expressed the belief that the science of human behavior and individuality can flourish only in a democracy.

Gesell's faith in human potential was tempered, however, by an equally firm belief in the role of biology in setting limits on human development. His concern for the health of the body ran counter to the prevailing emphasis in American child psychology on psychoanalysis, learning, conditioning, and cultural environment. It is ironic that the scholar who tried to synthesize biological and psychological definitions of man should be remembered only as a forefather of child behavior. Gesell was also a great humanist, who wrote about children with deep understanding and compassion based on memories of his own childhood. Living through a time when thinking men and women had to combine science and religion in their philosophic outlook, Gesell could conclude his 1949 edition of *Child Development* (a textbook combining *Infant and Child in the Culture of Today* and *The Child from Five to Ten*) with the heartfelt observation: "One of the great tasks of postwar education is to impart the life sciences and the physical sciences in a manner which will preserve both rational and spiritual values."

Bibliography
Boring, Edwin G., et al., eds. *History of Psychology in Autobiography*. Worcester, Mass.: Clark University Press, 1952. A brief autobiography that begins with Gesell's acknowledgment of Herman Melville's metaphor of the mat maker's loom—the shuttle, the warp, and the woof being like chance, necessity, and free will in the creation of an individual career. Gesell attributes much of his life to the interplay of these forces.
Cravens, Hamilton. "Child-saving in the Age of Professionalism, 1915-1930." In *American Childhood: A Research Guide and Historical Handbook*, edited by Joseph M. Hawes and N. Ray Hiner, 415-488. Westport, Conn.: Greenwood Press, 1985. An analysis and evaluation of Gesell and some of his important contemporaries, such as Henry Herbert Goddard, Lawrence K. Frank, and John Dewey.
Gesell, Arnold. *First Five Years of Life*. New York: Harper and Brothers, Publishers, 1940. Written with H. M. Halverson, Helen Thompson, Frances Ilg, B. M. Castner, Louise Ames, and Catherine Amatrude, this work refines the earlier studies of infants and young children.
Gesell, Arnold, Catherine S. Amatrude, Burton M. Castner, and Helen Thompson. *Biographies of Child Development: The Mental Growth Careers of Eighty-four Infants and Children*. New York: Paul B. Hoeber, 1939. In part 1, by Gesell, the lives of the children are described from about 1928 to 1938.
Gesell, Arnold, and Frances L. Ilg. *The Child from Five to Ten*. New York: Harper and Brothers, Publishers, 1946. Developmental characteristics of older children with chapters on hygiene, sex, play, and school life.
_____. *Infant and Child in the Culture of Today*. New York: Harper and Brothers, Publishers, 1943. Popular discussion of the role of the family in a democratic society, the individuality of growth patterns in children, and the developmental sequence from birth to five. Illustrations of the

Yale Guidance Nursery, lists of toys and play materials, and recommended books and music for children.

Gesell, Arnold, Frances L. Ilg, and Louise Bates Ames. *Youth: The Years from Ten to Sixteen*. New York: Harper and Brothers, Publishers, 1956. Continuation of the earlier volumes based on longitudinal studies of children in the Yale Clinic.

Lazerson, Marvin, and W. Norton Grubb. *Broken Promises: How Americans Fail Their Children*. New York: Basic Books, 1982. Good review of local, state, and federal policies and programs for children.

Bernard Mergen

JAMES GIBBONS

Born: July 23, 1834; Baltimore, Maryland
Died: March 24, 1921; Baltimore, Maryland
Area of Achievement: Religion
Contribution: As the most influential American archbishop of the late nineteenth century, Gibbons helped established Catholicism as an important and vital religion in modern American society.

Early Life

James Gibbons was born July 23, 1834, in Baltimore, Maryland, the eldest son in a family of five children. His parents, Thomas Gibbons and Bridget (Walsh) Gibbons, were Irish immigrants. When James was three, his family returned to Ireland because of his father's poor health. They resettled in New Orleans in 1853, six years after his father's death.

Upon his return to the United States, Gibbons worked as a clerk in a grocery store for two years. In 1855, he entered Saint Charles College, Ellicott City, Maryland. He moved on to Saint Mary's Seminary in his native Baltimore in 1857 and was ordained a priest of the Roman Catholic Church on June 30, 1861.

Throughout the Civil War, Gibbons pastored various congregations in the Chesapeake Bay area. In addition, he served as a volunteer chaplain at Forts McHenry and Marshall. His dedicated service earned for him much public admiration, and he was one of only three Catholic priests invited to pay their respects when the body of the assassinated President Abraham Lincoln passed through Baltimore.

Following the war, Gibbons' influence in the Catholic Church rapidly increased. In 1865, he was appointed secretary to the archbishop of Baltimore. A year later, he became assistant chancellor for that archdiocese. Gibbons was consecrated as bishop of North Carolina in 1868 and in the following year attended the Vatican I Council in Rome as the youngest bishop among the more than seven hundred in attendance. In 1872, Gibbons assumed the duties of the vacant Richmond see in addition to retaining his responsibilities in North Carolina. Despite the extraordinary demands on his time, he wrote his best-known work, *The Faith of Our Fathers* (1877), in 1876. This extremely popular book, written for the general public, presented an explanation and defense of Catholicism.

Photographs of Gibbons reveal an individual of slight but well-defined physical features, with a calm and peaceful demeanor. His unassuming appearance did not indicate the acumen and depth of the spiritual resources that enabled him to provide decisive leadership to the Catholic Church in America during the most volatile period in its history.

Life's Work

In 1877, at the age of forty-three, Gibbons became the ninth archbishop of Baltimore—a position he would hold until his death in 1921. The oldest archdiocese in the United States, it was also the most prestigious. Such a position made Gibbons the unofficial leader of American Catholics.

Gibbons was a highly effective administrator and spiritual leader, although he did not gain national attention until he presided over the Third Plenary Council in Baltimore in 1884. The council brought together American bishops and archbishops to enact legislation on doctrine, ecclesiastical governance, and parochial education. A major accomplishment of the council was the establishment of Catholic University in Washington, D.C. There, Gibbons provided distinguished leadership as both its first chancellor and its principal advocate.

Gibbons' work at the Third Plenary Council was highly acclaimed. He had diplomatically avoided many controversial social issues that would bitterly divide conservative and liberal Catholics throughout the remainder of the nineteenth century. His efforts prompted Pope Leo XIII to make Gibbons a cardinal in 1886. With this rapid rise to national prominence, Gibbons was thrust into the role of resolving a number of social issues. With the aid of his principal allies, Archbishop John Ireland and Bishop John J. Keane, Gibbons faced the pressing problems of organized labor and immigration.

Because of the deplorable working conditions of late nineteenth century America—for example, twelve-hour workdays and inadequate wages—the Knights of Labor was formed in 1869 to establish various labor unions. Its goals were primarily to limit working hours, improve working conditions, and increase wages. Since labor organizers were routinely fired by their employers, however, the membership and activities of the Knights of Labor became secretive. The pope had declared that membership in an organization requiring secret oaths and activities was incompatible with the Catholic faith. For this reason, as well as fear of Socialist tendencies, conservative Catholic leaders opposed the Knights of Labor. In 1884, Cardinal Elzéar Taschereau of Quebec obtained a ruling from the Vatican forbidding Catholics to belong to the labor organization. Conservatives argued that the ruling included the United States as well.

Gibbons fought for the laborers. He maintained that the prohibition applied only to Quebec and that it would be wrong for the Catholic Church to oppose the American labor movement. Although Gibbons and his liberal allies admired the achievements of capitalism, they believed that adequate wages, improved working conditions, and shorter working hours were demanded by the principles of Christian charity and justice. Furthermore, Gibbons warned that condemnation of the Knights of Labor would create an unnecessary conflict of conscience for Catholic laborers. A Catholic would be forced to choose between a union and the Church. Since the goals of the labor movement were just, Gibbons argued, opposition was uncalled for.

Gibbons backed a series of strikes in 1886 and a year later presented the pope with a lengthy document defending the Knights of Labor. In 1888, the Vatican removed its ban on the organization. This reversal represented a major victory for Gibbons and set a precedent for strong Catholic support of labor reform in the following years.

The great wave of immigration in the nineteenth century created a second pressing issue for Gibbons. During this time, the Catholic population in the United States increased from three million in 1860 to more than twelve million by 1895. This rapid growth inspired strong anti-Catholic sentiments within American society, as seen in the formation of such organizations as the Know-Nothing Party (1854) and the American Protective Association (1887). These groups claimed that Catholic teachings opposed democracy and the separation of Church and State, and they feared that priests would instruct their parishioners on how to vote based on orders from the Vatican. American society, they declared, was being attacked from an outside religious force.

Although such claims bore minimal influence on public opinion, they did create problems concerning how Catholics viewed their participation in American life. These attacks emphasized the ethnic differences that already existed among Catholics. For example, German Catholics tended to be rural, Midwestern, and conservative, whereas Irish Catholics tended to be urban, Eastern, and liberal. In response to these tensions, conservative Catholics began viewing American society as largely Protestant and hostile. They maintained that Catholics should not accommodate themselves to the larger culture but should preserve their religious and ethnic identity through traditional beliefs and customs.

Gibbons fought both the anti-Catholic claims and the conservative position. He countered that Catholicism was not opposed to democracy and could flourish in a nation where Church and State were legally separated. He believed that Catholics could, and must, simultaneously be good citizens and faithful members of the Church. As a liberal, he argued that Catholics must adapt to the American situation rather than preserve their traditional beliefs and ethnic customs. Catholics should be assimilated into American society by actively participating in its social, political, and educational institutions.

The liberal position that Gibbons advocated was popularly titled "Americanism." It was loudly condemned as heretical by its opponents and acclaimed as progressive by its supporters. The debate, however, was not decisive, since in 1895 Pope Leo XIII both praised the liberty of the Catholic Church in the United States and questioned whether the separation of Church and State was the most desirable situation. Although Gibbons had not won a clear victory, he clearly set the pattern for full Catholic participation in an increasingly pluralistic American society.

Summary

The lengthy career of this distinguished religious leader reflected the changing, often turbulent, character of American society at the close of the nineteenth century and beginning of the twentieth century. Gibbons' concern over labor and immigration reflected the problems of a nation that was simultaneously becoming prosperous and ethnically diverse. He brought a strong religious and moral commitment to the pressing political, economic, and social issues of his day.

Gibbons' range of interests was quite broad. He was routinely consulted on Church-State issues and provided advice to a variety of political leaders. Often invited to preach in Protestant churches, he worked toward improving relations between different religions and participated in the World Parliament of Religions in Chicago in 1893. The patriotism of Gibbons was unparalleled as he helped establish the National Catholic War Council at the United States' entry into World War I in 1917. His tireless will helped not only Catholics but all Americans as well to define the national character at a crucial time in history.

Bibliography

Browne, Henry J. *The Catholic Church and the Knights of Labor*. Washington, D.C.: Catholic University of America Press, 1949. Reprint. New York: Arno Press, 1976. An in-depth examination of the Knights of Labor controversy within the Catholic Church. Particular attention is directed toward the role Gibbons played in changing his Church's position on the labor organization.

Cross, Robert D. *The Emergence of Liberal Catholicism in America*. Cambridge, Mass.: Harvard University Press, 1958. A comprehensive overview of the various controversies between conservative and liberal Catholics in late nineteenth and early twentieth century America.

Dolan, Jay P. *The Immigrant Church*. Baltimore, Md.: Johns Hopkins University Press, 1977. Reprint. Notre Dame, Ind.: University of Notre Dame Press, 1983. Although this book concentrates on issues that divided German and Irish Catholics living in New York City in the mid-nineteenth century, it provides a good framework for understanding the various ethnic and immigrant issues that Gibbons and the Church faced.

Ellis, John Tracy. *American Catholicism*. Chicago: University of Chicago Press, 1956. An excellent concise introduction to the history of Catholicism in the United States.

Gibbons, James Cardinal. *A Retrospect of Fifty Years*. Baltimore, Md.: John Murphy Co., 1916. Reprint. New York: Arno Press, 1972. An autobiographical recounting of the major events that shaped the author's career.

McAvoy, Thomas T. *The Great Crisis in American Catholic History, 1895-1900*. Chicago: Henry Regnery Co., 1957. An extensive and excellent inquiry into the Americanism controversy.

_____, ed. *Roman Catholicism and the American Way of Life*. Notre Dame, Ind.: University of Notre Dame Press, 1960. A series of essays written by both Catholics and Protestants that review and evaluate the role of Catholicism in early twentieth century American society.

Marty, Martin E. *Pilgrims in Their Own Land*. Boston: Little, Brown and Co., 1984. Reviews the history of various religions in the United States. The chapter "Adapting to America" provides a concise and helpful framework for understanding the immigration and labor issues of the late nineteenth century.

Brent Waters

JOSIAH WILLARD GIBBS

Born: February 11, 1839; New Haven, Connecticut
Died: April 28, 1903; New Haven, Connecticut
Areas of Achievement: Physical chemistry and theoretical physics
Contribution: Gibbs established the theoretical basis for modern physical
chemistry by quantifying the second law of thermodynamics and developing heterogeneous thermodynamics. This and other work earned for him
recognition as the greatest American scientist of the nineteenth century.

Early Life

Josiah Willard Gibbs, later known usually as J. Willard Gibbs (to distinguish him from his father, who bore the same name), was the fourth child—
the only son among five children—of J. W. Gibbs, professor of sacred literature at Yale College Theological Seminary, and Mary Anna Van Cleve
Gibbs. Born in New Haven, Connecticut, Gibbs would live all of his life in
that city, leaving only to take one trip abroad, dying in the very house in
which he had grown up.

Well educated in private schools, Gibbs was graduated from Yale College
in 1858, receiving prizes in Latin and mathematics. In 1863, he took his
Ph.D. in engineering at Yale—one of the first such degrees in the United
States; his dissertation was entitled *On the Form of the Teeth of Wheels in
Spur Gearing.* For the next three years he tutored at Yale in Latin and natural philosophy, working on several practical inventions and obtaining a patent
for one of them, an improved railway brake. The foregoing points to a not
inconsiderable practical element in the chiefly theoretical scientist that Gibbs
would become.

In 1866, Gibbs embarked on a journey to Europe, where he attended lectures by the best-known mathematicians and physicists of that era, spending
a year each at the Universities of Paris, Berlin, and Heidelberg. What he
learned at these schools would form the basis for his later theoretical work.
His parents having died, and two of his sisters as well, he traveled with his
remaining sisters, Anna and Julia, the latter returning home early to marry
Addison Van Name, later Librarian of Connecticut Academy, in 1867.

Upon his return to New Haven in 1869, Gibbs began work at once on his
great theoretical undertaking, which he would not complete until 1878. He
lived in the Van Name household, as did his sister Anna; neither he nor she
was ever married. In 1871, he was appointed professor of mathematical physics at Yale—the first such chair in the United States—but without salary. He
was obliged to live for nine years on his not very considerable inherited income. When The Johns Hopkins University, aware of the significance of his
work, offered him a position at a good salary, Yale decided to offer Gibbs
two-thirds of what Johns Hopkins would pay; it was enough for Gibbs.

In 1873, he published his first paper, "Graphical Methods in the Thermodynamics of Fluids," which clarified the concept of entropy, introduced in 1850 by Rudolf Clausius. The genius of this insight was immediately recognized by James Clerk Maxwell in England, to whom Gibbs had sent a copy of the paper. The work was published, however, in a relatively obscure journal, *The Transactions of the Connecticut Academy of Arts and Sciences*, where almost all of Gibbs's subsequent writings would appear. In addition, his style was so terse, austere, and condensed as to be unreadable to all but a few readers who were already well acquainted with his underlying assumptions. Consequently, for most of his life Gibbs would remain largely unknown, especially in the United States, except among a small circle of his scientific colleagues.

This undeserved obscurity never seemed to trouble Gibbs. By all accounts, he was a genuinely unassuming and unpretentious man, tolerant, kind, approachable, and seemingly unconscious of his intellectual eminence. He was by no means gregarious and probably more than a little aloof; he had few really close friends, though he kept up a large correspondence. He attended church regularly. Physically, he was of slight build and owed a certain frailty in health to a severe case of scarlet fever in childhood. Yet he was strong enough to ride and was known as a good horseman. Photographs of him reveal a handsome but somewhat stern man with a well-trimmed, short beard. The photographic image leaves an apt impression of what he was in life: a gentleman, a professor, and a scientist of unimpeachable integrity.

Life's Work

Gibbs published yet another paper in 1873, "A Method of Geometrical Representation of the Thermodynamic Properties of Substances by Means of Surfaces." In 1876, the first 140 pages of his major work appeared (again in *Transactions*), the final 180 pages finally being published by that journal in 1878; both parts bore the title, "On the Equilibrium of Heterogeneous Substances." This work, of the utmost importance to science, never appeared in book form in English in Gibbs's lifetime. Its significance was appreciated by Maxwell, who incorporated some of its findings into his own books, but he unfortunately died in 1879. Continental Europeans perceived the general importance of Gibbs's discoveries, but had real difficulty reading Gibbs's text. (Gibbs himself rejected all suggestions that he rewrite his treatise as a readable book.) Hermann Helmholtz and Max Planck both duplicated some of Gibbs's work, simply because they did not know of it. A German translation of it, by the great scientist Wilhelm Ostwald, appeared only in 1892. French translations of various sections of the treatise were published in 1899 and 1903. Meanwhile, scientists came to perceive—in the words of physics professor Paul Epstein—that a "young investigator, having discovered an entirely new branch of science, gave in a single contribution an exhaustive treatment of it which foreshadowed the development of theoretical chemistry for a quarter of a century." Gibbs's was thus an achievement almost unparalleled in the history of science. Ostwald predicted that the result of Gibbs's work would determine the form and content of chemistry for a century to come—and he was right. A French scientist compared Gibbs, in his importance to chemistry, with Antoine Lavoisier. It should be mentioned that the editors of *The Transactions of the Connecticut Academy of Arts and Sciences* published Gibbs's work on faith alone as they were not able to understand it completely; they obtained the money for publishing the long treatise through private subscription.

Of special importance in Gibbs's work is its sophisticated mathematics. It is therefore not possible to summarize his discoveries in a brief article. There are two features, however, that must be noted. First, Gibbs succeeded in precisely formulating the second law of thermodynamics, which states that the spontaneous flow of heat from hot to cold bodies is reversible only with the expenditure of mechanical or other nonthermal energy. Consequently, entropy (S), equal to heat (Q) divided by temperature change (T), must continually be increasing. Prior to Gibbs, thermodynamics simply did not exist as a science.

Second, Gibbs derived from his more complex heterogeneous thermodynamics the "phase rule," which shows the relationship between the degrees of freedom (F) of a thermodynamic system and the number of components (C) and the number of phases (P), so that $F = C + 2 - P$. He showed how these relationships could be expressed graphically, in three dimensions. Often phase-rule diagrams proved to be the only practical key to the solution of hitherto insoluble problems concerning the mixing of components so that they would remain in equilibrium and not separate out and destroy the mixture. The phase rule helped make it possible to calculate in advance the temperature, pressure, and concentration required for stability—thus eliminating months and possibly years of tedious trial-and-error experiments. This would have important application in industry as well as in the laboratory.

Interestingly, after Gibbs's one major treatise on thermodynamics, he never wrote another important paper on the subject. He had said the last word, and he knew it. He did not, however, remain idle. Between 1883 and 1889, he published five papers on the electromagnetic theory of light. This work, too, was well received.

Meanwhile, he had begun to receive a certain amount of more or less perfunctory recognition at home: He was elected to the National Academy of Sciences in 1879 and to the American Academy of Arts and Sciences in 1880; in 1880 he received the Rumford Medal from the latter; in 1885 he was elected a vice president of the American Association for the Advancement of Science.

In the period between 1889 and 1902, Gibbs lectured on the subject of statistical mechanics but published almost nothing on the topic except for a brief abstract. This would be his major work during the final portion of his life; it would require about the same gestation period as did his investigation of thermodynamics. Simultaneously, however, he was lecturing and publishing papers on vector analysis and multiple algebra; the theory of dyadics which appeared in these works is regarded as his most important published contribution to pure mathematics. A book based on his lectures, *Gibbs' Vector Analysis*, was edited and published by a student, E. B. Wilson, in 1901.

That year, Gibbs was awarded the Copley Medal by the Royal Society of London for being the first to apply the second law of thermodynamics to the exhaustive discussion of the relation between chemical, electrical, and thermal energy and the capacity for external work. This was the highest honor for scientists prior to the founding of the Nobel Prize.

In 1902, Gibbs's final important work was published under the title *Elementary Principles in Statistical Mechanics Developed with Special Reference to the Rational Foundation of Thermodynamics*. In this brilliant study, Gibbs was as far ahead of his time as he had been with his first major treatise. The later work has been called "a monument in the history of physics which marks the separation between the nineteenth and twentieth centuries." Gibbs's perception of the role played by probability in physical events made his last work a true precursor to quantum mechanics, which did not develop fully until the 1920's.

During the year following the publication of his final gift to the world, Gibbs suffered from several minor ailments. One of these resulted in a sudden and acute attack from an intestinal obstruction, which led to Gibbs's untimely death on April 28, 1903.

Summary

Gibbs's contribution to American society occurred chiefly after his death. It is regrettable that few Americans had the capacity to recognize his achievements while he was alive, but it seems pointless to try to fix the blame for this. On the one hand, he himself declined to make his papers more accessible by revising them for a wider readership. On the other, physical chemistry was only beginning to develop in the United States. Few professors of either chemistry or physics had the background that would have enabled them to understand Gibbs's work; there were no grand figures such as Rudolf Clausius, James Clerk Maxwell, William Thomson (Baron Kelvin), or Wilhelm Ostwald in America to welcome the new young genius personally.

In addition, the chemical industry in the United States was conservative in the matter of adopting new methods derived chiefly from theory, while at the same time it was caught up in the chaos of a greatly expanding industrialism. There was virtually no one available to examine the implications for the chemical industry of Gibbs's new phase rule. Gradually, however, as the industry turned more and more to synthesizing new compounds and developing metal alloys, there came a demand for precisely the sort of tool that Gibbs long before had provided. The phase rule had an early application in alloys of iron and carbon to produce different types of steel. Another application involved the industrial synthesis of ammonia from nitrogen and hydrogen, and of nitric acid from ammonia. While most of these applications were first worked out in Europe, American industry finally learned how to reap the benefits of bringing theory to bear on practical processes. It finally came to recognize what it owed to Gibbs.

The United States thus reaped the practical benefits of Gibbs's work; it also had the honor of claiming as its own one of the world's greatest theoretical scientists.

Bibliography

Bumstead, H. A. "Josiah Willard Gibbs." In *The Collected Works of J. Willard Gibbs*, edited by H. A. Bumstead. 2 vols. New Haven, Conn: Yale University Press, 1948. With portrait. Reprinted, with some additions, from the *American Journal of Science* 4 (September, 1903). Also in a previous edition of *The Collected Works*, edited by W. R. Longley and R. G. Van Name. New York: Longmans, Green and Co., 1928. Written by a former student who knew Gibbs well, this basic source for all other biographies includes a useful list of Gibbs's publications in chronological order.

Crowther, J. G. "Josiah Willard Gibbs." In *Famous American Men of Science*, edited by J. G. Crowther, 227-297. Freeport, N.Y.: Books for Libraries Press, 1969. Reprinted with minor changes from first edition. New York: W. W. Norton, 1937. Two portraits, brief bibliography. Excellent psychological speculation about Gibbs's family and his social and academic life.

Jaffe, Bernard. "J. Willard Gibbs (1839-1903): America in the New World of Chemistry." In *Men of Science in America: The Role of Science in the Growth of Our Country*. New York: Simon and Schuster, 1944. Excellent discussion of American reception (or lack of it) of Gibbs, and the consequences for American society. Good explanation of phase rule and its application in industry.

Kraus, Charles A. "Josiah Willard Gibbs." In *Great Chemists*, edited by Eduard Farber, 783-803. New York: Interscience Publishers, 1961. Portrait. Good discussion of experimental work and of phase rule.

Rukeyser, Muriel. *Willard Gibbs*. Garden City, N.Y.: Doubleday, Doran, and Co., 1942. Portrait. Long text, reads almost like a novel, but offers good background detail that places Gibbs squarely within the context of the American culture of his time.

Seeger, Raymond John. *J. Willard Gibbs: American Mathematical Physicist Par Excellence*. Elmsford, N.Y.: Pergamon Press, 1974. Places greatest emphasis on details of mathematics and science. Includes useful chronology of life and work with a short bibliography.

Wheeler, Lynde Phelps. *Josiah Willard Gibbs: The History of a Great Mind.* Rev. ed. New Haven, Conn.: Yale University Press, 1962. The authorized biography. Same as revised edition of 1952 except for the addition of a forward by A. Whitney Griswold; the two revised editions, unlike the first edition of 1951, contain an appendix summarizing newly discovered family correspondence. Wheeler was a student of Gibbs in the 1890's, his account is comprehensive but rather genteel. Includes several portraits, a genealogical chart, a catalog of Gibbs's scientific correspondence, and an excellent bibliography of articles and books about Gibbs. Also includes text of Gibbs's first paper.

Donald M. Fiene

ROBERT H. GODDARD

Born: October 5, 1882; Worcester, Massachusetts
Died: August 10, 1945; Baltimore, Maryland
Area of Achievement: Rocketry
Contribution: As the deviser of the first successful liquid-fuel rocket and as a tireless explorer of the theoretical and practical problems of rocketry decades before the subject gained substantial support in the United States, Goddard stands as the great American pioneer of space travel.

Early Life

Robert Hutchings Goddard was born on October 5, 1882, in the central Massachusetts industrial city of Worcester. Nahum Goddard, then a bookkeeper for a manufacturer of machine knives, and his wife, the former Fannie Louise Hoyt, moved to Roxbury, Massachusetts, when Robert was only an infant but continued to spend considerable time at the family homestead until fifteen years later, when Mrs. Goddard's health dictated their return to Worcester. Various bronchial ailments plagued their only son, who, because of frequent absences from school, was not graduated from high school until his twenty-second year.

Like many boys of his time, Goddard devoured such prototypes of science fiction as Jules Verne's *From the Earth to the Moon* (1865) and H. G. Wells's *The War of the Worlds* (1898). Goddard dated the discovery of his vocation, however, from an experience which, like the story often told of George Washington, involved a cherry tree—but a story whose authenticity is not in doubt. On October 19, 1899, shortly after his seventeenth birthday, he climbed a cherry tree on the family property and, while in its branches, imagined a spaceship that might travel to Mars. He later claimed that when he descended from the tree, he was "a different boy," and for the remainder of his life he would solemnly celebrate the date as "Anniversary Day." Whenever possible, he visited the tree on October 19, as long as it stood.

Single-minded in his dedication to the idea of space flight, he entered the local engineering college, Worcester Polytechnic Institute, in 1904. Although he pondered space travel in his spare time, the nature of his collegiate work suggested to his physics professor the likelihood of a career in radio engineering. Upon graduation in 1908, he continued his study of physics at Clark University, also in Worcester; Clark had been founded as a graduate school and emphasized the natural and social sciences. Goddard taught physics briefly at Worcester Polytechnic Institute, but, upon receipt of his Ph.D. in physics in 1911, he accepted a research fellowship at Princeton University, realizing that his aptitude for research exceeded that for teaching.

In March of 1913, he learned that he had contracted his mother's illness, tuberculosis, and physicians gave him little chance to survive. He spent a year at home recuperating, and by 1914, was well enough to conduct a series of experiments with tiny rockets propelled by a smokeless powder of his own devising. The struggle with disease, however, had exacted its toll, leaving him nearly bald in his early thirties. He remained thin and frail throughout his life, and he developed a stoop while relatively young. The young scientist was of average height, his two most prominent facial characteristics being a trim brown mustache and expressive brown eyes under dark brows.

Rejecting offers from Princeton and Columbia, which he feared might not leave him sufficient time for research, he accepted a position as instructor in physics at Clark, an association which would last the remainder of his life.

Life's Work

The two world wars bounded, and greatly influenced, Goddard's working life. Of the 214 patents issued to him, the first two came in the summer of 1914, as World War I was beginning. One, for a cartridge-feeding mechanism, turned out to be impractical in rocketry; the second, for a liquid rocket-fuel, presaged his greatest accomplishment, still more than a decade of hard work away from fruition. Whereas science fiction had fired his imagination early, Goddard invariably approached his investigations in a matter-of-fact way and never seems to have wasted time on romantic but scientifically dubious schemes for space travel. At his time, weaponry, not space flight, occupied the American military, and Goddard, aware that the Germans had pursued applications of the Wright brothers' great invention more quickly than had Americans, and anxious that they not take the lead in rocket development, wrote to the United States Navy about his experiments. Although he provoked some interest, President Woodrow Wilson's declaration of American neutrality discouraged research in military rockets.

Furthermore, despite his success at sending his tiny powder rockets nearly five hundred feet into the air over Worcester by 1915, Goddard had not yet developed a suitable liquid fuel. When his university salary proved inadequate to support his research, he obtained a five-thousand-dollar grant from the Smithsonian Institution, and by the fall of 1918, he had devised a rocket which was capable of being fired from a trench and of delivering a payload three-quarters of a mile away. In November, he demonstrated his rockets at the army's proving grounds at Aberdeen, Maryland. Impressed that these rockets outperformed existing trench mortar, the army agreed to appropriate money for production. A few days later, however, Germany surrendered. It would require another global conflict to revive high-level interest in Goddard's rockets.

Returning to his first love, the goal of space travel, Goddard, under the auspices of the Smithsonian, published in 1919 a treatise explaining how rockets might ascend to the moon. This work, *A Method of Reaching Extreme Altitudes*, brought him unwelcome publicity as an eccentric professor, and references to him in the popular press as "moon man" stung this serious investigator. He was fortunate in his academic affiliation, however, for Clark granted him leaves of absence when necessary, and his work proceeded steadily. Between 1920 and 1923, he conducted experiments at the navy ordnance facility at Indian Head, Maryland. Back in Worcester in 1923, he was appointed director of laboratories at Clark in addition to his professorship. Clark took time out, in 1924, to marry Esther Kisk, who proved a devoted helpmate; after his death his widow would spend years editing his voluminous papers.

On March 16, 1926, on a farm in nearby Auburn, Goddard achieved his greatest success. The ten-foot rocket he sent up that day traveled for only two and one-half seconds and flew only 184 feet. His sponsor at the Smithsonian, Dr. Charles G. Abbot, was not impressed, for Goddard had talked in terms of hundreds of miles, and this rocket had attained a maximum altitude of forty-one feet. In retrospect, however, this short flight looms as momentous as that of the Wright brothers' airplane twenty-three years earlier at Kitty Hawk, North Carolina. This first successful flight of a liquid-propellant rocket established the feasibility of the spectacular space ventures that Goddard did not live to see.

His experiments having outgrown New England pastures, Goddard received the assistance of Colonel Charles A. Lindbergh, whose 1927 transoceanic flight had earned for him international fame. In 1929, Lindbergh talked philanthropist Harry Guggenheim into granting Goddard fifty thousand dollars for research on a larger scale. This largess enabled Goddard to spend much of the following decade at Roswell, New Mexico, improving his rockets. Clark issued another monograph on his work to date in 1936, but not until after his death would his major publication, *Rocket Development: Liquid-Fuel Rocket Research* (1948), appear. Unlike Hermann Oberth, his younger German contemporary, who independently achieved results comparable to Goddard's, the Clark professor shunned publicity and avoided joint projects with other scientists. As a consequence, he spent the latter part of his career laboring in obscurity while Oberth's work led directly to the V-1 and V-2 rockets of World War II.

During the war, Goddard worked for the navy in Maryland but found the required teamwork uncongenial. As the war dragged on, declining health and the knowledge that German rocketry was outdistancing that of the United States seized Goddard, and the American government's decision to concentrate on atomic research left him in a military backwater. In May of 1945, a few weeks after Germany's surrender, a physician detected a growth in Goddard's throat. Despite two operations at the University of Maryland Hospital in Baltimore, Goddard continued to fail. On August 10, 1945, America's rocket pioneer died; his body was returned to Worcester and buried on August 14—the day of Japan's surrender.

Summary

Assessing Goddard's achievement later that year, *Science* magazine credited him with investigating virtually every principle vital to the theory and practice of jet propulsion and rocket guidance. Nevertheless, most Americans did not know him until the early 1960's, when the successes of the American space program provoked interest in its historical background, and publications describing Goddard's life and work began to appear.

When his story was told, it was often with an emphasis on the solitariness and obscurity of his endeavors. His biographers have tended to depict him as a lonely hero, obliged to endure at first scorn and later neglect. Historians of rocketry and space travel, however, have pointed out the extent to which he imposed his plight upon himself. Retiring by nature, Goddard appears to have been driven further inward by the facetious tone of early journalistic accounts of his research. He conducted his experiments in a secretive and possessive manner, sharing his discoveries with only a few trusted assistants. Although a true scientist, Goddard evinced an inventor's interest in protecting his work by patent much more often than a scientist's desire to share his discoveries with fellow scientists in scholarly monographs. Pursued by both professional and amateur societies in his field, he generally remained aloof. As a result, it is likely that he fell behind other researchers in the 1930's and 1940's.

One of Goddard's biographers has noted that his brown eyes could radiate warmth and friendliness at times and turn cold and austere at others. Many anecdotes testify to his congeniality when at ease and among friends, but he seems to have been a man who coveted and cherished his professional isolation. Whatever the explanation of his proprietary attitude toward his work, he was a true pioneer in rocketry. He made original discoveries in many aspects of his subject, producing innovative igniters and carburetors, pumps and turbines, gyroscopic stabilizers and landing controls, jet-driven propellers and variable-thrust engines. His ceaseless dedication and the thoroughness of his research and testing complemented his sheer brilliance. Robert H. Goddard's legacy, so little recognized at the time of his death, is now manifest in the space age.

Bibliography

Bainbridge, William Sims. *The Spaceflight Revolution: A Sociological Study.* Seattle: University of Washington Press, 1976. Useful for its systematized information about the personal characteristics of space pioneers and for its insights into how and why the movement succeeded, this study stops short of explaining the often puzzling pattern of Goddard's professional behavior.

Braun, Wernher von, and Frederick I. Ordway III. *History of Rocketry and Space Travel.* Rev. ed. New York: Thomas Y. Crowell, 1969. This well-illustrated volume gives careful consideration to Goddard's achievements in relation to those of earlier and later theorists and practitioners. Contains a five-page chronology of Goddard's rocket tests from 1915 to 1941.

Dewey, Anne Perkins. *Robert Goddard: Space Pioneer.* Boston: Little, Brown and Co., 1962. A short, popular, illustrated life. Based on diaries and interviews with the scientist's widow, this book will serve the purposes of those seeking an intimate portrait of Goddard at home.

Goddard, Robert H. *The Papers of Robert H. Goddard.* Edited by Esther C. Goddard and G. Edward Pendray. 3 vols. New York: McGraw-Hill Book Co., 1969. Meticulously assembled from thousands of manuscript pages, this work is a highly competent chronological account of Goddard's career in his own words. Indispensable to the serious student of Goddard's life and work.

Lehman, Milton. *This High Man: The Life of Robert H. Goddard.* New York: Farrar, Straus and Giroux, 1963. Easily the best-written and most thorough of Goddard biographies. Gives some attention to the scientific context in which Goddard worked. Does not interpret Goddard but supplies most of the important facts in a well-constructed and readable narrative. The standard life until someone plumbs the wellsprings of his character.

Stoiko, Michael. *Pioneers of Rocketry.* New York: Hawthorn Books, 1974. For readers wishing a profile of Goddard, this book offers the chance to compare his career with those of four other pioneers, including the Russian Konstantin Tsiolkovsky and the German Hermann Oberth.

Winter, Frank H. *Prelude to the Space Age: The Rocket Societies, 1924-1940.* Washington, D.C.: Smithsonian Institution Press, 1983. The best source for Goddard's relations, or lack of them, with others who shared his interests. Suggests that Goddard's work would have been less often misunderstood and misinterpreted had he cultivated such relationships.

Robert P. Ellis

EDWIN LAWRENCE GODKIN

Born: October 2, 1831; Moyne, Ireland
Died: May 21, 1902; Brixham, England
Area of Achievement: Journalism
Contribution: As editor of *The Nation* and, later, of the *Evening Post*, Godkin was one of the most influential voices in post–Civil War American politics.

Early Life

Edwin Lawrence Godkin was born in Moyne, Ireland, on October 2, 1831, to Sarah Lawrence and James Godkin. The elder Godkin was a Protestant clergyman, journalist, and political activist of some note, a prominent figure in the Irish independence movement.

Godkin attended a series of Irish and English schools and in 1846 entered Queens College in Belfast, Ireland. There, he was introduced to the works of the Utilitarian philosophers Jeremy Bentham and John Stuart Mill, whose political and economic theories did much to shape Godkin's own views. Particularly attractive to Godkin was the Utilitarians' belief in *laissez-faire*, private property rights, and economic law as the basis for sound government. The young Godkin was also captivated with the idea of American democracy, though this view was always tempered by a distinctly aristocratic streak in his thought.

Upon his graduation in 1851, Godkin moved to London, where after a brief flirtation with law study, he began his journalism career as subeditor of *The Workingmen's Friend*, an entertainment magazine published by John Cassell. Godkin's first book, *The History of Hungary and the Magyars: From the Earliest Times to the Close of the Late War*, was published in 1853.

Hired as a special correspondent in Turkey for London's *Daily News*, Godkin covered the Crimean War from 1853 to 1855. The young correspondent's dispatches from the Turkish front, sharply critical of perceived incompetence in the British and Turkish military leadership, exhibit the penchant for faultfinding and polemics that marks his later writings. After his return to Great Britain, Godkin spent two years lecturing on the war and contributing articles to the liberal Belfast newspaper *The Northern Whig*.

Life's Work

In October, 1856, at the age of twenty-five, Godkin sailed to America, settling in New York. One of Godkin's first acquaintances in the United States was Frederick Law Olmsted, the distinguished writer, landscape architect, and political activist. Olmsted's liberal political opinions were close to those of Godkin, and the two men began a long friendship. Inspired in part by Olmsted's writings on the American South, Godkin traveled through the region in the fall of 1856. Reporting his experience in the London *Daily News*, Godkin expressed his dislike of the South—which he found rude and backward—and his aversion to slavery on both moral and economic grounds.

Returning to New York, Godkin studied law for a time and began contributing reportage to *The New York Times* and the *Evening Post*. His pieces offered perceptive, sometimes witty and biting commentary on American political affairs, usually taking a position intermediate between conservatism and radicalism.

On July 29, 1859, Godkin married Frances Elizabeth Foote, a member of a prominent New England family that included the writer and ecclesiastic Henry Ward Beecher and the novelist Harriet Beecher Stowe. A son, Lawrence, was born to the Godkins in 1860. The family spent two years in Europe, from 1860 to 1862, during which Godkin did little writing. When the Godkins returned to the United States, they found a country in a great upheaval. The Civil War had broken out, and President Abraham Lincoln had issued the preliminary Emancipation Proclamation. Godkin sided with the Union cause, though he criticized Lincoln for military inactivity in the early years of the conflict. For the next several years, Godkin wrote for a number of American newspapers, including Charles Eliot Norton's *North American Review*.

One of Godkin's more important essays, "Aristocratic Opinions on Democracy," was penned during this period. In it, Godkin argued that many of America's shortcomings, such as its people's coarseness of manners, could be attributed to the movement of populations to and from the country's less civilized frontier.

Godkin and Olmsted had for years sought to start their own periodical, free from the biases of the daily press. In 1865, their plan was realized. With the aid of a number of liberal and abolitionist financial backers, including Norton, the weekly New York–based newspaper *The Nation* was launched, with Godkin as its editor in chief. The first issued was published on July 6, 1865.

A journal of politics, literature, science, and the arts, *The Nation* was founded by its stockholders in part to promote the rights and societal assimilation of the newly freed slaves. Always fiercely independent, Godkin soon diverged from the goals of the paper's more liberal owners, opposing black suffrage and state support of the poor. On the reconstruction of the South, he took a moderate position between the mild policies of President Andrew Johnson and the more sweeping reforms proposed by the radicals. Godkin's disagreements with *The Nation*'s more radical stockholders produced a battle for control, and he assumed principal ownership of the paper in 1866.

Under Godkin's leadership, *The Nation* became one of the most influential publications of its era, distinguished by its superior writing and broad international scope; the paper won a large following among the country's scholars and decision makers. *The Nation*'s staff and contributors included many of the best-known historians, writers, and thinkers of nineteenth century America, among them Norton and Olmsted, the journalist John R. Dennett, the philosopher Charles Sanders Pierce, and the novelist Henry James and his brother, William, the philosopher and psychologist.

Godkin's own editorials set the tone of the paper, mixing astute observation and persuasive argument with humor, sarcasm, invective, and a sharp eye for governmental misconduct. Although Godkin is often remembered as liberal and progressive, his highly individual positions make him difficult to classify. He held government's true aim to be the promotion of virtue and culture, and he was therefore mistrustful of American democracy and popular rule, which he saw as leading to cultural vulgarization and political mediocrity. He pressed for civil-service reform, seeking to free the system from political favoritism, but opposed suffrage for blacks, women, and many immigrant groups. He resisted American territorial expansionism, but for reasons seemingly more economic than moral.

Godkin's personality and editorial style earned for him as many enemies as friends.He has been described by some contemporaries as mean-spirited and icy and by others as jovial and good-natured. Physically he was thick-set and of medium height. Pictures from his middle years depict a man of stately bearing, with chiseled features, full beard, and mustache.

Throughout its first decade, *The Nation* rose steadily in circulation, reaching a peak of about thirteen thousand in the mid-1870's. Circulation declined thereafter, a consequence to some extent of several unpopular political stands the paper had taken, including support for the presidential candidacy of Republican Rutherford B. Hayes.

On April 11, 1875, Godkin's wife, Frances, died, following a long illness. Godkin's younger daughter Elizabeth (born 1865) had died in 1873, and an infant son, Ralph, had died shortly after his birth in 1868. Grief-stricken, Godkin left his home in New York and moved to Cambridge, Massachusetts, relinquishing many of his editorial responsibilities at *The Nation*.

When Godkin moved back to New York several years later, *The Nation* was in severe financial difficulty. In 1881, Godkin was sold to the *Evening Post*, to be published as that paper's weekly edition. Godkin joined the *Evening Post* as associate editor under its new owner, Henry Villard, and editor in chief, Carl Schurz. Relations between Schurz and Godkin were strained, and Godkin eventually used his influence with the paper's owners to unseat Schurz and replace him as top editor in 1883. The *Evening Post* under Godkin in many ways resembled the *The Nation* of years previous: outspoken, independent, and reformist.

Godkin focused much of his editorial scrutiny during this period on American foreign policy, opposing the "annexation fever" and jingoism of the 1880's and 1890's. Godkin opposed American territorial expansion in a number of regions, including the Philippines, Cuba, Santo Domingo, Hawaii, and Samoa. He decried the United States' aggressive posture in disputes with Chile, Great Britain, and Spain.

Another target of Godkin's criticism was the New York City and State Democratic leadership at Tammany Hall, which was implicated in numerous corruption scandals during the latter part of the century.

In 1884, Godkin, a Republican of long standing, broke with the party and joined a number of independents (dubbed Mugwumps) in supporting Democratic presidential candidate Grover Cleveland. Godkin had been a vocal critic of the Republican presidential nominee, the congressman James G. Blaine, whom he accused of using political office for personal gain. The *Evening Post* continued to espouse the Mugwump cause throughout the decade.

Godkin was married in 1884 to Katherine B. Sands, of a wealthy and prominent New York and London family. In late 1899, in failing health and declining mental ability, Godkin was relieved of his duties with the *Evening Post*, staying on officially until January 1, 1900. Godkin traveled regularly to Europe in his later years and, in 1901, moved to England for good. He died there, at Brixham, on May 21, 1902.

Summary

Though it could hardly be called nonpartisan, Godkin's *The Nation* did set a new standard for independence and incisiveness. The publication's literary quality was virtually unrivaled. Among its other accomplishments, the paper's book reviews and literary notices were especially highly regarded.

Godkin himself influenced an entire generation of political thinkers and writers. He pressed doggedly for higher standards of governmental and municipal conduct, attacking corruption and cronyism wherever he perceived abuses. Godkin's forceful writings helped spur many regulatory reforms and served as an inspiration for twentieth century muckraking journalism. As an opponent of American militarism overseas, Godkin had a moderating effect on many international disputes. Yet he was not a pacifist or anti-imperialist. He believed, instead, that territorial annexation would disrupt free trade. He asserted, furthermore, that the absorption of new, non-Anglo-Saxon populations would contributed to the nation's moral decline.

While Godkin's reformist bent has earned for him the reputation of a progressive, he was in many ways conservative, looking back to older, more genteel traditions. The elevation of American manners and mores was perhaps his most cherished goal, an ideal that was often at odds with the values of an egalitarian society.

Bibliography

Armstrong, William M. *E. L. Godkin: A Biography*. Albany: State University of New York Press, 1978. An authoritative, well-written, and thoroughly researched work, the first full-scale Godkin biography since Ogden's work (below). Armstrong presents a variety of original material, painting Godkin in a less flattering light than have earlier biographers.

_____. *E. L. Godkin and American Foreign Policy: 1865-1900.* New York: Bookman Associates, 1957. A well-written account of Godkin's political milieu and his role in the key foreign policy debates of the day. Introduces many of the biographical themes explored more fully in Armstrong's later study of Godkin.

Fridlington, Robert. "Frederick Law Olmsted: Launching the Nation." *The Nation* 202 (January 3, 1966): 10-12. A useful summary of Olmsted's career, his social philosophy, and his relationship with Godkin. Describes the two men's efforts in founding *The Nation* and offers an insightful analysis of their shared political views.

Keller, Morton. *Affairs of State: Public Life in Late Nineteenth Century America.* Cambridge, Mass.: The Belknap Press of Harvard University Press, 1977. An excellent overview, thoroughgoing and well documented, of Godkin's era, its issues, and major figures. Numerous references to Godkin and *The Nation*.

Ogden, Rollo. *Life and Letters of Edwin Lawrence Godkin.* 2 vols. New York: Macmillan, 1907. Godkin's authorized biography, by his younger colleague at the *Evening Post*. Deferential and uncritical, this study is short on serious scholarship, but it has provided source material for many subsequent works.

Vanderbilt, Kermit. "Norton and Godkin: Launching *The Nation*." *The Nation* 200 (February 15, 1965): 165-169. Good background on the creation of *The Nation*. Useful description of Godkin's long relationship with his ideological ally and financial backer Charles Eliot Norton, one of *The Nation*'s founders and primary contributors.

Robert Pollie

GEORGE WASHINGTON GOETHALS

Born: June 29, 1858; Brooklyn, New York
Died: January 21, 1928; New York, New York
Area of Achievement: Engineering
Contribution: Goethals was chief engineer of the Panama Canal, which revolutionized maritime transportation and commerce.

Early Life

George Washington Goethals was born on June 29, 1858, in Brooklyn, New York. His parents were Dutch immigrants of modest means. Goethals attended public schools in Manhattan and Brooklyn prior to matriculation (at the age of fourteen) at City College. Three years later, in 1876, he won appointment to the United States Military Academy at West Point. He was commissioned a second lieutenant in the Army Corps of Engineers in 1880, having been graduated second in his class. (He was later upgraded to honor man when the actual honor man was convicted by court-martial of embezzlement.) Goethals valued his West Point education highly. Many years later, when he was offered a civilian job at an enormous increase over the salary that he had earned in the army, Goethals would decline, saying that all of his training and education had been at the public's expense and that he intended to serve his country, hoping thereby to repay that investment, as long as he was needed by his country.

Following commissioning, he was assigned to the United States Advanced Engineering School and then, in 1882, to Cincinnati to improve the Ohio River channel for navigation. This detail provided him with practical experience in lock and dam construction. A variety of engineering assignments followed. For example, he was in charge of the construction of the Muscle Shoals Canal on the Tennessee River. In this construction he designed and successfully completed a lock within a hydraulic system with a lift of twenty-six feet—an unprecedented height. He was chief engineer for a similar canal-hydraulic system near Chattanooga, Tennessee. In 1894, he was appointed assistant to the chief of engineers. During the Spanish-American War he was promoted to lieutenant colonel of volunteers (regular army major) and assigned as chief engineer of the Puerto Rican Army of Occupation. After that war he served in New England assisting in the design and construction of harbor defenses. His most important contribution related to the specific design for the fortifications near Newport, Rhode Island. Goethals was later made a member of the General Staff and was graduated from the United States Army War College.

Goethals married Effie Rodman of New Bedford, Massachusetts, in 1884, shortly before a stint as an instructor at West Point. She was the daughter of Captain Thomas R. Rodman. She bore him two sons—George R. and

Thomas R. Goethals. George went on to a successful military career (rising to the rank of colonel) and Thomas became a physician.

Life's Work

Goethals will always be remembered as the man who "built" the Panama Canal. While his distinguished assistants were as numerous as a regiment, it was Goethals who was ultimately responsible for recruiting and inspiring the huge army of workers; for conceiving the overall project; for laying out the many tasks; and for organizing, planning, and carrying through the work against the many obstacles posed by man, government, and nature. It was Goethals, for example, who fought to make the Panama Canal a lock canal and not a sea-level one. The problem of sanitation was mastered—with the invaluable help of William Crawford Gorgas—where earlier efforts had failed. Under Goethals, the Canal Zone was transformed from the vast graveyard it had been under Ferdinand de Lesseps and the French into a place where men could work and thrive.

The first work on the Panama Canal was begun in 1881 by the Panama Canal Company, a French chartered and financed business, under the direction of de Lesseps. De Lesseps had earlier been chief engineer for the Suez Canal project. De Lesseps had planned to construct a sea-level canal with no locks at a cost of 128 million dollars. Because of obstacles he could not overcome, his efforts ended with the bankruptcy of the French company and a major scandal in government. Only a small amount of work was actually accomplished. There followed over the next several years attempts to complete de Lesseps' plans for a sea-level canal. All failed. Matters stood at this point until the United States government determined to undertake the project.

The history of the United States' acquisition of the French company's charter to construct a canal and of the political complications that arose is fairly well-known and need not be recounted. It is sufficient to state that the United States in 1903 acquired the right to dig a canal across a new nation—Panama. President Theodore Roosevelt, well versed in the arguments among the supporters of a sea-level and the supporters of a lock canal, selected then Major George Goethals (junior to scores of other army engineers) to head the project. Goethals favored a lock canal. That Roosevelt came to the conclusion that a lock canal was superior to a sea-level canal reflects Goethals' persuasive arguments. Originally civilian engineers had been charged with the task. The planning and work of that group, especially of John Frank Stevens, proved to be extremely valuable to Goethals and to the Army Corps of Engineers. Goethals never failed to praise the work of his subordinates or, in this case, his predecessors—even when he found the hydraulic systems, the locks, dams, and spillways (all Goethals specialities) to be either as yet unplanned or flawed in design. When Goethals and the Army Corps of Engineers took over in 1907, he found that an awesome amount of work needed to be accomplished. The enormity of the task of digging the canal was far more staggering than were the technological difficulties which had to be overcome.

The Panama Canal as it was finally constructed works by raising a ship from the Caribbean Sea or from the Gulf of Panama in a lock chamber (of which there are twelve) eighty-five feet. Each chamber is 110 feet wide, built to accommodate the largest ship the navy had on the drawing boards, and one thousand feet long but capable of division into two chambers—one six and the other four hundred feet. These chambers are built in pairs so as to accommodate two-way traffic. Once raised, a vessel travels over Gatun Lake—a man-made, one-hundred-seventy-square-mile body of water eighty-five feet above sea level—to the opposite side of the isthmus. There it is lowered to sea level via the same process in reverse.

Completion of the canal took until 1914. The task called for the tearing away of the mountains in the canal channel, which involved moving hundreds of millions of cubic yards of earth. Creating Gatun Lake involved not only the damming of the Chagres River in order to control it but also the filling of the valleys with earth and water to a depth of eighty-five feet in many places. Building the enormous locks of concrete and steel was the most monumental task man had ever attempted. It was George Washington Goethals who made it a reality. He coordinated all the factors involved—sanitation, excavation, housing, commissary, labor, design, and construction. A man of great force and personality, he inspired complete confidence in the entire organization and brought it together in harmony. This effort served for years as a model of efficient labor and industrial harmony as well as sound engineering. Upon completion, Goethals received the formal thanks of the United States Congress for "distinguished service in constructing the Panama Canal."

President Woodrow Wilson appointed Goethals the first civil governor of the Panama Canal Zone. Following a two-year term, he was named state engineer for New Jersey. He resigned that post to accept recall to active duty with the United States Army when World War I erupted. During the war he was acting quartermaster general and director of purchase, storage, and supplies. As such he was responsible for the supply and transportation of all United States troops at home and abroad.

In 1919, he retired from active service and opened George Goethals and Company, a consultant engineering firm with offices in New York City. Among the major clients was the City of New York. Goethals and his company made a major impact upon the projects of the Port of New York Authority. He offered his expertise to help complete and operate the Holland Vehicular Tunnels under the Hudson River; the then-proposed George Washington Bridge, spanning the Hudson River; and the Goethals Bridge.

During his lifetime General Goethals was the recipient of many honors from educational and scientific institutions, including the National Geographic Society, the Civil Forum of New York, and the National Institute of Social Science. Goethals died after a prolonged illness in New York City on June 21, 1928. In his honor, flags in the Canal Zone were flown at half mast.

Summary

Goethals will always be remembered as the engineer who saw the Panama Canal become a reality. He is the most famous engineer ever to wear the uniform of the United States Army and one of the best-known graduates of West Point since the Civil War. His ability as director of the massive construction operations in Panama and as director of purchase, storage, and supplies in the United States Army in World War I is indicative of his greatness as an administrator as well as an engineer. His place in American and world history is secure.

Bibliography

Baker, Ray S. "Goethals the Man and How He Works." *Technical World Magazine* 21 (July, 1914): 656-661. Praises Goethals and describes his techniques in the administration of the entire range of the construction project that produced the Panama Canal.

Cameron, Ian. *The Impossible Dream: The Building of the Panama Canal.* William Morrow and Co., 1972. Contains facts and figures concerning the magnitude of the actual construction efforts—down to the number of tons of concrete poured as well as where it was poured.

Fast, Howard. *Goethals and the Panama Canal.* New York: Julian Messner, 1942. One of the best examinations of Goethals' achievements in Panama. It should be consulted by the serious student.

McCullough, David. *The Path Between the Seas: The Creation of the Panama Canal, 1870-1914.* New York: Simon and Schuster, 1977. Extremely reliable account of the construction of the Panama Canal. McCullough's tale of the pre–United States efforts are detailed and accurate. The role of the Army Corps of Engineers and of Goethals is placed in its proper perspective.

Mach, Gerstel. *The Land Divided: A History of the Panama Canal and Other Isthmian Canal Projects.* New York: Octagon Books, 1974. Perhaps the single most valuable work on the construction of the canal from inception to completion. Goethals' role is well detailed. Gives much credit to Goethals' predecessors, especially John Stevens.

Pepperman, W. L. *Who Built the Panama Canal?* New York: E. P. Dutton and Co., 1915. An older source yet very useful on the personnel involved in the undertaking. Gives major credit to Goethals as the man who orchestrated a seemingly impossible task.

Richard J. Amundson

SAMUEL GOLDWYN
Samuel Goldfisch

Born: August 27, 1882; Warsaw, Poland
Died: January 31, 1974; Beverly Hills, California
Area of Achievement: Motion pictures
Contribution: Working as an independent Hollywood producer with his own company and studio, Goldwyn made films that were known for their high quality and good taste, despite his own impoverished upbringing and limited education.

Early Life

Samuel Goldwyn was born as Samuel Goldfisch on August 27, 1882, in the Jewish ghetto in Warsaw, Poland. His parents, Abraham and Hannah Goldfisch, were Orthodox Jews who lived in poverty. It is not known how they earned a living.

Goldwyn's schooling stopped at age eleven, when he was put to work as an office boy in a Warsaw banking firm, earning five zlotys (one dollar) a week. An early encounter with anti-Semitism—in which a policeman called him "a dirty little Jew" and then beat him up, and robbed him of his money—impelled Goldwyn to escape from Warsaw at the age of twelve. He eventually made his way to the home of an aunt and uncle in England, where he worked at various jobs, until he was able to raise enough money to pay for a steerage ticket to the United States.

Arriving in New York in 1896, where an immigration official changed the spelling of his name from Goldfisch to Goldfish, Goldwyn was recruited to work in a glove factory in Gloversville (near Albany), New York. He began by sweeping floors, then became a glove-cutter, often working at the same bench for sixteen to eighteen hours a day, until at the age of sixteen, he was able to convince his employers to let him travel on the road as a glove salesman.

Goldwyn enjoyed great success as a salesman. Although he never entirely lost his Polish-Yiddish accent, and although he was neither well-read nor well educated, Goldwyn was a most convincing and energetic speaker who refused to take no for an answer. In addition, he had a winning smile and an impressive physical appearance—about six feet tall, slim, and always proudly erect—augmented by suits that were precisely tailored. In later years, Goldwyn became extremely vain about his wardrobe and appearance. He refused to carry anything—money, keys, or pens—in his pockets, so as not to mar the fit of his clothes.

As a result of Goldwyn's charm and tenaciousness, he was soon earning close to fifteen thousand dollars a year as a glove salesman. He became a sales manager in 1909 but was eager to improve himself further. Seeking to marry the boss's niece, Bessie Ginzberg, he lost out to Jesse L. Lasky, a vaudeville entrepreneur. Bessie, however, introduced Goldwyn to Lasky's sister, Blanche, whom he married in 1910.

Following the 1912 election of Woodrow Wilson, who promised to repeal the restrictive tariffs on imported products, Goldwyn became afraid that American-made gloves would be threatened by cheaper foreign competition. Looking for a new line of work, he saw potential in motion pictures.

Life's Work

At a time when most motion pictures were one- and two-reelers, lasting not much more than fifteen minutes, Goldwyn was one of a small group of people who believed that motion pictures had more to offer. Using his best salesmanship skills, Goldwyn convinced his brother-in-law, who had extensive contacts in show business, to establish the Jesse L. Lasky Feature Play Company. Goldwyn hired the actor Dustin Farnum to play the title role in a film adaptation of *The Squaw Man* (1914), a popular play about an Englishman in the Wild West. Lasky knew a young playwright, Cecil B. DeMille, who was eager to direct.

After much trial and error, *The Squaw Man* was released in February, 1914, and was an immediate hit, making a profit of roughly $200,000. More successes followed for the Lasky Company, which merged in June, 1916, with Adolph Zukor's Famous Players, to form the Famous Players–Lasky Company. Yet there was not room enough in the new company for both Goldwyn and Zukor. Lasky was forced to choose, and—perhaps because his sister had divorced Goldwyn in 1915—he chose Zukor. Famous Players–Lasky went on to become Paramount Pictures: Goldwyn, with the $900,000 he received as a settlement, went on to start a new company with Edgar and Arch Selwyn, two Broadway producers.

Looking for a new company name, Goldwyn (whose name then was still Goldfish) and the Selwyns thought of combining their two surnames. Sel-fish was one possibility, but Gold-wyn was more practical. The result was the Goldwyn Pictures Corporation, the sound of which was so pleasing to the company's president and chief stockholder (Samuel Goldfish) that in 1918 he legally changed his own name to match it: one of the few instances in which a man was named after a corporation, rather than vice versa.

The major reason that Goldwyn had been unable to work with Zukor and Lasky was that he was fiercely independent and accustomed to having things done his own way. It was inevitable, therefore, that Goldwyn would clash with his business partners in the Goldwyn Pictures Corporation. In March, 1922, for the second time in six years, Goldwyn was forced to resign from a company he had helped establish. The Goldwyn Pictures Corporation went on to merge with Marcus Loew's Metro Pictures Corporation in 1924, later becoming known as Metro-Goldwyn-Mayer. Samuel Goldwyn, having received one million dollars for his stock in Goldwyn Pictures, decided that he could not tolerate further partnerships and started his own company, known as Samuel Goldwyn Presents, in 1923.

Two years later, on April 23, 1925, Goldwyn married Frances Howard McLaughlin, a former actress, twenty-two years his junior. They moved from New York to Hollywood the next day, where they remained for the remainder of their lives. Goldwyn's wife was the only person in whom he seemed to have complete trust and confidence. She became his unofficial assistant producer and story consultant. Their only child, Samuel Goldwyn, Jr., later became a motion-picture producer himself.

From 1923 to 1959, Goldwyn independently produced eighty motion pictures. This output may be divided into three stages: the first, from 1923 to 1935, when he produced forty-one pictures, more than half of his life's work; the second, from 1936 to 1946, when he produced twenty-seven pictures, many of them enduring classics; and the third, from 1947 to 1959, when he produced only twelve pictures.

During the first period, from 1923 to 1935, Goldwyn's productions ranged from love stories (Ronald Colman and Vilma Banky were his most successful screen couple) to musical comedies (six of which starred Eddie Cantor) to sophisticated dramas, such as *Arrowsmith* (1931) and *Cynara* (1932). None of these films is acclaimed as a classic, but as a group they established Goldwyn's reputation in Hollywood as a producer who always aimed for top quality, regardless of cost.

The films produced during Goldwyn's second period, from 1936 to 1946, include those for which he is best known. He worked with screenwriter Lillian Hellman to make *These Three* (1936), based on a Hellman play which had been thought unproducible in Hollywood, and *The Little Foxes* (1941), nominated for eight Academy Awards. He adapted classic novels, such as Emily Brontë's *Wuthering Heights* (1847), in 1939, which helped make a star of Laurence Olivier, as well as more current literature, such as Sinclair Lewis' *Dodsworth* (1929), in 1936, and Sidney Kingsley's *Dead End* (1935), in 1937. As always, Goldwyn worked with many of Hollywood's best directors, including Howard Hawks in *Come and Get It* (1936) and *Ball of Fire* (1942) and John Ford in *The Hurricane* (1937). His own favorite director seemed to be William Wyler. Wyler and Goldwyn worked together eight times, culminating in Goldwyn's greatest success, *The Best Years of Our Lives* (1946), which won seven Academy Awards and the Irving Thalberg Memorial Award for Goldwyn.

During Goldwyn's final period, from 1947 (when he turned sixty-five) to 1959, fewer pictures were made, none of them particularly memorable. Included were several starring Danny Kaye, notably *The Secret Life of Walter Mitty* (1947) and *Hans Christian Andersen* (1952), and Goldwyn's final two productions, both of them musicals adapted from successful stage shows,

Guys and Dolls (1955) and *Porgy and Bess* (1959).

The failure of *Porgy and Bess* was a great disappointment to Goldwyn. After 1959, he ceased making pictures on his own and began renting his studio to other film and television producers. He suffered a stroke in 1969, which left him partially paralyzed. He died at his Beverly Hills home on January 31, 1974.

Summary

In spite of Goldwyn's success as a producer of high-quality motion pictures, he may be best known for his fractured phrases, unintentionally humorous, which have become known as Goldwynisms. Goldwyn is even included in Bartlett's *Familiar Quotations* for such memorable sayings as "Include me out" and "In two words: im-possible."

Yet Goldwyn's real achievements are of a different order. Even if most Goldwynisms are not apocryphal—and there is good reason to believe that many of them are—he ought to be judged not by what he said, but by what he put on the screen: There, his talents are indisputable. At a time when the major Hollywood studios regularly filled their yearly quotas with films of low quality, Goldwyn insisted on producing nothing but the very best. He did not always succeed in doing so, but it was never for lack of trying.

From the 1920's through the 1950's, the motion-picture industry was controlled largely by a handful of Hollywood studio heads who oversaw all aspects of a film: from production, to distribution, to exhibition. As an independent, Goldwyn ran counter to this trend. In so doing, however, he pioneered the way for the independent producer of the post-1960's New Hollywood.

For Goldwyn, being independent meant that he did not have to answer to anyone—bankers, stockholders, company officers—other than the public. It may sound peculiar that an uneducated, Jewish immigrant from Poland could have understood so well what the American public wanted to see. Goldwyn's artistic instincts, however, combined with a shrewd business sense, made him one of the most successful creators of one of the most distinctively American enterprises: the Hollywood motion picture.

Bibliography

Aberbach, David. "The Mogul Who Loved Art." *Commentary* 72 (September, 1981): 67-71. A balanced assessment of Goldwyn's career, noting his unusual combination of artistic taste and business shrewdness. There is also an attempt by Aberbach at a psychological interpretation of Goldwyn's accomplishments.

Easton, Carol. *The Search for Samuel Goldwyn*. New York: William Morrow and Co., 1976. This biography contends that Goldwyn, embarrassed by his humble origins, tried to hide them with elaborate (and deceitful) publicity.

Epstein, Lawrence J. *Samuel Goldwyn*. Boston: Twayne Publishers, 1981. This is the only book that examines Goldwyn's films in an analytic and thematic, rather than simply chronological manner. According to Epstein, Goldwyn deserves to be taken seriously as a film auteur.

Goldwyn, Samuel. *Behind the Screen*. New York: George H. Doran Co., 1923. These memoirs, surely ghostwritten, cover Goldwyn's first ten years in the motion-picture business but have little to do with Goldwyn himself. There is no mention, for example, of his birth in Poland or his marriage. Instead, the focus is on Goldwyn's famous Hollywood friends.

Griffith, Richard. *Samuel Goldwyn: The Producer and His Films*. New York: Museum of Modern Art Film Library, 1956. Reprint. New York: Garland Publishing, 1985. Published in conjunction with a series, "The Films of Samuel Goldwyn," at the prestigious Museum of Modern Art, this book gives a quick overview of the "Goldwyn touch," followed by a chronological examination of Goldwyn's work through 1955.

Johnston, Alva. *The Great Goldwyn*. New York: Random House, 1937. As indicated by the title, this is a flattering portrait of Goldwyn. The Goldwyn touch is defined, and Goldwyn's search for quality is seen as comparable to that of Gustave Flaubert. Originally published in *The Saturday Evening Post* (May-June, 1937).

Marill, Alvin H. *Samuel Goldwyn Presents*. South Brunswick, N.J.: A. S. Barnes and Co., 1976. This provides the most detailed examination (with complete credits, plot summaries, and critical reception) for all eighty of Goldwyn's independent productions, taken in chronological order.

Marx, Arthur. *Goldwyn: A Biography of the Man Behind the Myth*. New York: W. W. Norton and Co., 1976. As a Hollywood insider (Marx is the son of Groucho Marx), the author has written the most authoritative biography of Goldwyn. The book is especially good on Goldwyn's career within the larger context of the American film industry.

James I. Deutsch

SAMUEL GOMPERS

Born: January 27, 1850; London, England
Died: December 13, 1924; San Antonio, Texas
Area of Achievement: The labor movement
Contribution: Gompers helped create the first successful national organization of trade unions in the United States, the American Federation of Labor (AFL), and he led the AFL almost continuously from its creation in
1886 to 1924.

Early Life
Samuel Gompers was the son of Dutch parents who had emigrated to London in 1844. Gompers' father was a cigar-maker, and the family lived in poverty. Samuel's total formal education consisted of attendance, from the ages
of six to ten, at a free school provided by the Jewish community, plus some
free evening classes. Samuel left school because of the family's poor financial
condition, and, after a brief try at shoemaking, his father arranged for an
apprenticeship as a cigar-maker. Gompers worked in this trade until he
became a full-time union leader.

In 1863, the Gompers family followed relatives to the United States and
settled in New York City. Gompers married Sophia Julian in 1867. Although
they had many children, only five lived to reach adulthood. Sophia died in
1920, and Gompers remarried the next year. His second wife, Gertrude
Neuschler, was thirty years younger than he, and the marriage was an unhappy one.

Gompers was Jewish by birth, but he did not practice his religion; nor did
he exhibit any strong identification with other Jews. He had an attraction to
fraternal orders, including the Foresters, the Odd Fellows, and the Masons.
Gompers' father had been a union member in London, and father and son
joined the Cigar-makers' Union in 1864. Gompers, however, was more
involved with fraternal than with union activities until the early 1870's.

Hard times for skilled cigar-makers ultimately impelled Gompers into
active involvement with the union. The introduction of a new tool, the mold,
into the trade in 1869 simplified cigar-making and threatened the position of
the skilled workers. The long depression of 1873-1877 made the situation
worse. By 1872, Gompers had joined Adolph Strasser and Ferdinand
Laurrell in trying to remake the faltering Cigar-makers' Union. In 1875,
Gompers became president of a reorganized cigar-makers' local union in
New York City. Gompers then helped elect Strasser as president of the
national union in 1877. Together, they reconstructed the Cigar-makers'
Union on the model of British trade unions. This meant high dues; financial
benefits, such as a death allowance, sick pay, and out-of-work payments; and
centralized control of strikes. From 1880 onward, Gompers held office in his

local union, and, after 1886 and for the remainder of his life, in the national union.

In these early years, Gompers demonstrated the personal qualities that were to mark his later activities. He was pragmatic, indefatigable, honest, and totally devoted to the union cause, passing up many more lucrative job opportunities. Although short in stature and initially hampered by a stammer, Gompers became an accomplished speaker. Despite his meager formal education, he wrote extensively, including many articles as editor of the journal of the AFL. He gave his life to the labor movement, and he expected others to accept his leadership. Gompers rarely admitted a mistake or forgave an enemy.

Life's Work

As early as the 1870's, Gompers believed in the importance of a national organization to represent the trade unions of the country. Earlier efforts in the 1860's to create such an organization had failed. Gompers helped to form a weak federation of trade unions in 1881, and he was the leader, in 1886, in establishing a more powerful body, the AFL. He became its first president, and with the exception of 1894, he was reelected annually until his death. As president, Gompers developed his mature views on how the American labor movement should function, and he worked tirelessly to put them into practice.

Gompers believed that the labor movement must win acceptance by employers and the public as the representative of the workers' legitimate interests within the existing capitalist system. Any resort to violence or support of radicalism would lead to repression by the state. Thus, the labor movement must work within the law for goals understandable to most Americans: an improved standard of living, better opportunities for one's children, and security in one's old age.

Gompers was familiar with Socialist doctrine from his exposure to the movement in the 1870's. Although he retained certain elements of Marxism, particularly an intense belief in class as the determinant of political behavior, by 1880, he opposed the Socialists as being dangerous to the labor movement. He believed that the Socialists did not represent the views of most Americans on matters such as private property. Moreover, their demand for radical change threatened to stimulate repression. Since many workers were supporters of the two major political parties, the attempts of the Socialists to create an alliance between the trade unions and a radical third party were divisive. Gompers' struggles with the Socialists increased in intensity after 1890, and they were the major opposition to his leadership within the AFL.

For Gompers, legislation was not a major means for workers to win gains. Ultimately, this position flowed from his belief that politics was controlled by class interests. For Gompers, since the demands of workers would eventually conflict with the interests of other classes and since workers did not control the government and were unlikely to do so, political action would be dangerous for the labor movement. Gompers carried this idea to the point of opposing most labor legislation, because once the government intervened in the lives of workers, it would be more likely to do harm than good.

Rather than risk the danger of governmental intervention in labor matters, Gompers called upon workers to organize trade unions and to win their gains by this means. The trade union was the only institution in society fully under the control of the working class and responsive to its interests. This doctrine of voluntarism brought him into frequent conflict with social reformers, who pointed out that most workers were not members of trade unions. Strong opposition to Gompers' views also came from important elements within the labor movement—principally the weaker unions that saw little prospect of substantial immediate gains through their own efforts and who were therefore attracted to an alliance with middle-class reformers to secure labor legislation. This trend was most apparent during the two decades prior to World War I, known as the Progressive period.

On occasion, Gompers believed that political action might be necessary for limited objectives which were unachievable by trade-union action alone, or to protect the labor movement against assault. An example of the latter was the campaign by the AFL, from 1906 to 1914, to win relief from the use of the Sherman Anti-Trust Act against the labor movement. In such a case, however, labor had to follow a policy of rewarding friends and punishing enemies, without reference to party. Gompers argued that this practice would counteract the allegiance of workers to the two major parties and avoid the permanent commitment to any political party that Gompers wanted to avoid.

Despite his foreign birth, Gompers led the AFL in its demand for a restriction of immigration. He undoubtedly expressed the views of most trade unionists, who feared that the newcomers would accept lower wages and that the arrival of vast numbers of both skilled and unskilled workers would create an additional pool of labor that employers could use to crush strikes or to operate new machinery. The AFL consistently supported immigration restriction, beginning in 1897.

Gompers initially favored the organization of all workers. He opposed the tendency in some trade unions to bar immigrants, blacks, women, or the less skilled, since by doing so a nonunion work force that could weaken the labor movement would be created. Yet Gompers eventually yielded on this point and left the issue to individual unions.

Gompers also increasingly favored the organization of workers by craft, rather than through unions representing all the workers in an industry. Gompers believed that the creation of industrial unions would produce conflict with the existing craft unions, thus weakening the labor movement. Moreover, he argued that the craft unions could effectively organize the less skilled workers. In the event, however, this did not occur—and as a consequence, the scope of the American labor movement was severely limited. It took a split in the AFL in the 1930's and the subsequent formation of the Congress of Industrial Organizations (CIO) to make industrial unionism a significant force in the United States.

Gompers consistently supported the peaceful settlement of international disputes until 1916, when he embraced the concept of preparedness. Gompers strongly supported the war effort once the United States entered World War I in 1917. This shift in attitude reflects several of his basic beliefs. First, he contended that the nation overwhelmingly supported preparedness and then the war, and it weakened the labor movement to oppose popular opinion. Second, Gompers viewed the issue with his usual pragmatism: He correctly believed that the administration of Woodrow Wilson would cooperate with the AFL to maximize production during the war. Yet the gains for the labor movement could not be sustained after the war, in the face of the severe Red scare of 1919 and the political and economic conservatism of the 1920's. By the time of Gompers' death in 1924, the AFL was only slightly larger than it had been prior to the war.

Summary

Samuel Gompers' views strongly influenced the character of the American labor movement until the appearance of the CIO in the 1930's. Gompers' leadership was a combination of experience, tenacity, hard work, and the web of personal contacts which he had built in the labor movement. He could only persuade and implore; he could not command. Because Gompers was elected annually by the votes of the larger craft unions in the AFL, he had to represent their interests. Yet Gompers was too strong a personality to stay with a labor movement that he could not support. The AFL was not exactly what Gompers might have wanted, but it did reflect many of his basic views. Thus, he was able to develop, defend, and lead the organization for more than four decades.

Bibliography

Dick, William M. *Labor and Socialism in America: The Gompers Era*. Port Washington, N.Y.: Kennikat Press, 1972. Traces Gompers' relations with the Socialists over the course of his career.

Gompers, Samuel. *The Samuel Gompers Papers*. Vol. 1, *The Making of a Union Leader: 1850-86*. Edited by Stuart Kaufman. Urbana: University of Illinois Press, 1986-   . Excellent documentary history that covers Gompers' early life and career up to his accession to the presidency of the AFL. Other volumes to follow.

_____. *Seventy Years of Life and Labor: An Autobiography*. 2 vols. New York: E. P. Dutton and Co., 1925. Gompers' version of his life and times. Contains valuable information, but it must be used with care. Includes photographs.

Grob, Gerald. *Workers and Utopia: A Study of Ideological Conflict in the American Labor Movement, 1865-1900.* Chicago: Quadrangle Books, 1960. Examines Gompers' efforts to establish the AFL in competition with the Knights of Labor.

Livesay, Harold. *Samuel Gompers and Organized Labor in America.* Boston: Little, Brown and Co., 1978. Brief, interpretive, and readable study of Gompers.

Mandel, Bernard. *Samuel Gompers: A Biography.* Yellow Springs, Ohio: Antioch Press, 1963. Full-length biography that is rich in detail. Includes photographs.

Reed, Louis. *The Labor Philosophy of Samuel Gompers.* New York: Columbia University Press, 1930. Descriptive and analytical presentation of Gompers' views. The author sees a need for the AFL's type of unionism in the nineteenth century, but he believes that it became outdated in the twentieth century.

Taft, Philip. *The A.F. of L. in the Time of Gompers.* New York: Harper and Row, Publishers, 1957. Detailed account of the AFL; necessarily stresses Gompers' role. Generally supports the policies of the AFL and its leader.

Irwin Yellowitz

CHARLES GOODYEAR

Born: December 29, 1800; New Haven, Connecticut
Died: July 1, 1860; New York, New York
Area of Achievement: Invention
Contribution: Goodyear was the first man to vulcanize rubber, thereby rendering it usable for manufacturing numerous products.

Early Life

Charles Goodyear was born in New Haven, Connecticut, on December 29, 1800. He was the first child born to Amasa Goodyear and Cynthia Bateman Goodyear; their family later grew to include six children. Stephen Goodyear, an ancestor from London, had been one of a group of merchants who founded a colony in New Haven in 1638. Amasa Goodyear was also a merchant, selling hardware supplies to farmers, as well as an inventor. One of his patented farm tools was a hay pitchfork made from steel; it was a great improvement over the heavy cast-iron pitchforks that were used in the early 1800's.

Charles attended public schools in New Haven and Naugatuck, Connecticut, his father having moved the family in 1807 to a farm near Naugatuck to take advantage of a water-powered factory he had bought there. Charles helped his father, to whom he was a close companion, at both the factory and the farm. Contemporaries remembered him as a serious youth with a studious nature. An excellent Bible student, he considered being a minister, but when he finished public school at seventeen, he agreed with his father that he should enter the hardware business and was apprenticed, as a clerk, to a large Philadelphia hardware store run by the Rogers family.

Charles's tenure at the store was brief. He felt overworked, and his small, frail body soon wore out; ill health forced him to return to his father's house. Amasa Goodyear worked with his son as a business partner starting in 1826; together they sought to improve the farm tools of their era. During this time, in August of 1824, Charles married Clarissa Beecher, whose father was an innkeeper in Naugatuck.

Amasa Goodyear soon felt that his hardware sales were sufficiently good for him to open a branch store in Philadelphia. He sent his son to manage the new store; there the Goodyears sold only American-made goods, becoming the first United States hardware firm to eliminate British imports. Unfortunately, the young Goodyear's business sense was not acute. He often sold goods on credit, as did his father in Connecticut, and reached a point where his creditors became too numerous and he was deep in debt. Rather than declare bankruptcy (as the law allowed), he decided to pay off his debts gradually. When young Goodyear's creditors pressed for their money, he was put in debtor's prison for the first time. This was in 1830 in Philadelphia.

Charles Goodyear would spend time in and out of debtor's prison for the next ten years.

During one of the times Goodyear was out of prison, in 1834, he traveled to New York to try to secure bank loans to pay his debts. He was caught in a harsh rainstorm on the streets of Manhatten and entered the Roxbury India Rubber Company to get dry. Inside the store, he noticed a life preserver made with a faulty valve. He purchased it, hoping to redesign the valve and impress the firm's owners. Perhaps they would pay him for his invention. Goodyear spent the next few weeks on this project, but when he returned to the Roxbury Company with a perfected valve, he was surprised to learn of the great difficulties the firm was having with rubber goods.

Rubber goods had been produced and marketed in the United States since 1830. The demand for these products was high, especially in New England, where residents wore rubber boots and raincoats. The gum rubber that was used to make these items, however, was a sticky substance that melted in the summer and froze in the winter. When Goodyear first contacted the Roxbury Company, it was closing down. Goodyear came away from this encounter with the idea of curing rubber so it could be used more readily for clothing, life preservers, and other goods.

Life's Work

When Charles Goodyear returned to his Philadelphia home in the summer of 1834, he began what would be a five-year period of experimenting to cure rubber. Because he was not trained in chemistry, his experiments were conducted on a trial-and-error basis. He worked in the kitchen of his small cottage, or in prison when he was confined there. He was fortunate in that gum rubber was inexpensive and plentiful. Goodyear had no tools, so he worked the rubber with his hands. He first mixed it with a variety of substances (one at a time) to see if he could eliminate its stickiness. The good properties of rubber that he wished to retain were its elasticity and flexibility, along with its strength. Among the items Goodyear mixed with rubber were sand, ink, castor oil, witch hazel, and even salt, pepper, and sugar.

When Goodyear tried a mixture of rubber, magnesia, and quicklime, he thought he had a successful type of rubber. It appeared smooth and flexible and was no longer sticky. He jubilantly announced his news of a discovery to the press. He even produced some small items from the mixture to display at two institute fairs in New York in 1835, the New York American Institute and the New York Mechanics' Institute. Although both fairs awarded Goodyear prize medals for his discovery, it soon proved to be a failure. This treated or "tanned" rubber, as he called it, was destroyed when any acid (even a very weak acid) came in contact with it.

Goodyear was not discouraged by this failure; rather, he continued to mix other substances with gum rubber to find a useful compound. So intent was he to promote his products that he would dress all in rubber.

The hardships Goodyear and his family endured while he worked to perfect rubber were many. They often had no shelter, at one point living in an abandoned rubber factory on Staten Island, or no food—neighbors reported seeing the Goodyear children digging in their gardens for half-ripe potatoes. They never had money; Goodyear sold furnishings and even his children's school books to purchase supplies.

The only way the family survived was by Goodyear's finding a series of financial backers for his experiments. Among the men who funded him were Ralph Steele of New Haven and later William de Forest, who had been a tutor to young Charles and later would become his brother-in-law. De Forest's total investment in Goodyear's work rose to almost fifty thousand dollars. Another pair of backers, William and Emery Ryder of New York, had to withdraw all their funds when the economic panic of 1837 ruined them financially.

On June 17, 1837, Goodyear had obtained a patent for a procedure to treat rubber that he called the "acid-gas process." The bankruptcy of the Ryder brothers shortly thereafter, however, gave Goodyear another setback—only a temporary one, however, for he soon met John Haskins in New York, who next helped him. Haskins was the former owner of the Roxbury India Rubber Company; he still owned an empty factory in Roxbury, Massachusetts, and Goodyear and his family moved to nearby Woburn. Goodyear manufactured various rubber items using the acid-gas process; among the thin products he sold in 1838 were tablecloths and piano covers.

Goodyear had another meeting while he resided in Woburn. He became acquainted with Nathaniel Hayward, who had himself worked out a method of treating rubber. Hayward mixed gum rubber with sulphur and set the substance to dry in the sun; he called his process "solarization." Sharing their knowledge, Goodyear and Hayward began manufacturing what they believed to be permanent rubber products, no longer sticky and not likely to melt or freeze. As their reputation grew, the two men were awarded a United States government contract to produce 150 mailbags. After they had completed their order, they were disheartened to see that all the bags melted in the summer heat.

Ironically, although totally defeated (financially and publicly) by the mailbag disaster, Goodyear was very close to a successful curing of rubber. In the winter of early 1839, he accidentally dropped a piece of a ruined mailbag on the stove in his Woburn kitchen. He noticed that the sulphur-treated rubber did not melt, but charred as leather would when burned. Goodyear had worked long enough with rubber to realize he now had made a major breakthrough. The piece of charred rubber, when hung in the winter air overnight, also did not freeze.

The inventor still had a problem—no one, except his family, believed his new method was a success. Because of his past failures, the American press and any financial backers considered Goodyear a disturbed man who would never make a genuine discovery. It would be five more years before Charles Goodyear could slowly perfect his new treatment of rubber and have it patented on June 15, 1844. By that time, samples of Goodyear's new rubber had reached England, where one inventor, Thomas Hancock, had copied Goodyear's process. Hancock successfully obtained a British patent on this method of treating rubber, which he called "vulcanization," after the Roman god of fire, Vulcan.

Goodyear, however, did hold the American patent on vulcanization. When his countrymen began to realize that Goodyear finally had a truly usable product, he began to earn money. Royalties were paid to Goodyear by each company using his process to manufacture rubber goods in the United States.

Even after his great success with vulcanization, Charles Goodyear continued to spend large sums of money experimenting with rubber. After 1844, he concentrated on devising new rubber products. He also spent large sums of money promoting his products, especially in Europe. In 1855, Goodyear had built two elaborate exhibits abroad. In England, at the Crystal Palace Exhibition, he built a three-room Vulcanite Court completely furnished in rubber, at a cost of thirty thousand dollars. In France, at the Exposition Universelle in Paris, he constructed a similar exhibit for fifty thousand dollars. These expenditures, along with other debts, explain why Goodyear never became wealthy from his discovery of vulcanization.

Goodyear's wife Clarissa died in England in 1853, worn out by their lives of hardship and poverty; only six of their twelve children had survived to adulthood. Goodyear himself had always been a frail man, but in his final years he looked very old (although only in his fifties), and he had such severe gout and neuralgia that he could walk only with crutches for his last six years. He collapsed and died in New York City on July 1, 1860, on the way to see his gravely ill daughter in New Haven.

Summary

It is ironic that Charles Goodyear's experiments with rubber aided Americans and all mankind so greatly and his family hardly at all. He was able to renew his patent on vulcanized rubber during his lifetime, but his heirs were refused renewals. The Goodyear Rubber Company, organized decades after his death, merely used his name to promote their rubber tires; the company was founded by strangers.

The rubber tire, so vital to modern transportation, is considered one of the most important outcomes of Goodyear's invention, as well as many other products essential to a life of good quality: in medicine, telecommunications, electronics—indeed, virtually every modern industry. It is difficult to imagine what daily life would be like without the availability of vulcanized rubber.

Bibliography

Beals, Carleton. *Our Yankee Heritage: New England's Contribution to American Civilization*. New York: David McKay Co., 1955. Beals titles his chapter on Goodyear "Black Magic." In it, he emphasizes the inventor's personal life as well as his experimentation. This essay contains many details on Goodyear's family life not found in other sources. Beals also provides an analysis of Goodyear's character traits.

Chamberlain, John. *The Enterprising Americans: A Business History of the United States*. New York: Harper and Row, Publishers, 1963. Originally a series in *Fortune* magazine on famous American businessmen. In his lively and engaging account of Goodyear, the author places emphasis on the inventor's Yankee ingenuity. Includes a bibliography.

Fuller, Edmund. *Tinkers and Genius: The Story of Yankee Inventors*. New York: Hastings House, 1955. One book in a series called "The American Procession." The area on which Fuller focuses is New England and the mid-Atlantic states, from which many early inventors originated. The experiments made by Goodyear are explained simply but accurately and clearly; Fuller also shows Goodyear the man. Includes bibliography.

Gies, Joseph, and Frances Gies. *The Ingenious Yankees*. New York: Thomas Y. Crowell, 1976. The authors focus on how America's Yankee inventors helped transform a farming country into a powerful technological nation. A biographical sketch of Goodyear is included, as well as an extensive bibliography.

Patterson, John C. *America's Greatest Inventors*. New York: Thomas Y. Crowell, 1943. The author covers fully the lives and careers of eighteen inventors, including Goodyear. He includes interesting facts concerning Goodyear's work and personal difficulties, motivations, and thoughts.

Thompson, Holland. *The Age of Invention: A Chronicle of Mechanical Conquest*. New Haven, Conn.: Yale University Press, 1921. One volume in a series devoted to American life, history, and progress. It has a good-sized bibliography, as well as photographs and illustrations. Vivid descriptive passages of Goodyear at work are provided in the narrative of his life and work. Also details the workings of Goodyear's various experiments.

Wilson, Mitchell. *American Science and Invention: A Pictorial History*. New York: Simon and Schuster, 1954. A large volume which relies on period illustrations and photographs to describe the course of American invention. Concise and accurate on Goodyear's life as well as his discovery, with descriptions of how his experiments progressed. Also interesting on Goodyear's personal character.

Patricia E. Sweeney

WILLIAM CRAWFORD GORGAS

Born: October 3, 1854; Toulminville, Alabama
Died: July 4, 1920; London, England
Area of Achievement: Public health
Contribution: Gorgas, a dedicated humanitarian, led the effort that eliminated yellow fever as one of the major epidemic diseases throughout the world. This feat was accomplished through the diligent and practical application of scientific discoveries concerning the disease.

Early Life

William Crawford Gorgas was born October 3, 1854, in Toulminville, Alabama. His father, Josiah Gorgas, was an officer in the United States Army and a Northerner; his mother, Amelia (Gayle) Gorgas, was a Southerner. The sectional strife in the late 1850's caused Josiah Gorgas considerable anxiety, for both marriage and experience inclined him to the Southern side. Eventually, he resigned his commission and offered his services to the Confederacy. The family was soon living in Richmond, where Josiah was serving as chief of ordnance with the rank of general. His son, known as Willie while a child and W. C. as an adult, spent his early formative years intoxicated with the military romanticism of the rebellion. He never stopped wanting to be a soldier or wishing that the rebels had won.

When the war ended, the family settled in Brierfield, Alabama, where Josiah Gorgas invested his small remaining capital in a blast furnace. Willie got what schooling was available and was in fact fortunate that his father's business quickly failed. When the senior Gorgas obtained a position at the University of the South in Sewanee, Tennessee, his son entered as a preparatory student. In 1870, the young Gorgas went as a volunteer to fight a yellow fever epidemic in New Orleans, an experience that started his lifelong interest in the disease. He still wanted to be a soldier, and when he was graduated, his father, who wanted him to study law, reluctantly and unsuccessfully tried to get him an appointment to West Point. Gorgas decided to get into the army via the medical corps. In 1876, he entered Bellevue Hospital Medical College in New York. Although he had felt no initial call to the profession, he found that medicine fascinated him. After graduation and a year of internship at Bellevue Hospital, he realized his longtime ambition by becoming in June, 1880, a first lieutenant in the United States Army.

Gorgas was tested both physically and spiritually during his first two decades in the army. He was stationed at out-of-the-way posts in Texas, North Dakota, and Florida, where, as the only doctor in the area, he worked long hours serving the local civilian population as well as keeping up with his military duties. His small frame and frail appearance belied his toughness, and his devotion to military life never dimmed. He charted his own future course when in 1883, while stationed at Fort Brown, Texas, he violated orders by working with victims of a yellow fever epidemic. Having been exposed, he was kept at the task, and he met his future wife, Marie Doughty; she was the sister of the post commander, whom he treated and with whom, after contracting the disease himself, he convalesced. Gorgas and Miss Doughty were married the next year. His illness not only afforded him a bride, but also deepened his interest in yellow fever, which he continued to study over the next few years. Gorgas was soon recognized as an expert on the disease, though he was not impressed with the mosquito transmission theory which was gaining more and more attention. Little did the hardworking small-post army doctor know it, but yellow fever was about to become the center of his life.

Life's Work

When, in 1898, the Spanish-American War put large numbers of American soldiers into the Caribbean, the medical corps proved ill-prepared to handle the inevitable outbreaks of tropical disease. Already known for his work with yellow fever, Gorgas was assigned to the yellow fever camp at Siboney, near Havana. His best advice was the burning of everything that might have been in contact with victims—even buildings. Later in 1898, Major Gorgas was appointed sanitary officer of Havana. The city was littered with sewage and filth and was a pool of yellow fever infection, exporting the disease with trade goods to American ports. Gorgas went to work on the needed cleaning only to find that, contrary to expectations, yellow fever became increasingly common. This was, of course, a result of the arrival of more and more non-immunes. At first the bitterly disappointed Gorgas seemed headed for failure, but the solution to his problem was at hand.

An American medical commission headed by Walter Reed had come to Cuba to study the problem of yellow fever. With Gorgas as fascinated observer, the Reed Commission combined past discoveries with new experiments to answer the question of transmission. A number of investigators— most recently Carlos J. Finlay—had suggested mosquitoes as the carrier, but no one had actually been able to show such a transmission. Henry Rose Carter in Mississippi had, however, established that there was a period of development for the germ in the mosquito's system before it could be passed along. The Reed Commission was able to show conclusively that the mosquito had to bite an infected person within three days of the initial infection and that the mosquito itself was not dangerous for at least ten days. It was also determined that the carrier was the *Stegomyia fasciata* (called today *Aëdes aegypti*). This proved the vital information.

Despite the efforts of the Reed Commission, Gorgas remained dubious. The only real test, he believed, was to rid the city of the mosquito and see what happened. Reed agreed but believed that such an extermination was impossible. Gorgas first tried for a vaccine, but soon focused his attack on the insect. Studying its habits, he found that it preferred to live in and around human habitations and lay its eggs in fresh water held in artificial containers. It also had a fairly limited range. Dividing the city into zones, Gorgas assigned teams to eliminate or put a film of kerosene on all open water. Windows were screened and houses, especially those where a case of yellow fever had occurred, were fumigated. Civilian objections to such intrusions were gently but firmly put aside. The result was that October, 1901, was the first October in the recorded history of Havana without a case of yellow fever. A happy side effect of the campaign was that malaria cases were reduced by fully three-quarters as well. The surgeon general of the army recognized Gorgas' efforts by deciding that he should become the army expert on tropical diseases. In 1902-1903, he was sent to attend the world conference on tropical medicine at Cairo and to have a look at the antimalaria work done at Suez. He was also promoted to colonel.

These assignments were to help prepare him for a job in the planned construction of a canal across the Isthmus of Panama. The American Medical Association lobbied for his appointment to the Canal Commission, headed by Admiral John G. Walker, but he was merely appointed chief sanitary officer. Problems caused by disease had played a substantial part in the failure of the French effort to construct a canal in Panama, and Gorgas believed that he could prevent such problems. Admiral Walker and the other commissioners, however, considered the idea of mosquito transmission of disease foolish and were much more concerned with economy and avoidance of even the appearance of graft than with sanitation. Indeed, the sanitary staff was hopelessly inadequate in number, and its requests for supplies were often denied or reduced to a fraction of the amount requested. Pay scales were set so low that qualified medical personnel were uninterested in the positions.

Gorgas protested as strongly as his sense of military hierarchy and his courtly Southern demeanor would allow, but to no avail. During the first yellow fever season, the disease was at low ebb, but Gorgas knew that, as in Havana, the influx of nonimmunes would provide the raw material for an epidemic. In the spring and summer of 1905, the number of cases began to increase rapidly, and official reaction was to blame Gorgas. Fortunately, the American Medical Association sent Dr. Charles A. L. Reed to investigate and report to Secretary of War William Howard Taft. The report, which was made public, supported Gorgas totally, and in addition to other studies led President Theodore Roosevelt to reorganize the Canal Commission. The new chairman, however, Theodore P. Shonts, also rejected the mosquito transmission theory and tried to get rid of Gorgas. Although inclined to agree with Shonts and other doubters, the president sought the advice of several prominent physicians, all of whom maintained that Gorgas was the best man for the job and that mosquito transmission had been proved. Roosevelt ordered that Gorgas be given full support.

Gorgas quickly began to apply the lessons learned in Havana. By November, 1905, he had four thousand men, and although earlier his entire budget had been fifty thousand dollars a year, he was able to order ninety thousand dollars' worth of window-screen wire alone. Panama City and Colón were fumigated house by house, piped water was supplied to end the need for open household cisterns, and pools of standing water which could not be drained were regularly sprayed with kerosene. By the end of 1905, yellow fever was under control. Other diseases that had threatened, such as cholera and bubonic plague, were gone, and malaria was much reduced. Health care for workers was very good generally, and death rates would have been acceptable in virtually any American city. The arrival in April, 1907, however, of George W. Goethals as chief engineer, proved a beginning of renewed frustration for Gorgas. Goethals had been given extremely broad powers and used them dictatorially. His efforts at economy, Gorgas feared, would weaken the sanitary effort. The two rarely found common ground personally or professionally, but the sanitary foundation had been laid and morbidity rates did not increase.

Gorgas' success in the canal zone led to numerous honors. In 1907, he received the Mary Kingsley Medal and in 1908 was elected president of the American Medical Association. He was also granted many honorary degrees. An invitation came in 1913 to consult on the problem of pneumonia among miners in South Africa, and with the canal nearing completion, he received permission to accept. Although his visit was cut short in February, 1914, by his appointment as surgeon general of the United States Army— with promotion to the rank of brigadier general—his report proved the basis for a program that improved the miners' situation significantly.

As surgeon general, Gorgas was responsible for reforms that prepared the Army Medical Corps for World War I. He encouraged doctors to join the service and helped develop the Medical Reserve Corps which supplied many of the physicians needed when the United States entered the war in 1917. Between the beginning of American participation and the armistice, the number of doctors in the military service increased by more than thirty times its original amount. Sanitation in military camps proved a problem, and at times Gorgas faced strong criticism. He was able to defend himself by pointing out failures to follow basic regulations through ignorance or more often through pressure to enlist and train an army before the British and French were overwhelmed. He also became involved in a controversial political struggle over provision of higher rank for American medical officers and eventually saw the necessary legislation through Congress. On October 3, 1918, Gorgas turned sixty-four, and despite protests from friends and admirers, had to retire from active duty. He spent the rest of his life working on behalf of the Rockefeller Foundation trying to eliminate the remaining pockets of yellow fever in the world. After getting the program started in South America, he died in London on July 4, 1920, while on a journey that had been intended to take him to West Africa, where yellow fever was still often epidemic. King George V visited the hospital to bestow on Lieutenant General William C. Gorgas, the only son of a Confederate general officer to achieve a similar rank in the United States army, the Order of St. Michael and St. George. It was a high and fitting last honor.

Summary

Two quintessentially American qualities are the hallmarks of William Crawford Gorgas' career: practicality and hard work. Although he made none of the basic scientific discoveries needed to end the scourge of yellow fever, when those discoveries were made he took advantage of them. His dogged and eventually successful struggle to get the necessary support for his sanitation program saved thousands of lives among the work force that built the canal and was a key factor in making construction possible. He proved that controlling the mosquitoes that spread the disease would prevent epidemics. These lessons, when applied throughout the world, saved countless thousands more.

Gorgas' work as surgeon general of the army was also extremely successful. The American Expeditionary Force in World War I suffered almost twice as many combat deaths as deaths from disease. The army as a whole had fewer than twenty-five percent more deaths from disease than in battle. While to modern ears the latter may not sound like success, it was unprecedented for its day.

A gentle, soft-spoken man, Gorgas was widely admired and often loved. Although a brasher man might have gotten things done in a shorter time, his very courtesy made it very difficult to turn him away, and his gentleness masked an iron determination. His achievements helped to establish modern standards of public health, standards which have improved the quality of life in almost every part of the globe.

Bibliography
Duffy, John. *Sword of Pestilence: The New Orleans Yellow Fever Epidemic of 1853*. Baton Rouge: Louisiana State University Press, 1966. Although its subject predates Gorgas' activity, this short book gives an excellent picture of what a yellow fever epidemic meant before modern public health brought the disease under control.

Gibson, John M. *Physician to the World: The Life of General William C. Gorgas*. Durham, N.C.: Duke University Press, 1950. The most recent and scholarly biography of Gorgas, it contains some anecdotes of dubious authenticity and is flawed by racial and ethnic stereotypes.

Gorgas, Marie D., and Burton J. Hendrick. *William Crawford Gorgas: His*

Life and Work. Garden City, N.Y.: Doubleday, Page and Co., 1924. Written by Gorgas' daughter, this biography is overly kind to its subject but does contain interesting personal observations.

Gorgas, William Crawford. *Sanitation in Panama*. New York: D. Appleton and Co., 1915. Gorgas' own account of his program in the canal effort, this book, while not the easiest of reading, is the best source of information about Gorgas' ideas while he was working on the canal.

McCullough, David. *The Path Between the Seas: The Creation of the Panama Canal, 1870-1914*. New York: Simon and Schuster, 1977. Well-written study of the canal with a chapter on Gorgas' life and the problems of sanitation woven throughout. Excellent background for anyone interested in Gorgas or the canal.

Martin, Franklin H. *Fifty Years of Medicine and Surgery*. Chicago: Surgical Publications Co., 1934. A colleague and admirer of Gorgas, Martin supplies the observations of a trained colleague as well as personal commentary.

Fred R. van Hartesveldt

MARTHA GRAHAM

Born: May 11, 1894; Pittsburgh, Pennsylvania

Area of Achievement: Modern dance
Contribution: Graham's inventive choreography and striking performances
established dance as a crucial component of modernist art and as a vital
expression of American cultural life.

Early Life

The Allegheny Mountains of western Pennsylvania were home to three of
the most distinctive women artists of the twentieth century: Mary Cassatt,
the Impressionist painter, and Gertrude Stein, practitioner of experimental
literature, were drawn toward a transatlantic perspective, working primarily
from Paris, the central city of the Modernist movement. Martha Graham, the
daughter of a worldly physician specializing in mental disorders and a direct
descendant of the noted Puritan Myles Standish, remained in the United
States to create a new art form, "modern dance," a distinctively American
extension of one of the most fundamental forms of human expression.

As a child, Graham was word-struck, an avid reader and student of the
dictionary who impressed friends of her family with her serious demeanor
and sense of responsibility. When her family moved to Santa Barbara, California, in 1908, where cultural diversity and a congenial climate gave her a
new sense of light and space, she became aware of her inclination toward
what she described as "paganism," an impulse to channel her enormous energy into an outward world of performance as well as an inward one of discipline and introspection. In 1911, she saw a poster announcing a performance by Ruth St. Denis, one of the most famous exotic concert dancers in
the world. She convinced her father to take her to Los Angeles for the show,
and by its conclusion, she felt that she had been "elected" to her chosen
profession and life's work.

Graham's father felt that a career in dance was out of the question, and
she devoted herself to her studies at the Cumnock School, a preparatory
academy including a junior college which she attended. She pursued a curriculum which emphasized stagecraft and acting, and when her father died of
a heart ailment in 1914, she enrolled in Denishawn, a dancing school operated by her idol, Ruth St. Denis, and Ted Shawn. She was then twenty-two,
with little formal dance training and a tendency to be slightly overweight, and
a career in the theater seemed an unlikely possibility. Graham worked very
hard, a lifelong habit, and Shawn, impressed by her determination and the
intense concentration of her dancing, gave her a small role in a pageant presented in Berkeley. When Shawn volunteered for the Ambulance Corps as
the United States entered World War I, he invited Graham to live at the stu-

dio and teach classes. Upon his return to the school, he was sufficiently impressed by her ability and progress to create a dance for her, and in June, 1920, "Xochitl," an Aztec story about an emperor who is passionately aroused by the dancing of a peasant girl (Graham), was first performed. Graham continued to work with the Denishawn Company in 1922 and 1923, touring England and then the United States. She danced for two months in the Greenwich Village Follies of 1923, in New York City, and accepted a teaching position at the Eastman School of the Theater at Rochester, New York, in 1925, where she worked with Rueben Mamoulian. She resigned and moved to New York City in 1926, devoting herself to private teaching and choreography. In April, 1926, she gave her first independent recital in New York.

Life's Work

When Martha Graham's Dance Group made its debut on April 14, 1929, at the Booth Theater in New York, Graham was thirty-five years old. She stood five feet, two inches tall, and, in her studio, she seemed even smaller, with delicate limbs, a long neck, and hair falling in sheaths almost to her waist. On the stage, though, her carefully composed presence was riveting. One critic called her "severe as a cube," which suggested her compact power but neither her protean range nor the multiple versions of the self she projected through her dances. She was small-boned, almost gaunt, with exceptional elasticity in her joints. She stood very straight-spined, had the sturdy legs of a running back and the flaring lips of a seductress. Her searing eyes, riding between high cheekbones, had the questing brilliance of an explorer. To accentuate and mold her appearance, she designed and sewed her own costumes. As described by Ernestine Stodelle, they were

> generally ankle-length. Sometimes the material fell in huge folds, as in *Lamentations*, or clung to her legs, as did the form-fitting knitted tubing of *Ekstasis*. She used all kinds of weaves, rough or smooth, shining or dull; she used all kinds of stripes, broad and narrow often mixed, as in her vertically stripped black and white straight-lined sheath for *Primitive Canticles*. Under her hands, cloth behaved humanly. It moved with her body like its skin, or it stubbornly kept its own form, standing rigidly with each bend of the knee or thrust of the hip until it had a regal stature, like the overshirt, stiff as tapestry in *Imperial Gesture*.

"I am a dancer," the words that she often used to begin articles or addresses, was a typically forthright statement of her devotion to her work. Her commitment inspired other dancers, who shared her belief that "dancing is an affirmation of life through movement," and the total involvement of her company enabled her to present a series of works that shaped the attitude of the American public toward the art of dance. Her performances of *Primitive Mysteries* (1931), *Dithyrambic* (1931)—probably the most completely integrated and ambitious solo composition of her early career—and *Deep Song* (1937) marked her emergence as an artist of singular ability and as a person of growing celebrity and influence. Beginning with *Every Soul Is a Circus* (1939), she began to create dances which not only showcased her own ability but also presented large-scale dramatic conceptions.

Letter to the World (1940), a speculative interpretation of Emily Dickinson's inner life as suggested by her poems, was marked by her empathy for another woman whose art represented the objectification of her life. Her sense of Dickinson's poems is reflected in her statement that dance is "a graph of the heart." Similarly, her *Deaths and Entrances* (1943), a version of the life of the Brontë sisters, was built, as Louis Horst, her musical mentor and lifelong friend and collaborator of many years put it, "on dramatic scenes laid within the mind or heart of a woman faced with an urgency of decision or action . . . and with the dramatis personae of the group performing as symbols of her complex emotional reactions."

Her setting of Aaron Copland's Pulitzer Prize – winning score of *Appalachian Spring* in 1944 was a quintessential declaration of the pioneer spirit of the early days of the United States, in which she played "The Wife" to Erik Hawkins' character "The Husbandman" four years before her brief marriage to Hawkins. *Errand into the Maze* (1947) was inspired by the work of the contemporary poet Ben Belitt, and in the same year, she began a series familiarly known as "Martha's Greek Cycle." Beginning with *Night Journey* (1947), which dealt with the character of Zeus, continuing with *Clytemnestra* (1958), drawn from Robinson Jeffers' poem and described by John Martin as "a miracle of greatness," the series continued with *Alcestis* (1960), *Phaedra* (1962), *Circe* (1963), and concluded with *Cortege of Eagles* (1967), in which she played Hecuba, Queen of Troy, in the "signature piece of her last dancing days." The dances in this cycle presented Graham in the strength of her maturity, while her dancing still retained the astonishing vitality of an extended prime.

While fiercely, even fanatically resisting the limits imposed by advancing age, like any great athlete Graham had to make certain concessions. In 1959, she began to limit her movements to motions within the range of her resources. She reluctantly recognized that in some of her productions, younger members of her company might be better choices for the roles that she had created for herself. In her own work, she was now more an actress than a dancer, and in her position with her legendary company, perhaps more playwright than performer. In 1970, at the age of seventy-six, she was forced into a kind of retirement by the new Board of Directors and the reigning members of her company. Her life seemed bleak and desolate without the energizing necessities of creative work. After a two-year struggle with alcohol and illness, she reemerged as chief director of her school and presented, in 1973, *Mendicants of Evening*, in which she designed dances to an electronic score for the first time. An astonished critic commented, "The current season is a new dawn." More than a decade after that, Martha Graham is still reluctant to be separated from the art that defines her life. In ages hence, her name will remain synonymous with twentieth century dance in America.

Summary

Martha Graham is one of the masters of Modernism, the "great imaginative enterprise on which artists," as Hugh Kenner put it, "were to collaborate for half a century." Like Pablo Picasso's, her work was a summary of previous form and motion which was then transformed and extended into a new era. Like Albert Einstein, she developed new ways of seeing the interrelationship of time, space, and man's place in the universe. Like James Joyce, she made a familiar language new, fresh, and alive, demonstrating the eternal vitality of its essential parts. She understood that, as Whitman wrote Emerson in 1856, "Old forms, old poems, majestic and proper in their own lands here in this land are exiles," and while she did not reject classical ballet, she realized that it did not offer an American dancer means sufficient for the realization of all the body's possibilities. Respectful of the classical tradition, she wanted to use the most innovative and exciting work of avant-garde artists in the fields of music, language, and design. Graham was the dynamic center of an artistic revolution that created works fully expressive of the rhythms and themes of contemporary American life, uniting the contributions of Louis Horst and Norman Dello Joio (music), Isamu Noguchi (sets), and Jean Rosenthal (lighting).

Her exceptional awareness of her own body as an "instrument of thrilling wonder... a dynamo of energy," which could be "shaped, disciplined, honored and in time, trusted," helped to dissolve the mind/body separation still strong in America from Puritan days. She recognized the rigid, stylized methods of acting favored by cautious directors as quasi-European imitations and similarly rejected the undisciplined, excessive sloppiness of most vaudeville routines as an empty countermeasure. Her theatrical presentations abolished the limits of both by insisting on building technique "out of her own body-feeling," and by accepting the validity of the individual experience of the performer.

She lived in New York, in the Greenwich Village, Union Square, and Lower East Side neighborhoods—bohemian quarters glowing with creative energy. She drew dancers for her company from the entire continent, gathered their individual skills into an exceptional ensemble and animated them with her own fire. In addition to the dancers and choreographers she trained (people such as Sophie Maslow) in the new art of modern dance composition and performance, her work with actors such as Henry Fonda and Gregory

Peck led to an increased awareness in kinesthetics in American theater and moved Bette Davis to say, "I worshiped her, she was all tension—lightning," and to explain that Graham showed her how "the body via the dance could send a message." Or, as Charles Olson, the poet, put it, "he who possesses rhythm possesses the universe," emphasizing the crucial modernist preoccupation with the ordering of space, as well as a recognition of its vastness, both within and beyond the consciousness of an individual self.

Perhaps Graham's ultimate contribution is her genius for projecting the vital importance of dance and motion into human life. "The exhilaration of dance, its primordiality, expressivity," as Martin Pops points out, "sexualizes the world in perpetual enactment . . . providing final knowledge of the body." From the work of Isadora Duncan at the beginning of the century through the vibrant intensity of Michael Jackson in the century's ninth decade, some of the most exciting artists of American life—athletes, actors, acrobats, action-painters—have reminded society, that, in Olson's words, "to dance is enough to make a whole day have glory." Martha Graham's life and work are at the nucleus of an attitude that fed a great energy surge through this country as America moved to its position of prominence in the modern world.

Bibliography
Anderson, John Murray. *Out Without My Rubbers*. New York: Library Publishers, 1954. Memoirs by a noted dance critic which evoke the period of Graham's early dance experience and the beginning of her "school" in New York.
Armitage, Merle, ed. *Martha Graham*. New York: Dance Horizons, 1966. A compilation of impressions by Graham's coworkers and dance critics, including some of Graham's most pithy pronouncements.
Denby, Edwin. *Looking at the Dance*. New York: Horizon Press, 1968. Reflections and comments on the world of modern dance by one of the most esteemed critics of the art.
Graham, Martha. *The Notebooks of Martha Graham*. New York: Harcourt Brace Jovanovich, 1973. Fascinating accounts of Graham's productions, including her reflections on all of the arts as well as some comments on American culture.
Horst, Louis. *Pre-Classic Forms*. New York: Dance Horizons, 1968. This volume, plus Horst's scrapbooks, are useful in establishing the situation surrounding the performances to which Horst contributed.
Leatherman, Leroy. *Martha Graham: Portrait of the Lady as an Artist*. New York: Alfred A. Knopf, 1966. A good description of her work methods.
McDonagh, Don. *Martha Graham*. New York: Praeger Publishers, 1973. An incisive account of Graham's life and work up to 1973, including some candid appraisals of her strengths and limitations.
Stodelle, Ernestine. *Deep Song: The Dance Story of Martha Graham*. New

York: Shirmer Books, 1984. A perceptive, very informative account of Graham's life from a most sympathetic friend and admirer. Probably the best book about Graham written thus far, with excellent photographs, detailed descriptions of the dances, and intelligent commentary.

Leon Lewis

ULYSSES S. GRANT

Born: April 27, 1822; Point Pleasant, Ohio
Died: July 23, 1885; Mount McGregor, New York
Areas of Achievement: The military and government
Contribution: Grant became the preeminent general of the Civil War, demonstrating the persistence and strategic genius that brought about the victory of the North.

Early Life

Ulysses S. Grant, born Hiram Ulysses Grant on April 27, 1822, in Point Pleasant, Ohio, was the eldest child of Jesse Root Grant and Hannah Simpson Grant. His father had known poverty in his youth, but at the time of his first son's birth, he had established a prosperous tannery business. In 1823, Jesse moved his business to Georgetown, Ohio, where Grant spent his boyhood. He received his preliminary education at Georgetown, at Maysville Seminary in Maysville, Kentucky, and at the Presbyterian Academy, Ripley, Ohio. He did not show special promise as a student and lived a rather ordinary boyhood. His most outstanding gift turned out to be a special talent with horses, enabling him to manage the most fractious horse. He also developed a strong dislike for work at the tannery and a lifelong fondness for farming.

Jesse Grant secured an appointment for his son to the United States Military Academy at West Point in 1839. His son did not want to go but bowed to parental authority. Concerned about the initials on his trunk, "H.U.G.," he decided to change his name to Ulysses Hiram Grant. Arriving at West Point, Grant had his first skirmish with military bureaucracy. His congressman, evidently confusing Grant with his brother Simpson, had appointed him as Ulysses S. Grant. The army insisted that Ulysses S. Grant, not Ulysses H. or Hiram Ulysses, had been appointed, and eventually Grant surrendered. Grant wrote to a congressman in 1864: "In answer to your letter of a few days ago asking what 'S' stands for in my name I can only state *nothing.*"

He was graduated in the middle of his class in 1843. While at West Point, he developed a fondness for novels and showed a special talent for mathematics. Appointed a brevet second lieutenant in the Fourth United States Infantry, Grant served with distinction in the Mexican War (1846-1848). He fought in the battles of Palo Alto, Resaca de la Palma, and Monterrey under the command of Zachary Taylor, "Old Rough and Ready." Taylor impressed Grant with his informal attire and lack of military pretension, a style which Grant later adopted. He participated in all major battles leading to the capture of Mexico City and won brevet promotion to first lieutenant for bravery at Molino Del Rey and to captain for his behavior at Chapultepec. Although he fought with distinction, Grant believed that the Mexican War was unjust and later said that he should have resigned his commission rather than participate.

Grant married Julia Dent, the daughter of a St. Louis slaveholding family, on August 22, 1848. He had been introduced to his future wife in 1843, by her brother, a West Point classmate, while stationed at Jefferson Barracks, Missouri. The Mexican War, however, interrupted their romance. The Grants had four children, Frederick Dent, Ulysses S., Jr., Ellen Wrenshall, and Jesse Root, Jr. A devoted husband and father, Grant centered his life on his family. Indeed, the many surviving letters to his wife during absences caused by a military career provide the most poignant insights into the man.

Ordered to the Pacific Coast in 1852 with his regiment, Grant could not afford to take his wife and children. He grew despondent without his family, decided to resign his commission in 1854, and returned to live on his wife's family land near St. Louis to take up farming. For the remainder of Grant's life, rumors that he had been forced to resign on account of heavy drinking followed him. The next seven years were difficult for Grant. His attempt at farming did not work out, and he tried other occupations without real success. Finally, in 1860, he moved his family to Galena, Illinois, to work as a clerk in a leather-goods store owned by his father and operated by his two younger brothers.

Grant had never been a strident, political man. His father had been an antislavery advocate, yet Grant married into a slaveholding family. At once time, he owned a slave but gave him his freedom in 1858 at a time when Grant sorely needed money. His wife retained ownership of slaves throughout the Civil War. When news of the firing on Fort Sumter reached Galena, Grant believed that he had an obligation to support the Union. Because of his military experience, he assisted in organizing and escorting a volunteer company to Springfield, Illinois, where he stayed on to assist Governor Richard Yates in mustering in and organizing volunteer troops. Eventually, Yates appointed Grant colonel of the Twenty-first Illinois Volunteers, a disorganized and undisciplined unit. Grant quickly worked the regiment into shape, marched it to Missouri, and learned much about commanding volunteer soldiers.

Life's Work

On August 7, 1861, President Abraham Lincoln appointed Grant brigadier general, and Grant established headquarters at Cairo, Illinois, an important staging area for Union movement further south. On September 6, he occupied Paducah, Kentucky, near the strategic confluence of the Tennessee, Cumberland, and Ohio rivers. Grant's first battle followed shortly. He attacked Confederate forces at Belmont, Missouri, with mixed results. He lost control of his troops after initial success and had to retreat when Confederate reinforcements arrived.

Grant gained national prominence in February, 1862, when authorized to operate against Fort Donelson and Fort Henry, guarding the Cumberland and Tennessee rivers, obvious highways into the Confederate heartland. He moved his small army in conjunction with naval forces and captured Fort Henry on February 6 and immediately moved overland against Fort Donelson, twelve miles away. The Confederates attempted to escape encirclement on February 15 in a brief, but bloody, battle. On February 16, the Confederate commander asked Grant for surrender terms. His response brought him fame: "No terms except an unconditional and immediate surrender can be accepted." The Confederates surrendered on Grant's terms, and Lincoln rewarded him for the first significant Union victory with promotion to major general.

Grant's next major engagement, the battle of Shiloh, April 6-7, left him under a cloud. Surprised by Rebel forces, Grant suffered heavy losses but managed to rally his army on the first day. The second day, General Grant counterattacked and drove the Confederates from the field. This bloody engagement cast a long shadow, and Grant faced newspaper criticism, with rumors of his heavy drinking appearing in the press. Major General Henry W. Halleck arrived on the scene to take command of Grant's forces, placing him in a subordinate position with little to do. Grant considered leaving the army. He retained his humor, however, writing to his wife, "We are all well and me as sober as a deacon no matter what is said to the contrary." Halleck, however, was called to Washington to act as general in chief, and Grant resumed command. Although many had criticized Grant, Lincoln refused to relieve a fighting general, thus setting the stage for Grant's finest campaign.

Confederate control of the Mississippi River rested on extensive fortifications at Vicksburg, Mississippi, effectively barring Midwestern commerce. In the fall and spring of 1862-1863, Grant made a number of attempts against this bastion. The overland campaign through northern Mississippi came to grief when Confederate forces destroyed his supply base at Holly Springs, Mississippi, on December 20, 1862. Grant then decided to move down the Mississippi to attack the city. Ultimately, Grant bypassed the city, marching his army down the west bank of the river. At night, he sent steamboats past the batteries to assist in crossing the river from Louisiana into Mississippi. The general then launched a lightning campaign into the interior of the state to destroy Confederate communications before turning back against Vicksburg. Thoroughly confusing his opposition, he won five separate battles and besieged the city on May 19. On July 4, 1863, Grant accepted the surrender of his second Confederate army.

After a brief respite, Grant was given command of all Union forces in the West on October 18 and charged with rescuing Union forces besieged in Chattanooga, Tennessee. In a three-day battle (November 23-25), Grant smashed the Confederate forces and drove them back into Georgia.

In March, 1864, Lincoln promoted Grant to lieutenant general and gave him command of all Union armies. Grant left Halleck at Washington as chief of staff to tend to routine matters and established the beginning of a modern military command system. He stayed in the field with the Army of the Potomac, commanded by Major General George G. Meade. Grant made Union armies work in tandem for the first time. Using the telegraph, he managed troop movements across the country, keeping pressure on the Confederacy at all points. The two major efforts consisted of Major General William T. Sherman, moving against Atlanta, and Meade attacking Confederate forces in Virginia, commanded by the South's finest general, Robert E. Lee.

The final campaign opened in May, 1864, with the battle of the Wilderness (May 5-6). After a series of bloody engagements, Grant maneuvered Lee into Petersburg, Virginia, where siege operations commenced on June 16. While Grant held Lee at Petersburg, Sherman proceeded to gut the South, capturing Atlanta in September, then marching across Georgia and capturing Savannah in December. Grant then planned for Sherman to march his army up through the Carolinas into Virginia. On March 29, 1865, Grant launched his final campaign. He smashed Confederate lines at Petersburg, then tenaciously pressured the retreating Confederates, and accepted Lee's surrender at Appomattox Court House on April 9. Grant's magnanimous surrender terms attest to his humanity and sensitivity. Seventeen days later, the last major Confederate force surrendered to Sherman and the Civil War ended.

Lincoln's assassination on April 14 deeply affected Grant, but he believed that President Andrew Johnson would be able to reestablish the Union on an equitable basis. Grant busied himself with the reorganization of the army, threatening French forces operating in Mexico, marshaling forces to fight Indians, and seeking to avoid political questions. Yet he could not avoid the growing antagonism between Johnson and the radical Republicans. Increasing doubts about Johnson's Reconstruction policy brought the two men into conflict. In the face of growing Southern persecution of blacks, Grant came to believe that blacks had to be protected by the federal government. In 1868, the breach between Johnson and Grant became public, and Grant believed that it was his duty to accept the Republican nomination for president.

A reluctant candidate, Grant easily defeated his Democratic opponent. His military background, however, had left him with a distaste for the hurly-burly of politics, and his two-term presidency (March 4, 1869, to March 4, 1877) had many problems. Already convinced of the need to protect blacks, Grant sought in vain to advance Civil Rights for them. With the Force Acts (1870-1871), he succeeded in breaking up the first Ku Klux Klan, but by 1876, conservative Southerners had regained control and reasserted their dominance.

In foreign policy, Grant did much to normalize relations with Great Britain with the Treaty of Washington in May, 1871, which settled the *Alabama* claims arising out of the Civil War. His stubbornness and persistence, which had served him so well in war, however, proved to be an embarrassment in his unsuccessful attempts to annex Santo Domingo.

Grant made a number of unfortunate appointments to federal office, and official corruption even reached into the White House with the Whiskey Ring Scandal. Although Grant was not personally involved, these scandals tainted his second term. Plagued by corruption and politics, Grant resisted attempts to draft him for a third term in 1876.

After the presidency, Grant made a two-year journey around the world, indulging a passion for travel developed early in his life. This triumphant tour brought him worldwide renown. Restless after returning to the United States, he unsuccessfully sought a third term in 1880. He then moved to New York City to pursue business interests in connection with his son, Ulysses S. Grant, Jr., and became a silent partner in Grant and Ward. Ferdinand Ward turned out to be a swindler, and in 1884, Grant found himself penniless.

To support his family, Grant decided to write his memoirs. At about the same time, Grant learned that he had contracted cancer of the throat. He completed the manuscript only days before his death, on July 23, 1885. This work has become a literary classic and is recognized as one of the best military memoirs ever written.

Summary

Grant's boyhood had been ordinary, showing nothing of the extraordinary man he would become. He had not sought a military career and did not like things military. He detested military parades, disliked military dress, and rarely carried a weapon. He left the army in 1854 and suffered through seven years of disappointment. The outbreak of Civil War, for all its national trauma, rescued Grant from a life of obscurity.

This seemingly common man turned out to have a genius for war unmatched by his contemporaries. Grant perhaps had an advantage in that he had time to learn gradually the art of war. Grant made mistakes, learned from them, and never repeated them. He grew into the responsibilities of higher command. He also understood volunteer soldiers and their motivations for fighting.

Grant's military writings are extraordinary. His instructions are clear, brief, and to the point. Subordinates made mistakes, but not because of ambiguity of instruction. Grant became the finest general that the Civil War produced, indeed, the greatest American military figure of the nineteenth century.

The Grant presidency had many shortcomings. Not a politician, Grant never really understood presidential power and its uses. In this sense, he was a nineteenth century man: He believed that Congress decided policy and the president executed it. Had Grant viewed the presidency in the same manner that he perceived military command, his two terms might have been far different.

Grant returned to wartime form in the fight to complete his memoirs. This literary classic is really a gift to the ages as he again demonstrated that he was truly an extraordinary American.

Bibliography
Catton, Bruce. *Grant Moves South*. New York: Little, Brown and Co., 1960. This biography of Grant, covering his early Civil War career, is thoroughly researched and superbly written.

_____. *Grant Takes Command*. Boston: Little, Brown and Co., 1969. Catton continues his brilliant work, taking Grant from Chattanooga to Appomattox.

Garland, Hamlin. *Ulysses S. Grant: His Life and Character*. New York: Doubleday and McClure Co., 1898. This nineteenth century biography of Grant is among the best written. It is especially valuable because the author interviewed a number of Grant contemporaries.

Grant, Ulysses S. *The Papers of Ulysses S. Grant*. Edited by John Y. Simon. Carbondale: Southern Illinois University Press, 1967-   . Fourteen volumes of this comprehensive series have been published, following Grant through April 30, 1865. This work makes it possible to evaluate Grant's career using documentary sources and demonstrates that Grant's literary flair in his memoirs was not a fluke.

_____. *Personal Memoirs of U.S. Grant*. 2 vols. New York: Charles L. Webster and Co., 1885-1886. These volumes are magnificent from both a literary and a historical perspective. Grant's assessment of his life through the Civil War is powerful, compelling, and amazingly accurate.

Hesseltine, William B. *Ulysses S. Grant: Politician*. New York: Dodd, Mead and Co., 1935. This highly critical account of Grant's presidency reflects the historical scholarship of the 1930's.

Lewis, Lloyd. *Captain Sam Grant*. New York: Little, Brown and Co., 1950. This beautifully written biography examines Grant's life up to the Civil War. Catton takes over where Lewis left off.

McFeely, William S. *Grant: A Biography*. New York: W.W. Norton and Co., 1981. A well-written biography that uses modern standards to judge Grant harshly, emphasizing what Grant should have done to protect black civil rights during Reconstruction.

Porter, Horace. *Campaigning with Grant*. New York: Century Co., 1897. Written by a Grant staff officer, this account is excellent for a personal view of Grant during the last eighteen months of the war.

Young, John Russell. *Around the World with General Grant*. 2 vols. New York: American News Company, 1879. Although there is considerable padding in these volumes, they have real significance because of the author's numerous interviews with Grant.

David L. Wilson

ASA GRAY

Born: November 18, 1810; Sauquoit, New York
Died: January 30, 1888; Cambridge, Massachusetts
Area of Achievement: Science
Contribution: The leading botanical taxonomist in nineteenth century United States and the founder of the discipline of plant geography, Gray was the first advocate of Darwinian evolution in the United States.

Early Life

The son of Moses Gray, a tanner, and Roxana Howard Gray (New Englanders who had migrated to upstate New York after the Revolutionary War), Asa Gray was born on November 18, 1810, in Sauquoit, New York. Educated at local schools and academies, Gray entered the College of Physicians and Surgeons of the Western District of New York in 1826. Alternating attendance at the lectures at the medical school with apprenticeship with practicing physicians, Gray received his medical degree in January, 1831.

Slight, short, and clean-shaven until his middle age, Gray was physically agile and appeared ever-youthful. This physical agility was matched by his mental quickness. Complementing these traits was a self-assuredness which led him to abandon medical practice in 1832 to follow his dream of becoming a botanist.

Life's Work

Gray's interest in botany had been sparked by James Hadley, one of the faculty at the College of Physicians and Surgeons, but his real mentor was John Torrey, one of the outstanding American botanists. After a tryout in 1832, Torrey hired Gray the following year to collect specimens for him. Ultimately, Gray moved into the Torrey home and became Torrey's collaborator on his *Flora of North America* (1838-1843).

Finding employment as a scientist in the 1830's was not easy. For the first few years after he rejected a medical career, Gray supported himself through part-time teaching and library jobs. In 1836, he was selected as botanist on the United States Exploring Expedition but resigned the position in 1838, before the expedition ever sailed, disgusted by the delays which had plagued the venture. Instead, he became professor of botany (the first such professorship in the United States) at the University of Michigan, spending the next year in Europe purchasing books and equipment for the university. The university's financial problems resulted, however, in the suspension of his salary in 1840, before he had ever taught a class. Not until April, 1842, with his appointment as Fisher Professor of Natural History at Harvard University, with responsibility for teaching botany and maintaining the botanical gardens, did Gray obtain a stable and permanent institutional home. He remained at Harvard (which also indirectly supplied him with his wife, Jane Lathrop Loring, the daughter of a leading Boston lawyer who was a member of the Harvard Corporation) for the rest of his life.

Manifest Destiny helped shape the contours of Gray's scientific career: Overseas exploration and domestic reconnaissance and surveying during the two decades before the Civil War had resulted in a huge flow eastward of botanical specimens gathered by army engineers, naval explorers, and collectors accompanying the expeditions. Gray spent most of his professional life worrying about the nomenclature and taxonomy of these plants. Through either his own research or the coordination of the activities of other botanists, he was responsible for the description of flora gathered from Japan to Mexico.

By the 1850's, Gray was clearly the leading botanist in the United States. He was the cement that held together a huge network of amateur collectors. His publications included the *Manual of the Botany of the Northern United States* (1848) and extremely popular textbooks for college, high school, and elementary school students. A frequent visitor to Europe, he was well-known in international scientific circles.

The opportunity for Gray's greatest contribution to science came about because of his international reputation, but his connection with this flow of specimens enabled him to exploit fully the opportunity. Charles Darwin had written him in April, 1855, inquiring about the geographical distribution of Alpine plants in the United States. In response, Gray produced a statistical analysis of the flora of the northern United States, drawing on his wide knowledge of the botany of the Northern Hemisphere. This in turn encouraged Darwin in 1857 to let Gray in on his great secret—the theory of evolution.

At this point, Gray had in hand an extensive collection from Japan, gathered by Charles Wright during the North Pacific Exploring Expedition, as well as smaller collections from Matthew C. Perry's expedition, which opened in Japan. Gray discerned that the flora of Japan was much more similar to that of eastern North America than western North America or Europe. He rejected the possibility of separate creation and, applying Darwin's ideas, proposed instead that the similarities reflect the evolution of the flora from common ancestry under similar conditions. A single flora, Gray theorized, had stretched round the earth before the Ice Age; changing geological conditions resulted in the differences in Northern Hemispheric flora.

This public endorsement of Darwin in early 1859, the first in the United States, was followed by many others. Gray quickly became the leading American spokesman for Darwin's theory, and he negotiated the American publishing contract for *On the Origin of Species by Means of Natural Selection* (1859). Moreover, the review of this work in the *American Journal of*

Science, the leading American scientific journal of the day, was written by Gray. Time and again he debated the leading anti-evolutionist in the American scientific community, the Swiss-born Louis Agassiz, director of Harvard's Museum of Comparative Zoology. In 1860, in a series of articles in the *The Atlantic Monthly*, Gray defended Darwin from critics who charged that the theory of evolution was hostile to religion, taking a position on the compatibility of Darwinian evolution with theism which the author of the theory himself was unable ultimately to accept.

After his retirement from teaching in 1873, Gray continued his research and field trips. He spent six triumphant months in Europe in 1887, returning to the United States in October. A month later, he was taken ill and died in his home in Cambridge on January 30, 1888. He left behind the Harvard Botanic Garden, the Gray Herbarium, and a generation of botanists and collectors for whom he had provided training, guidance, and assistance.

Summary

Asa Gray was fortunate to be a botanist in the United States at a time when the expansionist drive of the nation resulted in its soldiers and sailors crisscrossing the North American continent and the Pacific Ocean. Describing the botanical fruits of these exploring and surveying expeditions was Gray's lifelong work. His skill helped set American botany on a par with its European counterparts. Prodded by Charles Darwin, he asked some important questions about plant distribution which led to the development of a new scientific field and further evidence for the evolutionary thought of Darwin.

Gray's greatest impact on American society, however, was as the defender of Darwin's theory of evolution. Gray, a member of the First Congregation Church of Cambridge, understood that if evolution was to be accepted by the deeply religious American scientific community of the mid-nineteenth century, it would have to be reconciled with a belief in the existence of God. Gray believed that Darwin's theory, whatever its scientific merits, had to be defended from accusations of atheism. His solution was to suggest that the Creator intervened by limiting or directing variations. Darwin could not accept such an interpretation, however, and Gray's vision died with him. If Darwin had made another choice, the intellectual, cultural, and philosophical history of the West might have taken a course much different from that which it subsequently followed.

Bibliography

Dupree, A. Hunter. *Asa Gray: 1810-1888*. Cambridge, Mass.: The Belknap Press of Harvard University Press, 1968. The standard biography, well documented, interpretive, and accurate. Views Gray within the context of the social and intellectual history of the United States.

Eyde, Richard H. "Expedition Botany: The Making of a New Profession." In

Magnificent Voyagers: The U.S. Exploring Expedition, 1838-1842, edited by Herman J. Viola and Carolyn Margolis, 25-41. Washington, D.C.: Smithsonian Institution Press, 1985. Discusses the problems surrounding the botanical activities of the expedition.

Goetzmann, William H. *Exploration and Empire: The Explorer and the Scientist in the Winning of the American West*. New York: Alfred A. Knopf, 1966. A well-researched history of American exploration in the nineteenth century and the scientific discoveries which were its by-product. Although Gray is mentioned only briefly, this book describes the context of much of his scientific efforts.

Gray, Asa. *Darwiniana*. Edited by A. Hunter Dupree. Cambridge, Mass.: Belknap Press of Harvard University Press, 1963. A collection of Gray's essays on evolution, first published in 1876. Essential for understanding Gray's attempt to reconcile evolution and religion.

_____. *The Letters of Asa Gray*. Edited by Jane Loring Gray. 2 vols. Boston: Houghton Mifflin Co., 1893. This collection, edited by Gray's widow, includes Gray's autobiography.

Loewenberg, Bert James. "The Reaction of American Scientists to Darwinism." *American Historical Review* 38 (1933): 687-701. Dated, but still useful. Focuses on three representative figures: Gray, Agassiz, and James Dwight Dana, who was an example of those scientists who initially rejected evolution but eventually changed their position.

Lurie, Edward. *Louis Agassiz: A Life in Science*. Chicago: University of Chicago Press, 1960. The essential biography of Darwin's chief American scientific opponent.

Rodgers, Andrew Denny, III. *American Botany, 1873-1892: Decades of Transition*. Princeton, N.J.: Princeton University Press, 1944. Discusses the evolution of American botany from a descriptive to an experimental science and Gray's role in that transition.

_____. *John Torrey: A Story of North American Botany*. Princeton, N.J.: Princeton University Press, 1942. A scholarly, although somewhat dated biography of Gray's mentor. Provides an excellent account of Torrey's scientific accomplishments and his role in developing American botany.

Marc Rothenberg

HORACE GREELEY

Born: February 3, 1811; Amherst, New Hampshire
Died: November 29, 1872; New York, New York
Areas of Achievement: Journalism and social reform
Contribution: A daring journalist and lecturer, Greeley engaged himself personally with a wide range of social issues—labor rights, abolitionism, territorial expansion, women's rights, and political reform—and his paper, the *New York Tribune*, became a medium for the best thought of his time.

Early Life

Horace Greeley's ancestors were among the founding families of New England, having arrived in 1640. The third of seven children of Zaccheus and Mary (Woodburn) Greeley, he was a frail boy, uncoordinated, with a very large head on a small frame. His mother was very protective of him, keeping him close as he was physically weak. She held great influence on him, and she urged him to read and study rather than risk injury in the rough-and-tumble world of children. Greeley could read at an early age, and with his delicate manners he became a favorite of teachers in Bedford, whose trustees were also impressed with the boy's brilliance. Some influential citizens even offered to underwrite Greeley at Phillips Academy in nearby Exeter. His parents declined the offer, as hard times seemed continually to press them to move from farm to farm, from Connecticut to Massachusetts and on to Westhaven, Vermont, all before Horace was ten years old. He continued with his self-education, aided and watched over by his mother. His ungainly appearance and odd wardrobe of baggy short trousers and a coat topped by equally odd slouching hats and caps did little to mitigate the impression made by the high-pitched, whining voice that came from his large, moonlike head. Youngsters called him "the ghost," and he became a subject for their merriment. Throughout his life he lacked social polish and a sense of dress.

At fifteen, Greeley was apprenticed to a small newspaper, the *Northern Spectator* of East Poultney, Vermont; there, he learned the rudiments of what was to become his life's work. He joined the local debating society, and, with his intense and serious attention to public affairs, he became a respected member of the community. The paper folded, however, and Greeley joined his family, which had moved to the Pennsylvania–New York border village of Erie, where his father had again taken up farming. There he helped with the farm and gained printing jobs in Erie, Jamestown, and Lodi, all towns in New York State. The struggle for existence, let alone success, in the dismal marginal area depressed him, and in 1831, with ten dollars, he set out on foot for New York City.

Life's Work

Finding employment in New York was difficult, but Greeley was willing to take on a job that no other printer would do: set up print for an edition of the New Testament with Greek references and supplementary notes on each book. This job, which strained Greeley's already weak eyesight, brought him to the attention of other printers. He began work on William Leggett's *Evening Post*, from which he was fired because he did not fit the model of "decent-looking men in the office." Greeley, however, was able to save some money and form a partnership with Francis Vinton Story, and later, Jonas Winchester. They did job-printing as well as printing *Bank Note Reporter* (1832) and the *Constitutionalist* (1832), which dealt with popular lottery printing. They attempted a penny paper called the *Morning Post* using patronage investment by H. D. Shepard and supply credit from George Bruce, but a general lack of business acumen caused the venture to fail. With the failure of the penny daily, Greeley turned to putting out a successful weekly, the *New-Yorker*, which, coupled with his other publications, made the partnership now called Greeley and Company a success in journalism although not in the cash box. The habit of newspapers to extend credit rather than work on a cash basis was not to be changed until James Gordon Bennett's *Herald* demanded it in the 1840's. Greeley's weekly was nonpartisan in politics, stimulating, well written, and well edited. Greeley also made extra money by selling his writing to other papers, such as the *Daily Whig*.

In 1836, Greeley married Mary Youngs Cheney, formerly of Cornwall, Connecticut, then a teacher in North Carolina. They had first met while virtual inmates of Sylvester Graham's boardinghouse; Cheney was a devoted follower of the Grahamite cause, while Greeley was simply a teetotaling vegetarian satisfying his curiosity about Graham's unique regimen for healthy living. They were an odd match. She was plain, dogmatic, humorless, supercilious, and uncommunicative; he was compassionate, outgoing, and egalitarian. From the first day of their marriage, on July 5, 1836, they did not get along.

As a matter of personal conscience, Greeley was never inclined to pyramid debt, and this contributed to the failure of his weekly. In addition, nonpartisanship was never Greeley's strong suit. Opinionated, he found advocacy-journalism more to his liking; therefore, he was more than willing to accommodate the proposition of Whig boss Thurlow Weed of Albany, New York, to put out a New York paper favoring the party. The result was the *Jeffersonian*, which brought Greeley a guaranteed salary of one thousand dollars per year and proved a success. More important, Greeley was mixing in state and national political circles. In 1840, the Whigs encouraged Greeley to publish another weekly, called the *Log Cabin*; because it had a guaranteed subscription list among the party faithful, the journal was an immediate success. Greeley edited the *Log Cabin* as well as his struggling *New-Yorker* until, on April 10, 1841, he combined the two publications using three thousand dollars, of which one-third was his cash, one-third was in supplies, and one-third was borrowed from James Coggeshall. The result was his *New York Tribune*. He had built a personal following through the political papers, and he now sought to capitalize on his name recognition.

As a conservative Whig daily, the *New York Tribune* was carefully structured, with sober news stories, minimal sensationalism, and a strong editorial section. Greeley turned over the business affairs to another partner, Thomas McElrath, while he concentrated on the journalism. Unlike Bennett, who was both a newsman and a businessman, Greeley was a man to whom opinions came first. His work was like an ongoing feature article. His Puritan background encouraged him to seek redress for the social wrongs that he saw everywhere. His belief in the rectitude of his moral cause made him impregnable to criticism. The common denominator linking many of his positions was his advocacy of the downtrodden and the oppressed. He strongly opposed the death penalty, which he saw as a violation of life and also a violence done by society against the weakest elements, who did not have the wherewithal to defend themselves; he led the fight for the rights of women and laboring classes, took up the cause of temperance as early as 1824, and championed the farming classes and frontier development. That he would join the cause against slavery was inevitable.

Both wage slavery and chattel slavery were regarded by Greeley as outrages against humanity, and he admonished the press to be as "sensitive to oppression and degradation in the next street as if they were practiced in Brazil or Japan." Greeley, however, was an economic nationalist where foreign trade was concerned, pushing for protective tariffs. In the matter of women's rights, he was not in favor of suffrage, but he championed virtually every other plea by the burgeoning women's movement of the mid-nineteenth century. These causes, which promoted confidence in the people, brought enormous success to the *New York Tribune*, both critical and financial. Despite his success, Greeley was always financially hard-pressed. He never held controlling interest in the paper and was indifferent to that fact until his last years. By then it was too late, as the brilliant talents that he had recruited and cultivated had acquired dominant interest. His intuitive sense of talent brought the iconoclastic Margaret Fuller to the paper and even to live in his home for a time. Charles A. Dana joined Greeley in 1847 and was followed by Bayard Taylor in the following year. George Ripley, in 1849, was given a free hand to develop the literary department. In a continual struggle with the *Herald* for circulation and dominance, the *New York Tribune* vigorously pursued talent to make the paper a complete publication. In the 1850's came James S. Pike as Washington correspondent and editorial writer, F. J. Ottarson as city editor, W. H. Fry as music editor, Solon Robinson as agricultural editor, and then Fry and Richard Hildreth as byline reporters. The quality and intensity of the paper's political reporting, though uneven, was unequaled in the Civil War years. The newspaper's circulation under Greeley grew enormously, reaching well over a quarter million per week. This number is incredible in that the paper attracted subscribers only in areas outside the South.

The paper took strong positions on virtually every topic. Though this might have doomed other newspapers, the compelling intelligence of Greeley and his staff kept the *New York Tribune* in the forefront. At first reserved in judgment, Greeley gained confidence as his paper matured. He opposed the Mexican War, supported the Wilmot Proviso limiting slavery, and reluctantly supported Zachary Taylor. Greeley was an avid abolitionist and, in 1850, during the course of the debate on the Compromise of 1850, he stated that rather than have slavery on free soil he would "let the Union be a thousand times shivered." The Kansas-Nebraska Act infuriated him. He inveighed against its supporters and called upon antislavery forces to arm themselves and ensure that Kansas be without slavery. Greeley considered himself an astute politician, but when he fell out with his influential friends William H. Seward and Thurlow Weed, he destroyed his chances for political success. He broke from Seward as a result of a dispute over the status of slavery in Kansas and from Weed because of the latter's refusal to support him for governor of New York. Greeley had been a member of the House of Representatives for a brief three months in 1848-1849, and he enjoyed the excitement of political action. He failed reelection in 1850, however, and even failed in his attempt to gain the lieutenant governorship of New York in 1854. Greeley wanted Seward's Senate seat in 1861 and attempted to gain nomination to the Senate again in 1863, but he was thwarted by Weed's forces. He also failed to gain candidacy for the House in both 1868 and 1870 as well as the office of state comptroller in 1869. The Weed-controlled state machine was determined to force Greeley out of political life forever in retaliation for his attack on Seward's presidential candidacy in 1860 in favor of Abraham Lincoln.

At the onset of the Civil War, Greeley was very inconsistent. At first he was vehement in opposition to slavery, secession, and concessions on the expansion of slavery, but, shortly after, he suggested that secession might be allowed if a majority of Southerners wished it. In a return to his earlier position, Greeley's paper took up the cry of "Forward to Richmond" in an article by Charles Dana that was often attributed to Greeley and which committed him to join the crusade. He allied himself with the Radical Republicans Thaddeus Stevens, Charles Sumner, and Salmon P. Chase and opposed all attempts by Lincoln to conciliate the South. His paper supported the John C. Frémont emancipation in Missouri and followed with an article, "The Prayer of Twenty Millions," on August 20, 1862, which attacked the Administration on Confiscation Act manipulation, which favored Southern slaveholders. He rejoiced at the passage of the Emancipation Proclamation. Greeley worked to undercut Lincoln in 1864 by suggesting a new candidate, but by September of that year his paper endorsed Lincoln's reelection. He had, in the interim, suggested that to save the nation from ruin a one-year armistice be declared during which the blockade would be lifted and each side would hold on to what it had gained. As a result of that suggestion, his judgment was questioned; his influence waned even more with his pronouncements on Reconstruction. He advocated full equality of the freedmen while at the same time calling for a general amnesty for Southerners. At a time when most politicians were "waving the bloody shirt," he signed the bail bond of Jefferson Davis in Richmond on May 13, 1867, and pushed for his freedom. Greeley's reputation and his paper's circulation both suffered. He supported the nomination of General Ulysses S. Grant but after two years turned against him. He committed himself to defeating Grant in 1872, determined to use both himself and his paper to develop an independent party. He feared the destruction of his paper, which by now was held by as many as twenty interests.

When the desperate Democrats made an alliance with liberal Republicans, Greeley was itching to become a presidential candidate. With enemies in all camps, he took up the crusade, which exhausted him physically and emotionally. He was pilloried by cartoonists, who mocked his odd build, his floppy hats and strange white duster fluttering in the wind as he waddled, and the chin whiskers circling his face. By October, it was clear that there was little prospect for victory or even a good showing. In the election, he carried only six border and Southern states, suffering the worst defeat of any presidential candidate to that time.

Greeley's wife, who had been ailing for years, died on October 30, 1872, five days before the disastrous election. His love for this irascible woman was enduring, and he felt totally alone. They had seen the death of five of their seven children, and now there were only the daughters Ida and Gabrielle to stand with him. He attempted to return to the *New York Tribune*, but it, too, rejected him and humiliated him. His mind snapped, and he was institutionalized in the home of Dr. George S. Choate of Pleasantville, New York, where he died on November 29. The death of this great public man was noted throughout the nation. After a monumental funeral, he was buried in Greenwood Cemetery. He was remembered by his printer union friends with a bust over his grave and other statues.

Summary

Horace Greeley was forever a child prodigy, a passionate friend of mankind, one who understood the uses of money but who held no commitment to either gaining it or keeping it, and one who was possessed of and by ideas and by any and all who harbored them. Politically, he was a vain naïf caught in a cynical world. He was a man who wanted greatness for his nation and for its people. He had a compelling need to communicate his ideas, and he attracted to his paper people who themselves had something to say. He loved to explain things to a nation that was moving too quickly to do its own thinking.

Whether the issue was corruption in politics, the plight of women, love and marriage, crime, the burdens of the laboring classes, or the complexities of socialism, Greeley had something to say about it in a way that the common man could understand. The people were his true family, and his *New York Tribune*, his lectures, his books, and his essays were the instruments by which he instructed this family.

Bibliography
Baehr, Harry, Jr. *The New York Tribune Since the Civil War*. New York: Dodd, Mead and Co., 1936. A useful book, especially the first section, which has some good illustrations of personalities associated with Greeley.
Commons, John Rogers. "Horace Greeley and the Working Class Origins of the Republican Party." *The Political Science Quarterly* 24 (September, 1909): 468-488. Provides insight into Greeley's approach to broadening the base of the party and his appeal to the laboring classes in nineteenth century America.
Greeley, Horace. *The American Conflict: A History of the Great Rebellion in the United States of America, 1860-'65*. 2 vols. Hartford, Conn.: O. D. Case and Co., 1864-1866. This is an involved personal overview of the events leading to the Civil War, and the war itself, by a less than disinterested observer who nevertheless maintained a reasonable objectivity.
_____. *An Overland Journey from New York to San Francisco in the Summer of 1859*. New York: C. M. Saxton Barker and Co., 1860. This, along with Greeley's other works, gives a sense of the charm and intelligence of the man.
_____. *Recollections of a Busy Life*. New York: J. B. Ford and Co., 1869. This book should be read by anyone who wants to know Greeley. He was such a public man that even academics presume to know him without reading what is an unsung but truly remarkable autobiography.
Hale, William Harlan. *Horace Greeley: Voice of the People*. New York: Harper and Brothers Publishers, 1950. A book that shows Greeley's intuitive understanding of the issues of his time.
Horner, Harlan Hoyt. *Lincoln and Greeley*. Urbana: University of Illinois Press, 1953. An examination of the curious relationship between Lincoln and the often presumptuous Greeley on issues of war and peace.
Isely, Jeter Allen. *Horace Greeley and the Republican Party, 1853-61: A Study of the "New York Tribune."* Princeton, N.J.: Princeton University Press, 1947. This work is necessary to an understanding of the making of the Republican Party and the exploitation of the Greeley paper toward that end.
Seitz, Don C. *Horace Greeley: Founder of the "New York Tribune."*

Indianapolis: Bobbs-Merrill Co., 1926. Seitz provides a journalistic biography of Greeley with some very useful information on the editor's family life.

Van Deusen, Glyndon G. *Horace Greeley: Nineteenth Century Crusader.* Philadelphia: University of Pennsylvania Press, 1953. This is the standard biography. Balanced, readable, well-documented; includes a general bibliography, "bibliography by chapter," and illustrations (a number of which are cartoonists' caricatures of Greeley).

Jack J. Cardoso

NATHANAEL GREENE

Born: August 7, 1742; Potowomut, Rhode Island
Died: June 19, 1786; Mulberry Grove plantation, Georgia
Area of Achievement: The military
Contribution: Greene was one of George Washington's most trusted subordinates throughout the Revolutionary War, playing a significant role both as a field commander and as the Continental army's quartermaster general.

Early Life

Nathanael Greene was one of the numerous descendants of the Quaker John Greene, who followed Roger Williams to Rhode Island in 1636 in search of religious freedom. He was born on August 7, 1742, in Potowomut (modern Warwick), Rhode Island. Because of his father's suspicion of learning, Greene was largely self-educated, his early reading being directed by a chance meeting with Ezra Stiles, later president of Yale College. The young Greene was five feet, ten inches tall and well built, with an oval face, blue eyes, a straight nose, a full, determined mouth, and a large forehead and firm double chin. A stiff right knee gave him a slight limp, but neither this nor periodic bouts of asthma prevented him from engaging in normal physical activity.

Like his brothers, Greene spent most of his youth working in the prosperous family forge and mills. In 1770, his father gave him control of the family forge in Coventry, Rhode Island, where he built his own house, including a library of 250 volumes. From early youth he had shown a fondness for dancing and an interest in things military; some time after his father's death, the Quaker meeting in Coventry dismissed him for attending a military parade.

Greene lived as a typical young man of his class, being elected to the Rhode Island General Assembly in 1770, 1771, 1772, and 1775. On July 20, 1774, he married Catharine Littlefield; they were to have two sons and three daughters. Greene was aware of the growing tensions between the American Colonies and the mother country, becoming convinced as early as October, 1775, that a break with Great Britain was necessary to preserve American liberties. He was instrumental in the formation of the Kentish Guards, a militia company organized in response to the Boston Port Act of 1774; he served as a private when some members indicated that a captain who limped would be a blemish on the company.

Life's Work

Greene's military career, which occupied the rest of his life, began when he was commissioned brigadier general of Rhode Island's three regiments on May 8, 1775. He took his troops to Boston, where he first met Washington, and on June 22 was appointed one of the eight brigadier generals of the Continental army. He commanded in Boston after the British evacuation in March of 1776; by May, he was supervising the building of fortifications on Long Island, though a three-week bout with fever kept him out of the battles there. He was made major general on August 9 and by mid-September was commanding his division during the retreat from New York. At this point, as commander of Forts Lee and Washington, Greene was confident that both could be held, and Washington took his advice. On November 16, Fort Washington surrendered, however, Fort Lee had to be evacuated, and Washington's army retreated through New Jersey.

Greene's division crossed the Delaware with Washington, and Greene led the left column against Trenton, capturing the Hessian artillery. In early January, he delayed Cornwallis while Washington made his night march to Princeton. At the battle of Brandywine on September 10, Greene's division covered four miles in forty-five minutes to aid the right wing, covered the retreat, and saved the artillery. Arriving late at the October 4 dawn attack on Germantown, Greene's left column fought in the two-hour battle and then protected the rear for five miles of the retreat, without losing a gun. On December 19, 1777, the army went into winter quarters at Valley Forge.

On February 25, 1778, Greene reluctantly agreed to become quartermaster general (officially appointed on March 2). A difficult job at best, it was much involved with the politicking and intrigue swirling around Washington and in the Continental Congress; the eddies alone could destroy a reputation, and Greene preferred military activity. Yet his realization of the importance of the work and his strong sense of obligation to Washington and the Revolutionary cause kept Greene in the position for eighteen months. During this time, he set up a system of supply depots and required monthly reports from his deputies. He was as effective as congressional politics, intercolonial squabbling, and inadequate financing allowed. On the march to Monmouth, for example, he picked good campsites and had them prepared with wood, straw, barrels of vinegar, latrines, and stone-walled springs, while seeing to the repair of equipment and the collection of fodder.

For the battle of Monmouth on June 28, Greene resumed his line command and led the right wing, pushing back Sir Henry Clinton's line. Sent to Rhode Island to further a projected Franco-American push, Greene commanded the right wing on August 11, when American troops were defeated while Count d'Estaing refused to disembark his four thousand French soldiers. Greene acted as peacemaker in the subsequent arguments and again as right wing commander in an unsuccessful engagement on August 29. The ensuing military lull did not extend to the quartermaster department, Greene administering approximately fifty million dollars in 1779; his effectiveness at supply helped to support the army during winter quarters in Morristown and to keep it mobile during the summer's maneuvering. When Congress adopted a plan to reorganize the department, Greene's resignation (the last of several) was accepted, on August 3. During September, while performing quartermaster duty until his successor took over, Greene also presided over the board of general officers which condemned Major John André to be hanged as a spy.

The war in the North wound down after 1778 as the British shifted their major operations to the South, taking Augusta and Charleston and setting up a chain of interior posts. After General Horatio Gates's defeat at Camden, Washington, on October 14, 1780, appointed Greene to the Southern command, and Congress ratified this to include control of all troops between Delaware and Georgia. In Philadelphia, Greene arranged for a medical department, engineers, artillery, clothing, horses, and equipment; in Richmond, he established cooperation with Governor Thomas Jefferson; in North Carolina, he ordered the building of boats and established cooperation with the patriot organizations. On December 2, in Charlotte, he took formal command, which was marked almost immediately by cooperation with the partisan leaders General Andrew Pickens, General Thomas Sumter, and Colonel Francis ("Swamp Fox") Marion, and by his use of able subordinates such as General Daniel Morgan, Colonel Otho H. Williams, and Colonel William Washington, with General Henry ("Light-Horse Harry") Lee's Legion as his intelligence arm. Throughout his tenure as the commander of the Southern Department, Greene made effective use of these brilliant and independent-minded leaders while maintaining good relations with political leaders in several states and paying his usual careful attention to the logistical details that made his strategy possible. A nationalist, the Rhode Islander felt no constraint in the South; more diplomatic as commander than he was as quartermaster general, he was able to get maximum cooperation from detached and independent forces.

American losses at Charleston and Camden had seriously reduced both numbers and morale, so Greene appointed good quartermaster officers and added to the strength of his forces, having about two thousand Continentals and between five hundred and a thousand partisans. Moving his camp to the Cheraw Hills, South Carolina, on the Pedee River, he once again faced Lieutenant General Cornwallis. Like Greene, Cornwallis did not have enough men to control the South, and his serious supply problems were never solved; although popular with his troops (with whom he shared privation and hardship) and fearless in battle, he did not plan in detail for long campaigns and often blundered.

Greene took the initiative and divided his army, sending off half under Morgan to the victory at Cowpens on January 17, 1781. Cornwallis burned his baggage and set off in pursuit. Both armies raced for the Dan River, but Greene had provided boats and Cornwallis had not. Greene, maneuvering while waiting for reinforcements, took a strong position near Guilford Courthouse on March 15; he used his forty-two hundred men well, but few were veterans. Cornwallis attacked with two thousand veterans, but although Greene retreated after three hours' hard fighting, Cornwallis lost a quarter of his force and had to withdraw toward the coast, unable to resume the offensive in the Carolinas. Greene was physically exhausted after six weeks with little sleep and no change of clothing, but after some rest he planned the best use of his limited resources: He was left with about 1,450 troops and the partisans. Cornwallis' subordinate Lord Francis Rawdon attacked Greene's new position (near Camden) on April 25; because of Colonel John Gunby's injudicious order to fall back, Greene was forced to make a general retreat from Hobkirk's Hill. Rawdon, however, his communications and supply lines threatened, was forced to move off. Greene's detachments took the British posts, Lee's Legion took Augusta; Greene besieged Ninety-six but Rawdon relieved the garrison on June 19. This was Rawdon's second Pyrrhic victory, for he had to abandon the post. Thus, by July Greene held nearly the entire lower South, having forced Cornwallis to leave the theater of operations. After the campaign's long marches and short rations, Greene took his army to camp at the High Hills of Santee for six seeks of recuperation, drill, and discipline.

The army moved out on August 23 and on September 8 surprised Lieutenant Colonel Alexander Stuart at Eutaw Springs, fighting a bloody battle against an army of equal size. The militia fought well, British regulars were pushed back in open fighting, and an American bayonet charge was successful. When, however, Lee's Legion and the artillery advanced beyond troops who stayed to enjoy the food and rum in the abandoned British camp, Greene was forced to leave the field. This indecisive battle, at best a draw, marked the end of the fighting in the lower South, as Stuart withdrew to Charleston. Congress later voted Greene thanks for the victory, along with a gold medal and a British standard, and Washington congratulated him in a letter.

With the onset of the cool season, Greene brought his army down from the Santee camp to besiege Charleston on January 2, 1782, holding a superior British force in the city until the end of the war. Supplying his army, aiding the restoration of civil government, and attempting to prevent mistreatment of loyalists occupied Greene until all troops began to leave in July of 1783. The legislatures of Georgia and of North and South Carolina had voted to grant him land in gratitude. Greene rode home to Rhode Island in November, but in 1784 had to return and sell the South Carolina plantation to settle claims made on him stemming from his arrangements for supplying the army before Charleston. (Congress granted, to his widow, the financial relief for which he had asked, in June, 1796.)

In the autumn of 1785, Greene moved his family to the Mulberry Grove plantation granted him in Georgia. He settled in to the life of a gentleman farmer, but on June 14, 1786, after walking in the afternoon sun, he developed head pains and inflammation, and died five days later. He was buried in the cemetery of Christ Episcopal Church in Savannah, and in 1902 reinterred under the Greene monument in Johnson Square in that city. The Marquis de Lafayette, a longtime friend of Greene, educated his son George Washington Greene in France until 1794; shortly after his return, at the age of nineteen, the boy drowned in the Savannah River. On June 28, 1796, Greene's widow married Phineas Miller; she died in 1814.

Summary

In many respects, Nathanael Greene exemplified the American experience. Descended from early English settlers fleeing religious persecution, he was continuing the economic and educationally upward mobility which characterized Colonial society when Lexington and Concord interrupted an essentially undistinguished life. Appointed a brigadier general despite an almost complete lack of experience, Greene quickly demonstrated his military value to Washington. Throughout the Revolution he held important commands, in all of them giving his country unstinting service despite personal and financial hardships. On many points he was somewhat ahead of general public opinion. Early in the conflict, he urged independence as a goal. He saw the need of a strong central government, and, equally in vain, advocated a large regular army, enlisted for the duration, with central command and adequate supply and financial support. In this he differed from both contemporary and historical opinion, which was that the traditional militia was an effective military force expressing the popular nature of American society without endangering American liberties. Military historians have come to see the Revolutionary patriot militias as a cross section of the Colonial yeomanry, the "nation-in-arms" proficient with weapons and familiar with its home terrain, fighting well with its own officers and in its own way. For example, its usual casual "desertions," to deal with farm and business needs, produced not only a constantly fluctuating troop strength but also far less pressure on slender resources than a consistently large regular army would have.

Yet a commander and quartermaster general was bound to concentrate on the militia's weaknesses, even when planning them into his tactics, as Greene placed mostly raw militia in his first two lines at Guilford Courthouse: He wanted then to retreat after a few volleys, knowing that militia usually broke and ran in the face of an enemy advance, particularly of a bayonet charge, "grim lines of scarlet-coated men emerging from the mist and heading straight toward . . . them with naked steel," write Mary and Franklin Wickwire. As quartermaster general, Greene was too preoccupied with shortages and inefficiencies to feel grateful that he had to provide for forces which were smaller than they would have been, had militiamen been metamorphosed into duration-of-the-war Continentals.

Quartermaster generals, however efficient, are rarely remembered except by the troops whom they contrive somehow to supply. Even secondary commanders, however much relied upon by their chiefs, do not decide strategy: While Washington accepted Greene's assurance that Fort Washington could be held, it was Washington's own decision to attempt to block British operations in New Jersey. As commander of the Southern Department after the Camden debacle, Greene came fully into his own, demonstrating great abilities in tactics and strategy, as well as what in a military leader is called "character": courage, determination, dominating one's opponent, taking the psychological initiative. Greene chose his subordinates well, dealt diplomatically with both political and partisan leaders, and achieved results truly remarkable in the light of his command, which consisted of a small and inadequately supplied army supplemented by independent partisan groups and undisciplined militia. In the South, Greene lost every major engagement he personally commanded, usually through the failure of troops at crucial points in the battle, when victory seemed imminent. Frustrating as these situations must have been to him—he had an impulsive temperament and was easily angered—he remained a cautious tactician, never risking a desperate continuation which might have won a battle but which might as easily have destroyed his force. Like Washington, he realized the necessity of retaining an army able to fight again; he was willing to retreat, even run, but always to return to the conflict. For despite his defeats, his Southern strategy achieved all the objectives of his campaigns; Cornwallis and Rawdon won battles but lost control of the lower South. By rapid movement, constant pressure on the enemy, the use of a variety of methods (raids, harassing supply lines, siege, battles), Greene kept Cornwallis off balance, prevented his controlling the lower South and protecting its loyalists, and possibly contributed to Cornwallis' decision to attempt a Virginia offensive rather than one in the Carolinas. That decision brought Cornwallis finally to Yorktown.

Bibliography
Alden, John R. *A History of the American Revolution*. New York: Alfred A. Knopf, 1969. A basic general history, providing the necessary perspective. Very clear section describing Greene's campaigns in the South.
Cook, Fred J. "Francisco the Incredible." *American Heritage* 10 (October, 1959): 22-25, 92-95. Vivid sketch of the exploits of the six-foot, eight-inch Peter Francisco, especially his participation in the battle of Guilford Courthouse, for which Greene presented him with an inscribed razor case.
Greene, Francis Vinton. *General Greene*. New York: D. Appleton and Co., 1893. Reprint. Port Washington, N.Y.: Kennikat Press, 1970. A biography as filiopietistic as one would expect from a late nineteenth century descendant of Greene, with occasional swipes at George Bancroft's work, which was hostile to Greene. Nevertheless, well written and reasonably objective,

with a nice balance of information on Greene's personal life and military career, the political background, and the prominent individuals whose lives intersected with his.

Greene, George Washington. *The Life of Nathanael Greene, Major-General in the Army of the Revolution.* 3 vols. New York: Hurd and Houghton, 1871. The late nineteenth century flavor of this work by Greene's grandson is amply compensated for by the author's intuitive grasp of his subject's character and development. Numerous quotations from primary sources. At seventeen, the author knew Lafayette, was a friend of Henry Wadsworth Longfellow, and spoke at length with Greene's brothers and contemporaries in their old age.

Higginbotham, Don. *The War of American Independence.* New York: Macmillan Publishing Co., 1971. A basic work on the Revolutionary War. A certain tendency to draw parallels between the Revolution and twentieth century warfare, stretching the comparisons slightly, does not really spoil the effective presentation of the overall military situation, specific battles, and also the general political background.

Ketchum, Richard M. "Men of the Revolution—III." *American Heritage* 23 (December, 1971): 48-49. A brief but comprehensive biographical sketch accompanied by Charles Willson Peale's portrait of Greene.

Miller, John C. *Triumph of Freedom 1775-1783.* Boston: Little, Brown and Co., 1948. A standard overview of the period, including an effective analysis of both Greene and Cornwallis.

Snow, Richard F. "Battles of the Revolution: Guilford Court House." *American Heritage* 24 (June, 1973): 17. A good summary of the military action at Guilford Courthouse, with color paintings of privates of the Delaware Regiment and the Seventy-first Regiment of Foot.

Thayer, Theodore George. *The Making of a Scapegoat: Washington and Lee at Monmouth.* Port Washington, N.Y.: Kennikat Press, 1976. A tendentious work attempting to prove, often without documentation, that Washington was so frustrated by defeat that he blamed Charles Lee. The author also contends that Washington blamed Greene for the loss of Fort Washington, and that Greene expressed indignation at the verdict of Lee's court-martial.

Wickwire, Franklin, and Mary Wickwire. *Cornwallis: The American Adventure.* Boston: Houghton Mifflin Co., 1970. A major study of Cornwallis, this work presents the war from the British perspective, with attention to the problems of the British political and military system. Although in style somewhat reminiscent of nineteenth century literature, thus giving a quaint flavor to the eighteenth century narrative coupled with twentieth century psychological insights, it is quite clear, explaining without explaining away Cornwallis' failures.

Marsha Kass Marks

D. W. GRIFFITH

Born: January 22, 1875; Floydsfork, Kentucky
Died: July 23, 1948; Hollywood, California
Area of Achievement: Motion pictures
Contribution: A genius in the exposition of complex plots through revolutionary filmmaking techniques, Griffith was the foremost figure in the development of the American film as an expression of American values and as a
commercially successful medium.

Early Life

David Wark Griffith was born January 22, 1875, in the family farmhouse at
Floydsfork in Oldham County, Kentucky, the second youngest of seven children. His mother, née Mary Oglesby, was the daughter of a wealthy Kentucky farmer who provided his daughter and her husband with a cottage and
employment on his farm. David's father, Jacob Griffith, who claimed descent
from Virginia planter aristocracy, was a romantic ne'er-do-well who, although he died when David was only seven years old, had a profound influence on his young son. Jacob Griffith had a checkered career. He had left his
home in Virginia as a young man and gone to Kentucky, where he studied
medicine as an apprentice for two years and briefly practiced it in Floyds-
burg. Unsuccessful and easily bored, he went off to fight in the Mexican War.
He then returned to Kentucky, married, and, in 1850, left his wife and three
children to escort a wagon train from Missouri to California toward the end
of the Gold Rush. After returning home, in 1853-1854, he served in the Kentucky legislature. His glory days, however, lay ahead. At the outbreak of the
Civil War he became a colonel under General Thomas "Stonewall" Jackson.
He was wounded on several occasions, and one of these wounds, improperly
treated, contributed to his later semi-invalidism and death. His most unusual
wartime experience was to lead a victorious cavalry charge from a buggy
since his wounds prevented him from riding a horse.

After the war, the Griffith family lived in the genteel poverty common
among many of their station at the time. Jacob Griffith dabbled again briefly
in Kentucky politics but spent most of his time regaling his family with tales
of his heroic experiences and of the Lost Cause. He also convinced the young
and impressionable David of his descent from Welsh kings. He read to his
family in his deeply resonant voice from Edgar Allan Poe, Sir Walter Scott,
and William Shakespeare and took his children to a magic-lantern show
which made a deep impression on the young David. By 1882, Jacob Griffith
was dead, a victim of his wartime wounds and heavy drinking. It was during
David's childhood years that his outlook was to be developed: He became a
romantic imbued with a sense of Southern gentility and convinced of his destiny to make his name in the literary and artistic world.

After the colonel's death, the family eventually moved to Louisville, where the young Griffith's mother opened a rooming and boarding house. Griffith took a variety of menial jobs to supplement the family's income. Most significant, he worked in the bookstore run by Bernard and Washington Flexner, members of a remarkable family of Jewish intellectuals. The shop was a gathering place for many local writers, including James Whitcomb Riley. David's literary appetite was further whetted by this experience. He also attended, as means would allow, this river town's numerous theaters and developed that intense interest so characteristic of youth. He was soon convinced that his destiny was to become a playwright, an American Shakespeare. He also developed an interest in acting as the means by which he could best learn stagecraft. By his early twenties, he had a job as an actor in a touring group of amateur players, much to his mother's dismay. In deference to his mother, he took the name Lawrence Griffith and began his theatrical career.

By the late 1890's, when Griffith began his theatrical career, he had developed the physical appearance he was to retain for most of the remainder of his life. Tall and thin with an aquiline nose, high forehead, and a moderately wide, thin-lipped mouth, he conveyed an aristocratic mien well suited to the stage actor. Later in life, he always wore a wide-brimmed hat.

Acting then, as ever, was an insecure profession. There were always more actors than roles, and anticipating the changing tastes of a fickle public was difficult. Thus, although Griffith acted, he took numerous other jobs as well. He worked in a steel mill and on a ship that carried lumber along the West Coast. He rode a freight train across country and begged for food. These experiences were important, however, for they acquainted the son of Southern aristocrats with the variety and conditions of men. In 1905, in San Francisco, he met a young actress, Linda Arvidson, who was to become his first wife. After the marriage, a year later in Boston, the two continued to act intermittently and maintained a hand-to-mouth existence. Griffith continued to write plays and sold one, *A Fool and a Girl*, in 1907 for seven hundred dollars. He also sold a poem and a short story for considerably lesser amounts and got an occasional acting role. In his early thirties, however, he was essentially a failure as an actor and writer. Yet his passion for both did not abate, and a chance meeting in 1908 which enabled him to utilize his talents successfully ignited a spark that was to develop into an obsession: a career in the fledgling motion-picture industry.

Life's Work

In the spring of 1908, in New York City, Griffith ran into an old friend, a fellow actor he had not seen for several years. As each recounted his experiences to the other, Griffith told his friend of the financial straits in which he and his wife then found themselves. The friend told Griffith that the motion-picture industry had been a lifesaver to him and suggested Griffith contact some of the numerous studios then operating in New York. Although Griffith knew little about this rapidly growing new industry, he took his friend's suggestion and found employment at the Edison Company. In his only film for Edison, Griffith worked under cinematographer-director Edwin S. Porter, the creator of the famous "chase" film *The Great Train Robbery* (1903). Griffith was to use the device of the chase in many of his own films, including *The Birth of a Nation* (1915), *Intolerance* (1916), *Way Down East* (1920), and *Orphans of the Storm* (1922). Griffith also learned from Porter the rudiments of the trick-shot or special effect, which he later incorporated into his films. At that time interested primarily in scriptwriting, Griffith turned to American Biograph Studios, where he and his wife then found employment, she as an actress and he as a writer and actor. Within weeks, however, Griffith was given his first opportunity to direct. Having found what, in combination with writing, proved to be his calling, Griffith started to work, immediately choosing the cast and crew of his first film, *The Adventures of Dollie* (1908). His most important choice was his cameraman, Billy (G. W.) Bitzer, who worked closely with Griffith throughout the heyday of the director's career.

Thus, in 1908, Griffith began his five-year tenure at Biograph, a period during which he developed his craft as a technician and storyteller, built up a talented crew of technical personnel headed by Bitzer, and created a stock company of players including Mary Pickford, Lionel Barrymore, Henry B. Walthall, Mae Marsh, Robert Harron, and, most important, the Gish sisters, Dorothy and the luminous Lillian—who was, for Griffith, the embodiment of virginal innocence and his favorite and most talented performer. During his years at Biograph, Griffith made more than four hundred films, none longer than two reels and of varying quality. Moving his operations to California and establishing his fame inside and outside the industry, Griffith became dissatisfied with Biograph's financial and creative restrictions. In October, 1913, he left Biograph, taking with him his players and certain technical and business personnel, and joined the recently allied Reliance-Majestic production company and the Mutual distributing company, for whom he made four films in 1914. Within less than a year he started to work on the first and best remembered of his masterpieces, *The Birth of a Nation*, the film which elevated the motion picture to art.

The Birth of a Nation is about two families, one from the South, the other from the North, during the Civil War and Reconstruction. Based upon two books by Thomas Dixon, an avowed racist, the scenario by Griffith was significantly different, less racist. The film, which when first shown ran two hours and forty-five minutes, is nevertheless pro-Southern, and its leading villains, especially in the section dealing with Reconstruction, are white abolitionists and carpetbaggers, blacks, and mulattoes. Indeed, it is the Ku Klux Klan, under the leadership of the film's Southern hero, which eventually prevails. For this reason, the film was at the time and has continued to be widely criticized. Nevertheless, it was the greatest film of its time and is considered one of the major films in history because of its impact on later filmmakers. Griffith's Civil War battle scenes, based on his study of the photographs by Matthew Brady, have never been improved upon. His attention to historical accuracy in set construction was also remarkable, and he set a standard few filmmakers have reached since. The film is also important for Griffith's ability to develop three-dimensional characters in what is essentially a spectacle film. Technically the film was far ahead of its time, and every film director since has been consciously or unconsciously influenced by it. Many of the features found separately in earlier Griffith films are found together in *The Birth of a Nation*: the close-up, the fade-out, the wide landscape shot, the use of moving cameras attached to vehicles in action scenes, and the action close-up of horses' hooves. Most important, Griffith was the first director-producer-writer to master the art of editing, enabling him to switch rapidly from place to place and character to character in a long, complex narrative and maintain the interest of the viewer. The film, which President Woodrow Wilson described as "history written by lightning," was a great critical and popular success, even as it was simultaneously attacked, vindicating Griffith's solicitation of additional financing when Reliance-Majestic ran short of funds. Unfortunately, Griffith enjoyed his greatest success with this, one of his very first feature films. At the peak of his creativity, he soon was to find that he was artistically and intellectually far ahead of his audience.

The success of *The Birth of a Nation* led Griffith to undertake immediately his magnum opus, *Intolerance*, which many film historians regard as the greatest film ever made, but which, at the time of its release in 1916, was a commercial failure. The theme is essentially the same as that of *The Birth of a Nation*: the damage wrought by hypocritical do-gooders who attempt to remold society in the image of what they think it should be without regard for the pain and suffering they cause. The scope of the film is, however, much larger, and this is what confused audiences. Griffith moves rapidly from twentieth century industrial America, to ancient Babylon, to Palestine at the time of Jesus, to sixteenth century France during the wars of religion. The segments of the film are bridged by a recurring scene of the universal mother forever rocking the cradle, reflecting Griffith's conviction of the endurance of love even during periods of evil and destruction. The spectacle of the film is revolutionary, especially the scenes of the walls and public buildings of Babylon. All the revolutionary technical innovations found in Griffith's first great film are here as well. In *Intolerance*, however, the subject matter was too obscure for the average viewer, and Griffith's editing confused more than excited.

Griffith continued to make films, though none of the scope and expense of *The Birth of a Nation* and *Intolerance*, with the partial exception of *Orphans of the Storm*, set during the French Revolution and notable for its action sequences, such as that of the storming of the Bastille. After 1916, Griffith became less independent because of the financial failure of *Intolerance* and found his creativity often stifled by the studios, even by United Artists, which he founded jointly with Douglas Fairbanks, Mary Pickford, and Charles Chaplin. One very significant additional film, however, was made. It was far more intimate than the aforementioned films and was made almost entirely on interior sets. This was *Broken Blossoms* (1919), a tragic tale set in the slums of London about the corruption and destruction of the virtuous and good.

Griffith reached the apex of his career by his early forties. From 1921 on, he found himself the prisoner of studio heads and their accountants. The independence which had fostered his creativity—his ability to work as director, producer, writer, and editor—was lost. He made his last film in 1931, a forgettable one called *The Struggle*. From that time until his death, Griffith was lost. He returned to Kentucky for several years, married a woman thirty-five years his junior (his first marriage had broken up during his Biograph days, although he did not get a divorce until 1936), and then returned to Hollywood in the late 1930's to work for Hal Roach on *One Million B.C.* (1940). When that film was completed, Griffith's name was mysteriously excluded from the credits. During the 1940's, he was a lonely, embittered man, often the recipient of praise and awards but unable to find employment in the city whose success he, more than any other, had assured; he was merely tolerated by many who had appropriated his innovations to their own use. Divorced for a second time in 1947, Griffith suffered a cerebral hemorrhage in the small hotel where he lived. He died at Temple Hospital on July 23, 1948.

Summary

D. W. Griffith was the foremost creative figure in the history of motion pictures. He developed the motion picture, America's greatest contribution to the arts, into a viable commercial and artistic medium. His influence on the evolution of the medium is incalculable, and it was recognized by many during his time, especially in the years during which he was ignored. He is a tragic figure in the history of American art. Beginning his career in an age when men of creative genius were allowed freedom in the application of their directorial, literary, and technical talents, he fell victim to the cupidity and timidity of an industry which he, more than any other, helped to create. To the end the Southern gentleman, he was unable to sacrifice his uncommon ideals to the demands of a medium which often has flourished on the trivial and the banal.

Bibliography
Croy, Homer. *Star Maker: The Story of D. W. Griffith*. New York: Duell, Sloan and Pearce, 1959. An anecdotal account of Griffith by a man who

himself was active in the film industry in its early years. Not always accurate, it is engagingly written and provides a satisfactory introduction to the subject.

Gish, Lillian, and Ann Pinchot. *The Movies, Mr. Griffith and Me*. Englewood Cliffs, N.J.: Prentice-Hall, 1969. A delightful autobiography by the actress most loved and admired by Griffith, and who reciprocated in affection and admiration for him.

Griffith, D. W. *The Man Who Invented Hollywood: The Autobiography of D. W. Griffith*. Edited by James Hart. Louisville, Ky.: Touchstone Publishing, 1972. The subject's own account of his life, essential for the serious student.

Henderson, Robert M. *D. W. Griffith: His Life and Work*. New York: Oxford University Press, 1972.

_____. *D. W. Griffith: The Years at Biograph*. New York: Farrar, Straus and Giroux, 1970. Readable and authorative accounts of Griffith's life by a man who has come to be recognized as the leading authority on the film pioneer.

Mast, Gerald. *A Short History of the Movies*. 2d ed. Indianapolis: Bobbs-Merrill Co., 1976. Includes a valuable evaluation of Griffith and his films within the context of the entire history, national and international, of filmmaking.

O'Dell, Paul, and Anthony Slide. *Griffith and the Rise of Hollywood*. New York: A. S. Barnes, 1971. A brief but useful volume in the International Film Guide Series. O'Dell emphasizes Griffith's artistic contributions to motion pictures, contributions he believes have been ignored by those who have concentrated only on his technical innovations.

Schickel, Richard. *D. W. Griffith: An American Life*. New York: Simon and Schuster, 1984. A massive biography that includes virtually every bit of information one could want to know about Griffith. Schickel, the film critic for *Time* magazine, has written numerous books on American film and the personalities prominent in its development. Though packed with information, this book is highly readable and incorporates more up-to-date material on Griffith.

Williams, Martin. *Griffith: First Artist of the Movies*. New York: Oxford University Press, 1980. A fine, brief treatment of Griffith and his films, this book provides the reader with an ideal introduction to the subject.

J. Stewart Alverson

DANIEL GUGGENHEIM

Born: July 9, 1856; Philadelphia, Pennsylvania
Died: September 28, 1930; Port Washington, New York
Areas of Achievement: Business and philanthropy
Contribution: Through daring business risks and tight family control over his ventures, Guggenheim created one of the first multinational corporations and went a long way toward his goal of controlling the mineral wealth of the entire world.

Early Life

Daniel Guggenheim was born July 9, 1856, in Philadelphia, Pennsylvania. His father was the greatest single influence in his life. Meyer Guggenheim had emigrated from Switzerland in 1848 to escape the restrictions placed on Jews in that country at that time. Daniel was the second of seven sons. When Daniel was born the family was still struggling. Meyer was a peddler who had gone into the manufacture and sale of stove polish and coffee essence. He made a large sum of money as a wholesaler during the Civil War. By the 1870's, Meyer had branched into the making of lye for domestic soap, had speculated in railroad stock, and had formed the firm of Guggenheim and Pulaski to import lace and embroideries from Switzerland and Saxony. Meyer was determined to earn enough money to provide for his family even after his death. His children were given a lax religious upbringing. His goal was that they should receive as good an education as could be had, so Daniel and his brothers were sent to a Catholic school.

Academically, Daniel did not shine; like his father, he was more concerned with things practical. At seventeen, he was sent to Switzerland to perfect his German and to study the embroidery business; he stayed there ten years. In 1877, M. Guggenheim and Sons was founded. Two years later, Meyer's worth was estimated at around $800,000. In 1881, he bought an interest in two lead and silver mines in Colorado. It was a gamble that was to set the course of Daniel's subsequent career (and those of his brothers) because the mines proved to be enormously rich. Daniel was recalled to man the New York office and all seven sons went into the mining business. By 1889, the entire Guggenheim family had moved to New York, the financial capital of the nation. From 1890 to 1923, it was Daniel, the most energetic and ambitious of the brothers, who directed the affairs of the Guggenheim interests.

In 1890, at the age of thirty-four, Daniel Guggenheim stood barely more than five feet tall. He was quick and very agile, bold and adventurous, possessed of truly demonic energy, and a born general. His manner was European; he was polished and self-assured. He believed in the essential virtue and inevitability of material progress. In his eyes there was an expression of such intensity that it appeared he was forever about to explode. His mania was for profits. Even at the end of his life, Guggenheim worked a sixteen-hour day. He was independent, autocratic, dynamic, and forward-looking. Morally, he was the typical Victorian—a devoted family man (he married in 1884), puritanical, and not in the least interested in society. His view of industrial management was unabashedly feudal.

Life's Work

The two Guggenheim mines in Colorado were followed by the construction of a smelter at Pueblo. As a result of favorable federal legislation which served to boost silver prices, a harsh labor policy, selective stockpiling, and the attainment of cheap railroad freight rates, profits from the smelter alone ran at five million dollars. Guggenheim's control over the Guggenheim interests, now all in mining, occurred as a result of a further piece of legislation, the McKinley Tariff Act of 1890. This placed a heavy duty on imported ores and motivated the Guggenheims to lease or buy mines in Mexico and to build smelters there. Guggenheim was sent to obtain the necessary concession from the Mexican government. It was the first, and by no means the last, occasion when the Guggenheims were able to use their industrial power to control poor countries. The result of Guggenheim's negotiations with President Porfirio Diaz was not only the right to operate in the country but also exemptions from import duty on machinery and from all municipal and state taxes. On his return to New York, Guggenheim was chosen to oversee the entire mining and smelting business and to plan future expansion.

The rise of the Guggenheims had excited the interests of others in the mining business. In 1889, Henry Huttleston Rogers, with the principal backing of William Rockefeller, began to form a huge trust to monopolize the smelting business in America. In 1898, the new trust became known as the American Smelting and Refining Company (ASARCO). The Guggenheims were invited to join but they refused. Guggenheim was convinced that his family's business was now too big to be squeezed out. By 1900, through a series of well-planned, astute moves, and aided by a two-month strike of ASARCO workers, the Guggenheims were able to flood the world market with cheap lead and silver, drive down prices and thus the value of ASARCO shares, and buy up those shares at low prices. Following merger negotiations and a series of court battles, Guggenheim emerged as chairman of the board and president of ASARCO, his brother Solomon became treasurer, three other brothers were board members, and the Guggenheims and their allies controlled fifty-one percent of the stock. Daniel Guggenheim was now firmly in control of mining and smelting in America.

In 1906, Guggenheim formed what came to be called the Alaska Syndicate with John Pierpont Morgan and Jacob Schiff. The discovery of Kennecott Creek, the richest copper deposit in the world at that time, excited the Guggenheims and their partners to the extent that they were willing to build the necessary two-hundred-mile railroad and the new harbor and acquire a steamship line to get the ore to the Guggenheim smelter at Tacoma, Washington. The necessity of buying coal mines to supply power to machinery and forests for construction purposes led the syndicate to attempt control over all the natural resources of Alaska. This led to the first great public controversy over Guggenheim business practices. Despite the efforts of Gifford Pinchot, chief of the United States Forestry Service, and others who argued that natural resources should belong to the nation as a whole, the conservationists got nowhere. Guggenheim had too many friends in the Administration and his brother Simon, United States senator from Colorado, also worked effectively for M. Guggenheim and Sons. Between the completion of the railroad in 1911 and the end of 1912, Kennecott paid three million dollars in dividends. By 1918, it had yielded more than seventy-two million dollars.

During this same period, the Guggenheim interests, with the aid of their consulting engineer, John Hays Hammond, bought up more mines in Mexico, constructed more smelters there, acquired Esperanza, the richest gold mine in Mexico, formed the Yukon Gold Company to dredge the gold-bearing sands of the Klondike and, after 1916, transferred the equipment to Malaya to dredge for tin; and got over the disaster of investment in Nipissing silver. The same period too, saw Daniel Guggenheim in partnership with Thomas Fortune Ryan and King Leopold of Belgium with exclusive rights to prospect for and develop all minerals in the Congo (modern Zaire), where gold and especially diamonds were found. Back in the United States, the Guggenheims bought Bingham Canyon, in Utah, which became the first open cast copper mine and the biggest copper operation in the world. Fully under way in 1910, the mine was run as a virtual slave-labor camp with specially imported cheap labor, and backed by the Utah state militia. Guerrilla warfare broke into open warfare between workers on the one side and company security men and state militia on the other. Some reforms followed, and, by 1935, profits from Bingham Canyon alone were estimated at $200 million. The year 1910 also saw the purchase of the Chuquicamata copper mine in Chile, nine thousand feet up in the Andes. It proved to be greater and richer than either Kennecott or Bingham Canyon. To exploit it, Guggenheim had to build a modern port, a road from the sea to his new mining town, an electric power plant, and fifty-five miles of aqueduct to bring in the nearest water.

By 1915, the Guggenheims controlled seventy-five to eighty percent of the world's silver, copper, and lead, and could dictate prices. Their mines were in full production to fill war orders. From 1915 to 1918, their copper interests alone paid $210 million in dividends. Public criticism of the Guggenheims as war profiteers grew until eventually, President Woodrow Wilson forced them to peg copper prices. Their reputation was not enhanced when, in a short strike at Kennecott, the company evicted striking workers from their bunkhouses into bitter thirty-below-zero weather.

Guggenheim's power in the industrial world was recognized by President Wilson in May, 1917, when he was chosen as one of two representatives of capital, the other being John D. Rockefeller, Jr., to meet the representative of labor to discuss industrial peace for the duration of the war. Guggenheim's public embrace of Samuel Gompers, the head of the American Federation of Labor, and his public endorsement of unionism, however, did not alter the policies of Guggenheim companies around the world.

The huge success of the Guggenheims was based on a business strategy devised by Daniel Guggenheim. First, they always went in for big development when the business barometer was low. Second, they used the cheap labor and raw materials of underdeveloped countries to depress their own country's wages and prices until they were so cheap that they could afford to buy them up and place them within their own monopoly. Third, in the metals industry, Guggenheim felt that there was no use competing unless one owned everything from mine mouth to finished product.

In 1922, Guggenheim was sixty-six years old. In that year, the board of ASARCO accused the Guggenheims of milking the company to further their own separate family interests. It voted the family out of control at a stockholders meeting. Not long after, Guggenheim retired and Simon, the ex-United States senator, became president of ASARCO, assisted by Guggenheim's son-in-law Roger Straus. The following year, Chuquicamata was sold by the family to Anaconda Copper.

During the next few years, Guggenheim and his brothers devoted their energies to redeeming the family image through philanthropy. In 1924, the Daniel and Florence Guggenheim Foundation was created for "the promotion, through charitable and benevolent activities, of the well-being of men throughout the world." Guggenheim's son, Harry, a World War I naval pilot, persuaded him to promote the neglected science of aeronautics; in 1925, the foundation granted $500,000 to New York University to establish the first school of aeronautics in the United States. The following year, the Daniel Guggenheim Fund for the Promotion of Aeronautics was established with $2.5 million. By 1930, the fund, almost single-handedly, had placed American aviation on a firm footing and had converted the public from apathy to enthusiastic support. Finally, convinced by Charles Lindbergh, the aviator, Guggenheim supported the experiments of an obscure physics professor in New England, Robert Hutchings Goddard. Following an initial grant from the foundation, the Daniel Guggenheim Fund for the Measurement and Investigation of High Altitudes enabled Goddard to establish the first United States rocket testing ground at Roswell, New Mexico.

When Guggenheim died, September 28, 1930, he had achieved not only a great reputation as a powerful industrialist, but also the admiration and affection of many.

Summary

Daniel Guggenheim was the head of an extraordinary industrial dynasty. Guided in the first instance by his father, he and his brothers developed a modest one-million-dollar fortune into one worth perhaps three hundred times that sum. The Guggenheims were a team, but, even though the contribution of his brothers is often much underrated, it was the driving ambition, ruthlessness, and boldness of vision provided by Daniel which, together with his undoubted ability and autocratic methods, made the Guggenheims into the controllers of most of the world's exploited mineral resources by 1915. It was said that, with one telegram, Daniel had the power to topple governments.

Bibliography

Baruch, Bernard. *My Own Story*. New York: Holt, Rinehart and Winston, 1957. The "boy wonder of Wall Street" was closely associated with Daniel Guggenheim for many years, and in this book he leaves portraits of Daniel and all of his brothers.

Bernstein, Marvin D. *The Mexican Mining Industry, 1890-1950*. New York: State University of New York Press, 1965. A comprehensive account of the development of the industry. Concentrates heavily on the Guggenheim interests and operations.

Cleveland, Reginald M. *America Fledges Wings: The History of the Daniel Guggenheim Fund for the Promotion of Aeronautics*. New York: Pittman Publishing Corp., 1942. A good account of the "foster father of United States aviation" stage of Guggenheim's life though, naturally, there is more material on Guggenheim's son Harry, who actually ran the fund.

Davis, John H. *The Guggenheims: An American Epic*. New York: William Morrow and Co., 1978. A well-balanced and informative account of the family to 1978. Daniel is dealt with in parts 1 and 2 and chapter 3 of part 3.

Lomask, Milton. *Seed Money: The Guggenheim Story*. New York: Farrar, Straus and Giroux, 1964. A work for a popular audience devoted largely to the philanthropic ventures of the family. Daniel is dealt with in chapters 2, 3, 6, and 8. Published by his grandson.

Marcosson, Isaac F. *Metal Magic: The Story of the American Smelting and Refining Company*. New York: Farrar, Straus and Giroux, 1949. A detailed account of the smelting and refining trust set up by Rockefeller to break the Guggenheims on the path to domination of metals in America but taken over by Daniel and his brothers in 1900. Published by Daniel's grandson.

O'Connor, Harvey. *The Guggenheims: The Making of an American Dynasty*. New York: Covici, Friede, 1937. Written by a socialist, labor journalist, and writer who also wrote about the Rockefellers, Astors, Mellons, and Carnegies. It takes a caustic view of Guggenheim business practices, favoring unions, independent miners, and smelter owners. It is the product of careful research and is in no way personally vicious. A good balance to Davis or Lomask.

Williams, Gatenby, and Charles Monroe Heath. *William Guggenheim*. New York: Lone Voice Publishing Co., 1934. Gatenby Williams was the pseudonym of William Guggenheim, youngest brother of Daniel, who left the company in 1901 and was forced to divorce his first wife, a California divorcée, by Daniel. His scholarly, contemplative temperament was overshadowed by the aggressiveness of his elder brothers, but his autobiography contains useful insights into the workings of the Guggenheim partnership and the building of its mining empire in the United States and Mexico.

Stephen Burwood

ALEXANDER HAMILTON

Born: January 11, 1755; Nevis, British West Indies
Died: July 12, 1804; New York, New York
Areas of Achievement: Politics and law
Contribution: Hamilton served as aide-de-camp to Washington during the American Revolution and was a delegate to the Philadelphia Convention of 1787 and signer of the Constitution. An early advocate of a strong national government, he coauthored *The Federalist* and was the United States' first secretary of the treasury.

Early Life

Alexander Hamilton was the illegitimate son of a Scottish ne'er-do-well and a woman previously arrested for adultery. He was probably born in 1755, although at times he claimed that his birth year was 1757. Hamilton spent his early years in abject poverty on the Caribbean island of his birth, Nevis. After his mother's death, he worked for a merchant family on St. Croix, where he flourished, as his unusual abilities brought him to the attention of his employers. Hamilton quickly rose to be something more than a clerk but less than a partner. By age sixteen, he was giving orders to ship captains, making decisions on when cargoes should be sold, and firing and hiring company lawyers. When not working, he studied on his own.

In 1773, Hamilton's employers, recognizing his precocious genius, sent him to the mainland for his first formal education. From 1773 to 1774, he lived with Elias Boudinot, a future president of the Continental Congress, and studied at a Presbyterian academy in Elizabethtown, New Jersey. In this period, Hamilton socialized with such future patriots and political leaders as William Livingston, Richard Stockton, Philip Schuyler, and Henry Brockholst Livingston. In 1774, Hamilton entered Kings College (now Columbia University) as a sophomore. In 1775, he anonymously published a pamphlet supporting the patriot cause; this was Hamilton's first political activity.

Life's Work

In March, 1776, Hamilton dropped out of college to become an artillery captain in the New York militia. He quickly came to the attention of senior officers, and in 1777 he joined George Washington's staff. Hamilton's relationship with the general was complex. The childless Washington often treated Hamilton as the son he never had. Hamilton, whose father was never present in his life, revered Washington, but at the same time he felt stifled working for "The Great Man," as his staff officers called him. As Washington's aide-de-camp, Hamilton had a unique view of the war and the politics of the Revolution. It was during this period that he became a committed nationalist, as he saw the states squabbling over issues while the national army went without adequate food and other provisions.

The young Hamilton was short, slim, and not particularly athletic. He was brilliant as an administrator but hardly suited to frontline command. Yet he longed for the opportunity to achieve battlefield glory. This desire strained his relationship with Washington, and in February, 1781, he resigned his position. In July, Hamilton returned with his rank of lieutenant colonel to command a battalion, and at Yorktown he was finally given his opportunity for combat glory. Hamilton led his battalion in a brief and heroic assault on a British position. He was thrilled with his exploit but bitter that the Congress never saw fit to award him a medal for his heroism. Shortly after the victory at Yorktown, Hamilton returned to civilian life.

In 1780, Hamilton was married to Elizabeth Schuyler. His father-in-law, General Schuyler, was one of the richest men in America and a powerful politician in New York. This family connection eliminated the taint of his illegitimate birth. In April, 1782, he began preparing for a career as a lawyer, and in July he was admitted to the bar. At first, Hamilton was ambivalent about his new profession, writing to the Marquis de Lafayette that he was "studying the art of fleecing my neighbours." Hamilton quickly threw himself into his law practice and was soon representing many of the wealthiest men in his state. Many of his clients were former loyalists who sought to regain property taken during the Revolution, yet Hamilton had few scruples about representing his former enemies. Between 1783 and 1789, he was involved in massive litigation over huge land claims in upstate New York. He also represented banks, shippers, and merchants. Hamilton's fundamentally conservative nature was reflected by his clients and his law practice.

During this period, Hamilton ventured into politics. The New York legislature chose him as a delegate to the Continental Congress (1782, 1783, 1787, 1788) and to the Annapolis Convention of 1786. Through his political connections, he served a short time as a collector of taxes for the Congress. In 1787, Hamilton was also elected to the New York legislature. With the exception of his election to the convention called to ratify the Constitution, this was the only popular election that Hamilton ever won. Although a brilliant political theorist, his personal style prevented him from being a popular candidate.

The Annapolis Convention of 1786 was called to negotiate a trade agreement among the American states under the Articles of Confederation. The convention failed: Most of the states did not bother to send delegations. The meeting at Annapolis led to a call for another convention, however, to be held in Philadelphia the following year. That convention would write the Constitution.

Hamilton was one of three delegates from New York to the Philadelphia Convention of 1787. He received the unanimous support of the state legislature. Even his political enemies (and he had many by this time) believed that

Hamilton was one of the ablest men in the state. At the beginning of the Convention, a fellow delegate wrote that "Colo. Hamilton is deservedly celebrated for his talents. He is a practitioner of the Law, and reputed to be a finished Scholar. . . . His manners are tinctured with stiffness, and sometimes with a degree of vanity that is highly disagreeable." While haughty and arrogant, Hamilton was also exceedingly handsome, with auburn hair, deep blue eyes, and a charming smile, especially when directed at women.

At Philadelphia, Hamilton was limited in his effectiveness. The other two New York delegates, John Lansing and Robert Yates, were opposed to a strong national government, which Hamilton supported. Thus, Hamilton was able to participate in debates, but his votes on the developing document were canceled by the rest of New York's delegation. In his first major speech, Hamilton argued for an extremely strong central government and a narrow and limited role for the states. Hamilton asserted his belief "that the British Govt. was the best in the world: and that he doubted much whether any thing short of it would do in America." He argued that the "hereditary interest of the King" prevented the dangers of corruption in England and that, for the American chief executive, "the English model was the only good one on this subject." His plan of government, which never received the support of any other delegates, called for a chief executive to serve for life and the appointment of state governors by the national government. This speech has led Hamilton's detractors to conclude that he was a monarchist. While that is perhaps an exaggeration, it is clear that Hamilton did favor a lifetime chief executive and that he leaned toward ruling over the people, rather than the people ruling themselves.

On June 29, Hamilton left the convention, in part because it was not headed in the direction he favored and in part because Yates and Lansing had outvoted him on most issues. Hamilton also wanted to return to his political base in New York and to the Continental Congress. Early in July, however, Yates and Lansing left the convention, and three days later, Hamilton returned. For the rest of the summer, Hamilton moved in and out of the convention. The rules of the convention required that each state have at least two delegates present in order to vote on the emerging document. Thus, Hamilton could debate but not vote. His most important contributions came in the debates that took place in September and in his work on the committee of style. At the end of the convention, he persuaded his fellow delegates to sign the document, even though New York as a state was not represented under the convention rules.

After the convention, Hamilton actively supported the new Constitution. In collaboration with fellow New Yorker John Jay and with Virginian James Madison, Hamilton planned and wrote a series of essays collectively known as *The Federalist* (1787-1788). All three authors wrote under the pen name Publius. Of the eighty-five separate essays, Hamilton wrote fifty-one and collaborated on another three. Madison's contributions, which included the famous numbers 10, 14, and 51, ended when he left New York in March, 1788, while Jay's writings were limited by illness. Hamilton continued the project without Madison and Jay, producing the last twenty-one essays on his own, including the powerful number 78, which explained the role of the judiciary in the constitutional system. *The Federalist* was written to convince New York voters to support the Constitution, but this goal was not really achieved. The majority of those elected to the New York ratifying convention opposed the Constitution. Neither the essays of Publius nor Hamilton's own speeches at the ratifying convention convinced the delegates to support the Constitution. Ultimately, New York ratified it by a slim three-vote margin, because a number of opponents of the Constitution concluded that with the ratification in Virginia and Massachusetts they had no choice but to ratify. While it was not persuasive in New York, *The Federalist* is generally considered to contain the single most important contemporary analysis of the Constitution and has been cited repeatedly by scholars and courts in the twentieth century.

With the organization of the new government, Hamilton became the nation's first secretary of the treasury. In his first two years in that office, Hamilton organized the nation's finances, established a mint and a system of creating money, and convinced the Congress and the president to support a national bank. He attempted to create a national program to support manufacturing and economic development, but this was defeated.

Hamilton's *Report Relative to a Provision for the Support of Public Credit* (1795), presented to the Congress in January, 1795, laid out a program for putting the nation on a sound financial footing. Hamilton urged that the national government pay off all foreign and domestic debt incurred by the Congress and the states during the Revolution and Confederation period. Two aspects of this report were particularly controversial. Hamilton recommended that all bondholders receive the face value of their bonds. This meant that speculators who had purchased war bonds at far below their original value would reap great profits, while those who had actually risked their money to support the American Revolution would not even get their original investment back. Hamilton also recommended that the national government pay off all unpaid state war debts. This proposal offended Virginia, which had paid off most of its debts and did not want to have to pay the debts of other states as well. Congressmen from states with small debts, such as Georgia, North Carolina, and Maryland, also opposed this plan. Representatives from states with large debts, including South Carolina, New York, and Massachusetts, naturally supported the plan.

Hamilton's goals in his debt-funding plan were not to aid one section of the nation and harm another. Nor did he seek to enrich speculators at the expense of patriotic investors who were forced, because of a postwar depression, to sell their bonds at low prices. Hamilton simply sought to put the nation on a sound economic footing. Nevertheless, high motives and sound economic policy were not enough to push through his proposal, and Congress adopted it only after much political maneuvering, which included an agreement to move the nation's capital from New York City to some place close to Virginia. Besides some political advantages, the Virginians hoped that the move would stimulate economic development in the Chesapeake region.

The creation of the Bank of the United States was Hamilton's second major accomplishment as secretary of the treasury. In the cabinet, Secretary of State Thomas Jefferson and Attorney General Edmund Randolph both opposed the bank. Congressional opposition was led by Madison, Hamilton's former collaborator on *The Federalist*. Hamilton's arguments in favor of the bank were more than economic. They were also constitutional. He asserted that the Constitution needed to be read broadly, and he argued that Congress must have the power to go beyond the specific "enumerated powers" in the Constitution through the "necessary and proper clause" of the document. In the cabinet debate, Hamilton prevailed and Washington signed the bank bill into law.

Hamilton's "Report on Manufactures," delivered to the Congress in December, 1791, argued in favor of stimulating manufacturing in the nation through tariff and tax policies. Hamilton's report detailed the types of manufacturing needed, including iron, leather, textiles, sugar, gunpowder, paper, and books. The report anticipated an America in which manufacturing, not agriculture, would be the dominant economic activity. This report was unacceptable, however, to the agrarian America of the 1790's.

In the cabinet, Hamilton proved a tireless and ruthless advocate of expanding national power. He came close to accusing Jefferson of treason when the secretary of state publicly indicated his disagreement with Hamilton. As a cabinet official, Hamilton helped organize the Federalist Party to support his economic and political policies. In 1794, he advocated the use of massive military force against hard-pressed western farmers who opposed his policy of taxing the producers of whiskey. Hamilton's role in the Whiskey Rebellion, was, in the end, almost comical. He led a large army into western Pennsylvania, where a handful of farmers were arrested and then released. Hamilton once again sought military glory, but this time he appeared to be an oppressor of the people; instead of glory, he won contempt.

In 1795, Hamilton left Washington's cabinet for the private practice of law. He quickly became one of the most successful attorneys in New York. In 1798, he became inspector general of the army when it appeared that a war with France was likely. This was his last public position. Once again, however, military glory eluded Hamilton, and he returned to law after the crisis with France ended. In his law practice, he was enormously successful, with clients begging for his services. In 1802, Hamilton earned nearly thirteen thousand dollars, an incredibly large sum for the period. Most of his law practice centered on marine insurance, banking law, and other litigation tied to commerce. Hamilton remained involved in politics, but his aggressive personal style and his penchant for intrigue served only to undermine the Federalist Party that he had helped to build in the early 1790's. Hamilton's public and private attacks on John Adams did little except to aid the fortunes of the Democratic-Republicans led by Jefferson and Aaron Burr. In 1804, he vigorously opposed Burr's attempt to gain the governorship of New York. Burr challenged him to a duel, which took place on July 11, 1804. Hamilton once again had an opportunity for glory on the field of combat. Once again, however, he was unsuccessful. He died, on July 12, of his wounds.

Summary

Hamilton was one of the great figures of the Revolutionary era. He was brilliant, charming, and a first-rate administrator. Yet he was also vain, overly ambitious, arrogant, and insecure over his status and place in the world. Hamilton's influence was undermined by his inability to get along with other leaders of the age. He was also something of a misfit. Reared in the West Indies, Hamilton was a monarchist when he first came to America. Although he quickly joined the patriot cause, his political views, as expressed in the Constitutional Convention and in Washington's cabinet, were almost always antirepublican; he had less faith in representative government than any of the other Founding Fathers. More than most public figures of the period, Hamilton favored a strong chief executive, if not a king. Hamilton was similarly out of step with America in his grandiose plans for the nation's economy. Nevertheless, the contributions of Alexander Hamilton to American politics, economics, and constitutional theory make him a towering figure of his age.

Bibliography

Bowen, Catherine Dinker. *Miracle at Philadelphia: The Story of the Constitutional Convention, May to September 1787*. Boston: Little, Brown and Co., 1966. Probably the best narrative history of the convention. Excellent for high school and undergraduate students. Good details on delegates to the convention.

Cooke, Jacob E. *Alexander Hamilton: A Biography*. New York: Charles Scribner's Sons, 1982. A short, readable biography by one of the nation's leading Hamilton scholars. An excellent place to begin.

_____, ed. *Alexander Hamilton: A Profile*. New York: Hill and Wang, 1967. Contains essays on Hamilton by a wide range of scholars, including those who liked him and those who did not.

Emery, Noemie. *Alexander Hamilton: An Intimate Portrait*. New York: G. P. Putnam's Sons, 1982. Much like the Flexner biography (below), although this volume gives more attention to Hamilton's later life.

Flexner, James Thomas. *The Young Hamilton: A Biography*. Boston: Little, Brown and Co., 1978. A superbly written study by the author of a leading biography of Washington. Focuses on Hamilton's early years and on his psychological development. A fascinating, accessible study.

Hamilton, Alexander. *The Reports of Alexander Hamilton*. Edited by Jacob E. Cooke. New York: Harper and Row, Publishers, 1964. Contains Hamilton's reports on public credit, the Bank of the United States, and manufacturers. Also contains Hamilton's constitutional arguments in favor of the bank. Excellent introduction by Cooke, a leading Hamilton scholar. Hamilton's reports are models of lucidity and can be read with profit by students and nonspecialists as well as by scholars.

Hamilton, Alexander, James Madison, and John Jay. *The Federalist*. Edited by Henry B. Dawson. New York: J. and A. McLeon, 1788. Reprint. Cambridge, Mass.: The Belknap Press of Harvard University Press, 1961. Various editions are available in both paperback and clothbound formats, generally including introductions by major scholars. The Federalist papers reveal much of Hamilton's political philosophy, although they should be read with care, since they were originally written to gain support for the Constitution and not as political theory.

Mitchell, Broadus. *Alexander Hamilton: A Concise Biography*. New York: Oxford University Press, 1976. Excellent one-volume study by one of Hamilton's major biographers. Mitchell is also the author of a more elaborate two-volume study of Hamilton. This book covers the same ground, with less detail.

Paul Finkelman

OSCAR HAMMERSTEIN II

Born: July 12, 1895; New York, New York
Died: August 23, 1960; Doylestown, Pennsylvania
Area of Achievement: Theater
Contribution: Working with such composers as Herbert Stothart, Jerome Kern, Sigmund Romberg, and especially Richard Rodgers, Hammerstein wrote books and lyrics which transformed the American musical into an integrated dramatic form and created a number of classics.

Early Life

Oscar Greeley Glendenning Hammerstein, named for his famous grandfather, Horace Greeley, and the minister who married his parents, was born in New York City on July 12, 1895, into a comfortable, middle-class environment. His father, William, was the son of the noted impresario Oscar Hammerstein and his first wife, Rose Blau. His mother, Alice Nimmo, was the daughter of Scottish immigrants, Janet and James Nimmo. Even though William Hammerstein managed the Victoria Theater, a leading vaudeville house, for his father, young Oscar saw very little of the flamboyant grandfather whose name he bore.

His interest in the theater began in 1902 when he made his debut in a Christmas entertainment at Public School No. 9; he began piano lessons at the age of nine. A happy childhood was marred by his mother's death in 1910. In 1912, Hammerstein entered Columbia University to prepare for a law career in accordance with his father's wishes. He joined the Pi Lamba Phi fraternity, played baseball, and maintained the grades he had always achieved. In 1914, his father died, but this bereavement did not affect him as deeply as the loss of his mother, to whom he had been devoted.

The following fall he joined the Columbia University Players, assuring his father's brother Arthur that this involvement would be strictly extracurricular. That same year he made his acting debut as a song-and-dance comic in the annual Columbia University Varsity Show. In his fourth year, he dutifully enrolled in Columbia Law School, attaining his B.A. at the end of the year. In 1916, he met the then fourteen-year-old Richard Rodgers, who later described Hammerstein at this time as "a very tall, skinny fellow with a sweet smile, clear blue eyes and an unfortunately mottled complexion."

Hammerstein's involvement with the Columbia Players continued even after he left the university and law. The 1917 varsity show, *Home James*, was written by Hammerstein and Herman Axelrod, but the *New York Herald* reviewer singled out young Hammerstein for his acting ability. The year 1917 was truly momentous in Hammerstein's life: He left law school, he was turned down by his draft board for being too thin, and he was able to persuade his uncle Arthur to give him employment as an assistant stagehand. In late summer, he married Myra Finn, and the following year their first child, William, was born. In 1919, he wrote two songs with Richard Rodgers for the Columbia Players and yet another in 1920. They were not to work together again for twenty-three years.

Life's Work

Hammerstein's career as a Broadway lyricist and librettist began, however, in 1920, when he wrote the book and lyrics for *Always You* (1920) to Herbert Stothart's music. More important, that year marked the beginning of a collaboration with Otto Harbach, whom he described as "the best play analyst I have ever met . . . and [a] born teacher." It was Harbach who taught him the importance of integrating all the elements of a show. Their musical, *Tickle Me* (1920), set to Stothart's music, was soon followed by such shows as *DaffyDill* (1922), *Wildflower* (1923), and *MaryJane McKane* (1923). Their 1924 show, *Rose Marie*, set to Rudolf Friml's tuneful music, was in a number of ways a break from the standard musical comedy formula of the day: "song, cue, song, cue." The songs now served to further the story, which even contained a murder, and the play ended with only two persons onstage instead of the usual assemblage of singers and dancers. It enjoyed a record-breaking run of one year, four months, and seven days. In 1925, Hammerstein and Harbach joined with composer Jerome Kern to create the first Hammerstein-Kern collaboration, *Sunny* (1925), which opened to good reviews. The following year, Hammerstein and Harbach wrote the lyrics to Sigmund Romberg's *Desert Song* (1926). During these productive years, the Hammerstein-Harbach collaboration gave birth to a series of highly popular songs, including "Who?," "The Desert Song," "The Riff Song," "One Alone," and "The Indian Love Call."

The Hammerstein-Kern collaboration attained its height in 1927 when they brought out *Show Boat*. Based on Edna Ferber's novel of the same title and set in the American South, it was the first really successful American musical play on a strictly American theme. The reviews were wildly enthusiastic, praising its "exceptionally tuneful score" and "gorgeous pictorial atmosphere." Hammerstein had written a folk play with characters and dialogue true to life, social problems mixed with humor, and lyrics that advanced the story line. Considered by many to be his masterpiece, it featured such songs as "Can't Help Lovin' Dat Man," "Make Believe," "Why Do I Love You," and notably "Ol Man River"—among the finest ever written for American musicals.

He followed it the next year with *The New Moon*, perhaps best remembered for the beautiful "Lover Come Back to Me" and the stirring "Stout-hearted Men," set to Sigmund Romberg's music. *Sweet Adeline*, written to Jerome Kern's score in 1929, was virtually a family affair, produced by uncle Arthur Hammerstein, directed by brother Reginald, and played at Hammerstein's Theater, a vast neo-Gothic structure recently built by Arthur.

While Hammerstein was becoming increasingly successful, his marriage to Myra was falling apart. Despite the birth in 1921 of a second child, Alice, the couple lived more or less separate lives, largely because of Myra's numerous affairs. She finally consented to a divorce in 1928. On May 13, 1929, Hammerstein married Dorothy Blanchard Jacobson, whom he had met en route to England. The new household at first consisted of Hammerstein, Dorothy, and her daughter Susan, who in 1950 would marry the actor Henry Fonda; Myra in time relinquished custody of Alice and Billy. Hammerstein disliked young children, but as they grew older he gave them stability and love, and they came to adore him. In March, 1931, a son, James, named for James Nimmo and James Blanchard, Dorothy's father, was born.

Generally speaking, the 1930's were comparatively unproductive years for Hammerstein. With the exception of *Music in the Air* (1932), a collaboration with Kern which produced the charming "I've Told Every Little Star," he spent most of this decade writing films. *Very Warm for May* (1939), written with Kern, was a Broadway failure, remembered only for one hit song, "All the Things You Are." His foray into English stage production turned out to be a mistake; his adaptation of a play staged at the Drury Lane Theater in London was a failure. Forsaking London, a rich Metro-Goldwyn-Mayer contract in hand, Hammerstein moved his family to Hollywood. The song "When I Grow Too Old to Dream," set to Romberg's music, was one of his very few lasting contributions as a Hollywood writer.

It was, however, during this period that Hammerstein's social conscience became manifest. Events in Germany convinced him of the evil of Nazism and, in 1936, he was one of the founders of the Hollywood League Against Nazism, becoming chairman of its cultural commission, which evolved the following year into an interracial commission. Throughout his life, he maintained an active interest in promoting understanding among persons of different races. His broad sympathies appear in *Show Boat*, in *Carmen Jones* (1942), in which he transplanted Georges Bizet's opera *Carmen* (1875) to the American South and substituted American blacks for Spanish Gypsies, in *South Pacific* (1949), in which he wrote against racial prejudice, and in *The King and I* (1951), set in nineteenth century Siam.

The fall of Paris in 1940 saddened him, recalling scenes of the city as he had known it as a small boy traveling with his family, as an adolescent, and as an adult living there for a few months in 1925. Now he composed a love poem to the captive city, which became the much-loved song "The Last Time I Saw Paris," which received the Motion Picture Academy Award after it was incorporated in the film *Lady Be Good* (1941). Kern wrote the music to Hammerstein's lyrics, one of the first times that the words preceded the composition of the music. In commenting on this practice later, however, Hammerstein said it seemed to make little sense. It had always been the other way around: score, then lyrics. Setting words to music was an almost infallible formula, and, when Hammerstein joined forces once more with Richard Rodgers in 1943, it became their regular mode of work.

The lean years ended in 1942 when Hammerstein's adaptation of Bizet's opera *Carmen*, retitled *Carmen Jones* and played by an all-black cast, was greeted enthusiastically by New York critics. *Variety* commented that "Hammerstein is now at the peak of his career." Little could the critic know what was to follow: in 1943, *Oklahoma!*, with 2,212 performances that year, a record that lasted for fifteen years; in 1945, *Carousel*, of which there were 890 performances; in 1945, the film *State Fair*; in 1947, *Allegro*, of which there were 315 performances; in 1951, *The King and I*, with 1,246 performances; in 1953, *Me and Juliet*; in 1955, *Pipe Dream*; in 1958, *Flower Drum Song*, of which there were 600 performances; and finally, in 1959, *The Sound of Music*, with 1,443 performances. The song "It Might as Well Be Spring" from *State Fair* also won an Academy Award (1945). From the Rodgers and Hammerstein collaboration came five musicals which are considered classics: *Oklahoma!*, *Carousel*, *South Pacific*, *The King and I*, and *The Sound of Music*.

Hammerstein died of cancer at the age of sixty-five on August 23, 1960, at his home in Doylestown, Pennsylvania. In tribute to him the lights on Broadway were blacked out for one minute at 9:00 P.M. the night of September 1. As taps were sounded in Duffy Square, a crowd of five thousand stood with bowed heads.

Summary

Hammerstein's contribution to the American musical theater is almost legendary. As early as 1932, his effort to transform the musical was recognized. In reviewing *Music in the Air*, Brooks Atkinson wrote in *The New York Times*, "At last the musical drama has been emancipated. . . . Without falling back into the cliches of the trade, Hammerstein has written sentiment and comedy that are tender and touching." Hammerstein was creating a new art form, removed from the trivial albeit melodious light opera or operetta, cohesive in form, no longer a parade of disconnected songs and dances interspersed with comedy routines but peopled with characters an audience could care about, expressing a concern for human beings of all races and persuasions, often tender, both sad and happy and never tasteless. The Pulitzer Prize committee in 1944 gave a special citation to Rodgers and Hammerstein for *Oklahoma!*

Hammerstein was expert in adapting the writings of others to the new form: *Show Boat* from the novel of the same title, *Oklahoma!* from Lynn Riggs's *Green Grow the Lilacs* (1931), *Carousel* from Ferenc Molnár's *Liliom* (1909), *South Pacific* from James Michener's *Tales of the South Pacific* (1947), *The King and I* from Margaret Landon's *Anna and the King of Siam*

(1944), and *The Sound of Music* from a German film about the von Trapp family.

Even his critics acknowledged that Hammerstein was a consummate craftsman. He labored over his writing, usually working in a standing position at a portable, "stand-up" writing desk. Hammerstein changed the course of the musical, its content and its form, turning it from the revue and chorus into the musical play. His lyrics dwelt on themes of racial tolerance, human dignity, joy, suffering, love, and the fraternity of all mankind. They were warm, charming, human, poetic, and quintessentially American.

Bibliography

Fordin, Hugh. *Getting to Know Him: A Biography of Oscar Hammerstein II*. New York: Random House, 1977. The best available account, based in large part on interviews with Hammerstein's widow, Dorothy, and children, this biography also has an introduction by Hammerstein's protégé, Stephen Sondheim.

Green, Stanley, ed. *Rodgers and Hammerstein Fact Book: A Record of Their Works Together and with Other Collaborators*. New York: Lynn Farnol Group, 1980. An invaluable compendium of facts, including casts of both Broadway and other companies, numbers of performances, and excerpts from reviews.

Hammerstein, Oscar, II. *Lyrics*. New York: Simon and Schuster, 1949. This volume contains only lyrics which the author wrote alone. It has besides a preface by Richard Rodgers a valuable autobiographical note on lyrics by Hammerstein.

Rodgers, Richard. *Musical Stages: An Autobiography*. New York: Random House, 1975. This autobiography of Hammerstein's most successful collaborator contains some reminiscences of note.

Rodgers, Richard, and Oscar Hammerstein II. *The Rodgers and Hammerstein Song Book: The Stories of the Principal Musical Plays and Commentary by Newman Levy*. New York: Simon and Schuster and Williamson Music, 1958. The title almost speaks for itself; this book is a mine of source material.

Sheean, Vincent. *Oscar Hammerstein I: The Life and Exploits of an Impresario*. Preface by Oscar Hammerstein II. New York: Simon and Schuster, 1956. The life of the grandfather of Hammerstein II with a note by the grandson. Written by a noted author, the book has a special value from interviews with the niece of Hammerstein I.

James A. Rawley